Fodor's Third Edition

China

The Guide for All Budgets, Completely Updated, with Many Maps and Travel Tips

Where to Stay, Eat,
and Explore

On and Off
the Beaten Path

When to Go,
What to Pack

Post-it® Flags,
Web Sites, and More

Fodor's Travel Publications • New York, Toronto, London, Sydney, Auckland
www.fodors.com

Fodor's China

EDITORS: Carissa Bluestone, Tania Inowlocki, Amy Karafin, Laura M. Kidder, Denise Leto

Editorial Contributors: Laurel Back, Kate and Tom Bryson, Denise Cheung, Eva Chui, Paul Davidson, Grace Fan, Denise Leto, Ke Ming Liu, Tobias Parker, George Vaughton, Lara Wozniak
Editorial Production: Tom Holton
Maps: David Lindroth, *cartographer*; Rebecca Baer and Bob Blake, *map editors*
Design: Fabrizio La Rocca, *creative director*; Guido Caroti, *art director*; Jolie Novak, *senior picture editor*; Melanie Marin, *photo editor*
Cover Design: Pentagram
Production/Manufacturing: Colleen Ziemba
Cover Photograph: © Dennis Cox/ChinaStock (Li River, Guilin)

Copyright

Third Edition

ISBN 0–676–90126–3

ISSN 1070–6895

Important Tip

Although all prices, opening times, and other details in this book are based on information supplied to us at press time, changes occur all the time in the travel world, and Fodor's cannot accept responsibility for facts that become outdated or for inadvertent errors or omissions. So **always confirm information when it matters,** especially if you're making a detour to visit a specific place.

Special Sales

Fodor's Travel Publications are available at special discounts for bulk purchases for sales promotions or premiums. Special editions, including personalized covers, excerpts of existing guides, and corporate imprints, can be created in large quantities for special needs. For more information, contact your local bookseller or write to Special Markets, Fodor's Travel Publications, 280 Park Avenue, New York, NY 10017. Inquiries from Canada should be directed to your local Canadian bookseller or sent to Random House of Canada, Ltd., Marketing Department, 2775 Matheson Boulevard East, Mississauga, Ontario L4W 4P7. Inquiries from the United Kingdom should be sent to Fodor's Travel Publications, 20 Vauxhall Bridge Road, London SW1V 2SA, England.

PRINTED IN THE UNITED STATES OF AMERICA

10 9 8 7 6 5 4 3 2 1

CONTENTS

Maps

ON THE ROAD WITH FODOR'S

The more you know before you go, the better your trip will be. Shanghai's best restaurant or Hong Kong's best open-air market could be just around the corner from your hotel, but if you don't know it's there, it might as well be on the other side of the globe. That's where this book comes in. It's a great step toward making sure your next trip lives up to your expectations. As you plan, check out the Web as well. Guidebooks have been helping smart travelers find the special places for years; the Web is one more tool. Whatever reference you consult, be savvy about what you read, and always consider the source. Images and language can be massaged to make places appear better than they are. And one traveler's quaint is another's grimy. Here at Fodor's, and at our on-line arm, Fodors.com, our focus is on providing you with information that's not only useful but accurate and on target. Every day Fodor's editors put enormous effort into getting things right, beginning with the search for the right contributors—people who have objective judgment, broad travel experience, and the writing ability to put their insights into words. There's no substitute for advice from a like-minded friend who has just come back from where you're going, but our writers, having seen all corners of China, are the next best thing. They're the kind of people you'd poll for tips yourself if you knew them.

Laurel Back has traveled and lived in more than 30 countries around the world. While working on her Masters, Laurel decided to tackle a Cultural Study of China. Laurel has now traveled twice to China and has participated in many cultural orientations with Chinese exchange students. She updated the Smart Travel Tips for the book.

Journalist and Hong Kong native **Denise Cheung** has written for a number of publications, including the *South China Morning Post* and *HK* magazine. She updated the dining section of the Hong Kong chapter.

Born in Hong Kong and raised in Australia, **Eva Chui** returned to her birthplace in 1995. She reported on the city's arts and popular-culture scenes as the entertainment editor for *HK* magzine and spent three years as a producer for Channel , Asia's No. 1 music-TV station. Currently, she divides her time between writing and working in the television and film industries in Hong Kong.

Paul Davidson updated the Shanghai, Eastern China, and Southwest China chapters. He currently lives in Yokohama, Japan.

Grace Fan, a graduate of Harvard University, has worked in China for four years, writing articles for *The New York Times, The Wall Street Journal, The Asian Wall Street Journal,* and *Gourmet* among other publications. In the interim, she updated the Northwest China and Mongolias chapters.

A native of Baoding, **Dr. Ke Ming Liu** is a graduate of the prestigious East China Normal University in Shanghai as well as Columbia University's Teacher College. She is a professor of linguistics at the City University of New York. She updated the Beijing and South Central China chapters.

Tobias Parker, who updated the Lodging section of the Hong Kong chapter for this edition, arrived in Hong Kong in 1996. He is the content manager for the Hong Kong Tourism Board's Web site.

George Vaughton, freelance writer, student of sinology and passionate traveler, updated the Northwestern and North Central chapters. He contributes articles to publications in Hong Kong as well as in Beijing, where he has lived since 1999.

Lara Wozniak is a U.S. lawyer and a Hong Kong-based associate editor at the *Far Eastern Economic Review,* a Dow Jones weekly magazine. She updated the Southeastern China chapter and the Hong Kong A to Z.

Don't Forget to Write

Your experiences—positive and negative—matter to us. If we have missed or misstated something, we want to hear about it. We follow up on all suggestions. Contact the China editor at editors@fodors.com or c/o Fodor's, 280 Park Avenue, New York, New York 10017. And have a fabulous trip!

Karen Cure
Editorial Director

China

RUSSIA

KAZAKHSTAN

ALTAI MTS.

MON

KIRGHIZSTAN

TIEN SHAN

TARIM BASIN

Ürümqi

XINJIANG

TAKLA MAKAN

GANSU

TAJIKISTAN

AFGHANISTAN

KUNLUN SHAN

QINGHAI

Xining

[JAMMU AND KASHMIR]

PLATEAU OF TIBET

H I M A L A Y A S

TIBET

SIC

Yarlung Zangbo

Lhasa
(Brahmaputra)

Nu (Salween)

Lancang

NEPAL

BHUTAN

(Mekong)

Kunming

BANGLA-DESH

YUNNA

INDIA

MYANMAR
(BURMA)

Bay of Bengal

THAILAND

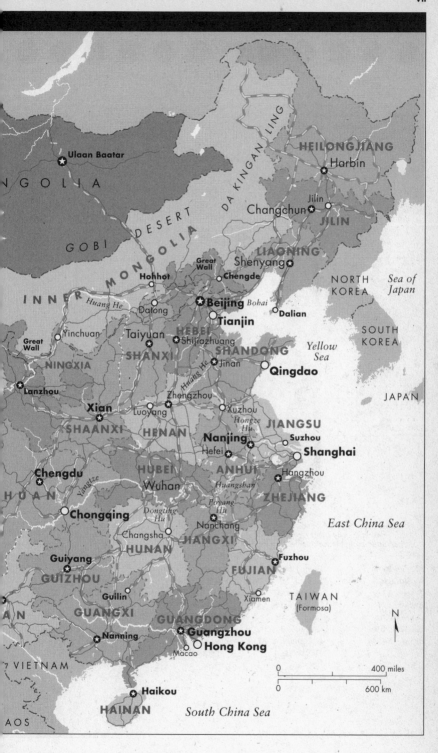

World Time Zones

Numbers below vertical bands relate each zone to Greenwich Mean Time (0 hrs.).
Local times frequently differ from these general indications,
as indicated by light-face numbers on map.

+11   +12 -   -11   -10   -9   -8   -7   -6   -5   -4   -3   -2

Algiers, **29**
Anchorage, **3**
Athens, **41**
Auckland, **1**
Baghdad, **46**
Bangkok, **50**
Beijing, **54**

Berlin, **34**
Bogotá, **19**
Budapest, **37**
Buenos Aires, **24**
Caracas, **22**
Chicago, **9**
Copenhagen, **33**
Dallas, **10**

Delhi, **48**
Denver, **8**
Dublin, **26**
Edmonton, **7**
Hong Kong, **56**
Honolulu, **2**
Istanbul, **40**
Jakarta, **53**

Jerusalem, **42**
Johannesburg, **44**
Lima, **20**
Lisbon, **28**
London
(Greenwich), **27**
Los Angeles, **6**
Madrid, **38**
Manila, **57**

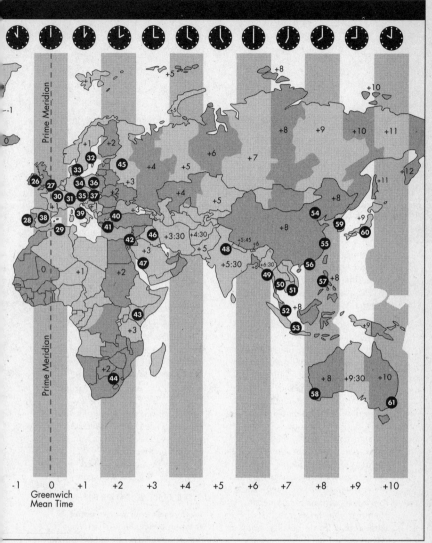

Mecca, **47**

Mexico City, **12**

Miami, **18**

Montréal, **15**

Moscow, **45**

Nairobi, **43**

New Orleans, **11**

New York City, **16**

Ottawa, **14**

Paris, **30**

Perth, **58**

Reykjavík, **25**

Rio de Janeiro, **23**

Rome, **39**

Saigon (Ho Chi Minh City), **51**

San Francisco, **5**

Santiago, **21**

Seoul, **59**

Shanghai, **55**

Singapore, **52**

Stockholm, **32**

Sydney, **61**

Tokyo, **60**

Toronto, **13**

Vancouver, **4**

Vienna, **35**

Warsaw, **36**

Washington, D.C., **17**

Yangon, **49**

Zürich, **31**

ESSENTIAL INFORMATION

AIR TRAVEL

Within mainland China all carriers are regional subsidiaries of the **Civil Aviation Administration of China** (CAAC). Reservations and ticket purchases can be made in the United States through the **U.S.-China Travel Service,** which has offices in Los Angeles and San Francisco; in Hong Kong at the **China National Aviation Corporation office** or **Air-China Travel Ltd.;** or in China through local **China International Travel Service** (CITS) offices(☞ *Individual city and regional chapters for addresses*).

The service on China's regional carriers has improved somewhat since the national airline, CAAC, was broken up into regional carriers. Flying, however, is still more expensive in China than it is in the United States. Flights between major cities generally offer first-class or business-class seating. The food is at best unremarkable. You can ask for vegetarian meals, but don't count on getting what you ordered. Generally, the best that can be said is that they get you where you're going. You can make reservations for domestic flights at your hotel travel desk, but some routes fill up quickly; book in advance.

➤ RESERVATIONS: **U.S.-China Travel Service** (U.S.: ☎ 800/332–2831 in the U.S.; Hong Kong: ✉ 34th floor, United Centre; 95 Queensway; Admiralty, Hong Kong, ☎ 852/2861–0288). **Air-China Travel Ltd.** (✉ Room 1604, Wheelock House, 20 Pedder St., Central, Hong Kong, ☎ 852/2801–9111).

BOOKING

When you book **look for nonstop flights** and **remember that "direct" flights stop at least once.** Try to avoid connecting flights, which require a change of plane. For more booking tips and to check prices and make on-line flight reservations, log on to www.fodors.com.

CARRIERS

Asiana flies to Beijing and Shanghai via Seoul on a local carrier. Air Canada has daily nonstop service between Shanghai and Vancouver. China Airlines goes to Beijing and Shanghai via Hong Kong on a local carrier. Korean Air flies to Beijing via Seoul. Northwest and United both fly to Beijing. Various Asian national airlines also fly to Hong Kong, Beijing, and Shanghai via their capital cities, usually at reasonable rates. China Eastern flies to Beijing and Shanghai.

➤ MAJOR AIRLINES: **Air Canada** (☎ 888/247–2262, WEB www.aircanada.ca). **Asiana** (☎ 800/227–4262, WEB www.flyasia.com). **China Airlines** (☎ 800/227–5118), WEB www.china-airlines.com. **China Eastern** (☎ 818/583–1500). **Korean Air** (☎ 800/438–5000, WEB www.koreanair.com). **Northwest** (☎ 800/225–2525, WEB www.nwa.com). **United** (☎ 800/241–6522, WEB www.ual.com).

CHECK-IN & BOARDING

Always **ask your carrier about its check-in policy.** Plan to arrive at the airport about two hours before your scheduled departure time for domestic flights and 2½ to 3 hours before international flights.

Assuming that not everyone with a ticket will show up, airlines routinely overbook planes. When everyone does, airlines ask for volunteers to give up their seats. In return, these volunteers usually get a certificate for a free flight and are rebooked on the next flight out. If there are not enough volunteers, the airline must choose who will be denied boarding. The first to get bumped are passengers who checked in late and those flying on discounted tickets, so **get to** the gate and check in as early as possible, especially during peak periods.

Always bring a government-issued photo I.D. to the airport; even when it's not required, a passport is best.

CUTTING COSTS

The least expensive airfares to China must usually be purchased in advance and are nonrefundable. It's smart to call a number of airlines, and when you are quoted a good price, book it on the spot—the same fare may not be available the next day. Always check different routings and look into using different airports. Travel agents, especially low-fare specialists (☞ Discounts & Deals, below), are helpful.

Consolidators are another good source. They buy tickets for scheduled international flights at reduced rates from the airlines, then sell them at prices that beat the best fare available directly from the airlines, usually without restrictions. Sometimes you can even get your money back if you need to return the ticket. Carefully read the fine print detailing penalties for changes and cancellations, and confirm your consolidator reservation with the airline.

➤ CONSOLIDATORS: Cheap Airlines (☎ 800/852-2608, WEB www. cheapairlines.com). Cheap Tickets (☎ 800/377-1000, WEB www. cheaptickets.com). Discount Airline Ticket Service (☎ 800/576-1600). Economy Travel (☎ 888/222-2110, WEB www.economytravel.com). Travelocity (☎ 877/811-9982, WEB www. travelocity.com). Unitravel (☎ 800/ 325-2222). Up & Away Travel (☎ 212/889-2345).World Travel Network (☎ 800/409-6753).

ENJOYING THE FLIGHT

For more legroom, request an emergency-aisle seat. Don't sit in the row in front of the emergency aisle or in front of a bulkhead, where seats may not recline. If you have dietary concerns, ask for special meals when booking. These can be vegetarian, low-cholesterol, or kosher, for example. On long flights, try to maintain a normal routine, to help fight jet lag. At night, get some sleep. By day, eat light meals, drink water

(not alcohol), and move around the cabin to stretch your legs. For additional jet-lag tips consult Fodor's FYI: Travel Fit & Healthy (available at bookstores everywhere).

If you're flying on local carriers while traveling within China, be prepared for less leg room and smaller seats.

FLYING TIMES

The flying time to Hong Kong or Beijing is between 20 and 24 hours from New York, including a stopover on the West Coast or in Tokyo; from 17 to 20 hours from Chicago; and 13 hours direct from Los Angeles or San Francisco.

HOW TO COMPLAIN

If your baggage goes astray or your flight goes awry, complain right away. Most carriers require that you file a claim immediately.

➤ AIRLINE COMPLAINTS: U.S. Department of Transportation Aviation Consumer Protection Division (✉ C-75, Room 4107, Washington, DC 20590, ☎ 202/366-2220, WEB www. dot.gov/airconsumer). Federal Aviation Administration Consumer Hotline (☎ 800/322-7873).

AIRPORTS

China's major airports are Beijing Airport, Hong Kong International Airport (known as Chek Lap Kok), and Shanghai Hongqiao International Airport. There is also a new international airport in Guilin.

➤ AIRPORT INFORMATION: Beijing Capital International Airport (☎ 010/ 6456-3604). Hong Kong International Airport (☎ 852/2181-0000). Shanghai Hongqiao International Airport (☎ 021/2153-7764). Guilin International Airport (☎ 077/3384-3922).

BIKE TRAVEL

Travel by bike is popular around Guilin in Guangxi province and in major cities. Biking around China independently is not a good idea, as foreigners are not permitted in many cities and can be penalized by police for trespassing. Biking within and around the cities is fine, as long as you don't mind maneuvering among the crowds of pedestrians, motorists, and other bicyclists. Large cities have wide bike lanes that are separate from regular traffic, which makes bike riding more convenient and safer.

In some cities, bikes can be rented just about everywhere, although your hotel and CITS are usually the best places to rent/inquire. When renting, you must show ID and pay a deposit. It's also prudent to **park your bike at guarded parking spaces** to avoid theft. Bike-repair shops are common. The U.S. company Backroads arranges bike tours in Guangxi and other parts of China.

➤ TOUR OPERATOR: **Backroads** (✉ 801 Cedar St., Berkeley, CA 94710-1800, ☎ 800/462–2848, WEB www. backroads.com).

BIKES IN FLIGHT

Most airlines accommodate bikes as luggage, provided they are dismantled and boxed. Airlines sell bike boxes, which are often free at bike shops, for about $5 (it's at least $100 for bike bags). International travelers can sometimes substitute a bike for a piece of checked luggage at no charge; otherwise, the cost is about $100. Domestic and Canadian airlines charge $25–$50.

BOAT & FERRY TRAVEL

Boat travel is relatively comfortable in China as well as a magnificent means of viewing the countryside, although the bathrooms leave much to be desired. For longer trips, first-class cabins with private bath/shower are available on Chinese boats and mandatory on luxury cruises. Larger boats are also equipped with viewing decks, large cabin windows, and restaurants that serve decent cuisine.

BUS TRAVEL

Long-distance bus travel can be a comfortable and economical means of transport in China, though bus drivers often don't speak English. Depending on the route, roads can be smooth or bumpy, and detours may take you over rocky terrain where roads don't even exist. You may be charged for insurance on more dangerous, mountainous routes. The more expensive bus companies, such as INTAC, are usually safer because drivers are held accountable for accidents by the government. If safety and comfort are a concern, **ask your hotel travel agent or CITS about the reputation of the bus company.** Most buses are equipped with a television (with programs in Chinese, of course). On long trips, drivers stop at concession stands where you can buy food and drink and use the bathroom.

CITS or your hotel can arrange bus tickets and provide bus schedules. You can also buy tickets in advance from the bus station. Unfortunately, bus stations only have schedules in Chinese and rarely have English-speaking staff. Many hotels now have shuttle buses for transport to and from the airport and downtown locations. There are public buses in every city, to almost every destination, usually for about Y1. However, unless you speak Mandarin, you're likely to get lost. If you decide to try it anyway, ask someone at your hotel which one to take to your destination.

➤ BUS INFORMATION: **CITS** in any city. **Hong Kong Tourist Association** (HKTA) information hot line (☎ 852/ 2807–6177).

BUSINESS HOURS

All businesses are closed on Chinese New Year and other major holidays.

BANKS & OFFICES

Banks, offices, government departments, and police stations (known as Public Security Bureaus, or PSBs) are open Monday–Saturday. Most open between 8 AM and 9 AM, close for lunch from noon to 2, and reopen until 5 or 6. Many branches of the Bank of China, China International Travel Service (CITS), and stores catering to foreigners are open Sunday morning. Some close on Wednesday afternoon.

MUSEUMS & SIGHTS

Museums are open 9 to 4 six days a week. They're usually closed on Monday.

SHOPS

Stores throughout China are generally open daily from 9 AM to 7 PM; those in touristy areas may stay open until 9 PM. Stores in Hong Kong generally open at 10. Outside Central, some shops stay open until 7:30 PM or 9:30 PM. Most are open on Sunday. Restaurants are usually open until 10 or 11.

CAMERAS & PHOTOGRAPHY

The Chinese love cameras and will be glad to take your picture—some may even want to be in them. However, you should always **ask before taking pictures of people.** Remember that at some sites, like the terra-cotta soldiers in Xian, photography is not allowed, and you risk a fine and/or camera seizure if you try to sneak a photo.

The *Kodak Guide to Shooting Great Travel Pictures* (available at bookstores everywhere) is loaded with tips.
➤ PHOTO HELP: **Kodak Information Center** (☎ 800/242–2424).

CUSTOMS

Before departing, **register your foreign-made camera or laptop with U.S. Customs** (☞ Customs & Duties). If your equipment is U.S.-made, call the consulate of the country you'll be visiting to find out whether the device should be registered with local customs upon arrival.

EQUIPMENT PRECAUTIONS

Don't pack film and equipment in checked luggage, where it is much more susceptible to damage. X-ray machines used to view checked luggage are becoming much more powerful and therefore are much more likely to ruin your film. Always **keep film and tape out of the sun.** Carry an extra supply of batteries, and **be prepared to turn on your camera or camcorder** to prove to security personnel that the device is real. Always **ask for hand inspection of film,** which becomes clouded after repeated exposure to airport X-ray machines, and **keep videotapes away from metal detectors.**

FILM & DEVELOPING

Kodak and Fuji film are available in China at reasonable prices. Film developing is also reasonable, although the quality tends to be inferior to that of American or European film developing agencies. Larger cities tend to offer higher-quality work—and one-hour film developing.

CAR RENTAL

Car rentals are not recommended and generally not available in China. Some local rentals are now possible in Beijing and Shanghai, but only for driving within the city (international tourists are forbidden from driving between most cities). It's better to hire a car with a driver for the day, and the costs in most Chinese cities are reasonable; depending on your travel needs, it's generally less expensive than renting a car. Given the dangers of driving in China (some would say it's only just short of suicidal), this is the most logical choice. In China check with your hotel concierge or local CITS office about hiring a car.

In Hong Kong the only major car rental companies are Avis and Hertz. Rates begin at $100 a day (which includes insurance) and $400 a week for an economy car with unlimited mileage.
➤ MAJOR AGENCIES: **Avis** (☎ 800/331–1084; 800/879–2847 in Canada; 02/9353–9000 in Australia; 09/525–1982 in New Zealand; 0870/606–0100 in the U.K., WEB www.avis.com). **Hertz** (☎ 800/654–3001; 800/263–0600 in Canada; 020/8897–2072 in the U.K.; 02/9669–2444 in Australia; 09/256–8690 in New Zealand, WEB www.hertz.com).

INSURANCE

When driving a rented car you are generally responsible for any damage to or loss of the vehicle as well as for any property damage or personal injury that you may cause. Before you rent, see what coverage your personal auto-insurance policy and credit cards provide.

REQUIREMENTS & RESTRICTIONS

In China your own driver's license is not acceptable. An International Driver's Permit is available from the American or Canadian Automobile Association, or in the United Kingdom, from the Automobile Association or the Royal Automobile Club.

SURCHARGES

Before you pick up a car in one city and leave it in another, **ask about drop-off charges or one-way service**

fees, which can be substantial. Note, too, that some rental agencies charge extra if you return the car before the time specified in your contract. To avoid a hefty refueling fee, **fill the tank just before you turn in the car,** but be aware that gas stations near the rental outlet may overcharge.

CAR TRAVEL

With the exception of Hong Kong, car travel in China, even when you're in the passenger seat, can be frightening. Cars speed to pass one another on one-lane roads, constantly blaring their horns. Taxis and pedicabs pass within inches of each other at intersections. Lanes and traffic rules seem ambiguous to those not accustomed to the Chinese style of driving. In larger cities, however, taxi driver identification numbers can be used to report bad behavior or bad driving, and thus tend to inspire more care. Many taxi drivers are also held liable for the condition of their vehicles, so they are less likely to take dangerous risks.

ROAD CONDITIONS

Road conditions in China, especially in the cities, are usually fine, and the construction of highways and expressways has done much to improve the efficiency and comfort of driving in China. In more rural areas, however, especially in the mountains of western China and the deserts of northwest China, roads can be very poor, narrow, and dangerous. Be sure to look into the conditions of roads before setting off.

RULES OF THE ROAD

Driving is on the right in mainland China. Traffic lights can be sparse but are obeyed. Road signs are also sparse except in cities. Traffic in the cities can move slowly, but pay attention nonetheless. Many street signs are in pinyin as well as Chinese characters. In Hong Kong, in British fashion, people drive on the left. Road signs are in English or pinyin, and speed limits are enforced.

CHILDREN IN CHINA

Cities have parks, zoos, and frequent performances involving acrobats, jugglers, and puppets. Most large international hotels in Hong Kong, Beijing, and Shanghai have baby-sitting services and may even offer special activities, though services may not be on a level with those in the West. In addition, travel can be rugged, familiar foods hard to find, and there are health risks and sanitation problems. It's not advisable to take children on trips outside the major cities.

Check with the CITS office in most cities for activities or tours. In Hong Kong check with the HKTA (☞ Visitor Information) for scheduled activities for children. *The Great Hong Kong Dragon Adventure,* an illustrated book about a dragon that flies children from place to place, is available at HKTA Visitor Information Centers.

For general advice about traveling with children, consult *Fodor's FYI: Travel with Your Baby* (available in bookstores everywhere).

FLYING

If your children are two or older, **ask about children's airfares.** As a general rule, infants under 2 not occupying a seat fly at greatly reduced fares or even for free. When booking, **confirm carry-on allowances** if you're traveling with infants. In general, for babies charged 10% of the adult fare you are allowed one carry-on bag and a collapsible stroller; if the flight is full, the stroller may have to be checked or you may be limited to less.

Experts agree that it's a good idea to use safety seats aloft for children weighing less than 40 pounds. Airlines set their own policies: U.S. carriers usually require that the child be ticketed, even if he or she is young enough to ride free, since the seats must be strapped into regular seats. Do **check your airline's policy about using safety seats during takeoff and landing.** And since safety seats are not allowed everywhere in the plane, get your seat assignments early.

When reserving, **request children's meals or a freestanding bassinet** if you need them. But note that bulkhead seats, where you must sit to use the bassinet, may lack an overhead bin or storage space on the floor.

LODGING

Most hotels in China allow children under a certain age to stay in their parents' room at no extra charge, but others charge for them as extra adults; be sure to **find out the cutoff age for children's discounts.**

PRECAUTIONS

If you're traveling with a child, be sure to take a generous supply of Pepto Bismol tablets, antibiotics such as Cipro, rehydration salts for diarrhea, motion sickness tablets, Tylenol, and vitamins. Children, like adults, will need some time to adjust to China's food, so be sure all food is thoroughly cooked. Boiled water is fine for children to drink; soybean milk, juices, and mineral water are also available.

SIGHTS & ATTRACTIONS

Places that are especially appealing to children are indicated by a rubber-duckie icon (🐤) in the margin.

COMPUTERS ON THE ROAD

Most hotels that serve foreigners allow modem hook-up from your room; you can usually access the Internet from computers in the hotel's business center as well (be prepared for very slow dial-ups). Bring a surge protector and a 220-volt adapter. While some outlets accept American plugs, it's a good idea to **carry several types of adapters** in case the Asian one (with diagonal prongs slanting inward) doesn't fit. Chinese sockets come in several different configurations.

CONSUMER PROTECTION

Whenever shopping or buying travel services in China, **pay with a major credit card,** if possible, so you can cancel payment or get reimbursed if there's a problem. If you're doing business with a particular company for the first time, **contact your local Better Business Bureau and the attorney general's offices** in your state and (for U.S. businesses) the company's home state as well. Have any complaints been filed? Finally, if you're buying a package or tour, always **consider travel insurance** that includes default coverage (☞ Insurance, *below*).

➤ BBBs: **Council of Better Business Bureaus** (✉ 4200 Wilson Blvd., Suite 800, Arlington, VA 22203, ☎ 703/276-0100, FAX 703/525-8277, WEB www.bbb.org).

CRUISE TRAVEL

Although cruises are cheaper in China, the boats are not always up to American luxury standards. Overbooking can also take away from your experience. The CITS in Wuhan can provide you with a list of 4- and 5-star ship models for Yangzi Three Gorges cruises. There are also U.S. companies that offer cruises in China as part of a package.

➤ CRUISE OPERATORS: **University Educational Inc.** (✉ 1985 Yosemite Ave., Suite 235, Simi Valley, California, 93063, ☎ 805/527-3748 or 800/525-0525, FAX 805/527-4219, WEB www.uet.com. **Chn-Asia Express Tours** (✉ 22 Main St., South River, NJ 08882, ☎ 732/432-9855 or 800/824-9965, FAX 732/432-7545).

CUSTOMS & DUTIES

When shopping, **keep receipts** for all purchases. Upon reentering the country, **be ready to show customs officials what you've bought.** If you feel a duty is incorrect or object to the way your clearance was handled, note the inspector's badge number and ask to see a supervisor. If the problem isn't resolved, write to the appropriate authorities, beginning with the port director at your point of entry.

IN AUSTRALIA

Australian residents who are 18 or older may bring home $A400 worth of souvenirs and gifts (including jewelry), 250 cigarettes or 250 grams of tobacco, and 1,125 ml of alcohol (including wine, beer, and spirits). Residents under 18 may bring back $A200 worth of goods. Prohibited items include meat products. Seeds, plants, and fruits need to be declared upon arrival.

➤ INFORMATION: **Australian Customs Service** (Regional Director, ✉ Box 8, Sydney, NSW 2001, Australia, ☎ 02/9213-2000, FAX 02/9213-4000, WEB www.customs.gov.au).

IN CANADA

Canadian residents who have been out of Canada for at least seven days may bring home C$750 worth of goods duty-free. If you've been away fewer than seven days but more than 48 hours, the duty-free allowance drops to C$200; if your trip lasts 24–48 hours, the allowance is C$50. You may not pool allowances with family members. Goods claimed under the C$750 exemption may follow you by mail; those claimed under the lesser exemptions must accompany you. Alcohol and tobacco products may be included in the seven-day and 48-hour exemptions but not in the 24-hour exemption. If you meet the age requirements of the province or territory through which you reenter Canada, you may bring in, duty-free, 1.14 liters (40 imperial ounces) of wine or liquor *or* 24 12-ounce cans or bottles of beer or ale. If you are 19 or older you may bring in, duty-free, 200 cigarettes and 50 cigars. Check ahead of time with the Canada Customs Revenue Agency or the Department of Agriculture for policies regarding meat products, seeds, plants, and fruits.

You may send an unlimited number of gifts worth up to C$60 each duty-free to Canada. Label the package UNSOLICITED GIFT—VALUE UNDER $60. Alcohol and tobacco are excluded.

➤ INFORMATION: **Canada Customs Revenue Agency** (✉ 2265 St. Laurent Blvd. S, Ottawa, Ontario K1G 4K3, Canada, ☎ 204/983–3500 or 506/636–5064; 800/461–9999 in Canada, WEB www.ccra-adrc.gc.ca).

IN CHINA

You will receive a short customs form either in the airplane or in the terminal on landing. Foreign currency for personal use has no restrictions. You are not allowed to bring in live animals, fresh produce, or printed matter deemed seditious or pornographic. The former is very broadly defined, of course, and would include anything that criticizes the Chinese government. They do not usually inspect your personal baggage for improper reading matter, but it could happen. It's best, for example, not to bring a book by a Chinese dissident with you. Customs inspection is usually fast and painless, unless of course you're suspected of bringing in the above-mentioned items.

On leaving, you are not allowed to take out of China antiques more than 150 years old and deemed valuable to the country.

IN NEW ZEALAND

Homeward-bound residents 17 or older may bring back $700 worth of souvenirs and gifts. Your duty-free allowance also includes 4.5 liters of wine or beer; one 1,125-ml bottle of spirits; and either 200 cigarettes, 250 grams of tobacco, 50 cigars, or a combination of the three up to 250 grams. Prohibited items include meat products, seeds, plants, and fruits.

➤ INFORMATION: **New Zealand Customs** (Custom House, ✉ 50 Anzac Ave., Box 29, Auckland, New Zealand, ☎ 09/300–5399, FAX 09/359–6730), WEB www.customs.govt.nz.

IN THE U.K.

From countries outside the European Union, including China, you may bring home, duty-free, 200 cigarettes or 50 cigars; 1 liter of spirits or 2 liters of fortified or sparkling wine or liqueurs; 2 liters of still table wine; 60 ml of perfume; 250 ml of toilet water; plus £145 worth of other goods, including gifts and souvenirs. If returning from outside the EU, prohibited items include meat products, seeds, plants, and fruits.

➤ INFORMATION: **HM Customs and Excise** (✉ Dorset House, Stamford St., Bromley, Kent BR1 1XX, U.K., ☎ 020/7202–4227, WEB www.hmce.gov.uk).

IN THE U.S.

U.S. residents who have been out of the country for at least 48 hours (and who have not used the $400 allowance or any part of it in the past 30 days) may bring home $400 worth of foreign goods duty-free.

U.S. residents 21 and older may bring back 1 liter of alcohol duty-free. In addition, regardless of your age, you are allowed 200 cigarettes and 100 non-Cuban cigars. Antiques, which the U.S. Customs Service defines as objects more than 100 years old, enter duty-free, as do original works of art done entirely by hand, including paintings, drawings, and sculptures.

You may also mail or ship packages home duty-free: up to $200 worth of goods for personal use, with a limit of one parcel per addressee per day (except alcohol or tobacco products or perfume worth more than $5); label the package PERSONAL USE and attach a list of its contents and their retail value. Do not label the package UNSOLICITED GIFT or your duty-free exemption will drop to $100. Mailed items do not affect your duty-free allowance on your return.

➤ INFORMATION: **U.S. Customs Service** (✉ 1300 Pennsylvania Ave. NW, Room 6.3D, Washington, DC 20229, WEB www.customs.gov; inquiries ☎ 202/354–1000; complaints c/o ✉ 1300 Pennsylvania Ave. NW, Room 5.4D, Washington, DC 20229; registration of equipment c/o Office of Passenger Programs, ☎ 202/927–0530).

DINING

In China, chopsticks are the utensil of choice. Be aware that the Chinese like to eat family style, with everyone sitting at a round table (which symbolizes union and perfection), burrowing their chopsticks into a common dish. It's considered bad manners to point or play with your chopsticks, or to place them on top of your rice bowl when you're finished eating (place the chopsticks horizontally on the table or plate). It is appropriate, however, to shovel rice into your mouth, to talk with your mouth full, and to stand up to reach for food across the table from you. Don't hesitate to spit bones directly onto the table: putting your fingers in your mouth is bad manners.

If you're invited to a formal Chinese meal, be prepared for great ceremony, many toasts and speeches, and a grand variety of elaborate dishes. Your host will be seated at the "head" of the round table, which is the seat that faces the door; it's differentiated from the other seats by a napkin shaped as a crown. The highest guest of honor will be seated to the host's right, the second highest guest of honor to the host's left. Don't start eating until the host takes the first bite, and then simply serve yourself as the food comes around. Be sure to **always let the food touch your plate before bringing it up to your mouth;** eating directly from the serving dish without briefly resting the food on your plate is considered bad form. It is an honor to be served by the person sitting next to you (though as a guest, you are not expected to do the same).

MEALS & SPECIALTIES

An old saying in China is "food is the first necessity of the people." Color, smell, taste, shape, sound, and serving vessel are all important aspects of the food being served. Vegetables are the main ingredients. Chinese food can be loosely divided into Northern and Southern styles. Food in northern China is based on wheat products and is often quite oily, with liberal amounts of vinegar and other flavorful spices such as garlic. Meat and vegetable dumplings, noodles, and filled buns are common. The cuisine in southern China is known for its use of fresh ingredients and liberal dosing of hot spices; remember you can always request a dish to be more or less spicy. Rice and rice by-products form the foundation of meals. Do **try as many different kinds of foods as you can;** food is an integral part of Chinese culture. If you're craving Western food, look for American fast-food chains in the major cities. Most higher-end restaurants have a "Western menu," but don't expect it to taste like the food back home.

The restaurants we list in this book are the cream of the crop in each price category.

MEALTIMES

Lunch in China is usually served in restaurants between 11 and 2, dinner from 5 to 10. Unless otherwise noted, the restaurants listed in this guide are open daily for lunch and dinner.

DISABILITIES & ACCESSIBILITY

There are few special facilities for people with disabilities, except in five-star hotels. Public toilets may be particularly problematic, as most are of the type you squat over, and buses, which are generally crowded, will be difficult to board. In most restaurants, museums, and other public spaces, people will be helpful and respectful to visitors with disabilities.

The Hong Kong Tourist Association has *A Guide for Physically Handicapped Visitors in Hong Kong*, which lists places with special facilities for people with disabilities and the best access to hotels, shopping centers, government offices, consulates, restaurants, and churches.

RESERVATIONS

When discussing accessibility with an operator or reservations agent, **ask hard questions.** Are there any stairs, inside *or* out? Are there grab bars next to the toilet *and* in the shower/tub? How wide is the doorway to the room? To the bathroom? For the most extensive facilities meeting the latest legal specifications, **opt for newer accommodations.**

TRAVEL AGENCIES

In the United States, the Americans with Disabilities Act requires that travel firms serve the needs of all travelers. Some agencies specialize in working with people with disabilities.

➤ TRAVELERS WITH MOBILITY PROBLEMS: **Access Adventures** (✉ 206 Chestnut Ridge Rd., Scottsville, NY 14624, ☎ 716/889–9096), run by a former physical-rehabilitation counselor. **Flying Wheels Travel** (✉ 143 W. Bridge St., Box 382, Owatonna, MN 55060, ☎ 507/451–5005 or 800/535–6790, FAX 507/451–1685, WEB www.flyingwheelstravel.com).

DISCOUNTS & DEALS

Be a smart shopper and **compare all your options** before making decisions. A plane ticket bought with a promotional coupon from travel clubs, coupon books, and direct-mail offers or on the Internet may not be cheaper than the least expensive fare from a discount ticket agency. And always keep in mind that what you get is just as important as what you save.

DISCOUNT RESERVATIONS

To save money, **look into discount reservations services** with toll-free numbers, which use their buying power to get a better price on hotels, airline tickets, even car rentals. When booking a room, always **call the hotel's local toll-free number** (if one is available) rather than the central reservations number—you'll often get a better price. Always ask about special packages or corporate rates.

When shopping for the best deal on hotels and car rentals, **look for guaranteed exchange rates,** which protect you against a falling dollar. With your rate locked in, you won't pay more, even if the price goes up in the local currency.

➤ HOTEL ROOMS: **Players Express Vacations** (☎ 800/458–6161, WEB www.playersexpress.com). **Steigenberger Reservation Service** (☎ 800/223–5652, WEB www.srs-worldhotels.com). **Travel Interlink** (☎ 800/888–5898, WEB www.travelinterlink.com). **Turbotrip.com** (☎ 800/473–7829, WEB www.turbotrip.com). **VacationLand** (☎ 800/245–0050, WEB www.vacation-land.com).

PACKAGE DEALS

Don't confuse packages and guided tours. When you buy a package, you travel on your own, just as though you had planned the trip yourself. Fly/drive packages, which combine airfare and car rental, are often a good deal.

ELECTRICITY

To use your U.S.-purchased electric-powered equipment, **bring a converter and adapter** or buy one in the airport before you leave. The electrical current in China is 220 volts, 50 cycles alternating current (AC); wall outlets take American-style plugs, with two flat parallel prongs; however, they may not take the converter's one oversized prong, used for grounding, now in general use in the United States.

In Hong Kong wall outlets use British-style three-pronged plugs. Sizes and shapes vary, so it is best to buy special adapters there, which will fit two-pronged American appliances or adapters.

If your appliances are dual-voltage, you'll need only an adapter. Don't use 110-volt outlets marked FOR SHAVERS ONLY for high-wattage appliances such as blow-dryers. Most laptops operate equally well on 110 and 220 volts and so require only an adapter. You may also want to bring a power-surge protector.

Although blackouts are not common in Chinese cities, villages occasionally lose power for short periods of time.

EMBASSIES

➤ AUSTRALIA: **Embassy of Australia–Beijing** (✉ 21 Dongzhimenwai Dajie, Beijing 100600, ☎ 010/6532–2331, FAX 010/6532–6718). **Australian Consulate–Guangzhou** (✉ Room 1509, Main Building, GITIC Plaza, 339 Huanshi Dong Lu, Guangzhou 510098, ☎ 020/8335–0909, FAX 020/8335–0718). **Australian Consulate–Hong Kong** (✉ 23/F Harbour Centre, 25 Harbour Rd., Wanchai, ☎ 0852/2827–8881, FAX 0852/2827–6583). **Australian Consulate–Shanghai** (✉ Level 22, CITIC Square, 1168 Nanjing Xi Lu, Shanghai 200041, ☎ 021/5292–5500, FAX 021/5292–5511).

➤ CANADA: **Canadian Embassy–Beijing** (✉ 19 Dongzhionenwai Dajie, Chaoyang District, Beijing, ☎ 010/6532–3536, FAX 010/6532–4311). **Canadian Consulate–Chongqing** (✉ Room 1705, Metropolitan Tower, 68 Zou Rong Lu, Yu Zhong District, Chongqing, ☎ 023/6373–8007, FAX 023/6373–8026). **Canadian Consulate–Guangzhou** (✉ Suite 801, China Hotel Office Tower, Liu Hua Lu, Guangzhou, ☎ 020/8666–0569, FAX 020/8667–2401). **Canadian Consulate–Hong Kong** (✉ 11th–14th Floor, 1 Exchange Sq., 8 Connaught Pl., Hong Kong, ☎ 0852/810–4321, FAX 0852/2810–6736). **Canadian Consulate–Shanghai** (✉ Tower 4, Suite 604, Shanghai Center, 1376 Nanjing Xi Lu, Shanghai 200040, ☎ 021/6279–8400, FAX 021/6279–8401).

➤ NEW ZEALAND: **New Zealand Embassy–Beijing** (✉ 1 Donger Jie, Ritan Lu, Chayangqu, Beijing 100600, ☎ 010/6532–2731). **New Zealand Consulate–Shanghai** (✉ 15 A Qihua Building, 1375 Huaihai Zhong Lu, Shanghai, ☎ 021/6433–2230).

➤ UNITED KINGDOM: **British Embassy–Beijing** (✉ 11 Guang Hua Lu, Jian Guo Men Wai, Beijing 100600, ☎ 010/6532–1061, FAX 010/6532–1937). **British Consulate–Chongqing** (✉ Suite 2801 Metropolitan Tower, 68 Zourong Rd., Chongqing 40010, ☎ 023/6381–0321, FAX 023/6381–0322). **British Consulate–Guangzhou** (✉ 2nd Floor, Guangdong International Hotel, 339 Huanshi Donglu, Guangzhou 510098, ☎ 020/8335–1354, FAX 020/8335–1321). **British Consulate–Macau** (✉ No. 1 Supreme Court Rd., Box 523, Hong Kong, ☎ 0852/2901–3000, FAX 0852/2901–3066). **British Consulate–Shanghai** (✉ Suite 301, Shanghai Centre, 1376 Nanjiing Xilu, Shanghai 200040, ☎ 021/6279–7650, FAX 021/6279–7651).

➤ UNITED STATES: **American Embassy–Beijing** (✉ 3 Xiu Shui Bei Jie, Beijing 100600, ☎ 010/6532–3431). **American Consulate–Chengdu** (✉ No. 4 Lingshiguan Rd., Chengdu 610041, ☎ 028/558–3992, FAX 028/558–9221). **American Consulate–Guangzhou** (✉ 1 Shamian Nanjie, Shamian Island, Guangzhou 510133, ☎ 020/8188–8911, FAX 020/8186–4001). **American Consulate–Shanghai** (✉ 1469 Huaihai Road, Shanghai 200031, ☎ 021/6433–1681, FAX 021/6433–1576). **American Consulate–Shenyang** (✉ 52 Shi Si Wei Lu, Heping District, Shenyang 110003, ☎ 024/2322–1198, FAX 024/2322–2374).

EMERGENCIES

If you lose your passport, contact your embassy immediately. Embassy officials can advise you on how to proceed in case of other emergencies. Your hotel may also be able to provide a translator if you need to report an emergency or crime to doctors or the police.

ETIQUETTE & BEHAVIOR

Be respectful and try not to get upset if things go wrong, especially when reserving tickets and hotel rooms. Be friendly but stern if you are having difficulties—raising your voice and threatening will only embarrass you in front of the Chinese, who feel that "face" is extremely important. It helps to learn a few words of Chinese, even if all you can say is thank you (shee-yeh shee-yeh) and hello (nee how). If you are stared at, simply smile back or treat it humorously. Playing with chopsticks is a sign of bad manners. Bowing the head and pressing the hands together is a sign of deep gratitude. Handshaking is the common greeting, but don't shake women's hands too firmly. Try to keep an open mind about anything that seems initially appalling, whether it's dog meat or Chinese toilets. The Chinese are generally a gracious people who will reciprocate kindness.

Don't photograph Tibetans without their permission—it's considered rude and an affront to their culture.

GAY & LESBIAN TRAVEL

China is still a conservative country when it comes to outward displays of affection. Although it's not unusual to see Chinese couples walking arm-in-arm in the bigger cities, Western couples, whether heterosexual or homosexual, may want to refrain from even these mild gestures. Homosexuality is not illegal but is considered a perversion or mental illness or, at the very least, improper behavior. There is a growing underground gay scene in Shanghai and other major cities, but discretion is wise. In Hong Kong, *Contacts,* a magazine covering the local gay scene, is available for HK$35 at the boutique Fetish Fashion. Propaganda is the largest gay and lesbian bar in Hong Kong.

➤ LOCAL RESOURCES: **Fetish Fashion** (⌧ Merlin Building, 32 Cochrane St., Hong Kong, ☎ 852/2544–1155). **Propaganda** (⌧ Lower Ground Floor, 1 Hollywood Rd., Hong Kong, ☎ 852/2868–1316).

➤ GAY- & LESBIAN-FRIENDLY TRAVEL AGENCIES: **Different Roads Travel** (⌧ 8383 Wilshire Blvd., Suite 902, Beverly Hills, CA 90211, ☎ 323/651–5557 or 800/429–8747, FAX 323/651–3678). **Kennedy Travel** (⌧ 314 Jericho Turnpike, Floral Park, NY 11001, ☎ 516/352–4888 or 800/237–7433, FAX 516/354–8849, WEB www.kennedytravel.com). **Now Voyager** (⌧ 4406 18th St., San Francisco, CA 94114, ☎ 415/626–1169 or 800/255–6951, FAX 415/626–8626, WEB www.nowvoyager.com). **Skylink Travel and Tour** (⌧ 1006 Mendocino Ave., Santa Rosa, CA 95401, ☎ 707/546–9888 or 800/225–5759, FAX 707/546–9891, WEB www.skylinktravel.com), serving lesbian travelers.

HEALTH

In China you can find an English-speaking doctor in most major cities. The best place to start is with your hotel concierge, then the local Public Security Bureau. The major cities have modern hospitals, but if you become seriously ill or are injured, it is best to try to get flown home, or at least to Hong Kong, as quickly as possible. **Check for medical coverage with your health insurer before you go.**

In Hong Kong English-speaking doctors are widely available. Hotels have lists of accredited doctors and can arrange for a doctor to visit your hotel room. Otherwise, consult the nearest government hospital. Check the "Government" section of the business telephone directory under "Medical and Health Department" for a list.

Make sure you **take enough of any prescription medication for the duration of your stay.** You should also carry a copy of your prescription with you in case you lose your medicine or are stopped by customs officials. If you wear contact lenses, take a couple extra pairs along in case you lose or rip a lens. **Wear plenty of sunscreen and a good pair of sunglasses,** even during winter.

FOOD & DRINK

In China the major health risk is traveler's diarrhea, caused by eating contaminated fruit or vegetables or drinking contaminated water. So **watch what you eat.** Carry a small bottle of antibacterial hand sanitizer and wash your hands frequently. Stay away from ice, uncooked food, and unpasteurized milk and milk products, and **drink only bottled water** or water that has been boiled for at least 10 minutes. Bottled water is widely available in most major cities in China. If you're going to rural areas, bring water purification tablets. Mild cases of diarrhea may respond to Imodium (known generically as loperamide) or Pepto-Bismol (not as strong), both of which can be purchased over the counter; however, keep in mind that these may complicate more serious infections. **Do *not* buy prescription drugs in China** unless absolutely necessary, as the quality control is unreliable. Ask your doctor for an antidiarrheal prescription to take with you, to use in emergencies. Drink plenty of purified water or tea—chamomile is a good folk remedy—and be sure to rehydrate yourself with a salt-sugar solution (½ teaspoon salt and 4 tablespoons sugar per quart of water).

Pneumonia and influenza are also common among travelers returning from China; many health professionals recommend inoculations before you leave. Be sure you're well rested and healthy to start with.

According to the National Centers for Disease Control (CDC) there is a limited risk of hepatitis A and B, typhoid, polio, malaria, tuberculosis, dengue fever, tetanus, and rabies in small cities and rural areas. In most urban or easily accessible areas you need not worry. However, if you plan to visit remote regions or stay for more than six weeks, **check with the CDC's International Travelers Hotline.** In areas where malaria and dengue, both of which are carried by mosquitoes, are prevalent, use mosquito nets, wear clothing that covers the body, apply repellent containing DEET, and use spray for flying insects in living and sleeping areas. Also **consider taking antimalarial pills** if you'll be staying in rural areas in warm weather. There is no vaccine that combats dengue.

MEDICAL PLANS

No one plans to get sick while traveling, but it happens, so **consider signing up with a medical-assistance company.** Members get doctor referrals, emergency evacuation or repatriation, hot lines for medical consultation, cash for emergencies, and other assistance.

➤ MEDICAL-ASSISTANCE COMPANIES: **International SOS Assistance** (WEB www.internationalsos.com; ✉ 8 Neshaminy Interplex, Suite 207, Trevose, PA 19053, ☎ 215/245–4707 or 800/523–6586, FAX 215/244–9617; ✉ 12 Chemin Riantbosson, 1217 Meyrin 1, Geneva, Switzerland, ☎ 4122/785–6464, FAX 4122/785–6424; ✉ 331 N. Bridge Rd., 17-00, Odeon Towers, Singapore 188720, ☎ 65/338–7800, FAX 65/338–7611).

SHOTS & MEDICATIONS

While currently no vaccinations are required to travel to China, during the summer months malaria is a serious risk in tropical and rural areas, as well as along the Yangzi River. If you'll be staying in cities for the duration of your trip, the risk of contracting malaria is small.

➤ HEALTH WARNINGS: **National Centers for Disease Control and Prevention** (CDC; National Center for Infectious Diseases, Division of Quarantine, Traveler's Health Section, ✉ 1600 Clifton Rd. NE, M/S E-03, Atlanta, GA 30333, ☎ 888/232–3228 or 877/394–8747, FAX 888/232–3299, WEB www.cdc.gov).

HOLIDAYS

National holidays include January 1 (New Year's Day), two days in late February–early March (Chinese New Year, also called Spring Festival), March 8 (International Women's Day), May 1 (International Labor Day), May 4 (Youth Day), June 1 (Children's Day), July 1 (anniversary of the founding of the Communist Party of China; in Hong Kong, the anniversary of the establishment of the Special Administrative Region), August 1 (anniversary of the founding of the Chinese People's Liberation Army), and October 1 (National Day—founding of the Peoples Republic of China in 1949) (☞ Festivals and Seasonal Events *in* Chapter 1).

INSURANCE

The most useful travel-insurance plan is a comprehensive policy that includes coverage for trip cancellation and interruption, default, trip delay, and medical expenses (with a waiver for preexisting conditions).

Without insurance you will lose all or most of your money if you cancel your trip, regardless of the reason. Default insurance covers you if your tour operator, airline, or cruise line goes out of business. Trip-delay covers expenses that arise because of bad weather or mechanical delays. Study the fine print when comparing policies.

If you're traveling internationally, a key component of travel insurance is coverage for medical bills incurred if you get sick on the road. Such expenses are not generally covered by Medicare or private policies. U.K. residents can buy a travel-insurance policy valid for most vacations taken during the year in which it's purchased (but check preexisting-condition coverage).

Always **buy travel policies directly from the insurance company**; if you buy them from a cruise line, airline, or tour operator that goes out of business you probably will not be covered for the agency or operator's default, a major risk. Before making any purchase, **review your existing health and home-owner's policies** to find what they cover away from home.

➤ TRAVEL INSURERS: In the U.S.: **Access America** (✉ 6600 W. Broad St., Richmond, VA 23230, ☎ 800/284–8300, FAX 804/673–1491, WEB www.etravelprotection.com), **Travel Guard International** (✉ 1145 Clark St., Stevens Point, WI 54481, ☎ 715/345–0505 or 800/826–1300, FAX 800/955–8785, WEB www.noelgroup.com).

➤ INSURANCE INFORMATION: In the U.K.: **Association of British Insurers** (✉ 51–55 Gresham St., London EC2V 7HQ, U.K., ☎ 020/7600–3333, FAX 020/7696–8999, WEB www.abi.org.uk). In Canada: **RBC Travel Insurance** (✉ 6880 Financial Dr., Mississauga, Ontario L5N 7Y5, Canada, ☎ 905/791–8700, 800/668–4342 in Canada, FAX 905/816–2498, WEB www.royalbank.com). In Australia: **Insurance Council of Australia** (✉ Level 3, 56 Pitt St., Sydney NSW 2000, ☎ 02/9253–5100, FAX 02/9253–5111, WEB www.ica.com.au). In New Zealand: **Insurance Council of New Zealand** (✉ Box 474, Wellington, New Zealand, ☎ 04/472–5230, FAX 04/473–3011, WEB www.icnz.org.nz).

INTERNET

Although the Internet (*īntèrlái* in pinyin) is still a novel concept for most Chinese outside of metropolitan areas, cybercafés and other types of computer centers are quickly spreading, especially in the large cities. Due to government restrictions, many Chinese still find browsing limited, but many professional Chinese these days do have E-mail addresses. Most major hotels in China have access to the Internet through their business centers, and some even allow you to use it from your room, provided your computer is equipped with the proper tools (modem, 220-volt adapter, Web browser, etc.) Be prepared for very slow dial-ups, and inquire about cost in cybercafés before going on-line.

Consider signing up for a free Internet-based E-mail account before you go.

LANGUAGE

The national language of China is Mandarin, known in China as Putonghua (*pǔtōnghuà*), "common language." Nearly everyone speaks Mandarin, but many also speak local dialects, some of which use the same characters as Mandarin with a very different pronunciation. In Hong Kong the main spoken language is Cantonese, although most people speak English.

All of the Chinese languages are tonal; there are four possible tones for every syllable, in addition to the basic sound of the syllable, and they make up part of a word's pronunciation. Each syllable has a different meaning depending on the pitch or musical inflection the speaker gives it. For example, in Mandarin the syllable *ma* can mean mother, horse, curse, or hemp plant—or, it can be a particle denoting a question—depending on the tone used. Thus, the sentence "Ma ma ma ma" translates as "does mother curse the horse?," a classic example of the complexity of the tonal Chinese language. Additionally, many Chinese characters are *homonyms*, which makes it difficult if not impossible for the foreign ear to understand what is being said. Since 1949 the government has revamped the teaching of Mandarin, introducing a simplified phonetic system known as pinyin, which uses the Roman alphabet to denote the pronunciations of the myriad Chinese characters (pinyin is taught alongside, and not instead of, ideograms). Names of sites in this book are given in pinyin with English translations, and lists of Chinese place names in the chapters provide the names of recommended sites in Chinese characters.

Although Chinese grammar is simple, it is still difficult for foreigners to speak Chinese and even harder to be understood. However, the Chinese will appreciate your making the effort to speak a few phrases understood almost everywhere. Try "Hello"— "*Ní hǎo*" (nee how); "Thank you"— "*Xiè xiè*" (shee-yeh, shee-yeh); and "Good-bye"—"*Zai jian*" (dzigh djyan). When pronouncing words written in pinyin, remember that "q" and "x" are pronounced like "ch" and "sh," respectively; "zh" is pronounced like the "j" in "just"; "c" is pronounced like "ts."

You can usually find someone who speaks English in the major cities. There are English signs almost everywhere in Hong Kong, but these are rare in the rest of China (with the exception of the Beijing subway). Fortunately, almost all cities have street signs written in pinyin. It can be difficult to get around China on your own without speaking the language. If you are not planning to go with a tour group, you can go from city to city and hire a local English-speaking guide from the CTS office at each stop.

➤ LANGUAGE RESOURCE: *I Can Read That! A Traveler's Introduction to Chinese Characters,* by Julie Mazel Sussman, China Books and Periodicals, Inc. (☎ 415/282–2994, FAX 415/ 282–0994, WEB www.chinabooks. com). *In the Know in China,* by Jennifer Phillips, Living Language/ Random House Inc. (☎ 800/726– 0600, WEB www.livinglanguage.com). **Business Companion: Chinese,** by Tim Dobbins and Paul Westbrook, Living Language/Random House Inc. (☎ 800/726–0600, WEB www. livinglanguage.com).

LODGING

The lodgings we list are the cream of the crop in each price category. We always list the facilities that are available—but we don't specify whether they cost extra: when pricing accommodations, always ask what's included and what costs extra. Also be aware that price may have little bearing on quality in China.

HOMESTAYS

Staying with a host family is a unique, inexpensive, and culturally rich experience. Generally your Chinese host family will speak enough English for basic communication, and you'll have the opportunity to experience life off of the beaten tourist path.

➤ ORGANIZATIONS: **American International Homestays, Inc.** (✉ Box 1754, Nederland, CO 80466, ☎ 800/876– 2048 or 303/642–3088, FAX 303/642–

3365, WEB www.commerce.com/ homestays). **ULink Travel Center** (✉ Box 938, He Ping Men, Beijing 100051, ☎ 010/6775–8655, FAX 010/ 6774–1523).

HOSTELS

No matter what your age, you can **save on lodging costs by staying at hostels.** In some 4,500 locations in more than 70 countries around the world, Hostelling International (HI), the umbrella group for a number of national youth-hostel associations, offers single-sex, dorm-style beds and, at many hostels, rooms for couples and family accommodations. Membership in any HI national hostel association, open to travelers of all ages, allows you to stay in HI-affiliated hostels at member rates; one-year membership is about $25 for adults (C$26.75 in Canada, £9.30 in the U.K., $30 in Australia, and $30 in New Zealand); hostels run about $10–$25 per night. Members have priority if the hostel is full; they're also eligible for discounts around the world, even on rail and bus travel in some countries.

➤ ORGANIZATIONS: **Australian Youth Hostel Association** (✉ 10 Mallett St., Camperdown, NSW 2050, Australia, ☎ 02/9565–1699, FAX 02/9565–1325, WEB www.yha.com.au). **Guangdong Youth Hostel Association of China** (✉ 185 Huanshix Rd., Guangzhou, Guangdong Province 510010, ☎ 8620/8666–6889, FAX 8620/8666– 5039). **Hostelling International— American Youth Hostels** (✉ 733 15th St. NW, Suite 840, Washington, DC 20005, ☎ 202/783–6161, FAX 202/ 783–6171, WEB www.hiayh.org). **Hostelling International—Canada** (✉ 400–205 Catherine St., Ottawa, Ontario K2P 1C3, Canada, ☎ 613/ 237–7884, FAX 613/237–7868, WEB www.hostellingintl.ca). **Youth Hostel Association of England and Wales** (✉ Trevelyan House, 8 St. Stephen's Hill, St. Albans, Hertfordshire AL1 2DY, U.K., ☎ 0870/8708808, FAX 01727/844126, WEB www.yha.org.uk). **Youth Hostels Association of New Zealand** (✉ Level 3, 193 Cashel St., Box 436, Christchurch, New Zealand, ☎ 03/379–9970, FAX 03/365– 4476, WEB www.yha.org.nz).

HOTELS

Major cities in China all have luxury hotels, and a recent wave of hotel construction is the cornerstone of China's new focus on tourism. Except for Hong Kong, Beijing, Shanghai, and Guangzhou, the service even in the best hotels might not measure up to international luxury standards. They will, however, have English speakers on staff, business centers, laundry service, foreign currency exchange, and a concierge who can arrange tours and transportation. Many also have exercise facilities, hairdressers, and restaurants.

Always **bring your passport when checking into a hotel.** The reception desk clerk will have to see it and record the number before you can be given a room. Sometimes unmarried couples are not allowed to stay together in the same room, but simply wearing a band on your left finger is one way to avoid this complication. Friends of the same sex, especially women, shouldn't have a problem getting a room together. There may, however, be regulations about who is allowed in your room, and it's also normal for hotels to post "visitor hours" inside the room.

All hotels listed have private bath unless otherwise noted. Remember that water is a precious resource in China and use accordingly.

➤ TOLL-FREE NUMBERS: **Best Western** (☎ 800/528–1234, WEB www.bestwestern.com). **Choice** (☎ 800/221–2222, WEB www.hotelchoice.com). **Clarion** (☎ 800/252–7466, WEB www.clarionhotel.com). **Days Inn** (☎ 800/325–2525, WEB www.daysinn.com). **Hilton** (☎ 800/445–8667, WEB www.hilton.com). **Holiday Inn** (☎ 800/465–4329, WEB www.basshotels.com). **Inter-Continental** (☎ 800/327–0200, WEB www.interconti.com). **Marriott** (☎ 800/228–9290, WEB www.marriott.com). **Nikko Hotels International** (☎ 800/645–5687, WEB www.nikkohotels.com). **Radisson** (☎ 800/333–3333, WEB www.radisson.com). **Renaissance Hotels & Resorts** (☎ 800/468–3571, WEB www.renaissancehotels.com). **Ritz-Carlton** (☎ 800/241–3333, WEB www.ritzcarlton.com). **Sheraton** (☎ 800/325–3535, WEB www.starwood.com). **Westin Hotels & Resorts** (☎ 800/228–3000, WEB www.westin.com).

MAIL & SHIPPING

Post offices are open from 8 AM to 6 PM Monday through Saturday. Public post offices are generally crowded, but large hotels have postal services open all day Monday through Saturday and Sunday 8 to noon.

OVERNIGHT SERVICES

➤ MAJOR SERVICES IN BEIJING: **DHL** (☎ 010/6466–5566). **FedEx** (☎ 010/6462–3183). **UPS** (☎ 010/6505–5005, FAX 010/6505–5115).

POSTAL RATES

A postcard to the United States costs Y4.2. A letter, up to 20 grams, costs Y5.40.

RECEIVING MAIL

Long-term guests can receive mail at their hotels. Otherwise, the best place to receive mail is at the American Express office. Most major Chinese cities have American Express offices with client mail service. Be sure to bring your American Express card, as the staff will not give you the mail without seeing it.

MONEY MATTERS

Costs vary widely from city to city. Standard museum entrance fees range between Y20 and Y50 and vary according to whether you're a local or a foreigner. A soft drink costs about Y10. A dumpling costs about Y10; a slice of pizza costs about Y50. Newspapers are about Y20; the *Herald Tribune*, printed in Hong Kong, is Y30. Prices throughout this guide are given for adults. Substantially reduced fees are almost always available for children, students, and senior citizens.

ATMS

ATMs using the Cirrus and Plus networks can be found all over Hong Kong, and are increasingly common in larger cities throughout China; at last count there were more than 100 ATMs in Beijing that accept MasterCard/Cirrus cards, and nearly 50 in Shanghai.

Before leaving home, **make sure your credit cards have been programmed**

for ATM use in China. Local bank cards often do not work overseas or may access only your checking account; **ask your bank about a Master-Card/Cirrus or Visa debit card,** which works like a bank card but can be used at any ATM displaying a Master-Card/Cirrus or Visa logo. These cards, too, may tap only your checking account; check with your bank about their policy.

CREDIT CARDS

Upscale hotels and restaurants, travel agencies such as CITS, tourist shops, and shopping centers will usually accept American Express, Master-Card, and Visa. Credit cards are less commonly accepted outside cities. Contact your credit card company before you go to inform them of your trip. Credit card companies have been known to put a hold on an account and send a report to their fraud division upon registering a purchase or cash advance in China. Be sure to copy your credit card numbers on a separate piece of paper and carry it in a place separate from your credit cards in case of theft.

Throughout this guide, the following abbreviations are used: **AE**, American Express; **DC**, Diner's Club; **MC**, MasterCard; and **V**, Visa.

➤ REPORTING LOST CARDS: **American Express** (☎ 202/554–2639 [call collect]). **Diner's Club** (☎ 303/799–1504 in the U.S. [call collect]). **MasterCard** (☎ 010/800–110–7309 in China). **Visa** (☎ 010/800–110–2911 in China).

CURRENCY

The Chinese currency is officially called the renminbi (RMB), or "People's Money." You can change money at most Bank of China branches, at the front desk of most upscale hotels, or at international airports. **Carry currency in several forms** (and in several different places) while abroad, such as cash, traveler's checks, and an ATM and/or credit card.

The Bank of China issues RMB bills in denominations of 2, 5, 10, 50, 100, 500, and 1,000 yuan. Yuan are commonly referred to as *kuài* (kwye); the abbreviation is Y. The exchange rates are approximately Y8.28 = $1 US, Y5.59 = 1C$, Y4.44 = 1$ Australian, Y11.96 = £1, Y3.71 = 1$ New Zealand, Y9.9 = 1 Irish punt, and Y1.1 = 1 South African rand. At press time, the exchange rates for the Hong Kong dollar (HK$) were 8.11HK$ = $1 US, 4.25 HK$ = 1$ Australian, 5.27 HK$ = 1C$, 3.5 HK$ = 1$ New Zealand, 9.34$ HK = 1 Irish punt, and 1.03 HK$ = 1 South African rand.

CURRENCY EXCHANGE

For the most favorable rates, **change money through banks.** Although ATM transaction fees may be higher abroad than at home, ATM rates are excellent because they are based on wholesale rates offered only by major banks. You won't do as well at exchange booths in airports or rail and bus stations, in hotels, in restaurants, or in stores. Generally speaking, you'll get a better deal when you exchange money within China, but do **purchase a small amount of renminbi prior to your trip.**

➤ EXCHANGE SERVICES: **International Currency Express** (☎ 888/278–6628 for orders, WEB www.foreignmoney. com). **Thomas Cook Currency Services** (☎ 800/287–7362 for telephone orders and retail locations, WEB www. us.thomascook.com).

TRAVELER'S CHECKS

Even though there is an increasing number of ATMs in China, your best bet is to take traveler's checks. **Take cash or exchange money in larger cities first if your trip includes rural areas** and small towns; take traveler's checks to cities. Lost or stolen checks can usually be replaced within 24 hours. To ensure a speedy refund, buy your own traveler's checks—don't let someone else pay for them: irregularities like this can cause delays. The person who bought the checks should make the call to request a refund. If you have been a member of AAA for at least a year, you can get traveler's checks for free. Be sure to keep your traveler's check receipts in a different place from your traveler's checks.

PACKING

Although the Chinese have become more fashion-conscious in the past few years, informal attire is still appropriate for most occasions. The streets are dirty, so you may prefer to bring older clothes and shoes. Sturdy, comfortable walking shoes are a must. A raincoat, especially a light Goretex one or a fold-up poncho, is useful for an onset of rainy weather. Summers are very hot and winters very cold in most of China, so pack accordingly. Avoid bringing clothes that need dry-cleaning. You will find it much easier to get around if you travel light, with no more than two or three changes of clothes, so bring clothes that you can layer should you need extra warmth. Clothes are also inexpensive in China, so you can always buy what you need. Most hotels have reliable overnight laundry, mending, and pressing services, so you can have your clothes washed frequently. Bring a more fashionable set of clothes to Hong Kong.

Eyeglasses, film, pantyhose, sundries, and over-the-counter medicines are widely available in Hong Kong but are harder to find in the rest of China. Pack the following essentials: alarm clock, contraceptives, dental floss, deodorant, mosquito repellent, shampoo, shaving cream and razors, sunglasses, sunscreen, tampons, toothbrush, and toothpaste. High-end hotels will generally provide a hair drier in the room. If you're planning a longer trip or will be using local tour guides, bring a few inexpensive items from your home country as gifts. American cigarettes are popular in China, but if you don't wish to promote smoking, bring candy, T-shirts, or small cosmetic items, such as lipstick and nail polish. **Do not give American magazines and books as gifts,** as this could be considered propaganda and get your Chinese friends into trouble.

Other useful items to have in China are a flashlight with extra batteries, English-language books and magazines, and a money belt. Bring a penknife to peel fruit and, if you're going to smaller cities and rural areas, water purification tablets.

In your carry-on luggage, **pack an extra pair of eyeglasses or contact lenses and enough of any medication** you take to last the entire trip. You may also ask your doctor to write a spare prescription using the drug's

generic name, since brand names may vary from country to country. In luggage to be checked, **never pack prescription drugs or valuables.** To avoid customs delays, carry medications in their original packaging. And don't forget to carry with you the addresses of offices that handle refunds of lost traveler's checks. Check *Fodor's How to Pack* (available in bookstores everywhere) for more tips.

CHECKING LUGGAGE

You are allowed one carry-on bag and one personal article, such as a purse or a laptop computer. Make sure that everything you carry aboard will fit under your seat or in the overhead bin. Get to the gate early, so you can board as soon as possible, before the overhead bins fill up. If you're flying within China on a local carrier, carry on as little as possible; flights can be very crowded and overhead bin space hard to get. Domestically, you're officially allowed one checked piece that weighs no more than 44 pounds (20 kilograms). Note that if you have a seat at the back of the plane, you'll probably board first, while the overhead bins are still empty. Be sure to lock your bags—for safety reasons and because some local carriers require that all checked bags be locked.

If you are flying internationally, note that baggage allowances may be determined not by piece but by weight—generally 88 pounds (40 kilograms) in first class, 66 pounds (30 kilograms) in business class, and 44 pounds (20 kilograms) in economy.

Airline liability for baggage is limited to $1,250 per person on flights within the United States. On international flights it amounts to $9.07 per pound or $20 per kilogram for checked baggage (roughly $640 per 70-pound bag) and $400 per passenger for unchecked baggage. You can buy additional coverage at check-in for about $10 per $1,000 of coverage, but it excludes a rather extensive list of items, shown on your airline ticket.

Before departure, **itemize your bags' contents** and their worth, and label the bags with your name, address, and phone number. (If you use your home address, cover it so potential thieves can't see it readily.) Inside each bag, **pack a copy of your itin-erary**. At check-in, **make sure that each bag is correctly tagged** with the destination airport's three-letter code. If your bags arrive damaged or fail to arrive at all, file a written report with the airline before leaving the airport.

PASSPORTS & VISAS

When traveling internationally, **carry your passport** even if you don't need one (it's always the best form of I.D.) and **make two photocopies of the data page** (one for someone at home and another for you, carried sepa-rately from your passport). If you lose your passport, promptly call the nearest embassy or consulate and the local police.

ENTERING CHINA

All U.S. citizens, even infants, need a valid passport with a tourist visa stamped in it to enter China for stays of up to 90 days. For Hong Kong you need only a valid passport.

GETTING A VISA

It takes about a week to get a visa in the United States. Travel agents in Hong Kong can issue visas to visit China. Costs range from about $35 for a visa issued within two working days to $50 for a visa issued over-night. **Note:** The visa application will ask your occupation. The Chinese do not like journalists or anyone who works in publishing or media. Ameri-cans and Canadians in these profes-sions routinely state "teacher" under "Occupation." U.K. passports state the bearer's occupation, and this can be problematic for anyone in the "wrong" line of work. Several years ago a British journalist on holiday in Beijing was detained for a day be-cause of his occupation. Before you go, contact the consulate of the Peo-ple's Republic of China to see how strict the current mood is.

➤ IN AUSTRALIA: **Chinese Embassy** (☎ 02/6273–4780, ext. 218 and 258, FAX 02/6273–9615, WEB www.chinaembassy.org.au).

➤ IN CANADA: **Chinese Embassy** (☎ 613/789–3434, FAX 613/789–1911, WEB www.chinaembassycanada.org).

➤ IN NEW ZEALAND: **Chinese Em-bassy** (☎ 04/472–1382, FAX 04/499–0419, WEB www.chinaembassy.org.nz).

➤ IN THE U.K.: **Chinese Embassy** (☎ 0171/636–2580, FAX 0171/636–2981, WEB www.chinese-embassy.org.uk).

➤ IN THE U.S.: **Chinese Embassy** (Room 110, 2201 Wisconsin Ave NW, Washington, DC 20007, ☎ 202/338–6688, FAX 202/588–9760, WEB www.china-embassy.org). **Chinese Consulate** (✉ Visa Office, 520 12th Ave., New York, NY 10036; ☎ 212/736–9301, automatic answering machine with 24-hour service; 212/502–0271, information desk open weekdays 2–4, FAX 212/502–0245, WEB www.nyconsulate.prchina.org).

PASSPORT OFFICES

The best time to apply for a passport or to renew is in fall and winter. Before any trip, check your passport's expiration date, and, if necessary, renew it as soon as possible.

➤ AUSTRALIAN CITIZENS: **Austra-lian Passport Office** (☎ 131–232, WEB www.dfat.gov.au/passports).

➤ CANADIAN CITIZENS: **Passport Office** (☎ 819/994–3500; 800/567–6868 in Canada, WEB www.dfait-maeci.gc.ca/passport).

➤ NEW ZEALAND CITIZENS: **New Zealand Passport Office** (☎ 04/494–0700, WEB www.passports.govt.nz).

➤ U.K. CITIZENS: **London Passport Office** (☎ 0870/521–0410, WEB www.ukpa.gov.uk) for fees and documenta-tion requirements and to request an emergency passport.

➤ U.S. CITIZENS: **National Passport Information Center** (☎ 900/225–5674; calls are 35¢ per minute for automated service, $1.05 per minute for operator service; WEB www.travel.state.gov/npicinfo.html).

REST ROOMS

Hotels, restaurants, and boats that often accommodate foreigners are usually equipped with Western toilets, but you are likely to encounter the standard model—squat toilets with or without a flush feature—in airports, train stations, trains, schools, parks, and other public spaces. Some cities' sanitation systems cannot handle toi-let paper, and a wastebasket is pro-vided for disposal. Be sure to carry toilet paper with you at all times, especially if you're taking a train or heading to the countryside. Moist towelettes are also invaluable.

SAFETY

There is little violent crime against tourists in China, partly because the penalties are severe for those who are caught—execution is the most common. Use the lock-box in your hotel room to store any valuables, but always carry your passport with you for identification purposes.

The traffic in Chinese cities is usually heavy and just as out of control as it looks. Be very careful when crossing streets or riding a bicycle. Respiratory problems may be aggravated by the severely polluted air in China's cities. Some residents as well as visitors find that wearing a surgical mask, or a scarf or bandana, helps.

LOCAL SCAMS

Pickpocketing is a growing problem. Keep valuables in a money belt or locked in a hotel safe. A general rule of thumb is **don't wear anything that will stand out,** that is, revealing or flashy clothes or expensive jewelry. If nothing else, you may be harassed by people politely asking if you will trade clothes or give them your watch!

SENIOR-CITIZEN TRAVEL

To qualify for age-related discounts, **mention your senior-citizen status up front** when booking hotel reservations (not when checking out) and before you're seated in restaurants (not when paying the bill). When renting a car, ask about promotional car-rental discounts, which can be cheaper than senior-citizen rates.

➤ EDUCATIONAL PROGRAMS: **Elder-hostel** (✉ 11 Ave. de Lafayette, Boston, MA 02111-1746, ☎ 877/426–8056, 𝖥𝖠𝖷 877/426–2166, 𝖶𝖤𝖡 www.elderhostel.org). Folkways Institute (✉ 14600 S.E. Aldridge Rd., Portland, OR 97236-6518, ☎ 503/658–6600 or 800/225–4666, 𝖥𝖠𝖷 503/658–8672, 𝖶𝖤𝖡 www.folkwaystravel.com).

SHOPPING

China has many things to buy; good souvenirs include Chinese medicines, silk, and tea. There are shops specializing in jade, old Chinese porcelain, and antique furniture, but **be alert for forgery when shopping.** Stick to Friendship Stores (formerly emporiums selling luxury goods for foreigners only, now more like an upscale department store chain) and shops attached to international hotels for some assurance of getting what you pay for. When you buy goods in established shops, you first pay the cashier and then present the receipt of sale to the store attendant, who will wrap your purchase.

With antiques, an item more than 100 years old will have an official red wax seal attached—but not all items with seals attached are more than 100 years old. The Chinese government has cleared only certain antiques for sale to foreigners. Save the bill of sale to show customs when you leave the country, or the antique will be confiscated. For exports, antiques must have been made after 1797.

Post offices in hotels usually have interesting Chinese stamps for sale. Ask about designs that were issued during the Cultural Revolution.

SMART SOUVENIRS

Around the tourist centers you'll find street merchants selling an array of cloisonné and jade jewelry, old Chinese coins (usually fake), fans, tea sets, chops (stone stamps that can be carved with your name in Chinese), embroidered silk robes and pillowcases, and other souvenirs. You can often bargain for these items. Areas frequented by tourists also abound with stores and street vendors selling art: scrolls, woodblock prints, paper cuts, and some contemporary oils.

STUDENTS IN CHINA

There are abundant and diverse opportunities for students to study in China through programs organized by both U.S. and Chinese universities. Campuses in China have facilities similar to those of their American counterparts, although the quality of Chinese classes varies. Classes are held Monday through Saturday. Dormitories are spartan and visiting rules apply. (If you're staying in a dormitory, it's generally difficult to make arrangements for friends or family to stay with you.) You'll find that relationships between students and teachers are hierarchical and classroom debate is not welcome. However, Chinese teachers generally will be very interested in you—so much so that they may delve into aspects of your life that you may regard as personal.

There are different visas for students staying in China for more than three months. If you're staying up to six months, you'll need an "F" visa; for more than six months but less than a year, an "X" visa; and for a year or longer, a "Z" visa. If for some reason you are issued the wrong visa, you can obtain the correct visa in China for a small fee. China also requires that anyone staying in China for more than a year must get a thorough physical, including a chest X ray and an HIV test. People who test positive for HIV are prohibited from entering China.

Students in China are entitled to discounts on museum and park fees, as well as 40% discounts on intra-continental air tickets if they have an official Chinese student card issued by their school.

➤ I.D.s & SERVICES: **Council Travel** (CIEE; ✉ 205 E. 42nd St., 15th floor, New York, NY 10017, ☎ 212/822–2700 or 888/268–6245, FAX 212/822–2699, WEB www.councilexchanges.org) for mail orders only, in the U.S. **NAFSA Association of International Educators** (✉ 1307 New York Ave. NW, 8th Floor, Washington, D.C. 20005–4701, ☎ 202/737–3699, FAX 202/737–3657, WEB www.nafsa.org. **Travel Cuts** (✉ 187 College St., Toronto, Ontario M5T 1P7, Canada, ☎ 416/979–2406 or 800/667–2887 in Canada, FAX 416/979–8167, WEB www.travelcuts.com).

TAXES

There is no sales tax in China. Hotels have a room tariff of 10% for service charges plus 5% tax. Airport departure tax is Y90 (about $11), payable in yuan only. Hong Kong's airport tax is HK$50 (about $6). Domestic flights require a Y50 ($6) airport construction fee, cash only.

TELEPHONES

AREA & COUNTRY CODES

The country code for China is 86; for Hong Kong, 852. To dial China direct from the United States or Canada, you must know the city code. Some important city codes are: Beijing, 10; Guangzhou, 20; Shanghai, 21. When dialing from within the country, add 0 before the city code. The country code is 1 for the United States and Canada, 61 for Australia, 64 for New Zealand, and 44 for the United Kingdom. To dial overseas direct, the international access code is 001.

DIRECTORY & OPERATOR ASSISTANCE

It's hard to find English-speaking operators in China, except through international directory assistance (dial 115). You can dial overseas direct from many hotel room and business center telephones. The international access code in China is 00. Hotels usually add a 30% surcharge to long-distance calls. In Hong Kong dial 1081 for assistance from English-speaking operators.

LONG-DISTANCE SERVICES

AT&T, MCI, and Sprint access codes make calling long distance relatively convenient, but you may find the local access number blocked in many hotel rooms. First ask the hotel operator to connect you. If the hotel operator balks, ask for an international operator, or dial the international operator yourself. One way to improve your odds of getting connected to your long-distance carrier is to travel with more than one company's calling card (a hotel may block Sprint, for example, but not MCI). If all else fails, call from a pay phone.

Most major hotels now have International Direct Dial (IDD) phones.The local access code in China is 11 for AT&T, 12 for MCI, and 13 for Sprint—dial these numbers after dialing the local operator (108), who will speak English.

➤ ACCESS CODES: **AT&T Direct** (☎ 800/874–4000). **MCI WorldPhone** (☎ 800/444–4444). **Sprint International Access** (☎ 800/793–1153).

PUBLIC PHONES

Most hotels have booths where you can place domestic and international calls. You pay a deposit of about Y200 and receive a card with the number of the booth. A computer times the call and processes a bill, which you pay at the end. Post offices have telecommunications centers where you can buy cards in denominations of Y20, Y50, and Y100 to make long-distance calls. Standard pay phones accept these cards and coins. The cards tend to be less expensive but only work in the province in which they're purchased.

TIPPING

Because the Chinese Government forbids asking for tips, tipping used to be unheard of, but now the custom is taking hold in hotels and restaurants. It's not necessary to tip taxi drivers, although you might let them keep small change. In Hong Kong taxi drivers charge you HK$5 per piece of baggage that they handle.

CTS tour guides are not allowed to accept tips. You can give guides and drivers small gifts. They often appreciate American cigarettes, but you also can offer American candy or T-shirts. If you hire a driver and guide independently, the tipping norm is $10 per day for the guide and $5 per day for the driver.

TOURS & PACKAGES

Because everything is prearranged on a prepackaged tour or independent vacation, you spend less time planning—and often get it all at a good price.

BOOKING WITH AN AGENT

Travel agents are excellent resources. But it's a good idea to collect brochures from several agencies as some agents' suggestions may be influenced by relationships with tour and package firms that reward them for volume sales. If you have a special interest, **find an agent with expertise in that area**; ASTA (☞ Travel Agencies) has a database of specialists worldwide.

Make sure your travel agent knows the accommodations and other services of the place being recommended. Ask about the hotel's location, room size, beds, and whether it has a pool, room service, or programs for children, if you care about these. Has your agent been there in person or sent others whom you can contact?

Do some homework on your own, too: local tourism boards can provide information about lesser-known and small-niche operators, some of which may sell only direct.

BUYER BEWARE

Each year consumers are stranded or lose their money when tour operators—even large ones with excellent reputations—go out of business. So **check out the operator.** Ask several travel agents about its reputation, and try to **book with a company that has a consumer-protection program.** (Look for information in the company's brochure.) In the United States, members of the National Tour Association and the United States Tour Operators Association are required to set aside funds to cover your payments and travel arrangements in the event that the company defaults. It's also a good idea to choose a company that participates in the American Society of Travel Agents' Tour Operator Program (TOP); ASTA will act as mediator in any disputes between you and your tour operator.

Remember that the more your package or tour includes the better you can predict the ultimate cost of your vacation. Make sure you know exactly what is covered, and **beware of hidden costs.** Are taxes, tips, and transfers included? Entertainment and excursions? These can add up.

➤ TOUR-OPERATOR RECOMMENDATIONS: **American Society of Travel Agents** (☞ Travel Agencies, *below*). **Cameron Tours** (✉ 6249 N. Kingston St., McLean, VA 22101, ☎ 703/538–7122 or 800/648–4635, 🌐 www.camerontours.com). **Chn–Asia Express Tours** (✉ 22 Main St., South River, NJ 08882, ☎ 732/432–7569, 🖷 732/432–7545). **Imperial Tours** ✉ 1802 N. Carson St., Suite 212–2296, Carson City, NV 89701, ☎ 888/296–5306, 🖷 800/380–6576, 🌐 www.imperialtours.net). **National Tour Association** (NTA; ✉ 546 E. Main St., Lexington, KY 40508, ☎ 859/226–4444 or 800/682–8886, 🌐 www.ntaonline.com). **United States Tour Operators Association** (USTOA; ✉ 342 Madison Ave., Suite

1522, New York, NY 10173, ☎ 212/599–6599 or 800/468–7862, FAX 212/599–6744, WEB www.ustoa.com).

TRAIN TRAVEL

Train tickets usually have to be purchased in the city of origin. If you do not speak Mandarin, it will be difficult to negotiate the ticket windows at the train station even though there is a special ticket counter just for foreigners, so buy tickets from the local CTS office or ask your hotel concierge to make the arrangements. Fares are more expensive for foreigners than for the Chinese. Make train reservations at least a day or two in advance, if you can. Boiled water is always available. Trains are always crowded, so arrive at the station two hours before departure. In Hong Kong there will be a queue to get on the train; on the mainland, it's every passenger for him- or herself.

CLASSES

The train system offers a glimpse of old-fashioned socialist euphemisms. Instead of first-class and second-class accommodations, you choose hard seat or soft seat, and for overnight journeys, hard sleeper or soft sleeper. The soft sleeper has four compartments with soft beds and is recommended if you're taking a long journey (though it is much more expensive than the hard sleeper). Note that theft on trains is increasing; on overnight trains, sleep with your valuables or else keep them on the inside of the bunk.

TRAVEL AGENCIES

A good travel agent puts your needs first. Look for an agency that has been in business at least five years, emphasizes customer service, and has someone on staff who specializes in your destination. In addition, **make sure the agency belongs to a professional trade organization.** The American Society of Travel Agents (ASTA), with more than 26,000 members in some 170 countries, is the largest and most influential in the field. Operating under the motto "Without a travel agent, you're on your own," it maintains and enforces a strict code of ethics and will step in to help mediate any agent-client disputes if necessary. ASTA also maintains a Web site that includes a directory of agents. (If a travel agency is also acting as your tour operator, *see* Buyer Beware *in* Tours & Packages)

➤ LOCAL AGENT REFERRALS: **American Society of Travel Agents** (ASTA; ✉ 1101 King St., Suite 200, Alexandria, VA 22314 ☎ 800/965–2782 24-hr hot line, FAX 703/739–7642, WEB www.astanet.com). **Association of British Travel Agents** (✉ 68–71 Newman St., London W1T 3AH, U.K., ☎ 020/7637–2444, FAX 020/7637–0713, WEB www.abtanet.com). **Association of Canadian Travel Agents** (✉ 130 Albert St., Suite 1705, Ottawa, Ontario K1P 5G4, Canada, ☎ 613/237–3657, FAX 613/237–7052, WEB www.acta.net). **Australian Federation of Travel Agents** (✉ Level 3, 309 Pitt St., Sydney NSW 2000, Australia, ☎ 02/9264–3299, FAX 02/9264–1085, WEB www.afta.com.au). **Travel Agents' Association of New Zealand** (✉ Level 5, Paxus House, 79 Boulcott St., Box 1888, Wellington 10033, New Zealand, ☎ 04/499–0104, FAX 04/499–0827, WEB www.taanz.org.nz).

➤ IN HONG KONG: In Hong Kong, **Phoenix Travel** (✉ Milton Mansions, 96 Nathan Rd., Room 6B; Tsim Sha Tsui, Kowloon, ☎ 852/2722–7378, FAX 852/2369–8884).

VISITOR INFORMATION

For general information before you go, including information about tours, insurance, and safety, call or visit the National Tourist Office in New York City, Los Angeles, London, or Sydney.

Within China, China International Travel Service (CITS) and China Travel Service (CTS) are under the same government ministry. Local offices, catering to sightseeing around the area (and to visitors from other mainland cities), are called CTS. CITS offices can book international flights.

➤ CHINA NATIONAL TOURIST OFFICES: **Australia** (✉ 19th floor, 44 Market St., Sydney, NSW 2000, ☎ 02/9299–4057, FAX 02/9290–1958, WEB www.cnto.org.au). **Canada** (✉ 556 W. Broadway, Vancouver, BC V5Z 1E9, ☎ 604/872–8787, FAX 604/873–2823, WEB www.citscanada.com.) **United Kingdom** ✉ 4 Glentworth St., London NW1, ☎ 0171/935–9427, FAX

0171/487–5842). **United States** (✉ 350 5th Ave., Suite 6413, New York, NY 10118, 212/760–8218, FAX 212/760–8809; ✉ 333 W. Broadway, Suite 201, Glendale, CA 91204, ☎ 818/545–7504, FAX 818/545–7506, WEB www.cnto.org).

➤ CHINA INTERNATIONAL TRAVEL SERVICE (CITS): **United States** (✉ 2 Mott St., New York, NY 10002, ☎ 212/608–1212 or 800/899–8618).

➤ U.S. GOVERNMENT ADVISORIES: **U.S. Department of State** (✉ Overseas Citizens Services Office, Room 4811 N.S., 2201 C St. NW, Washington, DC 20520, ☎ 202/647–5225 for interactive hot line, WEB www.travel.state.gov); enclose a self-addressed, stamped, business-size envelope.

WEB SITES

Do check out the World Wide Web when planning your trip. You'll find everything from weather forecasts to virtual tours of famous cities. Be sure to **visit Fodors.com** (www.fodors.com), a complete travel-planning site.

The government and regional tourist agencies in China sponsor a number of Web sites that can be accessed from the United States. Try www.chinatips.net, www.yahoo.com/cn, www.travelchinaguide.com, www.china.com, www.chinavista.com, www.english.ccnt.com.cn, and www.china.pages.com.cn. The China National Tourism Office is at www.cnto.org. You can also visit CITS at www.chinatravelservice.com or www.citsusa.com.

WHEN TO GO

Although temperatures can be scorching, summer is the peak tourist season, and hotels and transportation can be very crowded. Book several months in advance if possible for summer travel. The weather is better and the crowds not quite as dense in late spring and early fall, although you need to be prepared for rain. Winter is bitterly cold and not conducive to travel in most of the country. Avoid traveling around Chinese New Year, as much of China shuts down and the Chinese themselves travel, making reservations virtually impossible to get.

➤ FORECASTS: **Weather Channel Connection** (☎ 900/932–8437), 95¢ per minute from a Touch-Tone phone.

What follows are average daily maximum and minimum temperatures in Beijing and Hong Kong.

BEIJING

Jan.	34F	1C	May	81F	27C	Sept.	79F	26C
	14	−10		55	13		57	14
Feb.	39F	4C	June	88F	31C	Oct.	68F	20C
	18	−8		64	18		43	6
Mar.	52F	11C	July	88F	31C	Nov.	48F	9C
	30	−1		70	21		28	−2
Apr.	70F	21C	Aug.	86F	30C	Dec.	37F	3C
	45	7		68	20		18	−8

HONG KONG

Jan.	64F	18C	May	82F	28C	Sept.	85F	29C
	45	13		74	23		77	25
Feb.	63F	17C	June	85F	29C	Oct.	81F	27C
	55	13		78	26		73	23
Mar.	67F	19C	July	87F	31C	Nov.	74F	23C
	60	16		78	26		65	18
Apr.	75F	24C	Aug.	87F	31C	Dec.	68F	20C
	67	19		78	26		59	15

1 DESTINATION: CHINA

China's Dance

What's Where

Pleasures and Pastimes

Fodor's Choice

Festivals and Seasonal Events

CHINA'S DANCE

TAPED TO AN OLD SHOP WINDOW in Suzhou, a city more than 2,500 years old with its walls still intact, is an advertisement for cellular phones: A young Chinese woman holds a phone to her ear as she stands on the Great Wall, the long structure twisting off into the distance behind her. "Get connected," says the ad. "This is the new China."

Bamboo scaffolding and gleaming department stores, construction cranes looming over wooden villages, KFC and chopsticks, yak herders and cell-phone abusers within miles of each other, communism and capitalism coexisting— China has more paradoxes than it has dialects. To visit China now is to witness a country revolutionizing itself in the cities and struggling to stay alive in the countryside.

The third-largest country in the world, holding the world's largest population, China is chiefly challenged by questions of cohesiveness—how to bring a country speaking hundreds of different dialects together under one rule. Beginning with the Zhou dynasty (1100–771 BC), Chinese governors held the country together not only by force but by claiming a heaven-sent legitimacy known as the Mandate of Heaven. The mandate was a convenient claim of legitimacy, as anyone who led a successful rebellion could assert his victory was predicated upon the support of the gods. The traditional belief was that heaven would demonstrate disapproval of evil rulers through natural disasters like droughts and earthquakes, disease, and floods.

Today, as China's mesh of socialist and capitalist policies brings instability to the country, it is becoming unclear who holds the mandate. Are the heirs to Mao's revolution the conservative members of the Communist Party, or are President Jiang Zemin and other reformers intent on imbuing the national economy with a capitalist bent? Whatever the case, it's clear that as the country continues to modernize, especially with Hong Kong under its belt, communism appears to be taking the back seat to a still undefined front seat, neither capitalism in a Western sense nor communism as in the years of Mao. The Chinese government has found itself in an awkward situation. If it tries to clamp down, it will surely lose in the race for modernization. If it allows modernization to continue, its control is inevitably weakened.

Ranging from the Three Gorges Dam, a colossal project that is uprooting 2 million people, to the perpetual construction of skyscrapers crowding the cities' skylines, the Chinese landscape is quickly changing. In some respects, it's as if the people had been plucked from their traditional homes and transported 100 years into a future. Foreign companies and joint ventures have demanded that single men and women climb a corporate ladder at an accelerated pace; eating habits have changed from family style to a quick bite at McDonald's; grocery stores have begun to replace outdoor markets; bars and discos stay open all night. The country has become more modern, but what does that mean to a nation that looks back on more than 5,000 years of history?

The ancient philosophy of Confucianism laid a foundation for Chinese ethics and morals that still survives today, teaching respect, selflessness, obedience, and a sense of community. Unlike Americans, who prize their individuality and independence, the Chinese believe it is important to stay within and abide by a community. Shame is considered a much graver emotion than guilt: The Chinese judge themselves according to how they believe they are perceived by those whom they love and respect. As a new generation works the corporate life in cities away from home, how this undeniably Chinese characteristic will be affected is the subject of much debate.

The Chinese believe that, no matter where you were born, where you live, or what your native tongue, if you have Chinese ancestry, you are still Chinese. Their sense of pride about emerging as a colossal force in the global economy is combined with a deep sense of race that holds the country tentatively together. Paradoxically, China is busy buying up Western products, from french fries to Hollywood action movies. Nike is cool. Madonna is hip. This external desire for Western style coexists comfortably, though ironically, with a perennial internal nationalism. The Chinese have so internalized their landscape that, for example, the TV tower in Shanghai is for them comparable to the Jade Buddha Temple down the street as a sight not to be missed; advertisements in subway stations are celebrated as a new form of artistic expression; the elderly happily practice tai chi to the beat of rock music.

More than 70% of the mainland population lives along the eastern seaboard, leaving the westernmost provinces barren and nearly vacant, in part because only 20% of China's land is arable. In the 1970s peasants' lifestyles improved as a result of Deng Xiao Ping's policy of allowing profit after government quotas had been met, but small plots of land and an ever-increasing population meant the new policy only provided limited relief. People still flock to the cities, creating a large homeless population. Although China appears to be overhauling itself, many residents of the smaller cities and villages are still living the way they did 100 years ago. As in other countries experiencing rapid development, there is a profound division between the growing middle class and unemployed farmworkers.

Excursions to small towns reveal just how much China relies on basic human power. Farm laborers stand up with their tools and wave as a train passes, a girl wearing a Nike jacket carries buckets swinging from a yoke over her shoulders, herds of sheep carry goods down dirt roads into the village center, local buses are crowded full of men and women carrying raw animal furs, and everywhere cycles of every description carry people and goods. Even in the cities, a surplus of men work with hammer and nail to build a skyscraper. Perhaps these images will disappear in a few years, but for now they reveal a country in the throes of revolution still holding on quite tightly to tradition.

During a visit to China, often the best moments are the ones you invent on your own, not what the hotel or the China International Travel Service (CITS) recommends. In this way you can enjoy China's hidden secrets—nature walks, bustling markets, small villages. Of course, the consequence of making up your own itinerary is having to follow a very cryptic and archaic route, one where the roads may not be paved, the train does not show up, hotels are not where they are supposed to be, and People's Liberation Army officers creep up out of nowhere. There is little peace, little comfort, and incredible markups for foreigners; keep an open mind and an adventurous spirit.

— Angela Yuan

WHAT'S WHERE

China will reveal itself to the traveler who wants to see it all—snowcapped mountain ranges, cities packed full of bicycles and mopeds, Tibetan monasteries perched on hills, crystal blue rivers, creeks full of raw sewage, markets selling dried rats, charming friendly people who shout hello wherever you go, people who never look you in the face, people who say anything not to lose face. China is a country to be understood on many levels.

China slopes from west to east, creating three general tiers of land. The first tier, in the northwest, incorporates some of the world's highest mountain ranges (the peak being Everest's 29,000 ft, on the border of Tibet and Nepal). Most of China is made up of plateaus of roughly 3,000–6,000 ft, the country's second tier. The remaining plains and lowlands in the east harbor more than two-thirds of the population and the industrial community.

As you navigate in China, remember the Chinese words for directions: north is *bei*; south is *nan*; west is *xi*; east is *dong*; and middle is *zhong*. Street signs in cities are marked in both Chinese characters and pinyin (romanized Chinese).

Beijing
Red flags blowing over Tiananmen, the Summer Palace at dusk, the Great Wall seen from space, the endless steps and red-tile roofs of the Forbidden City—Beijing and the surrounding area are firmly rooted in grandeur. The Liao, Jin, Yuan, Ming, and Qing dynasties all chose it as their capital, for close to 2,000 years of imperial presence. The Chinese view the whole city as a historical and cultural museum, as much

of China's past has been demolished elsewhere. Although the wide avenues and huge blocks create a sterile feel, they embody the image those in control want to project; they're laid out so that the individual feels small in comparison to "order."

Eastern China

China's eastern provinces are the most densely populated and industrialized regions in the country. They are also home to some of China's most heavily visited spots. In Jiangsu province, Suzhou, with its meditative gardens, and in Zhejiang province, Hangzhou, with its serene lake, are often paired as "heaven and earth" by the Chinese and have attracted China's most illustrious poets and painters. The old Ming capital of Nanjing, in Jiangsu, is a city full of historic landmarks and Chinese architecture—a requisite stop for the sinologist. The Huangshan range in Anhui is one of China's best-known sacred mountain ranges, with marvelous views as well as an incredible number of people to go with them. Jingdezhen, in Jiangxi, is China's first and main producer of ceramics and porcelain; today it still turns out reproductions of ancient work of astonishingly high quality. Also in Jiangxi, the old hill resort of Lushan is a charming mountain village dotted with 19th-century European-style villas. Fujian's close proximity to Taiwan has created affluent cities, such as Xiamen and Fuzhou, backed by big businesses and industry.

Hong Kong

When the British handed back Hong Kong to China in July 1997, China acquired one of the world's most prosperous cities. Despite the financial downturn in the late 1990s, Hong Kong remains a city on the move. With all the political hype and foreboding for the future, the city is still intent on land-filling, hotel-expanding, bridge-building, business-dealing, and world-class shopping. Take the tram up to Victoria Peak and witness a city below that can inspire awe the way the Grand Canyon does. Equally spectacular are the blue waters and small islands surrounding the city. Cheung Chau, Lantau, and Lamma islands are speckled with fishing villages and lovely hiking areas. The formerly Portuguese port city of Macau is a delightful anomaly nearby. World-class hotels, Iberian architecture, and Macanese food specialties await the visitor.

Inner Mongolia and the Republic of Mongolia

Inner Mongolia, often confused with Mongolia, is an autonomous region of China; here the traditional Mongolian way of life has become mostly nonexistent as modernization hits fast. The Mongols invaded and conquered China on horseback in the 13th century, and today children in the Republic of Mongolia, China's northern neighbor, still learn to ride horses at the age of four or five. Racing, archery, and wrestling make up the annual Naadam Festival in Ulaan Baatar, the country's capital and most heavily populated city, where the surrounding grasslands fill up with riders in brightly colored dress. Bordering Siberia, Mongolia's huge territory (600,000 square mi) covers diverse geography ranging from the Gobi Desert to the pristine lake of Xowsgol to the Altai Mountain Range. Mongolia is home to a variety of cultural and historical museums as well as a few monasteries that survived the Stalinist purge.

North Central China

China's northern treaty ports—Qingdao, Tianjin, and Dalian—offer a counterpoint to nearby Beijing as major cities. Colonial architecture ornaments small neighborhoods in and around these ports. In Qingdao, you can even glimpse a fairly blue ocean past the German villa rooftops. Tianjin, a city full of foreign architecture, boasts one of the country's best antiques markets. The Qing and Song dynasties developed much of the inland provinces, investing cities such as Nanjing, in Jiangsu, and Kaifeng, in Henan, with historical and cultural merit; these cities may be among the most "authentically Chinese" places to visit in the country. The Great Wall snakes through Hebei and Shanxi provinces as well. Neither province is of great scenic or historic interest, but they do produce most of the country's coal.

Northeastern China

Dongbei, China's northeastern region of Heilongjiang, Jilin, and Liaoning, is home to the Manchus. A distinct ethnic group, the Manchus established the Qing Dynasty in 1644 and ruled China until 1911. The region is not as inviting as other provinces because of its cold and barren climate, but Harbin's winter ice festival draws visitors bundled up in –30°C (–22°F) weather to Heilongjiang—China's northernmost province. Just south is Jilin, home to the best Chinese ski resorts as well as China's largest nature reserve, where you can hike through thick forests up into the mountains to stand before a giant crater lake. Dalian, in Liaoning province, is among China's more "green" cities, where many parks and gardens line the colorful streets. The city has a strong colonial past, much of whose architecture survives to this day.

Northwestern China

The famed Silk Road ran through much of this region, beginning in Shaanxi province in the ancient capital of Xian and ending in Xinjiang's Kashgar, the westernmost city within China. Here you can sip Uighur tea while watching camels carry in goods from across the desert. In Gansu province yaks run aplenty in the charming, ethnically Tibetan town of Xiahe, nestled in the mountains and surrounded by grasslands. Ningxia is home to a large Hui population, beautiful sand dunes, and the Western Xia tombs, which sit among herds of goat and sheep. Qinghai, one of China's most remote provinces, is home to a large Tibetan population, as the region was formerly part of the Tibetan Autonomous Region. Although it is also known to house the country's most severe prisons (*laogai*), Qinghai, like Xinjiang, is a beautiful region full of mountain ranges and sweeping grasslands. At the eastern end of the region, the unforgettable terra-cotta soldiers stand sentinel after 2,000 years in Xian, which has other historic sights and pockets of delightful Muslim character as well.

Shanghai

Infamous in the 1920s for its gambling, prostitution, gangsters, and opium dens, Shanghai is regaining some of the reputation it lost after the Cultural Revolution. As one of the most Westernized cities in China, excluding Hong Kong, Shanghai is on the cutting edge of China's race for modernization. It's full of underground clubs, high-class restaurants, and upscale boutiques. Almost a quarter of the world's construction cranes stand in this city of 14 million; often it feels like half of those are on the street you happen to be walking down. On the other hand, architectural remnants of a strong colonial past survive along the charming, winding, bustling streets that make this city undeniably and intimately Chinese.

South Central China

Looking like sandcastles dropped from the sky, the karst rock formations of Guangxi province are among China's most spectacular landscapes. As industry and crowds overtake the city of Guilin, nearby Yangshuo is becoming the more desirable spot for karst mountain viewing. In Guizhou, one of China's more overlooked provinces, are the spectacular Huangguoshu Falls, set in the lush countryside where many of China's minorities make their home. In Hunan the cities of Shaoshan and Changsha—birthplaces of many Communist leaders, including Mao himself—draw steady streams of pilgrims. The industrial city of Wuhan, in Hubei province, is a port on the Three Gorges River cruise.

Southeastern China

The Chinese have a saying: In Beijing one talks, in Shanghai one shops, in Guangzhou (Canton) one eats. The infamous Qing Ping market of Guangzhou demonstrates how well this proverb reflects reality. From insects to dogs to indistinguishable rodents both live and dried, it appears the Cantonese eat anything and everything. The Cantonese tend to associate themselves with neighboring Hong Kong rather than faraway Beijing, sharing the same dialect, food specialties, and moneymaking ventures. Indeed, Guangzhou and the affluent region of Guangdong province have seriously tested Deng Xiao Ping's 1990 mandate: "To get rich is glorious." A frenzy and chaos define the city, a buzz and energy like no other. To the south lies Hainan Island, China's only real resort province. Surprisingly pristine beaches and great seafood dishes make the island province a popular vacation spot for mainlanders.

Southwestern China

In Sichuan province from Chengdu to Chongqing, locals gather in teahouses by day, dine on the spiciest food in China, and play mah-jongg long into the night—a relaxing way of life that has become tradition here. The Three Gorges boat cruise along the Yangzi River originates in Chongqing and shares—with Hubei province—some of the trip's most awesome river scenery. Just north of Vietnam and bordering Burma and Laos lies the ethnically diverse province of Yunnan, home to the Dai, Bai, Yi, and Naxi minorities. Backpackers relax in the ancient town of Dali below spectacular mountains before heading north to Lijiang and hiking past the waterfalls and through the valleys of Tiger Leaping Gorge. Another natural attraction, the Stone Forest, also stands in Yunnan. The Dai minority inhabits the tropical region of Xishuangbanna, where sparkling waters and junglelike flora evoke a bit of Southeast Asia.

Tibet

Tibet, hung from the Himalayas, was considered one of the most magical places in the world before the Chinese invasion of 1950. Though the autonomous region still holds a lofty place in Western imagination, Tibet has been largely stripped of its freedom and identity as a thriving Buddhist region. Nevertheless, Tibet remains a land of colorful people strengthened and characterized by the rugged terrain. The Potala Palace, in Lhasa, which only a handful of foreigners laid eyes on before the 1980s, stretches up its 1,000 rooms to the sky.

PLEASURES AND PASTIMES

Antiques Markets

Chairman Mao alarm clocks, calligraphy scrolls, porcelain, jade pieces, valuable coins, old Chinese locks, and a great number of fake antiques are spread carefully on tables that line the streets of most Chinese cities on a weekly, sometimes daily basis. Ask around for the date and time of the antiques market in your area and be mindful of rip-offs when you arrive. If you are seriously searching for antiques, it's best to get a local who speaks English to bargain for you while you wait unseen for the right price.

Bicycling

Most cities and popular tourist towns offer bicycle rentals for an average of a dollar a day. Mounting a Flying Pigeon and cruising down wide, tree-shaded bike lanes is an experience not to be missed.

Dining

Dining in China is best enjoyed in large groups so you can sample a variety of dishes. Usually the menus are divided into appetizers, meats, vegetables, seafood, soups, and so on. It's best to order from each category so you dine in true Chinese style—dishes at your elbows, across the table, in front of you, stacked up, and sometimes even on the ledge behind to make room for the next round. Although each province, indeed each city, in China has a distinctive way of cooking and eating, there are generally four regional categories of food found across the country.

Northern, or Mandarin, cuisine is characterized by fine cutting and pure seasoning, providing dishes with strong garlic, ginger, and onion flavors. Peking duck, served with pancakes and *hoisin* sauce, and Mongolian hot pot are also native to this region. An abundance of steamed bread (*mantou*) and flat pancakes are sold on the street and make good snacks.

Southern, or Cantonese, cooking is famous for dim sum, an eating experience found in Hong Kong, Guangdong province, and some larger cities with an overseas contingent. Bite-size dumplings, wonton, rice noodle dishes, sesame seed buns filled with bean paste, and a variety of other tasty snacks are pushed around on carts among patrons. Cantonese cooking tends to be the lightest and least oily of the four categories, though it can be just as exotic, with snake, turtle, monkey, rabbit, and a host of other animal and reptile specialties finding their way onto the menus.

Eastern, most notably Shanghainese, food is notorious for its heavy use of oil, though the freshest seafood, from hairy crabs to snails to shark's fin soup, are served in this region. Chicken and seafood dishes are simmered, boiled, or braised in their own juices, enhancing the natural flavors. Some wonderful *baozis* (steamed white bread filled with either vegetables, pork, or black bean paste) are sold on the streets of most cities and towns scattered throughout the region.

The spiciest of the four categories, Sichuan cooking loves to use that Chinese peppercorn and will keep you slugging back bottles of purified water. Chengdu is famous for its snacks, a variety of small dishes both hot and cold, served all day. Tea-smoked duck, marinated for more than 24 hours, peels right off the bone and melts in the mouth. Sichuan hot-pot restaurants have become so popular they are popping up as far away as Beijing.

In some cities restaurants commonly frequented by the locals provide a great enough variety and high enough quality to render them desirable choices—you can see how the populace eats without compromising your own expectations of taste and cleanliness. Other cities have a less developed dining culture; the local restaurants tend toward a Chinese version of fast food and provide fair to middling quality in a setting not quite up to many visitors' standards. Your best alternatives here usually lie with the city's high-class restaurants and the often excellent food served in the local hotels. Even the fancier venues are often quite affordable by Western standards. Most sizable hotels serving foreigners have a Western as well as a Chinese kitchen.

Early Morning

At 6 in the morning, no matter where you are in China, everyone is up and outside buying their daily vegetables, fruits, meats, eggs, and noodles in the local market. Vendors are out steaming, frying, boiling, and selling breakfast snacks to people on their way to work. Men and women practice tai chi in parks, along rivers, and in some unlikely places—the steps of a movie theater, an empty alley, the side entrance of a hotel—whenever the sun rises. Early morning in China is when the cities, towns, and villages come alive and should be experienced as much as possible, as every place has a different way of doing "business."

Hiking

Although this activity is unpopular with locals, China rewards the hiker with natural preserves, national parks, and sacred mountains. Songhuahu in Jilin, the Tiger Leaping Gorge, Emeishan, Huangshan, the Guilin-Yangshuo area, Xinjiang—practically every province has something to offer.

Teahouses

Along West Lake in Hangzhou, inside Chengdu's parks, on the fourth floor of a department store, on cobblestone streets, in subway stations, and along China's many rivers—teahouses are to China as cafés are to France. Relax, chat, and meditate over a pot of Oolong while sampling dried fruit snacks.

Wandering

Wandering and sometimes getting lost in China will reveal an inner logic to the city or town you are visiting. Here is where you get to experience China without a frame of propaganda around it. Encounter charming alleyways that twist behind major streets, hidden outdoor markets, friendly, responsive locals gesturing unintelligible messages, dramatic shifts from poverty to riches, and wild displays of the new and the old.

FODOR'S CHOICE

Hotels

Peninsula, Hong Kong, is simply one of the best and most famous hotels in the world, full of good taste and old-world style as well as all the latest conveniences ($$$$, Ch. 9).

Beijing Hotel, Beijing, the capital's oldest, has hosted such luminaries as Field Marshal Montgomery, Noël Coward, and Zhou Enlai ($$$, Ch. 2).

Ningwozhuang Guesthouse, Lanzhou, Gansu, is an old-fashioned villa set in beautiful gardens ($$–$$$, Ch. 5).

Karakorum Yurt Camp, Karakorum, Republic of Mongolia, set in open grassland, offers the chance to stay in a real yurt without having to rough it too much ($$, Ch. 12).

Victory, Guangzhou, Guangdong, a budget hotel composed of former colonial guest houses, stands on Shamian Island among restored old mansions ($, Ch. 8).

Man-Made Wonders

Bingling Si Shiku, Gansu, or Thousand Buddha Temple and Caves, are filled with Buddhist wall paintings and statuary from the 10th through 17th centuries (Ch. 5).

Changcheng (the Great Wall), Beijing, built by successive dynasties over two millennia, is a collection of many defensive installations that extends some 4,000 km (2,500 mi) from the East China Sea to Central Asia (Ch. 2).

Heping Fandian, Shanghai, also known as the Peace Hotel, is an Art Deco masterpiece right on the Bund (Ch. 6).

Longmen Shiku, Luoyang, Henan, the Dragon Gate Grottoes, are filled with thousands of Buddhist figures carved over several centuries (Ch. 4).

Ming Shisanling, Beijing, the Ming Tombs, in a valley northeast of Beijing, are the final resting place for 13 of the 16 Ming emperors; the approach is along a "spirit way" lined with weeping willow trees and imperial advisers, elephants, camels, horses, and other animals, all carved of stone (Ch. 2).

Mogao Ku, Dunhuang, Gansu, the extraordinary grottoes southeast of the small oasis town of Dunhuang, are home to caves that were painted by Buddhists from the 4th through the 10th centuries (Ch. 5).

Qin Shihuang Ling, Xian, Shaanxi, the tomb of the first Qin emperor, from the 3rd century BC, stands near an army of thousands of life-size **terra-cotta soldiers** with individual faces, buried as Qin's garrison in the afterlife and still being unearthed by archaeologists (Ch. 5).

Victoria Peak, Hong Kong, known in Chinese as Tai Ping Shan, or Mountain of Great Peace, offers a breathtaking panorama of sea, islands, and city on a clear day, as well as parklands for walking or hiking (Ch. 9).

Wangshi Yuan, Suzhou, Jiangsu, the Master of the Nets Garden, the finest in this city of gardens, was originally laid out in the 12th century (Ch. 7).

Yuyuan, Shanghai, a garden built in the 16th century, creates an atmosphere of peace amid the clamor of the city, with rocks, trees, dragon walls, bridges, and pavilions (Ch. 6).

Museums

Gansu Sheng Bowuguan, Lanzhou, Gansu, the Gansu Provincial Museum, though old-fashioned, has some excellent exhibitions on the Silk Road, especially pottery, porcelain, and bronzes (Ch. 5).

Hubei Sheng Bowuguan, Wuhan, Hubei, the Hubei Provincial Museum, contains Mao memorabilia and a fine collection of antiquities from 5th-century BC tombs (Ch. 10).

Nan Yue Wang Mu, Guangzhou, Guangdong, the Museum and Tomb of the Southern Yue Kings, displays a priceless collection of funerary objects from a 2nd-century BC tomb discovered in 1983 (Ch. 8).

Shaanxi Lishi Bowuguan, Xian, Shaanxi, Shaanxi History Museum, opened in 1992 and exhibits artifacts from the Paleolithic Age to 200 BC (Ch. 5).

Shanghai Bowuguan, Shanghai, an exquisitely displayed collection of Chinese art and artifacts, houses a world-renowned bronze collection (Ch. 6).

Zhongguo Lishi Bowuguan, Beijing, the Museum of Chinese History, is one of the world's best troves of Chinese art (Ch. 2).

Natural Wonders

Changbaishan, Jilin, the Changbaishan Nature Reserve, has mountainous forests, hiking, and hot springs (Ch. 3).

Hengshang Shan, Hengyang, Hunan, is one of China's Five Holy Mountains (Ch. 10).

Huangshan, Hefei, Anhui, a misty pine- and rock-covered mountain with peaks that have inspired emperors and artists for centuries, is networked with paths and stairways (Ch. 7).

Lijiang, Guilin, Guangxi, the Li River, is lined with evocative tree-covered karst mountains jutting up above both shores; the cruise to Yangshuo is spectacular (Ch. 10).

Tianchi Hu, Xinjiang, one of the prettiest lakes in China, with clear, clear water, is surrounded by mountains (Ch. 5).

Wuyi Shan Fengjingqu, Fujian, Wuyi Mountain Natural Reserve, has dramatic scenery with peaks, waterfalls, bamboo groves, and tea bushes (Ch. 7).

Palaces

Gugon Bowuguan (The Forbidden City), Beijing, was home to 24 emperors and two dynasties for 500 years; the 200-acre compound is filled with halls, courtyards, and lesser buildings, all stained imperial vermilion, decorated with gold on the outside, and furnished with exquisite screens, thrones, paintings, and more (Ch. 2).

Potala, Lhasa, Tibet, built in the 17th century on the foundation of the 7th-century original, the 11-story palace served as the spiritual and political headquarters of Tibet's theocracy (Ch. 13).

Yiheyuan (Summer Palace), Beijing, built in the mid-18th century, is a garden retreat on the northwest fringe of the city, where imperial families escaped summer heat in airy pavilions among trees and man-made lakes and aboard a marble boat (Ch. 2).

Restaurants

Dingshan Meishi Cheng, Nanjing, Jiangsu, with traditional latticework on the windows, serves excellent local Huaiyang cuisine ($–$$, Ch. 7).

Fortune Garden, Beijing, the city's foremost Cantonese restaurant, serves dishes such as roast suckling pig ($$$$, Ch. 2).

Tang Le Gong, Xian, Shaanxi, specializes in Tang dynasty imperial cuisine ($$$, Ch. 5).

Lijiacai (Li Family Restaurant), Beijing, in a tiny, informal space, serves imperial dishes whose recipes were handed down by a Qing court forebear ($$, Ch. 2).

Meilongzhen, Shanghai, dating from 1938, serves outstanding Sichuanese food in traditional surroundings ($$–$$$, Ch. 6).

Caigenxiang, Guangzhou, Guangdong, is a joy for vegetarians, with a choice of 200 dishes and 100 snacks ($, Ch. 8).

Temples and Monasteries

Gandan Khiid, Ulaan Baatar, Mongolia, houses a Tibetan Buddhist monastery and temples in buildings covered with golden roofs (Ch. 12).

Ganden, Lhasa, Tibet, an enormous monastery established in 1409 that became the foremost center of the Gelugpa sect of Tibetan Buddhism, draws pilgrims paying homage to its sacred sites and relics (Ch. 13).

Jokhang, Lhasa, Tibet, the most sacred building in Tibet, is a temple built in the 7th century that continues to attract worshipers (Ch. 13).

Laboleng Si, Xiahe, Gansu, Labrang Monastery, one of the two great Lamaist temples outside Tibet, was founded in 1710 and holds religious festivals several times a year (Ch. 5).

Linggu Si, Nanjing, Jiangsu, the Spirit Valley Temple, is entered through the 14th-century Beamless Hall, which is made entirely of brick (Ch. 7).

Liu Rong Si Hua Ta, Guangzhou, Guangdong, the Six Banyan Temple, is a landmark in the city with its trompe l'oeil 184-ft-tall pagoda and colorful, carved roofs (Ch. 8).

Tiantan, Beijing, the Temple of Heaven, holds the round altar where the emperor conducted sacrifices on the summer and winter solstices and the blue-roof Hall of Prayer for Good Harvests (Ch. 2).

Wenshu Yuan, Chengdu, Sichuan, a Buddhist monastery dating from the Tang dynasty, has buildings with exquisite carvings (Ch. 11).

Yufo Si, Shanghai, the Jade Buddha Temple, contains a 6½-ft-high statue of Buddha carved from white jade, as well as precious paintings and scriptures (Ch. 6).

FESTIVALS AND SEASONAL EVENTS

China has only three official holidays a year: Spring Festival, or Chinese New Year; National Day; and International Labor Day, for a grand total of five days off. These are high travel times for the Chinese, especially during Chinese New Year, and it's best to avoid them if at all possible.

Many of the most colorful festivals are celebrated by China's ethnic minorities, particularly in the region of Yunnan, an added bonus if your visit coincides with festival times.

The majority of China's holidays and festivals are calculated according to the lunar calendar and can vary by as much as a few weeks from year to year. Check a lunar calendar or with the CITS for dates more specific than those below.

WINTER

DEC. 25/JAN. 1➤ **Christmas and New Year's Day** are becoming an excuse for the Chinese to exchange cards, buy decorations (made in China), and eat out banquet style. In the big cities Christmas makes itself known by a ubiquitous paper Santa that is taped to almost every store. Some employees get a day off on New Year's.

JAN./FEB.➤ **Harbin's Ice Festival,** a tour de force of bigger-than-life ice sculptures of animals, landmarks, and legendary figures, is held from the beginning of January to late February. Although it can be as cold as –30°C, many visitors come to Zhaolin Park to check out the best ice festival China has to offer.

FEB.➤ **Chinese New Year,** China's most celebrated and important holiday, follows the lunar calendar and falls in early to mid-February. Also called Spring Festival, it gives the Chinese an official three-day holiday to visit family and relatives, eat special meals, and throw firecrackers to celebrate the New Year and its respective Chinese zodiac animal. Students and teachers get up to four weeks off, and many others consider that the festival runs as long as a month. It is a particularly crowded time to travel in China. Many offices and services reduce their hours or close altogether. Tickets and hotels may be unavailable for as much as a week.

FEB./MAR.➤ Following a lunar calendar, the **Tibetan New Year** is celebrated in Tibet, Gansu, and northern Sichuan provinces with processions, prayer assemblies, and yak butter sculptures and lamps.

FEB./MAR.➤ The **Spring Lantern Festival** marks the end of the Chinese New Year on the 15th day of the first moon. Colorful paper lanterns are carried through the streets, sometimes accompanied by dragon dances.

SPRING

APR.➤ The Dai minority, who live in the Xishuangbanna region of Yunnan, celebrate their own Lunar New Year, the **Water Splashing Festival,** usually in mid-April. Legend has it that the Dai people were subjected to demons by an evil ruler until one of his consorts lopped off his head with a single hair from his head. This produced an overflow of blood, which is now celebrated as the washing away of one's sins of the previous year. Minorities in colorful dress come from all over the region to enjoy three days of revelry, with activities ranging from boat races on the river to buffalo slaughter.

APR.➤ The **Third Moon Fair** (from the 15th to the 21st day of the third moon, usually April), attracts people to Dali, Yunnan province, from all over the province to celebrate a legendary sighting of the Buddhist goddess of mercy, Guanyin.

APR. 5➤ Not so much a holiday as a day of worship, **Qing Ming** (literally, "clean and bright"), or Remembrance of the Dead, gathers relatives at the graves of the deceased to clean the surfaces and leave fresh flowers.

MAY 1➤ **International Labor Day** is another busy travel time, especially if the holiday falls near a weekend.

MAY 4➤ **Youth Day,** though no longer a publicly celebrated holiday, commemorates the first mass student movement in 1919, which has come to symbolize a rejection of traditional political and religious ideas.

MAY➤ In Dali, of Yunnan province, the **Three Temples Festival,** on the 23rd to the 25th day of the fourth moon, is celebrated with walks to local temples and general merrymaking.

MAY➤ The **Birthday of Tun Hau,** goddess of the sea, is celebrated most heartily in Sai Kung, in Kowloon, where fishermen decorate their boats and gather at temples to pray for good catches for the coming year.

SUMMER

JUNE➤ **The Dragon Boat Festival,** on the fifth day of the fifth moon, celebrates the national hero Qu Yuan, who drowned himself in the 3rd century in protest against the corrupt emperor. Legend has it that people attempted to rescue him by throwing rice dumplings wrapped in bamboo leaves into the sea and frightening fish away by beating drums. Today crews in narrow dragon boats race to the beat of heavy drums, and rice wrapped in bamboo leaves is consumed.

JULY 1➤ Perhaps **July 1** will go down in history as the day China ended 150 years of shame and looked to the future with Hong Kong under its wing.

JULY➤ **The Torch Festival** is celebrated in the towns of Lijiang and Dali, in Yunnan, on the 24th day of the sixth moon.

AUTUMN

SEPT. 8➤ **Confucius's Birthday** may be overlooked in other parts of China, but there are celebrations aplenty in Qufu, his birthplace.

OCT. 1➤ **National Day** celebrates the founding of the People's Republic of China. Tiananmen Square fills up with flowers, entertainment, and a hefty crowd of visitors on this official holiday.

OCT.➤ **Mid-Autumn Festival** is celebrated on the 15th day of the eighth moon, which generally falls in early October. The Chinese spend this time gazing at the full moon and exchanging tasty moon cakes filled with meat, bean paste, sugar, and other delectable surprises.

OCT./NOV.➤ For 10 days the Xishuangbanna region of Yunnan shoots off rockets to celebrate the **Tan Ta Festival.** Special ceremonies take place in local temples in the area.

2 BEIJING
NORTHERN CAPITAL

Wide-eyed Chinese tourists converge on
Tiananmen Square each day at dawn to
watch a military honor guard raise China's
flag. As soldiers march forth from the vast
Forbidden City, these visitors, who usually
number in the hundreds, begin to take
pictures. They jockey for spots beneath the
fluttering banner. They pose before the Gate
of Heavenly Peace, its huge Chairman
Mao portrait gazing benignly from atop the
imperial doorway. This same shot, snapped
by countless pilgrims, adorns family albums
across the Middle Kingdom.

By George
Wehrfritz and
Diana Garrett,
with Bill Smith

Updated by
Keming Liu

THE DAILY PHOTOGRAPHIC RITUAL, the giddy throng gathered beneath the Forbidden City's ancient vermilion edifice, illustrates Beijing's position—unrivaled to this day—at the center of the Chinese universe. In spite of devastating urban renewal, parts of modern Beijing continue to convey an imperial grandeur. But the city is more than a relic or a feudal ghost. New temples to communism—the Great Hall of the People, Chairman Mao's mausoleum—convey the monumental power that still resides within the city's secret courtyards. If China is a dragon, Beijing is its beating heart.

Beijing's historic, cultural, and political preeminence dates back more than seven centuries. It first came to prominence after the Mongol conquest of northern China. In 1278 Kublai Khan, grandson of Genghis, made Beijing the capital of his Yuan dynasty. After the overthrow of the Yuan, the Ming emperor Yongle in 1406 relocated his court to this northern capital in a bid to secure the frontier from more attacks by nomadic herdsmen. Yongle mobilized 200,000 corvée laborers to construct his palace, a maze of interlinking halls, gates, and courtyards now known as the Forbidden City. Ming planners dug moats and canals, plotted Beijing's sweeping roadway grid and in 1553 constructed a massive new city wall to protect their thriving capital. The Ming also built China's grandest public works project: the Great Wall. The Ming Great Wall linked or reinforced several existing walls, especially near the capital, and traversed seemingly impassable mountains. Most of the most spectacular stretches that can be visited near Beijing were built by the Ming. But wall building drained Ming coffers and in the end failed to prevent Manchu horsemen from taking the capital—and China—in 1644.

This foreign dynasty, the Qing, inherited the Ming palaces, built their own retreats (most notably, the Summer Palace, on Kunming Lake), and perpetuated feudalism in China for another 267 years. In its decline, the Qing proved impotent to stop humiliating foreign encroachment. It lost the first Opium War to Great Britain in 1842 (and was forced to cede Hong Kong "in perpetuity" as a result). In 1860 a combined British and French force stormed Beijing and razed the Old Summer Palace, carting away priceless antiquities. After the Qing crumbled in 1911, its successor, Sun Yat-sen's Nationalist Party, struggled to consolidate power. Beijing became a cauldron of social activism. On May 4, 1919, students marched on Tiananmen Square to protest humiliations in Versailles, where Allied commanders negotiating an end to World War I gave Germany's extraterritorial holdings in China to Japan, not Sun's infant republic. Patriotism intensified. In 1937 Japanese imperial armies stormed across Beijing's Marco Polo Bridge to launch a brutal eight-year occupation. Civil war followed close on the heels of Tokyo's 1945 surrender and raged until the Communist victory. Chairman Mao himself declared the founding of a new nation, the People's Republic of China, from the rostrum atop the Gate of Heavenly Peace on October 1, 1949.

Like Emperor Yongle, Mao built a capital that conformed to his own vision. New, Soviet-inspired institutions rose up around—and in— Tiananmen Square. Beijing's city wall, the grandest rampart of its kind in China, was demolished to make way for a ring road. Temples were looted, torn down, closed, or turned into factories during the 1966– 76 Cultural Revolution. In the countryside, some sections of the Great Wall disappeared—pilfered by peasants brick by brick for use in nearby villages.

In recent years old Peking has suffered most from prosperity. Many ancient neighborhoods, replete with traditional courtyard homes lining narrow *hutong*, or alleys, have been bulldozed. In their place a new city of dreary apartment blocks and glitzy commercial developments has risen to house and entertain a citizenry often more interested in indoor plumbing than protecting Beijing's heritage. Preservationism has slowly begun to take hold, but CHAI (to pull down) and QIAN (to move elsewhere) remain common threats to denizens of Beijing's historic neighborhoods.

Beijing's 12 million official residents—plus another 2 million migrant workers—are a compelling mix of old and new. Early morning *taiqi* (tai chi) enthusiasts, bearded old men with caged songbirds, and amateur Peking opera crooners still frequent the city's many charming parks. Cyclists, most pedaling cumbersome, jet black Flying Pigeons, clog the roadways. But few wear padded blue Mao jackets these days, and they all must share the city's broad thoroughfares with trendy Chinese yuppies and their private cars. Beijing traffic has gone from nonexistent to nightmarish in less than a decade, adding auto emissions to the city's winter coal smoke and sparking the newest threat to social order—road rage.

Migrants to Beijing from impoverished rural areas typically work in construction, clean houses, run pedicabs, or collect garbage. Look for them selling fruit on street corners, sleeping at train stations, or loitering in department-store electronics departments to catch a glimpse of television.

Beijing still carries a political charge. It is the seat of China's bloated national bureaucracy, a self-described "dictatorship of the proletariat" that has yet to relinquish its political monopoly. In 1989 student protesters in Tiananmen Square tried—and failed—to topple this old order. The government's brutal response, carried live on TV, remains etched in global memory. More than 10 years later, secret police still mingle with tourists and kite fliers on the square, ready to haul away all those so brave or foolish as to distribute a leaflet or unfurl a banner.

Mao-style propaganda campaigns persist. Slogans that preach unity among China's national minorities, patriotism, and love for the People's Liberation Army decorate the city. The latest Singapore-style campaign is to encourage "civilized citizens." Provincial leaders, who manage increasingly independent regional economies, have all but abandoned such ideological measures; in Beijing they still flourish. The result is a mixture of new prosperity and throwback politics: socialist slogans adorn shopping centers that sell Gucci and Big Macs.

Pleasures and Pastimes

Biking

Beijing's pleasures are best sampled off the subway and out of taxis. In other words, walk or pedal. Rent bikes (available at many hotels) and take an impromptu sightseeing tour. Beijing is flat, and bike lanes exist on most main roads. Pedaling among the city's cyclists isn't as challenging as it looks: copy the locals—keep it slow and ring your bell often. Punctured tire? Not to worry: curb-side repairmen line most streets. Remember to park (and lock) your bike only in designated areas. Most bike parking lots have attendants and cost Y.20.

Dining

China's economic boom has revolutionized dining in Beijing. Gone are shabby state-run restaurants, driven out of business (or into the care of new management) by private establishments that cater to China's emerging middle class. You can now enjoy a hearty Cantonese or

Sichuan meal for under $5 per person—or spend $100 or more on a lavish imperial-style banquet. Hamburgers (or sushi, lasagna, and burritos) are available at numerous new eateries that target tourists, expatriates, and Chinese yuppies. Tips in hotel restaurants are included in the bill.

Peking duck and other local specialties remain popular. New eateries offer regional delights like spicy Sichuan tofu, Cantonese dim sum, Shanghai steamed fish, Xinjiang kabob—even Tibetan yak penis soup. One popular restaurant has commandeered a former palace, while dumpling shops offer dining under the stars in restored courtyard homes. Noisy pre-1949 Old Peking–style restaurants are the newest culinary trend.

CATEGORY	COST*
$$$$	over Y200
$$$	Y125–Y200
$$	Y60–Y125
$	under Y60

*per person for a standard three-course meal, excluding tax and tips

Lodging

China's 1949 Communist victory closed the doors on the opulent accommodations once available to visiting foreigners in Beijing and elsewhere. Functional concrete boxes served the needs of the few "fellow travelers" admitted into the People's Republic of China in the 1950s and '60s. By the late '70s China's lack of high-quality hotels had become a distinct embarrassment, to which opening to foreign investment was the only answer. Two decades later a multitude of polished marble palaces awaits your dollars with attentive service, improved amenities—such as business centers, health clubs, Chinese/Western restaurants, nightclubs, karaoke, beauty salons, and conference/banqueting facilities—and rising prices. Glitz and Western comfort, rather than history and character, are the main selling points for Beijing's near-identical hotels. If you're looking for Chinese-style accommodations enhanced by gardens and rockeries, consider the Bamboo Garden, Haoyuan, and Youhao guest houses (☞ Lodging, *below*).

As traffic conditions worsen, more business travelers are choosing hotels closer to their interests. The more distant hotels, such as the Lido, Friendship, Shangri-La, and Fragrant Hills, all offer shuttle-bus service into the city center (Friendship Store, Beijing Hotel, Lufthansa center). Booking rooms in advance is always advisable, but the current glut of accommodations means room availability is rarely a problem, whatever the season.

CATEGORY	COST*
$$$$	over Y1850
$$$	Y1200–Y1850
$$	Y750–Y1200
$	under Y750

*Prices are for a standard double room, including taxes.

Opera

Pop music has taken root in every Chinese city, but in Beijing it is still possible to see authentic Peking opera. Tragedy, warfare, palace intrigue—this is the stuff of the capital's traditional stage. Operas range from slothful to acrobatic; voices soar to near-shrill heights for female roles and sink to throaty baritones for generals and emperors. Costumes and makeup are without exception extravagant. Shortened performances catering to tourists are held at the Liyuan Juchang Theater. Full operas, and Beijing's enthusiastic opera crowd, can be seen several times each week at a number of theaters, including Chang'an Da Xiyuan (Chang'an Grand Theater).

Shopping

Modern supermarkets stock a wide range of imported food and drink, as well as most toiletries. Numerous "old goods markets" peddle everything from Chairman Mao kitsch to antique porcelain, jewelry, and furniture—plus a full selection of fakes. The Sunday flea market at Panjiayuan is the first stop for many portable antiques (wood carvings, statues, jade, old tile, and so on) entering Beijing from the countryside. Vendors, especially in the market's open-air rear section, are usually peasants who've journeyed to Beijing to sell items collected in their village. Antique rugs and furniture are perhaps Beijing's best bargain. A few dealers will arrange to ship larger items overseas.

Walking

Never bypass an intriguing alleyway. Strolls into the *hutong* frequently reveal ancient neighborhoods: mud-and-timber homes; courtyards full of children, chickens, and mountains of cabbage and coal; and alleys so narrow that pedestrians can't pass two abreast. This is Old Peking. See it before it vanishes. Should you ever get lost in the mazelike alleyways, you can always find a payphone or a rickshaw. Make sure you have a Chinese/English map with you so you can be directed somewhere—Tiananmen Square, for example—to regain your bearings.

EXPLORING BEIJING

Beijing rewards the explorer. Most temples and palaces have gardens and lesser courtyards that are seldom visited. Be curious. Even at the height of the summer tourist rush, the Forbidden City's peripheral courtyards offer ample breathing room, even seclusion. The Temple of Heaven's vast grounds are a pleasure year-round—and enchanting during a snowstorm.

Although the Forbidden City and Tiananmen Square represent the heart of Beijing from imperial and tourist perspectives, the capital lacks a definitive downtown area in terms of shopping (with the exception, perhaps, of Wangfujing) or business, as commercial and entertainment districts have arisen all over.

Outside the city, budget time for hiking. Explore the Ming Tombs or the Eastern Qing Tombs on foot and picnic in the ruins (a tradition among Beijing's expatriate community since the 1920s). Most upscale hotels offer elegant boxed lunches. If you've hired a car to the Great Wall, consider venturing a bit farther into the countryside where farming villages await. Don't be surprised when local farmers invite you into their homes for a rest and some tea.

Numbers in the text correspond to numbers in the margin and on the Beijing, Forbidden City, and Side Trips from Beijing maps.

Great Itineraries

IF YOU HAVE 3 DAYS

Begin day one at the dawn flag-raising ceremony in **Tiananmen Square.** Stroll past the Monument to the People's Heroes, circle **Chairman Mao's mausoleum,** and then head for the nearby ✕ **Grand Hotel** for coffee or breakfast. At 8:30 walk through the **Gate of Heavenly Peace** and spend the morning at the **Forbidden City.** Take the audio tour, which offers an entertaining south-to-north narration. Depart through the Gate of Obedience and Purity (the north gate) and walk west to **Beihai Park** for lunch at the food stalls. Explore the park. Arrive at the north gate before 1:30 for a half-day hutong tour, a guided pedicab ride through a mazelike neighborhood to the **Drum Tower.** Have dinner at the ✕ **Quanjude Peking Duck Restaurant,** south of Tiananmen Square. On day two visit the **Temple of Heaven,** the **Lama Temple,** and perhaps the **National Art Gallery** or **Museum of the Chinese People's Revolution.** Allow time for shopping at **Beijing Curio City, Silk Alley,** and the **Yihong Carpet Factory.** For dinner, eat Sichuanese at ✕ **Ritan Park.** Set aside day three for a trip to the **Ming Tombs** and the **Great Wall** at Mutianyu, where a Japanese gondola offers a dramatic ride to the summit. Bring a brown-bag lunch.

IF YOU HAVE 5 DAYS

For the first two days follow the itinerary above. On day three hire a car and visit the **Great Wall** at Simatai, where long, unrestored strands ascend steep crags. Be prepared for no-handrails hiking, tough climbs, and unparalleled vistas. On day four hire a car and visit the spectacular **Eastern Qing Tombs,** where a "spirit way" lined with carved stone animals and unrestored templelike grave sites rest in a beautiful rural setting. Wear walking shoes and bring a lunch. The drive takes five hours round-trip, so depart early. For an enjoyable day trip closer to Beijing, walk around Kunming Lake at the rambling **Summer Palace** on day five, and then spend a few hours at the nearby **Old Summer Palace,** now an intriguing ruin. Plan an evening to experience **Peking opera** or to relax at a club in the Sanlitun embassy area.

Tiananmen Square to Liulichang Antiques Market

The fame and symbolism of China's heart, Tiananmen, the Gate of Heavenly Peace, have been potent for generations of Chinese, but the events of June 1989 have left it forever etched into world consciousness. South of the square, a district of antiques shops and bookstores shows another side of Chinese culture.

A Good Walk

Start at the Renmin Yingxiong Jinianbei (Monument to the People's Heroes) in **Tiananmen Guangchang** ① (Tiananmen Square). Look to either side of the square for the monuments to the new dynasty—the individual is meant to be dwarfed by their scale. To the west lies the **Renmin Dahuitang** ② (Great Hall of the People), home to China's legislative body, the National People's Congress. The equally solid building opposite is host to the important **Zhongguo Lishi Bowuguan** ③ (Museum of Chinese History) and **Zhongguo Geming Lishi Bowuguan** (Museum of the Chinese Revolution).

Southward, straight ahead, between two banks of heroic sculptures, is the **Maozhuxi Jiniantang** ④ (Mao Zedong Memorial Hall), housing Chairman Mao's tomb. Beyond it stands **Qianmen** (Front Gate), the colloquial name for the **Zhengyangmen** ⑤ (Facing the Sun Gate), which affords great views of the city from the top. At street level, the Qianmen area remains as bustling as ever. Head down Qianmen Dajie, the large road leading south, for about 90 ft before turning right (west) and sharply left (south) down a parallel north–south avenue, Zhu Bao Jie (Jewelry Market Street). The old Beijing Silk Shop, at No. 5, will confirm you are on the right track. Here, in the **Dazhalan** ⑥ area, amid the silk and fur bargains of the present, continue traditions of commerce and entertainment stretching back to the Ming.

To escape the bustle into the calm of residential Beijing, take the second alley to your right, Langfang Ertiao; 65 ft in on the left is a three-story house with carved decorative panels. You'll see a number of such former inns and shops as you proceed west to the Meishijie (Coal Market Street) crossing, where you should head diagonally over to the Qudeng (Fetch Light) Hutong.

Beijing

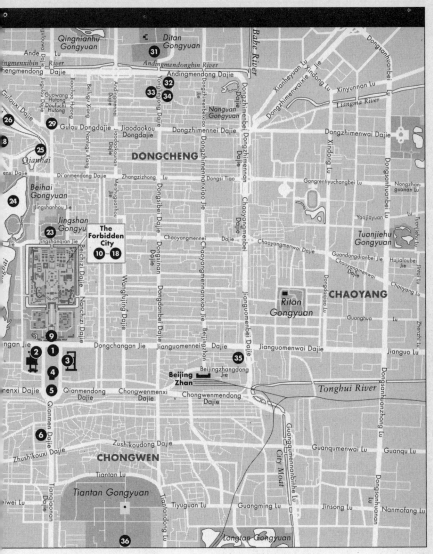

Follow Qudeng Hutong past traditional courtyard houses marked by wooden doorways, auspicious couplets, lintel beams (the more beams, the more important the original inhabitant), and stone door gods. At its end, veer right, then left and onto Tan'er (Charcoal) Hutong. At its close, turn left again down Yanshou Jie (Long Life Street), and the eastern end of **Liulichang Jie** ⑦ (Glazed-Tile Factory Street) will soon be apparent (look for the traditional post office). Continue along Liulichang and cross Nanxinhua Jie via the stone bridge to reach **Guanfu Tang Yishu Bowuguan** ⑧ (Guanfu Classical Art Museum).

TIMING

Allow three hours for the walk, longer if the museums arrest you and if serious antique/curio browsing is anticipated in Liulichang.

Sights to See

❻ **Dazhalan** (Large Wicker Gate). Popularly known for a gate that was lowered each night in Ming times to enforce a curfew, this district of close-packed lanes crowded with flags and sideboards was once filled with a cacophony of merchants, eateries, teahouses, wine shops, theaters, and brothels. Palace officials (and the occasional emperor in disguise) would escape here for a few hours' respite from the suffocating imperial maze. Traditional shops and crowded alleys still make Dazhalan one of Beijing's most interesting commercial areas, especially now that most shopping in the capital is conducted behind the glass screens of glitzy malls. Dazhalan's specialties include clothing, fabric, Chinese medicine, and Peking opera costumes. ⊠ *Zhubaoshi Jie, near Qianmen.*

❽ **Guanfu Tang Yishu Bowuguan** (Guanfu Classical Art Museum). This private museum contains a fine collection of imperial porcelain and furniture. The proprietor, Ma Yaodo, is a recognized authority on Chinese antiques. He offers occasional seminars (with English translation) on identifying and understanding traditional Chinese porcelain and furniture. Call to make reservations. ⊠ *53 Liulichang Xi Jie, Xuanwu District,* ☎ *010/6317–5059.* ▭ *Y20.* ☼ *Daily 9:30–5:30.*

❼ **Liulichang Jie** (Glazed-Tile Factory Street). The Ming factory that gave the street its name and the Forbidden City its yellow top was destroyed by the Qing, but renovation has restored the many book, arts, and antiques shops that crowded here in early Qing times. Be sure to visit the **Zhongguo Shu Dian** (China Bookstore; ⊠ Opposite No. 115) and the most famous shop on the street, **Rongbaozhai** (⊠ 19 Liulichang Xijie), which sells paintings, antiques, and calligraphy materials.

NEED A
BREAK?

Old shops line the sides of Liulichang, where high-rises and fancy restaurants are juxtaposed with ancient courtyards and teahouses. You can get a cup of tea upstairs at the **Jiguge** teahouse (⊠ 136 Liulichang Dong Jie), next to the stone pedestrian bridge. If you're hungry, the simple **Benshanxian** (⊠ 39 Nanxinhua Jie) restaurant is just over the bridge to the south. Employees lunch at the cafeteria in the **Renmin Dahuitang** (Great Hall of the People). You won't find many English-speakers (or forks) here, but you can order good and inexpensive food (by picture) and get friendly with the locals, with whom you'll share a long table.

❹ **Maozhuxi Jiniantang** (Mao Zedong Memorial Hall). Sentries here will assure that your communion with the Great Helmsman is brief. You'll be guided into a spacious lobby dominated by a marble Mao statue and then to the Hall of Reverence, where his embalmed body lies in state, wrapped in a Chinese flag inside a crystal coffin that is lowered each night into a subterranean freezer. In a bid to limit Mao's deification, a second-story museum, dedicated to the former Premier Zhou Enlai, former general Zhu De, and China's Vice Chairman before the

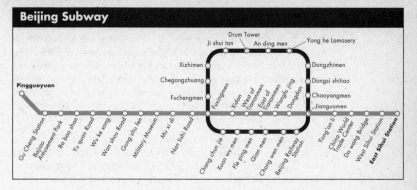

Beijing Subway

Cultural Revolution Liu Shaoqi (whom Mao persecuted to death during the Cultural Revolution), was added in 1983. The hall's builders willfully ignored the square's geomancy: the mausoleum faces north, boldly contradicting centuries of imperial ritual. Out back, where reverence turns to tack, hawkers still push "Maomorabilia." For genuine Cultural Revolution souvenirs, wait until Liulichang. ⊠ *Tiananmen Sq., Chongmen District,* ☎ *010/6513–2277.* 🖾 *Free.* ⊘ *Mon.–Sat. 8:30 AM–11:30 AM.*

❷ Renmin Dahuitang (Great Hall of the People). This solid edifice owes its Stalinist weight to the last years of the Sino-Soviet pact. Its gargantuan dimensions (205,712 square yards of floor space) exceed that of the Forbidden City. It was built by 14,000 laborers who worked around the clock for eight months. China's legislature meets in the aptly named Ten Thousand People Assembly Hall, beneath a panoply of 500 star lights revolving around a giant red star. Thirty-one reception rooms are distinguished by the arts and crafts of the provinces they represent. Call a day ahead to confirm that it's open. ⊠ *West side of Tiananmen Sq., Xuanwu District,* ☎ *010/6309–6156.* 🖾 *Y15.* ⊘ *Daily 8:30–3.*

❶ Tiananmen Guangchang (Tiananmen Square). The world's largest public square, and the heart of modern China, it owes little to the grand imperial designs of the Yuan, Ming, and Qing—and everything to the successor dynasty of Mao Zedong. Turn your back on the entrance to the Forbidden City, the Gate of Heavenly Peace, and the wonders of feudalism. Looking south, across the proletarian panorama, is the Great Helmsman's tomb. The old Imperial Way once stretched south from the Forbidden City. Where photographers now hustle for customers once stood quarters for the Imperial Guard and rice and wood stores for the imperial kitchen. Fires and demolition resulted in the beginnings of the square during the Republican era. The young protesters who assembled here in the 1919 May Fourth Movement established an honorable tradition of patriotic dissent.

At the square's center stands the tallest monument in China, the **Renmin Yingxiong Jinianbei** (Monument to the People's Heroes), 125 ft of granite obelisk remembering those who died for the revolution. Exhortations from Chairman Mao and Premier Zhou Enlai decorate it; eight marble reliefs line the base with scenes of revolution from 1840 to 1949. Constructed from 1952 to 1958, the monument marks the formal passing of Old Peking; once, the outer palace gate of the imperial city stood here.

As you leave the terrace southward, imagine mass Soviet-style parades with 600,000 marchers. At the height of the Cultural Revolution in 1967, hundreds of thousands of Red Guards crowded the square, chanting Mao's name and waving his Little Red Book. In June 1989 the square was the scene of tragedy when hundreds of student demonstrators and bystanders were killed by troops breaking up the pro-democracy protest. Known as "six-four" or "June 4th," the movement has become an albatross about the Chinese government's neck in regards to human rights and freedom of speech, a point of contention in Sino-American relations. Aside from the grand and tragic events here over the last 50 years, Tiananmen is truly a people's square, alive with local kite fliers and wide-eyed tourists from out of town. ⊠ *Bounded by Changan Jie on north and Xuanwumen Jie on south, Chongmen District.*

❺ **Zhengyangmen** (Facing the Sun Gate). From its top looking south, you can see that Zhengyangmen actually comprised two gates: the **Tian Lou** (Arrow Tower) in front was, until 1915, connected to Zhengyangmen by a defensive half-moon wall. The central gates of both structures opened only for the emperor's biannual trips to the Temple of Heaven to the south. Don't miss the evocative photo exhibition of Old Peking. Have some tea atop Zhengyangmen before heading up the Arrow Tower for views of the old Qianmen railway station, now the Railway Workers Cultural Palace. ⊠ *Xuanwumen Jie.*

★ ❸ **Zhongguo Lishi Bowuguan** (Museum of Chinese History). An extensive array of art and antiquities depicting China's cultural history is on display here. The collection, much of it borrowed from provincial museums, ranks among the world's best troves of Chinese art. Items include 3,000-year-old Shang oracle bones, priceless Zhou bronzes, Tang tomb relics, and imperial porcelains. Exhibitions are labeled in Chinese only. Bags must be checked (Y1) before you enter. ⊠ *South end of building on east side of Tiananmen Sq., Chongmen District,* ☎ *010/6512–8986.* ☒ *Y20.* ⊙ *Tues.–Sun. 8:30–3:30.*

Zhongguo Geming Lishi Bowuguan (Museum of the Chinese Revolution). Exhibits here relate China's official revolutionary history. The material, which includes rare photographs, documents, maps, and various medals awarded to "revolutionary martyrs," begins with the party's gestation during the May Fourth Movement (1919) and ends with the 1949 Communist victory. Explanations are in Chinese and English. All bags must be checked (Y1) before you enter. Call in advance to confirm your visit. ⊠ *North end of building on east side of Tiananmen Sq., Chongmen District,* ☎ *010/6512–9347.* ☒ *Y5.* ⊙ *Tues.–Sun. 8:30–5.*

Gugon Bowuguan (The Forbidden City)

★ It was from these nearly 200 acres at the heart of the Northern Capital that 24 emperors and two dynasties ruled the Middle Kingdom for more than 500 years. The city is known also as the Zijin Cheng (Purple City) because of the stately vermilion walls that enclosed the inner city, which begins at Wumen, north of Tiananmen. In imperial times, no buildings were allowed to exceed the height of these walls. Officially the site is now known as the Gugong Bowuguan (Old—as in former—Palace Museum), but Westerners usually just call it the Forbidden City. The city's walls towered above Old Peking and humbled everything in their view. Moats and gigantic timber doors protected each "son of heaven." Shiny double-eaved roofs, glazed imperial yellow, marked the vast complex as the royal court's exclusive dominion. Inside, ornate decor displayed China's most exquisite artisanship—ceilings covered with turquoise and blue dragons, walls draped with scrolls holding priceless calligraphy or lined with intricate cloisonné screens, thrones padded in delicate silks, floors of glass-smooth marble. Miraculously, the palace survived fire and war—and imperial China's final collapse.

Equally miraculous is how quickly the Forbidden City rose. The third Ming emperor, Yongle, oversaw 200,000 laborers build the complex in just 14 years, finishing in 1420. Yongle relocated the Ming capital to Beijing to strengthen China's vulnerable northern frontier, and Ming and Qing emperors ruled from inside the palace walls until the dynastic system crumbled in 1911.

The Forbidden City embodies architectural principles first devised three millennia ago in the Shang dynasty. Each main hall faces south, and looks upon a courtyard flanked by lesser buildings. This symmetry of *taoyuan,* a series of courtyards leading to the main and final courtyard, repeats itself along a north–south axis that bisects the imperial palace. This line is visible in the form of a broad walkway paved in marble and reserved for the emperor's sedan chair. All but the sovereign—even court ministers, the empress, and favored concubines—trod on pathways and passed through doors set to either side of this Imperial Way. 🚃 *Y55.* 🕑 *Daily 8:30–4.*

A Good Walk

Enter the Forbidden City through the **Tiananmen** ⑨ (Gate of Heavenly Peace), easily identified by its massive Chairman Mao portrait overlooking Tiananmen Square. Northward beyond the **Wumen** ⑩ (Meridian Gate), where the emperor made announcements, stands the outer palace, consisting of three halls used for high public functions. You'll first reach the **Taihedian** ⑪ (Hall of Supreme Harmony), then the **Zhonghedian** ⑫ (Hall of Complete Harmony), and after this the **Baohedian** ⑬ (Hall of Preserving Harmony). For a break from the Forbidden City's grand central halls, turn right beyond the hall to visit smaller peripheral palaces—once home to imperial relatives, attendants, and eunuchs and the scene of much palace intrigue. Next comes the **Zhenbaoguan** ⑭ (Zijin Cheng; Hall of Jewelry). Continue northward to Qianlong's Garden and the Concubine Well. Return via a narrow north–south passage that runs to the west of these courtyards. On the way is the **Zhongbiaoguan** ⑮ (Hall of Clocks and Watches). Walk northward from the nine-dragon carving and through the **Qianqingmen** ⑯ (Gate of Heavenly Purity) to enter the **Nei Ting** ⑰ (Inner Palace), the private rooms where the imperial family resided. Beyond the palace are the rocks, pebbles, and greenery of the **Yuhuayuan** ⑱ (Imperial Gardens). From here you can go back southward to Wumen.

TIMING

The walk through main halls, best done by audio tour, takes about two hours. Allow two more hours to explore side halls and gardens.

Sights to See

⑬ **Baohedian** (Hall of Preserving Harmony). The highest civil service examinations, which were personally approved by the emperor (who possessed superior knowledge of Chinese literature, rhetoric, and politics), were once administered in this hall. Candidates were selected from across China, and those who were successful served the imperial court. Behind the hall, a 200-ton marble relief of nine dragons, the palace's most treasured stone carving, adorns the descending staircase. It's the palace's most treasured stone carving.

⑰ **Nei Ting** (Inner Palace). Here, the emperor and his family carried on the rituals of their daily lives. The **Qianqinggong** (Hall of Heavenly Purity) holds another imperial throne; the **Jiaotaidian** (Hall of Union) was the venue for the empress's annual birthday party; and royal couples consummated their marriages in the **Kunninggong** (Palace of Earthly Peace). The emperor's family, however, didn't even stay in the same house with him; his many concubines provided him with their services on his order and by his preference.

24

Gugon Bowuguan (The Forbidden City)

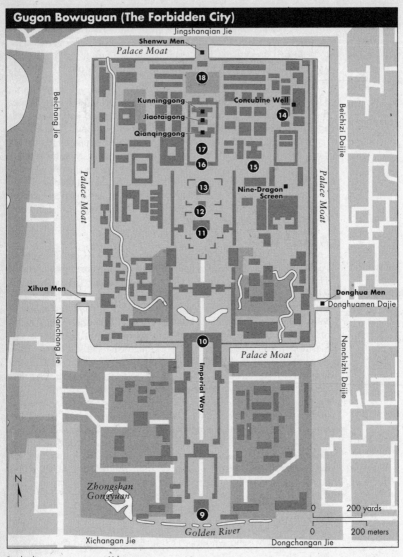

⓰ **Qianqingmen** (Gate of Heavenly Purity). Even the emperor's most trusted ministers never passed beyond this gate; by tradition, they gathered outside at dawn, ready to report to their sovereign.

⓫ **Taihedian** (Hall of Supreme Harmony). The building—used for royal birthdays, weddings, and Lunar New Year ceremonies—is fronted by a broad flagstone courtyard, the largest open area in the complex. Bronze vats, once kept brimming with water to fight fires, ring this vast expanse. The hall sits atop three stone tiers with an elaborate drainage system that channels rainwater through 1,100 carved dragons. On the top tier outside the hall, bronze cranes symbolize longevity, and an imperial sundial and grain measures invite bumper harvests. Inside, cloisonné cranes flank a massive throne beneath grand timber pillars decorated with golden dragons. Above the imperial chair hangs a heavy bronze ball—put there to crush any pretender to the throne.

⓽ **Tiananmen** (Gate of Heavenly Peace). This imposing structure was the traditional rostrum for the reading of imperial edicts. The Great Helmsman himself used it to establish the People's Republic of China on October 1, 1949, and again to review millions of Red Guards during the Cultural Revolution. Ascend the gate for a dramatic vantage on Tiananmen Square. Bags must be checked prior to entry, and visitors are required to pass through a metal detector. ✉ *Changan Jie at Tiananmen Guangchang,* ☎ *010/6513–2255.* ✉ *Y30.* ☉ *Daily 8–4:30.*

⓾ **Wumen** (Meridian Gate). At this U-shape doorway the emperor reviewed his armies and announced yearly planting schedules. Before entering, you can buy tickets to the Forbidden City and rent the accompanying Acoustiguide audio tour at the ticket office in the outer courtyard. ✉ *Y55; audio tour, Y30.* ☉ *Daily 8:30–4:30.*

⓲ **Yuhuayuan** (Imperial Gardens). Beyond the private palaces at the Forbidden City's northern perimeter stand ancient cypress trees, stone mosaic pathways, and a rock garden. You can exit the palace at the north through the park's **Shenwumen** (Gate of Obedience and Purity).

⓮ **Zhenbaoguan** (Zijin Cheng; Hall of Jewelry). Actually a series of halls, it has breathtaking examples of imperial ornamentation. The first room displays imperial candleholders, wine vessels, tea-serving sets, and—in the center—a 5-ft-tall golden pagoda commissioned by Qing emperor Qian Long in honor of his mother. A cabinet on one wall contains the 25 imperial seals, China's equivalent of the crown jewels in their embodiment of royal authority. Jade bracelets and rings, golden hair pins, and ornamental coral fill the second hall; and carved jade landscapes a third. ✉ *Y5.*

⓯ **Zhongbiaoguan** (Hall of Clocks and Watches). Here you'll find a collection of water clocks and early mechanical timepieces from Europe and China. Clocks astride elephants, implanted in ceramic trees, borne by a herd of goats, and mounted in a pagoda are among this collection's many rewards. Don't miss the temple clock, with its robed monks. ✉ *Y5.*

⓬ **Zhonghedian** (Hall of Complete Harmony). In this more modest building emperors greeted audiences and held banquets. It housed the royal plow, with which the emperor himself would turn a furrow to commence spring planting.

NEED A
BREAK?

A small snack bar, **Fast Food** (✉ North end of vendors' row between Tiananmen and Wumen), has noodles, set lunches, tea, and soft drinks.

The Muslim Quarter

Southeast of Liulichang is the lively Niu Jie (Ox Street) and its important mosque. Ethnic Hui—Han Chinese whose ancestors converted to Islam—make up most of the area's faithful. Their enclave, which occupies one of Beijing's oldest neighborhoods, has kept its traditional flavor despite ongoing urban renewal. Nearby is the extensive Buddhist Temple of the Source of Law, buried deep in a quiet hutong that houses a mixture of ancient and modern buildings.

A Good Walk

Begin at the **Niu Jie Qingzhensi** ⑲ (Ox Street Mosque). From the mosque walk south along the narrow Niu Jie (Ox Street) until you reach a crossroad. Turn left into **Nanheng Xijie** ⑳ (Southern Cross Street West), the center of commerce in the enclave. Continue eastward for 500 yards and turn left into Jiaozi Hutong just before you reach a large green building on your left. This is the headquarters of the Chinese Islamic Association (you should spot a red flag fluttering in front of the dome). Turn right immediately into the narrow Fayuansi Qian Jie, passing new apartments on your left and traditional courtyard houses on your right.

On the left you'll see the ancient temple of **Fayuansi** ㉑ (Source of Law Temple), which has an outstanding collection of bronze Buddha images. Continue eastward on Fayuansi Qian Jie until it ends at Qijing Hutong (Seven Well Alley). Turn right, cross Nanheng Xilu, and continue southward on Meng'er Hutong. Past a typical stretch of new highrise apartments, you'll find **Wanshou Gongyuan** ㉒ (Wanshou Park) on your right. Exit through the south gate and turn right on Baizhifang Dongjie (White Paper Lane East). Continue westward and turn right at Youannei Dajie, which becomes Niu Jie one block north.

TIMING

This walk takes about three hours, allowing for time in the mosque and the temple. Exploring alleys in this neighborhood, especially those running west from Niu Jie, is always rewarding.

Sights to See

㉑ **Fayuansi** (Source of Law Temple). The Chinese Buddhist Theoretical Institute houses and trains monks at this temple. Theoretical institutes in China are centers for the study of Buddhist teachings; they generally function within the boundaries of current regime policy. You can observe both elderly practitioners chanting mantras in the main prayer halls at Fayuansi, as well as robed students kicking soccer balls in a side courtyard. Before lunch the smells of vegetarian stir-fry tease the nose. The dining hall has simple wooden tables set with cloth-wrapped bowls and chopsticks. Dating from the 7th century but last rebuilt in 1442, the temple holds a fine collection of Ming and Qing statues, including a sleeping Buddha and an unusual grouping of copper-cast Buddhas seated on a thousand-petal lotus. ✉ *7 Fayuansi Qianjie, Xuanwu District,* ☏ *010/6303–4171 or 010/6353–4171.* ✐ *Y5.* ☉ *Thurs.–Tues. 8:30–11 and 1:30–4.*

⑳ **Nanheng Xijie** (Southern Cross Street West). Nanheng Xijie is filled with restaurants and shops catering to both the local Hui Muslims and newcomers from China's distant Xinjiang province. Restaurants serve Muslim dishes, including steamed meat buns, beef noodles, and a variety of baked breads; shops offer tea from across China; and street vendors sell flatbreads, fruit, and snacks. ✉ *Nanheng Xijie, Xuanwu District.*

⑲ **Niu Jie Qingzhensi** (Ox Street Mosque). Built during the Northern Song dynasty in 996, Beijing's oldest and largest mosque sits at the center of the Muslim quarter. Its exterior looks decidedly Chinese, with a traditional tile roof adorning its front gate. The freestanding wall opposite the mosque's main entrance is called a spirit wall, and was erected to prevent ghosts, who are believed not to navigate tight corners, from passing into the mosque. Today the main gate to the mosque is kept closed. Enter the mosque from the alley just to the south. Inside, arches and posts are inscribed with Koranic verse, and a Tower for Viewing the Moon allows imams to measure the beginning and end of Ramadan, Islam's month of fasting and prayer. Male visitors must wash themselves and remove their shoes before entering the main prayer hall. Women are confined to a rear prayer hall. At the rear of the complex is a minaret from which a muezzin calls the faithful to prayer. All visitors must wear long trousers or skirts and keep their shoulders covered. Women are not permitted to enter some areas. ⊠ *88 Niu Jie, Xuanwu District.* ☜ *Y10.* ☉ *Daily 8–sunset.*

㉒ Wanshou Gongyuan (Wanshou Park). Though smaller and more modern than Beijing's more famous parks, this one offers an attractive lawn and inviting shaded benches. Enter through the east gate and wander among the groups of old men with caged songbirds, mah-jongg (a chess-like game), and cards; roller-skating kids; croquet players; and qi gong practitioners. ⊠ *Between Meng'er Hutong and Baizhifang Dongjie, Xuanwu District.* ☜ *Y.20.* ☉ *Daily 6 AM–8:30 PM.*

North and East of the Forbidden City

Historic temples, parks, and houses that once lay within the walls of imperial Beijing now provide islands of tranquillity among the busy streets of this modern downtown area, most of which lies in the Dongcheng (East City) District.

A Good Tour

Start just north of the Forbidden City at the first in a series of parks, **Jingshan Gongyuan** ㉓ (Prospect Hill Park). From here you can walk through the greenery of **Beihai Gongyuan** ㉔ (North Lake Park), **Qianhai Gongyuan** ㉕ (Qianhai Lake Park), and **Houhai Gongyuan** ㉖ (Houhai Lake Park). Outside the park, visit the traditional courtyard of the **Song Qing-ling Guju** ㉗ (Soong Ching-ling's Former Residence), once the home of Sun Yat-sen's wife. Next, take a cab to **Gongwangfu** ㉘ (Prince Gong's Palace) to see how imperial relatives lived. Walk or take a cab to the **Gulou** ㉙ (The Drum Tower) and the nearby bell tower. Take a cab again to get to the **Gudai Qianbi Zhanlanguan** ㉚ (Museum of Antique Currency) to see rare Chinese coins, and to the **Ditan Gongyuan** ㉛ (Temple of Earth Park). Walk on to **Yonghegong** ㉜ (Lama Temple), Beijing's main Tibetan Buddhist temple; then to **Kong Miao** ㉝ (Temple of Confucius); and the neighboring **Guozijian** ㉞ (Imperial Academy), where Confucian scholars sat imperial examinations.

TIMING

If you want to do this all at once, it will take you a full day. The neighborhood is ideal for bike exploration.

A Good Bike Ride

A great way to explore Old Peking is by bicycle. The ride between Ditan Park and Coal Hill includes some of the city's most famous sights and finest hutong. Begin at **Ditan Gongyuan** ㉛ (Temple of Earth Park), just north of the Second Ring Road on Yonghegong Jie. Park your bike in the lot outside the south gate and take a quick walk. Next, ride south along Yonghegong Jie until you come to the main entrance of **Yonghegong** ㉜ (Lama Temple). Running west, across the street from the temple's main gate, is Guozijian Jie. Shops near the intersection sell

Buddhist statues, incense, texts (in Chinese), and tapes of traditional Chinese Buddhist music. Browse them before riding west to **Kong Miao** ㉝ (Temple of Confucius) and the neighboring **Guozijian** ㉞ (Imperial Academy). The arches spanning Guozijian Jie are the only ones of their kind remaining in Beijing.

Follow Guozijian Jie west until it empties onto Andingmennei Dajie. Enter this busy road with care (there's no traffic signal) and ride south to Guloudong Dajie, another major thoroughfare. Turn right (west) and ride to the **Gulou** ㉙ (The Drum Tower). From here detour through the alleys just north to the Zhonglou. A market of tiny noodle stalls and restaurants links the two landmarks. Retrace your route south to Di'anmenwai Dajie (the road running south from the Drum Tower), turning onto Yandai Jie, the first lane on the right. Makers of long-stem pipes once lined the lane's narrow way (one small pipe shop still does). Sadly, much of the area is slated for redevelopment.

Wind northwest on Yandai Jie past guest houses, bicycle repair shops, tiny restaurants, and crumbling traditional courtyard houses toward Houhai Park. Turn left onto Xiaoqiaoli Hutong and find the arched bridge that separates **Houhai** ㉖ and **Qianhai** ㉕ lakes. Before the bridge, follow the trail along Houhai's north shore, traveling west toward **Song Qing-ling Guju** ㉗ (Soong Ching-ling's Former Residence). Circle the lake until you arrive at Deshengmennei Dajie. Follow it south to the second alley, turning east (left) onto Yangfang Hutong, which leads back to the arched bridge. Park your bike in the first alley off Yangfang Hutong, Dongming Hutong, and walk toward the lake. At the footpath and market that hugs its banks, turn left and walk about 100 yards to find a tiny lane lined with antiques and curio shops.

After bargain hunting, ride along Yangfang Hutong past the stone bridge and follow Qianhai Lake's west bank. Sip a soda, beer, or tea at the teahouse pavilion on the lake. Continue along the lane to Qianhai Xijie, then fork right (northwest) just after a restaurant sign bearing a large heart. Nearby, but difficult to find, is **Gongwangfu** ㉘ (Prince Gong's Palace), 300 yards north of the China Conservatory of Music. Look for the brass plaque.

TIMING

Allow a half day for this ride, longer if you expect to linger at the sights or explore the parks on foot.

Sights to See

㉔ **Beihai Gongyuan** (North Lake Park). Immediately north of Zhong-nanhai, the tightly guarded residential compound of China's senior leaders, the park is easily recognized by the white Tibetan stupa perched on a nearby hill. Near the south gate is the **Tuan Cheng** (Round City). It contains a white-jade Buddha, said to have been sent from Burma to Qing emperor Qian Long, and an enormous jade bowl given to Kublai Khan. Nearby, the well-restored **Yongan Si** (Temple of Eternal Peace) contains a variety of Buddhas and other sacred images. Climb to the stupa from Yongan Temple. Once there, you can pay an extra Y1 to ascend the Buddha-bedecked **Shangyin Tang** (Shangyin Hall) for a view into forbidden Zhongnanhai.

The lake is Beijing's largest and most beautiful public waterway. Amusement park rides line its east edge, and kiosks stock assorted snacks. On summer weekends the lake teems with paddle boats. In winter it's Beijing's most popular ice-skating rink. The **Wu Long Ting** (Five Dragon Pavilion), on Beihai's northwest shore, was built in 1602 by a Ming dynasty emperor who liked to fish and view the moon. The halls north of it were added later. Among the restaurants in the park is **Fangshan,** an elegant establishment open since the Qing dynasty. ✉ *South Gate, Weijin Lu, Xicheng District.* ☎ *010/6404–0610.* ☞ *Y10; extra fees for some sights.* ◷ *Daily 9–dusk.*

㉛ Ditan Gongyuan (Temple of Earth Park). In the 16th-century park are the square altar where emperors once made sacrifices to the earth god and the Hall of Deities. ✉ *Yonghegong Jie, just north of Second Ring Rd., Dongcheng District,* ☎ *010/6421–4657.* ☞ *Y1.* ◷ *Daily 6–dusk.*

㉘ Gongwangfu (Prince Gong's Palace). This grand compound sits in a neighborhood once reserved for imperial relatives. Built during the Ming dynasty, it fell to Prince Gong, brother of Qing emperor Xianfeng and later an adviser to Empress Dowager Cixi. With nine courtyards joined by covered walkways, it was once one of Beijing's most lavish residences. The largest hall, now a banquet room, offers summer Peking opera and afternoon tea to guests on guided hutong tours (☞ Beijing A to Z). Some literary scholars believe this was the setting of *The Dream of the Red Chamber,* China's best-known classic novel. ✉ *Xicheng District,* ☎ *010/6618–0573.* ☞ *Y5.* ◷ *Daily 8:30–4:30.*

㉚ Gudai Qianbi Zhanlanguan (Museum of Antique Currency). This museum in a tiny courtyard house showcases a small but impressive selection of rare Chinese coins. Explanations are in Chinese only. Also in the courtyard are coin and curio dealers. ✉ *Deshengmen Tower south bldgs., Bei'erhuan Jie, Xicheng District,* ☎ *010/6201–8073.* ☞ *Y5.* ◷ *Tues.–Sun. 9–4.*

㉙ Gulou (The Drum Tower). Until the late 1920s the 24 drums once housed in this tower were Beijing's timepiece. Sadly, all but one of these huge drums have been destroyed, and the survivor is in serious need of renovation. Kublai Khan built the first drum tower on this site in 1272. You can climb to the top of the present tower, which dates from the Ming dynasty. Old photos of Beijing's hutong line the walls beyond the drum; there's also a scale model of a traditional courtyard house. The nearby **Zhonglou** (Bell Tower), built in 1747, offers worthwhile views from the top of a long, narrow staircase. The huge 63-ton bronze bell, supported by lacquered wood stanchions, is also worth seeing. ✉ *North end of Dianmen Dajie, Dongcheng District.* ☞ *Y6 each tower; Y10 combined.* ◷ *Daily 9–4:30.*

㉞ Guozijian (Imperial Academy). Once the highest academic institution in China, it was established as a school for boys in 1306 and evolved into a think tank devoted to the Confucian classics. Scholars studied here to prepare for imperial exams. ✉ *Guozijian Lu next to Temple of Confucius, Dongcheng District,* ☎ *010/6406–2418.* ☞ *Y6.* ◷ *Daily 9–4:30.*

㉓ Jingshan Gongyuan (Prospect Hill Park). This park was built around Meishan (Coal Hill), a small peak formed from earth excavated for the Forbidden City's moats. The hill was named for an imperial coal supply supposedly buried beneath it. Climb a winding stone staircase past peach and apple trees to Wanchun Pavilion, the park's highest point. It overlooks the Forbidden City to the south and the Bell and Drum towers to the north. Chongzhen, the last Ming emperor, is said to have hanged himself on Coal Hill as his dynasty collapsed in 1644. ✉ *Jingshanqian Dajie at Forbidden City, Dongcheng District,* ☎ *010/6404–4071 or 010/6403–2244.* ☞ *Y3.* ◷ *Daily 9–4:30.*

㉝ Kong Miao (Temple of Confucius). This austere temple, which honors China's greatest sage, has endured close to eight centuries of additions and restorations. Stelae and ancient musical instruments are the temple's main attractions. The Great Accomplishment Hall houses Confucius's funeral tablet and shrine, flanked by copper-color statues depicting China's wisest Confucian scholars. A selection of unique musical instruments are played only on the sage's birthday. A forest of stone stelae, carved in the mid-1700s to record the *Thirteen Classics,* philosophical works attributed to Confucius, lines the west side of the grounds. ⊠ *Guozijian Lu at Yunghegong Lu near Lama Temple, Dongcheng District,* ☎ *010/8401–1977.* ☐ *Y10.* ☉ *Daily 8:30–5.*

㉕–㉖ **Qianhai Gongyuan and Houhai Gongyuan** (Qianhai and Houhai Lake Parks). The parks surrounding these two lakes are popular for their markets. Near Qianhai's southwest entrance antiques shops line the alley leading from the north gate of Beihai Park (☞ Beihai Gongyuan). You can get to another curio market on Houhai's western shore by walking (or biking) along Qianhai's eastern shore and crossing the bridge to Houhai. Visit early on weekend mornings to view the produce and dry goods market at Houhai's northern end. ⊠ *North side of Dianmen Xi Lu, north of Beihai Lake, Xicheng District.*

㉗ **Song Qing-ling Guju** (Soong Ching-ling's Former Residence). Soong Ching-ling (1893–1981) was the wife of Sun Yat-sen, the Nationalist revolutionary who founded the Republic of China in 1911. Unlike her younger sister, Soong Meiling, who married Nationalist strongman Chiang Kai-shek, Ching-ling sided with the Chinese Communists in 1949 and was hailed as a key supporter of the revolution. Her former residential compound is a wonderful example of traditional courtyard architecture. A small museum documents her eventful life and work in support of impoverished women and children. Exhibits are labeled in English as well as Chinese. ⊠ *46 Houhai Beiyan, Xicheng District,* ☎ *010/6403–5997 or 010/6404–4205.* ☐ *Y8.* ☉ *Tues.–Sun. 9–4.*

★ **㉜** **Yonghegong** (Lama Temple). This Tibetan Buddhist temple is Beijing's most visited religious site. Its five main halls and numerous galleries are hung with finely detailed *thangkhas* (painted cloth scrolls) and decorated with carved or cast Buddha images—all guarded by young lamas (monks). Originally a palace for Prince Yongzheng, it was transformed into a temple after he became the Qing's third emperor in 1725. The temple flourished under Yongzheng's successor, Emperor Qianlong, housing some 1,500 resident monks. Unlike most "feudal" sites in Beijing, the Lama Temple survived the 1966–76 Cultural Revolution unscathed.

You'll walk past trinket stands with clattering wind chimes to reach the temple's five main halls. The Hall of Heavenly Kings has statues of Maitreya, the future Buddha, and Weitou, China's guardian of Buddhism. In the courtyard beyond, a pond with a bronze mandala represents a Buddhist paradise. In the Hall of Harmony sit Buddhas of the Past, Present, and Future. Note the exquisite silk thangkha of White Tara—the embodiment of compassion—hanging from the west wall. The Hall of Eternal Blessing contains images of the Medicine and Longevity Buddhas. Beyond, courtyard galleries display numerous statues depicting Tibetan deities and dharma guardians, some passionately entwined.

A large statue of Tsong Khapa (1357–1490), founder of the Gelugpa order, sits in the Hall of the Wheel of Law. Resident monks practice here on low benches and cushions. A rare sand mandala is preserved under glass on the west side of the building. The temple's tallest building, the **Wanfuge** (Pavilion of Ten Thousand Fortunes), houses a breathtaking 85-ft Maitreya Buddha carved from a single sandalwood block. White-and-gold blessing scarves drape the statue, which wears a massive string of prayer beads. English-speaking guides are available at the temple entrance. ⊠ *12 Yonghegong Dajie, Beix-*

(Old Summer Palace), which once outshone its newer rival, offers quieter walks among splendid ruins. Don't miss the two summer palaces even if you have to skip other sights. If you have another day, there are several more places of interest on this side of town: the **Zhenbaoguan** ㊸ (Treasure House) craft museum; **Zhongyang Dianshita** ㊽ (Central Radio and Television Tower); the 16th-century **Wanshousi** ㊾ (Temple of Longevity); and the **Beijing Zhanlan Guan** ㊿ (Beijing Exhibition Hall) planetarium.

Sights to See

㊴ **Baitasi** (Temple of the White Pagoda). This 13th-century Tibetan stupa, the largest of its kind in China, dates from Kublai Khan's reign and owes its beauty to a Nepalese architect (name lost to history) who built it to honor Sakyamuni Buddha. Once hidden within the structure were Buddha statues, sacred texts, and other holy relics. Many of the statues are now on display in glass cases in the **Miaoying** temple, at the foot of the stupa. A local qi gong association also runs a traditional clinic on the premises. ⊠ *Fuchenmennei Dajie near Zhaodengyu Lu; turn right at first alley east of stupa, Xicheng District,* ☎ *010/6616–6099.* ▭ *Y10.* ☾ *Daily 8:30–4:30.*

㊲ **Baiyunguan** (White Clouds Taoist Temple). This Taoist temple serves as a center for China's only indigenous religion. Monks wearing blue-cotton coats and black-satin hats roam the grounds in silence. More than 100 of them now live at the monastery, which also houses the official All-China Taoist Association. Visitors bow and burn incense to their favorite deities, wander the back gardens in search of a qi gong master, or rub the bellies of the temple's three monkey statues for good fortune.

In the first courtyard, under the span of an arched bridge, hang two large brass bells. Ringing them with a well-tossed coin is said to bring wealth. In the main courtyards, the **Laolu Tang** (Shrine Hall for Seven Perfect Beings) is lined with meditation cushions and low desks. Nearby is a museum of Taoist history (explanations in Chinese). In the western courtyard, the temple's oldest structure is a shrine housing the **Liushi Huajiazi** (60-Year Protector). Here the faithful locate the deity that corresponds to their birth year, bow to it, and light incense, then scribble their names, or even a poem, on the wooden statue's red cloth cloak as a reminder of their dedication. A trinket stall in the front courtyard sells pictures of each protector deity. Also in the west courtyard is a shrine to Taoist sage Wen Ceng, depicted in a 10-ft-tall bronze statue just outside the shrine's main entrance. Students flock here to rub Wen Ceng's belly for good fortune on their college entrance exams. ⊠ *Lianhuachidong Lu near Xibianmen Bridge, Xuanwu District.* ▭ *Y5.* ☾ *Daily 9–4:30.*

㊿ **Beijing Zhanlan Guan** (Beijing Exhibition Hall). This impressive if slightly grubby planetarium is a favored field-trip destination for Beijing area students. Programs change frequently. Call in advance to check schedules and reserve seats. ⊠ *138 Xizhimenwai Dajie at Beijing Zoo, Xicheng District,* ☎ *010/6831–2517 or 010/6835–3003.* ▭ *Y12 per show.* ☾ *Daily 9–5.*

㊸ **Biyunsi** (Temple of Azure Clouds). Once the home of a Yuan dynasty official, the site was converted into a Buddhist temple in 1331 and enlarged during the 16th and 17th centuries by imperial eunuchs who hoped to be buried here. The temple's five main courtyards ascend a slope in ☞ **Xiangshan Gongyuan** (Fragrant Hills Park). Although severely damaged during the Cultural Revolution, the complex has been attentively restored.

The main attraction is the Indian-influenced Vajra Throne Pagoda. Lining its walls and five pagodas are gracefully carved stone-relief Buddhas and bodhisattvas. The pagoda once housed the remains of Nationalist China's founding father, Dr. Sun Yat-sen, who lay in state here from 1925 to 1929, when his mausoleum was completed in Nanjing. A hall in one of the temple's western courtyards houses about 500 life-size wood and gilt arhats—each sitting or standing in a glass case. ⊠ *Xiangshan Gongyuan, Haidian District,* ☎ *010/6259–1155.* ✆ *Park, Y3; temple, Y10.* ⊙ *Daily 8:30–3:30 (winter), 8–4 (summer).*

④ **Dazhongsi** (Big Bell Temple). The two-story bell here is cast with the texts of more than 100 Buddhist scriptures. Believed to date from Emperor Yongle's reign, the 46-ton relic is considered a national treasure. The temple also houses the **Guzhong Bowuguan** (Ancient Bell Museum), a collection of bells from various dynasties and styles. ⊠ *1A Beisanhuanxi Lu, Haidian District,* ☎ *010/6255–0843 or 010/6255–0819.* ✆ *Y10.* ⊙ *Daily 8:30–4:30.*

❸ **Lu Xun Bowuguan** (Lu Xun House and Museum). Lu Xun, one of China's most celebrated modern writers, lived here in the 1920s. His best-known works are *Diary of a Madman* and *The True Story of Ah Q*. In the small courtyard garden, he wrote novels and short stories that typically depict the plight of poor, uneducated people in prerevolutionary China. The rooms around the courtyard display documents and artifacts relating to Lu Xun's life and literature. ⊠ *Fuchenmennei Dajie, Xicheng District, next to Baitasi,* ☎ *010/6459–8343 or 010/6615–6549.* ✆ *Y5.* ⊙ *Tues.–Sun. 9–3:30.*

④ **Wanshousi** (Temple of Longevity). A Ming empress built this temple to honor her son in 1578. Qing emperor Qianlong later restored it as a birthday present to his mother. From then until the fall of the Qing, it served as a rest stop for imperial processions traveling by boat to the Summer Palace and Western Hills. Today Wanshou Temple is managed by the Beijing Art Museum and houses a small but exquisite collection of Buddha images. The Buddhas in the main halls include Sakyamuni sitting on a thousand-petal, thousand-Buddha bronze throne and dusty Ming-period Buddhas. ⊠ *Xisanhuan Lu, Haidian District,* ☎ *010/6841–3380 or 010/6841–9391.* ✆ *Y10.* ⊙ *Tues.–Sun. 9–4.*

④ **Wofosi** (Temple of the Sleeping Buddha). Although the temple was damaged during the Cultural Revolution and poorly renovated afterward, the Sleeping Buddha remains. Built in 627–629, during the Tang Dynasty, the temple was later named after the reclining Buddha that was brought in during the Yuan Dynasty (1271–1368). An English-language description explains that the casting of the beautiful bronze, in 1321, enslaved 7,000 people. The temple is inside the **Beijing Botanical Gardens**; stroll north from the entrance through the neatly manicured grounds. ⊠ *Xiangshan Lu, 2 km (1 mi) northeast of Xiangshan Park, Haidian District.* ✆ *Temple Y5; gardens Y5.* ⊙ *Daily 8:30–4.*

④ **Wutasi** (Five-Pagoda Temple). Hidden behind trees and set amid carved stones, the temple's five pagodas reveal obvious Indian influences. Indeed, the Five-Pagoda Temple was built during the Yongle Years of the Ming Dynasty (1403–1424), in honor of an Indian Buddhist who came to China and presented a temple blueprint to the emperor. Elaborate carvings of curvaceous female figures, floral patterns, birds, and hundreds of Buddhas decorate the pagodas. Also on the grounds is the **Beijing Shike Yishu Bowuguan** (Beijing Art Museum of Stone Carvings), with its collection of some 1,000 stelae and stone carvings. ⊠ *24 Wuta Si, Baishiqiao, Haidian District,* ☎ *010/6217–3836.* ✆ *Y2.5 includes admission to museum and pagodas.* ⊙ *Daily 8:30–4:30.*

㊷ Xiangshan Gongyuan (Fragrant Hills Park). This hillside park west of Beijing was once an imperial retreat and hunting ground. From the eastern gate you can hike to the summit on a trail dotted with shady pavilions and small temples. If you're short on time, ride a cable car to the top. Avoid weekends to avoid the crowds. ⊠ *Haidian District,* ☎ *010/ 6259–1155.* ⊡ *Y5; cable car, Y50.* ☉ *Daily 6 AM–7 PM.*

★ **㊺ Yiheyuan** (The Summer Palace). This expansive, parklike imperial retreat dates from the Yuan dynasty, when engineers channeled spring water to create a series of man-made lakes. It was not until the Qing that the Summer Palace took on its present form. In 1750 Emperor Qianlong commissioned the retreat for his mother's 60th birthday. Construction of palaces, pavilions, bridges, and numerous covered pathways on the shores of Kunming Lake continued for 15 years. The resort suffered heavy damage when Anglo-French forces plundered, then burned, many of the palaces in 1860. Renovation commenced in 1885 using funds diverted from China's naval budget. Empress Dowager Cixi retired to the Summer Palace in 1889 and seven years later imprisoned her nephew, Emperor Guangxu, on the palace grounds and reclaimed control of the government. She controlled China from the Summer Palace until her death in 1908.

Enter the palace grounds through the **Donggongmen** (East Palace Gate). Inside, a grand courtyard leads to the **Renshoudian** (Hall of Benevolent Longevity), where Cixi held court. Just beyond, next to the lake, the **Yulantang** (Hall of Jade Ripples) was where Cixi kept the hapless Guangxu under guard while she ran China in his name. Cixi's own residence, the **Leshoutang** (Hall of Joyful Longevity), sits just to the north and affords a fine view of Kunming Lake. The residence is furnished and decorated as Cixi left it. Cixi's private **theater,** just east of the hall, was constructed for her 60th birthday at a cost of 700,000 taels of silver. The **Long Corridor** skirts Kunming Lake's northern shoreline for 2,388 ft until it reaches the **marble boat,** an elaborate two-deck pavilion built of finely carved stone and stained glass. Above the Long Corridor on **Wanshou Shan** (Longevity Hill), intersecting pathways lead to numerous pavilions and several Buddhist prayer halls. Below, Kunming Lake extends southward for 3 km (2 mi), ringed by tree-lined dikes, arched stone bridges, and numerous gazebos. In summer you can explore the lake by paddleboat (inexpensive rentals are available at several spots along the shore). In winter, walk—or skate— on the ice. Although the palace area along Kunming Lake's north shore is usually crowded, the less-traveled southern shore near Hump-backed Bridge is an ideal picnic spot. ⊠ *12 km (7½ mi) northwest of downtown Beijing, Haidian District,* ☎ *010/6288–1144.* ⊡ *Y30; additional fees at some exhibits.* ☉ *Daily 7–7.*

★ **㊻ Yuanmingyuan** (Old Summer Palace). Once a grand collection of palaces, this complex was the emperor's summer retreat from the 15th century to 1860, when it was looted and systematically blown up by British and French soldiers. The Western-style buildings—patterned after Versailles in France—were added during the Qing dynasty and designed by Jesuits. Catholic missionaries carried the gospel into China in 1583 and settled in Guangdong Province (it was on their map that Chinese intellectuals saw their country's position in the world for the first time). In 1597 the missionary Matteo Ricci was appointed director of Jesuit activities in China, and in 1601 he finally achieved his goal of being admitted to Beijing, the capital.

Beijing has chosen to preserve the vast ruin as a "monument to China's national humiliation." Beijing students take frequent field trips to the site and (encouraged by their teachers, no doubt) scrawl patriotic slogans on the rubble. A large lake, ideal for summer boating or winter ice-skating, is in the center of the grounds. ✉ *Qinghuan Xi Lu, Haidian District,* ☎ *010/6255–1488 or 010/6254–3673.* 🎫 *Y10; extra fees for some sights.* ⊙ *Daily 7–7.*

47 **Zhenbaoguan** (Treasure House). Ceramics, stone carvings, lacquerware, and other traditional craft items are on display in this small museum run by the China National Art and Craft Museum. The museum is on the fifth floor of the Parkson department store. A shopping area outside the exhibition hall sells quality reproductions of priceless antiques. ✉ *101 Fuxingmennei Dajie, Xuanwu District,* ☎ *010/6607–3677.* 🎫 *Y8.* ⊙ *Daily 9:30–4.*

48 **Zhongyang Dianshita** (Central Radio and Television Tower). On a clear day this needlelike tower offers an awe-inspiring perspective on eastern Beijing and beyond. An outdoor viewing platform hangs 1,325 ft above the ground. Elevators take visitors there first, then down a few floors to an indoor deck where drinks and snacks are served. Another two levels down is a Chinese restaurant with simple set meals. This tower rests on the foundation of the **Altar of the Moon,** a Ming dynasty sacrificial temple. ✉ *11 Xisanhuanzhong Lu, Haidian District,* ☎ *010/6847–5809, 010/6845–0715, or 010/6843–7755 ext. 377.* 🎫 *Y50.* ⊙ *Daily 8:30 AM–10 PM.*

DINING

With the demise of staid, state-run canteens, where quality gave way to quantity and canteen workers took precedence over diners, Beijing dining has undergone an even greater revolution than other sectors of the economy. Countless small, private restaurants mushroomed across the city in the 1980s and 1990s. Even now, almost every day sees the opening of another bold venture into culinary capitalism. Most Beijingers frequent these cheap and cheerful places, which sometimes double as bars and karaoke venues.

Peking duck is the most famous dish of the capital, though it is normally available only in specialist or larger restaurants. Imperial-style banquets offer a contrast to staples like noodles and *jiaozi* (meat- and vegetable-filled dumplings). Vying with the local dishes are authentic specialties from such faraway regions as Guangdong, Hunan, Sichuan, Yunnan, Xinjiang, and even Inner Mongolia and Tibet. Western restaurants and fast-food outlets—both Chinese versions and the global franchises—have also taken root.

Against all this competition from inside and outside China, traditional-style Beijing dining is making a comeback. Waiters (the tradition extends to a male-only staff) whisk dishes through crowded, lively restaurants furnished with wooden menu boards and lacquered square tables. Doormen, dressed (like the waiters) in traditional cotton jackets, loudly announce each arrival and departure.

Casual attire is acceptable in most Beijing restaurants.

American

$$ ✕ **Frank's Place (Wanlong Jiuba).** Frank's looks like a typical American bar. In addition to great hamburgers, the menu includes chili, fried chicken, and Philly cheese steaks. ✉ *Gongrentiyuguan Dong Lu, across from Workers' Stadium, Chaoyang District,* ☎ *010/6507–2617. Reservations not accepted. AE, MC, V.*

Chinese

$$$$ ✗ **Fortune Garden.** Arguably Beijing's best Cantonese restaurant, For-
★ tune Garden offers all the southern favorites: roast suckling pig, bone-
less duck, a selection of steamed dim sum, and fresh vegetables stir-fried
in oyster sauce. ⊠ *Palace Hotel, 8 Jinyu Hutong, Wangfujing,
Dongcheng District,* ☎ *010/6512–8899 ext. 7900. AE, V.*

$$$$ ✗ **Four Seasons.** In the Jianguo Hotel, the Four Seasons offers a delicious two-person Peking duck set meal plus a full menu of traditional
Chinese dishes. The decor is elegant but understated. Tables are set with
silver, fine china, and white linen. Nightly performances of traditional
Chinese string music add to the intimate atmosphere. ⊠ *Jianguo Hotel,
5 Jianguomenwai Dajie, Chaoyang District,* ☎ *010/6500–2233. AE,
DC, MC, V.*

$$$–$$$$ ✗ **Fangshan.** In a traditional courtyard villa on the shore of Beihai Lake
★ you can sample China's imperial cuisine. Established in 1925 by three
royal chefs, Fangshan serves dishes once prepared for Qing emperors
based on recipes garnered from across China. Each of the 11 intimate
dining rooms is adorned with calligraphy and antique furniture. The
extensive menu includes a variety of fish, vegetable, and meat dishes—
including mainstays like sweet-and-sour pork—plus several delicious
soups. Fangshan is best known for its filled pastries and steamed
breads—traditional snack foods developed to satisfy Empress Dowa-
ger Cixi's sweet tooth. You can also order one of the banquet-style set
meals. Be sure to make reservations two or three days in advance. ⊠
*Beihai Gongyuan, Xicheng District (enter through east gate, cross
stone bridge, and bear right),* ☎ *010/6401–1879 or 010/6404–1184.
Reservations essential. AE, DC, MC, V.*

$$$ ✗ **Daijiacun (Dai Village) Restaurant.** Lively song and dance comple-
ment a rich variety of dishes from Yunnan province. Coconut, chili,
and pineapple feature heavily. Rice wine, wild mushrooms, rice steamed
in bamboo tubes, and spicy chicken cooked inside a pineapple are all
popular. For a real culinary adventure, try Daijiacun's snake, scorpions, or silkworms. After your meal at either location, Dai dancers invite you to join the festivities. ⊠ *13 Tiyuguan Lu, Chongwen District,*
☎ *010/6714–0145;* ⊠ *Guandongdian Nanjie, Chaoyang District,* ☎
010/6594–2454. Reservations essential. AE, DC, MC, V.

$$ ✗ **Afunti.** Beijing's largest and best-known Xinjiang Muslim restaurant
has become a popular and boisterous dinner-show venue. Uzbek mu-
sicians and belly dancers entertain you and later encourage you to per-
form on your table! Afunti offers a variety of Xinjiang kebabs, hotpot,
baked flat bread, and handmade noodles. ⊠ *166 Chaonei Dajie,
Dongcheng District,* ☎ *010/6525–1071 or 010/6525–5551 ext. 3055.
Reservations essential. AE, V.*

$$ ✗ **Jinghua Food Court.** In a restaurant set around a large courtyard
perfect for summer dining, Jinghua's chefs serve a wide range of stir-
fried dishes, delicate meat-filled pastries, and cold snacks that capture
the flavor of Old Peking. Look for a traditional gateway behind a giant
copper teapot, 200 yards south of the northwest gate to Longtan Park.
⊠ *8A Longtan Xilu, Chongwen District,* ☎ *010/6711–5331. No
credit cards.*

$$ ✗ **Lijiacai** (Li Family Restaurant). This tiny eatery is in such demand
★ that it sometimes takes weeks to book a table. The restaurant's impe-
rial dishes are prepared and served by members of the Li family in a
cozy, informal atmosphere. Li Li established the restaurant in 1985 (after
flunking her college entrance exams), using recipes handed down from
her great-grandfather, once a steward for the Qing court. Since then,
her renditions of China's culinary classics, like deep-fried scallops, *gong-
bao* chicken (spicy, with peanuts), and Mandarin (sweet-and-sour)

38

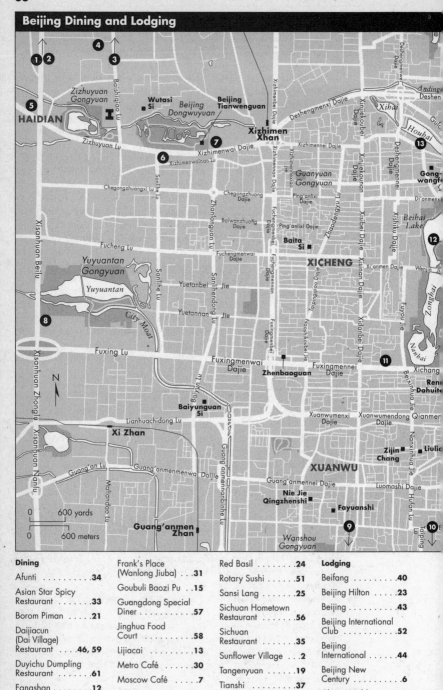

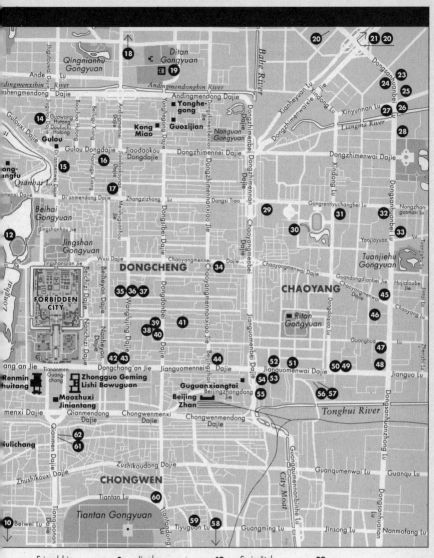

fish, have won the family business international renown. ⊠ *11 Yang-fang Hutong, Denei Dajie, Xicheng District,* ☎ *010/6618–0107. Reservations essential. No credit cards.*

$$ ✕ **Quanjude Kaoyadian.** This establishment has served succulent Peking duck since 1852. Nationalized after the 1949 Communist Revolution, it since has opened several branches across Beijing. Each serves the same traditional feast: cold duck tongue, sautéed webs, sliced livers, and gizzards to start; a main course of roast duck, to be dipped in plum sauce and wrapped with spring onion in a thin pancake; and duck soup to finish. Three Quanjude branches are within a few blocks of each other near Qianmen. The palatial seven-story Da Ya (Big Duck) has 40 dining rooms seating up to 2,000 people. Lao Ya (Old Duck), just south of Tiananmen Square, offers four garishly decorated floors with private rooms. The more intimate Bing Ya (Sick Duck) is named for its proximity to the Capital Hospital. *Big Duck:* ⊠ *14 Qianmen Xi Dajie, Chongwen District,* ☎ *010/6301–8833. AE, DC, MC, V. Old Duck:* ⊠ *32 Qianmen Dajie, Chongwen District,* ☎ *010/6511–2418. AE, DC, MC, V. Sick Duck:* ⊠ *13 Shuaifuyuan, Wangfujing, Dongcheng District,* ☎ *010/6525–3310. AE, DC, MC, V.*

$$ ✕ **Sichuan Restaurant.** This is a branch of a longtime favorite eating place of cadres—see the picture on the wall of Deng Xiaoping. Take refuge from the crowds of shoppers on Wangfujing while you enjoy a combination of Sichuan standards heavy with hot chilies and more subtly spiced dishes such as sautéed eggplant. Specialties include sizzling rice crust, hot pepper soup, and cold noodles. ⊠ *37A Donganmen Dajie, Wangfujing, Dongcheng District,* ☎ *010/6513–7591. No credit cards.*

$$ ✕ **Sunflower Village.** This restaurant exploits a peculiar nostalgia for the "10 lost years" of the Cultural Revolution (1966–76). Decorated with murals of Chairman Mao, Sunflower Village seeks to emulate the rustic atmosphere of a rural commune. Its food recalls the fare dished out to millions of urban Red Guards sent by Mao to "learn from the peasants" in the countryside. Menu items range from stir-fried corn and pine nuts and tasty *wotou* (steamed cornbread) to various fresh grasses or fried cicada larvae. More standard northern dishes, like braised tofu, hotpot, or stewed fatty pork, are also offered. ⊠ *26 Wanquanhe Lu, Haidian District,* ☎ *010/6256–2967. No credit cards.*

$$ ✕ **Tangenyuan.** Easily combined with a trip to Ditan Park, Yonghegong, or Kong Miao, this is the ideal place for a lively group dinner and an Old Peking experience. Rickshaws rush you to the door of a courtyard-style building. Inside is a re-creation of traditional streets and a small stage where acrobats, Peking opera singers, and magicians entertain you, sometimes a little too loudly. The food is traditional, served in large quantities, with presentation given not much attention. ⊠ *1A East Gate, Ditan Gongyuan, Dongcheng District,* ☎ *010/6428–3358. Reservations essential. No credit cards.*

$$ ✕ **Tianshi.** The chefs at this Taiwan-managed Buddhist vegetarian restaurant have mastered the art of concocting faux-meat dishes from soybean and other vegetarian ingredients. Even dedicated carnivores will recognize the tea-marinated "duck," crisp-fried "chicken," and sweet-and-sour Mandarin "fish." The look and taste is extraordinary. Tianshi also serves a wide variety of teas and even alcohol-free beer and an assortment of (nondairy) fruit shakes. Upstairs, the main dining hall's decor melds fake Ionic columns with real modern art to create a trendy, pop feel. A ground-floor cafeteria offers inexpensive lunch platters, muffins, and doughnuts. ⊠ *57 Dengshikou Dajie, Dongcheng District,* ☎ *010/6524–2349. AE, DC, MC, V.*

$$ ✕ **Tibet Shambala.** Diners here sit in small whitewashed rooms draped with banners and Buddhist thangkha paintings. Specialties include: *momos* (yak dumplings); *tsampa* (barley flour paste, usually mixed with yak butter); *thukpa* (noodles with lamb, onions, turnips, and coriander); and yak penis with caterpillar fungus (no explanation required). ✉ *301 Xinjiang Xiao Lu, Baishiqao, Haidian District,* ☎ *010/6842–2631. Reservations not accepted. No credit cards.*

$ ✗ **Duyichu Dumpling Restaurant.** History has it that this Shandong-style dumpling house won fame when Qing emperor Qianlong stopped in on his way back to the Forbidden City after a rural inspection tour. A plaque hanging on the wall, supposedly in Qianlong's own hand, attests to the restaurant's flavorful fare. Today the Duyichu's large, raucous dining hall is decidedly proletarian. But the dumplings and assorted Shandong dishes still command applause. Expect to wait for a seat during the dinner rush. Customers share large round tables. ✉ *36 Qianmen Dajie, Chongwen District,* ☎ *010/6511–2093 or 010/6511–2094. Reservations not accepted. No credit cards.*

$ ✗ **Goubuli Baozi Pu.** Juicy *baozi* (steamed dumplings) are the specialty of this traditional eatery in a very busy district of Beijing directly north of Tiananmen and Jingshan Park. No trip to China is complete without trying the *goubuli baozi*—dog-doesn't-even-want-to-bother dumpling—filled with meat and scallions and a unique sauce. ✉ *155 Di'anmenwai Dajie, north of Jingshan Park, Dongcheng District,* ☎ *010/6404–3097. Reservations not accepted. No credit cards.*

$ ✗ **Guangdong Special Diner.** Across the street from the Sichuan Hometown Restaurant, the Guangdong Special Diner is popular with locals and foreign diplomats alike. The predominantly Cantonese menu offers an assortment of soups, steamed dishes, and stir-fries (less firey than typical Cantonese fare). ✉ *Yonganxili Produce Market, alley south of Jianguomenwai Dajie, opposite Friendship Store, Chaoyang District,* ☎ *010/6500–7185. Reservations not accepted. No credit cards.*

$ ✗ **Old Beijing Noodle King.** Close to the Temple of Heaven, this restaurant re-creates traditional fast food in a lively Old Peking atmosphere. Waiters shout across the room to announce customers arriving or leaving. Try the tasty noodles, usually eaten with a thick sesame- and soy-based sauce. Look for the rickshaws parked outside. ✉ *Chongwenmen Dajie, Chongwen District, west side of Chongwenmen, north of Temple of Heaven east gate,* ☎ *010/6705–6705. Reservations not accepted. No credit cards.*

$ ✗ **Sichuan Hometown Restaurant.** This bargain eatery serves hearty fare from China's most populated province, Sichuan, that goes heavy on the spices (images of three succulent red peppers adorn the manager's business card). The restaurant has indoor seating in a narrow dining hall as well as tables on the alley, by day a thriving fruit market. ✉ *Southeast of Friendship Store at Yonganxili Market, Chaoyang District,* ☎ *010/6595–7688. Reservations not accepted. No credit cards.*

European

$$ ✗ **Metro Café.** This informal restaurant offers a standard assortment of Italian pastas. Although service is inconsistent, the food is usually very good, and the outdoor tables are wonderful (if you can get one) on mild evenings. ✉ *6 Gongrentiyuguan Xilu, Chaoyang District,* ☎ *010/6501–3377 ext. 7706. AE, V.*

$$ ✗ **Moscow Café.** In times past the Moscow Café, built in the 1950s, was Beijing's best Western restaurant. Its massive Stalinesque ballroom and Russian menu attracted the city's Communist elite, intellectuals, and East Bloc foreign residents. Today the neon-lighted ballroom is gaudy and threadbare. But a side wing still serves passable braised beef, chicken Kiev, oxtail casserole, borscht, and other Russian dishes. ✉ *135 Xizhimenwai Dajie, Xicheng District,* ☎ *010/6835–4454. Reservations not accepted. No credit cards.*

Japanese

$$$ ✕ **Rotary Sushi.** At this informal self-service restaurant you'll find a full range of sushi and sashimi. Grab a dish as it inches past you on the conveyor belt. ✉ *17 Jianguomenwai Dajie, Chaoyang District,* ☎ *010/6711–5331. AE, DC, MC, V.*

$$ ✕ **Sansi Lang.** This affordable sushi bar could pass muster with any salary-man. The menu offers sushi, sashimi, tempura, cold soba noodles, and a variety of delicious set meals. Seating is in booths or, upstairs, in private tatami rooms. ✉ *52 Liangjiu Lu, Liangmaqiao, opposite Kempinski Hotel, Chaoyang District.* ☎ *010/6464–5030. AE, MC, V.*

Thai

$$$$ ✕ **Red Basil.** Understated Thai accents adorn the Red Basil's dining area, which is elegantly furnished in hardwood and leather. But the clientele, both expatriates and well-heeled Chinese, come for the food. House favorites include spicy glass noodles with shrimp, and, in a bow to Beijing, a rich Thai red curry with Beijing roast duck. ✉ *Sanyuan Dongqiao, Sanhuan Beilu, Chaoyang District, opposite Jingxin Plaza,* ☎ *010/6460–2339 ext. 44. AE, MC, V.*

$$$ ✕ **Borom Piman.** Guests must part with their shoes in the entry hall to accommodate traditional Thai seating around low tables. The food, too, is traditional, with Thai curries, crab cakes, glass noodles, and spicy hot prawn soup, all of which make for superior dining. ✉ *Holiday Inn Lido Hotel, Jichang Lu, Chaoyang District,* ☎ *010/6437–6688 ext. 2899. Reservations essential. AE, MC, V.*

$$–$$$ ✕ **Asian Star Spicy Restaurant.** Chefs from Thailand, India, and Indonesia offer an eclectic but authentic menu, including Thai green chicken, Indonesian fried rice, and deep-fried shrimp cakes. Spicy dishes are rated with chili symbols, but even a mild curried chicken is best accompanied by plenty of ice water or a *lassi* (yogurt drink). Batik-patterned walls and a giant mural of Hong Kong's skyline brighten the decor. ✉ *26 Dongsanhuan Beilu, Chaoyang District,* ☎ *010/6582–5306. Reservations essential. AE, DC, MC, V.*

LODGING

Beijing is as well supplied with glitzy, comfortable hotels as any modern metropolis. What it lacks in variety it makes up for in quantity. Grandiose lobbies, air-conditioned elevators, coffee lounges, and 15th-floor guest rooms—all lacking in Chinese flavor—are the norm. Most major hotels have facilities such as business centers, health clubs, Chinese and Western restaurants, nightclubs, karaoke, and beauty salons. Gone are the days of surly service, when hotel staffs were often unwilling to interrupt their meals or naps to attend to a guest. Today most hotels will book restaurants, taxis, cars with drivers, and travel tickets.

Some traditional courtyard houses, on the other hand, have been converted into small hotels—a quiet alternative to the Western-style establishments. Courtyard hotels usually have a more distinct Chinese character, but those in older buildings may be lacking in the range and standard of facilities. Often managed by entrepreneurs who bought the courtyard houses from people who once lived there, these hotels are not necessarily glamorous dwellings of rich families, but simply a modern invention. Given that fewer and fewer old courtyards exist in China, courtyard hotels are often favored by savvy travelers who go to China for its history. Because of the smaller number of rooms in courtyard hotels, reservations are important.

Contemporary Hotels

$$$$ ★ ⌧ **China World.** One of the finest hotels in Beijing, the China World is Shangri-La's flagship China hotel and part of the prestigious China World Trade Center, home to offices, luxury apartments, and premium retail outlets. The center's conference and banquet facilities are popular for large-scale gatherings, and the hotel has an executive floor. The restaurants cover most cuisines, from Indian to Italian. ⌧ *1 Jianguomenwai Dajie, Chaoyang District, 100004,* ☎ *010/6505–2266 or 010/6505–0828,* FAX *010/6505–3167,* WEB *www.shangri-la.com. 700 rooms, 56 suites. 20 restaurants, 2 bars, deli, beauty salon, massage, health club, dance club, car rental. AE, DC, MC, V.*

$$$$ ⌧ **Grand.** Standing on the north side of Chang'an Avenue is this luxury hotel whose roof terrace overlooks Beijing's Forbidden City. A former imperial palace, the Grand blends the traditions of China's past with modern comforts and technology. The Red Wall Café, Ming Yuan dining room, Rong Yuan Restaurant, and Old Peking Grill provide a range of cuisines, from authentic Chinese to European. The third floor has a spectacular atrium decorated in marble with Chinese art and antiques. There's a shopping arcade and a fully equipped spa. Even if you don't stay here, try to make it to the rooftop terrace for sunset drinks overlooking the yellow roofs of the Forbidden City. ⌧ *35 Dongchangan Jie, Dongcheng District, 100006,* ☎ *010/6513–7788,* FAX *010/6513–0048,* WEB *www.grandhotelbeijing.com/eng. 217 rooms, 40 suites. 5 restaurants, pool, sauna, spa, health club, bicycles, shops, car rental. AE, DC, MC, V.*

$$$$ ⌧ **Great Wall Sheraton.** A reproduction of said wall was built just outside this Sheraton near the Sanlitun embassy area. The hotel has comfortable rooms, an executive floor, conference and banquet facilities, a ballroom, a theater, and a Chinese garden. In the ground-floor teahouse, jazz is performed every weekday evening; on weekends you can listen to piano and Chinese music—ranging from Mozart to Chinese Peking Operas. The health center is small but thorough. One of the restaurants serves French cuisine. ⌧ *10 Dongsanhuan Beilu, Chaoyang District, 100026,* ☎ *010/6590–5566,* FAX *010/6590–5504,* WEB *www.sheraton.com. 800 rooms, 200 suites. 4 restaurants, bar, pool, sauna, health club, dance club, theater. AE, DC, MC, V.*

$$$$ ⌧ **Swissôtel.** This hotel is a joint venture between Switzerland and the Hong Kong and Macau Affairs Office of the State Council (hence its Chinese name—Gang'ao Zhongxin—the Hong Kong Macau Center). The Hong Kong connection means Hong Kong Jockey Club members can place bets here; it was also one of the first hotels in Asia to provide facilities for people with disabilities. In the large lobby you can enjoy excellent jazz every Friday and Saturday evening. Among the many restaurants here, the Italian is particularly good. ⌧ *Dongsishiqiao Flyover Junction (2nd Ring Road), Chaoyang District, 100027,* ☎ *010/ 6501–2288,* FAX *010/6501–2501. 424 rooms, 30 suites. 7 restaurants, bar, pool, sauna, gym, car rental. AE, DC, MC, V.*

$$$ ★ ⌧ **Beijing.** The forerunner of them all, the Beijing Hotel is the capital's oldest, born in 1900 as the Hotel de Pekin. Within sight of Tiananmen Square, it has housed countless foreign delegations, missions, and friends of China, such as Field Marshal Montgomery from Britain and the American writer Edgar Snow. Room 1735 still bears a sign indicating where China's longtime premier Zhou Enlai stayed and worked. The central section retains its old-fashioned splendor. The west wing—now the Grand Hotel—was added in 1955 and the east wing in 1974. ⌧ *33 Dongchangan Jie, Dongcheng District, 100004,* ☎ *010/6513–7766,* FAX *010/6513–7307,* WEB *www.cbw.com/hotel/beijing. 850 rooms, 100 suites. 5 restaurants, bar, pool, sauna, health club. AE, DC, MC, V.*

$$$ ☖ **Beijing Hilton.** Surrounded by high-rises, bars, and restaurants, this comfortably elegant Hilton lies at the northeast corner of Beijing's imperial grid pattern. Among its restaurants, Genji has top-notch sushi and the excellent Louisiana serves Cajun cuisine. ✉ *1 Dongfang Lu, Dongsanhuan Beilu, Chaoyang District, 100027,* ☎ *010/ 6466–2288,* FAX *010/6465–3052,* WEB *www.hilton.com. 363 rooms, 24 suites. 6 restaurants, bar, pool, sauna, bicycles, dance club, car rental. AE, DC, MC, V.*

$$$ ☖ **Beijing International Club.** This chic hotel in a prime location mixes classical Chinese elegance and fine modern furnishings. The hotel is a favorite with the foreign business community. The grand piano, dark wood, and bookcases in its Press Club Bar create the mood of a private London club. ✉ *21 Jianguomenwai Dajie, Chaoyang District, 100020,* ☎ *010/6460–6688,* FAX *010/6460–3299. 273 rooms, 20 suites. 3 restaurants, bar, pool, sauna, business services, meeting room, car rental. AE, DC, MC, V.*

$$$ ☖ **Beijing New Century.** Forty minutes from Beijing's International Airport, the New Century enjoys great views of the Summer Palace, Beijing Zoo, and the Great Wall. The facilities in the hotel are equally impressive. Seven restaurants serve Chinese, Japanese, and Western cuisine, and sports facilities include a tennis court, gym, bowling alley, golf training course, sauna, and indoor swimming pool. The 32-story highrise in north Beijing's Haidian District, near the Capital Gymnasium, is a joint-venture hotel with Japan. ✉ *6 Shoudu Tiyuguan Nanlu, Haidian District, 100044,* ☎ *010/6849–2001,* FAX *010/6849–1107,* WEB *www.newcenturyhotel.com.cn. 700 rooms, 24 suites. 10 restaurants, bar, pool, sauna, tennis court, bowling, gym, car rental. AE, DC, MC, V.*

$$$ ☖ **Gloria Plaza.** In a good location just behind the New Otani Changfugong and Scitech, this well-managed Hong Kong–run hotel is owned by China's Ceroils group. It has good facilities for banquets and functions, as well as excellent Vietnamese fare on the second floor. ✉ *2 Jiangguomen Nandajie, Chaoyang District, 100022,* ☎ *010/6515–8855,* FAX *010/ 6515–5273,* WEB *www.gphbeijing.com. 423 rooms, 20 suites. 5 restaurants, bar, pool, sauna, gym, dance club, car rental. AE, DC, MC, V.*

$$$ ☖ **Jianguo.** Despite its 1950s-style name ("build the country"), this is actually a U.S.–China joint venture. Wonderfully central and close to the diplomatic compounds and southern embassy area, the hotel is a favorite of journalists and frequent visitors to Beijing. Nearly half the rooms have balconies overlooking busy Jianwai Dajie. The Jianguo has maintained its friendly and cozy feel, and Western classical music, including opera, is performed Sunday morning in the lobby. Justine's is one of the best French restaurants in Beijing. ✉ *5 Jianguomenwai Dajie, Chaoyang District, 100020,* ☎ *010/6500–2233,* FAX *010/6501–0539. 400 rooms, 70 suites. 4 restaurants, bar, pool, beauty salon, car rental. AE, DC, MC, V.*

$$$ ☖ **Kempinski.** The hotel forms part of the Lufthansa Center, together with a luxury department store, offices, and apartments. It's within walking distance of the Sanlitun embassy area and dozens of bars and restaurants. The hotel, which has a ballroom and six meeting rooms, provides excellent service to its many business guests. The 18th floor houses a gym and a swimming pool, while in the basement a Western instructor leads aerobics classes. ✉ *50 Liangmaqiao Lu, Chaoyang District, 100016,* ☎ *010/6465–3388,* FAX *010/6465–3366. 500 rooms, 114 suites. 11 restaurants, 2 bars, pool, gym, bicycles, car rental. AE, DC, MC, V.*

$$$ ☖ **Radisson SAS.** This standard, comfortable, and pleasant Radisson chain hotel is near the international exhibition center in northeast Beijing. The restaurants—one open-air—offer outstanding food, including a good-value Western-style Sunday brunch with music. ✉ *6A Beisanhuan*

Donglu, Chaoyan District, 100028, ☎ 010/6466–3388, FAX 010/6465–3181, WEB www.radisson.com. 360 rooms. 3 restaurants, bar, pool, sauna, gym, bicycles, dance club, car rental. AE, DC, MC, V.

$$$ 🏨 **Traders'.** Inside the China World Trade center complex, the independently managed Traders' stands just behind the China World Hotel. The hotel regularly serves business travelers. ⊠ 1 Jianguomenwai Dajie, Chaoyang District, 100004, ☎ 010/6505–2266, FAX 010/6505–0828. 567 rooms, 20 suites. 2 restaurants, bar, health club, car rental. AE, DC, MC, V.

$$$ 🏨 **Zhaolong.** Handy to the Sanlitun embassy area and pub land, the Zhaolong was a gift to the nation from Hong Kong shipping magnate Y. K. Pao, who named it for his father. It has many amenities plus a theater and banquet facilities. ⊠ 2 Gongren Tiyuchang Beilu, Chaoyang District, 100027, ☎ 010/6597–2299, FAX 010/6597–2288. 260 rooms, 20 suites. Bar, pool, sauna, gym, bicycles, dance club, theater, car rental. AE, DC, MC, V.

$$ 🏨 **Fragrant Hills.** This rather unusual garden-style hotel takes its name
★ from the beautiful park on which it's set. In the western suburbs of Beijing, Fragrant Hills was a favored retreat of emperors through the centuries. Designed by the Chinese-American architect I. M. Pei, the hotel opened in 1983. It has a large lake and a miniature stone forest. The lobby forms a traditional courtyard; rooms extend along a hillside, and each has a balcony overlooking the park. The outdoor swimming pool is covered for year-round use. The hotel is peaceful, affording marvelous walks in the nearby woods. ⊠ Fragrant Hill Park, Haidian District, 100093, ☎ 010/6259–1166, FAX 010/6259–1762. 200 rooms, 27 suites. 3 restaurants, bar, pool, sauna, dance club, car rental. AE, DC, MC, V.

$$ 🏨 **Holiday Inn Crowne Plaza.** Perhaps the best of Beijing's Holiday Inns, the Crown Plaza is near the Wangfujing shopping area, 10 minutes' walk from the Forbidden City, and 15 minutes' walk from Tiananmen Square. The hotel has an art gallery and a salon on the second floor where Western classical and traditional Chinese music are performed. ⊠ 48 Wangfujing Dajie, Dongfeng District, 100006, ☎ 010/6513–3388, FAX 010/6513–2513, WEB www.holiday-inn.com. 500 rooms, 50 suites. 5 restaurants, bar, pool, sauna, bicycles, car rental. AE, DC, MC, V.

$$ 🏨 **Holiday Inn Lido.** Northeast of the city center, close to the airport, the Lido is one of the largest Holiday Inn hotels in the world. Designed as a fully self-sufficient facility, the hotel is within Lido Place, a commercial/residential complex that is home to a number of Beijing's expats and multinational companies. The Lido is a haven for foreigners: the complex has a deli, bakery, supermarket, offices, apartments, and a full range of sporting, leisure, and entertainment facilities. The wide variety of restaurants includes Borom Piman (Thai), Bauernstube (German), Pinocchio (Italian), The Texan Bar & Grill, and the Patio Coffee Shop. ⊠ Jichang Lu at Jiangtai Lu, Chaoyang District, 100004, ☎ 010/6437–6688 or 800/810–0019, FAX 010/6437–6237, WEB www.holiday-inn.com. 726 rooms, 66 suites. 9 restaurants, bar, pool, beauty salon, massage, sauna, gym, dance club. AE, DC, MC, V.

$$ 🏨 **Jinglun.** Just 10 minutes' drive from Tiananmen Square, the Jinglun is a well-appointed business and leisure hotel at a competitive price. It's known for good Chinese food at its fourth-floor restaurant and its outdoor café, which serves drinks and barbecue beside a fountain from spring through autumn. ⊠ 3 Jianguomenwai Dajie, Chaoyang District, 100020, ☎ 010/6500–2266, FAX 010/6500–2022, WEB www.jinglunhotel.com. 400 rooms, 4 suites. 6 restaurants, bar, beauty salon, pool, massage, sauna, gym, bicycles, baby-sitting, travel services, car rental. AE, DC, MC, V.

$$ 🏨 **Kunlun.** At this 28-story property topped by a revolving restaurant, impressive presentation and a full range of facilities make up for occasional lapses in service. A magnificent Chinese landscape painting greets you in the spacious lobby. On the second floor, one of Beijing's best hotel discos, the Glass House, attracts trendy locals and foreign students. ✉ *2 Xinyuan Nanlu, Chaoyang District, 100004,* ☎ *010/6590-3388,* FAX *010/6590-3214,* WEB *www.hotelkunlun.com. 1,000 rooms, 50 suites. 9 restaurants, bar, pool, sauna, gym, bicycles, car rental. AE, DC, MC, V.*

$$ 🏨 **Mövenpick.** The Mövenpick has a fantastic outdoor pool and good food that includes Swiss, Japanese, barbecue, and Mongolian hotpot (served inside a traditional felt yurt). Horse rides in nearby woods attract Beijing expats for weekend breaks from city smog. ✉ *Xiao Tianzhu Village (Box 6913), Capital Airport, Shunyi County, 100621,* ☎ *010/6456-5588,* FAX *010/6456-5678. 408 rooms, 35 suites. 5 restaurants, 2 bars, pool, sauna, gym, dance club. AE, DC, MC, V.*

$$ 🏨 **New Otani Changfugong.** Managed by the New Otani Group from Japan, this hotel combines that country's signature hospitality and attentive service with a premium location in downtown Beijing (near the Friendship Store and the old observatory). The hotel offers authentic Chinese meals that are unforgettable, and the main restaurant serves delicious (and expensive) Japanese food. The hotel is popular with businesspeople and large groups from Japan. It's accessible for people with disabilities. ✉ *26 Jianguomenwai Dajie, Chaoyang District, 100022,* ☎ *010/6512-5555,* FAX *010/6513-9810,* WEB *www.newotani. co.jp/en. 500 rooms, 20 suites. 2 restaurants, bar, pool, beauty salon, massage, sauna, tennis court, gym, bicycles, car rental, parking. AE, DC, MC, V.*

$$ 🏨 **Palace.** The Palace Hotel (Beijing Wuangfu Fandian) is a beautiful combination of ultramodern facilities and traditional Asian luxury. A waterfall cascades down through the spacious lobby, which is decorated with Chinese antiques. The hotel is in the center of Beijing's business and commercial districts. Discreet and more intimate than other residences in the area, the hotel has deluxe rooms and a presidential suite and abundant business and recreation facilities. The large ballroom on the second floor has seen many prestigious events, such as the government's New Year's celebration. ✉ *8 Dongdanbeidajie, Jinyu Hutong, Dongcheng District, 100006,* ☎ *010/6559-2888,* FAX *010/6512-9050. 511 rooms, 20 suites. 5 restaurants, bar, deli, pool, beauty salon, sauna, tennis court, health club, dance club, car rental. AE, DC, MC, V.*

$$ 🏨 **Scitech.** This is part of the Scitech complex, which consists of an office tower, a hotel, and a luxury shopping center. The hotel enjoys a good location on busy Jianguomenwai Dajie opposite the Friendship Store. The interior, facilities, and service are pleasant if not spectacular. There is a small fountain in the lobby, with a teahouse on one side. ✉ *22 Jianguomenwai Dajie, Chaoyang District, 100004,* ☎ *010/6512-3388,* FAX *010/6512-3542. 300 rooms, 15 suites. Pool, sauna, gym, dance club, car rental. AE, DC, MC, V.*

$$ 🏨 **Shangri-La.** Set in delightful landscaped gardens in the western part of the city (30 minutes from the commercial and business centers), the Shangri-la is a wonderful retreat. A 24-hour business center offers a full range of services such as banking and Internet facilities. The hotel has a fine variety of cuisine from seven different restaurants: Peppino (Italian), Nishimura (Japanese), and Shang Palace (Cantonese), to name a few, and is equipped to host large conferences and banquets. ✉ *29 Zizhuyuan Lu, Haidian District, 100084,* ☎ *010/6841-2211,* FAX *010/6841-8002,* WEB *www.shangri-la.com. 657 rooms, 21 suites, 15 1- to 3-bedroom apartments. 4 restaurants, bar, pool, beauty salon, health club, dance club, car rental. AE, DC, MC, V.*

$–$$ ⊡ **Continental Grand.** In the Asian Games village in north Beijing, this massive structure came into being for the 1990 Games. It has modern facilities for conferences and functions, though service could be improved. The Olympic sports center across the road is a great health club; guests have access for a fee. ⊠ *8 Beichen Donglu, Andingmenwai, Chaoyang District, 100101,* ☎ *010/6491–5588,* ℻ *010/6491–0106. 1,000 rooms, 50 suites. 20 restaurants, bar, sauna, dance club, car rental. AE, DC, MC, V.*

$–$$ ⊡ **Friendship.** The Friendship's name is telling: it was built in 1954 to house foreign experts, mostly Soviet, who had come to help build New China. Beijing Friendship Hotel is one of the largest garden-style hotels in Asia. The style is classic and elegant, with traditional Chinese architecture. It offers a full range of amenities, including 14 restaurants, a business center, conference halls, and recreational facilities that include tennis courts, an Olympic-size pool, a driving range, and a theater. ⊠ *3 Baishiqiao Lu, Haidian District, 100873,* ☎ *010/6849–8888,* ℻ *010/6849–8866,* ⓦⒺⒷ *www.cbw.com/hotel/friendship. 800 rooms, 32 suites. 14 restaurants, bar, pool, sauna, driving range, tennis courts, dance club, theater, car rental. AE, DC, MC, V.*

$–$$ ⊡ **Minzu.** At its birth in 1959, the Minzu (Nationalities) Hotel was labeled one of the Ten Great Buildings in Beijing. This paean to the unity of China's different peoples has welcomed many prominent foreign visitors over the years. It's been renovated into yet another shiny pleasuredome but maintains its original appeal. The hotel lies on western Changan Dajie, 10 minutes' ride from Tiananmen Square and next to the Nationalities' Cultural Palace. ⊠ *51 Fuxingmennei Dajie, Xicheng District, 100031,* ☎ *010/6601–4466,* ℻ *010/6601–4849,* ⓦⒺⒷ *www.minzuhotel.com. 600 rooms, 52 suites. 4 restaurants, bar, sauna, car rental. AE, DC, MC, V.*

$ ⊡ **Beifang.** Built in 1953, this small hotel distinguished by its Chinese architecture is in the city center near Wangfujing. The restaurant serves northern Chinese (Beifang) food. ⊠ *45 Dongdan Beidajie, Dongcheng District, 100005,* ☎ *010/6525–2831,* ℻ *010/6525–2928. Restaurant. AE, DC, MC, V.*

$ ⊡ **Beijing International.** This white monolith, built in the mid-1980s, symbolized the takeoff of China's tourist industry. It offers most facilities and acceptable service. Opposite the old train station, it's only a few minutes' ride from Tiananmen Square. ⊠ *9 Jianguomennei Dajie, Dongcheng District, 100005,* ☎ *010/6512–6688,* ℻ *010/6512–9961. 1,008 rooms, 42 suites. 2 restaurants, bar, pool, bowling, gym, shops, car rental. AE, DC, MC, V.*

$ ⊡ **Jingguang New World.** Modern China's obsession with blue glass finds its most monstrous expression in this 53-story building. The Jingguang Center houses the hotel plus offices, shops, and luxury apartments. It's hard to miss on the eastern Third Ring Road, not far from Jianguomenwai Dajie. The restaurants serve Cantonese, Korean, and Western food. ⊠ *Jingguang center, Hujialou, Chaoyang District, 100020,* ☎ *010/6597–8888,* ℻ *010/6597–3333. 426 rooms, 20 suites. 4 restaurants, 2 bars, pool, beauty salon, sauna, gym, dance club, car rental. AE, DC, MC, V.*

$ ⊡ **Jinghua.** Cheap, adequate, and friendly, this backpacker retreat lies at the southern edge of Beijing, on the Third Ring Road. Rooms have showers, telephones, and air-conditioners. The hotel also has dorms. ⊠ *Xiluoyuan Nanlu, outside Yongdingmen, Fengtai District, 100077,* ☎ *010/6722–2211,* ℻ *010/6721–1455. 168 rooms, 14 dorm rooms with 110 beds. No credit cards.*

$ ⊡ **Qiaoyuan.** Long a backpacker favorite, the Qiaoyuan went predictably upmarket after its 1996 renovation. In the far south of the city, it is well connected by bus (Yongdingmen station) to the Beijing (old) railway station. Due to the backpacker legacy, numerous inexpensive restaurants outside the hotel offer simple but tasty Chinese as well as Western food. Plenty of bike rental places are nearby. ✉ *135 Dongbinhe Lu, Youanmen Wai, Fengtai District, 100054,* ☎ *010/6303–8861,* FAX *010/6318–4709. 440 rooms. Restaurant. AE, DC, MC, V.*

Traditional Hotels

$$ ⊞ **Zhuyuan Binguan** (Bamboo Garden Hotel). This charming small hotel
★ was converted from the residence of Sheng Xuanhuai, a high-ranking Qing official, and later, of Mao's henchman Kang Sheng, who lived here after after the 1949 Revolution. A powerful and sinister character, responsible for "public security" during the Cultural Revolution, Kang nevertheless had fine taste in art and antiques. The Bamboo Garden cannot compete on comfort and facilities with the high-rise crowd, but its lovely courtyards and gardens bursting with bamboo make it a genuine treasure. You can take an interesting 10-minute hutong stroll from the hotel to the old Drum Tower. ✉ *24 Xiaoshiqiao Hutong, Jiugulou Dajie, Dongcheng District, 100009,* ☎ *010/6403–2229,* FAX *010/6401–2633. 40 rooms, 1 suite. Restaurant, bar, beauty salon, sauna, bicycles. AE, DC, MC, V.*

$$ ⊞ **Ziyu Binguan** (Purple Jade Hotel). A colorful gateway, decorated with dragons and supported by red pillars, marks the entrance to a compound combining ancient and modern styles. With full services and Western-style rooms in its main block, this hotel also has traditional rooms set around small courtyard gardens. Though quite far out in Beijing's western suburbs, the Ziyu is convenient to the Beijing West Railway Station, the Summer Palaces, and Xiangshan. ✉ *55 Zhongguan Lu, Haidian District, 100037,* ☎ *010/6841–1188,* FAX *010/6841–1355. 316 rooms, 6 suites. 2 restaurants, bar, beauty salon, sauna, business services, travel services. AE, DC, MC, V.*

$ ⊞ **Haoyuan.** Tucked away in a hutong close to a busy shopping street and the Palace Hotel, the Haoyuan has rooms surrounding two tranquil courtyards. In summer you can sit under the date trees and listen to the evening chorus of cicadas. The hotel's small restaurant serves good traditional dishes. ✉ *53 Shijia Hutong, Dongsinan Dajie, Dongcheng District, 100010,* ☎ *010/6512–5557,* FAX *010/6525–3179. 17 rooms. Restaurant. No credit cards.*

$ ⊞ **Lüsongyuan.** In 1980 China Youth Travel Service set up this delightful
★ courtyard hotel on the site of an old Qing Mandarin's residence, a few lanes south of the Youhao Guesthouse. The traditional wooden entrance is guarded by two *menshi* (stone lions). Inside are five courtyards, decorated with pavilions, rockeries, and plants. Rooms are elegant, with large window panels. Though it calls itself an International Youth Hostel, the hotel has no self-service cooking facilities; but it is cheap and has a great Chinese restaurant. ✉ *22 Banchang Hutong, Kuanjie, Dongcheng District, 100009,* ☎ *010/6401–1116,* FAX *010/6403–0418. 38 rooms. Restaurant, bar. No credit cards.*

$ ⊞ **Youhao Guesthouse.** Behind a high gray wall with a wrought-iron
★ gate, deep in hutong land near the Drum Tower, the lovely Youhao (Friendly) Guesthouse forms a small part of the large traditional compound where Nationalist leader Chiang Kai-shek once stayed. From each comfortable room in the two-story guest house, you have a view of either the spacious front courtyard or the back garden where there are trees, flowers, and Chinese-style corridors. The main building is used for karaoke, but other pleasures remain, such as a Roman-style folly and rockery gates. There are some intriguing hutong houses nearby. ✉ *7 Houyuanensi, Jiaodaokou, Dongcheng District, 100009,* ☎ *010/6403–1114,* FAX *010/6401–4603. 30 rooms. 2 restaurants. No credit cards.*

NIGHTLIFE AND THE ARTS

Until the late 1970s the best night out most Beijingers could hope for was dinner at a friend's apartment followed by a sing-along. Since then China's economic boom has brought countless karaoke venues and small discos, which form the backbone of Beijing's nightlife. More affluent people head for the huge new cabaret and restaurant complexes around Third Ring Road. Some restaurants compete with the clubs by offering live music, belly dancers, or other floor shows. Prostitution (illegal in China) is common in many bars and clubs, which may have back rooms for that purpose. Peking opera, strangled almost to death in the Cultural Revolution (1966–76), has revived just enough to generate some interest among the older generations.

The Arts

The arts in China took a long time to recover from the Cultural Revolution, and political works are still generally avoided. Film and theater reflect an interesting mix of modern and avant-garde Chinese and Western influences, though language is a barrier for foreign visitors. The film industry has actually experienced a slow-down of late, being as it is in competition with the new hip-hop culture and with—of course—karaoke; as a result, discount tickets to theaters are often available. Modern dance and commercial art galleries are flourishing.

Recent theatrical productions include works by Ionesco, Lao She, and contemporary Taiwanese writers, and a Chinese stage version of *The Sound of Music* (officials usually require foreign plays to be adapted for "Chinese taste"). People under 60, who grew up in Communist China, are as likely to listen to Western opera as Peking opera; they'll watch performances of the latter only at the Chinese New Year temple fairs. A few theaters maintain the grand tradition, staging shows for audiences of elderly enthusiasts and foreign visitors.

Acrobatics

Chaoyang Juchang (Chaoyang Theater; ✉ 36 Dongsanhuan Beilu, Hujialou, Chaoyang District, ☎ 010/6507–1818) has nightly, spectacular individual and team acrobatic displays employing bicycles, seesaws, catapults, swings, and barrels. At the **Tiandi Juchang** (Universal Theater; ✉ Dongsishi Qiao, Chaoyang District, ☎ 010/6502–3984) the mostly young performers of the China Acrobatics Troupe run through their nightly repertoire of breathtaking, usually flawless stunts.

Music and Variety

Beijing Yinyueting (Beijing Concert Hall; ✉ 1 Beixinhua Jie, Xicheng District, ☎ 010/6605–5846 or 010/6605–7006), Beijing's main venue for Chinese and Western classical music concerts, also has folk dancing and singing, and many celebratory events throughout the year. **Tianqiao Le Chaguan** (Tianqiao Happy Teahouse; ✉ 113 Tianqiao Shichang, Xuanwu District, ☎ 010/6304–0617), in an old, traditional theater, re-creates the Chinese variety shows that were so popular before 1949, including opera, acrobatics, cross talk, jugglers, illusionists, and contortionists.

Peking Opera

Chang'an Da Xiyuan (Chang'an Grand Theater; ✉ 7 Jianguomennei Dajie, Dongcheng District, ☎ 010/6510–1155) stages weekend matinee performances of traditional stories, with full operas in the evenings. **Guanghe Juchang** (Guanghe Theater; ✉ 46 Qianmenroushi Jie, Qianmen Dajie, Chongwen District, ☎ 010/6702–2463) stages plays and films as well as operas. Full operas in a traditional setting are presented at **Huguang Huiguan** (Huguang Guildhall; ✉ 3 Hufangqiao, Xuanwu District, ☎ 010/6351–8284). Performances at **Lao She Chaguan** (Lao She Teahouse; ✉ 3rd floor, 3 Qianmenxi Dajie, Chongwen District, ☎ 010/6303–6830, FAX 010/6301–7529) vary, but usually include Peking opera and a variety of other folk arts, such as acrobatics, magic, or comedy. In the popular **Liyuan Juchang** (Liyuan Theater; ✉ Qianmen Hotel, 175 Yongan Lu, Chongwen District, ☎ 010/6301–6688 ext. 8860, FAX 010/6303–2301), a Peking opera venue for tourists, performances include acrobatics as well as singing with English subtitles.

Theater

At the **Zhongyang Shiyan Huajuyuan Xiao Juchang** (China Experimental Performance Small Theater; ✉ 45 Maoer Hutong, Dianmen, Dongcheng District, ☎ 010/6403–1099 or 010/6403–1109), lesser-known directors and actors put on avant-garde theater and Chinese dramatizations of such works as *Romeo and Juliet, Death of a Salesman,* and *A Streetcar Named Desire*. **Beijing Zhanlanguan Juchang** (Beijing Exhibition Center Theater; ✉ 135 Xizhimenwai Dajie, Xicheng District, ☎ 010/6835–4455), in a Soviet-style building inside the Exhibition Center complex, stages Chinese and Western plays, opera, and ballet. At **Zhongguo Mu'ou Juyuan** (China Puppet Theater; ✉ 1 Anhuaxili, Chaoyang District, ☎ 010/6425–4849), traditional stories acted out by shadow and hand puppets provide lively entertainment for children and adults alike.

Nightlife

Beijing has about a dozen regular venues for local rock and jazz bands, and outdoor music festivals are occasionally held in summer. Bars open virtually all night in the three main bar areas. Several aircraft-hangar-size nightclubs present laser shows, cage dancers, and other live performances. Mandopop, Cantopop, techno, and Latin American are all popular, and sometimes mixed. Underground punk clubs and even ecstasy bars make up the radical fringe. (Drug use, however, is rare, the risk being jail without a fair trial.) Censorship always lurks just below the surface: in 1999, in the lead-up to 50th-anniversary celebrations, several popular bars, music venues, and discos were temporarily closed to prevent their giving the capital a bad image.

Ordinary Chinese people make no real distinction between bars and restaurants. Locals' "bars" are simple restaurants (often without tablecloths or toilets) that serve a limited range of bottled or draft beer, Chinese liquor, and sometimes wine; some have karaoke. Wealthier people—usually men—go to karaoke lounges or nightclubs, some of which have dancers or hostesses. Most of the bars that have sprung up are Western (especially American) style and try to attract foreigners as well as affluent locals.

Bars

At **Arcadia** (Tian Cheng; ✉ Bldg. 3, Jindu Apartments, Fangchengyuan Block 1, Fangszhuang, Fengtai District, ☎ 010/6764–8272), modern abstract decor, live Chinese rock bands every Friday and Saturday, and a mainly Chinese clientele create a different atmosphere from the more popular expat bars. **CD Cafe** (CD Kafei; ✉ Dongsanhuan Lu, Chaoyang District, ☎ 010/6501–6655 ext. 5127), next to one of Beijing's major roads, has jazz and blues bands performing standard numbers in a large, informal setting. The crowd is mixed, with Chinese and foreigners of all ages. At **Goose and Duck** (Eya Jiuba; ✉ Ritandongyi Jie, Chaoyang District, ☎ 010/6509–3777), you can enjoy an English draft beer while you listen to folk, country, and easy-listening music played by Chinese and Western musicians Tuesday–Saturday.

Minder Cafe (Mingdaxi Canting; ⊠ Dongdaqiao Xiejie, Chaoyang District, ☎ 010/6599–6066), packed with revelers dancing to the resident band every weekend, is Beijing's best-known meeting place for young expats. One of the trendiest bars in Beijing is **On Off** (Shang Xia Xian; ⊠ Xingfu Zhonglu, Chaoyang District, ☎ 010/6415–8083). The **Sanwei Bookstore** (Sanwei Shuwu; ⊠ 60 Fuxingmennei Dajie, Xicheng District, ☎ 010/6601–3204) has the traditional Chinese arrangement of a bookstore with an adjacent café. In the past these attracted writers who sipped tea while listening to Peking Opera and talking about their work. Here, the upstairs houses a popular bar; Friday is jazz night, and Saturday sees Chinese classical music played on instruments such as the *pipa* and the *guzheng*. The American-style bar **Schiller's** (Xile Jiuba; ⊠ Liangmaqiao Lu, Chaoyang District, ☎ 010/6461–9276), named for the German poet, is popular with Beijing's younger expats.

Nightclubs
Hotspot (Ridian; ⊠ Sanhuan Donglu, Chaoyang District, ☎ 010/6531–2277) is frequented by affluent, trendy young Chinese; the lively venue offers frenetic disco dancing, cage dancers, and karaoke singers in an industrial atmosphere created by a tin entrance tunnel, matte black decor, and steel balustrades. At **Nightman** (Caite Man; ⊠ 2 Xibahenanli, Chaoyang District, ☎ 010/6466–2562) multilevel black-tiered seating and dancing areas house young Chinese and Westerners enjoying nonstop dancing to hip-hop, techno, and everything else served up by the imported DJs.

OUTDOOR ACTIVITIES AND SPORTS

The Chinese don't do sports the way Americans do. Exercise is not a daily avocation, although a few older people do tai chi in the morning and some young men jog. Golf, tennis, and swimming are limited to a few serious competitors. Recently, golf has attracted the devotion of a few nouveau riche "Daquan" (entrepreneurs); weekend golf outings are often as much for business deal–making as for pleasure. There are very few sports clubs open to the Chinese public, and those that are are often poorly managed in terms of hygiene and maintenance. Clubs in large hotels catering to expats are generally well run.

Golf

Beijing Chaoyang Golf Club. Just beyond the Third Ring Road in downtown Beijing, this short nine-hole course takes less than two hours to play and caters to Japanese expats. The course is convenient and—by Beijing standards—inexpensive. Facilities include a driving range and practice green. ⊠ *Shangsi Lu, Chaoyang District*, ☎ *010/6507–3380 or 10/6500–1149.* ▣ *Greens fee: Y600 weekends, Y400 weekdays.* ◷ *Course, daily 9–6; driving range, daily 9–9:30.*
Beijing Country Golf Club. Known as the farmer's course, this Japanese-managed complex offers two 18-hole courses reclaimed from wheat fields. ⊠ *35 km (22 mi) northeast of Beijing in Shunyi County*, ☎ *010/6944–1005 or 010/6940–1390.* ▣ *Greens fee: Y975 weekdays, Y1,310 weekends. Rental clubs, caddies available.* ◷ *Mar.–Nov., daily 7–5.*
Beijing International Golf Club. Nestled on a hillside above the Ming Tombs, this spectacular 18-hole course is Beijing's finest. Long (par 72), challenging, and meticulously groomed, it has hosted professional tournaments. Facilities include a restaurant, pro shop, and driving range. ⊠ *46 km (29 mi) north of Beijing near Changping*, ☎ *010/6076–2288.* ▣ *Greens fees: Y650 weekdays, Y1,100 weekends. Caddies (required): Y120. Rental clubs available.* ◷ *Mar.–Nov., daily 7–5.*

Health Clubs

Most high-end hotels in Beijing have extensive fitness centers. Usually these are open to the general public. Typical facilities include a lap pool; a weight room with step machines, treadmills, exercise bikes, and modern weight-lifting machines; and even squash, racquetball, and tennis courts.

Great Wall Sheraton Fitness Center offers a modern weight room, an indoor lap pool, a sauna, evening aerobics (Monday, Wednesday, and Friday), and tennis courts (Y70 per hour, reservations required). ☎ *010/ 6590–5566 ext. 2251.* ✉ *Y150.* ☉ *Daily 6 AM–10 PM.*

New Otani Health Club offers a lap pool, a well-equipped exercise room, a tiny indoor track, tennis (Y30 per hour during the day, Y40 per hour after 6:30 PM, reservations required), sauna baths, and steam rooms. ☎ *010/6512–5555 ext. 85.* ✉ *Y120.* ☉ *Daily 7 AM–11 PM.*

Shangri-La Health Club has an indoor lap pool, a weight room, tennis courts (reservations required), and Ping-Pong. ☎ *010/6841–2211 ext. 2833.* ✉ *Y150; tennis courts: weekends Y120 per hour, weekdays Y180 per hour.* ☉ *Daily 6 AM–10:30 PM; tennis courts daily 9 AM–11 PM.*

SHOPPING

The arrival of numerous modern shopping malls, department stores, and groceries is squeezing Beijing's traditional markets. But, for now, most people still rely on street stalls for their produce, meat, dry goods, and other household items. The city's trendiest shopping district, Wangfujing, offers shoppers (and window-shoppers) an array of swank boutiques and department stores. For a more traditional flavor—and bargain reproduction antiques—try the Sunday market at Panjiayuan.

Department Stores

The **Beijing Friendship Store** (✉ 17 Jianguomenwai Dajie, ☎ 010/6500–3311), a longtime tourist favorite, sells the widest range of traditional Chinese goods and handicrafts under one roof, including hand-drawn tablecloths, silk and cashmere goods and clothing, porcelain, watercolor paintings, traditional Chinese medicine, jade and gold jewelry, rugs (both silk and wool), and groceries. The **Lufthansa Center** (✉ 52 Liangmaoqiao, Chaoyang District, ☎ 010/6465–1188), among Beijing's top department stores, stocks cosmetics, consumer electronics, wool and cashmere clothing, and new rugs; a Western grocery store occupies the basement.

Specialty Stores

Arts and Antiques

Antiques began pouring out of China more than a decade ago despite strict rules banning the export of precious "cultural relics." According to Chinese law, nothing that predates the death of Qing emperor Qianlong (1795) can be legally exported. The same holds for religious items, including Buddha statues and Tibetan thangkhas, certain imperial porcelains, and any item deemed important to China's Communist Revolution. Although many antiques—from Tang dynasty tomb art to priceless Zhou dynasty bronzes—are smuggled out of China, export of many genuine antiques is likely to be illegal unless they have been bought from a licensed shop (they should have a special customs sticker carrying a Temple of Heaven symbol).

MARKETS

Beijing Curio City (✉ Dongsanhuan Nanlu, Chaoyang District, exit 3rd Ring Rd. at Anjiayuan Bridge, ☎ 010/6774–7711 or 010/6773–6021 ext. 63) is a four-story complex housing scores of kitsch and curio shops and a few furniture vendors. Prices are high (driven by tour groups), so don't be afraid to low-ball. **Chaowai Market** (✉ Shichangjie, Chaoyangmenwai Dajie, Chaoyang District), Beijing's best-known venue for affordable antique and reproduction furniture, houses scores of independent vendors who sell everything from authentic Qing chests to traditional baskets, ceramics, carpets, and curios. Be sure to bargain; vendors routinely sell items for less than half their starting price. **Houhai Market** (✉ At Houhai Gongyuan) is a small lane lined with tiny antiques shops. It can be tough to find on weekends, when a surrounding produce market fills the neighborhood with shoppers. Follow the footpath that hugs the shore on the west bank of Houhai Lake. Look for a sign (in English) advertising ANTIQUES.

In **Liangmahe Market** (✉ 49 Liangmaqiao Lu, just north of Kempinski Hotel, Chaoyang District) stalls offer curios, antiques, collectibles, and fakes. Prices are higher than at Chaowai, so good bargaining skills are imperative. Toward the north of the market are several shops selling high-quality antiques. One of these, the **Hua Yi Classical Furniture Company,** has a warehouse/factory complex outside Beijing that is open to the public. Ask a salesperson to accompany you. **Liulichang Jie** (✉ Liulichang, Xuanwu District) occupies a narrow street that has been carefully restored to its Ming-era grandeur. Its classical architecture is as much an attraction as the art and antiques shops. Artists come here for the selection of brushes, paper, and ink stones. The Sunday market at **Panjiayuan** (✉ Huaweiqiaoxinan Jie, Dongsanhuan, Chaoyang District) is Beijing's liveliest. Vendors, many from faraway provinces, fill hundreds of open-air stalls with a dizzying array of collectibles, as well as lots of junk. Old clocks, new porcelain, jade, bronzes, tomb art, wood carvings, Tibetan rugs, "Maomorabilia"— it's all here. The market is grubby, so dress down. Arrive at sunrise to beat the crowds. Many stalls also do business on Saturday.

STORES

If time permits, compare shops before making a purchase. For collectibles, try the **Beijing Jewelry Import & Export Corporation** (✉ 229 Wangfujing Dajie, ☎ 010/6525–4889). **The Beijing Painting Gallery** (✉ 289 Wangfujing Dajie) deals in contemporary art. **Han's Gallery** (✉ Ritan Dongyijie) is a small private venue specializing in contemporary Chinese painters and antique embroidery. The **Huaxia Arts & Crafts Store** (✉ 293 Wangfujing Dajie) has a selection of crafts.

Books

Many hotel kiosks sell international newspapers and magazines. Some hotels, such as the Great Wall Sheraton, Kempinski, and China World, sell books on China and foreign novels. **Beijing Friendship Store** has a small but well-stocked bookstore with a good selection on Chinese history and culture. It also stocks foreign news magazines, imported fiction, and a few children's books. For more variety, try **Foreign Languages Bookstore** (✉ 235 Wangfujing Dajie, Dongcheng District, ☎ 010/6512–6922), which stocks foreign-language novels, textbooks, tapes, maps, art books, academic texts, and dictionaries.

Clothing

Silk Alley (✉ Jct. Xiushui Nanjie and Xiushui Dongjie) has long been popular with both expatriates and fashion-conscious Chinese. If you start at the south end of Silk Alley near the Beijing Friendship Store, you can follow the alley north to browse open-air clothing stalls specializing in silks, cashmere, and made-for-export apparel. Depending on the season (and what happens to fall off the truck) you can find everything from Esprit sportswear to designer women's suits to North

Face jackets. Beware of hawkers who troll the area with pirate CDs, VCDs, and CD-ROMs; these illicit copies are often damaged or virus-tainted. Made-for-export clothing abounds in **Yabao Market** (⊠ West side of Ritan Lu), also known as the Russian Market; the quality is often inferior to that found at Silk Alley. Russians and Eastern European traders buy here for export. Popular items include cotton apparel, fur coats, and bedding. Some vendors only deal in bulk. Another market known for its export-quality clothing runs along **Gongren Tiyuchang Beilu,** west of Gongren Tiyuchang Donglu, and then continues along Sanlitun Lu in the Sanlitun diplomatic quarter. Come here to stock up on cotton and linen. Some children's clothing is also available.

Fabric, Embroidery, and Drawn Work

Most department stores sell silk, satin brocades, and wools. Beijing's best yardage shop, the **Yuanlong Embroidery and Silk Store** (⊠ 55 Tiantan Lu, Chongwen District, across from north gate of Temple of Heaven Park, ☎ 010/6701–2859) has sold silks and yard goods for more than a century. It also offers custom tailoring and shipping. For hand-painted fabric, try the **Baizihfang Embroidery Factory** (⊠ A44 Liren Jie, Xuanwu District, ☎ 010/6303–6577). The **Golden Peacock Art World** (⊠ 13 Dongtucheng Lu, Chaoyang District, ☎ 010/6421–4757) has drawn work among other art products. The **White Peacock Art World** (☞ Rugs, *below*) has a wide range of arts and crafts including drawn work.

Jewelry

Everything from porcelain to toilet paper is sold at the **Hongqiao Market** (⊠ Tiantan Lu, between Chongemenwai Lu and Tiyuguan Dajie, ☎ 010/6711–7630), but the main attraction, on the third floor, is freshwater pearls. The market offers a good selection at affordable prices. The **Shendege Gongyipin Shangdian** (Shard Box Store; ⊠ 1 Ritan Beilu, Chaoyang District, ☎ 010/6500–3712) specializes in silver, jade, coral, and turquoise jewelry worn by China's national minorities. Many pieces are one-of-a-kind items from Tibet or Yunnan. The store takes its name from traditional jewelry boxes, which were often made from pottery shards.

Rugs

Antique Chinese, Mongolian, Tibetan, and Central Asian rugs are sold in many of Beijing's antiques shops. Many offer shipping services. The walls and floors of the **Beijing Carpet Import & Export Corporation** (⊠ 1st floor, Hong Kong Macao Center, Dongsishitiao, Chaoyang District, ☎ 010/6501–2568) are covered with a large selection of wool and silk carpets in modern and traditional Chinese and Middle Eastern designs, a few antique, in a variety of sizes and prices. The **Beijing Qianmen Carpet Factory** (⊠ 44 Xingfu Dajie, Chongwen District, in bomb shelter behind theater, ☎ 010/6715–1687; call before visiting) outlet offers a small selection of older rugs.

The **Beijing Yihong Carpet Factory** (a.k.a. the Women's Carpet Cooperative; ⊠ 35 Juzhang Hutong, Chongwen District, ☎ 010/6712–2195), a back-alley showroom, is managed by women from a state-owned carpet factory. Its showroom is stacked with dusty rugs from Mongolia, Xinjiang, and Tibet. Cleaning and repairs are free. Although it's primarily an outlet for old rugs, new items are on sale as well, and copies of old designs can be made to order, usually within weeks. The **White Peacock Art World** (⊠ Beibinhe Lu, Deshengmenwai Dajie, Haidian District, ☎ 010/6201–3008) carries a large selection of new rugs in silk and wool; it will also make rugs to order. Among department stores with good new rug selections are the Beijing Friendship Store and the Lufthansa center.

Stamps and Coins

For new Chinese stamp sets, visit the **Wangfujing Post Office** (⌧ 2 Xu-anwumendong Dajie at Wangfujing Dajie). For old stamps try the **Yuetan Schichang,** where stamp traders occupy stalls along the west side of Yuetan Gongyuan (Yuetan Park). Coins are sold at many antiques and curio shops. Old coins and paper currency are traded outside the **Gudai Qianbi Zhanlanguan** (Museum of Antique Currency).

Supermarkets

For Western groceries, several new branches of **Park 'n' Shop** (⌧ COFCO Plaza, Basement, 8 Jianguomennei Dajie, ☎ 010/6526–0816; ⌧ Full Link Plaza, Basement 2, 18 Chaowangmenwai Dajie, ☎ 010/6588–1168) have Beijing's best selection. The **Lido Supermarket** (⌧ Jichang Lu, Jiangtai Lu, Chaoyang District, ☎ 010/6437–6688 ext. 1541), at the Holiday Inn Lido, is another option. There's a smaller supermarket at **Scitech Plaza** (⌧ 22 Jianguomenwai Dajie, Chaoyang District, ☎ 010/6512–4488).

Wangfujing

Wangfujing Dajie, Beijing's premier shopping street, underwent a huge face-lift in the period leading up to Communist China's 50th anniversary. Many of the tiny shops that were once its hallmark have been replaced by glitzy malls and department stores. Still, Wangfujing retains much of its charm, and several shops that survived the modernization drive remain well worth a browse.

Begin at the corner of Dengshikou and Wangfujing Dajie, walking south. On the northwest corner is the Century Plaza department store. To the south, on the west side of Wangfujing Dajie, find the **China Star Silk Store** (⌧ 133 Wangfujing Dajie, ☎ 010/6525–7945), where you can order a *qipao,* a traditional silk dress. The **Beijing Sports Department Store** (⌧ 201 Wangfujing Dajie) has the city's best selection of sporting gear, including ice skates for winter. Just south is an official condom and birth control outlet, reputedly Beijing's first sex shop when it opened in the 1980s. Across Wangfujing is the **Luwu Jewelry and Craft Store** (⌧ 268 Wangfujing Dajie), where merchants sell silk, jade, wood, and other souvenirs. Back on the west side, just south of the crossroads, the **Foreign Language Book Store** (⌧ 235 Wangfujing Dajie) contains four floors of books, maps, videotapes, CDs, and school supplies. This is one of the best places to buy English-language books, maps, postcards, VCDs, and CD-ROMs about China. As you continue south, on your left is the giant **Sun Dongan Plaza** shopping center, which is full of designer shops but makes a concession to Old Peking with a traditional-style shopping street on the second floor. Wangfujing's grand dame, the **Beijing Department Store** (⌧ 255 Wangfujing Dajie, ☎ 010/6512–6677) continues to attract large crowds, despite the allure of Sun Dongan and the even bigger Oriental Plaza complex (which begins at the southern end of Wangfujing and stretches a block east to Dongan Dajie). On the opposite side of the road is the **Chengguzhai Antique Store** (⌧ 194 Wangfujing Dajie, ☎ 010/6522–0673), which sells more handierafts than antiques.

SIDE TRIPS FROM BEIJING

Changcheng (Great Wall)

60–120 km (37–74 mi) north and west of Beijing.

Built by successive dynasties over two millennia, the **Changcheng** (Great Wall) isn't actually one structure but a collection of many defensive installations. Erected to repel marauding nomads, they extend

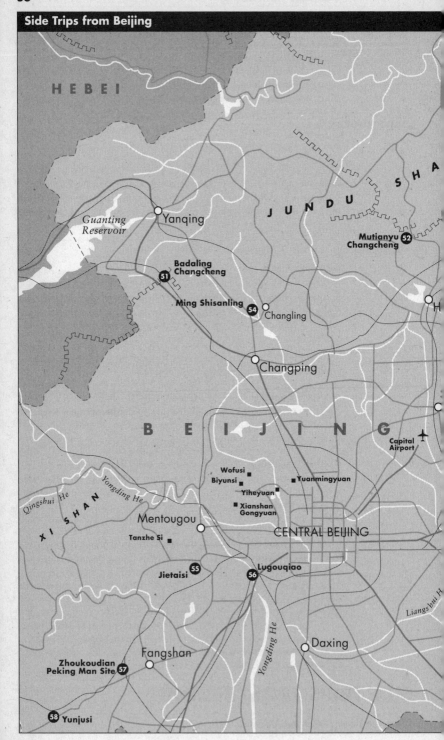

HEBEI

Guanting
Reservoir

Yanqing

JUNDU SHA

Mutianyu 52
Changcheng

Badaling 51
Changcheng

Ming Shisanling 54
Changling

H

Changping

BEIJING

Wofusi
Biyunsi
Yuanmingyuan
Yiheyuan
Xianshan
Gongyuan

Capital
Airport

Mentougou

Qingshui He

Yongding He

XI SHAN

Tanzhe Si

CENTRAL BEIJING

Jietaisi 55

Lugouqiao 56

Liangshui H

Yongding He

Zhoukoudian
Peking Man Site 57

Fangshan

Daxing

58 Yunjusi

Bai He

Miyun
Reservoir

53
Simatai
Changcheng

HEBEI

N

Xinglong

Miyun

Huairou

Qing
Dongling

59

Shunyi

Jmji He

Pinggu

SHI

Sanhe

HEBEI

Chaobai He

Dachang

ai He

Xianghe

TANJIN

0   20 miles

0   30 km

some 4,000 km (2,480 mi) from the East China Sea to Central Asia. Built of wood, the earliest walls and signal towers have long since disappeared. The more substantial brick-and-earth ruins that snake across the mountains north of Beijing date from the heyday of wall building, the Ming dynasty.

China's first wall builder, Qin Shihuang, began fortifying the northern border after he established the Qin dynasty in 221 BC. His work, which stood far to the north of the present-day wall, extended some 5,000 km (3,100 mi) from Liaoning province, in the east, to Gansu, in the west. By some accounts, Qin mustered nearly a million people, or about a fifth of China's total workforce, a mobilization that claimed countless lives and gave rise to many tragic folktales. (In one, a woman hears of her husband's disappearance and goes to the worksite to wait for his return, believing her determination will eventually bring him back. In the end, she turns into a rock, which to this day stands at the head of the Great Wall in the beautiful seaside town of Qinhuangdao, some 480 km [300 mi] east of Beijing.)

Later dynasties repaired existing walls or built new ones. The Ming, which took power in 1386, committed vast resources to wall building as a defense against increasingly restive northern tribes. The Ming wall, which is about 26 ft tall and 23 ft wide at its base, could accommodate six horsemen riding abreast. It incorporated small wall-top garrisons linked by beacon towers used for sending smoke signals or setting off fireworks to warn of enemy attack. In the end, however, wall building failed to prevent the Manchu invasion that toppled the Ming in 1644.

That historical failure hasn't tarnished the Great Wall's image. Although China's official line once cast it as a model of feudal oppression—focusing on the brutality suffered by work crews and the vast treasures squandered on the useless fortification—the Great Wall is now touted as a national patriotic symbol. "Love China, Restore the Great Wall," declared Deng Xiaoping in a 1984 campaign that kicked off the official revisionism. Since then large sections of the Great Wall have been repaired and opened to visitors.

51 **Badaling Changcheng.** Close to Beijing, 9 km (5½ mi) above the giant Juyongguan garrison and an hour by car from downtown, the Badaling Fortress is where visiting dignitaries go for a quickie photo-op. Its large sections of restored wall rise steeply to either side of the fort in rugged landscape. Convenient to the Ming Tombs, Badaling is popular with group tours and often crowded. People with disabilities find access to the wall at Badaling better than elsewhere in the Beijing area. ⊠ *Yanqing County, 70 km (43 mi) northwest of Beijing,* ☎ *010/6912–1235 or 010/6912–1338.* ◎ *Y25; cable car, Y80 one-way, Y100 round-trip.* ◎ *Daily 6:30 AM–sunset.*

★ **52** **Mutianyu Changcheng.** A bit farther from downtown Beijing, the Great Wall at Mutianyu is more spectacular and (usually) less crowded than Badaling. Here, a long section of restored wall is perched on a high ridge above serene wooded canyons. Views from the top are truly memorable. The lowest point on the wall is a strenuous one-hour climb above the parking lot. As an alternative, you can take a cable car on a breathtaking ride to the highest restored section, from which several hiking trails descend. If you don't plan to hike, phone ahead to make sure the gondola is running. ⊠ *Huairou County, 90 km (56 mi) northeast of Beijing,* ☎ *010/6162–6873 or 010/6162–6506.* ◎ *Y20; cable car, Y80 one-way, Y100 round-trip.* ◎ *Daily 7 AM–sunset.*

★ **53** **Simatai Changcheng.** Remote and largely unrestored, the Great Wall at Simatai is ideal if you're seeking adventure. Near the frontier garrison at Gubeikou, this section of wall traverses towering peaks and hangs precariously above cliffs. In some places stairways are crumbling and the trail is so steep that the journey is more a crawl than a hike. Several trails lead to the wall from the parking lot. The hike takes about two hours. A cable car serves a drop-off point about 40 minutes on foot from the wall. If you want a quieter, easier, but less spectacular hike, head west from the small lake below the wall, toward the restored Jinshanling section. ✉ *Near Miyun, Miyun County,* ☎ *010/6903–5025 or 010/6903–1051.* 🎫 *Y20; cable car, Y40 one-way, Y60 round-trip.* ⊘ *Daily 8–5.*

Ming Shisanling

★ ❺❹ *48 km (30 mi) north of Beijing.*

A narrow valley just north of Changping is the final resting place for 13 of the Ming dynasty's 16 emperors (the others were buried in Nanjing). Ming monarchs would journey here each year to kowtow before their clan forefathers and make offerings to their memory. The area's vast scale and imperial grandeur convey the importance attached to ancestor worship in ancient China.

The road to the Ming Shisanling (Thirteen Ming Tombs) begins beneath an imposing stone portico that stands at the valley entrance. Beyond, a **shen lu** (spirit way; 🎫 Y16, ⊘ daily 9–5:30), once reserved for imperial travel, passes through an outer pavilion and between rows of stone sculptures—imperial advisers and huge, serene elephants, lions, horses, and other creatures—on its 7-km (4½-mi) journey to the burial sites.

The road leads to **Changling,** the grand tomb built for Emperor Yongle in 1427. Architecturally, it matches the design of Yongle's great masterpiece, the Forbidden City, which he built after moving the Ming's imperial capital north to Beijing.

Changling and a second tomb, **Dingling,** were rebuilt in the 1980s and opened to the public. Unfortunately, both complexes suffer from over-restoration and crowding. Do visit, if only for the tomb relics on display in small museums at each site, but allow ample time for a hike or drive northwest from Changling to the six *unrestored* tombs lying a short distance farther up the valley. Here, crumbling walls conceal vast courtyards shaded by ancient pine trees. At each tomb, a stone altar rests beneath a stele tower and burial mound. In some cases the wall that circles the burial chamber is accessible on steep stone stairways that ascend from either side of the altar. At the valley's terminus (about 5 km [3 mi] northwest of Changling), the Zhaoling tomb rests beside a traditional walled village. This thriving hamlet is well worth exploring.

Picnics amid the Ming ruins have been a favored weekend activity among Beijing-based diplomats for nearly a century. Ignore signs prohibiting this, but do carry out all trash. ✉ *Near Changping, Changping County.* 🎫 *Restored tombs, Y30; unrestored tombs, free.* ⊘ *Daily 9–5:30.*

Jietaisi

❺❺ *35 km (22 mi) west of Beijing.*

On a wooded hill west of Beijing, Jietai Temple is one of China's most famous ancient Buddhist sites. Its four main halls occupy terraces on a gentle slope up to Ma'an Shan (Saddle Hill). Originally built in AD 581, the temple complex expanded over the centuries and grew to its current scale in a major renovation conducted by Ming-era devotees from 1436 to 1450. The temple buildings, plus three magnificent bronze Buddhas in the Mahavira Hall, date from this period. To the right of this hall, just above twin pagodas, is the Ordination Terrace, a platform built of white marble and topped with a massive bronze Sakyamuni seated on a lotus flower. Tranquil courtyards, where ornate stelae and well-kept gardens bask beneath the Scholar Tree and other ancient pines, augment the temple's beauty. Many modern devotees from Beijing visit the temple on weekends. ⊠ *Mentougou County.* 🚇 *Y10.* ☉ *Daily 7:30–6.*

En Route   Farther along the road past Jietai Temple, **Tanzhe Si** (Tanzhe Temple) is a Buddhist complex nestled in a grove of *zhe* (cudrania) trees. Established around AD 400 and once home to more than 500 monks, Tanzhe was heavily damaged during the Cultural Revolution (it has since been restored). The complex makes an ideal side trip from Jietai Temple or Marco Polo Bridge. ⊠ *Mentougou County, 10 km (6 mi) past Jietai Temple, 45 km (28 mi) west of Beijing.* 🚇 *Y13.* ☉ *Daily 8:30–4.*

Lugouqiao

56 *16 km (10 mi) southwest of Beijing's Guanganmen Gate.*

Also known as Marco Polo Bridge because it was praised by the Italian wayfarer, this impressive span is Beijing's oldest. Built in 1192 and reconstructed after severe flooding during the Qing dynasty, its 11 segmented stone arches cross the Yongding River on what was once the imperial highway that linked Beijing with central China. The bridge's marble balustrades support nearly 500 carved stone lions that decorate elaborate handrails. Note the giant stone slabs that comprise the bridge's original roadbed. Carved imperial stelae at either end of the span commemorate the bridge and surrounding scenery.

The Marco Polo Bridge is best remembered in the 20th century as the spot where invading Japanese armies clashed with Chinese soldiers on June 7, 1937. The assault began Japan's brutal eight-year occupation of eastern China, which ended with Tokyo's surrender at the end of World War II. The bridge has become a popular field-trip destination for Beijing students. On the Beijing side of the span is the **Kangri Zhanzheng Jinianguan** (Memorial Hall of the War of Resistance Against Japan). Below the bridge on the opposite shore, local entrepreneurs rent horses (asking price Y120 per hour, but you should bargain) and lead tours of the often-dry riverbed. ⊠ *Near Xidaokou, Fengtai District.* 🚇 *Y10.* ☉ *Daily 8:30–6.*

Zhoukoudian Peking Man Site

57 *48 km (30 mi) southwest of Beijing.*

This area of lime mines and craggy foothills ranks among the world's great paleontological sites (and served as the setting for Amy Tan's *The Bonesetter's Daughter*). In 1929 anthropologists, drawn to Zhoukoudian by apparently human "dragon bones" found in a Beijing apothecary, unearthed a complete cranium and other fossils dubbed homo erectus pekinensis, or Peking Man. These early remains, believed to be nearly 700,000 years old, suggest (as do similar homo erectus discoveries in Indonesia) that man's most recent ancestor originated in Asia, not Europe. A large-scale excavation done in the early 1930s unearthed six skullcaps and other hominid remains, stone tools, evidence of fire, plus a multitude of animal bones, many at the bottom of a large sinkhole believed to be a trap for woolly rhinos and other large game. Sadly, the Peking Man fossils disappeared under mysterious circumstances during World War II, leaving researchers only plaster casts to contemplate. Subsequent digs at Zhoukoudian have yielded nothing equivalent to Peking Man, although archaeologists haven't yet abandoned the search. Trails lead to several hillside excavation sites. A small museum showcases a few (dusty) Peking Man statues, a collection of Paleolithic artifacts, and some fine animal fossils, including a bear skeleton and a saber-toothed tiger skull. ⊠ *Zhoukoudian*, ☎ *010/6930–1272.* 🎫 *Y21.* ☉ *Daily 9–4:30.*

Yunjusi

58 *121 km (75 mi) southwest of Beijing.*

Yunju Temple is best known for its collection of 14,278 stone tablets carved with Buddhist scriptures between the 6th and 17th centuries. A small pagoda at the center of the complex commemorates Jing Wan, the Tang-era monk who carved the earliest 146 stone tablets and ordered that the work continue after his death. Many of these tablets were once stored in caves carved into the cliffs on Shijing Mountain, behind the temple. Today these carvings are stored in rooms built along the temple's southern perimeter.

Four central prayer halls, arranged along the hillside above the main gate, contain impressive Ming bronze Buddhas. The last in this row, the Dabei Hall, displays a spectacular Thousand-Arm Avalokiteshvara. This 13-ft-tall bronze sculpture image—which actually has 24 arms and five heads and stands in a giant lotus flower—is believed to embody boundless compassion. A group of pagodas, led by the 98-ft-tall Northern Pagoda, are all that remain of the original Tang complex. They are nonetheless remarkable for their Buddhist reliefs and ornamental patterns. Heavily damaged during the Japanese occupation and again by Maoist radicals in the 1960s, the temple complex remains under renovation. ⊠ *Off Fangshan Lu, Nanshangle Xiang, Fangshan County.* ☎ *010/6138–2101 or 010/6138–1612.* 🎫 *Y16.* ☉ *Daily 8–6.*

Qing Dongling

★ **59** *125 km (78 mi) east of Beijing.*

Modeled on the Ming Tombs, the Qing Dongling (Eastern Qing Tombs) replicate the Ming spirit ways, walled tomb complexes, and subterranean burial chambers. But they're even more extravagant in their scale and grandeur. The ruins contain the remains of five emperors, 15 empresses, and 136 imperial concubines, all laid to rest in a broad valley chosen by Emperor Shunzhi while on a hunting expedition. By the Qing's collapse in 1911, the tomb complex covered some 18 square mi of farmland and forested hillside, making it the most expansive burial ground in all China.

The Eastern Qing Tombs are in much better repair than their older Ming counterparts. Although several of the tomb complexes have undergone extensive renovation, none is overdone. Peeling paint, grassy courtyards, and numerous stone bridges and pathways convey a sense of the area's original grandeur. Often, visitors are so few that you may feel as if you've stumbled upon an ancient ruin unknown beyond the valley's farming villages.

Of the nine tombs open to the public, two are not to be missed. The first, **Yuling,** is the resting place of the Ming's most powerful sovereign, Emperor Qianlong, who ruled China for 59 years during the 18th century. Beyond the outer courtyards, Qianlong's burial chamber is accessible from inside Stela Hall, where an entry tunnel descends some 65 ft into the ground and ends at the first of three elaborately carved marble gates. Beyond, exquisite carvings of Buddhist images and sutras rendered in both Sanskrit and Tibetan adorn the tomb's walls and

ceiling. Qianlong was laid to rest, along with his empress and two concubines, in the third and final marble vault, amid priceless offerings
looted by warlords early in the 20th century.

Dingdongling was built for the infamous Empress Dowager Cixi (1835–
1911). Known for her failure to halt Western imperialist encroachment,
Cixi once spent funds allotted to strengthen China's navy on a traditional stone boat for the lake at the Summer Palace. Her burial compound, reputed to have cost 72 tons of silver, is the most elaborate (if
not the largest) at the Eastern Qing Tombs. Many of its stone carvings
are considered significant because the phoenix, which symbolized the
female, is level with, or even above, the imperial (and male) dragon—
a feature, ordered, no doubt, by the empress herself. A peripheral hall
paneled in gold leaf displays some of the luxuries amassed by Cixi and
her entourage, including embroidered gowns, jewelry, a selection of imported cigarettes, and even a coat for one of her dogs. In a bow to tourist
kitsch, the compound's main hall contains a wax statue of Cixi sitting
Buddha-like on a lotus petal flanked by a chambermaid and a eunuch.

The Eastern Qing Tombs are a three- to four-hour drive from the capital. Poor roads and road construction slow the journey. But the rural
scenery is dramatic, and the trip is arguably the best full-day excursion
outside Beijing. ⊠ *Near Malanguan, Hebei.* ☎ *Y32.* ⊘ *Daily 8:30–5.*

BEIJING A TO Z

*To research prices, get advice from other travelers, and book travel ar-
rangements, visit www.fodors.com.*

AIR TRAVEL

Beijing Capital International Airport is 27 km (17 mi) northeast of the
city center. Recently expanded, it's now extremely efficient.

Departing international passengers must pay a Y90 airport tax (payable
only in RMB) before check-in. Passengers on domestic flights must pay
Y50. Coupons are sold at booths inside the terminal and collected at
the entrance to the main departure hall. After checking in, plan on long
lines at immigration, especially in the morning.

➤ AIRPORT INFORMATION: **Beijing Capital International Airport** (☎ 010/
6456–3604).

AIRPORT TRANSFERS

The easiest way to get from Capital Airport to Beijing is by hotel shuttle. Most major hotels have representatives at the airport able to arrange a car or minivan. Departing visitors should prebook transportation
through their hotels.

The taxi queue is just outside the terminal beyond a small covered parking area. The line (usually long) moves quickly. Do not accept rides
from drivers who try to coax you away from the line. These privateers
simply want more cash. At the head of the line, a dispatcher will give
you your taxi's number, useful in case of complaints or forgotten luggage. Insist that drivers use their meters, and do not negotiate a fare.
If the driver is unwilling to comply, feel free to change taxis. Most of
the taxis serving the airport are large-model cars. Flag fall is Y12
(good for 3½ km) plus Y2 per additional kilometer. Passengers are expected to pay the Y10 toll for the airport expressway. If you're caught
in rush-hour traffic, expect standing surcharges. In light traffic it takes
about 30 minutes to reach Beijing's eastern district; during rush hour,
allow at least 45. For the city center expect a one-hour cab ride. After
11 PM, taxis impose a 20% late-night surcharge, but there are no extra
charges for luggage.

The airport bus (Y12) terminal is outside the arrivals area (buy tickets from the booth, which is easy to spot, before you exit, then cross the road to the buses). There are two routes (A or B), clearly marked in English and Chinese. On board, stops are often announced in English and Chinese (if not, the drivers on these routes speak basic English). Route A runs between the airport and the Beijing railway station, stopping at the airport expressway/Third Ring Road intersection, Lufthansa center, Kunlun Hotel, Great Wall Sheraton Hotel, Dongzhimen subway station/Second Ring Road, Hong Kong Macau Center (Swissôtel), Chaoyangmen subway station, and one block north of the Beijing train station/Beijing International Hotel. Route B runs from the airport to the CAAC ticket office on Changan Dajie. It travels west along the Third Ring Road, following it south to Changan Jie. Stops include the SAS Hotel, Asian Games Village, Friendship Hotel, and Shangri-La Hotel.

BIKE TRAVEL

Beijing is made for pedaling. All of the city's main boulevards and many secondary streets have wide, well-defined bike lanes often separated from other traffic by an island with hedges or trees. If a flat tire or sudden brake failure strikes, seek out the nearest street-side mechanic (they're everywhere), easily identified by their bike parts and pumps.

BUS TRAVEL TO AND FROM BEIJING

Beijing is served by four long-distance bus stations. They are: Dongzhimen (northeast), Haihutun (south), Beijiao, also called Deshengmen (north), and Majuan (east). Long-distance buses are usually quite basic—much like an old-fashioned school bus—although some overnight buses now boast two cramped decks with reclining seating or bunks. The four long-distance bus companies are equally good.

➤ Bus Information: **Beijiao** (north; ✉ Deshengmenwai Dajie, Xicheng District, ☎ 010/6204–7095 or 010/6204–7096). **Dongzhimen** (northeast; ✉ Dongzhimenwaixie Jie, Chaoyang District, ☎ 010/6468–6792, 010/6467–1346 or 010/6460–8131). **Haihutun** (south; ✉ Yongwai Chezan Lu, Fengtai District, ☎ 010/6726–7149 or 010/6722–4641). **Majuan** (east; ✉ Guangqumenwai Dajie, Chaoyang District, ☎ 010/6771–7620 or 010/6771–7622).

BUS TRAVEL WITHIN BEIJING

Getting on or off a Beijing city bus is often, quite literally, a fight. Buses are hot and crowded in summer and cold and crowded in winter. If you choose the bus—and you shouldn't—watch your belongings very carefully.

EMBASSIES

➤ Australia: (✉ 21 Dongzhimenwai Dajie, Chaoyang District, ☎ 010/6532–2331, FAX 010/6532–3101).

➤ Canada: (✉ 19 Dongzhimenwai Dajie, Chaoyang District, ☎ 010/6532–3536, FAX 010/6532–4972).

➤ Republic of Ireland: (✉ 3 Ritan Donglu, Chaoyang District, ☎ 010/6532–2691, FAX 010/6532–6857).

➤ New Zealand: (✉ 1 Dong'er Jie, Ritanlu, Chaoyang District, ☎ 010/6532–2732 or 010/6532–2733, FAX 010/6532–4317).

➤ South Africa: (✉ Suite C801, Lufthansa Center, 50 Liangmaqiao Lu, Chaoyang District, ☎ 010/6532–0172, FAX 010/6465–1965).

➤ United Kingdom: (✉ 1 Guanghua Lu, Chaoyang District, ☎ 010/8529–6077 or 010/8529–6600, FAX 010/6532–1937).

➤ United States: (✉ 3 Xiushui Beijie, Chaoyang District, ☎ 010/6532–3431 ext. 229 or 010/6532–3831 ext. 264, FAX 010/6532–2483).

EMERGENCIES

In case of an emergency, call your embassy first; embassy staff members are available 24 hours a day to help handle emergencies and facilitate communication with local agencies. Asia Emergency Assistance Center (AEA) has 24-hour emergency and pharmacy assistance. International Medical Clinic (IMC) has 24-hour emergency and pharmacy services, as well as a dental clinic. Probably the best place for nonemergency treatment is the Beijing United Family Health Center.

You can file a complaint as a tourist with Beijing Tourism Quality Supervision, or call the taxi complaint number. Often the police (☎ **110**, toll-free) do not speak much English.

➤ CONTACTS: **Asia Emergency Assistance Center** (AEA; ✉ 2-1-1 Tayuan Diplomatic Office Bldg., 14 Liangmahe Nanlu, Chaoyang District, ☎ 010/6462–9112 during office hrs; 010/6462–9100 after hrs). **Beijing Tourism Quality Supervision** (☎ 010/6513–0828). **Beijing United Family Health Center** (✉ 2 Jiangtai Lu, Chaoyang District, near Lido Hotel, ☎ 010/6433–3960). **Fire** (☎ 119). **International Medical Clinic** (IMC; ✉ Beijing Lufthansa Center, Regis Office Bldg., Room S110, 50 Liagmaoqiao Lu, Chaoyang District, ☎ 010/6465–1561 or 010/6465–1562). **Police** (☎ 110). **Medical Emergency** (☎ 120). **Traffic Accident** (☎ 122).

ENGLISH-LANGUAGE MEDIA

For books in English, try Foreign Languages Bookstore, and The Friendship Store. Most major hotels sell international newspapers and magazines, plus books about China.

➤ BOOKSTORES: **Foreign Languages Bookstore** (✉ 235 Wangfujing Dajie, Dongcheng District, ☎ 010/6512–6922). **The Friendship Store** (✉ 17 Jianguomenwai Dajie, Chaoyang District, ☎ 010/6500–3311).

PEDICAB TRAVEL

Pedicabs were once the vehicle of choice for Beijingers laden with a week's worth of groceries or tourists eager for a street-eye city tour. Today many residents are wealthy enough to bundle their purchases into taxis, and the tourist trade has moved on to the tight schedules of air-conditioned buses. But pedicabs still can be hired outside the Friendship Store on Jianguomenwai Dajie and near major tourist sites such as Liulichang and Beihai Park. Be sure to negotiate the fare in advance, clarifying which currency will be used (Y or US$), whether the fare is considered a one-way or round-trip (some drivers will demand payment for a round-trip whether or not you come along), and whether it is for one person or two. Fares start at Y10.

SUBWAY TRAVEL

Beijing's two subway lines are packed during rush hour but offer convenient travel on off-hours. One line circles Beijing beneath the Second Ring Road and the other runs east–west from the city center to the western suburbs. The lines meet at Fuxingmen. The subway runs from 5 AM to midnight daily. Fares are Y3 per ride for any distance. Unlike many subway systems in the West, Beijing's subway has limited stops. It's a quick way of getting around the city, but it may not always be the most convenient. Note, however, that stations are marked in both Chinese and English.

TAXIS

There are three classes of taxis in Beijing. The cheapest—but endangered—species is the *miandi* (bread-loaf van), a tiny minivan usually painted yellow. These vehicles cost Y10 at flag fall and must travel 10 km (6 mi) before the Y1.5-per-kilometer meter kicks in. Although miandi are certainly a bargain, they're often filthy and falling apart. They're also banned from certain roads, so cross-city trips in them can take longer than in bigger cabs. A second, and better, grade of taxi is the *xiali*, a domestically produced car reminiscent of the first Honda hatchbacks. Tall people find xialis cramped. Flag fall for these taxis is Y10 for the first 4 km (2½ mi) and Y1.2 per km thereafter. A 20% night-time surcharge is added after 11 PM. At the top end are the sedans found waiting at the airport, major hotels, and large tourist sites. They're clean, comfortable, and still cheap compared with Western cabs. Flag fall is Y12 for the first 3½ km (2 mi) and Y1.6–Y3 per kilometer thereafter, depending on the vehicle. A 20% nighttime surcharge kicks in at 11 PM. Be sure to check that the meter has been engaged to avoid fare negotiations at your destination.

➤ CONTACTS: **Taxi Complaints** (☎ 010/6835–1150).

TOURS

Every major hotel offers guided tours to sites outside Beijing. Among the hotel-based travel agencies are China Swan International Tours and Beijing Panda Tour. China International Travel Service (CITS) is the official government agency. New travel agencies are springing up all the time in Beijing; ask at your hotel about alternatives to CITS.

The Beijing Hutong Tourist Agency offers the only guided pedicab tours of Beijing's back alleys. This half-day trip winds its way through what was once Beijing's most prestigious neighborhood, stops at the Drum and Bell Towers, and finishes with tea at Gongwangfu. These tours offer a glimpse of buildings usually closed to the public. Advance reservations are recommended. Tours begin on Di'anmen Xidajie near the back entrance of Beihai Park, start at 9 and 2 daily, and run about Y180 per person.

➤ FEES & SCHEDULES: **Beijing Hutong Tourist Agency** (✉ 26 Di'anmen Xidajie, ☎ 010/6612–3236, FAX 010/6400–2787). **Beijing Panda Tour** (✉ Holiday Inn Crowne Plaza, 48 Wangfujing Dajie, ☎ 010/6513–3388 ext. 1213). **China International Travel Service** (CITS; ✉ 28 Jianguomenwai Dajie, Chaoyang District, ☎ 010/6515–8562, FAX 010/6515–8603). **China Swan International Tours** (☎ 010/8391–3058).

TRAIN TRAVEL

Beijing is served by four stations: the Beijing Main and Beijing West stations (both of which have International Passenger Booking offices for foreigners), and the Beijing North and South stations. Tickets are sold up to five days in advance. Book early to ensure a seat. Ticket office hours are 5:30 AM–7:30 AM, 8 AM–5:30 PM, and 7 PM–12:30 AM. You can now make ticket reservations or get general information from the Beijing Railway Bureau. Most domestic routes depart from the massive Beijing Xi Zhan (West Station), Beijing's most modern. Some major-city routes still depart the Beijing Zhan (Main Station), as do international routes to Hong Kong or Siberia. Tickets can be purchased at all stations for trips that leave from that station. Trains are directed to different stations depending on the intricate rail system and not on their travel destinations.

➤ TRAIN INFORMATION: **Beijing Railway Bureau** (☎ 010/6321–1114). **Beijing Xi Zhan** (West Station; ✉ Lianhuachi Dong Lu, Haidian District, ☎ 010/6321–4233, 010/6321–4269, or 010/6321–4522). **Beijing Zhan** (Main Station; ✉ Beijing Zhan Jie, Dongcheng District, ☎ 010/6563–4422 or 010/6563–4238). **FESCO Travel Service** (✉ Level 1, China World Trade Center, Jianguimenwai Dajie, ☎ 010/6505–3330).

WALKING AROUND BEIJING

Beijing is sprawling. City blocks are very large. To avoid arriving exhausted at sites that appeared deceptively close on the map, walk around sites rather than between them. Ration your foot time for Beijing's intriguing back alleys.

VISITOR INFORMATION

China International Travel Service (☞ Tours) maintains offices in many hotels and at some tourist venues. The free magazines *City Edition, Metro Weekly, Beijing Scene,* and *Beijing This Month* (the city's official tourist publication, published for the Information Office of the Beijing Municipal Government and Beijing Tourism Administration) all have useful guides to entertainment, the arts, and expat events in Beijing. Pick them up at your hotel or one of the expat bars. Check www.xianzai.com for a weekly Internet listing of events in Beijing. Useful maps giving names in both Chinese and English can be bought at many hotels. Chinese name cards for hotels and other destinations are handy for showing taxi drivers.

3 NORTH CENTRAL CHINA

SPIRITUAL AND TEMPORAL LEGACIES

From the quiet seaside of Beidaihe to the antiques markets in Tianjin to the ancient Buddhist grottoes at Luoyang, a trip through this region is a trip through Chinese history. At inland sites, see where Confucianism, Buddhism, and various Chinese empires put down their roots. On the coast—notably Qingdao, Tianjin, and Beidaihe—you can see where Westerners arrived and began to open up China, leaving European architecture as their earliest legacy.

By David
Murphy

Updated by
George
Vaughton

DOMINATED BY THE YELLOW RIVER in the south and the Great Wall in the north, this is the cradle of Chinese civilization: Many dynasties have made their capitals here. It is also the seat of religion and philosophy; there are ancient Buddhist grottoes at Luoyang and Datong, and the birthplace and mansion of Confucius at Qufu. On the coast, foreign influences, from the Bavarian architecture in Qingdao to the lovely seaside resort of Beidaihe, established by vacationing diplomats and missionaries at the end of the 19th century, lend the region a cosmopolitan tinge.

Han Chinese civilization originated along the banks of the Yellow River near where the cities of Luoyang and Zhengzhou now stand, in the small but populous province of Henan. The name of the province, which literally translates as "south of the river," is a constant reminder of the river's importance. Traces of what was, 36 centuries ago, the capital of the Shang dynasty can still be faintly seen in modern-day Zhengzhou, Henan's capital. Archaeological finds suggest that another capital in the same area predated even this early city. The river itself still holds a certain fascination, largely for its potential destructive power.

West of Zhengzhou, Henan harbors the starting point of another aspect of Chinese civilization. Buddhism, brought to China in the 1st century AD, found its first home in White Horse Temple, on the outskirts of present-day Luoyang. The religion, once it was translated and adjusted a bit to Chinese sensibilities, gained enormous popularity, inspiring Henan's extraordinary Dragon Gate Grottoes. In the 6th and 7th centuries AD, artisans carved thousands of Buddhist figures into a stretch of mountain faces near Luoyang. Time has not been kind to these astounding artworks, but despite foreign looting and the ravages of wind and rain, they remain one of the region's most important, and most impressive, sights.

Northward in Shanxi, Datong has its own similarly impressive grottoes. About 50,000 statues were cut into a one-kilometer length of cliffs in the 5th century, and it is now Shanxi's most important site. This region was the cultural and political center of the state of Qin. As a northern frontier on the Great Wall, it had the important job of defending the state from nomadic tribes of the north. These days Shanxi's strategic importance lies in its coal mines.

Jutting out into the Yellow Sea, the Shandong Peninsula has long been the beneficiary and victim of the Yellow River, which makes the region fertile for farming and susceptible to flooding. The holy Mt. Tai and the birthplace of Confucius, at Qufu, are two of Shandong's sites with deep relevance for Asian history. Across China, Korea, and Japan, the old sage's influential teachings are still clearly evident. Old colonial settlements on the coast brought in the first railroads and missionaries to China. In particular, Qingdao's crumbling Bavarian architecture and seaside strolls are charming.

An industrial powerhouse and trading way station, Tianjin is one of China's new engines of capitalism. But unlike Hong Kong or Shanghai's shiny environs, Tianjin still evokes the more gritty side of enterprise. Even the old neighborhoods that were once European concessions are sooty and bursting with chaotic storefronts. Tianjin does offer interesting antiques, a great dumpling restaurant, and a quiet riverside stroll.

The southern flatlands of Hebei are crowded with industrial towns. But Chengde, an old imperial retreat in the mountains, has a fantastic collection of Chinese architecture in a variety of styles including Han, Mongol, Qing, Tibetan, and others. On the Bohai Gulf, today's leaders hold Communist Party getaways and policy brainstorming sessions at Beidaihe. Beidaihe also has a number of sanatoriums for the common people and a tasteful resort for foreigners. Up the coast at Shanhaiguan, the Great Wall starts west from the sea to climb its first mountain.

Pleasures and Pastimes

Dining

Along the coast, seafood predominates on restaurant menus, and you'll often be asked to choose your fare while it's still swimming in the tank. In addition to Chinese, Japanese, and Korean food, the occasional German or Austrian eatery remains in towns like Tianjin and Qingdao, remnants of long-gone colonies and trade concessions.

CATEGORY	COST*
$$$$	over Y210
$$$	Y125–Y210
$$	Y60–Y125
$	under Y60

*per person for a main course at dinner

Lodging

Most of the large cities have expensive hotels with all the creature comforts and business facilities you might need. Towns like Luoyang, Datong, Chengde, and Shanhaiguan still have good accommodations but are a bit rough on the edges. Luoyang in April is particularly crowded.

CATEGORY	COST*
$$$$	over Y1,000
$$$	Y620–Y1,000
$$	Y415–Y620
$	under Y415

*per standard double room, excluding tax

Nightlife

One of the best things to do is hit the seafood markets of coastal towns like Beidaihe and Qingdao. Point and eat is the name of the game. Towns with a fast-paced business culture or Western influence, like Tianjin or Qingdao, have a more active nightlife than other parts of the region. Snacking reaches its apex in Kaifeng, a short ride east of Zhengzhou, where the considerable local Muslim population sets up a nightly porkless market stretching for blocks around the center of town.

Shopping

Some of the best shopping for antiques is in Tianjin's sprawling antiques market. Everything from painted ceramics to bronze ware, jewelry, embroidered cloth, and Mao kitsch covers every inch of space in these back-to-back stalls. Foreigners are not allowed to take many real antiques out of the country. Pushcart owners in Zhengzhou quickly and expertly convert long, flat pieces of grass into various cute-looking insects.

Exploring North Central China

Great Itineraries

The best way to explore North Central China is by train. Overnight sleepers connect Beijing with such destinations as Qingdao and Luoyang. Shorter trips include Beidaihe, Chengde, Datong, and Tianjin.

The ancient grottoes of **Datong,** the summer palace of **Chengde,** or the quiet seaside of **Shanhaiguan** make a good two- or three-day side trip from Beijing. Alternatively, in the south near **Luoyang** visit the fantastically carved Dragon Gate Grottoes, and if it's spring, get a glimpse of budding peonies before heading back east on a sleeper train to Taishan, one of China's holiest mountains, near **Jinan,** and then continuing east six hours by train to explore **Qingdao**'s older neighborhoods for a day.

In **Datong** see the fantastic Buddhist grotto carvings, move on to **Chengde**'s mountain resort and surrounding temples and then to seaside **Beidaihe/Shanhaiguan,** where you can see the Great Wall, relax at a resort, and eat fish like an emperor. In **Luoyang** be sure to see the Baima Temple, China's first Buddhist temple, as well as the martial arts Shao Lin Temple, between Luoyang and Zhengzhou. End up by going past Zhengzhou into **Kaifeng,** an ancient capital that has managed to hold on to its small neighborhoods and vibrant culture.

Follow the first three-day itinerary and continue south to **Qingdao,** exploring the old German sections of town and perhaps Mt. Lao, to the east. Catch a train west to the birthplace of Confucius at **Qufu** and then go farther west to **Kaifeng** and **Luoyang.**

When to Tour North Central China

The spring and fall are the best seasons in North Central China. In the summer months it can be unpleasantly hot, particularly in grimy cities like Tianjin and Zhengzhou. Although this makes the beach most tempting, be warned—Beidaihe in July can be as crowded as a Beijing bus. March and April are good months in Luoyang, famed for its peonies.

TIANJIN

The Tianjin municipality has a population of more than 9 million and a thriving seaport with an extensive hinterland that includes Beijing, only two hours away. Numerous multinational businesses, including nearly 1,000 from the United States alone, have set up here. Most are in the new satellite city, known as Teda (Tianjin Economic Development Area), to the south of old Tianjin.

Tianjin is one of China's four municipalities, meaning it reports directly to China's State Council instead of to a provincial government. (The others are Beijing, Shanghai, and Chongqing.) The city occupies the banks of the Hai River, 50 km (31 mi) from where it flows into the Gulf of Bohai. A large number of European-style buildings survive here, a legacy of European and Japanese colonialism, and in spring and autumn Tianjin's narrow, leafy streets offer an alternative to the wide avenues of nearby Beijing.

Tianjin signifies "the point where the Son of Heaven forded the river" and refers to the route taken by the Ming dynasty emperor Yongle to a key battle in the south, where he succeeded in establishing his reign, beginning in 1403. Thereafter Tianjin grew in stature and was viewed as the gateway to the imperial capital of Beijing.

The Second Anglo-Chinese war, in 1858, forced Beijing to sign the Treaty of Tianjin, which made the city a treaty port similar to Shanghai. Concessions were established by the British and the French, followed by the Belgians, the Germans, the Italians, the Russians, the Austro-Hungarians, and the Japanese. The city they called Tientsin became a major international port and manufacturing center, producing the Tientsin carpets that are still a major export. In the first part of the 20th century it was a temporary home for engineer Herbert Hoover in his prepresidential career, Sun Yat-sen, Zhou Enlai, and the last emperor, whose parties in the Astor Hotel were re-created here in the movie *The Last Emperor.*

In modern times Tianjin was badly damaged in the 1976 Tangshan earthquake but was rebuilt in time to benefit from the Open-Door policy. Its port is the biggest in northern China, and the new California-like suburb of Teda contains some of China's most successful joint ventures among its 3,000 foreign-funded enterprises.

Exploring Tianjin

An official count reckons there are more than 1,000 buildings in Tianjin surviving from the colonial period. The old quarter is a virtual museum of European architecture.

A Good Walk

From the Hyatt Regency Hotel, at the crossing of Jiefang Beilu and Qufu Dao head north along the riverside promenade, Tai'erzhang Lu. A block away is the Astor Hotel, worth a quick visit as the occasional home of the last emperor. Continue along the promenade, where you'll find groups of pigeon fanciers comparing and selling birds and other people playing Chinese chess. As well as lawns with topiary animals, fountains, and small cafés, the promenade has an inimitable view across the river of surviving 19th-century European-style colonial mansions. Make a detour on Chengde Dao to see a collection of Chinese art in the **Yishu Bowuguan** (Art Museum) ①, then continue along the waterfront to Beima Lu. Follow it for a block to reach **Gu Wenhua Jie** (Culture Street) ②. Explore the shops and the Tianhou Gong, then take the main road, Dongma Lu, south until it becomes Heping Lu. Turn right on Rongji Dajie to **Shi Pin Jie** (Food Street) ③, where you can stop for lunch. Return to Heping Lu. In British concession times, this was Cambridge Road, lined with fashionable shops and banks, many of which are still here, albeit with different owners. One classic reminder is the **Quanyechang Baihuoshangchang** (Quanyechang Department Store) ④, modeled after Harrod's. Two blocks farther on is Zhongxin Park, with playgrounds and tree-shaded benches and surrounded by some grand old buildings. From here you can take the modern avenue Yingkou Dao heading north back to the promenade, or south to **Xikai Jiaotang** (St. Paul's Catholic Church) ⑤.

TIMING

This walk should take about 3½ hours, plus an hour if you include lunch, and as long as you like browsing the museum, culture street, and cathedral.

Sights to See

❷ **Gu Wenhua Jie** (Culture Street). During foreign concession days the area in the north of the city was a traditional "Chinatown." In the 1980s Tianjin's mayor decided to restore some of the old buildings with their carved wooden facades and ornate balconies hung with silk-banner advertisements. Some contain shops selling antiques, reproductions, carpets, swords, paintings, books, coins, and assorted craft items. Others are restaurants serving such local delicacies as *baozi* (dumplings filled with meat) and soup. At one end of the street is the **Tianhou Gong** (Tianhou Temple), dedicated to the goddess of seafarers, with prayer pavilions set in garden courtyards. ⊠ *Beima Lu.* ⊑ *Free.* ☉ *Daily 9* AM– *11* PM.

North Central China

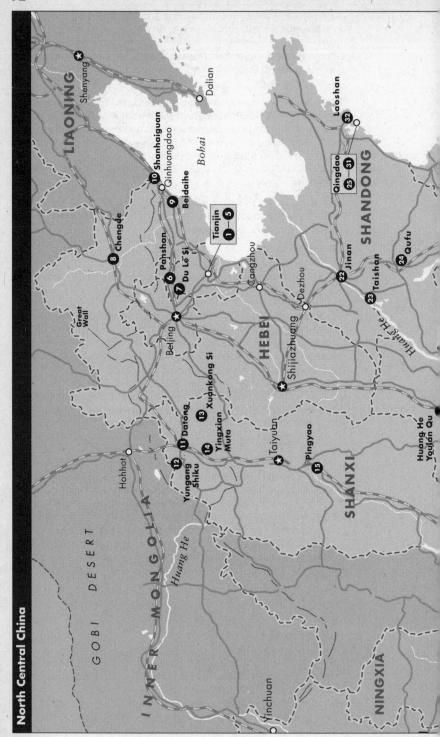

LIAONING

Shenyang ★

Dalian

Shanhaiguan
10 Qinhuangdao
9 Beidaihe

Bohai

Laoshan
32

Qingdao
25—31

SHANDONG

Chengde
8

Panshan
6
7 Du Le Si

Tianjin
1—5

Cangzhou

Dezhou

Qufu
24

Great
Wall

Beijing ★

HEBEI

Shijiazhuang

Jinan
22
23 Taishan

Xuankong Si

Datong
11
13

Yingxian
14 Muta

Taiyuan ★

Pingyao

Huang He
Youlan Qu

Yungang
12 Shiku

15

SHANXI

Huang He

I N N E R   M O N G O L I A

Hohhot

Huang He

G O B I   D E S E R T

NINGXIA

Yinchuan

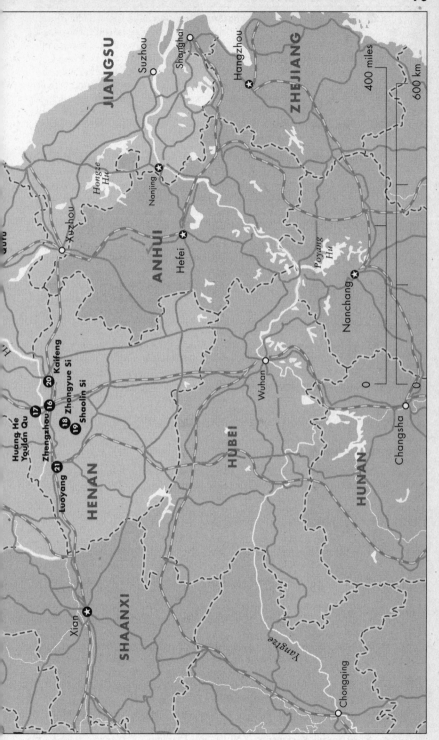

❹ **Quanyechang Baihuoshangchang** (Quanyechang Department Store). Built in the 1920s and modeled after London's Harrod's, this was a landmark of the old British concession. Its handsome facade restored, today it's an upmarket store with imported brand-name fashions, Chinese luxury items, and a selection of arts and crafts. Other grand colonial buildings in the neighborhood that have been renovated include City of London–style banks now used by Chinese financial institutions, apartment blocks, and trading houses that now contain the offices of multinational firms. Many have candy-stripe window awnings. ✉ *Heping Lu at Binjiang Dao.* ◷ *Daily 10–10.*

❸ **Shi Pin Jie** (Food Street). Actually more of a food city, this three-story block contains more than 100 shops selling food and drink from all over China and around the world. The dishes range from donkey meat and burnt rice to pizzas and hamburgers. The complex has pagoda roofs and city gate–like entrances bearing the characters for "People's lives depend on food." ✉ *Rongji Dajie.* ◷ *Daily 6 AM–midnight.*

❺ **Xikai Jiaotang** (St. Paul's Catholic Church). Built by French Jesuits in 1917, this extraordinary building is a landmark, with its twin domed towers and tan-and-cream brickwork. Amazingly, it survived the Cultural Revolution with no more than a broken window and in recent years has been beautifully restored. It is regularly full for Sunday services and well attended at daily morning mass. ✉ *Xining Dao.* ◷ *Mon.– Sat. 9 AM–11 AM and 2 PM–4 PM.*

❶ **Yishu Bowuguan** (Art Museum). The setting of this collection is itself a prime exhibit, being a restored colonial mansion that recalls the architecture of the Belle Epoque. Attractively displayed are some fine examples of traditional Chinese paintings and calligraphy on the first floor; folk art, particularly elaborate giant paper kites, on the second; and temporary exhibitions on the third. ✉ *12 Chengde Dao,* ☎ *022/2312– 2770.* ◩ *Y5.* ◷ *Tues.–Sun. 8:30 AM–11 AM and 1:30 PM–4 PM.*

Dining and Lodging

$$$ ✕ **Ganbeiyiding.** This street-front restaurant furnished with wooden tables and lattice chairs serves set Japanese meals. The open-plan dining area and kitchen gives an entertaining and informative view of the chefs in action, while smaller rooms upstairs have karaoke facilities. ✉ *12 Zhangde Dao,* ☎ *022/2331–0439. AE, DC, MC, V.*

$$ ✕ **Tianjin Kaoya Dian.** Here are five floors serving Peking duck. The ground floor serves cheap roast duck fast-food style. Prices shoot up in the room where Mao Zedong chewed the crisp fat on August 13, 1958. His likeness is on the door to the room, and photographs of the occasion hang on the walls. The restaurant decor varies from the plastic bucket seats on the ground floor to elegant wood-paneled rooms on the upper floors. ✉ *146 Liaoning Lu,* ☎ *022/2730–3335. No credit cards.*

$–$$ ✕ **Bader Brauhaus.** On the third floor of Kiesslings Bakery (founded in 1911), this tastefully furnished restaurant has wood floors and walls hung with scenes from old Tianjin. Behind the bar, which occupies the middle of the floor, two large copper vats contain the house's special brew. The menu lists dishes from 10 countries and includes tortillas and Wiener schnitzel. On the floor below is a hot-pot restaurant. ✉ *33 Zhejiang Lu,* ☎ *022/2332–1603. No credit cards.*

$ ✕ **Goubili Restaurant.** Tianjin's most famous restaurant is the proud purveyor of the Tianjin-style *baozi* (steamed dumpling filled with chopped meat and vegetables). The ground floor of the three-story restaurant serves fast food (fast baozi). The second and third floors are a mixture of large dining areas and smaller, more exclusive rooms. Both serve

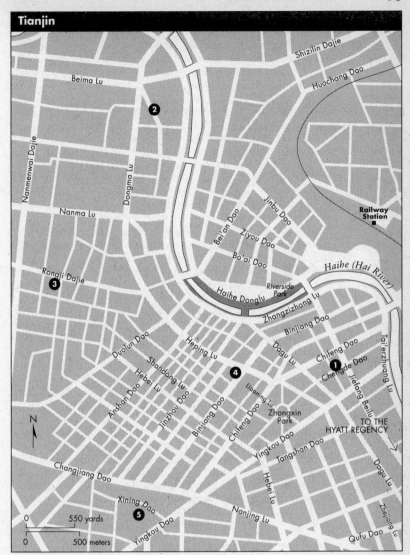

Tianjin

regular Chinese food as well as baozi. ⊠ *77 Shandong Lu,* ☏ *022/2730–2540. No credit cards.*

$$$$ ⌂ **Crystal Palace.** Near the International Exhibition Center in the He Xi District, this modern seven-story hotel sits on a corner of Youyi Lu, in front of Yingbing Lake. Plainly furnished standard rooms come with satellite TV. Chinese, Japanese, and Western cuisines are served at the restaurants. ⊠ *28 Youyi Lu, 300061,* ☏ *022/2835–6666,* ℻ *022/2835–8886. 346 rooms. 3 restaurants, bar, tennis court, gym, business services. AE, DC, MC, V.*

$$$$ ⌂ **Holiday Inn.** In this hotel on the banks of the Hai River comfortable standard rooms are equipped with satellite TV. The restaurants serve Chinese, Japanese, and Western food. ⊠ *288 Zhongshan Lu, 300141,* ☏ *022/2628–8888,* ℻ *022/2628–6666,* 🖳 *www.basshotels.com/holiday-inn 265 rooms. 3 restaurants, bar, pool, gym. AE, DC, MC, V.*

$$$$ ⌂ **Hyatt Regency Tianjin.** One of the more established high-class hotels in Tianjin, the Hyatt backs onto the Hai River. Old-style green Chinese tiles gird the upper floors of this Hong Kong–managed hotel, making it something of a landmark. Inside is a spacious three-story atrium lobby. Standard rooms are bright, clean, and comfortable and are equipped with a business desk, minibar, and satellite TV. The restaurants serve Chinese, Japanese, and Western cuisines. ⊠ *219 Jiefang Beilu, 300042,* ☏ *022/2330–1234,* ℻ *022/2331–1234,* 🖳 *www.hyatt.com 428 rooms. 5 restaurants, bar, gym, business services. AE, DC, MC, V.*

$$$$ ⌂ **New World Astor.** Facing the Hai River, the Astor, the oldest hotel in Tianjin (founded in 1863). It has played host to such luminaries as Sun Yat-sen, Herbert Hoover, and Puyi, China's last emperor. Rooms have satellite TV and minibar. The restaurants offer Chinese, Italian, and international cuisines. ⊠ *33 Tai'erzhuang Lu, 300040,* ☏ *022/2331–1688,* ℻ *022/2331–6282. 195 rooms, 28 suites. 3 restaurants, bar, gym, business services. AE, DC, MC, V.*

$$$ ⌂ **Sheraton Hotel.** Its own gardens surround this hotel with an adjacent apartment building in the quiet He Xi District. The comfortable rooms are decorated in light colors and are equipped with a business desk, minibar, and satellite TV. The restaurants serve Japanese, Chinese, and Western food. ⊠ *Zi Jinshan Lu, 300074,* ☏ *022/2334–3388,* ℻ *022/2335–8740,* 🖳 *www.sheraton.com. 230 rooms. 3 restaurants, bar, pool, tennis court, bowling, gym, business services. AE, DC, MC, V.*

Nightlife

Sgt. Pepper's (⊠ 62 Jiefang Beilu, ☏ 022/2312–8138) offers live music and a great bar and grill just behind the riverside stretch of expensive hotels.

Shopping

Department Stores

The **International Market** (⊠ South end of Binjiang Dao, ☏ 022/2304–1740) has a wide variety of goods and is open daily 9:30–9. **Isetan** (⊠ 209 Nanjing Lu, ☏ 022/2722–1111), a Japanese department store open daily 10–8:30, has five floors of mostly Western and Japanese cosmetics, household wares, consumer durables, and clothes.

Districts

Binjiang Dao is the center of shopping in Tianjin. Department stores and upscale Western boutiques are concentrated at the northern end of the street. To the south these give way to market stalls selling clothes and a few other bargains.

Side Trips from Tianjin

❻ Panshan. This range of peaks at the northern end of the Tianjin municipality is noted for its pine trees and beautiful scenery. One of China's 15 famous mountains, Panshan was home in the past to numerous monasteries and temples. ⊠ *75 km (46 mi) east of Beijing; trains and buses run from Tianjin.*

❼ Du Le Si (Du Le Temple). This 1,000-year-old temple in Jixian county houses a 52-ft statue (among the largest clay statues in China) of Guanyin, goddess of mercy, that stretches to the octagonal ceiling three floors up. Buddhist murals cover the walls on the ground floor. ⊠ *3 hrs (100 km/62 mi) north of Tianjin municipality by train.*

Tianjin A to Z

To research prices, get advice from other travelers, and book travel arrangements, visit www.fodors.com.

AIRPORT

Tianjin Airport is a half hour southeast of the city center. There are regular flights to and from Hong Kong and other major Chinese cities as well as South Korea.

➤ AIRPORT INFORMATION: **Tianjin Airport** (☎ 022/2490–2929).

TAXIS

Taxis are the easiest way to get around. The meter starts at Y10.

TRAIN TRAVEL

There are a half dozen departures to and arrivals from Beijing every day. Trains run regularly to Jinan, Nanjing, Shanghai, Qingdao, and other cities.

➤ TRAIN INFORMATION: **Tianjin Train Station** (☎ 022/2430–6444).

VISITOR INFORMATION

➤ TOURIST INFORMATION: **CITS** (⊠ 22 Youyi Lu, opposite Friendship Store, ☎ 022/2835–8499, FAX 022/2835–0823).

HEBEI

Hebei wraps itself around the cities Beijing and Tianjin, with mountains to the north and plains to the south. This was China's old frontier, and the Great Wall wanders among the mountains. There are no major cities of note in the bleak and industrial flatlands. Several small towns rich in history, with refreshing clean air, do make excellent short trips from Beijing: Chengde, with its palace and temples, and the seaside resorts of Beidaihe and nearby Shanhaiguan, where the Great Wall meets the sea.

Chengde

❽ *4½ hrs (175 km/109 mi) by train northeast of Beijing, 7 hrs (470 km/291 mi) southwest of Shenyang.*

At Chengde, in the Yanshan Mountains northeast of Beijing, lies the largest intact imperial garden complex in China, built in the 17th and 18th centuries as an emblem of national unity. The town of Chengde itself is interesting only as a typical small Chinese community.

Bishu Shanzhuang (the Mountain Resort for Escaping the Summer Heat)—now known simply as the Mountain Resort—was begun by the Qing emperor Kangxi in the late 17th century. He hoped it would serve as an emblem to encourage minority groups in a newly united

China to stay together. Enclosed by a 10-km (6-mi) wall, its interconnected palaces (whose architecture also reflects China's diversity), lakes, and trails sit in a landscape originally manipulated to resemble China's various ecozones. Ideally you could walk from the lakes and lush forests of southern China to the Mongolian steppes in an afternoon. Replicas of famous temples representing China's different religions stand on hillsides surrounding the palace as though paying homage to the court.

Beginning with Kangxi and continuing under his son, construction went on for 89 years. The Mountain Resort gradually became a more and more important focus for politics, as the emperor moved the throne and seat of government to Chengde every summer. At its height the complex had nearly 100 buildings within its walls and 12 temples on the surrounding hillsides. Today numerous buildings remain; some have been restored but many have grass coming up through the cracks. Only eight of the temples are open for visitors (two of the originals were demolished and another two are dilapidated).

Many palace buildings are unpainted wood, reflecting Kangxi's disdain for fame and wealth (although he didn't forgo grand hunting parties and orgies). Various palace rooms have been restored into dioramas, with period furniture, ornaments, and costumed mannequins frozen in time. The surrounding landscape of lakes, open grasslands, and cool forests is lovely for a stroll. Mountains in the northern half of the park and a giant pagoda in the center afford panoramas of the city of Chengde to the south and the temples to the north and east. The Mountain Resort and the temples are so big that even with a massive influx of summer tourists they don't feel crowded. ⊠ *Center of town; several entrances.* ☞ *Y50.* ☉ *Daily 5:30 AM–6:30 PM.*

Viewing Chengde's eight **temples** from the mountain or from the large pagoda in the summer palace, it looks as though Emperor Kangxi built a Disneyland for China's religions. The architectural styles range from Han to Manchu, Mongolian, Tibetan, Buddhist, and others. The temples are somewhat run down, but restoration efforts are under way. **Puning Si** (⊠ Northeast of Mountain Resort, ☞ Y30, ☉ daily 8–5) contains the largest wooden statue in the world—a 72-ft Avalokitesvara with 42 arms—and is the only working temple among the eight. The **Putuozongcheng Miao** (⊠ North of Mountain Resort, ☞ Y20), modeled on the Potala Palace in Tibet, is the largest temple in Chengde. It's open daily 8–6. **Pule Si** (⊠ East of Mountain Resort, near the base of the cable car, ☞ Y20, ☉ daily 8–5:30) is in the best shape, with fresh paint and shiny new tiles on a circular pavilion. Guardian demons brandishing strange weapons glare down with bulging eyes at the gate.

A cable car and a hiking trail lead up to **Bangzhong Shan** (Club Peak), an improbably balanced rock, fatter at the top and skinny at the bottom, that resembles a club standing on end. It juts up from the ridgeline east of the Mountain Resort. ⊠ *East of Mountain Resort.* ☞ *Cable car, Y35.*

Dining and Lodging

$–$$ ✕ **Qianlongxing.** Originally an offshoot of a nearby dumpling restaurant, this thriving upscale eatery has become one of the most popular in Chengde. The picture menu carries delicacies ranging from mushrooms with chicken to scorpions and camels' paws. ⊠ *8 Zhongxing Lu,* ☎ *0314/203–9766. No credit cards.*

$$ ☷ **Yunshan Hotel.** Modern and clean, this hotel has a few staff members who speak English and can help arrange tours of nearby temples and the Mountain Resort. A good Chinese restaurant, a Western restaurant, a gift shop, and a business center make this one of the choice hotels in Chengde. ⊠ *6 Nan Yuan Donglu, 067000,* ☎ *0314/215–6171,* FAX *0314/215–4551. 230 rooms. 2 restaurants, bar, hair salon, business services. AE, DC, MC, V.*

$–$$ 🏨 **Huilong Hotel.** Near the train station, this hotel has a grand marble lobby and clean, modern rooms. The restaurant serves Muslim dishes such as lamb kebabs, and karaoke rooms provide entertainment. ⊠ *1 Xinjuzhai, Chezhan Lu, 067000,* ☎ *0314/208–5369,* FAX *0314/208–2404. 112 rooms. AE, DC, MC, V.*

$ 🏨 **Mongolian Yurts Holiday Inn.** Open from April through November only, these "yurts" are concrete and have beds and TVs. Although bearing no relation to the international Holiday Inn hotel chain, this place does make for an unusual night. Best of all, it is inside the Mountain Resort with its quiet and clean air, not the busy streets of Chengde. ⊠ *Just inside the Wanshuyuanmen (eastern) entrance to Mountain Resort, 067000,* ☎ *0314/216–3094,* FAX *0314/216–3094. Restaurant. No credit cards.*

$ 🏨 **Xinhua Hotel.** At this shabby concrete building in the center of town near the bus station the rooms are quiet, airy, and reasonably clean. The hotel is a bit tired, but at least you don't have to go far to refuel: the restaurant downstairs has good regional cooking. ⊠ *4 Xinhua Beilu, 067000,* ☎ *0314/206–5880. 204 rooms. Restaurant, meeting room, travel services. No credit cards.*

Beidaihe

➒ *4 hrs (260 km/160 mi) east of Beijing by express train, 5 hrs (395 km/245 mi) southwest of Shenyang, 1 hr (35 km/22 mi) by minibus southwest of Shanhaiguan.*

The seaside resort town of Beidaihe with its long beach, cool pine forests, and excellent seafood draws major crowds from July through September. Missionaries and diplomats from European powers first converted what had been a fishing village into a vacation destination, building villas here in the late 19th century to enjoy bathing on the long Mediterranean-style beaches. Now many members of the Communist Party elite have their summer homes here, while the government has built sanatoriums and other facilities for loyal workers to take a break from China's choking cities. The town center is small; it's easy to reach quiet spots along the seashore on foot or by bicycle.

The main attraction in Beidaihe is the **beach.** Walk along it for hours, wiggle your toes in the sand, breathe the clean seaside air, and pinch yourself: this is China, too. At several points along the coast perch pavilions for viewing rocks shaped like animals or the sea.

North of the middle beach is **Lianfengshan Gongyuan** (Lianfeng Hill Park), where quiet paths through pine forest lead to **Guanyin Si** (Guanyin Temple), a quiet place to relax in the woods. There are also good views of the sea from the top of Lianfeng Hill. ⊠ *West-central side of town.* 🎟 *Y15.* 🕙 *Daily 8–5.*

Qinhuang Gong (Emperor Qin Shi Huang's Palace), a 20th-century replica built in homage to the first Qin dynasty emperor's inspection of Beidaihe, has well-constructed rooms with mannequins in period costumes that include colorful robes, impressive weapons, and embroideries. 🎟 *Y15.* 🕙 *Daily 8–5.*

Dining and Lodging

Seafood restaurants line the beach, and you only need point at the most appetizing thing squirming in red buckets for the waiter to serve up a delicious fresh meal. More good seafood restaurants cluster on Haining Lu near the beach.

$–$$ ✕ **Kiesslings.** The only nonstandard Chinese eating place here, originally an Austrian restaurant for foreigners, has good baked goods for breakfast. It's open from June through August only. ⊠ *Dongjing Lu, Middle of town, just behind Guesthouse for Diplomatic Missions,* ☎ *0335/404–1043.* ⊙ *Daily 8 AM–10 PM. No credit cards.*

$$ 🏨 **Jinshan Hotel.** On a quiet, less developed section of the beach, this hotel spreads among five large two-story buildings linked by tree-lined paths. The rooms are clean and quiet with a TV and two double beds. The CITS office is in the hotel, but the hotel staff's English might not be up to directing you to it. Nevertheless, either can organize tours with English-speaking guides. Few of the hotel's facilities are open outside high season. ⊠ *4 Dongsan Lu, 066100,* ☎ *0335/404–1338,* 🅵🅰🆇 *0335/ 404–2478. 267 rooms. 2 restaurants, gym, nightclub, business services, travel services. No credit cards.*

$–$$ 🏨 **Beidaihe Waijiao Renyuan Binguan** (Beidaihe Guesthouse for Diplomatic Missions). Specifically catering to foreigners, the guesthouse has several staff members who speak English remarkably well. The multibuilding complex is set among cypress and pines in a peaceful spot overlooking the sea, not far from Beidaihe's main intersection. Among its accommodations is a "building for distinguished guests," with suites for dignitaries. Rates for more expensive rooms include breakfast. ⊠ *1 Baosan Lu, 066100,* ☎ *0335/404–1807 in Beidaihe; 010/6532– 4336 in Beijing. 150 rooms. Restaurant, air-conditioning, tennis court. No credit cards.*

Shopping

Vendors of tourist trinkets will undoubtedly find you, but if you want to run the gauntlet, Haining Lu near the beach has big souvenir shops selling everything from seashell necklaces to water guns to lacquered lobsters.

Shanhaiguan

⑩ *1 hr (35 km/22 mi) by minibus northeast of Beidaihe, 5 hrs (280 km/174 mi) east of Beijing, 5 hrs (360 km/223 mi) southwest of Shenyang.*

Shanhaiguan is, depending on your point of view, where the Great Wall meets the sea or where it climbs its first mountain. Long, long ago this was China's frontier, and an impressive wall still surrounds the old town, though the warriors on the battlements are now mannequins. The town has myriad narrow, mildly interesting streets, but most of Shanhaiguan's attractions are in the nearby countryside, just a 10- to 15-minute taxi ride away.

The **Tianxiadiyiguan** (First Gate Under Heaven) is the impressive north-facing portal of this fortress-town. It was built in 1381 under the Ming dynasty and defended China's northern frontier until the Manchus overran it in 1644. The top has views of the town and, through binoculars, of the Great Wall snaking up nearby mountains. ⊠ *Northeast side of wall.* 🎫 *Y35.* ⊙ *Daily 6:30 AM–7 PM.*

The **Changcheng Bowuguan** (Great Wall Museum) has a good collection of photographs of the wall from across China and cases full of military artifacts, but all the captions are in Chinese. ⊠ *Between CITS and Bank of China just south of First Gate Under Heaven.* 🎫 *Y5.* ⊙ *Daily 7 AM–8 PM.*

Legend has it that the Great Wall once extended all the way into the Bohai Sea, ending with a giant carved dragon head. The original wall fell into such disrepair that the seaside fortress at what today is called **Lao Long Tou** (Old Dragon Head) was reconstructed from archaeological digging and historical records only with much difficulty. The final battlement of the Great Wall juts out into the sea, waves smashing at its base. The park's rebuilt army garrisons, lookouts, and beach make a pleasant stroll. ☎ *Y30.* ☉ *Daily 8–5.*

After tracing a line inland from the sea, connecting with the walled town of Shanhaiguan, and passing through a few kilometers of farmland farther, the Great Wall suddenly heads for the sky at **Jiao Shan** (Jiao Mountain). The steep and precipitous section has been thoroughly rebuilt on its lower stretches, but it's a tough hike up on a hot day. As the ridge levels off, the reconstruction has basically ceased, leaving an earthen mound with occasional stretches of intact flagstones. There's a **cable car** (Y10) if you don't want to climb. ✉ *10-min taxi ride northwest of town.*

Yangsai Hu is a deep blue reservoir with arms jutting in between steep mountains outside town. It has an aviary, a cable car leading up one side of a hill and down the other if you don't want to follow the tree-lined path around it to the water's edge, and a few pavilions connected by concrete trails dotting the landscape. ✉ *15-min taxi ride northwest of town.* ☎ *Y30.*

Beyond the reservoir is **Changshou Shan** (Longevity Mountain), which has giant characters affirming a long life elegantly carved and painted onto the rocks. ✉ *East of Yangsai Hu.*

Down the coast from Dragon Head is **Mengjiangnu Miao,** a shrine commemorating the story of a woman whose husband died in slavery building the Great Wall. She wept as she searched for his body, and in sympathy the Great Wall is said to have split open before her, revealing the bones of her husband and others buried within. Overcome with grief, she threw herself into the sea. The temple has good views of the mountains and sea, and for some reason houses an old jet-fighter aircraft. ✉ *10-min taxi ride northeast of town.* ☎ *Y30.* ☉ *Daily dawn–dusk.*

Dining and Lodging

Shanhaiguan has a street of acceptable restaurants, Dong Dajie, near the Jingshan Hotel. Beware of the "guides" in this area whose only guidance will be to lead you to the restaurants that employ them.

$ ✕ **Mongolian Hotpot.** This small restaurant with only four tables is sometimes crowded with revelers. The friendly owners will fill you to the hilt on cheap hotpot—thinly sliced meat dipped into boiling broth with an array of sauces and vegetables. ✉ *West side of Nandajie, just south of main crossroads,* ☎ *no phone. No credit cards.*

$ 🏨 **Jingshan Hotel.** Built to resemble a Qing mansion, this hostelry consisting of gray-brick buildings around courtyards is the cleanest, most comfortable retreat in Shanhaiguan. Conveniently near the First Gate Under Heaven, the hotel is quite shiny on the outside, but the rooms are a little tired. The restaurant is above average; the management doesn't harass customers the way owners do on the nearby street of restaurants. The staff will arrange air and train reservations if you can communicate with them. ✉ *8 Dong Dajie, 066200,* ☎ *0335/505–1130. 120 rooms. No credit cards.*

Hebei A to Z

To research prices, get advice from other travelers, and book travel arrangements, visit www.fodors.com.

AIR TRAVEL

Beidaihe and Shanhaiguan are served by a small airport at the industrial port of Qinhuangdao. There are frequent flights to Dalian and fewer flights to other Chinese cities.

➤ AIRPORT INFORMATION: **Qinhuangdao Airport** (☎ 0335/505–1976).

BIKE TRAVEL

Renting bicycles is particularly worthwhile in Beidaihe, given the long coast, but the traffic in Shanhaiguan and Chengde puts you in mortal danger.

BOAT AND FERRY TRAVEL

Aboard a boat is certainly the most comfortable way to travel here. Small cruise ships serve the port of Qinhuangdao (between Beidaihe and Shanhaiguan). Overnight boats with comfortable sleepers and good restaurants go to Dalian, Qingdao, Tainjin, and Shanghai. Boat schedules are available at CITS offices; hotels can make reservations for you. Qinhuangdao CITS serves Beidaihe and Shanhaiguan as well as Qinhuangdao.

➤ BOAT AND FERRY INFORMATION: Qinhuangdao CITS (✉ 100 Heping Dajie, ☎ 0335/323–1111).

BUS TRAVEL

Long-distance buses are uncomfortable and slow, but they're the only transport linking Chengde with Beidaihe and Shanghaiguan. Several buses a day make this trip, all departing in the early morning.

An excellent minibus service runs between Beidaihe, Qinhuangdao, and Shanghaiguan. Buses leave every 30 minutes and cost Y5 for the somewhat circuitous ride, with frequent stops between Beidaihe and Shanhaiguan. The bus station in Beidaihe is at the intersection of Heishi Lu and Haining Lu, and that in Shanhaiguan is in front of the train station. Buy tickets on the bus.

TAXIS

The half-hour taxi ride between Beidaihe and Shanhaiguan costs about Y100. Within all three towns taxis are cheap and will take you to nearby attractions.

TRAIN TRAVEL

Trains running between Beijing, Tianjin, and Shenyang pass through Beidaihe and Shanhaiguan quite frequently, but not all of them stop. The train station in Beidaihe is somewhat outside town; if you arrive late at night the taxi drivers charge exorbitant rates. The ride from Beijing can take as many as seven hours or as few as 4½.

Chengde is on a northern rail line between Beijing and Shenyang. Beijing is between five and seven hours away, Shenyang more than 12. No trains run between Chengde and Beidaihe/Shanhaiguan.

TRANSPORTATION AROUND HEBEI

In general, Chengde, Beidaihe, and Shanhaiguan are all small enough to explore on foot.

VISITOR INFORMATION
In Beidaihe and Shanhaiguan contact CITS in Qinghuangdao, or in the Beidaihe Guesthouse for Diplomatic Missions. In Chengde contact CITS or Yunshan Hotel.

➤ TOURIST INFORMATION: **Beidaihe Guesthouse for Diplomatic Missions** (✉ 1 Baosan Lu, Beidaihe, ☎ 0335/404–1287). **Qinhuangdao CITS** (✉ 100 Heping Dajie, Qinhuangdao, ☎ 0335/323–1111). **Yunshan Hotel** (✉ 6 Nan Yuan Donglu, Chengde, ☎ 0314/215–6171).

SHANXI

Shanxi was at or near the center of Chinese power from about 200 BC until the fall of the Tang dynasty in the early 10th century. Since then it has remained relatively backward, a frontier area used as a defense against predatory northern neighbors; nevertheless, its very lack of development has allowed a large number of historic sites, such as Datong's grottoes, to survive.

Today trucks and even donkey carts heavily laden with coal dominate the roads of Shanxi, providing a constant reminder that the province produces one-third of China's coal. It wasn't until the Japanese occupation that serious exploitation of the coal reserves began, but the mountainous terrain in Shanxi also worked against the Japanese, providing plenty of cover for Chinese guerrillas fighting the anti-Japanese war.

Datong

⑪ *275 km (170 mi) west of Beijing; 724 km (449 mi) by plane west of Dalian.*

Datong, in the heart of China's coal-mining region, is drab and polluted, but it has some good restaurants and shopping areas, as well as a few historic buildings. The city's most important sites are the nearby grottoes (☞ Side Trips from Datong, *below*), where China's ancient history is deeply rooted.

In northern Shanxi near the border with Inner Mongolia, Datong lies close to the old Chinese frontier with the Mongolian and Turkic clans who lived beyond the Great Wall. Datong was a heavily defended city, and the countryside around it contained chains of watchtowers where, at the approach of enemy troops, huge bonfires were lighted and the warning passed on, giving defenders time to prepare for attacks.

The old city area, a square within the confines of the still partially surviving city walls, is neatly divided into quarters. The chief areas of interest are within this square.

Originally a screen wall in front of the gate of the palace of the 13th son of the first emperor of the Ming dynasty, the impressive ceramic tiled **Jiu Long Bi** (Nine Dragon Screen) is about 150 ft long and is decorated with colorful depictions of, well yes, nine dragons. ✉ *East of Da Dong Jie and Da Bei Jie intersection,* ☎ *0352/205–4788.* 🎫 *Y6.* ☺ *Daily 8–6.*

The **Huayan Si** (Huayan Monastery), originally built in the 12th century, is in the western part of the old city. Divided into an Upper Monastery and a Lower Monastery, it has very well-preserved statues, frescoes, built-in bookshelves, and ceilings. The main hall of the Upper Monastery is one of the largest Buddhist halls extant in China and houses five gilded Buddha statues seated on lotus thrones. The Bhagavat Storage Hall of the Lower Monastery was used for storing Buddhist scriptures and today houses religious statues. ✉ *Xiasipo Hutong, off Da Xi Jie,* ☎ *0352/205–3629.* 🎫 *Y10.* ◷ *Daily 8–6.*

The **Shanhua Si** (Shanhua Monastery), set in peaceful grounds, dates originally from the Tang dynasty. The four surviving buildings provide important material for the study of Tang and Song dynasty architecture. The main hall contains statues of 24 divine generals. ✉ *Off Da Nan Jie,* ☎ *0352/205–2898.* 🎫 *Y10.* ◷ *Daily 8–6.*

Train spotting is possible only through a CITS (☞ Visitor Information, *below*) tour of the **Datong Jiche Cheliang Chang** (Datong Locomotive Works), which made steam engines until the late 1980s, the last factory in China to do so. These black workhorses, reputedly modeled on a 19th-century British steam locomotive, can still be seen on minor lines or in rail yards away from the boom areas of China. A visit to the works—which now makes diesel engines—includes a ride on one of the old steam engines. ✉ *Daqing Lu, western suburbs.*

Dining and Lodging

$–$$ ✕ **Yong He.** Serving the best food in Datong, this restaurant has the same menu on all three floors, but the ground floor—stylish and wood paneled—also serves hotpot, which is what you need to eat if you are in Datong in winter. The regular menu contains a full range of excellent Chinese food, including Peking duck, and seafood, including turtle, crab, and crayfish. A new branch opposite the Yungang Hotel serves similar food plus Dim Sum, but no hotpot. ✉ *Xiao Nan Jie, at the entrance of Shanhua Monastery,* ☎ *0352/204–7999. Reservations essential. No credit cards.*

$ ✕ **Hong Ya.** This two-story family-run restaurant has a few specialties, including Peking duck. ✉ *1 Yingbin Donglu,* ☎ *0352/502–5566. No credit cards.*

$ 🏨 **Hongqi.** Just across from the train station, this is one of the best located hotels in Datong. Rooms are simple but clean, and Chinese and Western cuisine is available in the restaurant. ✉ *11 Zhanqian Jie, 037005,* ☎ *0352/281–6823,* 🅵🅰🆇 *0352/281–6671,* 🆆🅴🅱 *www.dthongqi. com/newpage2.htm. 100 rooms. Bar, 3 restaurants, hair salon, sauna, billiards, dry cleaning, business services. AE, DC, MC, V.*

$ 🏨 **Yungang.** In the south of the city, this is where most foreigners stay in Datong. Standard rooms are small but adequate and have TVs. Datong's main CITS office is in the hotel complex. The restaurant serves Chinese food. ✉ *21 Yingbin Donglu, 037008,* ☎ *0352/502–1601,* 🅵🅰🆇 *0352/502–4927. 160 rooms. Restaurant, bar, nightclub. AE, DC, MC, V.*

Shopping

Although far from any of China's booming coastal regions, Datong's main shopping street, Da Xi Jie, has its share of fashionable clothing chains and department stores. The most modern department store is the six-story **Hualin Market** (✉ Xiao Nan Jie, ☎ 0352/204–4876), which sells groceries and just about every household item you might want.

Side Trips from Datong

★ ⑫ The **Yungang Shiku** (Yungang Grottoes), the oldest Buddhist caves in China, are Datong's most famous site. Built mainly in the latter part of the 5th century, the grotto complex, containing various religious icons, from huge Buddha statues to scores of intricate carvings, stretched over 15 km (9 mi) from east to west. Today only a kilometer of this survives, encompassing 53 major grottoes. Most are now railed off at the front, but visitors can peer in for a better look. ✉ *16 km (10 mi) west of Datong.* 🎫 *Y35.* ◷ *Daily 9–6.*

⑬ The 1,400-year-old **Xuankong Si** (Hanging Monastery) is attached precariously to the side of a sheer cliff face in the Hengshan Mountains, one of China's five sacred mountain ranges. The all-wooden monastery holds China's three traditional belief systems within its buildings: Taoism, Buddhism, and Confucianism. In one temple there are statues of Laozi, Sakyamuni, and Confucius. ✉ *Near Hunyuan, 75 km (46 mi) south of Datong, via CITS tour or private car.* 🎫 *Y35.* ⊙ *6 AM–7 PM.*

⑭ Built around AD 1100, the octagonal **Yingxian Muta** (Yingxian Timber Pagoda) is thought to be the oldest wooden building in China. Reflecting the dangers of the bad old days in Shanxi, it began life as a watchtower and waited 400 years before being converted into a temple. In something of an architectural trick, the pagoda's 220 ft appear to contain five floors but in fact hold nine. Whatever its construction, it has been strong enough to survive three powerful earthquakes, although most of the statues and relics inside were destroyed by the upheavals of the Cultural Revolution. A notable survivor is the huge statue of Sakyamuni on the ground floor. ✉ *Yingxian, 70 km (43 mi) south of Datong.* 🎫 *Y35.* ⊙ *Daily 8–7.*

⑮ Billed as the last fortress city in China and declared a World Heritage Site by UNESCO in 1997, the dusty old town of **Pingyao** offers a good sampling of Yuan, Ming, and Qing dynasty architecture. A visit here is best spent strolling or bicycling through old sections of town viewing wonderfully carved and painted eaves. The top of the city wall affords views of the street layout within and the plains beyond. ✉ *300 km (186 mi) south of Datong—1 hr by plane, 4½ hrs by car, 11 hrs by train southwest of Beijing.*

Shanxi A to Z

To research prices, get advice from other travelers, and book travel arrangements, visit www.fodors.com.

TAXIS
Taking a taxi is the easiest mode of transportation in Datong.

TRAIN TRAVEL
Daily trains link Datong with Beijing. Datong is also on the route to Inner Mongolia to the north and Lanzhou in the west.

VISITOR INFORMATION
➤ TOURIST INFORMATION: **CITS** ✉ (Railway station, ☎ 0352/712–4882; ✉ Yungang Hotel, 21 Yingbin Donglu, ☎ 0352/510–1326, FAX 0352/510–2046).

HENAN

Henan is both a source of pride and a sore point for the nation. The Huang He (Yellow River) area supports the popular conception of China's "5,000-year history," a ubiquitous phrase in any discussion of Chinese culture; but the economy of the current province is in sad shape. The Shang dynasty, established in the 17th century BC, set its capital in Henan, moving it to several different cities throughout its 600-year reign. The northern Song dynasty also returned the capital to this region, occupying Kaifeng. This city, just west of Zhengzhou, remains one of Henan's most enchanting. Threatened by invaders in the 12th century AD, the Song fled south, leaving Kaifeng and the surrounding region to their own devices.

Henan's fertile land supported a growing population, which in the end may have been its downfall. Apart from the periodic flooding of the Yellow River, which wreaks havoc on crops and lives, the steady increase in population has made Henan the home of some of the nation's most impoverished people. Refugees of a sort, fleeing the poverty of their home regions, the majority of China's millions of migrant workers come from Henan and Sichuan.

The area's most famous sight, the **Longmen Shiku** (Dragon Gate Grottoes), is close to Luoyang; you might start in Luoyang, visit Shaolin Temple on the way from Luoyang to Zhengzhou, spend the night in Zhengzhou, and go on to Kaifeng the next afternoon.

Zhengzhou

🔟 *110 km (68 mi) east of Luoyang, 610 km (378 mi) south of Beijing.*

Archaeological finds indicate that the region around this city has been populated since the Neolithic period. It was the Shang dynasty capital for a time and became an important transportation and economic center under the Sui and Tang dynasties, when canals connecting the Yellow River to the northwest terminated in Zhengzhou's great grain market. When the Song moved their capital east to Kaifeng, the city's importance waned.

In the 20th century Zhengzhou once again became an important transportation center. It was the site of one of the chief railway strikes of the 1920s and, later, of a major wartime disaster. When Chiang Kai-shek's retreating Nationalist army blew up the dams on the Yellow River in a vain attempt to stop Japanese military progress into the country, millions suffered from the ensuing floods. The Nationalists also moved Zhengzhou's industry to avoid its falling into Japanese hands. After 1949 the Communist government rebuilt industry in what was at that point only an administrative and commercial center. The heavy industrialization of recent years has given an otherwise nondescript provincial capital a level of pollution, traffic, and noise befitting a major urban center. Cultural attractions, unfortunately, have not kept pace.

Zhengzhou, along with Luoyang, provides a suitable base for exploring some of China's oldest and best-known sights. The area around Zhengzhou is one of the most important in Chinese ancient history. Sights are organized below in order of their proximity to the central restaurant and hotel district along Jinshui Lu.

☽ If you're lucky, you can catch a glimpse of some city ruins in the far eastern section of **Zijingshan Gongyuan** (Zijingshan Park). The park also has a playground for children, a minimally functional miniature golf course, and several pretty wooden pagodas. It's a worthwhile escape from the noise of the city, especially if you are traveling with children. ⊠ *Jinshui Lu between Zijingshan Lu and Chengdong Lu, entrance at intersection of Jinshui Lu and Zijingshan Lu.* 🎫 *Free.* ☽ *Daily 5 AM–11 PM.*

Renmin Gongyuan (People's Park) provides a relaxing alternative to the city's dusty streets. It contains a small lake with a large island and some ageing carnival rides, and provides a favorite dawn and dusk tai chi venue for the local populace. ⊠ *Jinshui Lu between Erqi Lu and Minggong Lu, entrance on Erqi Lu just south of Jinshui Lu.* 🎫 Y2. ☽ *Daily 8–dusk.*

Zhengzhou's **Henan Bowuguan** (Henan Museum of China), housed in a striking and innovative pyramid-shaped building, has an excellent collection of archaeological finds from this area as well as others. You can see some of the Neolithic remains found on the Yellow River, Shang bronzes found in and around the city itself, and other ancient artifacts such as earthenware pots and ceramics from various dynasties. ⊠ *8 Nongye Lu,* ☎ *0371/385–0860.* ⊡ *Y20.* ⊙ *Daily 8:30–6.*

Zhengzhou was the site of one of several important and bloody railway strikes that took place in the early 1920s. On February 7, 1923, striking railway workers halted the busy rail line to Wuhan, angering the regional strongman Wu Peifu as well as the British business community in Wuhan. Wu ended the strike by ordering his troops to fire on a crowd of demonstrators and then publicly executing the strike leaders. Fifty-two people were killed and more than 300 wounded; more than 1,000 workers were fired. The event shook the confidence of the two-year-old Chinese Communist Party and put a damper on the burgeoning Chinese labor movement for the next two years. This early Communist martyrdom is commemorated in the **Er Qi Ta** (February 7 Pagoda), whose fresh colors and distinctive shape ornament a major traffic circle a short way from the train station. Inside, documents and pictures concerning the strike and Communist history in Zhengzhou are on display, but few are labeled in English. ⊠ *Junction Er Qi Lu, Renmin Lu, and Zhengxing Jie,* ☎ *no phone.* ⊡ *Y5.* ⊙ *Daily 8:30– noon and 2–5:30.*

Dining and Lodging

$$–$$$ ✕ **Yuexiu.** Zhengzhou's most famous restaurant, the YX (as it's informally known) is aware of its foreign clientele. It offers Western classical music from a string quartet near the bar and lounge section, and from a small shop in back it sells not only Chinese books but framed calligraphy scrolls that non-Chinese speakers can also enjoy. Aside from the main dining area there is a selection of themed private rooms, each decorated in a particular Chinese or Western style. It serves up a tasty selection of some favorite Cantonese foods, including more daring specialties like snake gall. ⊠ *Renzhai Bei Jie, East Section, between Jingqi Lu and Jingba Lu,* ☎ *0371/383–7666,* 𝖥𝖠𝖷 *0371/393–2222. No credit cards.*

$–$$ ✕ **Yangguang.** This restaurant specializes in delicious Chaozhou cuisine from the south of China, which emphasizes fresh flavors and elaborate presentation. ⊠ *28 Shangcheng Lu, east of Chengdong Lu,* ☎ *0371/632–2688. No credit cards.*

$$$–$$$$ ⌂ **Crowne Plaza Zhengzhou.** At the edge of Zhengzhou's restaurant row, set back from the street behind a tall fountain, this appealing hotel provides everything you would need during a stay in Zhengzhou. The Shang Palace restaurant, on the first floor, tends toward formality and serves a variety of excellent Chinese dishes in a tasteful and quiet environment. Mama Mia's Pizzeria claims actual American-style oven-baked pizzas, and the downstairs Patisserie serves fine coffee and a variety of cakes and cookies. Geared toward foreign business travelers, the hotel has a friendly staff whose English tends to be quite good. ⊠ *115 Jinshui Lu, 450003,* ☎ *0371/595–0055,* 𝖥𝖠𝖷 *0371/599–0770,* 𝖶𝖤𝖡 *www.crowneplaza.com/hotels/cgoch. 177 rooms, 44 suites. Restaurant, bar, pool, gym, nightclub, business services, meeting room, travel services. AE, DC, MC, V.*

$–$$ ⌂ **Asia.** Walk out the door and see the February 7 Pagoda. This hotel has an excellent location if you plan to do much sightseeing outside Zhengzhou: it's close to the train and long-distance bus stations. The facilities in the hotel are excellent, and the staff is very helpful. Each room comes with satellite TV, International Direct Dial (IDD) telephone, and a minibar. ⊠ *165 Jiefang Xi Lu, 450003,* ☎ *0371/696–8866,* 𝖥𝖠𝖷 *0371/696–9877. 159 rooms, 15 suites. 3 restaurants, bar, minibars, hair salon, sauna, gym, billiards, dance club, business services, meeting room. AE, DC, MC, V.*

$–$$ ⊞ **Golden Sunshine.** This hotel has business-class tourists in mind. Directly north of the railway station, it makes up for its distance from most restaurants by offering a Western eatery as well as an excellent Chinese restaurant that prepares specialties from various regions. Each room comes with IDD telephone and TV. ✉ *86 Erma Lu, 450003,* ☎ *0371/696–9999,* FAX *0371/699–9534. 383 rooms, 17 suites. 3 restaurants, bar, hair salon, billiards, business services. AE, DC, MC, V.*

$ ⊞ **Friendship.** The best buy for budget travelers, the Friendship offers few outstanding facilities but has good service at a good price. It's a few blocks north of the February 7 Pagoda. ✉ *97 Jinshui Lu, 450053,* ☎ *0371/622–8807,* FAX *0371/622–4728. 116 rooms, 4 suites. 2 restaurants, bar, hair salon, sauna, shops, business services. No credit cards.*

$ ⊞ **Haitian.** Occupying most of a high-rise off Jinshui Lu, this hotel has great service and an enjoyable indoor environment even though the street outside is not the most attractive. The rooms are very light. A major travel service has its offices on two floors of the building. ✉ *288 Chengdong Beilu, North Section, 450003,* ☎ *0371/595–9988,* FAX *0371/596–1603. 40 rooms, 8 suites. Restaurant, bar, hair salon, business services, meeting room. AE, DC, MC, V.*

$ ⊞ **Henan Province Henan.** Tending toward monumental Soviet style, this is a clean building with minimal facilities. It is a better buy if you are traveling with several people; the cost of singles here is on a par with the rates of other modestly priced hotels. Neither of the two restaurants serves Western fare. ✉ *26 Jinshui Lu, 450003,* ☎ *0371/394–3117,* FAX *0371/394–4619. 500 rooms. 2 restaurants. No credit cards.*

$ ⊞ **International Hotel Zhengzhou.** A bit bland on the outside, the International Hotel has two restaurants, one Chinese and one Western, that are quite decent, if lacking in character. Each room comes with IDD telephone, satellite TV, and a minibar. ✉ *114 Jinshui Lu, East Section, 450003,* ☎ *0371/595–6600,* FAX *0371/595–1526. 216 rooms, 9 suites. 2 restaurants, bar, minibars, pool, gym, nightclub, business services, travel services. AE, DC, MC, V.*

$ ⊞ **Red Coral.** This hotel close to the railway station caters mainly to businesspersons who value its convenient location. It is tastefully decorated and offers an excellent range of facilities. ✉ *20 Erma Lu, 450003,* ☎ *0371/698–6688,* FAX *0371/699–3222,* WEB *www.redcoralhotel.com. 155 rooms, 12 suites. 2 restaurants, pool, bowling, dance club, business services, travel services. AE, DC, MC, V.*

Nightlife

In Zhengzhou the few bars that spring up now and then tend to have a short and uncertain life span. **Cola Planet** (✉ 105 Jian Kang Lu, 1st Floor, Fazhan Building, ☎ no phone) serves coffee by day and transforms into a bar and disco by night. For a relaxed evening check out the **Target Bar** (✉ 10 Jing Liu Lu, ☎ no phone), which serenades customers with jazz through the week and rap on weekends.

Shopping

Zhengzhou has several night markets where the local Muslims set up food stands and local merchants peddle wares. You can find anything from baby clothes to the most recent publications here, but the main attraction is usually the people. The **Erqi Area Night Market** (✉ Along small side streets off Minzhu Lu, 1 block west of Erqi Lu) starts doing business around 7 PM and keeps going until the crowd gets tired—usually around 10 PM.

The best shopping for regional crafts and reproductions of famous archaeological finds can be found at the sights outside Zhengzhou. The local **Friendship Store** (✉ 96 Erqi Beilu, ☎ 0371/622–0082) sells prints and antiques. The **Henan Museum Shop** (✉ Nongye Lu, in

Henan Provincial Museum, ☎ no phone) sells local art, reproductions of its own exhibits, carved jewelry, and the like. The **Jin Bo Da Shopping Center** (✉ 200 Erqi Lu, ☎ 0371/624–8054) is the best department store in town. The **Shaolin Monastery** (☞ Shaolin Si, *below*) is surrounded by stands selling everything from art reproductions to little martial arts figurines.

Side Trips from Zhengzhou

⓱ A short ride from the city, the clean and relaxing **Huang He Youlan Qu** (Yellow River Park) offers an impressive view of the river. Exhibits document the importance of the river as both the origin of ancient civilization and a major destructive force in recent times. Its flooding has claimed millions of lives over the years. Several dams now harness the river's power for hydroelectric use. To get to the park, catch a minibus from outside the train station or ask at your hotel travel or information desk about rides. ✉ *30 km (19 mi) northwest of Zhengzhou.* ✆ *Y10.* ☉ *Daily 8:30–dusk.*

⓲ One of the lesser-known attractions in this area, **Zhongyue Si** (Temple of the Central Peak) stands amid beautiful mountains. Officially, it is the local Taoist temple, but China has a long tradition of intermingling religions. Like most temples of its kind, Zhongyue in fact bears as much significance to Buddhists as to Taoists: locals come to pray, and who they pray to is completely up to them. You can stop in on the way to or from Shaolin Monastery. ✉ *60 km (37 mi) southwest of Zhengzhou; accessible by minibus or hired car.* ✆ *Y10.* ☉ *Daily 8:30–dusk.*

☝ ⓳ If you like martial arts, you'll want to see where it started in China— at **Shaolin Si** (Shaolin Monastery). Chinese combat martial art is thought to have been invented here by Buddhist monks who needed some diversion from their meditation. Amid gorgeous hills checkered with large patches of farmed land, the site actually extends up and down a fairly long street, including far more than just the temple. The large temple has a bamboo grove surrounded by stone stelae and a pavilion illustrated with scenes from the Confucian *Classic of Filial Piety.* Across the street, something resembling a wax museum portrays famous martial artists in various fighting positions and battle arrays. Children tend to enjoy this bit. The martial arts school at the temple often has performances and competitions, so you may get to see actual monks and other students showing off their skills. Farther up the hill, famous monks of the past are commemorated in the Forest of Pagodas. ✉ *70 km (43 mi) southwest of Zhengzhou; accessible by minibus or hired car.* ✆ *Y60; 1 ticket buys entry to all sights.* ☉ *Daily 8:30–5:30.*

★ ⓴ Once the capital of the Song dynasty, **Kaifeng,** east of Zhengzhou, was abandoned by the court in the 12th century when northern invaders forced the Song south to Hangzhou. Amazingly, it has managed to retain many of its attractions, as well as large chunks of its city wall, without having been turned into a heavy industrial center or a tourist trap. It's a relatively quiet, friendly city that has preserved its neighborhood feel. The Muslim population has a strong influence, and two mosques in white-and-green tile, complete with Middle Eastern onion domes, have been built in the last few years. Older, Chinese-style mosques, as well as Buddhist temples, dot the side streets. The Muslims also run one of the busiest food and wares markets.

The city's most famous sight stands near Tieta Hu (Tieta Lake). The **Tie Ta** (Iron Pagoda) is not made of iron but of brick covered with tiles that look like iron. You can climb to the top on a narrow pitch-black staircase that leads to several small windows. You can also see the lake and wander around the pretty surroundings. ⊠ *Northeast corner of town, near No. 3 bus terminus.* ☎ *Park Y20, pagoda Y5.* ⊙ *Daylight hrs.*

🔄 **Longting Gongyuan** (Dragon Pavilion Park), Kaifeng's major park, includes three lakes and a pavilion. It is a favorite family outing spot. ⊠ *North end of Zhongshan Lu.* ☎ *Y10.* ⊙ *Daily 8–5.*

The **Xiangguo Si** (Xiangguo Temple), originally built in the 6th century, was most recently rebuilt in the 18th century and houses some old artifacts. A food and souvenirs market has sprung up around it. ⊠ *Ziyou Lu.* ☎ *Y20.* ⊙ *Daily 8–5.*

Near the middle of town, the **Yangqing Guan** (Yangqing Taoist Temple) is a two-story structure with a strikingly ornate exterior around an unusually bare interior. A shop displays some calligraphy scrolls. ⊠ *Off Yingbin Lu.* ☎ *Y10.* ⊙ *Daily 8:30–5:30.*

Luoyang

㉑ *3½ hrs (430 km/267 mi) by train west of Zhengzhou, 7 hrs (320 km/198 mi) by train northeast of Xian.*

First established by the Zhou in the 12th century BC, Luoyang became the dynastic capital in 771 BC. Although well known as one of the "ancient capitals," Luoyang became more important for its religious and artistic history. Not only did it serve as capital to 10 successive dynasties, it also welcomed and built a temple for the first monk to bring Buddhism to the Middle Kingdom. Under instructions from the emperor of the Northern Wei dynasty, cave temples were constructed slightly south of the city. These temples are now regarded as some of the most important monuments to Buddhist art. Buddhism's incorporation into indigenous beliefs and everyday lives was so complete that even restrictions and periodic purges by various dynasties as well as by modern governments have not kept people from praying to the arhats. In fact, with increased government openness—fueled perhaps partly by a desire to attract tourists, particularly those from Taiwan, Hong Kong, and Singapore—Buddhism seems to be on the rise again today.

The art that Buddhism fostered once adorned Luoyang's many temples and monasteries, but the city reached its cultural apex centuries ago, and for hundreds of years its symbolic importance as a name associated with religious and dynastic powers carried more weight than the fact of its existence. Nowadays it is a growing industrial center. The city itself holds few important sights, but you'll need about a day to see the chief places of interest around Luoyang. If you can get here in April, you should give yourself an afternoon to see the blooming peonies that are Luoyang's pride, second only to the Buddhist grottoes. All sights but Wangcheng Park lie outside the city proper.

🔄 Spring means peonies in Luoyang. Stroll through the peony show in **Wangcheng Gongyuan** (Park of the Royal Town) during the third week of April every year, when Luoyang is crowded with visitors from the region. Families come out to enjoy the sight, and college students skip class and take the seven-hour train ride from Xian to participate. At other times of year, the park is a restful if unremarkable recreation area. It has a small zoo in the back, as well as a playground for kids. ⊠ *Just northwest of Zhongzhou Zhonglu and Wangcheng Lu,* ☎ *no phone.* ☎ *Y3, but Y15 during peony show.* ⊙ *Daily 8:30–dusk.*

The **Gumu Bowuguan** (Ancient Tombs Museum) stands north of the city atop Mangshan Mountain, which was viewed as an auspicious site. The museum displays 22 of the thousands of ancient tombs found in the area. The underground tombs come from dynasties from the Han to the Song. ⊠ *4 km (2½ mi) north of city; tour or minibus.* 🖼 *Y15.* ⊙ *Daily 8:30–6.*

East of town is the site of the original Buddhist temple. **Baima Si** (White Horse Temple)—named for the white horses believed to have carried the first scriptures from India to China—became a focal point for China's powerful fascination with this imported religion. The temple has been destroyed several times over, and the buildings we see now date from the Ming and Qing dynasties. Statues of white horses stand to either side behind the central hall as emblems of its origins. ⊠ *13 km (8 mi) east of city; accessible by minibus or hired car.* 🖼 *Y25.* ⊙ *Daily 8:30–6.*

South of the city lies **Guanlin** (Grove of Guan), a large enclosure with tree-lined paths between its many prayer halls. Not far from the Dragon Gate Grottoes, it provides a peaceful setting for an afternoon walk as well as a glimpse of contemporary Buddhist practice. ⊠ *7½ km (4½ mi) south of town; accessible by minibus or hired car,* ☎ *no phone.* 🖼 *Y15.* ⊙ *Daily 8:30–6.*

★ To the southeast, the **Longmen Shiku** (Dragon Gate Grottoes) are a tribute to Buddhism's immense force in the Chinese past. Carved during two successive dynasties over several centuries, these thousands of Buddhist figures are ranged along the mountainside overlooking the Luo River. Although some of the grottoes are labeled in English, you rarely get more than a dynasty name and an uninformative blurb. The Chinese blurbs are not much better. The atmosphere of the site is part artwork, part ruins—exposure to the elements has done its bit to wear away the intricacy of the work. The real damage was done by the English and other Western enthusiasts of the 19th century who decided to take some of the artwork home with them. Many figures now stand headless, their faces decorating European museums or private collectors' shelves. You can visit the caves on your own or take one of numerous guided tours offered by CITS and the local hotels. ⊠ *16 km (10 mi) southeast of town; accessible by taxi, Buses 53, 60, and 81, and private minibuses with the same numbers.* 🖼 *Y50.* ⊙ *Daily 8–6.*

Dining and Lodging

$–$$ ✕ **Yaxiang Lou.** The Elegant Scent restaurant is one of the better dining options in Luoyang outside the big hotels. It serves a variety of Chinese dishes, and specializes in Cantonese-style cuisine. ⊠ *4 Anhui Lu,* ☎ *0379/492–3030. No credit cards.*

$ ✕ **Zhen Butong.** The name means "truly different"; not surprisingly, it is the only restaurant around that specializes in real "Luoyang flavor." The house specialty is a "water banquet," named for the rapidity of each successive course, but perhaps also referring to the soupy sauces in which each dish swims. These include both spicy entrées and a soothing dessert that tastes something like a Middle Eastern version of rice pudding. You don't have to order a whole banquet to enjoy some of its component parts. ⊠ *369 Zhongzhou Donglu,* ☎ *0379/395–2338. No credit cards.*

$$ 🏨 **New Friendship Hotel.** Don't be confused by the addresses—the New Friendship is in fact neighbor to the Friendship Guesthouse. Not surprisingly, they quite resemble each other. This one's main attraction is the Suzhou-style garden out back, whose arched bridges, small pavilions, and peony blossoms outdo those at the Guesthouse. ⊠ *6 Xiyuan Lu, 471003,* ☎ *0379/491–3770,* 🗷 *0379/491–2328. 133 rooms, 4 suites. 2 restaurants, gym, nightclub, recreation room, travel services. AE, DC, MC, V.*

$$ ⌗ **Peony Hotel.** This joint-venture hotel lies a short walk from Wangcheng Park, where Luoyang's peony festival takes place. Its rooms are fresh, and its small restaurant serves fairly good Western food as well as some excellent Chinese dishes. More than half its guests are foreign tourists and businesspeople. The staff is friendly, and the atmosphere is tasteful and quiet. ✉ *15 Zhongzhou Xi Lu, 471003,* ☎ *0379/485–6699,* FAX *0379/485–6999. 188 rooms, 6 suites. Restaurant, bar, recreation room, travel services. AE, DC, MC, V.*

$–$$ ⌗ **Peony Plaza.** This towering edifice opened with much pomp in the center of town. Although it's obviously built to cater to business travelers and upscale tourists, it also offers some great weekend deals and tour prices. The building is light, clean, and well furnished, with a professional and energetic staff. A revolving restaurant on the 25th floor gives a great view of the city. ✉ *2 Nanchang Lu, 471003,* ☎ *0379/ 493–1111,* FAX *0379/493–0303. 143 rooms, 20 suites. 2 restaurants, bar, pool, gym, recreation room, business services, convention center, meeting room, travel services. AE, DC, MC, V.*

$ ⌗ **Friendship Guesthouse.** A joint venture, the Friendship has tasteful amenities and a lovely courtyard out back whose artificial lake, curved bridge, and rock arrangement are inspired by the gardens of Suzhou. ✉ *6 Xiyuan Lu, 471003,* ☎ *0379/491–2788,* FAX *0379/491–3808. 125 rooms, 13 suites. 2 restaurants, food court, pool, hair salon, sauna, business services, travel services. AE, DC, MC, V.*

Nightlife

Locals head to the outdoor market that springs up between Jinguyuan Lu and Kaixuan Lu and bustle around the shopping district on Zhongzhou Donglu in the old city. For dancing, drinking, and entertainment, you're best off staying in your hotel.

Shopping

The tricolor pottery associated with the Tang dynasty developed here. The lot in back of the Longmen Grottoes has many Tang-style figurines. The Ru ceramics of the Song dynasty are also local; the greenish glaze has a distinctive thick, opaque quality. Reproductions of these creations are sold at hotel shops and specialty stores. For everyday goods, try the **Luoyang Department Store** (✉ 21 Zhongzhou Zhonglu, ☎ 0379/ 323–3531). The **Meitao Cheng** (✉ Jian Donglu, ☎ 0379/393–1817) carries regional products. **Wenwu Shangdian** (✉ Zhongzhou Donglu, ☎ no phone) specializes in antiques, including calligraphy, pottery, and jewelry.

Henan A to Z

To research prices, get advice from other travelers, and book travel arrangements, visit www.fodors.com.

AIR TRAVEL

Luoyang is not as convenient to reach by plane as Zhengzhou. There are flights to Xian on weekdays and to major cities several times a week. Book through the travel offices in the Peony Hotel or in the Friendship hotels or through CAAC at the Luoyang Airport.

Zhengzhou Airport is about 40 minutes' ride from town and offers daily flights to major Chinese cities. Tickets can be purchased at the central CAAC office or at CAAC outlets in the major hotels.
➤ AIRLINES & CONTACTS: **Central CAAC office, Luoyang** (✉ Daobei Lu, ☎ 0379/231–0121). **Central CAAC office, Zhengzhou** (✉ 3 Jinshui Lu, ☎ 0371/696–4789).

BUS TRAVEL BETWEEN CITIES IN HENAN

From the long-distance bus station in Kaifeng (just south of Baogong Lake on Yingbin Lu; take Bus 4, 6, 10, 12, or 13) buses run to Zhengzhou every hour on the half-hour until 6:30 PM. An hourly service is available to Luoyang.

The Luoyang bus station is right across from the train station and provides buses to Zhengzhou (every 20 minutes), three hours away, and to Shaolin Temple, about 1½ hours away.

The long-distance bus station in Zhengzhou is directly across from the train station and offers buses to just about everywhere in China. The easiest places to reach by bus are Luoyang (every 20 minutes) and Kaifeng (every hour).

BUS TRAVEL WITHIN CITIES IN HENAN

Kaifeng's bus system covers all points of interest in the city. Bus 4 goes from the effective center of town at Gulou to the long-distance bus station.

A number of buses run the route down Luoyang's main drags, Zhongzhou Xi Lu and Zhongzhou Donglu; these are crowded at rush hour but are otherwise not bad. Public buses go out to the Buddhist grottoes and to White Horse Temple, but private minibuses are usually more comfortable.

Zhengzhou is a rather sprawling metropolis, and buses are a convenient way of getting around it. Public buses do not run to the out-of-town sights, but you can catch minibuses at the train station, or ask at your hotel information desk—many hotels run their own services.

CAR TRAVEL

It may be convenient to hire a car for a tour of the sights surrounding Zhengzhou and Luoyang. Check with a major hotel for hiring information. Kaifeng is smaller and best handled by bus or on foot.

EMERGENCIES

In Luoyang and Zhengzhou it is best to contact the police and hospitals through your hotel.
➤ HOSPITALS: **Henan People's Hospital** (✉ Weiwu Lu, ☎ 0371/558–0114). **Second People's Hospital of Luoyang** (✉ 288 Zhongzhou Zhonglu, ☎ 0379/326–4500).

TAXIS

Kaifeng's friendly drivers have red taxis and pedicabs. Luoyang has vans and four-doors that congregate mostly on Zhongzhou Lu, east and west. These are easy to flag down and aren't expensive. Unless you know how much a ride should cost, it is usually to your advantage to make sure the driver follows the meter, rather than agreeing on a price beforehand. Canary yellow minivans and dark red four-doors roam the streets of Zhengzhou, particularly around the hotel and restaurant strip of Jinshui Lu.

TOURS

In Kaifeng the sights are within the city proper and don't require minibus hauls out of town. You're best off just getting a map and exploring the sights on your own.

Hotels in Luoyang offer minibus service out to the Longmen Grottoes and White Horse Temple. Other guided tours of the area can be arranged with CITS and include Mangshan and the ancient tombs.

Most hotels in Zhengzhou offer their own buses to Shaolin Temple and the Yellow River, and some will create custom tours if you want to see more of what lies between Zhengzhou and Luoyang. There are no guided city tours.

TRAIN TRAVEL

Kaifeng is easily accessible by rail: any train going east out of Zhengzhou will pass through here. Getting out is harder: the train station can't guarantee seats, and the place is often crowded and unruly. Leaving Kaifeng, it's best to take a bus.

Luoyang is on the rail line between Xian (six–seven hours) and Zhengzhou (about three hours). Trains run often to and from these destinations. The double-decker "tourist trains" are the most comfortable option.

Zhengzhou is one of the best-connected cities in China, lying on the intersection of both north–south and east–west lines. You can buy tickets to most major Chinese cities. Foreigners are encouraged to go to ticket windows Numbers 1 or 2; you can also go to the advance booking office to avoid the crowds. Some hotels will book tickets for you.
➤ TRAIN INFORMATION: **Advance booking office** (✉ 193 Erqi Lu, Zhengzhou).

TRAVEL AGENCIES

In Zhengzhou, it's best to stick with the hotel travel agencies— every major hotel has one.
➤ LOCAL AGENT REFERRALS: **CITS** (✉ 99 Dayuankengyan Jie, Kaifeng, ☎ 0378/595–5743; ✉ Jiudu Xilu, Luoyang, ☎ 0379/431–3701; ✉ 50 Jinqi Lu, Zhengzhou, ☎ 0397/595–2072). **Haitian Hotel** (✉ 288 Chengdong Lu, North Section, 8th floor, Zhengzhou, ☎ 0379/595–9988). **Peony Hotel** (✉ 15 Zhongzhou Xi Lu, Luoyang, ☎ 0379/485–6699).

VISITOR INFORMATION

Hotels and the CITS offices are the best source of visitor information in all three cities.

SHANDONG

As the birthplace of Confucius (born in Qufu) and site of two of China's holy mountains (Taishan and Laoshan), Shandong is home to some of China's most important cultural sights. Along with the city of Qingdao, these are among the province's highlights. It is also the *laojia* (old home) of many current inhabitants of the northeastern provinces of Liaoning, Jilin, and Heilongjiang (☞ Chapter 4) who escaped from poverty and war into Shandong in the decades after 1911 or colonized the area in Mao Zedong's postrevolution China.

The Yellow River, hard hit by drought in recent years, enters the Yellow Sea on the Shandong coastline. To the north lies the Bohai Gulf, and on land Shandong is bordered by Hebei, Henan, Anhui, and Jiangsu provinces. Shandong is one of the most populous provinces in China (population 87 million), and although Qingdao is relatively prosperous, many cities and much of the countryside are still very poor.

Jinan

㉒ *6 hrs (355 km/220 mi) by train south of Beijing; 6 hrs (305 km/189 mi) by train west of Qingdao.*

The old city of Jinan was given a new lease on life by the construction of a railway line linking it to the port city of Qingdao around the turn of the century. German, English, and Japanese concessions operated here, and a good number of buildings survive from this era in the downtown area. Jinan is a pleasant city, and the locals are friendly—something for which Shandong people in general enjoy a good reputation.

Today's city center, the most interesting part of Jinan, where European influence lingers, is laid out in a grid to the south of the railway station. An exploration of the city should begin here.

Zhongshan Gongyuan (Sun Yat-sen Park) is a quiet retreat from the city traffic. Early in the morning small groups of elderly people gather here to do tai chi, watched over by birds in cages they hang on nearby trees while they exercise. ⊠ *138 Jing San Lu.* ☜ *Y2.* ☉ *Daily 6 AM–8 PM.*

Qianfoshan (Thousand Buddha Mountain), on the southern outskirts of the city, is still the focus of religious festivals though most of the Buddhas have been lost to the ravages of time and the Cultural Revolution. The mountain does offer a good view of Jinan—air quality permitting. ⊠ *18 Jing Shiyi Lu, off Qianfoshan Lu beside Qilu Hotel.* ☜ *Y15.* ☉ *Daily 6 AM–7 PM.*

One interesting architectural legacy of the foreign occupation is an imposing redbrick **Protestant church,** with its landmark twin towers. Built in 1927, it is still in use. ⊠ *425 Jing Si Lu.*

Dining and Lodging

$–$$ ✕ **Jinsanbei.** Customers here choose their meals in a novel way: ingredients—meat, fish, vegetables, and so on—are stocked in open coolers off the lobby, and live fish are in nearby tanks. After you take your pick, the staff carries it to the kitchens while you retire to the large wood-paneled dining room to wait for the meal. ⊠ *5 Qianfoshan Lu,* ☎ *0531/296–1616. No credit cards.*

$–$$ ✕ **Luneng Shaoezai.** This Mongolian barbecue–style restaurant is very popular with locals. It presents a vast buffet of fresh seafood, meat, vegetables, and flavorings for customers to combine as they please and deliver to the kitchen for cooking. ⊠ *Jing Si Lu, in Linxiang Dasha complex,* ☎ *0531/601–1888. No credit cards.*

$–$$ ✕ **Shandong Danlian Seafood Restaurant.** At this simple open-plan restaurant specializing in seafood, customers can choose their meal from the selection of live (in tanks) and frozen seafood displayed in the lobby. ⊠ *86 Jing Ba Lu,* ☎ *0531/290–1618. No credit cards.*

$ ✕ **A Fun Ti Hometown Music Restaurant.** This delightful Xinjiang-style restaurant serves up a culinary and audio feast. Customers can sample Muslim-influenced dishes from China's western regions while listening to live music also of central Asian origin. In the late evening tables are cleared aside and eating gives way to dancing. ⊠ *18 Chaoshan Jie,* ☎ *0531/612–7228. No credit cards.*

$$$ ☶ **Hotel Sofitel.** This glittering tower, opened in 1999, is easily the most upscale hotel in Jinan. The luxurious rooms all have minibars and satellite TV, while the restaurants serve up a choice of Western, Japanese, Cantonese, or Shandong cuisines. ⊠ *66 Luoyuan Dajie, 250063,* ☎ *0531/606–8888,* ℻ *0531/606–9999,* ⓦⓔⓑ *www.accor-hotels-china. com/jinan 326 rooms. 3 restaurants, bar, minibars, pool, gym, business center. AE, DC, MC, V.*

$$–$$$ ☶ **Guidu.** On a side street off Wei San Jie, this modern hotel has rooms that are clean, tastefully decorated, and equipped with satellite TV, a business desk, and a minibar. The restaurants serve Chinese and Western food. ⊠ *1 Sheng Ping Lu, 250001,* ☎ *0531/690–0888,* ℻ *0531/*

690–0999. 225 rooms, 15 suites. 2 restaurants, bar, minibars, night-club, business services. AE, DC, MC, V.

$$–$$$ ⚏ **Qilu.** At this lavish hotel on the fringes of the city near Thousand Buddha Mountain, standard rooms are decorated in light colors and come with satellite TV and minibar. The restaurants serve Chinese, Japanese, and Western food. ⊠ *Qian Foshan Lu, 250014,* ☎ *0531/296–6888,* Ⓕ *0531/296–7676. 225 rooms. 4 restaurants, bar, minibars, gym, nightclub, business services. AE, DC, MC, V.*

Nightlife

There is little in the way of conventional nightlife in Jinan. What exists is concentrated in a short strip near the Qilu Hotel.

The popular **Boiling Point Bar** (⊠ 9 Qianfoshan Lu, ☎ no phone) is furnished in timber, has a dance floor in the middle, a dart board on the wall, and a cooler full of imported beers. **Shandong Elite Teahouse** (⊠ 9 Qianfoshan Lu, ☎ no phone) serves all kinds of tea at polished dark wooden tables in an exquisite traditional Chinese teahouse setting, decorated with lattice wooden paneling, vases, and musical instruments.

Shopping

The best department store in Jinan is the **Yin Zuo** (Silver Plaza; ⊠ Luo Yuan Dajie), with a shiny seven floors of everything from domestic appliances to cosmetics, plus a basement supermarket and Chinese fast-food outlets.

Side Trips from Jinan

㉓ The top of **Taishan** (Mt. Tai) is 5,067 ft above sea level. It is one of China's five holy Taoist mountains. The walk up—on cut-stone steps—by open mountainside, steep crags, and pine woods takes three to four hours. Some people stay overnight to watch the sun rise, but the classic sunrise over cloud-hugged mountainside seen in photos is actually a rare sight. Confucius is said to have climbed the mountain and commented from its height, "The world is very small." Much later Mao Zedong climbed it and even more famously said, "The East is red." At the foot of the mountain is the unremarkable town of Taian. ⊠ *About 50 km (30 mi) south of Jinan.*

㉔ **Qufu** is the birthplace of the great sage himself. A good percentage of Qufu's population claim to be descendants of Confucius. The **Confucius Temple, Confucius Family Mansion,** and the **Family Graveyard** are the focus of today's visitors. Confucius has been honored in Qufu almost consistently since his own time 2,500 years ago. Money was regularly sent from Beijing by the emperors to augment and keep up the extensive buildings devoted to his memory. ⊠ *3 hrs by car (110 km/68 mi) south of Jinan.*

Qingdao

12 hrs by train or 2 hrs by plane (540 km/335 mi) southeast of Beijing; 6 hrs by train (310 km/192 mi) east of Jinan.

Qingdao was a sleepy fishing village until the end of the 19th century when Germans, using the killing of two German missionaries in the vicinity as a pretext, set up another European colony on the coastal fringe of China. The German presence lasted only until 1914, but the city continued to build in the German style, and large parts of the old town make visitors feel as if they have stumbled into southern Germany. Today it is one of China's most charming cities and home to the country's best-known brewery, Tsingtao (the old-style Romanization of Qingdao), founded in 1903. East of the main harbor, Tsingtao still does a fair im-

Qingdao

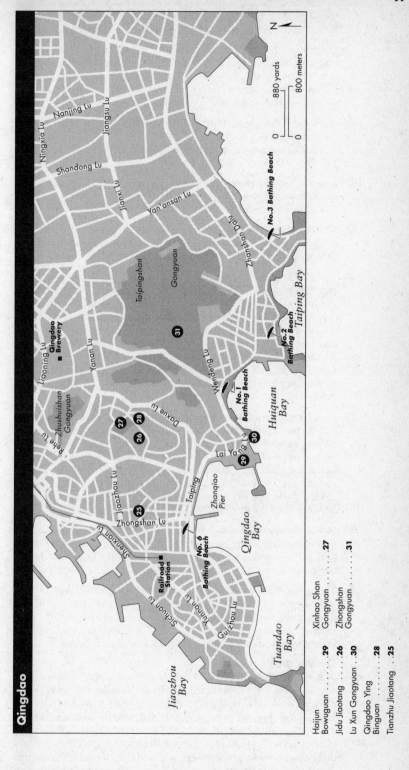

Ningxia Lu
Nanjing Lu
Jiangsu Lu
Jiaxu
Shandong Lu
Yan'ansan Lu
Taipingshan
Gongyuan
Zhanshan Dalu
No.3 Bathing Beach
Taiping Bay
Liaoning Lu
Qingdao Brewery
Yanan Lu
Zhushuishan Gongyuan
31
Wendeng Lu
No.2 Bathing Beach
Rehe Lu
Daxue Lu
No.1 Bathing Beach
Huiquan Bay
27 **28**
26
30
Jiaozhou Lu
Lai Yang
29
Zhongshan Lu
Taiping
Zhanqiao Pier
25
Qingdao Bay
Sianxian Lu
Railroad Station
No. 6 Bathing Beach
Yunnan Lu
Guizhou Lu
Sichuan Lu
Tuandao Bay
Jiaozhou Bay

N

0 ———— 880 yards
0 ———— 800 meters

pression of a good German lager and produces a sweet black stout as well. The city is also nursery to a growing wine industry.

Qingdao, with its seafront promenades, winding colonial streets, parks, and red-tile roofs, is made for strolling. The main shopping areas are around Zhongshan Lu; nearby is the city's landmark building, a twin-spired Catholic church. Don't miss the fascinating wholesale fresh seafood markets, along the edge of the city's smaller harbor.

㉕ A landmark in Qingdao is the **Tianzhu Jiaotang** (Catholic church), with its towering 200-ft twin steeples and red-tile roof. Originally named St. Emil Church, it was built by the Germans in 1934. ⊠ *15 Zhejiang Lu.* ☞ *Y5.* ☉ *Mon.–Sat. 8–5, Sun. 9–5.*

㉖ Qingdao's **Jidu Jiaotang** (Protestant Church) has a bell tower with a clock. It was built in 1910 at the southwest entrance of Xinhao Park. ⊠ *15 Jiangsu Lu.* ☞ *Y3.* ☉ *Daily 8:30–4:30.*

㉗ One of the best views of old Qingdao is from the three red mushroom-shape towers on the top of Xinhao Shan in **Xinhao Shan Gongyuan** (Xinhao Hill Park). ⊠ *Off Daxue Lu.* ☞ *Park Y2, towers Y12.*

㉘ The old **Qingdao Ying Binguan** (German governor's residence) was a public hotel until 1996 when it became a museum. Built in 1903 as the official residence of the governor-general of the then-German colony of Qingdao, it is set on a hill in mature gardens overlooking the old city. The interior is warm, with wood paneling and a wide stair-case leading from the ground-floor foyer to the guest rooms. Among the famous leaders who stayed here were Mao Zedong; his wife, Jiang Qing; Zhou Enlai; Deng Xiaoping; and Cambodia's Prince Sihanouk. ⊠ *26 Longshan Lu, just below Xinhao Hill Park.* ☞ *Y10.* ☉ *Daily 8:30–4:30.*

㉙ In the upper yard of the **Haijun Bowuguan** (Navy Museum) is an in-door exhibition documenting the history of the Chinese navy and dis-playing an extensive collection of uniforms and plaques presented by visiting navies. Outdoors in the lower yard stands a range of military equipment, including Russian-made fighter aircraft, fixed turret and anti-aircraft naval guns, rockets, tanks, ground artillery, naval vessels (in-cluding three moored in the adjacent harbor), and even an old biplane. ⊠ *8 Lai Yang Lu,* ☎ *0532/286–6784.* ☞ *Y20.* ☉ *Daily 8:30–7:30.*

㉚ **Lu Xun Gongyuan** (Lu Xun Park), built in 1929, faces onto Huiquan Bay, combining traditional Chinese garden art with the rocky coast-line. In 1950 it was named for the distinguished Chinese writer and commentator Lu Xun. ⊠ *West end of No. 1 Bathing Beach.* ☞ *Y2.*

㉛ **Zhongshan Gongyuan** (Sun Yat-sen Park), named for Dr. Sun Yat-sen, is the largest park in the city. Its Oriental cherry path, osmanthus gar-den, and other exotic plant gardens are best visited in spring. The park is also home to the Qingdao Zoo. ⊠ *28 Wendeng Lu, north of Hui-quan Dynasty Hotel.* ☞ *Y5.* ☉ *Daily 5 AM–9 PM.*

Dining and Lodging

$$$ ✕ **Dunhuang Baochixian.** This upscale restaurant presents diners with a bewildering array of seafood, from fresh fish to sharks' fin soup and abalone, cooked in the southern Cantonese and Chaozhou styles by a Hong Kong chef. A full range of stir-fried dishes is also available. ⊠ *102 Xiang Gang Zhonglu,* ☎ *0532/588–7556. AE, MC, V.*

$–$$ ✕ **Chunhelou.** Established in 1891, this restaurant specializes in Shan-dong cuisine, steamed dumplings, and traditional snacks. Downstairs is fast-food style, while the second floor is smarter with more of an emphasis on seafood. ✉ *146 Zhongshan Lu,* ☎ *0532/282–4346. No credit cards.*

$ ✕ **Dou Lia Shun.** This seafood restaurant across from the Catholic church has big fish tanks and a courteous staff. A new interior and high ceilings make it airy and quiet. Dark and pale beers are brewed on site. ✉ *26 Zhejiang Lu,* ☎ *0532/288–1717. No credit cards.*

$ ✕ **Gaoli.** One of the better Korean restaurants in the city serves on-table barbecues, and its other dishes are relatively cheap. ✉ *2 Huiquan Lu,* ☎ *0532/386–5301. No credit cards.*

$ ✕ **Mingtian Coffee Language.** This elegant and comfortable coffee shop is decorated entirely with materials imported from Taiwan, and specializes in the flavored milk teas so popular on the island. Chinese snacks and set meals are also served, but no alcohol is permitted. ✉ *82 Hong Kong Central Rd.,* ☎ *0532/592–3101. No credit cards.*

$ ✕ **Yiqinglou.** Immensely popular with locals, this restaurant requires diners to choose live seafood from tanks, or from a huge array of demonstration plates of mixed meat, vegetables, and fish. An identical meal is then prepared by the chefs and presented at the table. ✉ *90 Hong Kong Central Rd.,* ☎ *0532/588–3388. No credit cards.*

$$$$ 🏨 **Grand Regency.** Extravagantly modern, the hotel has a huge foyer and an immense ballroom made with materials imported from Italy, England, and South Africa. Rooms are tastefully decorated and spacious. The only drawback is the relatively poor view due to the hotel's location in the industrial and commercial district. All rooms offer in-house movie channels and satellite TV. The restaurants serve Cantonese, French, Japanese, and international fare. ✉ *1 Taiwan Lu, 266071,* ☎ *0532/588–1818,* FAX *0532/588–1888,* WEB *www.grh-ohm.com. 448 rooms. 4 restaurants, 2 bars, minibars, pool, tennis court, gym, nightclub, business services. AE, DC, MC, V.*

$$$$ 🏨 **Haitian.** Overlooking Qingdao's Number 3 Bathing Beach, this hotel has clean, modern rooms with minibar, satellite TV, and a good coastal view. The restaurants serve Chinese, Japanese, Korean, and Western fare. ✉ *48 Xiang Gang Xi Lu, 266071,* ☎ *0532/387–1888,* FAX *0532/387–1777,* WEB *www.hai-tian-hotel.com. 606 rooms. 4 restaurants, bar, minibars, pool, gym, business services. AE, DC, MC, V.*

$$$$ 🏨 **Huiquan Dynasty.** This modern hotel overlooks the Number 1 Bathing Beach and the sea east of the downtown area. In the newest part, a high-rise tower, every guest room has a private balcony overlooking the Yellow Sea. The revolving restaurant—serving Chinese and Western breakfast and evening meals—on the 25th floor affords views of the beautiful old city of Qingdao. Spacious and comfortable standard rooms come with color TV with in-house movies. The restaurants serve Chinese, Japanese, and Western cuisine. ✉ *9 Nanhai Lu, 266003,* ☎ *0532/288–6688,* FAX *0532/287–1122. 409 rooms. 4 restaurants, bar, minibars, pool, tennis court, gym, nightclub, business services. AE, DC, MC, V.*

$$$$ 🏨 **Shangri-La.** This top-class hotel opened in late 1997 with standard Shangri-La facilities. Though situated in a commercial rather than a tourist district, it is nevertheless only a block from the scenic coastline, and close to some of the best shopping and eating in town. ✉ *9 Xiang Gang Zhonglu, 266071,* ☎ *0532/388–3838,* FAX *0532/388–6868,* WEB *www.shangri-la.com 402 rooms. 2 restaurants, bar, in-room data ports, in-room fax, minibars, refrigerators, pool, tennis court, gym, business services. AE, DC, MC, V.*

$$–$$$ 🏨 **Dongfang.** In the university area within walking distance of downtown, this hotel has good views of colonial Qingdao from its comfortable guest rooms. All are equipped with satellite TV. The restaurants serve Chinese and Western food. ✉ *4 Daxue Lu, 266003,* ☎ *0532/286–5888,* FAX *0532/286–2741,* WEB *www.hotel-dongfang.com. 141 rooms. 2*

*restaurants, bar, minibars, tennis court, gym, nightclub, business ser-
vices. AE, DC, MC, V.*

$$–$$$ ☑ **Oceanwide Elite.** This modern, elegant hotel built in a semi-German
style sits right on the seafront promenade. Rooms range from the elegant wood-paneled Presidential Bedroom to a standard, simply furnished, spic-and-span room. ☒ *29 Taiping Lu, 266001,* ☎ *0532/288–
6699,* FAX *0532/289–1388, 82 rooms, 6 suites. 2 restaurants, gym,
nightclub. AE, DC, MC, V.*

Nightlife and the Arts

The **International Beer Festival,** in August, is Qingdao's biggest event
of the year, with fireworks and gallons of beer for tasting. There are
also several **harvest festivals,** including the **Taidong Radish Festival**
and the **Sugar-Coated Haws Festival,** both in January. The **Cherry Festival** takes place in April and May. In early September the **Mt. Daze
Grape Festival** celebrates the fruit of the vine.

Shopping

The North end of Zhongshan Lu has a cluster of antiques and cultural
artifacts shops. The **Ju Bao Zhai Art Shop** (☒ 169 Zhong Shan Lu, ☎
0532/282–4184) offers a selection of porcelain, metal, and stone wares.
The largest antique shop on the street is the **Qingdao Art and Craft Store**
(☒ 212 Zhongshan Lu, ☎ 0532/281–7948), with four floors of porcelain, scroll paintings, silk, gold, and jade and other stones.

Department stores include **Fada Mansion** (☒ Junction of Zhongshan
Lu and Hunan Lu, ☎ 0532/296–1818) and **Parkson** (☒ 46 Zhongshan Lu, ☎ 0532/202–1085). The Japanese-owned **JUSCO** (☒ 72 Xiang
Gang Zhonglu, ☎ 0532/571–9600) has the best supermarket and
mall in town.

Side Trips from Qingdao

③② The holy **Laoshan,** which rivals Shandong's other famous mountain,
Taishan, rises to a height of more than 3,280 ft above sea level. A repository of Taoism, during its heyday it had nine palaces, eight temples,
and 72 convents. With sheer cliffs and cascading waterfalls, the beautiful mountain is widely recognized in China as a source of the country's best-known mineral water. The mountain area covers 400 square
km (154 square mi), but paths to Laoshan proper lead from the Song
dynasty Taiqing Palace. Tourist buses to Laoshan leave from the main
pier in Qingdao. ☒ *40 km (25 mi) east of Qingdao.*

Near Laoshan, **Huadong Winery,** Shandong's best winery, is not yet
as famous as the province's brewery but has already won a string of
prizes. The winery's equipment comes from France and the United States,
and the vines were bought from France in the mid-1980s. The chardon-
nay is on a par with any good American wine, perhaps because the
wine-growing area of Shandong is on the same latitude as California's
Napa Valley. Tours are only available through CITS.

Shandong A to Z

*To research prices, get advice from other travelers, and book travel ar-
rangements, visit www.fodors.com.*

AIR TRAVEL

Regular flights link Jinan airport and Hong Kong and other major Chinese cities. The airport is 70 km (43 mi) northeast of Jinan.

Qingdao airport is 30 km (19 mi) from the city center. Direct flights
link Qingdao with Osaka and Seoul, as well as Hong Kong and other
major Chinese cities. Flights can be booked through hotels or at CAAC.

➤ AIRPORT INFORMATION: **Jinan Airport** (☎ 0531/597–3853). **Qingdao Airport** (☎ 0532/471–5139).
➤ AIRLINES AND CONTACTS: **Qingdao CAAC** (✉ 29 Zhongshan Lu, ☎ 0532/289–5577, FAX 0532/287–0747).

BOAT AND FERRY TRAVEL

During the summer months, several boats a week link Qingdao with Shanghai. Ask at CITS or buy tickets at the passenger ferry terminal.
➤ BOAT AND FERRY INFORMATION: **CITS** (✉ 9 Nanhai Rd., Qingdao, ☎ 0532/288–0390). **Ferry Terminal** (✉ Xinjiang Jie near Friendship Store).

BUS TRAVEL

Regular buses link Qufu with Jinan, three hours away, and Taian, two hours away. Taian is about an hour from Jinan by bus. Buses ply the route between Qingdao and Jinan every 20 minutes, taking four to five hours. The bus terminals in Qingdao and Taian are opposite the respective train stations. In Qufu the bus station is south of the town center, at the intersection of Shen Dao and Jingxuan Lu.

TRAIN TRAVEL

Jinan station is on the Beijing–Shanghai rail line and the Beijing–Qingdao line, so there is no shortage of trains. The trip to Beijing takes about 5½ hours. Trains link the Qufu station with Jinan and Beijing. Taian station is on the main Beijing–Shanghai rail line with onward connections in either direction.

Direct trains link Qingdao with Beijing, Shanghai, Shenyang, Yantai, Xian, and Lanzhou.
➤ TRAIN INFORMATION: **Jinan Station** (☎ 0531/242–8862). **Qufu Station** (☎ 0537/442–1571). **Taian Station** (☎ 0538/824–6222).

4 NORTHEASTERN CHINA

INDUSTRY AND WILDERNESS

Northeastern China has the huge urban centers of modern China—some booming, some going bust—and a giant wilderness contiguous with Siberia. Also known as Manchuria, it has witnessed the rise of the Manchu dynasty, Russian adventurism, Japanese invasion, Chinese resistance, and Cold War hostility, and retains the architectural stamps of each. From Harbin's Ice Lantern Festival to the port of Dalian ("Hong Kong of the north") to the wilderness outside the cities, northeast China rewards travelers willing to leave the tourist trail with a surprising diversity.

T HE NORTHEAST, OR MANCHURIA—what the Chinese call Dongbei—consists of the provinces of Liaoning, Jilin, and Heilongjiang.
This land was home to China's last imperial house, the Qing, who
conquered Beijing in 1644 and ruled China until the 1911 Republican
revolution. The Qing were Manchus, who still survive as a distinct ethnic group in the Northeast.

By David
Murphy

Updated by
George
Vaughton

Until 1911 Han were forbidden to settle in Manchuria, and the area,
though agriculturally rich, was sparsely inhabited. In the 1920s,
driven by war and poverty, people flocked from neighboring Shandong across the Bohai Gulf to work as farmers or in the many Japanese factories that had been established in the puppet state of
Manchukuo. After the 1949 Communist Revolution, China's new
leader, Mao Zedong, encouraged people to fill the empty parts of
China. This created another massive flood of settlers, again mostly
from Shandong. As a result, many in these three northeasterly
provinces claim Shandong as their *laojia* (ancestral home). Most outsiders who come here are on business. Tourism facilities are not as
plentiful as they are in other parts of the country, but the resulting
peace and quiet can be a blessing.

Pleasures and Pastimes

Dining

The variety and value of food to be encountered in this region are as
good as anywhere in China. Cheap, clean restaurants are the best bet.
The high turnover gives you a better chance of avoiding stomach bugs.
The more expensive ones, unless very popular, are rarely worth it. Every
city has its own special local dish. Many outlets specialize in dishes
from other provinces, notably Sichuan. The coastal city of Dalian has
some of the best seafood in China. Farther north, hotpot is a great favorite; you can choose from any number of ingredients and spices to
cook food at your own table. Snacks, including yogurt, are available
at street corners.

If you want to take a break from Chinese food, you'll find Korean and
Japanese street-front and hotel restaurants in many cities. For Western food, it's better to stick to the restaurants in leading foreign-man-
aged or joint-venture hotels, which often have excellent-value
Western-style buffet lunches.

CATEGORY	COST*
$$$$	over Y250
$$$	Y100–Y250
$$	Y15–Y100
$	under Y15

Per person for a main course at dinner

Lodging

Nearly all hotels in this region are relatively modern and without any
special character. Most state-run hotels have musty rooms, poor service, and inadequate facilities—particularly for the price charged.
Some even impose extra charges on foreigners. Western–, Hong Kong–,
or Singaporean–managed hotels are far better. Occupancy is as low as
30% in some top-class hotels, and special deals are available; fax
ahead to request the hotel's best rate.

CATEGORY	COST*
$$$$	over Y1100
$$$	Y800–Y1100
$$	Y500–Y800
$	under Y500

Prices are for a standard double room with bath in high season.

Nightlife

In good weather the entire Chinese population seems to empty onto the streets or gather in public places at evening time. Young and old carry on a wide range of activities, from ballroom dancing to badminton, in the public squares and thoroughfares. Taking a stroll around these areas at night is hard to beat if you enjoy people-watching. Conventional nightlife is patchy. The karaoke plague is widespread, but there are signs that it has peaked.

Shopping

Markets are fun to look around and curios may take your fancy. Bargaining is advisable at all stalls and is possible in many stores.

Exploring Northeastern China

Of Dongbei's three provinces, Jilin and Heilongjiang are heavily agricultural, while Liaoning, the more southerly of the three, is industrial, home to many of China's big state-owned enterprises, which were built up during the 1950s and '60s. Most of Dongbei's cities are industrial and not especially pleasant to visit. However, ancient tombs in Shenyang and the Ice Festival in Harbin make these two worth the trip. The isolated Changbaishan Nature Reserve is dramatic and pristine, but getting there takes some planning.

Great Itineraries

The itineraries below are based on train journeys, but a combination of rail and flight is possible on any tour of this region.

Numbers in the margin correspond to points of interest on the Northeastern China and Dalian maps.

IF YOU HAVE 3 DAYS

Dalian, a former colonial center and today one of China's smartest cities, makes an excellent weekend trip from Beijing. Comfortable overnight sleeper trains are available from Beijing, departing at nightfall. Spend your days here in pure relaxation—having a round of golf, lounging on the beach, or taking a stroll along the coast roads—and at night indulge in the seafood extravaganza that is dining in Dalian.

IF YOU HAVE 5 DAYS

From **Dalian** take the train to **Changchun** (about eight hours), spend a day here exploring the history of the Japanese occupation of the area, and on the way back take a look at **Shenyang,** one of China's great industrial cities. The historical heritage here is of an older vintage, and the palace, pagodas, and tombs easily make for a couple days of sightseeing. From Dalian there are departures to Beijing (train, plane) and Shandong (boat, train).

IF YOU HAVE 8 OR MORE DAYS

Spend a couple of days in **Harbin,** which, even when the Ice Lantern Festival is not happening, has a rich architecture tradition, a picturesque shopping district, and some interesting markets. Then move south by train (four or five hours between cities) to stay two days each in **Changchun,** then **Shenyang,** and finally **Dalian,** on the tip of the Liaodong peninsula. From here you can take tours to spectacular nature reserves like Changbaishan. These four cities combined give a very full flavor

Habarovsk

Nenjiang

Yichun

Hegang

Jiamusi

Amur

Heilong Jiang

Wusuli Jiang

Qiqihar

Daqing

H E I L O N G J I A N G

Songhua Jiang

Jixi

Xingkai Hu

(Ozero Hanka)

1 Harbin

Baicheng

Fuyu

Mudan-
jiang

RUSSIA

Di'er Songhua Jiang

Changchun

2

4

**Jilin
City**

**5 Beidahu
Ski Resort**

Dunhua

Vladivostok

N E I M O N G O L
(INNER MONGOLIA)

6

Song Hua Hu

Yanji

J I L I N

Liaoyuan

**Changbaishan
Nature Reserve**

3

Tumen Jiang

Hunjiang

Shenyang

7

N

Fuxin

Fushun

Sea of Japan

Liaoyang

8

Jinzhou

Anshan

L I A O N I N G

*Liaodong
Wan*

Dandong

Yalu Jiang

**NORTH
KOREA**

0   100 miles

0   150 km

Korea Bay

⭐ Pyongyang

**Lushun
Prison**

14 **Jin Shi Tan**

13

Dalian

9 – 12

Bohai

⭐ Seoul

**SOUTH
KOREA**

Inchon

Yantai

N D O N G

Qingdao

*Huang Hae
(Yellow Sea)*

Taejon

Kwangju

Taegu

Pusan

of today's China: Harbin, with the intriguing flavor of a border town and a blend of cultures; Changchun, the standard Chinese provincial city; Shenyang, both hugely industrial (though on the decline) and rich in history; and Dalian, the up-and-coming coastal resort and typical East Chinese boom town. Visit **Jilin** if you have extra time.

When to Tour the Northeast

Late April and May are the best times to visit the region; the emergence of natural colors in springtime is a relief from the unrelenting grayness of the winter. Just before late September–early November is next best, when the countryside takes on rich natural hues and the climate remains comfortable. The area also has a number of winter attractions, primarily the outstanding Ice Lantern Festival in Harbin, but also the ice-covered trees of Jilin and several emerging ski resorts. In many cities, restaurants and other service- or visitor-oriented businesses close early in winter. Summer is hot and humid. Good hotels have air-conditioning, but many taxis and most offices do not.

HEILONGJIANG

With a relatively small population and an area of nearly 470,000 square km (181,500 square mi), Heilongjiang (Black Dragon River) is making a name for itself as an outdoor destination, with an emphasis on fishing and bird-watching. It was one of the points where imperial European expansion (in this case czarist Russia) met imperial China in the 19th century. Heilongjiang belonged to the vast swath of empty territory in east Asia that was colonized in the 20th century by European Russians and Han Chinese. Native tribes that survived in the Heilongjiang, for example the Oroqen, are now happy modern citizens of the People's Republic of China (PRC), according to the official press: it's difficult to infer from the prominent government reports what the true sentiment is.

The province is renowned for its rich black soil and is a major producer of grain. The Heilong River (Heilongjiang), known to the Russians as the Amur, provides the boundary between the province and Russia, though even today the border is not fully delineated.

Harbin

❶ *16 hrs (1,000 km/621 mi) northeast of Beijing by train and just over 2 hrs by plane.*

Harbin, on the banks of the Songhua River, takes its name from the Manchu word *alejin,* suggesting fame and reputation. It's the capital of the province and was once a Russian railway terminus for the line to Vladivostok. The city bounced between the Russians and the Japanese until after World War II. Today Russians are again on the scene— as tourists and traders. Winters are cold; temperatures average close to −20°C (−4°F) in January, the coldest month, and can plunge to −38°C (−36°F).

In winter the frozen water of the Songhua is bringing fame to Harbin, in the form of ever more intricate ice carvings. Massive blocks of ice are taken from the river by mechanical excavators and transported to Zhaolin Park. There artists carve the blocks into more than 1,000 fantastic ice sculptures, many with colored lanterns placed inside. Exhibitions regularly include versions of the Great Wall, famous pagodas, and the Xian warriors. The festival usually begins on January 5.

The **Daoli** District contains numerous buildings dating from the era of Russian domination in Harbin. Many have been restored in recent years, along with the cobblestone streets. The area centered on **Zhongyang Dajie** has been revitalized as a commercial district. A good stroll is down Zhongyang Dajie to the river embankment and the huge **Fanghong Jinian Ta** (Flood Control Monument), a column commemorating the construction of a flood-control embankment along the banks of the river. People practice tai chi here in the morning and *yang ge* (a rhythmic traditional dance) in the evenings. You can turn right down the **esplanade** (a favorite kite-flying spot) on the banks of the Songhua or left through the **night market** (mostly clothes), which runs parallel to the river and then winds around to Tongjiang Jie and the junction of Youyi Lu.

Zhaolin Gongyuan (Zhaolin Park) is where the bulk of Harbin's ice sculptures are displayed during the Ice Festival. At other times of year it's a pleasant place to stroll—you can barely hear the honking horns from here. Its weekend outdoor amusement park includes a Ferris wheel. ⊠ *Youyi Lu and Shangzhi Dajie, Daoli District.* ☜ *Y2.* ☉ *May–Sept., daily 7 AM–9 PM; Oct.–Apr., daily 8–7.*

About five minutes' walk east of the Flood Control Monument, **Dao Wai Jie Yu Shi Chang** (Dao Wai Street Fish Market) is not very well stocked in winter, but during the rest of the year a wide range of tropical fish (in jam jars and trays) are on sale here, as well as caged birds, flowers, teapots, raw tobacco, and much more. ⊠ *Dao Wai Jie, east of Flood Control Monument.*

☾ **Youle Yuan** (Youle Park) has kiddie rides, an indoor children's playground, and a large roller coaster. The pavements around it are lined with stalls selling Buddhist tokens, trinkets, and joss sticks for use in the nearby temples. ⊠ *Dongda Zhi Jie.* ☜ *Y2 (Y5 during the Ice Festival).* ☉ *May–Sept., daily 8 AM–9 PM; Oct.–Apr., daily 8–5.*

In winter, Harbinites build snow sculptures at **Taiyang Dao.** The area is home to a small military museum and an amusement park. It is a favorite walking and jogging spot for locals. ⊠ *North of city, across river, to right-hand side of bridge.*

Harbin has quite a few surviving Christian **churches,** many of them architectural as well as cultural novelties. Several of the establishments listed below are active places of worship, and although they charge no entry fee they are officially open only during service times. However, you may be able to talk the caretakers into letting you look around at other times. The **Russian Orthodox church** (⊠ 268 Dongda Zhi Jie, ☉ Sat. 2 PM service), built of redbrick with cupolas, stands in its own square, a reminder of the time when Russians dominated Harbin. Across the street from the Russian Orthodox church is a rather unimpressive, but active **Catholic church** (⊠ 211 Dongda Zhi Jie). Farther up the road, also in its own grounds, the busy **Protestant church** (⊠ 252 Dongda Zhi Jie; ☉ Wed., weekends, service times vary), built in 1910 by German missionaries, is a thriving center for the Harbin Protestant community. The elaborate Catholic **Wuhao Siguan Church** (⊠ 47 Sheke Jie, Nangang District) was built in 1922 and reopened in 1980 following a pause for the Cultural Revolution.

The most impressive church in Harbin is the 1907 **St. Sofia's Cathedral** (⊠ Zhaolin Jie, ☜ Y10), which until the 1960s served the more than 100 Russian residents of Harbin. The cathedral was closed down when the Russians were forced to leave China during the Cultural Revolution. The building's huge green onion dome atop a redbrick nave is striking in its incongruity with its surroundings. Until recently the cathedral was contained by a tight square of old six-story workers' apartments and a timber yard; but these have now been cleared away, and the cathedral stands resplendent in the center of a paved square. Despite the attention the physical structure has received, it no longer functions as a religious building. It's actually the Harbin Architecture Arts Center, housing an exhibition of photographs documenting the city's turbulent 20th-century history.

Dongda Zhi Jie is also the location of a cluster of **temples.** The Ji Le Si (Ji Le Temple; ✉ 9 Dongda Zhi Jie, 🎫 Y10, ☯ Daily 8–4:30) is a rather average Buddhist temple of the kind found in most cities, but worth a look if you haven't seen one before. The neighboring **Qiji Futu Ta** (Seven Layer Pagoda; ✉ 2 Dongda Zhi Jie, 🎫 Y20, ☯ Daily 8–4) contains some elegant examples of Chinese Buddhist architecture. The pick of the bunch is the **Pu Zhao Si** (Pu Zhao Temple; ✉ 1 Dongda Zhi Jie), an active place of Buddhist worship and home to a number of monks and nuns. It is only officially open to the public on the first and fifteenth day of each lunar month (for prayers), but offers a rare glimpse of a working monastery.

Dining and Lodging

In Harbin particularly—though the practice can be seen elsewhere in the Northeast—red lanterns are hung outside Chinese restaurants to denote cost and quality. The greater the number—the maximum is usually five—the higher the cost and quality. Blue lanterns denote Hui (a Muslim minority) restaurants.

$$–$$$ ✕ **Portman Western Restaurant.** This is Harbin's latest entrant in the competition to serve good European cuisine. The interior is cozy, with comfortable upholstered chairs and dark wooden fittings. The menu has mainly Russian dishes, with an emphasis on river and lake fish, and the international drinks list is extensive. A live pianist plays during weekend evenings. ✉ 63 Xiqi Daojie, off Zhongyang Dajie, ☎ 0451/468–6888. No credit cards.

$$ ✕ **Huamei Restaurant.** Opposite the Modern Hotel on Zhongyang Dajie, this novel restaurant was built in the 1920s by Russian expatriates. Of the three floors, by far the best is the second, with its wooden floor and high, ornate ceiling supported by Greek-style columns. The walls are hung with pastoral Russian scenes. Cold dishes include caviar and sour cucumber and thick slabs of white bread accompanied by plates of jam. The main courses are Russian, Chinese, and French—chicken and fish au gratin, braised mutton chops, and shashlik à la russe are among the main courses. Huamei is also open as a café between meals, with inexpensive (Y2) coffee served thick and sweet, with enough sugar to keep you buzzing for a week. ✉ 112 Zhongyang Dajie, Daoli District, ☎ 0451/467–5574. No credit cards.

$$ ✕ **Million Land House Restaurant.** This large open-plan restaurant is one of the best in Harbin. It serves some excellent seafood, including pearl fish cooked in a light batter and dipped in salt; scallops; and North Pole shrimp, which is first cooked and then frozen before being served. Also on the menu are frozen tofu and hotpot. ✉ 169 Zhongshan Lu, Nangang District, ☎ 0451/261–1111. No credit cards.

$$ ✕ **Shun Feng.** This 24-hour restaurant, immensely popular with locals, is plainly furnished with wooden tables and chairs. It has a glossy picture menu and specializes in beef hotpot, although plenty of other meats, vegetables, and seafood are available. ✉ 107 Wen Chang Jie, Nangang District, ☎ 0451/268–8888. No credit cards.

$–$$ ✕ **Lao Du Yi Chu.** This time-honored restaurant has been serving jiaozi (dumplings) to the people of Harbin since 1929, and many locals claim it is still the best place to go if you want the real thing. Look for the big "1" sign outside. ✉ 25 Xi Shisan Daojie, off Zhaoyang Dajie, ☎ 0451/461–5895. No credit cards.

$$$$ 🏨 **Shangri-La.** Ideally situated for a winter trip to Harbin, this luxurious hotel overlooks the stretch of the Songhua River on which a large portion of the Ice Festival takes place. The stylish green and gold rooms come complete with minibar, electronic safe, color TV, IDD phone, and computer/fax lines. ✉ *555 Youyi Lu, Daoli District, 150018,* ☎ *0451/485–8888,* FAX *0451/462–1777,* WEB *www.shangri-la.com. 300 rooms and 46 suites. 2 restaurants, bar, indoor pool, tennis court, gym. AE, DC, MC, V.*

$$$–$$$$ 🏨 **Holiday Inn.** At this modern hotel in the Daoli District standard rooms are a little dark but otherwise comfortable. They are equipped with a minibar and color TV with movie channels. The restaurants serve Chinese and Western food. ✉ *90 Jingwei Jie, Daoli District, 150010,* ☎ *0451/422–6666,* FAX *0451/422–1661,* WEB *www.holiday-inn.com/harbincn 143 rooms. 2 restaurants, bar, gym, nightclub, business services. AE, DC, MC, V.*

$$ 🏨 **Gloria Inn.** Large and modern, this hotel occupies an impressive building constructed in the old neoclassical European style near the Flood Control Monument. Standard rooms are bright and comfortable and are equipped with a minibar, refrigerator, and satellite TV. There is a Cantonese restaurant and a coffee shop serving Western and Asian food. ✉ *257 Zhongyang Dajie, Daoli District, 150010,* ☎ *0451/463–8855,* FAX *0451/463–8533,* WEB *www.giharbin.com. 304 rooms. 2 restaurants, nightclub, business services. AE, DC, MC, V.*

$–$$ 🏨 **Modern Hotel.** The rooms in this Russian-era hotel are comfortable, with high ceilings and drapes suspended to create a four-poster effect on the beds. Try to get a room overlooking fashionable Zhongyang Dajie (unless you are a light sleeper). There are also cheaper simply furnished rooms. ✉ *89 Zhongyang Dajie, 150010,* ☎ *0451/461–5846,* FAX *0451/461–4997. 133 rooms. 2 restaurants, bar, business services. AE, DC, MC, V.*

$–$$ 🏨 **Lungmen Hotel.** An excellent value, the Lungmen is directly opposite the main railway station. The rooms are clean and quiet and have minibars, Internet connections, and satellite TV. Rooms in the newer building are nicer, though more expensive, than those in the original structure. ✉ *85 Hongjun Jie, 150001,* ☎ *0451/642–6810,* FAX *0451/ 363–9700,* WEB *www.lmhotel.com.cn. 252 rooms. 2 restaurants, bar, gym, business services. AE, MC, V.*

$ 🏨 **Hong Kong Palace Hotel.** Overlooking Zhaolin Park, this friendly hotel has the same owner as Beijing's Jianguo Hotel. Rooms are clean and bright, with a minibar and satellite TV. The restaurant serves Chinese food, and the café offers Western and Southeast Asian food. ✉ *212 Shangzhi Jie, 150010,* ☎ *0451/469–1388,* FAX *0451/461–0894. 106 rooms. 2 restaurants, business services. MC, V.*

Nightlife

Harbin nightlife is fairly quiet. One place that's worth a visit is the **Log-cabin Bar** (✉ 24 Zhongxuan Jie, Nangang District, ☎ 0451/264–9797), which is tastefully decorated, has good beer, pool tables—and no karaoke facility. Local musicians playing various styles (country and western, rock) provide the entertainment. One of the nicest cafés in northern China, **Russia** (✉ 57 Xitou Daojie, Daoli District, ☎ 0451/456–3202) is the ideal spot to defrost after a day on the Ice. Housed in a Russian-era building near the north end of Zhongyang Dajie, it serves perfect coffee and crepes in an old-world setting.

Shopping

Besides the area around Zhongyang Dajie and the night market near the Flood Control Monument, a couple of other places in Harbin have some interesting shopping. The outdoor **Minmao Shi Chang** (Minmao Market) deals mostly in clothes but also sells souvenirs, antiques, fishing rods, and an inordinate number of binoculars, telescopes, and hand-held periscopes. Soviet-era stamps, watches, ginseng, Russian babushka dolls, and dried penises—several varieties (they're traditional medicine, mind you)—are also available. The market is busiest on the weekends, and many Russians come from the border city of Khabarovsk to buy goods for resale at home. The touts and money-changers speak Russian to foreigners.

A massive bomb shelter built at a time of high tension between China and Soviet Russia is now home to a booming shopping center in the **Nangang** District (✉ Dongda Zhi Jie), where clothes, leather, and household goods are available.

Heilongjiang A to Z

To research prices, get advice from other travelers, and book travel arrangements, visit www.fodors.com.

AIR TRAVEL
Regular flights link Harbin with major Chinese cities including Beijing and Shanghai.

TAXIS
Taxis are the easiest way to get around Harbin. Flag fall is Y10, and all the cabs have meters. In Daoli District going by foot gives you more time to appreciate the area's unique architecture.

TRAIN TRAVEL
There are regular rail connections between Harbin and Changchun (four hours) and points south, including Shenyang, Dalian, and Beijing. Keep in mind that no one at the general inquiries line is likely to speak English; travelers generally buy tickets through hotels and travel agents, which charge a commission.
➤ INFORMATION: **Rail Inquiries** (☎ 0451/642–0115).

VISITOR INFORMATION
➤ TOURIST INFORMATION: **CITS** (✉ 2 Tielu Jie, Nangang District, 11th Floor of the Hushi Building, to the south of the train station entrance, ☎ 0451/367–2074, 𝔽𝔸𝕏 0451/367–1789).

JILIN

Jilin is the smallest of the three provinces that together make up the Chinese region of Dongbei. It is bordered by North Korea to the southeast, Liaoning to the south, Inner Mongolia to the west, and Heilongjiang to the north. It has a population of about 27 million, the bulk of whom are Han; many ethnic Koreans live in the Korean border area.

Changchun

❷ *12 hrs by train (850 km/527 mi) or 1½ hrs by plane from Beijing.*

Changchun (Long Spring) is a name based more in hope than reality, given the long, cold winters of China's northeast. Under Japanese rule from 1931 to 1945, Changchun was renamed Xinjing (New Capital) when it was made capital of the puppet state of Manchukuo. It's now the provincial capital of Jilin. After the 1949 revolution Changchun was established as China's very own motor city—home to First Auto Works (FAW), and more recently FAW's large joint-venture Volkswagen plant (joint ventures are one of the few ways foreign companies are allowed to operate in China), which dominate industry here. Chinese president Jiang Zemin worked here as a factory director in the late 1930s. Today the pleasant city of some 6.8 million has wide avenues, lined with evergreen trees, which make for pleasant walks, notably in the areas around Xinfa Lu and Renmin Guangchang.

In **Weihuanggong** (the Puppet Emperor's Palace), Puyi, China's last emperor before the 1911 revolution, was set up by Japan to be the nominal head of the state of Manchukuo. Appropriately, the palace of the puppet emperor has a puppet feel to it. The buildings are more suited to a wealthy merchant than to the successor to a nearly 300-year-old dynasty and offer no sense that power resided here. Puyi's former house is now a museum documenting his life from childhood through his role as a pawn of the Japanese and then after the 1949 Revolution to his conversion as a citizen of the new China. Photos are on display in an adjacent courtyard house—one shows Hitler and the Manchukuo economic minister shaking hands during the latter's trip to Europe. Some torture instruments, including a bed of nails, depict the savagery of the Japanese war in China. There are also details on the notorious Camp 731, where crude experiments were carried out on prisoners of war. ⊠ *5 Guangfu Beilu,* ☎ *0431/566–7139.* ▩ *Y20.* ☉ *May–Sept., daily 8:30–5; Oct.–Apr., daily 8:30–4:30.*

The **Changchundianying Zhipianchang** (Changchun Film Studio), home to a large slice of China's movie industry, contains screen props of palaces, castles, and scenery. If you're lucky you may even get to see scenes being filmed. ⊠ *28 Huxi Lu, Chaoyang District,* ☎ *0431/762–8737.* ▩ *Y20.* ☉ *Daily 8–4.*

Changchun Dianying Cheng (Changchun Film City) is a glitzier themepark version of the Film Studio. It's divided into thematic areas, including a huge indoor "undersea world" aquarium, traditional Chinese and European architecture zones, a dinosaur world, and a children's cartoon park. ⊠ *92 Zhengyang Jie, Luyuan District,* ☎ *0431/595–3511.* ▩ *Y80 all-inclusive, or Y15 for park entry plus Y15–Y30 per attraction.* ☉ *Daily 8:30–5.*

Bai Quan Di Yi Ke Daxue (Bethune First Medical University) is named for Canadian surgeon Norman Bethune, who was with the Republicans in 1930s Spain before working with the Communists at their base in Yanan in Shaanxi province. Built between 1933 and 1936, the university was modeled on Tokyo's parliament building; during the Japanese occupation it housed the Manchukuo Parliament. The fourth floor houses a small museum dedicated to this regime, but all captions are in Chinese. The ground-floor shop stocks a range of ginseng and medicinal products. The prize of the tour is on the first floor, where a collection of specimens of human body parts, in row upon row of formaldehyde jars, is stored. It's interesting, though not for the squeamish. ⊠ *2 Xin Min Dajie, next to Wenhua Guangchang and opposite the Bethune Hospital.* ▩ *Free; Y8 for the museum.* ☉ *Daily 9–7.*

Banruo Si (Banruo Monastery) was established in 1921, turned into a cardboard-box factory in 1966 at the beginning of the Cultural Revolution, and restored to its role as a monastery after 1982. Forty Buddhist monks now live here. The Grand Hall occupies the center of a courtyard complex that includes the reception, meditation, dining, and head monk's halls. In the Great Hall you can write down a prayer, strike a bell, and hope your prayer is answered. Inside the main gate are two drum towers. The drums are sounded on the arrival of an important visitor. ⊠ *Changchun Lu, Nanguan District.* ☉ *Daily 8–3.*

A monument in the center of **Renmin Guangchang** (People's Square)—actually a circular green area—commemorates the Soviet liberation of Changchun from the Japanese in 1945. It's a great place for people-watching in the evening or early morning. ☒ *Bounded by Renmin Lu, Changchun Lu, Minkang Lu, and Xian Lu.*

Around **Xinfa Lu,** on pleasant tree-lined avenues—good for strolling—are a number of buildings dating from the Japanese era, now occupied by the current provincial government.

Dining and Lodging

$$–$$$$ ✕ **Tongda Restaurant.** Marked by garish plastic greenery draped from ceiling beams, this restaurant nevertheless serves good northeastern cuisine, including stewed pork, and such southern imports as spare ribs steamed in lotus leaves. A specialty of the house is braised ginseng root and deer penis. ☒ *60 Tongzhi Jie, Chaoyang District, 130021,* ☎ *0431/ 563–2682. No credit cards.*

$$–$$$ ✕ **Ben Tu Feng.** One of a growing number of Japanese eateries in town, this charmingly decorated little restaurant offers a range of authentic sushi, sashimi, tempura, and udon noodles, all served by Japanese exchange students from the city's universities. ☒ *4 Ming De Lu,* ☎ *0431/566–2899. No credit cards.*

$$–$$$ ✕ **Tai Shan Hotel Korean Restaurant.** On the ground floor of the Tai Shan Hotel this dimly lit open-plan restaurant serves familiar Korean food, including spring onion pancakes and ginseng chicken soup. ☒ *35 Tongzhi Jie, Chaoyang District, 130021,* ☎ *0431/563–4991. AE, DC, MC, V.*

$–$$ ✕ **Eastern King of Dumpling Restaurant.** Walk the length of this unpretentious restaurant, which has several sections, to see the chefs rolling the dough and preparing the fillings for the thousands of tasty jiaozi served here daily. You can mix your own dip with mustard, garlic, chili, soy sauce, and vinegar. Prepare to be amazed at the accuracy and flourish with which waiters refill your tea from a pot with a 3-ft spout. ☒ *59 Gongnong Lu,* ☎ *0431/560–2847. No credit cards.*

$$$$ 🏨 **Shangri-La.** Changchun's best hotel is modern, centrally located,
★   stylish, and charming throughout. The wood paneling in the public areas and the friendly staff give it a slightly old-fashioned feel. All rooms have a color TV and in-house movies, minibar, refrigerator, 24-hour room service, a full-size executive desk, and fax, phone, and computer outlets. There are both Chinese and Western restaurants. ☒ *9 Xian Dalu, 130061,* ☎ *0431/898–1818,* FAX *0431/898–1919,* WEB *www.shangri-la.com. 458 rooms. 3 restaurants, bar, room service, pool, tennis, bowling, gym, business services. AE, MC, V.*

$$$ 🏨 **Changchun Nobel.** This 25-floor hotel is the only one in northeastern China that has a Thai restaurant. The lobby gleams with its polished stone floor and pillars. The elegant rooms have color TVs with in-house movie channels and 24-hour room service. ☒ *135 Renmin Lu, 130021,* ☎ *0431/562–2888,* FAX *0431/566–5522. 300 rooms. 3 restaurants, bar, pool, bowling, gym, business services. AE, DC, MC, V.*

$$ 🏨 **The Swiss Belhotel.** Its revolving hotpot restaurant is worth a visit for the view it offers of the city. Standard rooms are spacious, well furnished, and have color TVs with in-house movies, minibar and refrigerator, and an executive desk. ☒ *39 Chuang Ye Da Jie, 130011,* ☎ *0431/598–8888,* FAX *0431/598–9999,* WEB *www.swiss-belhotel.com. 230 rooms. 2 restaurants, bar, pool, tennis court, gym, business services. AE, DC, MC, V.*

$ 🏨 **South Lake Hotel.** This postrevolution hotel has high ceilings and the musty smell of Chinese state-run hostelries. The rooms are average, but the hotel is set in huge wooded grounds peppered with guest buildings and villas, which you can also rent. Many of the villas are occupied by VW staff from the FAW factory. Top leaders stay here when they come to Changchun. ☒ *2 Nanhu Dalu, 130022,* ☎ *0431/568– 3571,* FAX *0431/568–2559. 250 rooms. AE, DC, MC, V.*

Nightlife and the Arts

The **Cultural and Entertainment Center** (✉ Near junction of Renmin Lu and Jiefang Lu) frequently puts on plays (in Chinese).

A number of bars in Changchun have live music. Be warned, though, that establishments here can close down as suddenly as they appear. The **Happy Hour Bar** (✉ 19 Longli Lu, behind the Nobel Hotel, ☎ 0431/567–2769) sees a lively crowd of Chinese, Koreans, and Westerners mix at its bars and small dance floor. Many of the Happy Hour clientele head to the **New Millennium Club** (✉ 34 Guilin Lu, ☎ 0431/566–4409) disco later in the evening, where African DJs (mainly exchange students) keep the show going well into the early hours. **Second Home** (✉ Across from Shangri-La, ☎ 0543/896–9086, ☉ Daily 7 PM–10 PM) is a favorite for foreigners; on weekends you'll see a crowd of German autoworkers ordering Johnny Walker Black by the bottle and singing Bayern Munich football songs.

Outdoor Activities and Sports

Changchun is home to the **Jilin Tigers** (✉ Changchun Renmin Dajie), one of the stars of the CNBA (China National Basketball Alliance); they compete against the likes of the Beijing Lions, Guangzhou Rams, and Shanghai Nanyang. The season runs from November through March, and games are played two or three evenings a week.

Shopping

DEPARTMENT STORES

The most modern department store in Changchun, **Changchun Mall** (✉ 2 Liaoning Lu, ☎ 0431/271–1601, ☉ Daily 9–8:30), is opposite the railway station. The upscale **Charter Shopping Center** (✉ 99 Chongqing Lu, next to the Shangri-La, ☎ 0431/896–3423) stocks everything from brand-name perfumes to imported electronic goods. The **Friendship Store** (✉ Ziyou Lu, ☎ 0431/569–9278) sells Chinese paintings and furniture.

MARKETS

The best place for souvenirs in Changchun is the **Jilin Guwu Cheng** (Jilin antiques market; ✉ 15 Chongqing Lu, second floor of the Heping Da Shijie Building). The entire floor is taken up with stamps and phone cards, metal and ceramic badges from the Cultural Revolution, coins, banknotes, and secondhand cameras. There are also paintings, calligraphy posters, carved jade, wood and walnut carvings, wall clocks, phonographs, and a whole shop dedicated to Mao paraphernalia.

Guilin Lu Shichang (Guilin Road Market; ✉ Guilin Lu, Chaoyang District) is a large indoor market for one-stop shopping. Meat, fruit, and vegetables are displayed in open stalls, as are fish (from Dalian), cigarettes, spices, alcohol, canned foods, and household hardware. In the Guangfu Lu vicinity is **Pifa Shichang,** a large indoor wholesale market selling everything from household furniture to Pepsi, which is made locally. The streets nearby are lined with stalls. The **French Bakery** (✉ 33 Guilin Lu, ☎ 0431/562–3994) makes a range of good breads, pizza, and fruit tarts. Take away, or eat in with a coffee.

Side Trips from Changchun

Jingyue Hu (Clear Moon Lake) was built by the Japanese as a reservoir to serve Changchun. It lies in a large pine-wooded area where horse riding and boating facilities are available. A hotel and villas are concentrated near the entrance to the area; on the far side of the lake is a practice ski slope. ✉ *20 mins southeast of city center by car.*

Changbaishan Nature Reserve

★ ❸ *300 km (186 mi) southeast of Changchun or Jilin.*

The main attraction in this huge forest reserve is **Tianchi** (Heavenly Pool), a lake in the crater of a now-extinct volcano, on the Chinese–North Korean border. Sacred to Korean culture, it draws thousands of South Korean visitors every year and has spectacular views, particularly in autumn and winter. The area is part of the Yanbian Korean Autonomous Prefecture and is home to large numbers of ethnic Koreans. (Certain areas in China with a high percentage of ethnic minorities are granted "autonomous" status, meaning they have [limited] powers to decide on local issues independently of central government.) The lower slopes are densely wooded, but vegetation becomes sparse higher up. Bathing in hot springs and hiking are just two of the activities possible here. Three-day CITS tours are available from Changchun or Jilin between early June and early September. You can also hire a car from Baihe, the small town nearest Changbaishan. In summer accommodations are available in the reserve (expensive) or in Baihe (cheaper), but the reserve is open year-round, as long as the road isn't iced over.

Jilin City

❹ *2½ hrs by car or train (95 km/59 mi) east of Changchun.*

Jilin City, on the banks of the winding Songhua River, is the second-largest city in the province (but small by Chinese standards). Although it's an industrial center, local authorities are making a determined effort to draw tourists by promoting winter activities. Ski resorts around the city, an ice festival, and the phenomenon of ice-rimmed trees are all being peddled as worthy attractions.

The city is set in picturesque lake and mountain scenery, such as that in **Bei Shan Gongyuan** (North Mountain Park). On the south side of the park's lake are a number of pavilions. The main attraction here is the **Guan Di Si** (Guan Emperor Temple), founded in 1701 and named 50 years later by the emperor Qian Long for one of his predecessors. Among several lesser temples nearby are the **San Wang Miao** (Three Kings Temple) and the **Yao Wang Miao** (King of Medicine Temple). ⊠ *West side of city behind Beishan railway station,* ☎ *0432/484–3283.* ⌑ *Y5.*

Jilin has made a virtue out of ugly industrial development in the form of its **rime trees.** A hydroelectric plant, which supplies power to Jilin's industries, takes in cold water from the Songhua River and expels warm water. The vapor, which rises from the river as it flows along in the depths of winter, freezes on the trees overhanging the river bank, resulting in the sort of picturesque scene beloved by Japanese, Korean, and Chinese tourists. ⊠ *Take Bus 9 from roundabout north of Xiguan Hotel on Songjiang Lu to hydroelectric plant.*

The twin spires of the Gothic-style **Catholic Church** reach nearly 150 ft. Catholics first arrived in Jilin in 1898 and began construction of the church in 1917. Its doors opened in 1926, and it still serves the local Catholic community, who come in large numbers for the main Christian festivals. ⊠ *3 Song Jiang Lu,* ☎ *0432/202–5142.*

Dining and Lodging

$$–$$$$ ✕ **Yang Guang Yan Yuan.** The ground floor of this establishment—one of the most popular in town—serves snacks and quick meals, while upstairs is a more formal dining room. Hundreds of plates of ingredients and tank-fulls of live seafood are displayed, complete with

prices, for you to select and send off to the kitchen. ⊠ *1 Yangguang Lu,* ☎ *0432/253–0888. No credit cards.*

$$ ✕ **Dong Sheng Xing Islamic Restaurant.** This two-story restaurant serves traditional Hui food, such as lamb, beef, and noodle dishes. ⊠ *Tianjin Lu (opposite Xin Hua Theater),* ☎ *0432/243–1016. No credit cards.*

$$ ✕ **Xin Xing Yuan Dumpling Restaurant.** Jiaozi and northeastern dishes are the specialty in this white two-story restaurant. Try the entire banquet of dumplings, which include many unusual shapes and fillings. ⊠ *115 He Nan Jie,* ☎ *0432/202–4393. No credit cards.*

$$$ ⊡ **The Century Swiss-Belhotel.** The most upscale hotel in Jilin offers sumptuous accommodation just south of the town center. Cozy rooms and a whole suite of relaxation facilities—including a Finnish sauna and Turkish steam bath; Thai, Korean, Chinese, and Japanese shiatsu massage; and a 100-ft indoor heated swimming pool—make for a very comfortable stay (especially after working it on the night club's dance floor). ⊠ *77 Jilin St., 132013* ☎ *0432/464–9888,* ℻ *0432/464–9000,* 𝖶𝖤𝖡 *www.swiss-belhotel.com. 166 rooms and suites. 3 restaurants, bar, business center, gym, pool, squash. AE, DC, MC, V.*

$$$ ⊡ **Jilin Crystal Hotel.** On the banks of the Songhua River and near the foot of scenic Longtan Mountain, this seven-story hotel (also known as Rime Hotel) has a short, sloping roof. Rooms are equipped with TVs and minibars. ⊠ *29 Longtan Dajie, 132021,* ☎ *0432/398–6200,* ℻ *0432/398–6501. 113 rooms. 3 restaurants, bar, pool, bowling, gym. AE, DC, MC, V.*

$ ⊡ **Jiangcheng Hotel.** This seven-story hotel has the huge gleaming lobby common in China's newer hotels. It stands beside Qingnian Park on the banks of the Songhua River. Rooms have TVs. ⊠ *4 Jiangwan Lu, 132001,* ☎ *0432/245–7721,* ℻ *0432/245–8973,* 𝖶𝖤𝖡 *www.jlcta.com.cn. 111 rooms. Restaurant, gym, business services. AE, DC, MC, V.*

Shopping

Jilin Department Store (⊠ 179 Jilin Dajie, ☎ 0432/245–5489) has four floors of household goods and food. **East Shopping Building** (⊠ 131 Henan Lu, ☎ 0432/202–4831) is an all-purpose shopping center with an emphasis on domestic appliances and clothing.

Side Trips from Jilin City

❺ Beidahu Ski Resort, 65 km (40 mi) from the city center, has five slopes. Snow stays on the ground here from December to mid-March. The resort has a small hotel and restaurants that serve Western and Hui food. ⊠ *Wu Li He Town, Yong Ji County,* ☎ *0432/420–2222.*

The Songhua River flows from the Changbaishan Mountains into long, narrow **❻ Song Hua Hu** (Song Hua Lake) before continuing on its way about 24 km (15 mi) southeast of the city center. It was built as a reservoir between 1937 and 1943. Boating facilities are available on the lake amid beautiful natural surroundings. Tours are available through CITS.

Jilin A to Z

To research prices, get advice from other travelers, and book travel arrangements, visit www.fodors.com.

AIR TRAVEL

Changchun Airport is 10 km (6 mi) west of the city center. Regular flights link it with Beijing, Shanghai, Guangzhou, Shenzhen, and less frequently, Hong Kong and Irkutsk, in Siberia. Jilin City airport is 25 km (15 mi) outside the city and has scheduled flights to Beijing, Shanghai, and Guangzhou, as well as to Shenyang, Dalian, and Harbin.

➤ AIRPORT INFORMATION: **Changchun Airport** (☎ 0431/798–7841). **Jilin City Airport** (☎ 0432/351–3000).

BUS TRAVEL

Express buses link the Linjiang long distance bus station (west of the Yinhe hotel) in Jilin with Changchun's long distance bus station (south of Weixing Square, at the southern extreme of Renmin Dajie) every half hour. The trip costs Y30 and takes around 90 minutes.

EMERGENCIES

Dial 120 to call the hospital in Changchun. You can find medicines at the state-owned medicine shop, which is open 24 hours and stocks Chinese-style Western medicines, or at the Lobby shop, which stocks some Western medicines. In a medical emergency, consult your hotel; most operators at emergency numbers will not speak English.
➤ CONTACTS: **Changchun Hospital emergency line** (☎ 120). **Lobby shop** (✉ Shangri-La Hotel, 9 Xian Dalu, Changchun). **Medicine shop** (✉ Tongzhi Jie, Changchun).

TAXIS

In both Changchun and Jilin taxis are inexpensive and the most convenient means of transportation. For longer trips outside the cities, check with the hotels or tour operators.

TRAIN TRAVEL

The Changchun railway station is about 15 minutes north of downtown. Trains link it with Harbin, Jilin, Shenyang, Dalian, and Beijing regularly. The Jilin City train station is served by trains from Beijing, Shenyang, Dalian, Harbin, and Changchun.
➤ TRAIN INFORMATION: **Jilin City train station** (Off Yanan Yu, ☎ 0432/454–529).

VISITOR INFORMATION

➤ TOURIST INFORMATION: **CITS** (✉ 7th floor of the Yinmao Dasha building, 14 Xinmin Dajie, Changchun, ☎ 0431/560–9039; ✉ 4th floor of the Jiangcheng Hotel, Jilin City, ☎ 0432/243–6810, FAX 0432/243–6811).

LIAONING

Home to a large percentage of China's state-owned industry, Liaoning was better off than many during the postrevolution period, when steel mills and a wide range of manufacturing industries were set up. Then it was China's powerhouse. Nowadays state-owned industry is in terminal decline, teetering under the strong winds of market reform. Unemployment is rife, and the province has so far failed to attract the levels of investment that have allowed the other great industrial center, Shanghai, to create new jobs to replace old ones. The one success story in Liaoning, Dalian is blessed by natural and administrative advantages—among them a port and preferential tax breaks—but it too is being limited by the poverty of its hinterland.

Shenyang

❼ *2 hours (280 km/174 mi) by express train southwest of Changchun; 9 hours (600 km/372 mi) by express train northeast of Beijing.*

The modern provincial capital, Shenyang (formerly Mukden) became the capital of Manchuria under the warrior king Nurhachi in the 16th century. In 1644 when the Manchus took Beijing and founded the Qing dynasty, which ruled China until the 1911 revolution, Manchuria remained a place apart from the rest of China, and Mukden remained its capital. Mao Zedong's new China added to the industry the Japanese had established here, and Shenyang was a key city in the industrial drive of the 1950s and '60s. With the switch to market reforms Shenyang lost its edge to the busy coastal cities. Today it is a place of high unemployment and industrial decay.

Although not a particularly beautiful place, Shenyang has something to offer in the way of imperial tombs, pagodas, and the old Imperial Palace, predecessor of Beijing's Forbidden City.

The **Gugong** (Imperial Palace) was home to the Manchu emperors before they conquered the rest of China and established themselves in Beijing. Dating from the early 17th century, it is very similar to the capital's Forbidden City, but smaller, less crowded, and of greater architectural variety. ⊠ *171 Shenyang Lu,* ☎ *024/2484–4192.* ☞ *Y35.* ☉ *Daily 8:30–5:30).*

Zhongshan Guangchang (Sun Yat-sen Square) makes for a great after-dinner stroll, weather permitting. It's overlooked by a huge fiberglass statue of the late Chairman Mao surrounded by heroic workers, peasants, and soldiers. Mao's majestic wave is interpreted by the local kids as the Chairman trying to flag down a taxi. ⊠ *Nanjing Jie and Zhongshan Lu.*

The sight of stern, gray Gothic-style **Nanguan Catholic Church of the Sacred Heart of Jesus,** set amid the apartment blocks and hutongs of urban China, is arresting. Built in 1878, it burned during the Boxer Rebellion in 1900. Its spires rise 120 ft into Shenyang's gray sky. ⊠ *40 Nan Le Jiao Lu, Xiao Nan Da Jie, Shenhe District.* ☎ *024/2484–3986.* ☉ *About 5:30 AM–about 6 PM.*

The courtyard of the Buddhist **Ci En Fozhao Si** (Loving Kindness Buddhist Temple) has seen a lot. Founded during the Tang dynasty, it was rebuilt in the Qing, and then during the Cultural Revolution it was converted into a factory. The reforms of the 11th Party Congress in 1977 paved the way for its restoration, though the factory did not finally pull out until 10 years later. Monks now live in this pleasant temple, and worshipers burn incense in bronze containers and bow to the Buddhist statues in the halls. The alleys around the monastery are lined with stalls selling Buddha statues, trinkets, and incense. ⊠ *Ci En Si Hutong, Da Nan Jie.* ☉ *Daily 7–4.* ☞ *Free.*

The old city of Shenyang was ringed by **pagodas,** which are now well within the urban area. Although they're in various stages of disrepair, they provide oases of calm and architectural delight amongst the modern industrial chaos. Beautifully secluded in the northeast of the city is the **Sheli Ta** (Sheli Pagoda; ⊠ Alley 45, Tawan Jie, ☞ Y4, ☉ Daily 8:30–4:30), a thousand-year-old Buddhist tower and temple courtyard. (Chinese temples generally take the form of a large rectangular courtyard, within which are various halls, gateways, and gardens.) Side buildings house a photographic exhibition of Chinese pagodas and stupas, which is interesting despite the Chinese-only captions. The **Beita** (Northern Pagoda; ⊠ 27 Beita Jie, off Chongshan Donglu, ☞ Y5, ☉ Daily 8–5) is one of the best preserved of the lot, and has a small museum with an impressive model of the ancient city of Shenyang.

Set in parkland in the north of the city, **Beiling** (North Tomb) is the burial place of Huang Taiji (1592–1643), founder of the Qing dynasty. Inside the entrance a short avenue is lined with stone animals surrounded by pine trees, good feng shui tokens. The burial mound is at the rear of the complex and can be viewed from the top of the wall that encircles the two large central courtyards. Some of the outer buildings house souvenir shops, while another contains the 400-year-old bodies of a government official and his wife on open display. ✉ *Taishan Lu, north side of city,* 🎟 *Y3 for park; Y10 for tomb area.*

Dining and Lodging

$$ ✕ **Dong Lai Shun.** Cook your own beef, squid, shellfish, rice noodles, green vegetables, or a host of other dainties in a copper hotpot of constantly boiling water placed on your table in this clean, reasonably priced restaurant. Hotpot is a winter favorite in the north of China, though it is eaten year-round. You can also choose cold plates and enjoy the sesame sauce, soy, chili, bean curd sauce, and sour mustard dips that come with the hotpot. ✉ *23 Huanghe Nan Dajie, Heping District,* ☎ *024/8685–5555. No credit cards.*

$$ ✕ **Na Jia Guan.** This local specialty restaurant, just west of the Gugong, serves up the traditional cuisine of the Manchu people, the original inhabitants of northeast China. Dishes tend to be hearty and meat-based, with plenty of pickles and stewed dishes. ✉ *90 Shenyang Lu, Shenhe District,* ☎ *024/2485–7761. No credit cards.*

$–$$ ✕ **Lao Bian Dumpling Restaurant.** In business for 170 years and now in the hands of the fourth generation of the founding family, this spartan two-story restaurant is famous in Shenyang for its jiaozi. ✉ *57 Beishi Yi Lu, Heping District,* ☎ *024/2272–1819. No credit cards.*

$$$$ 🏨 **Traders Shenyang Hotel.** Part of the rapidly growing Shangri-La hotel chain, the Traders Shenyang is modern and centrally located. Comfortable, tastefully furnished standard rooms are equipped with minibar, refrigerator, executive desk, and satellite TV. ✉ *68 Zhong Hua Lu, Heping District, 110001,* ☎ *024/2341–2288,* 🖷 *024/2341–1988,* 🌐 *www.shangri-la.com. 92 rooms. 2 restaurants, bar, gym, nightclub, business services. AE, DC, MC, V.*

$$$ 🏨 **Gloria Plaza.** This modern hotel stands opposite the North Railway Station in Shenyang's commercial district, just 10 minutes from the Imperial Palace. Standard rooms are bright and comfortable, and all are equipped with satellite TV, minibar, and refrigerator. The restaurants serve Chinese food; a café serves Western dishes. ✉ *32 Yingbin Jie, Shenhe District, 110013,* ☎ *024/2252–8885,* 🖷 *024/2252–8533,* 🌐 *www.gloriahotels.com. 289 rooms. 2 restaurants, gym, business services. AE, DC, MC, V.*

$$$ 🏨 **Shenyang Marriott Hotel.** The first luxury hotel to open in Shenyang, the Marriott overlooks the Yun River, not far from the U.S. Consulate. Sumptuous rooms come complete with satellite TV, minibar, and electronic safe. ✉ *388 Qing Nian Da Jie, Shenhe District, 110003,* ☎ *042/ 2388–3456,* 🖷 *024/2388–0677,* 🌐 *www.marriotthotels.com. 435 rooms, 43 suites. 2 restaurants, bar, room service, pool, tennis court, gym, baby-sitting, laundry service, business services, travel services. AE, DC, MC, V.*

$ 🏨 **Liaoning Guesthouse.** The lobby and dining room interiors in this hotel possess real character. Built by the Japanese in 1927 to a European design, they have wood paneling and tiled and wooden floors, high ceilings, and a strong hint of the style of 18th-century Europe. Japanese visitors like it for its good feng shui. The hotel restaurants serve Shandong, Liaoning, and Western food. At press time the guesthouse was undergoing renovation; be sure to call in advance to confirm that it's open. ✉ *97 Zhongshan Lu, on Zhongshan Sq., Heping District, 110001,* ☎ *024/2383–9166,* 🖷 *024/2383–9103. 3 restaurants, tennis court, exercise room, billiards. AE, DC, MC, V.*

Shopping

Wu Ai Shichang (Five Loaves Wholesale Market; ✉ Re Nao Lu, Shenhe District, ⏱ 3 AM–1 PM) is a great place to see the free market in oper-

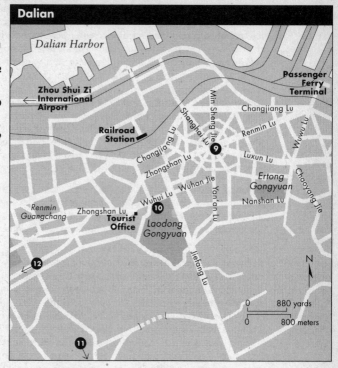

ation. It contains literally acres of stalls—mostly clothes but also shoes and light consumer goods. Most things are made locally.

Tai Yuan Jie Market (⊠ Next to Traders Hotel) mainly sells clothing, some electronic goods, and CDs. The **Gong Yi Meishu Shangdian** (⊠ Taiyuan Jie) has crafts and artworks—scroll paintings, tea sets, vases, small and large pieces of jade, and other tourist pieces—on the fourth and fifth floors. The **Cashmere Building** (⊠ 67 Sanjing Jie, Shenhe District, ☎ 024/2284–6759) carries a reasonable collection of cashmere garments.

Side Trips from Shenyang

The road out of Shenyang in the direction of Dalian puts you on the first highway in China, built in the early 1980s. Along it, in the town of **Liaoyang**, the **Baita** (White Tower) is worth a look. Built in the time of the local Liao Kingdom during China's Song dynasty about AD 1000, the White Tower is an impressive octagonal structure with a tier of 13 eaves and Buddhist statues and reliefs carved around it. Repaired several times since it was first built, it was last restored in 1986 but does not bear the kitschy new look of so much restoration in China. To get here, contact CITS for a price quote (which will run on the high side) and then hire a taxi for a little less; you can ask the driver to use the meter. The cheapest option is to go by bus, which leaves from the long-distance bus station south of the Wu Ai Shichang. ⊠ *Road to Dalian, 30 km (18 mi) south of Shenyang.*

Dalian

4 hrs by train (350 km/217 mi) south of Shenyang; 12 hrs by train, 1 hr by plane (450 km/279 mi) east of Beijing.

Dalian is easily one of the most charming cities in China. Lying at the tip of the Liaodong peninsula between the Yellow Sea and the Bohai

Sea, this small city is at once a postcard from China's past and a sign-post to the country's future. In the 19th century, Russia, seeking an ice-free port, established a trading center here but lost it to Japan in their 1904–05 war. Other Europeans traded here later on, and the resulting combination of Russian, Japanese, and Western European architecture that survives in public buildings and houses gives Dalian a unique atmosphere. After the 1949 revolution the Soviet Union continued to wield enormous influence in China and retained control of Dalian and Port Arthur, which they had taken over when the Japanese surrendered at the end of World War II (strategically the Russians have always been hampered by the lack of an ice-free port in the east). When Stalin died in 1955, much of the pressure on China was relaxed, and these two cities were returned to the Chinese.

Dalian is a great city for walking. Its wide, colonial-era streets and public squares and parks, including Zhongshan Square, Renmin Square, and Laodong Park, are its most striking features. With the sea on three sides, it has something else that is rare in a Chinese city—relatively clean air.

But more tangible than history are the present economic boom and rising wealth that give Dalian the sort of sophistication for which Shanghai is frequently noted. Many of the large colonial buildings have been renovated, new hotels are springing up, and Japanese and Korean fashions dominate the streets. The city's special economic status (a package of tax and investment breaks to attract foreign companies) and general economic health are often attributed to the charismatic and politically savvy former mayor Bo Xilai, son of Long March veteran Bo Yibo. The source of the area's economic boom is its good port facilities (Dalian is also China's biggest shipbuilding center) and the Dalian Economic and Trade Development Zone, 25 minutes from the city, where Japanese, Korean, European, and U.S. companies are based.

❾ Zhongshan Guangchang (Sun Yat-sen Square) is actually a large circle at the center of Dalian where in good weather locals gather in the evenings to practice genteel ballroom dancing and the lazy version of badminton that is common throughout China. Scenes from the movie *The Last Emperor* were filmed in the square, which is encircled by stately colonial-era buildings, most of which are today occupied by banks.

❿ Rong Sheng Dixia Shichang (Rong Sheng Underground Market) has everything from flat fish to salmon steaks, plus shrimp, octopus, sea cucumber, turtle, tortoise, lobster, crab, eels, barnacles, and scallops, as well as stalls of fresh fruit and canned goods. The upper part of the two-level underground complex is dedicated to household furniture. ☒ *Wuhui Lu, east of the north entrance to Laodong Gongyuan.* ☉ *Daily 9–6.*

⓫ The **Dalian Senlin Dongwuyuan Yesheng Fangyangyuan** (Dalian Forest Zoo Safari Park) is where Dalian proudly shows off its Siberian tigers in natural surroundings, together with around 4,000 other animals of over 60 species. The park occupies an expansive parkland setting. Some areas are accessible on foot, others by safari bus only. ☒ *Between the city center and the beach (main entrance on Bin Hai Lu),* ☎ *0411/ 249–5072.* ☒ *Y40.* ☉ *Daily 7:30–4.*

⓬ Next to a small beach in Xinghai Park, **Haiyang Shijie** (Ocean World Aquarium) has a 380-ft plexiglass walk-through tunnel where you can get a full view of the more than 200 varieties of resident fish. ☒ *508 Zhongshan Lu,* ☎ *0411/468–5136.* ☒ *Y35.* ☉ *May–Sept., daily 9–4; Oct.–Apr., daily 8–6.*

Dining and Lodging

$$–$$$$ ✕ **Tian Tian Yu Gang.** One of the best in a chain of nine restaurants around the city serving excellent Dalian seafood, Number 4 offers sea cucumber sautéed and served with asparagus, carrots, and cucumber; abalone—raw or braised; and prawn and crab. The entrance is guarded by fish tanks and basins from which you can choose your meal. There's an open dining area on the ground floor, and upstairs are a half dozen private dining rooms. ⊠ *10 Renmin Lu,* ☎ *0411/280–1122. No credit cards.*

$$–$$$ ✕ **Le Café Igosso.** This offbeat Japanese-owned Italian restaurant is decorated in cream colors and serves pizza, pasta, and cappuccino. There's jazz at night and outdoor seating on a veranda in the summer. The manager plays saxophone and his partner, who runs the kitchen, plays bass. ⊠ *45 Nanshan Lu,* ☎ *0411/265–6453. AE, DC, MC, V.*

$$–$$$ ✕ **Market Place.** On the first floor of the Holiday Inn, overlooking busy Chang Jiang Lu, this restaurant has a German chef and serves the best Western food in town. It runs special theme menus, such as traditional Italian, New Zealand lamb, or barbecue. ⊠ *18 Shengli Guangchang,* ☎ *0411/280–8888. AE, DC, MC, V.*

$$ ✕ **Sorabol.** The staff here prepares delicious Korean food right at your table. Among the offerings are the traditional *boolgogi* (marinated beef and vegetables barbecued at the table) and *boolgahlbi* (marinated beef served on and off the bone). The restaurant has both private rooms and open booths. Wooden floors and surroundings and friendly service give the place a warm feel. ⊠ *18 Qiyi Jie,* ☎ *0411/263–1460. AE, DC, MC, V.*

$$ ✕ **Taiyang Cheng.** For reasonable late-night food, try the restaurants here. Like many Chinese restaurants, the ground floor serves fast-food and cheap eats, while upstairs is a more upscale dining room. Order from the menu, or choose your own live seafood from tanks to the side. ⊠ *109 Youhao Lu,* ☎ *0411/264–3232. DC, MC, V.*

$$$$ 🏨 **Shangri-La Dalian.** Rooms at this modern high-rise are tastefully decorated and comfortable; all come with minibar, refrigerator, executive desk, and color TV with movie channels. Several floors are given over to the Horizon Club, which has its own business center and offers complimentary breakfast, cocktails, and express check-in and check-out. The restaurants offer Chinese, Japanese, or Western food. ⊠ *66 Renmin Lu, 116001,* ☎ *0411/252–5000,* FAX *0411/252–5050,* WEB *www.shangri-la.com. 563 rooms. 3 restaurants, bar, deli, in-room fax, indoor pool, hot tub, tennis court, gym, shops, baby-sitting, business services, airport shuttle, car rental. AE, DC, MC, V.*

$$$ 🏨 **Holiday Inn.** Just two minutes' walk from the railway station, this hotel is among the best lodging values in Dalian. The red-front 23-story building was one of the first high-rises in the city (1988). All rooms have TV, in-house movie channels, and a minibar. ⊠ *18 Shengli Guangchang, 116001,* ☎ *0411/280–8888,* FAX *0411/280–9704,* WEB *www.holiday-inn.com. 405 rooms, 26 suites. 3 restaurants, 2 bars, pool, beauty salon, sauna, exercise room, shop, baby-sitting, dry cleaning, concierge, business services, car rental. AE, DC, MC, V.*

$$–$$$ 🏨 **Furama Hotel.** Next door to the Shangri-La, the Furama has executive-floor rooms, offices, apartments, and suites. Its massive atrium lobby decked out in marble links its two towers. Spacious, comfortably furnished standard rooms are equipped with minibar and in-house movie channels. The restaurants serve Chinese, Western, and Japanese cuisines. ⊠ *60 Renmin Lu, 116001,* ☎ *0411/263–0888,* FAX *0411/280–4455,* WEB *www.furama.com.cn. 832 rooms, 28 suites. 6 restaurants, 3 bars, pool, tennis court, gym, squash, business services. AE, DC, MC, V.*

$ Grand Hotel. This modern hotel houses the Dalian International Exhibition Center, which hosts trade fairs. The plain, red-carpeted rooms come with color TV and minibar; some have a view of the harbor. ⊠ *1 Jiefang Jie, 116001,* ☎ *0411/280–6161,* FAX *0411/280–6980,* WEB *www.grand-hotel-cn.com. 248 rooms. Restaurant, 2 bars, barbershop, gym, massage, business services, airport shuttle. AE, DC, MC, V.*

Nightlife and the Arts

THE ARTS

The **Er Tong Le Yuan** (Children's Palace; ⊠ Renmin Guangchang) hosts occasional photographic and painting exhibitions. The new eight-story **Dalian Wenhua He Meishu Guan** (Dalian Culture and Art Mansion; ⊠ Shidao Nan Jie) is home to the city's dance and theater ensembles.

Spring Festival (Chinese New Year: January or February) is the big annual holiday; traditional festivities include a fireworks display. An ice lantern and **ice sculpting** show also takes place at Bingyugou (2½ hours drive northeast of Dalian) over the Chinese New Year. **Acacia Flower Festival** (last week in May) culminates with a song-and-dance performance in Laodong Gongyuan (Labor Park) in celebration of the blooming lotus.

NIGHTLIFE

Nawei Senlin Bar (⊠ Renmin Lu, West of the Furama Hotel, ☎ 0411/281–2329), a bar by night and a teashop by day, is frequented by young Chinese and some foreigners. The **Dalian New Friendship Nightclub** (⊠ 6 Renmin Lu, 10th floor, ☎ 0411/282–5888 ext. 385), has singers with a backup band (Western and Chinese rock music) and a dancing show. The strobe-lit dance floor of **JJ's** (⊠ 4 Wuwu Jie, ☎ 0411/270–5518), with a capacity of about 1,200, is packed on weekends with young Chinese rocking to a DJ.

Outdoor Activities and Sports

The 36-hole **Dalian Golden Pebble Golf Course** (⊠ Dalian Jin Shitan State Tourist and Vacation Zone, ☎ 0411/790–0543), on the coast, a half hour northeast of the city center, is open to the public, but you must make reservations in advance.

Shopping

The **Ti Yu Chang outdoor market** (Xigang District) sells food, clothes, and electronic goods and is busiest on weekends. Five minutes' walk from the Holiday Inn lies the commercial district around **Qingni Jie,** where you'll find department stores, markets, and fast-food outlets.

The **Dalian Friendship Shopping Center** (⊠ 6–8 Renmin Lu) is a modern department store stocking a wide range of men's and women's clothing, cosmetics, and luxury goods. **Wenwu Zongdian Shop** (⊠ 229 Tianjin Jie, ☎ 0411/263–4955) sells quality Chinese wood carvings, scrolls, pottery, and interesting lamps and lampshades; you can bargain here.

Side Trips from Dalian

The 32-km-long (20-mi-long) road that winds south of Dalian along the peninsula has some attractive views and a number of good beaches, including Lao Hu and Fujiazhuang. Local couples drive out here following their marriage ceremony to use the coastline and sea as backdrops for wedding photographs.

⓭   **Lushun Prison,** built in the early years of this century by the Russians and later used by the Japanese to hold Chinese prisoners, now houses a museum documenting the Japanese occupation of China. ⊠ *139 Xiangyang Jie, Lushun, 42 km (26 mi) north of Dalian,* ☎ *0411/661–4409.*

⑭ **Jin Shi Tan** (Golden Stone Beach), a series of small coves strung along the coast, is near the Dalian Golden Pebble Golf Course. ⊠ ½ *hr northeast of city center.*

Liaoning A to Z

To research prices, get advice from other travelers, and book travel arrangements, visit www.fodors.com.

AIR TRAVEL
Dalian airport is 30 minutes northwest of the city center. There are regular flights to Beijing, Shanghai, Guangzhou, Hong Kong, and Tokyo.

AIRPORTS
➤ AIRPORT INFORMATION: **Dalian airport** (international, ☎ 0411/364–5892 or 0411/362–6151; domestic, ☎ 0411/364–5892 or 0411/362–6151).

BOAT AND FERRY TRAVEL
Frequent passenger service links Dalian with Yantai, in Shandong; Tianjin, and Shanghai.
➤ BOAT AND FERRY INFORMATION: **Dalian Marine Co.** (☎ 0411/462–3064).

CONSULATE
➤ UNITED STATES: **U.S. Consulate** (⊠ 52 Shisi Wei Lu, Heping District, Shenyang 110003, ☎ 024/2322–1198, FAX 024/2322–2374).

EMERGENCIES
The below emergency contact numbers are for the city of Dalian.
➤ CONTACTS: **Ambulance** (☎ 119). **Hospital** (☎ 120). **Police** (☎ 110).

TAXIS
The most convenient mode of transport in Dalian is taxi. Flag fall is Y10, though you may have to ask that the meter be used. You can negotiate a price for longer trips outside the city. There are three tram lines (5 mao flat fare, equivalent to Y.50).

The easiest way to get around Shenyang is by taxi. Flag fall is Y8.

TRAIN TRAVEL
From Dalian station the overnight train to and from Beijing has two-berth sleeper cabins and four-berth hard sleepers, making it more comfortable than most other trains in China. Regular services link Dalian with Shenyang and beyond.

Shenyang has two train stations: Bei Huo Che Zhan (North Railway Station, and Nan Huo Che Zhan (South Railway Station).
➤ TRAIN INFORMATION: **Dalian station** (⊠ Shengli Guangchang, Zhongshan District, ☎ 0411/254–2993). **Bei Huo Che Zhan** (North Railway Station; ☎ 024/2204–3522). **Nan Huo Che Zhan** (South Railway Station; ☎ 024/2206–3222).

VISITOR INFORMATION
➤ TOURIST INFORMATION: **CITS**; ⊠ 1 Changtong Jie, Dalian, 116011, ☎ 0411/369–1165, FAX 0411/368–7868; ⊠ 113 Huanghe Nan Dajie, Shenyang, ☎ 024/8680–9383, FAX 024/8680–6986).

5 NORTHWESTERN CHINA

TERRA-COTTA SOLDIERS
AND THE SILK ROAD

Home to the fabled Silk Road, Northwestern China encompasses some of the most stunning and inhospitable landscapes in the nation. To the east, Shaanxi's Xian harbors the magnificent terra-cotta warriors of the country's first emperor. Gansu province's Mogao caves contain an unrivaled collection of Buddhist art. The Western Xia tombs stand among grazing flocks in Ningxia. The source of China's vital Huang He (Yellow River) is in the grasslands of eastern Qinghai, while snowcapped mountains form the province's western edge. The oil-rich and politically troubled province of Xinjiang extends to China's westernmost frontier.

By Jan
Alexander,
Anya
Bernstein,
Christopher
Knowles

Updated and
revised by
Grace Fan

HOME TO MANY OF THE NATION'S most haunting and memorable sites—not least a vast, life-size army of soldiers built to outlast death—northwestern China also encompasses the fabled Silk Road. The legendary east–west trade artery brought silks, spices, and other precious goods from the nation's great ancient capital of Chang'an to Rome more than two millennia ago.

The provinces of Shaanxi, Gansu, Ningxia, Qinghai, and Xinjiang extend more than 1,000 mi, starting in the nation's heartland, where fertile farmland is abundant, and winding west past barren mountains and eerily desolate grasslands to the "wild west" of China's dusty frontier reaches. It is a territory rich in history and its paradoxes, including magnificent Buddhist lamaseries in two of the poorest provinces in the nation and seething ethnic unrest in the troubled but wildly colorful border region of Xinjiang.

The Silk Road starts in Xian (formerly Chang'an), capital of Shaanxi province and the seat of Chinese imperial power for more than a millennium. Heir to some of the oldest civilizations known to man, Chang'an birthed 12 dynasties, including the reign of China's first emperor, Qin Shihuang, and the illustrious Tang dynasty, from the 7th to 9th centuries AD—the most hallowed era of the nation's history. During this Chinese renaissance, travel along the Silk Road flourished, bringing Persians, Arabs, Japanese, Mongols, Greeks, and other foreigners in great numbers to the most cosmopolitan city of the ancient world. Turkish costumes swept the city, birds from tributary countries fluttered about court aviaries, Chinese women rode horses, and polo was all the rage.

After the collapse of the Tang in the 9th century, Chang'an steadily declined in importance until the city became little more than a dusty provincial metropolis in the 20th century, overshadowed by tales of its former glory. In 1974 all this changed, when local peasants accidentally unearthed one of the greatest archaeological finds of the 20th century— the terra-cotta army of Qin Shihuang—with rich treasures still unexcavated in Qin's nearby booby-trapped tomb. Today an infusion of foreign capital and glitzy hotels has transformed Xian into the most modern city on the Silk Road.

Shaanxi is also home to the Communist pilgrimage site of Yanan, 260 km (161 mi) north of Xian, where Mao's Communists camped for a decade at the height of their civil war in the 1930s and '40s against the Nationalists.

Going westward, the caravans of the Silk Road wound their way through the largely barren strip of Gansu province, historically the last frontier of the nation, where the Great Wall ends. During the Han dynasty, horsemen patrolled the borders of this natural corridor, which provided an essential military and communications link between China and the fiercely contested northwestern territories. Tibetans, Mongols, Han Chinese, Kazakhs, and the Xiongnu tribes poured through in ensuing centuries, battling for control of shifting territory. Today the province's population still comprises more than a dozen different ethnicities. Bordered by mountains and dominated by bleak deserts, however, Gansu continues to be one of the most impoverished regions of China despite recent attempts by the government to industrialize it. But the province is also heir to some of the most stunning religious sites of the Silk Road, including the oasis town of Dunhuang, which has the world's richest repository of Buddhist shrines, and the famed Labrang Monastery, where Tibetan Buddhist pilgrims come to pray in the tiny town of Xiahe.

To the north, nestled in between Shaanxi and Gansu, lies Ningxia, the quietest of China's five autonomous regions. Once the capital of the 11th-century Kingdom of the Xia, Ningxia has never played a terribly significant political or geographic role in China's history, having been passed back and forth between various administrative regions. Today the province is a pleasant place with a large Muslim Hui population that remains largely untrafficked by tourists. The Silk Road wound through the southern part of present-day Ningxia, en route from Chang'an to Lanzhou, the capital of Gansu.

Southwest of Gansu, on the northeast border of Tibet, lies Qinghai, a province of grasslands and desert locked in by mountains and pitted with strange moonlike craters. Historically a part of Tibet until the 18th century, when a Qing dynasty emperor lopped it off and claimed it as Chinese terrain, this remote region lay too far south and inland to experience any major Silk Road traffic. Even today, despite an influx of Han Chinese into its metropolises, much of the province remains unpopulated.

Since 1949 Qinghai's desolate beauty has had a shadow cast over it by its notorious political role as the nation's Siberia. Intellectuals and political prisoners were sent here in droves in a whole series of Communist crackdowns, including the Hundred Flowers campaign in the late 1950s, the Cultural Revolution, and present-day incarcerations. But the province is much more than a forbidding series of prisons and *laogais* (the word literally means "reform through labor" and accordingly, many inmates are forced to work in factories without pay to make goods for export). Home to one of the six renowned temples of the Tibetan Buddhist Yellow Hat sect, Qinghai continues to share a strong cultural heritage with Tibet. Away from the industrializing cities, under an epic sky and vast open plains, seminomadic herders clad in brown robes slashed with fluorescent pink sashes still roam the grasslands, herding yak and goats the way their ancestors did for centuries before them—on horseback.

From Gansu the Silk Road crosses into Xinjiang (New Dominion), an immense territory half the size of India divided in ancient times into 36 different kingdoms. Xinjiang now comprises fully a sixth of China's total area. Here, in a province populated by at least 13 different ethnic groups—including Uighurs, Mongols, Kazakhs, Uzbeks, and Tatars—you may feel you've crossed over into another land. It is a region of extremes—stunning mountain ranges, sapphire blue lakes, blasted terrain, and the deadly sweep of the Taklamakan Desert. Positioned in an area of strategic importance to the Chinese, Xinjiang has always been politically volatile as well.

China's influence first extended to Xinjiang in the 1st century AD under the Han dynasty, when the opening of the Silk Road thrust the territory to the forefront of the nation's economic and military concerns. As the dynasty waned, local warlords and kings reasserted sovereignty over their former terrain. This pattern of Chinese conquest followed by loss of military control occurred again in the Tang and Qing dynasties. In 1884 Xinjiang was officially declared a Chinese province by the Qing government, but when the Qing fell in 1911, the area was once again left to local warlords. In 1945 a Kazakh named Osman established an independent state—the Turkestan Republic—but it was short-lived, and in 1949 the Communist army moved in and claimed the territory as its own.

Since the '50s the Chinese government has flooded the area with Han Chinese in an attempt to dilute the minority populations and quell ethnic dissent. But many Uighurs, who comprise a majority of Xinjiang's populace, still consider the Chinese to be invaders. Over the past few decades, most recently in the late '90s, Uighur separatists have increasingly resorted to violent means, including gun trafficking, bus bombings, riots, and even assassination to make their point. A swift crackdown by the Chinese military, however, ensures that the territory, despite rising tensions, remains under Chinese control. The discovery of valuable oil deposits in Xinjiang, notably near Turpan and in the Taklamakan Desert, has only cemented China's resolve to hold on to the vast region.

Nowadays many cities in Xinjiang, notably the capital, Ürümqi, and even the small city of Yining, in the northwest, are quickly "catching up" with modern China, with the attendant slapped-together buildings, traffic, and air pollution. Still, religion and tradition continue to play crucial roles in the inhabitants' lives. Special festivals, ethnic music, cuisine, and traditional costumes—far from disappearing— have become a source of ethnic pride. Xinjiang also has the spectacular Karakorum Highway, where ancient caravans wound their way over three mountain ranges and through the Valley of Blood into present-day Pakistan. Outside the city of Turpan, abandoned oasis cities of the Silk Road such as Kharakhoja and Yarkhoto can be explored. At the Sunday bazaar in Kashgar—a bustling city rich with color and traditions—veiled women in resplendent colors bargain over bolts of cloth and old Uighur men squat by the roadside, haggling for hours over the price of sheep.

Pleasures and Pastimes

Dining

In northwestern China, much of the cuisine—like much of the population—is Muslim, though good Chinese cooking can also be found all across the region. The particular dishes vary from city to city but invariably include grilled mutton kebabs, *lamian* (hand-pulled noodles sprinkled with diced tomatoes, green peppers, and chili peppers), and different types of *nan* (flat breads).

Another common dish is Mongolian hotpot. The price is usually reasonable, and the buffet has ingredients to suit every palate: meat, seafood, chicken, bean curd, mushrooms, vegetables, and noodles. You pick the ingredients, add them yourself to a simmering pot filled with a spicy stew, and mix your own seasonings. You can make a satisfying meatless meal out of hotpot (though the soup is invariably a meat-based one unless you specifically request that it not be); otherwise, it is often difficult to stick to a vegetarian diet in western China, unless you frequent Chinese restaurants.

Of all the cities in this region, Xian unquestionably offers the best and most exciting variety of foods, both Chinese and Muslim. Shaanxi province doesn't have its own regional cuisine, but restaurants tend to focus on noodles and *jiaozis* (dumplings) rather than rice, and they serve a colossal number of meat-based dishes. Still, vegetables and fresh fruit are also available. A Xian Muslim specialty is *yangroù paomo,* a spicy lamb soup poured over broken pieces of nan. Other popular Muslim street foods are *heletiao* (buckwheat noodles marinated in soy sauce and garlic) and *roùjiamo* (pita bread filled with beef or pork and topped with cumin and green peppers).

Outside Xian, the farther west you go, the less variety there is. Gansu, Ningxia, and Xinjiang don't offer much in the way of culinary surprises, but in Xinjiang, where temperatures can reach scorching levels, you'll find a variety of local ices, ice cream, and *bingshui* (a refreshing apricot or peach juice mixed with water). In Kashgar a popular drink for locals is an iced sour yogurt drink ladled from huge basins. The outdoor food stalls near the Sunday market are also worth checking out, where a lush display of tomatoes, red and green peppers, and other food items all piled together rises majestically from a boulder of solid ice. Fruit in Xinjiang is plentiful as well. Grapes from Turpan and melons from the oasis town of Hami are famous throughout China.

In Qinghai the many Tibetan restaurants serve such traditional staples as yak butter tea, yak meat, and *stemba,* a dough made by combining yak butter, yak cheese, sugar, boiling water, and barley flour; it's eaten with the fingers. Yak penis is a delicacy served when available.

Restaurant hygiene practices in northwestern China have been improving with modernization, but still fall below Western standards—and they're worse outside the major cities. Outside the provincial capitals, the cleanest restaurants, not surprisingly, tend to be in the major hotels. It's an unfortunate dilemma, as the best way to sample northwestern cuisine, and get a taste for the region's lively street life at the same time, is to head to small family-owned restaurants or the local night markets to try the street food. Use common sense and check for clean tabletops and dinnerware before dining, even in recommended eateries. There still isn't a strong sense of quality control, and restaurants that were excellent six months ago could suddenly plummet into the nether regions of more dubious fare.

Dress is casual everywhere except in the luxury hotel restaurants in Ürümqi. Unless otherwise indicated, reservations are not necessary. Tipping is not necessary, although diners may consider adding a 10% tip in higher-priced restaurants.

CATEGORY	COST*
$$$	over Y120
$$	Y40–Y120
$	under Y40

per person for a main course at dinner.

Festivals

At the Labrang Monastery in Xiahe (Gansu), the **Monlam** (Great Prayer Festival) is held on the 13th, 14th, and 15th days of the first month of the Tibetan new year. Monks assemble to hold philosophical debates, and Tibetan pilgrims flock in droves to the monastery to celebrate Tibet's most important religious ceremony. The same festival is celebrated at the Ta'Er Monastery, outside Xining in Qinghai. Remarkable sculptures are carved out of frozen yak butter as part of the festivities. There are also many ethnic festivals at both places, especially during the summer. Traditional ethnic music and dancing take place then, as well as special events, often including contests on horseback.

Dates for holidays based on the Muslim calendar vary slightly from year to year. The **Rozi Festival** (February) ends the monthlong fast of Ramadan, the Muslim New Year. The Kazakh **Nawiriz Festival** (mid-March) has special events on horseback—horse races, lambskin tussling, and contests in which young men chase young women on horseback. The **Korban Festival** (mid-April; 70th day after the Rozi Festival on the Muslim calendar) is the Sacrifice Festival, to mark the time when Allah asked the prophet Abraham to sacrifice his son as a test of loyalty; Muslim families slaughter sheep and have a feast. The Mongolian **Naadam Fair** (July or August), at Sayram Lake, includes horse races, competitions in archery and wrestling, dancing, and music. At the height of the grape harvest season, Turpan stages the 10-day-long **Grape Festival** (end of August), with traditional Uighur music and dancing nightly around the city.

Lodging

The major capital cities (Xian, Lanzhou, and Ürümqi) generally have the best hotels in the region, with comfortable and well-appointed rooms in the more upscale establishments. Some hotels in lower price categories also offer good service and accommodations, though others can be downright grubby. Outside Xian, an English-speaking staff is a rarity.

Aside from the capital cities, hotels in the western provinces tend to be fairly run down, not the cleanest, and subject to plumbing problems such as brown water, lack of hot water, or lack of any water. Even so, prices are no longer rock-bottom, except for dorm rooms. The situation is gradually improving, however, as the Silk Road becomes more popular and a rush of new hotels intensifies the competition.

If you're staying in the mountains or near a lake between May and October, nomadic families may offer inexpensive accommodations in a yurt. There is rarely plumbing but plenty of ambience. Expect to pay about Y20 per person per night, plus a few yuan extra for meals.

CATEGORY	COST*
$$$$	over Y800
$$$	Y600–Y800
$$	Y300–Y600
$	under Y300

Prices are for a standard double room with bath in peak season.

The Outdoors

Outside Shaanxi, the northwestern region is a nature-lover's paradise. Stunning mountain ranges, vast grasslands, and the harsh but desolate beauty of the Taklamakan Desert offer the chance to experience a region that has never been tamed by humankind, even at the beginning of the 21st century. CITS and a number of foreign travel outfitters now organize intriguing adventure trips: biking, mountain climbing, horseback riding in the lake areas, rafting down rivers on inflatable goatskin rafts, and riding camels through the desert. Some of the mountains have the potential to develop skiing trails, but there are no lifts as of yet.

Exploring Northwestern China

Northwestern China and the Silk Road start at the land-locked province of Shaanxi in the geographical heart of the nation and stretch across some of the country's most beautiful and undeveloped regions to China's western borders. Northwestern China is a long way from anywhere else and merits a stay of two weeks at the very least, but even a few days can be rewarding if you plan wisely.

Great Itineraries

A pared-down list of must-see sites on the Silk Road would have to include the terra-cotta warriors in Xian, Dunhuang's Mogao Caves, the lost city of Jiaohe and other Silk Road sites outside Turpan, and Kashgar's vibrant Sunday Bazaar. The Thousand Buddha Caves outside Lanzhou are also well worth the trip, as is a bus or jeep ride from Kashgar down the Karakorum Highway to China's border with Pakistan.

Numbers in the text correspond to numbers in the margin and on the Northwestern China, Xian, and Lanzhou maps.

IF YOU HAVE 3 DAYS

Begin with a flight to ⚀ **Xian** to see the terra-cotta warriors, the Great Mosque, and the Ming dynasty city walls. The next day, fly to ⚀ **Dunhuang** and hire a car to visit the Mogao Caves outside the city. At sunset head to Singing Sand Mountain to see the most spectacular sand dune vistas on the Silk Road. On the following day return to Xian. If time permits, visit the Shaanxi Provincial Museum and take a walking tour of the city to catch the Great Goose Pagoda, Small Goose Pagoda, Xian Forest of Stone Stelae Museum, the Bell Tower, and the Drum Tower.

As an alternative, if the Wild West of China attracts you, head to Xinjiang to see the buried cities of the Silk Road. Arrive in ⛴ **Ürümqi** and visit the Xinjiang Museum and the Erdaoqiao Market. At night stop by the Wuyi Night Market to sample the smoky lamb kebabs and spicy hotpot of Uighur cuisine. The next day go to **Turpan** in the morning by bus or hired car; in the afternoon visit the Jiaohe Gucheng, outside the city. On the last day visit the Flaming Mountains, Bezeklik Thousand Buddha Caves, Atsana Tombs, Gaochang Gucheng, Karez Irrigation Tunnels, and Emin Ta. Return to Ürümqi in the evening.

IF YOU HAVE 7 DAYS

Arrive in ⛴ **Xian** and follow the itinerary for the first two days, above. On the third day fly into ⛴ **Ürümqi** and follow the alternative three-day itinerary above for Ürümqi. Another option is to start with the three-day itinerary above for Ürümqi. On the fourth day take a bus or hire a car to **Heavenly Lake,** return in the afternoon to Ürümqi, and take the evening flight to ⛴ **Kashgar.** The next day visit the Id Kah Mosque, the Kashgar Sunday Market, and the Tomb of Abakh Hoja. On day six visit the Cave of the Three Immortals and the Mor Pagoda; return to Ürümqi on the evening flight. Leave Ürümqi on the seventh day.

IF YOU HAVE 15 OR MORE DAYS

Spend the first two days in ⛴ **Xian,** seeing the terra-cotta warriors and the sights on the walking tour of the city. On day three fly to ⛴ **Xining** and see the Ta'Er Monastery. On day four hire a car to visit ⛴ **Qinghai Lake** and Bird Island. In the morning of day five take the four-hour train ride to ⛴ **Lanzhou** and visit the Gansu Provincial Museum. On day six hire a car to see the Thousand Buddha Caves outside Lanzhou, and return to Lanzhou in the evening. On day seven fly to ⛴ **Dunhuang** and visit the Mogao Caves and Singing Sand Mountain. On the following day fly to **Ürümqi** to visit the museum and market. Take the evening flight to ⛴ **Kashgar.** Spend days 9 through 11 in Kashgar; try to time your visit to coincide with the Sunday Bazaar. Hire a jeep to take the **Karakorum Highway** from Kashgar down to the border city of **Tashkurgan** and nearby ⛴ **Karakuli Lake.** Stay overnight in a yurt at Karakuli Lake and return to Kashgar the next day. On the 12th day return to Ürümqi by plane and take the bus to ⛴ **Turpan.** Spend the next two days visiting the ancient city of Jiaohe, Flaming Mountains, Bezeklik Thousand Buddha Caves, Atsana Tombs, Gaochang Gucheng, Karez Irrigation Tunnels, and Emin Ta. On day 15 take the bus back to Ürümqi.

Adventure Trips

Many trips that take you hiking through mountains, horseback riding along Sayram Lake, bicycling through ancient Silk Road routes (you have to bring your own bicycle), or seeing the Taklamakan Desert on camelback can be arranged through **CITS** (⊠ 51 Xinhua Beilu, Ürümqi, Xinjiang 830002, ☏ 0991/282–1428, ℻ 0991/2810–0689 or 0991/281–0689, 🕸 www.xinjiangtour.com).

Qinghai's **CITS** (⊠ 156 Huanghe Lu, Xining, next to Qinghai Binguan, ☏ 0971/614–4888 ext. 2439 or 0971/614–3711) runs 10-day tours to the source of the Yellow River and 12-day hikes in the 20,000-ft-high Anyemaqen Mountains (sacred to the Tibetans), 800 km (500 mi) southwest of Xining.

In Ningxia, **Sha Po Tou Travel Agency** (⊠ 1/F, Zhongwei Binguan, Zhongwei 7017510, ☏ 0953/701–2961, ℻ 0953/701–8841) offers adventure tours, including rafting trips down the Yellow River on inflatable animal-skin rafts, camel rides into the Tengger Desert to tour the Ming dynasty Great Wall, and sand skiing on desert dunes.

Most of these trips take off only in the high season—May–October. Prices vary according to the number of people in the group. Expect to spend approximately Y1,000 per person per day, including food, lodging, transportation, and English-speaking guide.

When to Tour Northwestern China

The best time to visit this area is from early May to late October, when the weather is warm. This is the high tourist season, when many festivals take place and the land is in bloom with grasses and flowers.

SHAANXI

One of the oldest habitations of Chinese people, Shaanxi was also home of the first unifier of China, Qin Shihuang—first (and penultimate) emperor of the Qin dynasty. Because of the prestige of its capital city, then called Changan, the province grew in importance until it reached new heights of prosperity and artistic productivity during the Tang. The great trade caravans of the Silk Road set off from here, and as a locus of Asian trading routes, the city prospered. At the same time, the Muslim, Buddhist, and, to a lesser extent, Christian influences from the West added to the vibrant, diverse culture encouraged during the Tang.

As China's focus turned inward and the outside seemed to grow more and more distant, the capital was moved east. With a slackening of trade and a clampdown on religious and cultural diversity, Shaanxi's assets became its losses. Minority Muslim unrest caused major rebellions in the 14th and 17th centuries, and the harsh repression of uprisings caused thousands of deaths during the late Qing. The complex web of irrigation canals that sustained the populace fell into disrepair, and the province was ravaged by famine. These cultural conflicts and natural disasters ensured that it would never again reach the heights it had known in the 10th century.

The late 19th and early 20th centuries saw poverty and famine sweep this once-prosperous area; millions died as the country was wracked by military unrest and, finally, civil war. In the late 1920s the young Communist Party started a countrywide effort to win over Chinese peasants; the state of disaffection and despair in this province gained them enthusiastic recruits. When the embattled Communists embarked on their Long March in 1934, it was from Shaanxi that they chose to emerge. They set up a camp in Yanan that would last them for more than 10 years of intermittent Japanese and Guomindang (GMD) conflict. It was here that much party theory was first hammered out and that Mao Zedong consolidated his power over the party. In 1947 the Communists were finally routed by the GMD and fled the province, only to return in triumph two years later.

Xian

7 hrs by train southwest of Luoyang; approximately 2 hrs by plane northwest of Nanjing.

Haunting in sweep, artistry, and scale, the magnificent life-sized terracotta army of China's first emperor is justly considered one of the 20th century's greatest archaeological finds. The emperor Qin, acceding to the throne in 221 BC at the age of 38, ruled China with an iron hand until his death just 11 years later. He not only ruled it, he created it. At the time of his accession, the lands we now call China were splintered

Northwestern China

KAZAKHSTAN

Lake Balkhash

Alakol

Altay

35 **Sayram Hu**

Karamay

34 **Yining**

Shihezi

Changji

Ysyk-Kol

Ürümqi **32** **33** **Tianchi Hu**

43 **Putao Gou**

KYRGYZSTAN

Turpan **38** **39** **Bozikeli Qian**

Jiaohe **42** **40**
Gucheng **41** **Atsana-**
Karakhoja M

Aksu

Gaochang
Gucheng

Korla

Artux Sugun

Kashgar **36**

XINJIA

Mor Ta

TADZHIKISTAN

X   I   N   J   I   A   N   G

Lop Nor

37 **Tashkurgan**

Hotan

Qiemo

K

Karakorum
Shankou

U

PAKISTAN

N

L   U   N   S   H

HOH · XIL   SHAN

N

XIZANG ZIZHIQU
(TIBET AUTONOMOUS REGION)

INDIA

Q   I   N   G   S   H   A   N   G   A   O   Y   U   A   N
(PLATEAU OF TIBET)

31 **Tangg**
Shank

H
I
M
A
L
A
Y
A

TANGGULA   SHAN

N

0   100 miles

0   150 km

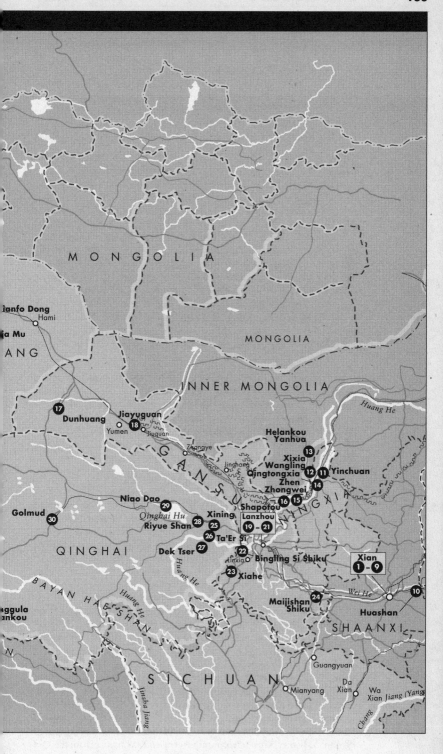

into numerous small kingdoms. Qin took it upon himself to "unite"—
that is, to conquer—a huge territory during his lifetime. He imposed military unity and instigated a series of bureaucratic reforms to centralize
the country's governmental systems as well. He standardized money and
measurements, divided the country into administrative units under central control, started construction on the Great Wall, and burned any books
he could find that challenged state decrees—including many of the ancient classics. His son inherited the throne, but the dynasty crumbled four
years after Qin's death. Nevertheless, his conquered lands and his administrative ideas formed the foundation of what China would become.

The area met with changing fates for the next millennium. The Han
dynasty, which overthrew the Qin, established its capital just northwest of modern-day Xian, but when in AD 23 the Later Han moved its
capital to Luoyang, the region's prestige declined. In the 6th century
the Sui dynasty returned to Xian—then called Chang'an, meaning
"eternal peace." Over the next centuries, under the Tang dynasty,
Chang'an became one of the largest and most cultured cities in the world.
A complex web of communication systems united the capital with the
rest of the country. It also became an important center for what is considered China's most cultured and artistic dynasty. Not surprisingly,
the Silk Road flourished during this period as well, bringing Turkish
fashions to court, rare birds to royal aviaries, and foreigners from as
far as Persia and even Rome to the city. The name Xian, which translates as "western peace," was given during the Ming, a less idealistic
time. Much of the city lies on a grid that focuses on what used to be
its exact center, where the bell tower stands.

More recently, in 1936, Xian "hosted" Chiang Kai-shek when his
own general, Zhang Xueliang, had him arrested. Zhang used the arrest to convince Chiang to join the Communist Party in opposing the
Japanese invasion of China. Chiang agreed—although Zhang later
paid heavily for the betrayal; accused by Chiang of treason, Zhang was
eventually confined to house arrest for decades. Today Xian contains
a wealth of cultural artifacts and architecture, chiefly concentrated in
the southeastern and western quarters.

A Good Walk

Start at the **Da Qingzhen Si** ① (Great Mosque). The Muslim neighborhood around the mosque is also a great place to wander and shop.
Head east and south to pass under the **Gulou** ② (Drum Tower). Next,
follow Xida Jie east to the **Zhonglou** ③ (Bell Tower), which stands in
the exact center of Xian, where Dongda Jie turns into Xida Jie and the
north–south axis street of Nan Da Jie (south) and Bei Da Jie (north)
comes into view. From here you can go south on Nan Da Jie and east
to the **Xian Beilin** ④ (Xian Forest of Stelae Museum). Exiting, turn west
(right) onto Sanxue Jie, which will quickly lead you to **Shu Yuan
Men** ⑤ (Calligraphy Yard), a small pedestrians-only street with old-fashioned architecture where shops sell calligraphy brushes, imitation
terra-cotta soldiers, and other esoterica. At the crossing with Nan Da
Jie, notice the impressive Ming dynasty **Nanmen** ⑥ (South Gate) on
your left. This gate is one of the city wall's access points. Here you can
climb up on the top and stroll along the 32-ft-wide walls. You can even
take a minibus along the top if you don't feel like walking. Just south
of the South Gate is the pleasant **Xiao Yan Ta** ⑦ (Small Goose Pagoda).
Farther south and east, the excellent **Shaanxi Lishi Bowuguan** ⑧
(Shaanxi History Museum) contains terra-cotta warriors from the Qin
tomb farther outside town, among other important dynastic relics. Southeast of the museum, you can visit the **Da Yan Ta** ⑨ (Great Goose
Pagoda), one of the best-known pagodas in the country.

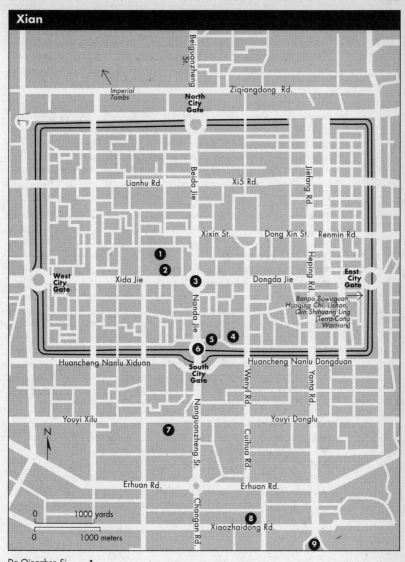

Xian

Imperial Tombs

North City Gate

Beiguanzheng St.

Ziqiangdong Rd.

Lianhu Rd.

Xi5 Rd.

Beida Jie

Jiefang Rd.

Xixin St.

Dong Xin St.

Renmin Rd.

West City Gate

Xida Jie

Nanda Jie

Dongda Jie

Heping Rd.

East City Gate

Banpo Bowuguan, Huaqing Chi, Lishan, Qin Shihuang Ling (Terra-Cotta Warriors)

Huancheng Nanlu Xiduan

South City Gate

Huancheng Nanlu Dongduan

Weny Rd.

Yanta Rd.

Youyi Xilu

Nanguanzheng St.

Cuihua Rd.

Youyi Donglu

N

Erhuan Rd.

Erhuan Rd.

Changan Rd.

Xiaozhaidong Rd.

0   1000 yards
0   1000 meters

The chief places of interest in the Xian vicinity—**Banpo Bowuguan** (Neolithic village), **Huaqing Chi** (Huaqing hot spring), the **Imperial Tombs,** several *si* (temples), and, especially, the **Qin Shihuang Ling** (Tomb of Qin Shihuang) and the **Qin Shihuang Bing Ma Yong Bowuguan** (Museum of Qin Terra-cotta Warriors)—lie outside the city and can be visited on tours or by minibus.

Sights to See

★ **Banpo Bowuguan** (Banpo Neolithic Village). Accidentally unearthed in 1953, this settlement 6 km (3½ mi) east of the city holds the remains of the earliest Yangshao culture yet discovered. The matriarchal village of 200–300 people was populated from around 4500 BC to 3750 BC, and though villagers survived mainly by fishing, hunting, and gathering, there is evidence of animal domestication (pigs and dogs, and perhaps cattle or sheep) as well as farming in the surrounding areas.

This was also one of China's earliest pottery sites, with kilns reaching temperatures of 1,000°C (1,800°F) to produce cooking ware as well as ceremonial containers, many of which are decorated with animal designs. Five pottery kilns were unearthed here, as well as more than 40 dwellings and more than 200 graves. Banpo is part village, part museum: an attempt has been made to re-create the conditions of the ancient village to give a sense of the past. Unfortunately, the re-created "village" seems to boast little if any historical value. The Disneyfied section to the side of the dig is fronted by a modern reddish-clay hut with two unmistakable breasts protruding out of the side wall. Inside, there's not much, other than locals paid to dress up in traditional garments and play musical instruments. The museum displays actual archaeological finds, including 6,000-year-old bone needles and stone axes. ⊠ *139 Banpo Lu, off Changdong Donglu, 6 km (3½ mi) east of city; bus 11 from train station,* ☎ *029/729–5646.* ⊡ *Y20.* ⊙ *Daily 8–6.*

❶ **Da Qingzhen Si** (Great Mosque). This lushly gardened mosque with four graceful courtyards may have been established as early as AD 742, during the Tang, but the remaining buildings date mostly from the 18th century. Amazingly, it was left standing during the Cultural Revolution and has been significantly restored since then. Stone tablets mark the various pavilions, often bearing inscriptions in both Chinese and Arabic. Be sure to look above the doors and gates: there are some remarkable designs here, including 3-D Arabic script that makes the stone it's carved in look as malleable as cake frosting. The northern lecture hall holds a handwritten Koran from the Ming. Non-Muslims are not allowed in the prayer hall, as the mosque is still an active place of worship. The bustling **Muslim Quarter,** in the small side streets surrounding the mosque, is the center of the city's Muslim community, with shops and a lively market. In the alleyway called Hua Jue Xiang leading to the mosque, crowded tourist stands sell everything from prayer beads to jade paperweights; it's a fine place to pick up souvenirs. A few blocks west, the bustling Islamic market street **Da Mai Shi Jie** has peddlers hawking a pointillistic array of dried fruits and candies, as well as tiny noodle and kebab stalls. Look for the seaweed-green Islamic archway on the north side of Xida Jie, one block west of Da Xue Xi Jie. ⊠ *30 Hua Jue Xiang, off Beiguangji Jie, 5 mins north of Gulou, small side street on left with sign in English: Great Mosque,* ☎ *029/ 727–2541.* ⊡ *Y12.* ⊙ *Summer, daily 8–7; winter, daily 8–6:30.*

❾ **Da Yan Ta** (Great Goose Pagoda). Four kilometers (2½ mi) southeast of the city wall's south gate, on the former grounds of the Da Ci'En Si (Temple of Great Maternal Grace), this impressive 209-ft-high Buddhist pagoda was originally constructed in the 7th century AD but was rebuilt during the Qing, in a Ming style. Parts have been restored since

1949. Here the Tang dynasty monk Xuan Zang (600–664), one of the best-known travelers of the Silk Road, spent 11 years translating more than 600 Buddhist scriptures that he had brought back with him from India. In 652 he asked the emperor that a stone stupa be built to house the scriptures. The emperor partly obliged, with a five-story brick and wood edifice, originally called the Scripture Pagoda. It was directly connected to the imperial palace during the Tang and in fact houses the tumulus of the emperor Qin Shihuang. In 703, five more stories were added to the pagoda; a fire later burned down three stories. Inside the pagoda, statues of Buddhist figures in Chinese history line the various chambers. The pagoda also houses the **Tang Dynasty Arts Museum,** on the eastern side of the temple grounds, which collects originals and reproductions from that era of high artistic production. Walk behind the pagoda to see a courtyard of pavilions, erected in 1999, commemorating Xuan Zang's trip. In 2001, the entranceway to the pagoda was extended; the new square is graced with a statue of the eminent monk. ⊠ *Yanta Lu,* ☎ *029/525–5141.* 🎫 *Y20; additional Y15 to enter the pagoda.* ⊙ *Daily 8:30–6.*

❷ **Gulou** (Drum Tower). Originally built in 1380, this 111-ft-high Ming dynasty building, which used to hold the alarm drums for the imperial city, marks the southern end of the Muslim Quarter. The tower was renovated during the Qing Dynasty and again in the 1950s. The second and third floors hold exhibits of calligraphy and peasant paintings (brightly colored folk paintings of rural subjects). Both the street on which the tower is located and the side street running left directly after the tower are restored market streets on which ubiquitous peddlers offer anything from Chinese Muslim–style clothing to seals engraved on the spot, in Chinese or English, by old men bent over their metal picks. The drum in the tower sounds twice a day, at 8 AM and 6 PM, after the bell in the tower is rung. ⊠ *Bei Yuan Jie,* ☎ *029/727–4580.* 🎫 *Y12.* ⊙ *Daily 8–7.*

Huaqing Chi (Huaqing Hot Spring). The Tang dynasty equivalent of a Beverly Hills spa, this spring once provided natural hot water for 60 pools, as well as private baths. It stands amid elegant gardens east of the city overlooked by Li Shan (Black Horse Mountain). Unfortunately, it has almost run dry, save for two fountains from which a trickle of water is siphoned out to allow tourists to bathe their hands and face (Y5). The imperial history of the spring is said to extend back to the 8th century BC, when the Zhou rulers first discovered the pleasures of warm water. Later rulers, notably China's first emperor, Qin Shihuang, also came to bathe. The site is most famously linked, however, to Tang emperor Xuanzang, who built a walled palace here for his favorite concubine, Yang Guifei, in 747. Standing in front of a lake, a voluptuous white statue of Yang is a magnet for Chinese tourists who like to pose before it for photos.

In 1936 the Xian Incident occurred here, when Guomindang leader Chiang Kai-shek was taken prisoner by his subordinate Zhang Yueliang, "The Young Marshal." Zhang was deeply troubled by the Japanese military threat to China and Chiang's preoccupation with his civil war with the Communists. At dawn on December 12, his army stormed Chiang's headquarters at the hot springs where Chiang was sleeping. After a brief chase into the hillside, they captured the shivering, barefoot, and pajama-clad generalissimo, who purportedly didn't even have time to put in his dentures. On the orders of Stalin himself, Zhang released Chiang on Christmas Day. Chiang angrily court-martialed Zhang and sentenced him to 10 years in prison (later changed to house arrest). The incident nevertheless eventually prompted Chiang's Nationalists to work more closely with Mao's Communists until the end of World War II.

Chiang's threadbare headquarters and the bedroom from which he fled are in the buildings to the side of the hot spring. The spot on the hill where he was captured is marked as well. ⊠ *Northern foothills of Li Shan, 30 km (19 mi) east of Xian,* ☎ *029/381–2004.* 🖃 *Y30.* ☉ *Summer, daily 7–7; winter, daily 7:30–6.*

Imperial Tombs. This series of tombs north and west of the city can be seen most conveniently on a day tour organized by a travel agency or hotel. The **Qian Ling** (Qian Tomb; ⊠ 85 km [53 mi] northwest of Xian) is the burial place of the Tang emperor Gao Zong and his wife, Empress Wu, whose 21-year reign after his death was marked by an effective acquisition of power through such age-old means as political intrigue and murder. **Zhang Huai Mu and Yong Tai Gongzhu Mu** (Prince Zhang Huai and Princess Yong Tai's Tombs; ⊠ Near Qian Tomb) hold murals and engravings, although the princess's have stood the test of time better than the prince's. Both of these royals—he, the second son of Empress Wu; she, Emperor Gao Zong's granddaughter—fell out of favor with the empress. The princess was killed and the prince exiled; both were posthumously rehabilitated and their remains returned to Xian.

Many of the most important artifacts in the **Zhao Ling** (Zhao Tomb; ⊠ 70 km [43 mi] northwest of Xian) have been transported to other sites, notably the Philadelphia and Xian museums, but the tomb itself, built for the second Tang emperor, is still a sight to see. Tai Zong died in AD 649 and was buried surrounded by his retainers and relatives. A small museum holds murals and examples of tricolor Tang pottery.

The largest Han dynasty tomb around—about 154 ft high—the **Mao Ling** (Mao Tomb) was built for the Han's strongest leader, Emperor Wu. The emperor was interred with retainers and horses, clad in a burial garment of jade and gold. ⊠ *40 km (25 mi) west of Xian.*

Lishan. This small mountain east of the city has several pavilions along its paths, as well as the local Taoist temple and Han dynasty beacons. It's an inviting stroll if your tour stops at Huaqing Hot Springs and you want to get away from the crowds. A cable car at the bottom provides easy access to the summit. ⊠ *30 km (19 mi) east of Xian.*

❻ **Nanmen** (South Gate) is the most impressive access point of Xian's 39-ft-high Ming dynasty city walls. The south gate of the city wall hosts a small market during the day. This is also one of the points at which the city wall can be climbed; take a stroll along this ancient structure for a panoramic view of the old city of Xian inside and of the new city sprawling outside. The walls mark the original site of Tang dynasty walls; the present ones were built at the beginning of the Ming and renovated in the 1980s. Enterprising locals have started a minibus service (Y10) that zips you to the far end of the south wall and back. Although many city walls in China were torn down during the 20th century, these remained standing; small caves were hollowed out in them and used as storage and protection areas during the Japanese invasion. ⊠ *South end of Nan Da Jie.* 🖃 *Y10.* ☉ *Daily 8–6.*

★ **Qin Shihuang Ling** (Tomb of Qin Shihuang). The first Qin emperor started construction on his enormous, richly endowed tomb, said to be booby-trapped with automatic crossbows, almost as soon as he took the throne. According to ancient records, this underground palace with 100 rivers flowing with mercury took 36 years and 700,000 workers to build. Though the tomb was rediscovered to the east of the city in the 1970s, the government cordoned it off without touching it due to lack of sophisticated machinery—and reportedly executed any local foolish enough to attempt a treasure-seeking foray. In 1999 a team of archaeologists finally began initial excavations in honor of the nation's 50th anniversary, and—as anticipated—unearthed some fabulous treasures. Just a mile away from Qin's tomb, the **Bing Ma Yong,** an army of thousands of hand-shaped, life-size terra-cotta warriors was buried. Complete with weapons and horses, they were to be Qin's garrison in the afterlife. Each of the thousands of soldiers has individual facial features, including different moustaches, beards, and hairstyles. After the fall of the Qin to the Han—during which the soldiers were damaged—the terra-cotta army was forgotten, only to be found again in 1974, when some farmers digging a well unexpectedly came up with a piece of sculpture. Only a part of the entire area has been excavated, and the process of unearthing more warriors continues. In fact, no one is sure just how many warriors there are or how far their "tomb" extends beyond the 700-ft-by-200-ft section being excavated.

You can see what they've dug up so far in three vaults—at the impressive **Qin Shihuang Bing Ma Yong Bowuguan** (Museum of Qin Terra-Cotta Warriors)—about a mile from Qin's tomb. The government has spared no expense to make Xian's star attraction a modern one, and new touch-screen computer displays and other exhibits installed in 1999 make this museum one of the nation's finest. The first vault holds about 6,000 warriors, though only 1,000 have been painstakingly pieced together by archaeologists. The warriors stand unapproachable in their original pits and can only be seen from the walkways erected around the digs. Those in the front ranks are well shaped and fully outfitted except for their weapons, whose wooden handles had decayed over the centuries (the bronze blades were still sharp upon excavation). Be sure to walk around the entire pit: in the back, a less fully excavated section dramatically displays half-formed figures, some headless or limbless, emerging from the hard earth. Pit 2 offers a glimpse of Chinese archaeologists still working on excavating an estimated 1,000 soldiers. In 1999, they discovered the first tri-color figures of the site here: look closely and you can still see pink on the soldiers' faces and patches of dark red on their armor. Vault 3 has 68 warriors and a chariot.

Nearby, an imposing sand-colored pavilion, also erected in 1999, now houses two miniature **bronze chariots** unearthed in the western section of the tomb. Found in 1980, these chariots have intricate detail on their finely crafted surfaces. In the atrium leading to the bronze chariots, look for the massive bronze urn—it's one of the treasures unearthed by archaeologists in their May 1999 excavation of an accessory pit near Qin Shihuang's mausoleum. On the second floor, rotating exhibits are held as well.

Apparently, photographs and videos are now allowed inside the vaults, a change from previous years when guards brusquely confiscated your film if they noticed your camera. There is also a 360-degree movie on the making of the terra-cotta warriors. Postcards and other souvenirs are available in the shops outside the vaults and the movie, or from hawkers outside the main gates, who sell them for under half the museum's price. CITS and practically every hotel arrange tour buses out, or you can go solo on public Buses 306 or 307, which leave from the train station. ✉ *30 km (19 mi) east of Xian,* ☎ *029/391–1954.* ✐ *Y65 (includes movie).* ☉ *Summer, daily 7:30–6; winter, daily 8–5.*

★ ❽ **Shaanxi Lishi Bowuguan** (Shaanxi History Museum). The works in this imposing two-story museum, built in Tang dynasty style, are arranged chronologically; included are artifacts from the Paleolithic and New

Stone ages, later Zhou dynasty bronzes and burial objects, and several terra-cotta warriors taken from the tombs outside town. This is the closest you can get to these statues, which are displayed here behind glass. The exhibits, which have English labels, also show Han, Wei, and northern Zhou dynasty relics, ending with more recent technological displays from the Sui, Tang, Ming, and Qing, as well as impressive bronze and jade artworks and religious statues. Foreigners enter through a door to the left of the main gate. ⊠ *91 Xiaozai Donglu,* ☎ *029/525–4727.* ⊑ *Y35.* ⊘ *Daily 8:30–6.*

❺ Shu Yuan Men (Calligraphy Yard). The government renovated this walk-way for tourism in 2000; it's now also known as Wen Hua Jie (Cul-tural Street). The houses on the lively, bustling pedestrian street are built in a traditional style. A good place to buy gifts, the sides of the road have peddlers and shops selling various wares—calligraphy brushes and artworks including scrolls and watercolors. ⊠ *Two blocks north of Nan-men; look for the traditional red archway.*

Si (temples). A number of temples near Xian are worth a visit. To the south, **Daxingshan, Caotang, Huayan, Xiangji,** and **Xingjiao** were all built to house Buddhist scriptures or to commemorate famous monks. Several schools of Buddhism begun in this area grew to renown and popularity throughout Asia. To the northwest, **Famen Si** (Famen Tem-ple), originally built in the 3rd century AD, was renovated in 1981. It turned out to hold a crypt that housed thousands of coins and various sacrificial objects of jade, gold, and silver. These can be viewed at the museum on the temple grounds. All these temples are best seen on an organized tour.

❹ Xian Beilin (Xian Forest of Stelae Museum). The first thing you see as you walk through the mammoth pagoda-style entranceway here is the impressive Forest of Stone Stelae, in a quiet courtyard shaded with trees. As the name suggests, there is no shortage here of historical stone tablets, on which imperial edicts and poems were engraved, starting as early as the Han dynasty. More than 1,000 stelae bear inscriptions ranging from descriptions of administrative projects to artistic renditions of land-scape, portraiture, and even calligraphy. One of the world's first dic-tionaries and a number of Tang dynasty classics are housed here. One, known as the *Popular Stela,* dates from AD 781. It records the inter-action between the emperor and a traveling Nestorian priest, Raban. After presenting the empire with translated Nestorian Christian texts, Raban was allowed to open a church in Xian. The rest of the museum holds Silk Road artifacts, including stone sculptures from the Tang dy-nasty. ⊠ *15 San Xue Jie, west of Duanlu Men,* ☎ *029/721–0764.* ⊑ *Y30.* ⊘ *Summer, daily 8:15–6; winter, daily 8:15–5:15.*

❼ Xiao Yan Ta (Small Goose Pagoda). Once part of the 7th-century AD Da Jianfu Temple and Monastery, this 15-tier pagoda south of the city's south gate was built by Empress Wu Zetian in 707 to honor her de-ceased predecessor, Emperor Gao Zong. The pagoda housed Buddhist texts brought back from India by the pilgrim Yiqing in the 8th cen-tury. A tremendous 16th-century earthquake lopped off the top two stories of the original pagoda, but they were rebuilt. The other build-ings were actually constructed during the Ming and have also been re-built at various times. The grounds are pleasant, and the pavilions are a good place to relax and stroll. Near the entrance a pavilion houses a small arts shop that sells local imitations of ancient styles as well as more modern paintings that still bear the marks of their Chinese ori-gin. There are some excellent reproductions here at reasonable prices. ⊠ *Youyi Xilu, west of Nanguan Zhengjie,* ☎ *029/525–3455.* ⊑ *Y10.* ⊘ *Daily 8:30–6.*

❸ **Zhonglou** (Bell Tower). The Bell Tower was first built in the late 14th century to mark the center of the city. Subsequent changes in city organization have displaced it from this prominent position, but the city still revolves around it. Despite its lack of centrality, it marks the point where Xida Jie (West Main Street) becomes Dongda Jie (East Main Street) and Beida Jie (North Main Street) becomes Nanda Jie (South Main Street). You can cross to the tower, which stands in the middle of a traffic circle, through an underground passage from the north side of the street and climb up to see its centuries-old pillars and roofs, as well as an art exhibition on its upper floor. The tower was renovated in the Qing dynasty. The large iron bell that gives the tower its name is rung at 8 AM and 6 PM daily. ⊠ *Junction of Dongda Jie, Xida Jie, Beida Jie, and Nanda Jie.* 🎟 *Y15.* ⊙ *Daily 7–7.*

Dining and Lodging

$$$ ✕ **Tang Le Gong.** Using recipes preserved from ancient times, the Tang
★ Le Gong specializes in Tang dynasty imperial cuisine—a taste you're not likely to find back home at your local Chinese restaurant. Book in advance for an unusual evening of entertainment: a full-length imperial banquet, complete with Tang dynasty singing and dancing. Dinner begins at 7, and the performance at 8:30. ⊠ *75 Changan Beilu,* ☎ *029/526–1620. Reservations essential. AE, MC, V.*

$–$$ ✕ **De Fa Chang Restaurant.** If you think dumplings are just occasional snack food, think again. This is one of Xian's fanciest and most famous restaurants, first opened in 1936 and moved to a central location in 1999. With red lanterns hanging outside and neon lighting at night, this four-story behemoth attracts large groups of locals, who sometimes exit singing. Its claim to fame is its dumpling banquet, which even President Jiang Zemin has sampled. The restaurant also serves a tempting hotpot, which comes out flaming in an intricate brass pot, as well as an array of tiny dessert dumplings, stuffed with everything from minced carrots to crushed sweetened walnuts. ⊠ *Beidajie, north side of Zhonglou Guangchang,* ☎ *029/721–4060. No credit cards.*

$–$$ ✕ **Xian Fanzhuang.** The oldest and largest restaurant in the city, the Xian specializes in local foods with a Muslim flavor as well as "small eats"—street food spruced up for the visitor. Suited businessmen and T-shirt-clad college students alike head to the bustling first-floor cafeteria for quick service. The second floor is a proper restaurant, where more intricate dishes—from fresh steamed carp to roasted duck—are prepared. The private rooms on the third floor host banquets. ⊠ *298 Dongda Jie,* ☎ *029/727–3821 (ask for restaurant). No credit cards.*

$–$$ ✕ **Laosun Jia.** Otherwise known as the Xian Muslim Restaurant, this
★ traditional, family-run affair, crowned by a green dome and crescent moon, serves some of the best local Islamic specialties in lamb and beef. The first floor has a snack bar, while the second floor has a more formal atmosphere and friendly service. The decor is nothing to write home about, but two more branches have opened up around town, commercial evidence that the food is worthwhile. ⊠ *364 Dongda Jie, southeast corner of Dongda Jie and Duanlumen,* ☎ *029/724–0936. No credit cards.*

$ ✕ **Jiefang Lu Jiaozi Guan.** *Jiaozi* generally refers to boiled dumplings with meat fillings. This restaurant, which makes large succulent jiaozis with more than 200 different fillings at low prices, has become so popular for its handmade delights that it's opened up five more branches around town. Service is friendly and prompt. The restaurant offers a couple of nonmeat dumplings. ⊠ *302 Jiefang Lu,* ☎ *029/744–2132. Reservations essential. No credit cards.*

$$$$ **ANA Grand Castle Hotel.** Right outside the old city's south gates, this classy hotel—with its white walls and black-tipped pavilion roof mod-

eled after the Great Goose Pagoda—is luxurious and less expensive than its competitors. It's a good base for touring the old city. ✉ *12 Xi Duan Huan Cheng Nanlu, 710068,* ☎ *029/723–1800,* FAX *029/723–1500. 293 rooms, 18 suites. 3 restaurants, hair salon, gym, business services, travel services. AE, MC, V.*

$$$$ 🏨 **Grand New World.** This luxurious hotel benefits from its proximity to an access point in the city wall as well as from its association with the Xian Cultural Center, which holds performances of plays and Xian-style operas in the hotel's theater. The courtyard, with statues of historic figures, is an escape from the busy street outside. Several bus routes run on Lianhu Lu going to more central parts of town. ✉ *48 Lianhu Lu, 710002,* ☎ *029/721–6868,* FAX *029/721–9754,* WEB *www.newworldhotels.com/sianw. 469 rooms, 22 suites. 3 restaurants, pool, tennis court, gym, business services, travel services. AE, MC, V.*

$$$$ 🏨 **Hyatt Regency Hotel.** Former presidential couple Bill and Hillary Clinton stayed here when they visited Xian in 1998. The deluxe establishment, a few steps away from the town's chicest boutiques and bars, provides excellent service and high-quality Chinese food, as well as data ports in all rooms. It's a short ride from the best Xian sights, as well as within walking distance of the East Gate of the city wall. ✉ *158 Dongda Jie, 710001,* ☎ *029/723–1234,* FAX *029/721–6799,* WEB *www.hyatt.com. 382 rooms, 22 suites. 2 restaurants, bar, café, tennis court, gym, nightclub, laundry service, dry cleaning, business services, meeting room, airport shuttle. AE, MC, V.*

$$$$ 🏨 **Royal Xian.** This Japanese-owned hotel, with its rectangular modernist facade and splashing fountains in front, has reasonable service and standard amenities. A Nikko Hotel, it caters to Asian tour groups. ✉ *334 Dongda Jie, 710001,* ☎ *029/723–5311,* FAX *029/723–5887,* WEB *www.nikkohotels.com. 420 rooms, 29 suites. 2 restaurants, bar, driving range, gym, nightclub, laundry service, business services, meeting room, travel services. AE, MC, V.*

$$$$ 🏨 **Sheraton.** Never mind the dusty blue-glass facade: this is a joint venture with high-quality standards and well-appointed rooms. Unfortunately, it's some distance from town (staying here adds roughly 30 to 40 minutes to a terra-cotta warriors excursion), but it has the convenience of a CITS branch on site. ✉ *12 Fenghao Donglu, 710001,* ☎ *029/426–1888,* FAX *029/426–2188. 438 rooms, 17 suites. 4 restaurants, bar, pool, gym, business services, travel services. AE, MC, V.*

$$$$ 🏨 **Shangri-La Golden Flower Xian.** Its golden glassy veneer shields a well-lit property with excellent service and facilities. One of the most imposing and upscale hotels in the city, the Shangri-La maintains the chain's usual strict quality. The hotel offers bicycle rentals and tours of the area. Its only disadvantage is its location outside the old city walls, a 10-minute cab ride from the city center (without traffic). ✉ *8 Changle Xilu, 710032,* ☎ *029/323–2981; 800/942–5050 in the U.S.,* FAX *029/ 323–5477,* WEB *www.shangri-la.com/eng/hotel/15/. 389 rooms, 57 suites. 2 restaurants, 2 bars, indoor pool, gym, nightclub, business services, meeting room. AE, MC, V.*

$$$–$$$$ 🏨 **Bell Tower Hotel.** The service isn't what it used to be at this former Holiday Inn–managed hotel, though prices remain high. Still, rooms are clean and comfortable, and the hotel has the most desirable address in the city, directly across from the Bell Tower. Upstairs, there's a branch of CITS and the Golden Gate Travel Service. You can rent bicycles here or set up tours of the area, and the hotel is home to some of Xian's best Western food. ✉ *110 Nanda Jie, 710001,* ☎ *029/727– 9200 ext. 2809,* FAX *029/721–8767. 309 rooms, 11 suites. 2 restaurants, bar, baby-sitting, dry cleaning, laundry service, business services, meeting room, travel services. AE, MC, V.*

$–$$ 🏨 **Liging.** The Liging is probably the best choice for a hotel in its price range. Rooms are relatively clean and comfortable, and the service is friendly. Its trump card is its location, just a stone's throw from the Bell Tower. ⊠ *6 Xida Jie, 710002,* ☎ *029/728–8731 or 029/721–8895,* FAX *029/728–8731 ext. 303. 100 rooms, 3 suites. Restaurant, business services, travel services. No credit cards.*

$ 🏨 **Jiefang.** Across from the railway station, the Jiefang is a standard Chinese hotel that caters mostly to Chinese guests, with relatively clean if small rooms. Its service is lackadaisical at best, but it's very convenient if you're coming in late at night or want to be at the hub of Xian excursion possibilities. CITS has a ticketing office upstairs. ⊠ *181 Jiefang Lu, 710005,* ☎ *029/742–8946,* FAX *029/742–2617. 313 rooms, 8 suites. 3 restaurants, hair salon, massage, sauna, laundry service, business services, travel services. No credit cards.*

Nightlife and the Arts

The **Shaanxi Provincial Dance and Song Assembly** (⊠ 5 Wenyi Beilu, ☎ 029/785–2664) stages traditional performances in colorful ethnic regalia; check with CITS for times. The **Shaanxi Provincial Drama Assembly** (⊠ 59 Beida Jie, ☎ 029/727–1515) has periodic performances of regional-style traditional opera and plays.

One of the busiest parts of town in the evening is the **Muslim Quarter,** where crowds converge to shop, stroll, and eat virtually any night of the week. It's a great place to check out the local scene.

In the late 1990s a spurt of Western-style bars and discos hit Xian, mainly grouped in a strip on Dongda Jie, between the Grand Hyatt and the Hotel Royal Xian. Although many went under after a 2000 nationwide crackdown on nightspots, prostitution, and gambling, the most chic and sleekest club in town is still the metal-sheathed **Bar 1+1** (⊠ 285 Dongda Jie, ☎ 029/721–6265 or 029/726–3128), which is a magnet for beautiful people; hordes pack the dance floor even on weekdays to vogue to Japanese techno, bathed in red neon laser lights. Kitsch mixes with cool at Xian's other popular hangout, **China City** (⊠ 4/F, Nanda Jie, entrance on Fen Xiang Lu, ☎ 029/721–0215 or 721–4395), where local singers croon soft-pop standards.

If you're looking for quieter haunts to while away the afternoon or evening, Xian's new **De Fu Xiang Café Street** is another popular choice among locals. Here, over a dozen almost-identical Western-style cafés offer your choice of tea or cappuccino in double-decker surroundings with pine wood floors. To find De Fu Xiang, walk south on Nanda Jie and take a right at Fen Xiang. After five minutes or so, you'll see the café street, marked by a neon-lit archway on the left-hand side. One of the street's more popular cafés is the pleasant **Jie Chu Ta Chi** (Touch Café; ⊠ 22 De Fu Xiang, ☎ 029/721–8019), where you can drink Colombian coffee or one of a variety of teas while tinkering with an assortment of puzzles and brain-teasers.

Shopping

Predictably, Xian swarms with terra-cotta references in various flavors and styles: aside from postcards and picture books, you can get imitation terra-cotta warriors at virtually every tourist site in town. Made with detail that quite resembles the original, these range in size from those that fit in the palm of your hand to others that stand eye to eye with an upright adult and can be shipped home for you.

But there is more to buy here than Qin reminders. The **Art Carving Factory** (⊠ 8 Nanxin Jie, ☎ 029/721–7332) carries local art wares. All kinds of crafts and souvenirs can be bought at the **Friendship Store** (Youyi Shang Dian; ⊠ 1A Nanxin Jie, ☎ 029/721–0551). The **Jade Carving**

Factory (✉ 173 Xi Yi Lu, ☎ 029/745–2570) sells sculptures by local jade workers. The **Overseas Chinese Department Store** (✉ 297 Dongda Jie, ☎ 029/721–7673) has two floors of local artists' wares. A bit outside town but well worth the trip, the **Xian Chinese Painting Institute Shopping Center** (✉ Naner Huan Lu at Lingyuan Lu, ☎ 029/526–4775228) displays and sells local artworks.

Xian also has a number of market streets where peddlers sell foods, replica antiques, and more. You can sometimes find lovely souvenirs here. The **Dajue Xiang market** (✉ Hua Jue Xiang), on the alley that leads into the entrance of the Great Mosque, is one of the best places to find souvenirs. Expect the antique dagger or beautiful porcelain bowl you're eyeing to be fake, however, no matter how hard the vendor insists your find is "genuine Ming dynasty." **Fangu Jie** and the area around the **North Gate** also have antiques sellers. One of the liveliest food markets is the covered **Nan Shi Jie,** off Dongda Jie, where everything from fresh fruit to turtles and monkey testicles are sold.

Side Trip from Xian

A few hours east by train from Xian lies one of China's five Famous ⑩ Mountains, **Huashan.** The 7,218-ft mountain has some lovely scenery, including tall, sloping pines whose distinctive tufts of green are reminiscent of a Dr. Seuss creation, and granite walls that rise shockingly out of the surrounding flatter lands. This is not a trip for the fainthearted: hiking the main trail takes a good seven to nine hours one-way, some of it along narrow passes on sheer cliffs. For the less athletically inclined, there is a cable car ride to North Peak three-quarters up the main trail (Y55, Y100 round-trip); frequent minibuses (Y10) run from Huashan Village to the cable car station, located just a few kilometers southeast of the village. From Xian, you can take a train (1¾–3 hrs, Y10) to Huashan Village, at the base of the mountain. Note: the Huashan train station is confusingly located 15 km (9 mi) outside Huashan Village, in the neighboring town of Mengyuan; frequent minibuses (Y3) link both places. Alternately, buses (2 hrs, Y12) run direct to Huashan Village hourly from the Xian bus station. Inquire at CITS for new hotels in the area, as several upmarket hotels catering to foreigners (with prices to match) are opening up; a decent budget option with relatively clean and comfortable rooms is the **Xiyue Fandian** (✉ Yuquan Lu, ☎ 0913/436–3145).

Shaanxi A to Z

To research prices, get advice from other travelers, and book travel arrangements, visit www.fodors.com.

AIR TRAVEL

You can book tickets at CAAC, through CITS, or your hotel travel desk. For Hong Kong flights you can take the domestic carrier or Dragonair.

➤ AIRLINES AND CONTACTS: **CAAC** (☎ 029/870–8486). **CITS** (✉ 32 Changan Beilu, ☎ 029/727–9200 ext. 2842, FAX 029/526–1454). **Dragonair** (✉ 12 Fenghao Donglu, in the Sheraton Hotel, ☎ 029/426–2988).

AIRPORTS

Around 40 km (25 mi) northwest of town, Xian's Xianyang Airport has daily or almost daily service to Beijing, Shanghai, Guangzhou, Chengdu, and Ürümqi, and several flights a week to Hong Kong and Macau. It's also connected internationally, with daily flights to Japan.

Taxis to and from the airport should cost Y120–Y160. China Northwest Airlines also runs an hourly shuttle-bus service (Y25) between the airport and its booking office from 5 AM–6 PM daily.

➤ AIRPORT INFORMATION: **Xian Xianyang Airport** (☎ 029/870–8450). **China Northwest Airlines shuttle service** (✉ 296 Laodong Nanlu, ☎ 029/870–2299).

BIKE TRAVEL

Many Xian hotels rent bicycles for a song. In good weather this is a great way to see the city—all the sights within the city walls are close enough to bike to, and you might want to ride around to the park that surrounds the moat.

BUS TRAVEL

Xian's bus center stands directly south of the Bell Tower; just about every bus in the city passes through here. City maps show bus routes and numbers. From here you can also catch convenient, and less crowded, buses to out-of-town sights. Buses run frequently and traverse the city, but they're very crowded, and the driving tends to be a little fast and loose. It's best to stick to the cabs, which are plentiful, cheap, and easily hailed.

The long-distance bus station, across from the train station on Jiefang Lu, has buses to Huashan every hour from 6 AM–4 PM daily (2 hours, Y12) and other Shaanxi destinations, as well as Henan stops.

CAR TRAVEL

Because so many of the sights lie outside the city proper, hiring a taxi or hotel car with a driver is convenient and allows you the freedom to leave when you like instead of waiting for the rest of the tour. Ask for a rental car at your hotel; major hotels provide car services.

EMERGENCIES

In case of an emergency, contact your hotel manager for assistance. If you speak Chinese (or are traveling with someone who does), the following numbers may prove useful: Police ☎ 110, the fire department ☎ 119, and the first aid hotline ☎ 120.

➤ CONTACTS: **Xian Medical University Affiliated Hospital No. 1** (✉ 1 Jiankang Lu, ☎ 029/522–7604).

INTERNET SERVICES

Most major hotels in town have Internet access, though the rates are sometimes exorbitant. The most centrally located place is Internet Club 169, where you can pay Y12 for an hour. Cheaper Internet places have also sprung up on Dongda Jie, including the popular and crowded Mu Wei Jiu Ba, where going online is Y3 an hour; and Internet 169 Bar, where surfing the Web costs Y10 an hour. Nanda Jie south of the old city walls (Nan Guan Zheng Jie) has a number of Internet cafés. If you have your own laptop, you can also get online with a public access Internet number. The telephone number, user name, and password is 163; all you pay for is the phone time.

➤ CONTACTS: **Internet Club 169** (✉ 2/F, China Telecom Bldg., Bell Tower Sq., ☎ 029/723–2017, FAX 029/723–2047). **Internet 169 Bar** (✉ 213 Dongda Jie, ☎ 029/728–1449). **Mu Wei Jiu Ba** (✉ 2/F, 341 Dongda Jie, ☎ 029/721–1245).

TOURS

Every hotel offers its own guided tours of the area, usually dividing them into eastern area, western area, and city tours. More upscale hotels have special English-language tour guides, but their availability often depends on the number of people in your group. You don't have to stay at the hotel to participate in a tour. CITS (☞ Visitor Information) arranges similar tours.

➤ TOUR-OPERATOR RECOMMENDATIONS: **CITS** (✉ 32 Changan Beilu, ☎ 029/727–9200 ext. 2842, FAX 029/526–1454).

TRAIN TRAVEL
FARES AND SCHEDULES

The train station, Xian Zhan, lies on the same rail line as Lanzhou (10 hours), the next major stop on the Silk Road; Dunhuang (24 hours); and Ürümqi (35 hours). Off the Silk Road, other major stops are Beijing (13½ hours), Shanghai (17 hours), Guangzhou (28 hours), Chengdu (15 hours), and Kunming (36 hours). Going east you can also connect to Luoyang, Zhengzhou (8 hours), and Nanjing (14 hours). The main Huashan stop is about an hour out of Xian on the train. The foreigners' ticket window upstairs above the main ticket office is open daily 8:30–11:30 and 2:30–5:30. First order your destination at one of the windows on the far left, then take the receipt and line up on the other side of the room. CITS will book tickets for a fee, as will Golden Bridge Travel Agency (☞ Travel Agencies); both need three days' notice.

➤ TRAIN INFORMATION: **Xian Zhan** (✉ Huancheng Beilu Dong Duan and Jiefang Lu, ☎ 029/727–6076).

TRAVEL AGENCIES

CITS offers good basic tours of the area all year, and books hotels, train, and plane tickets. Across the hall from CITS, Golden Bridge Travel Agency has similar services and can book hotels for a discount, but be prepared to bargain hard for lower prices.

➤ LOCAL AGENT REFERRALS: **Golden Bridge Travel Agency** (✉ Bell Tower Hotel, 2nd floor; 227 Nanda Jie, ☎ 029/725–7275, FAX 029/725–8863). **Xijing Travel Agency** (✉ 77 Qingnian Lu, North Building, 3/F, ☎ 029/721–7951).

VISITOR INFORMATION
➤ TOURIST INFORMATION: **CITS** (✉ 32 Changan Beilu, ☎ 029/727–9200 ext. 2842, FAX 029/526–1454).

NINGXIA

The smallest of China's five autonomous regions is something of an enigma, with little known about it outside its own borders. With an area of 66,400 square km (25,600 square mi) and a population of a mere 5.6 million, it is surrounded by the provinces of Gansu and Shaanxi and the huge autonomous region of Inner Mongolia. A third of the population is composed of minorities, most of them Hui (Muslim Han), but also significant numbers of Mongols and Manchurians.

An arid region traditionally inhabited by nomads, most of Ningxia is high, flat plateau, and the rest lowland plain along which the Yellow River flows, providing water for the network of canals that have been in use for many hundreds of years. The climate of Ningxia is continental, characterized by very cold winters and warm summers that are rarely excessively hot. The annual rainfall is less than 8 inches.

With the exception of a couple of comparatively brief periods, the region has been under Chinese control since the Qin dynasty. Ningxia was part of various administrative regions until 1928, when it became a province. In 1958 the government turned the area into the Autonomous Region of Ningxia Huizu Zizhiqu.

Ningxia's capital, Yinchuan, is quite lively. The remoter areas offer insight into the lesser-known aspects of Chinese life—ancient water wheels are still used for irrigation, and in some areas leather rafts continue in use.

Yinchuan

⑪ *540 km (335 mi) southwest of Hohhot (10 hrs by train); 850 km (530 mi) southwest of Beijing (20½ hrs by train).*

Once the capital of the 11th-century Western Xia dynasty, Yinchuan stands amid a network of irrigation canals thought to have been in constant use since the Han dynasty. It's close to the Yellow River to the east and the Helan Mountains to the west. The town is actually divided in two: the New Town, site of the railway station, and the Old Town, about 5 km (3 mi) southwest.

All ancient Chinese cities had their drum and bell towers, which were used to announce the beginning and end of the hours of curfew. Yinchuan's **Gulou** (Drum Tower), having survived the destructive phases of Chinese history, stands on the main street not far from the post office. Of interest to history buffs may be the black-and-white photography exhibition of Communist history on show here in four rooms: amid the pictures of Ningxia Communist Party members, there are some fine photos, including a haunting one of Deng Xiaoping in his youth and one of Chiang Kai-shek and his wife. ⊠ *Gulou Jie,* ☎ *0951/602–4652.* ⚏ *Y2.* ⊙ *Summer, daily 8–noon and 3–6; winter, daily 8–noon and 2:30–6. (If there is no one at the entrance, go to Yuhuang Ge, and ask the ticket attendant to open the door.).*

Close to the Drum Tower, the **Yuhuang Ge** (Yuhuang Pavilion) is a restored 400-year-old house containing a small museum. On the first floor is an exhibition of contemporary landscape paintings; head upstairs to look at artifacts from the New Stone Age to the Qing Dynasty, including coins, sculptures, pottery, and brassware. ⊠ *2 Yuhuang Ge Bei Jie,* ☎ *0951/602–4652.* ⚏ *Y4.* ⊙ *Summer, daily 8:30–noon and 3–6:30; winter, daily 8:30–noon and 2:30–6.*

In the northern suburbs is a pagoda that has stood here since the 5th century. The current **Haibao** (Treasure) or **Haibao Ta** (North Pagoda) dates from 1771, when it replaced an earlier one destroyed by an earthquake in 1739. Forming part of a temple complex, it has 11 stories and is 177 ft high, offering fine views across the town to the Yellow River. Although actually rectangular in shape, it has niches designed to create the illusion that it's 12-sided. Walk to the back of the pagoda for the large golden reclining Buddha. ⊠ *Jinning Jie,* ☎ *0951/503–8045.* ⚏ *Y5.* ⊙ *Daily 8–6.*

In a former monastery, **Ningxia Bowuguan** (Ningxia Museum) houses a fine collection of Western Xia and Zhou dynasty artifacts, ceramics, and sculptures, as well as materials illustrating Hui Muslim culture, some Stone Age petroglyphs from the Helan Mountains, and a collection of Ming and Qing paintings. Of the monastery itself the most obvious remaining part is the pagoda, known as the towering **Xi Ta** (West Pagoda), with its glazed-tile roof. It was built in about 1050 during the Western Xia dynasty. The museum offers car service to the Western Xia Tombs and Helanshan Petroglyphs at some of the cheapest rates in town. ⊠ *32 Jinning Nan Jie,* ☎ *0951/503–6497.* ⚏ *Y15.* ⊙ *Daily 9–noon and 2–5.*

The modern, busy **Nanguan Si** (Nanguan Mosque) is interesting for its purely Arabic architectural style. ⊠ *Just south of Nanguancheng Lu.* ⊙ *Daily 8–noon and 2–5.*

The restored red **Nanmen** (South Gate), built in classical Chinese style, is all that remains of the city wall. ⊠ *Zhongshan Jie.* ⚏ *Y2.* ⊙ *Daily 8–8.*

Dining and Lodging

You can eat tolerably well in the hotel restaurants, but in Yinchuan you're almost better off eating at the smaller places on the street, such as the Hanmin Canting, the Yingbinlou, or the Huanying. A great food alley to try is Zhong Xin Xiang, between Jiefang Xi Jie and Xinhua Dong Jie, near the Yuanheng Hotel. The local food is essentially Islamic, with lamb and beef dishes, dumplings and pastries, and blended teas. But regional specialties include several tasty cold vegetarian dishes as well: try the *zhima bocai* (sesame spinach) or *kuku cai* (bitter greens marinated in vinegar and spiced with garlic and red peppers). *Hongshao ji eu* ("red-cooked" river fish) is another popular dish, made with fish caught from the Yellow River.

$–$$ ⊞ **Hongqiao Da Jiu Dian** (Rainbow Bridge Hotel). Centrally located, the Hongqiao Da Jiu Dian is possibly the best hotel of its price category in town. The resplendent gold-trimmed lobby has subtle touches of white marble and rose, the staff is friendly, and the rooms are comfortable and well priced. ⊠ *16 Jiefang Xi Jie, 750001,* ☎ *0951/691–8888,* ℻ *0951/691–8788. 142 rooms, 12 suites. 3 restaurants, sauna, miniature golf, business services. AE, MC, V.*

$ ⊞ **Ningfeng Hotel.** This good, modern hotel boasting a cozy white marble lobby has comfortable rooms and reasonable facilities. ⊠ *236 Jiefang Dong Jie, 750004,* ☎ *0951/602–8898,* ℻ *0951/602–7224. 132 rooms, 11 suites. 3 restaurants, bar, hair salon, massage, shop. No credit cards.*

Shopping

Ningxia is well known for its **carpets.** You can also buy the local **teas.** The main shopping street is Gulou Lu.

Side Trips from Yinchuan

★ ⑫ Lying at the foot of the Helan Mountains 35 km (22 mi) west of Yinchuan, the **Xixia Wangling** (Western Xia Tombs) have a certain dramatic appeal. Because this dynasty, which lasted 189 years (1038–1227) before being exterminated by the Mongols, was not included in the imperial annals, little is known about many aspects of it, including the occupants of the tombs. Despite the shortness of its history, however, the dynasty invented its own written language (similar to Chinese), minted new currency, possessed a strong military, and developed a flourishing culture and new artistic style. Stunning artifacts unearthed from the tombs—including horse and cow sculptures, gold masks, patterned tiles, and simple but striking glazed ceramics, as well as several dioramas of the surrounding region—are housed in the impressive yellow-pavilioned Xixia Museum on site; unfortunately, there are no English captions. In a wing opposite the museum, plaster sculptures depicting well-known scenes from Xixia history have been erected; avoid these if you can, and head over to the tombs. The founder of the dynasty, Li Yuanhao, is believed to have built 72 tombs for himself and his relatives. Only one of the circular brick mounds is open to the public; to gain entry, you have to book a tour with a travel agency. ⊠ *Hire a taxi, book a CITS tour or a car from the Ningxia Museum, or take bus no. 17 from bus station to terminus, then taxi.* 🚌 *Y30.* ☉ *Daily 8–5.*

⑬ **Helankou Yanhua** are also called Helanshan Yanhua (Petroglyphs of the Helan Mountains). Etchings of goggling human masks, fleet-footed deer, crouching tigers, sexual intercourse, and even a witch draining energy from a human captive appear in these New Stone Age petroglyphs, chiseled into the rocks at the base of the Helan Mountains between 3,000 and 10,000 years ago. The site opened to the public in 2000 after an international conference was convened by local archaeologists to call attention to the historic value of the petroglyphs; no paved road to the site existed beforehand. Over 3,200 petroglyphs have been discovered here so far, as well as a Qing Dynasty inscription commemorating the renovation of the Helanshan Pass by soldiers. Go, if only for the breathtaking scenery: steps have been carved into the slopes of the mountains, and as you wind past overhanging shrubbery to gaze down at the barren white plain of rocks at the base of the mountains, mountain goats occasionally cross the path. ⌧ *70 km (44 mi) northwest of Yinchuan, via hired taxi or car from the Ningxia Museum or a CITS tour,* ☎ *0139/9519–2603.* 🎫 *Y20.* ☉ *Daily 8–6.*

Qingtonxia Zhen

⑭ *80 km (50 mi) south of Yinchuan (1–1½ hrs by train).*

Qingtongxia Zhen (Old Qingtongxia) is an ancient town that contains one of the most famous sites in Ningxia, that of a group of **108 Dagobas.** Aligned in 12 rows forming a giant triangle on the shores of a lake in the middle of arid semidesert land, these Tibetan-style sacred pagodas were built in the Yuan (Mongol) dynasty. Nobody knows why they were placed here: maybe in celebration of some great event or as thanks for the water of the lake.

Zhongwei

⑮ *160 km (100 mi) southwest of Yinchuan (2½–3 hours by train).*

A market town on the fringes of the desert, Zhongwei is close to the Yellow River. Here the **Gao Si** (Gao Temple) was originally built in the 15th century and has been rebuilt and expanded several times since. Essentially constructed of wood, it was designed to cater to all the main religions and beliefs of China, with chapels and shrines to Buddhism, Confucianism, and Taoism.

Outside the town it's possible to see relics of ancient ways of life. As in other parts of China, irrigation techniques using water wheels have been in operation since the Han dynasty. They have become largely obsolete, but examples can still be found close to the village of **Xiaheye,** on the far side of the Yellow River. With luck you will be able to make the crossing using a leather raft, made from sheep or cow skin wrapped around a wooden frame, of a type that was once used to transport goods over distances of up to 2,000 km (1,240 mi).

Shapotou

⑯ *21 km (13 mi) west of Zhongwei (1 hr by bus).*

Shapotou lies on the edge of the Tengger Desert, where several thousand hectares of green fields have been reclaimed from drifting sand dunes. The site was first founded in 1956 around the Shapotou Desert Research Center, when researchers were looking for a way to keep sand dunes from covering the railway line; they solved the problem by planting straw checkerboard bales into the sand. Since the late 1990s, Shapotou has been turned into the region's main tourist attraction. Inside a sprawling complex of a Chinese amusement park, lined with lush fields and trees amidst desert scenery, you can ride camels and horses, sail down the Yellow River on an animal-skin raft or motorboat (followed by a camel ride back to the park), or sled down a golden mountain of sand, amid other carnival attractions. Near Shapotou, shimmering rice paddies and muddy plots dot the landscape: among the peasant laborers, mules, and oxen working the land, you may see the occasional camel plowing the fields as well. Independent minibuses leave from the Zhongwei bus station about every half hour, 7–5 daily. The trip takes *about an hour and costs Y3.5. ☎ 0953/701–2961. ➥ Y20; additional fees for some attractions. ◷ Daily 24 hrs.*

Ningxia A to Z

To research prices, get advice from other travelers, and book travel arrangements, visit www.fodors.com.

AIR TRAVEL
Direct flights link Yinchuan daily to Beijing and Xian, and several times a week to Shanghai, Chengdu, Nanjing, Lanzhou, Urumqi, Xiamen and Guangzhou.

AIRPORTS
CAAC runs a shuttle-bus service (Y15) to the airport, which is 21 km (13 mi) outside the city.
➤ AIRPORT INFORMATION: **CAAC** (✉ Ming Hang Bldg., Nan Men square, ☎ 0951/691–3456; ✉ 93 Jiefang Dong Jie, ☎ 0951/609–3722).

BUS TRAVEL
FARES AND SCHEDULES
From Yinchuan buses go daily to Lanzhou and Xian every 20 minutes as well as to the other towns in the province, such as Zhongwei (3½ hours). The bus station is in the south of town.
➤ BUS INFORMATION: **Yinchuan bus station** (✉ Zhongshan Jie, near Nan Men, ☎ 0951/603–1571).

CAR RENTAL
Cars with drivers can be hired through CITS.
➤ CONTACTS: **PSB** (✉ 5 Jinning Bei Jie, Yinchuan, ☎ 0951/602–2888).

MONEY MATTERS
CURRENCY EXCHANGE
In Yinchuan you can change money in the major hotels or at the Bank of China.
➤ EXCHANGE SERVICES: **Bank of China** (✉ 80 Jiefang Xi Jie, ☎ 0951/504–1115).

TOURS
In Zhongwei, Sha Po Tou Travel Agency has some intriguing tours, including camel-riding in the Tengger Desert and camping by the Ming Dynasty Great Wall, as well as sheepskin rafting down the Yellow River.
➤ TOUR-OPERATOR RECOMMENDATIONS: **Sha Po Tou Travel Agency** (✉ 1/F, Zhongwei Binguan, 33 Gulou Xi Jie, ☎ 0953/701–2961, FAX 0953/701–8841).

TRAIN TRAVEL
FARES AND SCHEDULES
Direct trains link Yinchuan with Datong (15 hours), Hohhot (10 hours), Lanzhou (8 hours), Beijing (20½ hours), Shanghai (39 hours), Xian (13 hours), and Xining (11 hours). From Yinchuan station there are several trains a day to Qingtongxia Zhen (1½ hours) and Zhongwei (2½ hours). Direct trains link Zhongwei to Shanghai (36 hours), Beijing (23 hours), Lanzhou (5½ hours), Jiayuguan (12 hours), Hohhot (12½ hours), Xian (11 hours), and Yinchuan.
➤ TRAIN INFORMATION: **Yinchuan Station** (✉ Xingzhou Lu, eastern part of New Town, ☎ 0953/504–6271).

TRANSPORTATION AROUND NINGXIA
Buses and minibuses around Yinchuan link the old and new towns. Taxis are widely available.

VISITOR INFORMATION

➤ TOURIST INFORMATION: CITS (✉ 3/F, 116 Jiefang Xijie, Yinchuan, 750001, ☎ 0951/504–8006, FAX 0951/504–3466).

GANSU

Gansu is the long, narrow corridor province that links central China with the desert regions of the northwest. It has an area of 451,000 square km (174,130 square mi) and a population consisting of Hui, Mongol, Kazakh, and Tibetan peoples.

Despite its length, the geography of Gansu is not as variable as you might expect. It has an average altitude of between 3,300 and 9,900 ft, with the highest peak reaching 19,000 ft. Although the eastern part of the province is a loess area through which flows the Yellow River, and much of the south and west is steppe land, what was for long the poorest province in China is essentially rugged and barren. The climate is of the continental kind, with cold and dry winters and hot summers.

Historically Gansu has been a vital conduit between China and the western world, the beginning of the Silk Road along which merchants for centuries transported their wares until shifting power and maritime trade rendered it obsolete. Gansu first became part of China proper in the Qin dynasty (221–206 BC). Buddhism made its way into China through here as early as the first century BC. The oasis towns that were strung along the desert areas became the provision stations for pilgrim and merchant alike—as the merchants made their fortunes from silk and other luxuries, so the oasis towns became significant shrines.

Gansu became the edge of China, the last link with the Middle Kingdom and therefore with civilization. The Great Wall, the most solid representation of ancient Chinese opinion of the outside world, passed through Gansu to the great fortress at Jiayuguan, beyond which lay Dunhuang, and then perdition. And yet Gansu has never been the most compliant of provinces. The influence of Islam was considerable here, and 19th-century rebellions were savagely put down. The decline of the Silk Road brought terrible suffering and poverty, from which the area has only very recently begun to recover as tourism boosts the local economy.

There has also been considerable industrial and mining expansion. Agriculture is important, but conditions are difficult, despite irrigation. Horses are reared here as well as sheep, pigs, and cattle; wheat, melons, cotton, and millet are important crops. Still, outside of its major cities, Gansu remains one of China's most impoverished and undeveloped provinces.

Dunhuang

 900 km (558 mi) northwest of Lanzhou (16 hrs).

Dunhuang, a small oasis town, is in many ways the most important destination on the Silk Road. Here, just outside of town, you can see an extraordinary array of wall paintings in caves that form part of Mogao Ku, considered the richest repository of Buddhist shrines in the world.

Dunhuang (Blazing Beacon) was made a prefecture in 117 BC, during the Han dynasty. At that time it was at the very edge of the Chinese empire, on the fringes of "barbarian" desert country. Its earthen "beacons" were a sort of extension of the Great Wall, used for sending signals between garrisons.

Buddhism entered China via the Silk Road at about the same time as Christianity was beginning to take hold in the Western world. As Dunhuang was the point of entry to the Chinese world, it was not long before a temple was established here. By AD 366 the first caves were being carved at the Mogao oasis. The carving continued until the 10th century; the works were subsequently left undisturbed for nearly a thousand years until adventurers from Europe and America began to plunder the area at the end of the 19th century. The paintings' and carvings' miraculous state of preservation is due to the dry desert conditions.

Dunhuang remained an important center until the end of the Tang dynasty, after which the spread of Islam and the temporary decline of Chinese influence in the region brought an end to centuries of creative energy. Indeed, Dunhuang became known as Shazhou (Sand Town). But the paintings survived; even more astounding was the discovery by Sir Aurel Stein in 1907 of one cave, seemingly deliberately sealed by departing priests at this period of decline, that revealed a stack of early Buddhist sutras, including one written on paper and dated AD 406, many centuries before paper was in use elsewhere, and one of the earliest printed documents, the Diamond Sutra of 868, which is now in the British Museum. The discovered papers did not concern only religious matters; there were also many items relating to local administration. The Chinese took umbrage at the European Sinologists' depredations, with the result that there are next to no documents to be seen at Dunhuang. The murals and statuary are all still in place. Modern Dunhuang still exudes the sleepy air of a dusty frontier town, although it has begun to change with the influx of tourists.

The surprisingly small **Dunhuang Bowuguan** (Dunhuang Museum), with a pink tri-camel sculpture in front, has three sections. One displays the items discovered in Cave 17 by Stein and his French colleague Pelliot. Another deals more in the practical items found in the region (silks and old textiles), while the third is devoted to sacrificial and funeral items. The museum sometimes closes without warning for staff weddings and other events. ⊠ *8 Yangguan Donglu,* ☎ *0937/882–2981.* 🎟 *Y10.* ⊙ *Daily 8–6:30.*

Across the Donghe River, west of town, the elegant but solitary-looking nine-tiered **Bai Ma Ta** (White Horse Dagoba) was established in 384 AD during the Northern Wei dynasty by a Kuchean monk to commemorate the death of his brave white horse. In the back corner of the lot that encloses the dagoba, look for a rusted iron door that leads to the remains of the ancient city walls of Shazhou. Unfortunately, there's nothing but fields of dirt left to see now: the ancient city walls were knocked down by the Red Guards during the Cultural Revolution, as was the temple that surrounded Bai Ma Ta. ⊠ *3 km west of the city center.* 🎟 *Y13.* ⊙ *Daily 9–6.*

South of Dunhuang, the oasis gives way to desert. Here, among the gorgeous sweep of sand dunes known as *Ming Sha Shan* (Singing Sand Mountain) is nestled **Yueyaquan** (Crescent Moon Lake), a lovely crescent-shaped pool of water that by some freak of the prevailing winds never silts up. The dunes themselves are the main attraction, named for the light rattling sound that the sand makes when wind blows across the surface— "rumbling sands," noted Marco Polo. Forty kilometers (25 mi) in length and 20 km (12 mi) wide, the tallest peak of the dunes is 5,600 ft above sea level. The half-hour climb to the summit is hard work but worth it for the views, particularly at sunset. Camel rides are available for Y30–40, and in summer, the latest innovation is paragliding (Y20). ⊠ *Take Dingzi Lu, continue about 5 km (3 mi) south of town.* 🎟 *Y30.*

★ The magnificent Buddhist **Mogao Ku** (Mogao Grottoes) lie southeast of Dunhuang. At least 40 caves are open to the public (a flashlight is a useful item for your visit), the earliest dating from the Northern Wei period (AD 386–534: caves 246, 257, 259); followed by the Western Wei (AD 535–556: cave 249); the Sui (AD 581–618: caves 244, 420, 427); Tang (AD 618–907: caves 17, 96, 130, 148, 172, 209, 323, 329); and Five Dynasties (AD 907–960: caves 16, 98). These are just a selection of some of the most interesting—there are plenty of others. Which caves are open on a given day depends on the local authorities. If a particular cave is closed, you can request that it be opened; whether that will happen is another matter. Don't miss caves 96 and 130—usually included on the regular tour—with stunning statues of a 108- and 78-ft-high Buddha.

In creating the paintings, the artists plastered the surfaces of the cave walls first with mud and then with layers of dung, straw or hair, and still more mud. The final surface was prepared with china clay, and mineral paints were applied (to both walls and statues), the colors of which have changed as they oxidized over the centuries. The monks who worshiped in these grottoes lived in small, unadorned caves in the cliff to the right of the painted caves as you look at them. The whole of the cliff was carved out eventually, so several of the caves were painted over in later dynasties. The art is definitely under threat, as the extra oxidation from huge numbers of tourists is fading the colors. A fine museum on site funded by a Japanese preservation organization contains reproductions of eight of the caves, where the art can be studied in full light. A smaller auxiliary exhibition space opposite the real caves has excellent rotating exhibitions on the history and art of individual caves. ✉ *25 km (15 mi) southeast of town; take minibus or taxi (Y50–80 round-trip);* ☎ *0937/886–9056.* 🎫 *Tour of 10 caves, exhibition space, and museum, Y80; additional Y20 for an English-speaking guide.* ☉ *Guided tours only, daily 9–5.*

Southwest of Dunhuang are the **Xi Qianfodong** (Western Thousand Buddha Caves). Considered to be of less importance than those at Mogao, they do nonetheless contain paintings from the Northern Wei and Tang dynasties. ✉ *30 km (18 mi) southwest of town; take taxi.* ☉ *Daily 9–noon and 2–5.*

Dining and Lodging

Aside from the hotel dining rooms, the night market just off Yangguan Donglu—though less exciting than night markets in Xinjiang—is worth a visit, for spicy hotpot, cold beer, and charred but flavorful lamb kebabs. Near the bus station, enterprising individuals have started a few small restaurants around Dingzi Lu with banana pancakes and chocolate milk shakes. Try John's Information Café with outdoor café tables, or Shirley's Café just across the street. There are also a host of small Chinese restaurants on this street.

$$$$ ✕🏨 **Silk Road Dunhuang Hotel.** Outside town just a half-mile from
★ the desert, this stone fortress of a Hong Kong joint-venture hotel, with its enormous grounds, is easily the most luxurious place to stay in Dunhuang, and one of the most elegant hotels on the entire Silk Road. Designed in the manner of a traditional *siheyuan* or Chinese courtyard house, it has desert rock gardens, stone tiles, and light-wood ceilings. The large, spacious rooms have historical touches like Ming reproduction furniture and traditional wooden shower buckets. The friendly staff speaks only a little English and can be disorganized. The hotel arranges some great tours, including a camel ride to the sand dunes of Mingshashan at sunrise, followed by breakfast. *West side of Dunyue Lu, 736200,* ☎ *0937/882–5388,* 📠 *0937/882–5211,* 🌐 *www.the-silk-road.com/dunhuang. 294 rooms, 6 suites. 2 restaurants, gym, shops, laundry, business services, travel services. AE, MC, V.*

$$–$$$ ✕🏨 **Dunhuang Binguan.** The first hotel built to cater to the influx of foreigners after 1976, this mid-range hotel is aging but provides reasonable comfort and facilities in a good location. The professional staff speaks decent English, and there's a travel agency on the first floor. ✉ *14 Yangguan Donglu, 736200,* ☎ *0937/882–2538,* 🖷 *0937/882–2195. 145 rooms, 15 suites. 4 restaurants, hair salon, gym, shops, travel services, business services. MC, V.*

$$ 🏨 **Dunhuang International Hotel.** At the southern edge of town, this towering white monolith with black-speckled marble floors is a Hong Kong joint-venture, with pleasant and clean rooms that are good value, though bathrooms tend to be on the smallish side. ✉ *28 Mingshan Lu, 736200,* ☎ *0937/882–8638,* 🖷 *0937/882–1821. 170 rooms, 6 suites. 2 restaurants, hair salon, gym, shops, laundry, business services. V.*

$$ 🏨 **Grand Sun Hotel Dunhuang.** Don't be put off by the gaudy metallic sun motif glitzing up this hotel's shiny white-marble lobby. The rooms here are spacious and well-appointed, with all the modern conveniences. The older wing, once a separate hotel, was annexed when the new 12-story Grand Sun building was constructed in 1997. ✉ *5 Shazhou Beilu, 736200,* ☎ *0937/882–9998,* 🖷 *0937/882–2019. 220 rooms, 22 suites. 4 restaurants, bar, hair salon, sauna, massage, shops, billiards, laundry, business services, travel services, gym. AE, MC, V.*

Nightlife and the Arts

There isn't exactly a rockin' night scene in Dunhuang. The cafés on Dingxi Lu, which are often open past midnight, draw backpackers eager to check their E-mail or just hang out. However, these are open only in high tourist season. There is also the occasional performance of song or dance at various hotels. Check with CITS (☞ *below*).

Outdoor Activities and Sports

You can hire a bicycle easily from any of several outlets and bike around town or to the sand dunes to watch the sunset.

Side Trip from Dunhuang

★ ⑱   The once-impressive old fort of **Jiayuguan,** 5 km (3 mi) outside the town of the same name, and some 280 km (174 mi) southeast of Dunhuang, stands in a dramatic spot guarding a pass between two mountain ranges. It was the westernmost point of the Great Wall during the Ming dynasty. The fort was built in 1372 with 33-ft-high walls and a circumference of well over 770 yards. In the vicinity of Jiayuguan you can visit (reconstructed and new-looking) parts of the Great Wall, rock paintings from the Warring States period, and tombs in the desert. History aside, it's only worth a day trip here if you're en route to or from Dunhuang by rail. On the other hand, the city itself is laid back, and the silver light of the sun flooding down from an immense sky can be transcendental. ✉ *Gansu Lu, 240 km (149 mi) northwest of Jiayuguan.*

Lanzhou

900 km (558 mi) southeast of Dunhuang; 450 km (279 mi) northwest of Xian.

Built on the banks of the Yellow River, the capital of Gansu extends along the base of a narrow gorge whose walls rise to 5,000 ft. A city with a long history, Lanzhou has been nearly ruined by rampant industrialization and is now one of the most polluted urban areas in the world—a pity, as the locals are unusually friendly and many of the streets are wide and graciously shaded by trees.

Founded more than 2,000 years ago, Lanzhou was already a substantial town by the middle of the Han dynasty, soon developing into one of the most important centers along the Silk Road. Following the

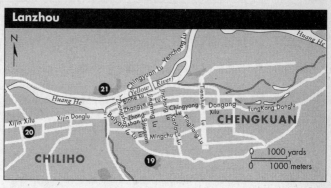

decline of the Han, Lanzhou became capital of a series of tribal kingdoms. In a narrow corridor between mountains, its strategic location, through which all traffic heading northwest or southeast must pass, has continued to invest it with considerable importance. After 1949 Lanzhou became the second-largest city in the region as the Chinese government turned it into an important industrial center. It is also a key railway junction linking the northwest with central, north, and northeastern China.

19 Wuquan Shan (Five Spring Mountain), named for the springs at its foot in the south of the city, rises to 5,250 ft. On it, from **Wuquanshan Gongyuan** (Five Spring Park), you can see impressive views of the city below, though the five springs have dwindled to only a trickle. In the park are a number of monuments. The Chongqing (Temple of Reverent Solemnity) dates from 1372. In it is a large bronze bell, 10 ft high and weighing 5 tons, that dates from 1202. A 16-ft bronze Buddha is from 1370. Behind Wuquanshan is Lanshan, towering over 6,600 ft and accessible by chair lift. ⊠ *Bus No. 8 from Jiuquan Lu in town center.* ☎ *Y5.* ☉ *Daily 8–6.*

★ **20** The old-fashioned but nonetheless excellent **Gansu Sheng Bowuguan** (Gansu Provincial Museum) has exhibits on three floors, including a perfectly reconstructed 26-ft-long prehistoric elephant on the first floor, and relics from the Silk Road on the second. Among the most memorable are the 7,000-year-old pottery shards from the Dadiwan culture (the earliest Neolithic site so far discovered in China) decorated with what are probably the earliest pictograms. There are also examples of decorated wares that indicate contact between China and Rome at least as far back as 2,200 years ago, as well as early textiles and magnificent tri-colored Tang porcelain. The most famous item is the elegant bronze "Flying Horse," considered a masterpiece of ancient Chinese art, and found in an Eastern Han tomb at Wuwei (a city in Gansu). With its hoof delicately poised on the wings of a bird, its image is much used as a symbol of the area. Among the other items on display are collections of early Yangshao pottery, Zhou bronzes, a Chinese minorities exhibition, and a Han dynasty tomb reconstruction. ⊠ *3 Xijin Xilu,* ☎ *0931/233-3346.* ☎ *Y15.* ☉ *Tues.–Sun. 9–4.*

21 The **Baitashan Gongyuan** (Mountain of the White Pagoda Park), a public park laid out in 1958, covers the slopes on the Yellow River's north bank close to the ancient crossing place used by merchants and travelers for centuries. The park is named for the white dagoba that was built at the summit of the hill during the Yuan dynasty (1271–1368) and rebuilt in the 15th century. In the pleasant park are some interesting pavilions and terraces. ⊠ *Zhongshan Qiao.* ☎ *Y2.* ☉ *Daily 7–7.*

Dining and Lodging

The best restaurants in Lanzhou are in the hotels; a good one to try is the elegant Chinese restaurant in the Lanzhou Hotel. Lanzhou's "Food Street," along Nongmin Xiang to the north of the Lanzhou Hotel, is lined with a variety of small restaurants.

$ ✕ **Wan He Huo Guo Lou.** If you're a fan of hotpot, head here: locals tout Wan He Huo Guo Lou as the best in town. Despite curt service and flotsam on the floors, hordes of diners crowd the place nightly. Red-suited waiters run to tables with huge pots of freshwater fish simmered with red chili peppers and other spices, all extraordinarily flavorful and succulent due to the eaterie's secret recipe. The traditional hotpot meal follows. Prices are low; unfortunately, there's no English menu. ⊠ *2/F, 118 Gaolan Lu,* ☎ *0931/872–2170.*

$$$–$$$$ ⊡ **Lanzhou Legend.** Also known as the Feitian Hotel, the Legend is plush and expensive, with service to match the high prices. The rooms are well furnished, though on the small side. It is right in downtown Lanzhou. ⊠ *599 Tianshui Lu, 730000,* ☎ *0931/888–2876,* FAX *0931/ 888–7876. 384 rooms, 22 suites. 2 restaurants, bar, sauna, massage, shop, billiards. AE, MC, V.*

$$–$$$ ⊡ **Ningwozhuang Guesthouse.** Before tourism took off, the best ac-
★ commodation in cities like Lanzhou was villa-style guest houses set in beautiful gardens. This is one of those—old-fashioned, now veering toward the shabbier side of gentility, but still gracious and secluded. Once reserved only for visiting cadres, the rooms in the old building are solidly furnished; the newer VIP building has spacious and more modern rooms in pale green, with a touch of glitz. ⊠ *366 Tianshui Lu, north of Nanchang Lu, 730000,* ☎ *0931/826–5888,* FAX *0931/827–8639. 200 rooms, 33 suites. 5 restaurants, bar, pool, hair salon, massage, sauna, tennis court, shops, bowling, laundry service, business services. AE, MC, V.*

$$ ⊡ **Lanzhou Friendship Hotel.** Off the beaten path in the western part of the city (near the Lanzhou Museum), this hotel with its pagoda top and splashing fountains was originally built in the 1950s and has been extensively renovated. Don't be deterred by the red neon KTV sign as you walk in: The spacious rooms have been tastefully modernized, and there is a tennis court and a garden with a miniature golf course. ⊠ *16 Xijin Xilu, 730000,* ☎ *0931/233–3051,* FAX *0931/233–0304. 400 rooms, 46 suites. 5 restaurants, bar, miniature golf, tennis court, shops, business services, travel services. V.*

$–$$ ✕⊡ **Lanzhou Hotel.** Once just another concrete Sino-Stalinist block in the center of town this fan-shaped hotel, built in 1956, has been extensively remodeled and now has a black-marble lobby, pleasant service, and clean, standard-size rooms that are good value; an older wing houses shabbier rooms with worn red carpets for half the price. At the hotel's Chinese restaurant, you can sample the best of local cuisine, from hand-rolled dumplings and roasted lamb shank (served with a side of spices and raw garlic bulbs) to more esoteric entrées like camel's feet soup. ⊠ *434 Donggang Xilu, 730000,* ☎ *0931/841–6321,* FAX *0931/ 841–8608. 476 rooms, 50 suites. 5 restaurants, sauna, massage, shops, business services, travel services. MC, V.*

Nightlife and the Arts

Ask CITS (☞ *Gansu A to Z*) or your hotel about opera or acrobatics performances. There are a few karaoke parlors scattered around the center; but the booming bar/café scene on Zhongshan Lu is where the city's trendy now head for dates. A cozy little place to try is **Impression: Sunrise** (⊠ 191 Zhongshan Lu, ☎ 0931/330–3520, ⊘ noon–1 AM), which serves imported Carlsberg and Corona beer for Y15–20, as well as a variety of teas and coffee. Next door, Da Shanghai is popular with locals as well.

Bingling Si Shiku

★ ㉒ *90 km (56 mi) west of Lanzhou.*

Near Yongjing, the Bingling Si Shiku (Thousand Buddha Temple and Caves) site, filled with Buddhist wall paintings and statuary—including one impressive 89-ft tall Buddha carved into a cliff face—is Lanzhou's most important sight. It is definitely worth the trip, despite a lengthy boatride upstream from the Liujiaxia Dam to the Yellow River to get here. Though the art is disappointing compared to the Mogao caves at Dunhuang, the 200-ft-high canyon is stunning, dominated by spectacular cliff formations of porous rock. The caves were first decorated in AD 420, but the best work, as at Dunhuang, was executed during the later Song and Tang dynasties. It became a Tibetan monastery during the Yuan (Mongolian) dynasty. There are more than 700 statues and several hundred square yards of wall painting; the finest paintings are in Caves 3, 4, 11, 70, 82, and 114, where the largest Buddha (Maitreya, the Buddha of the Future) sits. To see caves 169 (the oldest cave) and 172, considered the most magnificent caves of all, costs a separate and outrageous entrance fee of Y300.

The canyon is located along one side of the Yellow River; seasonal rains occasionally flood the river, prohibiting access to the caves, but when water levels are low, the journey through a gorge lined by water-sculpted rocks and capped by rising peaks and an immense sky is spectacular. When the canyon is dry, You can also travel 2.5 km (1½ mi) up the canyon to see the small community of Tibetan lamas at the Upper Temple of Bingling. The temple itself is run down and nothing special, but the twists and turns of the upper gorge are breathtaking, and the monks are friendly. If the walk is too arduous, catch a jeep ride on the dry riverbed for Y5 (or a boat ride, if there is water) from enterprising locals. Travel agencies also sell all-inclusive round-trip ferry ride plus entrance fee, Y150 (speedboat trip plus entrance fee, Y230) at the Liujiaxia boat dock. ⊠ *CITS or private travel agent; or local bus from Lanzhou's West bus station, 7:30 or 8:30 AM, then ferry at Liujiaxia boat dock; fast boat, Y80, 3 hrs; slow boat, Y30, 8 hrs.* ☎ *Y20.* ☉ *Daily 8–5 (subject to water level).*

Xiahe

㉓ *250 km (155 mi) southwest of Lanzhou (5–6 hrs by bus).*

This tiny town blessed with an extraordinary clarity of light is nestled amid hills downed with light-green grass—one of the most interesting
★ excursions possible from Lanzhou. Xiahe is home to the **Laboleng Si** (Labrang Monastery), one of the most important Tibetan institutions, a member of the Gelupka (Yellow Hat) sect, and one of two great Lamaist temples outside Tibet (the other being the Ta'Er Monastery in Qinghai). Founded in 1710, it once had as many as 4,000 monks, a number now much depleted due in large part to the Cultural Revolution, when monks were forced to return home and temples were destroyed. Though the monastery reopened in 1980, the government's policy of restricted enrollment has kept the number of monks down to about 1,500.

Since the late 1990s, Xiahe has experienced a dizzying rise in the number of backpackers and tourists. Even monks clad in traditional fuchsia robes now watch TV, play basketball, and listen to pop music, and the town's one main street is crowded with cafés flaunting English-language menu signs. Despite these signs of encroaching modernity, Xiahe is still a place of tremendous atmosphere, attracting large numbers of Tibetan pilgrims who come to study and to spin the 1,147 prayer wheels of the monastery daily, swathed in their distinctive costume of heavy woolen robes slashed with brightly colored sashes.

Although partly gutted by fire in 1985, the temple looks much as it always has. It's divided into a number of institutes of learning (including law and medicine), as well as the **Gongtang baota** (Gongtang Pagoda), the **Qi Dao Tang** (Prayer Hall), and the **Ser Kung Si** (Golden Temple).

Apart from the religious festivals during the Tibetan New Year and the month after, when pilgrims and nomads congregate by the thousand, a daily highlight (a feature of most Tibetan monasteries) is the gathering of monks on a lawn for religious debate, when fine points of theology are discussed in the liveliest fashion. Soft-drink bottles are thrown into the air, the monks charge at each other in groups, hissing good-naturedly, and the older monks supervise everyone, including the Tibetan pilgrims gathering to watch, with a benevolent air. The debate takes place after lunch in the afternoons; ask at the ticket office for times. ⊠ *1.5 km (1 mi) west of long-distance bus station.* ▧ *Free; guided tours, Y25.* ☉ *Daily 8–7.*

Maijishan Shiku

★ ㉔   *300 km (186 mi) southeast of Lanzhou (8 hrs by train and bus).*

The Maijishan Grottoes (Corn Rick Mountain caves) are among the four largest Buddhist caves in China. The site is dramatic, a steep outcrop of rock into which have been carved several dozen grottoes dating from the 4th century onward. The caves, between 100 and 230 ft above the foot of the mountain, are reached by wooden steps. An earthquake in the 8th century split the site in two, east and west. The western caves are the best preserved, having been left untouched since the Song dynasty. Early Western influences are seen in some of the work (for example in cave 100), while the finest work is generally considered to be that in cave 133, which has engravings dating from the Wei and Zhou periods. The eastern caves are less well preserved, but there is fine work here, too, most notably in caves 4, 7, 13, 102, and 191. A flashlight is essential; you should either join a tour or obtain a private guide in order to get the best out of the visit. The caves are best reached by train (7 hours, Y26–Y52) to Tianshui and then bus (45 min, Y25 round-trip) the remaining 30 km (19 mi). ⊠ *Due east of Tianshui.* ▧ *Door Ticket, Y10; Caves, Y30; English language tour, Y70.* ☉ *Daily 8–6.*

Gansu A to Z

To research prices, get advice from other travelers, and book travel arrangements, visit www.fodors.com.

AIR TRAVEL
There are daily flights from Dunhuang to Jiayuguan, Lanzhou, Beijing, Ürümqi, and Xian.

From Lanzhou, there are flights daily to Beijing, Guangzhou, Shanghai, Chengdu, Ürümqi, and Xian. Within Gansu, there are flights twice daily to Dunhuang and three times a week to Jiayuguan.

AIRPORTS
Dunhuang's airport is 13 km (8 mi) east of town. The CAAC office, open daily 8–11:30, 3–6 is in town. CAAC runs a shuttle bus service (Y6) to and from the airport; a taxi ride costs Y20–Y30.

Lanzhou's airport is about 90 km (56 mi) north of the city. CAAC Office runs a shuttle bus to and from the airport (Y25) if there are enough passengers.

➤ AIRPORT INFORMATION: **Dunhuang CAAC** (✉ 12 Yangguan Donglu, ☎ 0937/882–2389. **Lanzhou CAAC** (✉ 520 Donggang Xilu, ☎ 0931/888–9666).

BUS TRAVEL

Dunhuang's long-distance bus station is in the south of town. Buses go to Jiayuguan (7 hours) and other local destinations.

Buses leave Lanzhou's East Bus Station every afternoon for Yinchuan (12 hrs) and Xian (15 hrs). From the West Bus Station in the north-west part of the city, buses go to Jiayuguan (16 hrs) in the afternoon. Buses for Xiahe (5–6 hrs) leave twice a day; the slow bus is at 7:30 AM and the fast bus is at 8:30 AM.

➤ BUS INFORMATION: **Dunhuang bus station** (✉ Dingzi Lu, ☎ 0937/882–2174). **Lanzhou East Bus Station** (✉ Ping yuang Lu (next to Jiaotong Fandian), ☎ 0931/841–8411). **Lanzhou West Bus Station** (✉ 458 Xijin Donglu, ☎ 0931/233–3285).

CAR RENTAL

Cars with drivers can be hired through CITS (☞ see Tours, *below*).

➤ CONTACTS: **Dunhuang PSB** (✉ Xi Dajie, ☎ 0937/882–2425). **Lanzhou PSB** (✉ 310 Wudu Lu, ☎ 0931/846–2851).

MONEY MATTERS

➤ EXCHANGE SERVICES: **Bank of China** (✉ 90 Dong Da Jie, Dunhuang, ☎ 0937/261–4812; ✉ 589 Tianshui Lu, Lanzhou, ☎ 0931/883–1988).

TOURS

In Dunhuang, CITS (☞ Visitor Information) can arrange multiday tours to both the northern and southern Silk Road, as well as day tours of Moggao Ku and Mingshashan; The Dunhuang Tourist Agency also arranges tours, and books train and plane tickets. If you want to ride a camel to watch the sunset at Ming Sha Shan, sand-sled or sand-bathe, head to the Silk Road Dunhuang Hotel.

CITS in Lanzhou can arrange trips to Bingling Si and Xiahe; the friendly Western Travel Agency offers similar tours.

➤ TOUR-OPERATOR RECOMMENDATIONS: **Dunhuang Tourist Agency** (✉ 1/F, Dunhuang Hotel, ☎ 0937/882–2195). **Silk Road Dunhuang Hotel** (✉ Dunyue Lu, ☎ 0937/882–5388).

Western Travel Agency (✉ 1/F, Lanzhou Hotel, ☎ 0931/841–6321).

TRAIN TRAVEL

The railway station serving Dunhuang is in the small town of Liuyuan, 130 km (81 mi) away: don't be fooled by the name of the train station, which was changed to "Dunhuang Station" to attract more tourists. There are trains to Jiayuguan (3 hrs) and Lanzhou (12½ hrs), as well as Chengdu (46 hrs), Beijing (37 hrs), Shanghai (41 hours), Turpan (8 hrs), Ürümqi (10 hrs), and Xian (24 hrs). Buses leave regularly for Dunhuang (about every hour 8 AM to 4 PM, though drivers often wait until all the seats are filled; once on the road, the journey takes 2–3 hours.

Lanzhou's train station is fairly central, toward the southwest of the city. Trains go to Beijing (24 hrs), Shanghai (27 hrs), Xian (10 hrs), Chengdu (26 hrs), Ürümqi (24 hrs), Guangzhou (42 hrs), Hohhot (17½ hrs), Qingdao (37 hrs) and Xining (4 hrs). Within Gansu, trains go northwest to Jiayuguan (10 hrs) and Liuyuan (for Dunhuang; 12½ hrs). CITS books tickets three days in advance for trains out of Lanzhou and Dunhuang; otherwise, buy the tickets at the train station.

➤ TRAIN INFORMATION: **Lanzhou train station** (☎ 0931/881–3644). **Liuyuan train station** (☎ 0937/882–3095).

TRANSPORTATION AROUND GANSU

For getting around in the immediate vicinity of Dunhuang, you should rent a bicycle, the best way to navigate the town. If the desert sun gets too hot for you, taxis, easily hailed, will cost you Y10 for the first 10 km (6 mi). The alternative is to use minibuses, which leave when full for various places around and outside town.

In Lanzhou taxis are readily available. Otherwise, the public bus system is good—you can get maps at CITS, railway and bus stations, and bookshops—though, as always in China, be wary of pickpockets or bag-slashers in crowded buses.

VISITOR INFORMATION

➤ TOURIST INFORMATION: CITS (⊠ 32 Mingshan Lu, Dunhuang, ☎ 0937/882–2474; (⊠ 18 Nongmin Xiang, Lanzhou, ☎ 0931/881–3222).

QINGHAI

A remote province on the northeast border of Tibet with sweeping grasslands locked in by mountain ranges, Qinghai is known to the rest of China mostly as the nation's Siberia, a center for prisons and laogai. Yet the province shares much of the majestic scenery of Xinjiang, combined with the rich legends and culture of Tibet. With the exception of the eastern area around Xining, Qinghai, formerly known as Amdo, was part of Tibet until the early 18th century. The mountains and forests of Qinghai are home to wild deer, wild yaks, and the endangered snow leopard.

Qinghai's relative isolation from the rest of the mainland may change in the next decade, however, with the central government's planned construction of the highest railway in the world—the multibillion-dollar Qinghai–Tibet railway—to be laid along the world's highest plateau at an elevation of higher than 12,000 ft. The project to connect the "roof of the world" to Qinghai was attempted before, but the government abandoned its effort in 1984 after savage weather and the icy terrain made construction efforts near impossible. The new rail initiative, announced in 2000, is part of the Communist Party's ambitious campaign to develop China's northwest and encourage foreign investment. Officials have already admitted that construction of the railway will have a "devastating impact" on the surrounding environment, but they claim they are seeking ways to minimize the damage. The project is scheduled to start sometime in 2002; officials estimate that the railway, which currently terminates in Golmud, will take six years to complete, eventually span over 1,700 km (1,100 miles), and end in Lhasa.

For now, the province continues to be sparsely populated, with a little more than 5 million people, not counting prisoners. About 57% of the population are Han Chinese, and about 21% are Tibetan. The rest are Mongolian, Hui, and Salar (the two latter are Muslim ethnic minorities). The 14th Dalai Lama himself was born in the northeastern part of Qinghai, in a mountainous peasant village a day-trip away from Xining.

Xining

➎ *1,370 km (849 mi) southeast of Ürümqi (28 hrs by train); 225 km (140 mi) west of Lanzhou (4 hrs by train).*

Qinghai's capital, Xining (Western Peace), started out as a remote Chinese military garrison in the 16th century, guarding the western borders. It was also an important center for trade between China and Tibet. A small city by Chinese standards, with a population slightly more than 1 million, today's Xining is no longer cut off from the rest of China.

An airport and rail links to Beijing, Shanghai, Xian, and Lanzhou ensure that the population now has a steady diet of Coca-Cola and Ritz crackers. Modernization has hit hard, in fact: the city is an industrial vision straight out of Dickens—heavy gridlock, black clouds of smoke, workers toting shovels, and stripped-down antiquated tractors clanking noisily down side streets. Glitzy office towers and Hong Kong–style boutiques are starting to spring up alongside faded Communist billboards glorifying policemen and soldiers, but the city remains at heart a desolate mix of the curiously old and curiously new, a frontier town revving up for the future but without the capital to pull it off.

Xining is not without its occasional charms, of course: green-domed mosques rise gracefully from clusters of modern bathroom-tiled buildings—evidence of the city's ample population of Hui and Uighurs. Still, Xining functions most frequently as a convenient stopping-off point for visits to the important Ta'Er Monastery, just outside the city, and the stunning bird sanctuary of Bird Island, 350 km (217 mi) away on the shores of China's largest saltwater lake, Qinghai Hu (Green Lake).

Xining lies on the Tibetan plateau at an altitude of nearly 7,000 ft. It's not high enough to cause serious altitude sickness, but you may feel light-headed during your first day or two here. Eating light and getting plenty of rest and water will help ease altitude discomfort. The weather is moderate in the city, with cool summers and very little rainfall. In winter the temperature averages around -1°C (30°F), with sunshine. The winter can be very cold in the surrounding mountains.

Start your visit early in the morning with a walk or taxi ride to the **Beishan Si** (North Mountain Temple), at the northwest end of town. The modern Buddhist temple, which is still in use, sits at the top of a hill and offers a sweeping view of town. ⊠ *Just north of intersection of Qilian Lu and Chanjiang Lu.* ☉ *Dawn–dusk.*

From Chanjiang Lu and Xi Jie you can stroll through the **market stalls** starting at Xi Jie, as it crosses the Nan Chuan (South River). Vendors hawk everything from goldfish to socks alongside the river promenade, but the once-picturesque cityscape has largely been engulfed by a modern plaza boasting kebab stands and various construction projects.

In and around the **Qinghai Bingguan** (Qinghai Guest House) are a number of restaurants where you can stop for lunch. ⊠ *On western side of river, walk south about 15 mins from where Xi Jie crosses Huanghe Lu.*

If you've ever wanted to see what the outside of a laogai (prison factory) looks like, here is your chance. Follow Nanshan Lu east to Nantan Jiedao (South Beach District). After about 300 yards watch for a road turning to the right. You'll see two grim-looking compounds on the left, both laogai. Pass the gate of the second one, **Qinghai Pimao Beifu Chang** (Qinghai Hide and Garment Factory). Right next door to the entrance gate is another door leading to the factory shop, where the goods made by inmates of this prison are displayed for sale. You can walk or take a taxi back along Nanshan Lu to the Qinghai Guest House. ⊠ *40 Nanshan Lu,* ☎ *0971/824–7342.*

Dining and Lodging

$$–$$$ ✕ **Zheng Pai Ming Ren Yu Cha.** With red lanterns and a log-lined facade, this cozy 24-hour two-decker teahouse is one of the nicest spots in town to relax, with hardwood floors, small, intimate dark corners, and an eager-to-please staff. Regular green and oolong teas start at Y10–Y20 a pot and climb to a dizzying Y180 for the name brands. Walk to the north end of Bei Da Jie and make a left. ⊠ *6 Bei Da Jie,* ☎ *0971/ 824–7075. No credit cards.*

$-$$ ✕ **Shang Yi Da Xia.** This popular Muslim restaurant is in downtown Xining, a few doors east of the Bank of China tower. It has a small, crowded dining room, but excellent hotpot and kebabs. ✉ *190 Dongguan Lu,* ☎ *no phone. No credit cards.*

$ ✕ **The Cafe.** In a huge hall with large round tables, Chinese style, it has an excellent Mongolian hotpot buffet—all you can eat for Y35. ✉ *Xining Hotel, 348 Qi Yi Lu,* ☎ *0971/823–8701. No credit cards.*

$ ✕ **Tibetan Restaurant.** The aroma of yak butter permeates this small, bare-bones restaurant with orange tablecloths, where a big bowl of noodles can be had for just Y3. It's down the street from the Xining Hotel. ✉ *348–29 Qi Yi Lu,* ☎ *0971/823–8701. No credit cards.*

$-$$ 🏨 **Jian Yin Hotel.** A handsome, pink-marble foyer entrance greets you at the newest hotel in town, opened by the China Construction Bank. Not surprisingly, given its origins, everything shouts money here: from the silver-and-chrome facade to the tan leather couches down to the marble ball revolving inside the lobby's rock-lined pool. The rooms are about the same as everywhere else in town, but with an extra layer of shininess and glitz. ✉ *55 Xida Jie, 810000,* ☎ *0971/826–1885,* 🖷 *0971/826–1551. 160 rooms, 20 suites. 2 restaurants, hair salon, massage, sauna, shops, bowling, laundry service, business services, meeting room, travel services. No credit cards.*

$-$$ 🏨 **Qinghai Hotel.** A gigantic pink box of a hotel, the Qinghai has shiny marble floors and a somewhat impersonal feel, with rooms that are a tad more expensive than those at the Xining Hotel, but no cleaner or more comfortable. The hotel has a shopping arcade, a small Bank of China branch, and a CITS office. ✉ *158 Huanghe Lu, 810001,* ☎ *0971/614–4888,* 🖷 *0971/614–4145. 330 rooms, 62 suites. 4 restaurants, hair salon, massage, gym, bowling, laundry service, business services, meeting room, travel services. No credit cards.*

$ **Qinghai Minzu Binguan** This centrally located hotel with its white marble facade and friendly staff is a good value. The fixtures generally work in the clean bathrooms, and the standard rooms exude a cheerful air despite the shabbiness of the yellow curtains and worn red rugs. A friendly branch of China Youth Travel Service (CYTS) is in the back of the hotel on the first floor; there is also a clinic here. ✉ *1 Huayuan Bei Jie (at Dongda Jie),* ☎ *0971/822–5951,* 🖷 *0971/822–5892. 96 rooms, 8 suites. 2 restaurants, business services, travel services. No credit cards.*

Shopping

Xining is a good place to find Tibetan and Chinese crafts at reasonable prices. **Native Arts and Crafts** (✉ Qinghai Hotel, 2nd-floor arcade, 20 Huanghe Lu) has vests, hats, and toys in designs using the techniques of traditional Tibetan folk embroidery; brass gongs; jewelry; and some Chinese jade and porcelain objects. **Ba Chang Ge** (✉ 30 Bei Da Lu) has Chinese antique porcelain, jade figurines from the region, and Tibetan folk embroidery.

Side Trips from Xining

Trips can be arranged through various travel agencies, including CITS (☞ Visitor Information, *below*) at the Qinghai Hotel. The government travel agency has something of a monopoly on transportation of tourists to the scenic spots outside Xining, and traveling with CITS or one of its offshoots seems to be the surest way to get around without being turned away by the police for entering an area without clearance.

㉖ The magnificent **Ta'Er Si** (Ta'Er Monastery, also known as Pagoda Lamasery or Kum Bum) is southwest of Xining. Built in 1560, it is one of the six great monasteries of the Tibetan Buddhist sect known as Yellow Lamaism—now the dominant sect in Tibet—and reputedly the birthplace of the sect's founder, Tsong-Kha-pa, as well. A great reformer who lived in the early 1400s, Tsong-Kha-pa formulated a striking new doctrine at a time of great religious Tibetan strife; his reform movement (known as the Dge-lugs-pa, literally "virtuous") stressed a return to monastic discipline, strict celibacy, and moral and philosophical thought over magic and mysticism. Tsong's followers were easily identified by their hats: hence the name *Yellow Hat Sect*. Still a magnet for Tibetan pilgrims, Ta'er Si boasts a dozen prayer halls, an exhibition hall, 20,000 religious paintings and embroideries, and the monks' quarters, all in a complex that covers nearly a quarter of a square mile. The **Kumbum Festival,** a religious fair at which monks perform 500-year-old songs and activities—including the Devil Dance to purge bad spirits—is held five times a year at the monastery, in February, May, July, November, and December. In winter frozen yak butter is carved into extraordinary Buddhist scenes and exhibited on the 15th day of the lunar New Year. Shops right outside the main gate of the monastery sell beads, prayer scarves, brass gongs, and even some sacrificial yak skulls. ⊠ *Huangzhong, 26 km (16 mi) southwest of Xining. Minibuses (Y3–Y4) leave from the left side of Xining Gymnasium on Xi Dajie, just west of Ximen (West Gate) every 10–20 mins for the 45-min trip; cars can also be hired through CITS.*

27 **Dek Tser,** a peasant village in Ping'an County, is the birthplace of the 14th Dalai Lama, the exiled spiritual leader of Tibetan Buddhism. The long, winding, and rocky road up to the high mountain village is not for the fainthearted. Behind the wooden door next to the old Hong Ya School (which is still marked in Chinese characters) live two great-nieces of the Dalai Lama. One teaches at the school. Across the road a few feet farther uphill, a wall encloses a temple painted in bright colors. If you knock on the great-nieces' door, they'll let you in to see the temple, past a yard filled with pigs, chickens, donkeys, sheep, and cows. ⊠ *32 km (20 mi) east of Ta'Er Si.*

28 **Riyue Shan** (Sun Moon Mountain), in Huangyuan County, has two pagodas—the Sun and the Moon—on adjoining peaks, each with friezes depicting the story of a 7th-century Chinese princess, Wen Cheng: she married the Tibetan emperor against her will as a result of the wiles of Ludong Zan, the Tibetan prime minister. The site is nice enough, amid grasslands and gently rolling mountains with a desolate beauty, but not worth a visit on its own. It's often a stop on the Qinghai Lake trip. Yak rides are available here (Y5). ⊠ *11 km (7 mi) west of Xining.*

29 **Niao Dao** (Bird Island) is the main draw at **Qinghai Hu** (Green Lake or Qinghai Lake), China's largest inland saltwater lake, which lies in the northeastern part of Qinghai province and the Tibetan Plateau. The eerily electric-blue lake has a circumference of 360 km (223 mi) and is surrounded by four mountain ranges. From late spring to early fall, the grasslands and rolling hills surrounding the lake are green and covered with yellow rapeseed flowers. Wild yaks roam here. Beyond the hills the area is ringed with snowcapped mountains. An estimated 100,000 birds flock in the spring and summer to breed at Niao Dao, on the western side of the lake. Egrets, speckle-headed geese, cormorants, gulls, and black-neck cranes are among the birds who settle on the various shores and fill the air with clucks, coos, squawks, and screeches. You can see the breeding birds only from a couple of special viewing areas cordoned off from the sites themselves—but the sight is nevertheless astounding. The best times to view the birds are May and June. The name *Bird Island* is a bit misleading: the site was once an island, until the lake receded and made the shore part of the mainland. ⊠ *7- to 8-hr drive, about 300 km (186 mi) northwest of Xining.*

DINING AND LODGING

Several small restaurants line the main road beside Qinghai Hu. The restaurants serve Qinghai Lake's only fish—the so-called naked carp (wulin huangyu)—yak meat, and other local delicacies. Lunch costs about Y25–Y30 per person.

$ 🏨 **Birds' Islet Hotel.** Decent and relatively clean accommodations with 24-hour hot water can be had in this generic white, blue-glassed hotel. There are no private baths. The second-floor restaurant serves very good food, including Qinghai Lake's naked carp, fresh vegetables, and other local delicacies. ✉ *51 Bayi Xilu, Bird Island, about 20-min walk from Bird Island observation sites;* ☎ *0971/812–5416. 27 rooms, 20 dorm rooms. Restaurant. No credit cards. Closed Sept.–Mar.*

Golmud

➌⓪ *675 km (419 mi) west of Xining.*

Golmud, in central Qinghai province, is a forlorn wasteland of a city—the largest metropolitan area in the world, covering nearly 49,000 square mi. That's just a little less than ½ square mi of space per person, as the population is a mere 120,000. It lies on a dry, windy plateau. On the horizon is a long stretch of dry earth with mud craters that look like those on the moon. The plateau is inhospitably cold in winter and desolate all year. Although the area has a number of famous landscapes nearby, including pasture lands, glaciers, and the Tanggula Mountain Pass, most trips require a permit. Golmud serves primarily as a jumping-off point for the stunning but arduous overland trip to Lhasa on the highest highway in the world.

Lodging

$ 🏨 **Golmud Hotel.** Once the only hotel in town that admitted foreigners, the Golmud is divided into a budget guest house and a more upscale hotel. Two branches of CITS are here. ✉ *160-219 Kunlun Lu,* ☎ *0979/412–061, FAX 0979/416–484. 188 rooms, 15 suites. 3 restaurants. No credit cards.*

$ 🏨 **Qinggang Binguan.** Spacious and carpeted rooms can be found at this shiny new hotel, which is the only other place in town that receives foreigners; an indoor swimming pool and a branch of CITS number among the amenities. ✉ *108 Kunlun Lu,* ☎ *0979/421–808, FAX 0979/423–988. 108 rooms. 2 restaurants, business center, meeting rooms, shop, indoor pool. No credit cards.*

Side Trips from Golmud

➌① The chief reason to visit Golmud is to travel over the spectacular **Tanggula Shankou** (Tanggula Mountain Pass), which can be visited June–September, into Tibet on a sleeper bus that is liable to break down several times before arriving in Lhasa, extending the scheduled 26-hour journey by 15 to 20 more hours. The bus costs about Y200, but add in the requisite official tourist permit all foreigners are compelled to purchase, and the price jumps to roughly Y1,660; the fare includes the bus ticket, plus a hired vehicle and mandatory tour guide for three days in Lhasa. CITS usually rounds up foreigners from the Golmud Hotel and takes them to the Tibet bus station on Xizang Lu. The bus leaves every day around 4 PM.

Qinghai A to Z

To research prices, get advice from other travelers, and book travel arrangements, visit www.fodors.com.

AIR TRAVEL

Several flights a week link Xining with Beijing, Shanghai, Guangzhou, Xian, and Ürümqi, and three flights a week go to Lhasa (Y1,290, not including travel permit).

AIRPORTS

The Xining airport (Xining Jichang), 30 km (19 mi) southeast of Xining, takes about a half hour to reach by taxi.

BUS TRAVEL

The daily bus (Y80) between Golmud and Xining takes anywhere from 18 to 20 hours. Buses leave Xining from the main bus station, opposite the train station twice a day. Purchase bus tickets for Lhasa from CITS in Golmud; the buses (26–28 hours) officially run each day, if weather conditions permit, departing from the Tibet bus station at around 4 PM.

➤ BUS INFORMATION: **Xining main bus station** (✉ Jianguo Lu (across the river from the train station), ☎ 0971/814–9506). **Tibet bus station** (✉ Xizang Lu, ☎ no phone).

EMERGENCIES

➤ CONTACTS: **PSB** (✉ 35 Bei Da Jie, just north of Xining Hotel, Xining, ☎ 0971/824–8190; ✉ Golmud Hotel, Golmud, ☎ 0979/412–375).

Qinghai People's Hospital (✉ 2 Gonghe Lu, east side of Xining, ☎ 0971/817–7911). **Xining Number 2 People's Hospital** (✉ 29 Tongren Lu, northwest end of Xining, ☎ 0971/614–3314).

TRAIN TRAVEL

Daily trains link Xining with Lanzhou (4 hrs), Xian (14 hrs), Golmud (17 hrs), and Shanghai (40 hrs). Every other day, trains run between Xining and Beijing (33½ hrs) and Qingdao (41 hrs). Tickets can be purchased in Xining from CITS or at the railway station. From Golmud a train also runs direct to Lanzhou (21 hrs).

➤ TRAIN INFORMATION: **Xining railway station** (✉ East of town just beyond Qilian Lu, ☎ 0971/814–9793).

TRANSPORTATION AROUND QINGHAI

The best ways to get around both Xining and Golmud are on foot or by taxi. For day trips, catch a taxi in town and negotiate the fare to your destination in advance, or hire a car and driver from CITS.

VISITOR INFORMATION

To arrange travel permits for Tibet, head to CITS (open daily 8:30–12:30 and 2–6); permits can be processed within 24 hours. The agency also arranges tours to Lhasa.

➤ TOURIST INFORMATION: **CITS** (✉ 156 Huanghe Lu, 300 ft north of Qinghai Binguan, Xining, ☎ 0971/614–4888 ext. 2439; ✉ 14 Jianguo Lu, Xining, ☎ 0971/817–8814; ✉ 2/F Golmud Hotel, 160–219 Kunlun Lu, Golmud, ☎ 0979/413–003, FAX 0979/412–764). **China Youth Travel Service Qinghai** (✉ 136 Huzhu Xilu, Xining, ☎ FAX 0971/817–8096).

XINJIANG

The vast Xinjiang Uighur Autonomous Region, covering more than 966,000 square km (375,000 square mi), or half the size of India, is the largest province in China and one of the most resource rich and ethnically diversified. It borders Mongolia, Kazakhstan, Kirghizstan, Tadzhikstan, Afghanistan, and Kashmir. About 40% of Xinjiang's 19.25 million people are Han Chinese, about 47% are Uighur (a people of Central

Turkic origin), and the remainder are Kirghis, Kazakhs, Tajiks, Uzbeks, Hui, Mongols, Heibei, Manchus, Tatars, Daur, and Russians.

Historians believe the area was first settled by nomadic Turkic tribes in the 3rd century BC. In the 1980s archaeologists discovered dozens of tombs in various parts of Xinjiang, with bodies that had been buried about 3,000 years before yet remained remarkably preserved, thanks to the arid desert climate. Many of the mummies, believed to be forefathers of the Uighurs, had northern European features, including fair hair and skin. The theory is that they intermarried with other peoples and gradually evolved into a tribe of mostly dark-haired people. Even today, fair coloring and blue or green eyes are not uncommon among Uighurs.

In the Qin and Han dynasties (221 BC–AD 220) Xinjiang was inhabited by a variety of tribes, with anywhere from 36 to 50 walled states. Genghis Khan's troops conquered part of the region in 1218. By the time the Qing dynasty came to power in 1644, the area was under constant dispute among four different Mongol tribes that roamed the areas north of the Tian Shan (Heavenly Mountains), while the areas south of the mountains were inhabited by the Uighur people, ruled by descendants of the Mongol khans. The Muslims declared independence during the Tang dynasty (AD 618–970) and held on to it until the 19th century.

Although territorial wars continued throughout most of Xinjiang's history, and climatic conditions on the vast desert were not always hospitable to travelers, the region nevertheless became the most important crossroad for trade between China, Europe, and the ancient Persian empire.

In this century the Uighurs continued to resist Chinese rule. In 1933 they succeeded briefly, seizing power from a warlord governor and claiming the land as a separate republic, which they named East Turkistan. China tightened its grip after the revolution, however, encouraging Han settlers to emigrate to the province to dilute the Uighur population. In 1949, the entire province was home to only 6% Han; Today the capital, Ürümqi, is about 73% Han. The Uighurs live mostly in the less industrialized areas, and many complain that business and government are dominated by the Han Chinese. Since the breakup of the Soviet Union, the Uighurs have seen their Muslim neighbors in the Central Asian countries gain independence and have renewed their own efforts, sometimes resorting to violent means, only to be repressed in a series of crackdowns that have resulted in countless arrests and a few hundred executions.

In the last five years, as the insurgency has continued to grow, the government has aggressively stepped up religious persecution, banned Islamic publications, sentenced scores of Uighurs to life imprisonment after forced confessions, and arbitrarily executed prisoners accused of being terrorists or separatists. The most explosive clashes between separatists and authorities occurred in 1997, when hundreds of Uighurs in Yining city rioted against Chinese rule for two days. Bombs exploded aboard buses in both Urumqi and Beijing. Xinjiang is currently the only region in China where political prisoners have been executed in recent years. The party is hoping that its new "Develop The West" campaign will pour money into the local economy, encourage even more Han immigration to the region, and sap ethnic tensions; in the next five years Xinjiang is slated to spend $12 billion on 70 major infrastructure projects.

Although the territorial dispute may never be resolved, today much of Xinjiang is wide open to foreign visitors. The roads are bumpy, but the landscapes are magnificent. The Uighurs and other so-called minority groups are generally eager to introduce foreigners to their traditional music, cuisine, and celebrations.

One quirky side effect of China's rule is that Xinjiang is officially in the same time zone as Beijing. Clocks run on "Beijing time," so in winter it's almost 9 AM when the sun rises. Hours stated here are Beijing time. Unofficially, clocks run on "Xinjiang time," which is an hour earlier than Beijing time.

The majority of the people in Xinjiang speaks Mandarin, but the predominant language is Uighur, a Turkic-derived language. Little English is spoken. A few Uighur words to remember: Hello: *Yahshimu siz* (*yah*-shee-moo siz). Thank you: *Rachmad* (rak-*mad*). How much?: *Kanche pul?* (kan-che *poll*). Market: *Bazargha* (ba-*zaar*-ga). Goodbye: *Heri hosh* (her-*ee* hosh).

Xinjiang has a desert climate, with very little rainfall. It gets very cold in winter and very hot in summer, especially in the Turpan Basin, although the temperature can drop by as much as 20 degrees at night. Xinjiang's average annual rainfall is only six inches. Winter lasts from around November through April. The sun is strong all year, so pack sunglasses, sun hats, and sunscreen.

Ürümqi

32 *1,530 km (949 mi) southwest of Ulaan Baatar; 2,250 km (1,400 mi) northwest of Beijing.*

Xinjiang's capital and largest city, Ürümqi has the distinction of being the most landlocked city in the world—the nearest sea is 2,240 km (1,389 mi) away. It is a new city by Chinese standards, built on pasture land in 1763. Originally the city was little more than barracks for Qing dynasty troops. The Qing emperors called the city Dihua (Enlightening and Civilizing). In 1884, when the Chinese declared the region a province and named it Xinjiang (New Territories), Dihua became the capital. In 1954, five years after the Revolution, the city was renamed Ürümqi, or "beautiful pastures" in Mongolian.

A sleepy and dusty trading post for light industrial goods and farm produce in the mid-1980s, Ürümqi has grown to a modern city, with a population of just over 2 million, and new buildings constantly under construction. Nevertheless, the occasional peasant does walk a sheep along its downtown streets. About 3 km (2 mi) from the center of town is the Erdaoqiao District, an Uighur area where some residents still live in adobe huts and drive donkey carts.

Exploring Ürümqi

Start your tour of Ürümqi with a 15-minute walk up a stone path to the top of **Hong Shan** (Red Mountain), a hill about a half mile above sea level that offers a panoramic view of the city. At the top is an array of incongruously grouped objects, including a Big Buddha and the **Zhenglong Ta** (Zhenglong Pagoda), built by the emperor in 1788 to suppress an evil dragon. There's also an entire **amusement park,** including bumper cars, gondolas, and a Ferris wheel, but the rides aren't included in the regular admission price. ⊠ *North end of Xinhua Beilu; 45-min walk or 10-min taxi ride from center; entrance halfway up hill, on east side.* 🎫 *Y10.* ☉ *Sunrise–sunset.*

In the Uighur section south of the center of town is the **Erdaoqiao Shichang** (Erdaoqiao Market). Once the streets here were lined with adobe dwellings and full of donkey carts, flocks of sheep, men in embroidered skullcaps, and women in heavy brown wool veils and leggings; with modernization, the area has sprouted several bathroom-tiled buildings, but the rakish, laid-back atmosphere remains. The main market is in a covered alleyway. You can bargain for Uighur crafts, such as embroidered caps and vests and decorated knives. Farther down the passageway are several shops selling carpets, animal pelts, and fur hats, as well as food vendors. If you're heading to Kashgar, the Sunday Bazaar has a far better selection of crafts at lower prices. ⊠ *About 5 km (3 mi) south of center, ½ block north of Tuan Jie Lu, between Xinhua Nanlu and Jie Fang Lu.*

Don't miss the exhibition of nearly a dozen 3,000-year-old mummies at the superb **Xinjiang Bowuguan.** The mummies were excavated from tombs in various parts of Xinjiang, including those from the ancient Silk Road cities of Loulan, Hami, and Cherchen, and the Atsana graves in Turpan. In addition, the museum has intriguing fragments of silk brocade, wool rugs, pottery, and even hemp-cloth documents discovered in the tombs along with the corpses. There are also some fine examples of minority costumes, crafts, musical instruments, and architecture, including a few yurts and stuffed sheep and yaks. The museum shops have fairly good selections of carpets, Chinese jewelry, porcelain, and Uighur musical instruments (cash only). ⊠ *59 Xibei Lu,* ☎ *0991/453–6436.* 🎫 *Y12.* ☺ *Weekdays 9:30–5:30, weekends 10:30–5:30.*

Dining and Lodging

Ürümqi is a fine place to try both Uighur and Chinese cuisine. The row of restaurants on Hongqi Lu, in the boutique district, serves everything from Beijing-style dumplings to the traditional Uighur specialties of grilled lamb and vegetable kebabs, flat bread, *lamian* (pulled noodles seasoned with tomatoes, green peppers, and red chili peppers), and spicy hotpot. Farther north, the cluster of restaurants on Jianshe Lu is also worth checking out. To get the real flavor of Ürümqi nightlife, head to the bustling night market on Wu Yi Lu near the Hong Ju Fu Hotel; among the dazzling variety of foods and fruits there are heaps of fresh seafood, crabs, and dark little escargots marinated in chilies (piled beside the Mongolian hotpot stands). There's also a night market just outside the Renmin Hotel. Unless otherwise stated, restaurants are open noon to 3 and 6:30 to 9.

$–$$ ✕ **Kashgari's.** Decorated with Uighur tapestries and other ornaments, this hotel restaurant has background music that evokes images of snake charmers. The Uighur cuisine is prepared with an imaginative flourish, using local ingredients such as Turpan raisins. ⊠ *Holiday Inn, ground floor, 168 Xinhua Beilu,* ☎ *0991/281–8788. AE, MC, V.*

$–$$ ✕ **Pearl Palace.** A bit out of the way, this Chinese seafood restaurant, complete with tanks full of fresh catches that are flown in daily, is worth the trip. Private rooms are available for large parties. Try the special fresh-baked *mianbao* (slightly sweet bread filled with a paste of nuts and mushrooms). ⊠ *Hotel World Plaza, 2 Beijing Nanlu.* ☎ *0991/383–6400 ext. 3138. Reservations essential. AE, MC, V.*

$–$$ ✕ **Xi Wang Mu.** A memorable Chinese restaurant, it serves a number   ★ of regional specialties from around the country. Try the Shanghai-style fish (a whole poached fish with ginger slivers) and chicken with Sichuan black-bean sauce. There's also a delicious shark's-fin soup. ⊠ *Holiday Inn, 2nd floor, 168 Xinhua Beilu,* ☎ *0991/281–8788. Reservations essential. AE, MC, V.*

$ ✕ **Shang Jian Jiu.** Instantly recognizable by the Jaeger Beer sign out front, this is a noisy, friendly place with an excellent all-you-can-eat Mongolian hotpot buffet for lunch and dinner. ⊠ *Luoyang House, 18 Jianshe Lu,* ☎ *0991/481–5690. No credit cards.*

$ ✕ **Da Han San Guan.** At one of the cleaner choices on a little street known as Restaurant Alley, the noodles are tasty, and there are fresh-roasted sunflower seeds to munch on while you wait for your food. ⊠ *33 Jian Shi Lu,* ☎ *no phone. No credit cards.*

$ ✕ **Hotpot Place.** This unassuming but clean hotpot restaurant with a cheerful staff is a quick and convenient pit stop for lunch. Ordering is easy: Just point at the mushrooms, lamb chunks, and other ingredients already pre-skewered on kebab sticks. ⊠ *18 Jianzhu Xilu, off side street near Holiday Inn,* ☎ *0991/230–2295. No credit cards.*

$$$$ ⊞ **Holiday Inn.** The first foreign-owned hotel in all of western China, the Holiday Inn continues to be one of the leading hotels in Ürümqi—with prices to match. It has the usual luxuries, good restaurants, nicely appointed rooms, and an English-speaking staff, though some fixtures are aging. Silks, the disco, is popular among both visitors and locals, as is Unicorns, the lobby bar, which has live entertainment nightly. ⊠ *168 Xinhua Beilu, 830002,* ☎ *0991/281–8788,* FAX *0991/281–7422,* WEB *www.holiday-inn.com/hotels/urcch. 360 rooms, 22 suites. 3 restaurants, bar, deli, refrigerators, indoor pool, hair salon, gym, shops, billiards, dry cleaning, laundry service, business services, meeting room, travel services, airport shuttle. AE, MC, V.*

$$$ ⊞ **Hong Fu Da Jiu Dian.** One of the newest hotels in town, owned by the nearby China Telecom, the dusty rose-marble Hong Fu is also one of the most upscale, offering spacious, elegant rooms with beautiful mahogany furniture and touch-sensitive light switches, all in a good location. The night market on Wuyi Lu is just steps from the hotel entrance. ⊠ *26 Huang He Lu, 830000,* ☎ *0991/588–1588,* FAX *0991/582–3188. 343 rooms, 18 suites. 6 restaurants, gym, massage, sauna, laundry service, business services, meeting room. AE, MC, V.*

$$$ ⊞ **Tunhe Da Jiu Dian** (Tunhe Hotel). A bright-yellow sign splashed across the front of a tall white tower greets visitors at the centrally located Tunhe, which opened in 2000. The lobby here is elegant, and spacious light-color rooms offer all the standard amenities, including Internet outlet ports. There is also an in-house clinic. ⊠ *52 Changjiang Lu, 830000,* ☎ *0991/587–6688,* FAX *0991/587–6689. 277 rooms, 20 suites. 3 restaurants, hair salon, massage, sauna, gym, billiards, nightclub, babysitting, laundry service, business services, meeting room, travel services. AE, MC, V.*

$$$ ⊞ **World Plaza.** A huge high-rise built near the airport in the early 1990s, the World Plaza looks old for its age. Inside, though, it's perfectly comfortable, with an eager-to-please staff and tasteful rooms decorated with grey satin-striped comforters. The second floor has a spacious and classy Internet café (Y8 per hour), with drinks and sandwiches available, but slow computers. Note that the hotel is a trek from the city center. ⊠ *2 Beijing Nanlu, 830011,* ☎ *0991/383–6400,* FAX *0991/383–6399. 352 rooms, 32 suites. 3 restaurants, café, refrigerators, indoor pool, hair salon, massage, gym, billiards, dry cleaning, laundry service, travel services, airport shuttle. AE, MC, V.*

$$–$$$ ⊞ **Silk Road Hotel.** This friendly hotel is at the south end of town, about 10 km (6 mi) from downtown Ürümqi—a 10-minute walk from Erdaoqiao Market. A pleasant place to stay if you want to get away from the hustle-and-bustle of the city center, rooms are clean and comfortable, and the staff is professional. ⊠ *52-1 Yanan Lu, 830001,* ☎ *0991/255–8899,* FAX *0991/255–7788,* WEB *www.silkroad-hotel.com. 98 rooms, 9 suites. 3 restaurants, bar, pool, sauna, massage, tennis court, basketball, bowling, billiards, business services. AE, MC, V.*

$ ⊞ **Xinjiang Hotel.** Near the train station, this hotel, with its dark lobby and fluorescent lighting, is unprepossessing, but it has clean rooms for moderate prices, and the staff is usually amiable. The Chinese restaurant here is popular with locals for its roast duck; to the left of the hotel entrance, the inexpensive self-serve Chinese fast food eaterie has a range of tasty street food, noodles, and vegetable dishes. ⊠ *107 Changjiang Lu, 830002,* ☎ *0991/585–2511,* FAX *0991/581–1354. 55 rooms, 12 suites. 3 restaurants, business services, travel services. No credit cards.*

$ ☒ **Xinjiang Jian Zhu Da Xia.** (Xinjiang Construction Building Hotel). Popular with Chinese tourists, this small hotel a few blocks away from Hong Shan has clean, modern rooms with green-striped comforters, 24-hour hot water, and friendly if erratic service. ☒ *38 Hong Shan Lu, 830092,* ☎ *0991/232–4268,* FAX *0991/232–4231. 30 rooms. Restaurant, laundry service, business services, travel services. No credit cards.*

Nightlife

Karaoke is the most popular form of nighttime entertainment in China's cities, and Ürümqi is no exception. The bars seem to come and go every few months, scattered all over the downtown district. The action doesn't begin until after 10 PM.

Silks Disco (☒ Holiday Inn, 168 Xinhua Beilu) starts jumping after about 10 PM, especially from Thursday through Sunday, with strobe lights and Western disco recordings. The **Rock & Roll Café** (☒ 1–108 Xinhua Beilu) plays rock music until the wee hours and tries to look like a Hard Rock Cafe.

Shopping

Stores are open 10 to 6 daily.

An extensive **outdoor food market** sells local fruits, nuts, bread, and small cakes, along with handmade noodles and kebabs, in the alley beside the **Xinjiang Jinxin Hotel** (☒ Renmin Lu, east of Xinhua Nanlu at Jie Fang Nanlu), a lodging that doesn't admit foreigners.

Ürümqi is not known for its Uighur handicrafts in the way that Kashgar and Turpan are, but the **Erdaoqiao Market** (☞ Exploring Ürümqi, *above*) has a good selection of handicraft items, fruit (fresh and dried), and carpets brought in from other parts of Xinjiang.

Ürümqi Carpet Factory (☒ 40 Jin Er Lu, ☎ 0991/581–3338) sells carpets made in the factory workshop based on Central Asian patterns. You can tour the factory any time during the day, after which a guide will usher you into the showroom and try to talk you into buying something. You can arrange shipment at an extra charge. **Xinjiang Antique Store** (☒ 325 Jie Fang Nanlu, ☎ 0991/281–5284) has a good selection of Uighur handicrafts and Chinese bric-a-brac, including jade, jewelry, carpets, ink brushes, bronze ware, and porcelain.

Tianchi Hu

★ ㉝   *115 km (71 mi) northeast of Ürümqi (2–3 hrs by bus).*

About three hours' ride from Ürümqi is the not-to-be-missed Tianchi Hu (Heavenly Lake), possibly the prettiest lake in China, surrounded by snow-sprinkled mountains. The water is crystal clear, with a sapphire tint, untouched by swimmers or fishermen. Taiwanese tourists come here to commune with the Buddhist goddess of mercy. Others come for the hiking and horseback riding, or simply to spend a day enjoying nature. In summer white flowers dot the hillsides. Tourism, however, is starting to leave its imprint here. A ferry (Y20) now allows tourists to circle the lake, and garish new hotels are being built in the area.

Kazakh families still set up traditional yurts along the shores of Heavenly Lake from early May to late October, bringing their horses, sheep, and cashmere goats. The Kazakh people have a long history as horse breeders and are known as skilled riders. Most of the yurt dwellers are able to furnish horses—and a guide—for a day of riding around the lake. The more business-minded ones are erecting clusters of yurts to cater to tour groups. From Urumqi, buses (Y25 round-trip) to Tianchi leave at 9 in the morning from both north and south gates of Renmin

Gongyuan (People's Park) in the summer; add Y15 to take the bus back if you want to stay overnight.

Dining and Lodging

There are some excellent small **restaurants** without names along the western shore, near the hotels, that will prepare whatever they have on hand for lunch and dinner and produce a fresh and delicious array of stir-fried meat, vegetables, and noodles. Ask to move your table outside, and you can enjoy the view while you eat. Prices for dinner for two will be Y30–Y50. Only cash is accepted.

There is a cluster of **hotels** at the western shore of the lake. You will not find any luxury accommodations here. Showers and toilet are shared, and some hotels have dorm beds only.

You can also stay in a **yurt** for about Y20 per person per night; Y40 for lodging and three meals (soup made mostly from flour, hard-as-rock sheep cheese, and tea with either salt or fried flour in it; if you bring your own tea bags, your host will provide plain boiled water). The sleeping quarters are communal, and there's no plumbing. However, you'll have a rewarding glimpse into the way your Kazakh hosts live. Yurts are made from hides or canvas stretched over a wooden frame. The interior is colorfully decorated with handmade rugs and blankets, neatly hung along the walls and lining the floor. There is usually a wood-burning stove in the center, for cooking and keeping the yurt warm at night. Most accommodate four people.

$$ ☒ **Shui Xin Hotel.** The Shui Xi has private guest rooms (with shared baths) and a restaurant open for lunch and dinner. ☒ *Western shore of lake, near stop for bus from Ürümqi. 12 rooms. Restaurant. No credit cards.*

$ ☒ **Shui Shou Shan Zhuang.** This group of yurts and cabins, run by the water-management company, offers sterile-looking but clean accommodations set off from the rest of the pack at the southeastern side of the lake. To cater to karaoke-crazed guests, some yurts are even equipped with a fully functional KTV lounge in a common room sheathed with yellow satin, which can make sleeping difficult. The toilets are communal but clean; there are sinks but no showers. ☒ *Southeastern side of lake, 15–20-min trek from bus stop on paved road,* ☎ *0994/325–1007. 6 cabins, 5 yurts. Restaurant. No credit cards.*

Yining

34 *700 km (434 mi) west of Ürümqi.*

The city of Yining is the main stop in Ili Prefecture, a rich farming valley in northern Xinjiang near the border of Kazakhstan. Yining itself is too industrialized to be charming, but all around the city are the apple orchards for which Ili is famous, and in summer local Uighurs and Kazakhs perform traditional folk dances in the orchards. The countryside on the outskirts of Yining is a pleasant area to explore. Take a taxi to the Yili River bridge, 6 km (4 mi) from the town center, then walk or take a horse carriage over the bridge. Just across the river is a rustic village where the dirt roads are lined with birch trees. The houses have blue-painted doors that open into courtyards filled with grapevines.

35 From Yining you can take a three-hour bus ride to **Sayram Hu** (Sayram Lake), in nearby Bole Prefecture. In summer you can circle the lake on horseback with a guide (about Y50 a day). It's a pretty ride, with the grasslands in bloom and the snowcapped mountains in the distance. In July or early August, Sayram Lake's shore swarms with Kazakhs gathering for the **Naadam Fair.** They sell handicrafts, perform traditional music and dance, and stage a number of games and races on horseback. "Sheep polo" is a popular spectator sport. Here the men from the village slaughter and skin a sheep, then race around a ring on horseback, each contestant trying to grab the sheepskin from whoever has it and ride a complete circle around the ring with it. The game can go on for hours. In another version of the game, known as the "girl chase," village men try to capture women on horseback.

Dining and Lodging

A yurt is the preferred place to stay at Sayram Hu. Yurts cost about Y20 a night per person, with accommodations similar to those at Heavenly Lake.

$ **Huacheng Hotel.** Once just a backpacker place close to the bus station, the Huacheng now boasts newly renovated doubles with 24-hour hot water, bathrooms, and air-conditioners, though dorm rooms continue to be dilapidated. A long way from the center of town, the hotel has some amenities, including a 24-hour Chinese restaurant. ⊠ *Ahe Mai Ti Jiang Jie, No. 7 Alley, No. 5 835000 Yining, south of bus station,* ☎ *0999/812–5050,* FAX *0999/812–1640. 158 rooms, 10 suites. 3 restaurants, hair salon, sauna, business services, travel services. No credit cards.*

$ **Yili Binguan** (Yili Guest House). Located in a lushly gardened complex, the Yili has modest and rather sterile looking rooms in the main building; but newer rooms in the west wing come with more amenities including spacious bathrooms and great views. ⊠ *22 Ying Bin Lu, 835000 Yining,* ☎ *0999/802–3799,* FAX *0999/802–4964. 200 rooms. No credit cards.*

$ **Youyi Binguan** (Friendship Hotel). Like the other two hotels, the Youyi has renovated its rooms in recent years, and most rooms now offer clean bathrooms, 24-hour hot water, and air-conditioners. It's a popular choice among backpackers. ⊠ *Sidaling Jie, Lane 3, No. 7, 835000, South of bus station,* ☎ *0999/802–3901,* FAX *0999/802–4631. 155 rooms, 6 suites. No credit cards.*

Kashgar

③⑥   *675 km (419 mi) southwest of Yining; 1,175 km (729 mi) south of Ürümqi (24 hrs by train).*

The area that is now Kashgar (known as Kashi in Chinese) has been a center for trade between China and the outside world for 2,000 years. A Buddhist kingdom was first established in Kashgar in the 1st century AD and thrived until Islam arrived and took hold in the 10th century. Today Kashgar is a hub for merchants coming in on the fabled Karakorum Highway through the Kunjerab Pass from Pakistan and the Turogart Pass from Kirgiziya. When these two treacherous mountain passes are open, between May 1 and October 30, Kashgar becomes a particularly colorful city, abuzz with visitors.

The population—1.3 million in the town and surrounding area—is 93% Uighur. Kashgar sits on a fertile desert oasis; on the farmland that surrounds the town are fields of cotton and orchards. As the desert in this area is thought to be full of untapped oil reserves, as well as large deposits of precious stones and minerals, Chinese and foreign-driven industrial development is on the way. Yet Kashgar still has fine examples of traditional Uighur architecture. In the center of town are some old houses with ornately carved and painted balconies.

Start in the town square, which is filled with photographers with outdoor stands. The landmark in the square is the **Id Kah Emin** (Ai Ti Ga Er Qingzhen Si in Chinese), one of the largest mosques in China. The ornate structure of yellow bricks is the result of many extensions and renovations to the original mosque, which was built in 1442 as a prayer hall for Shakesirmirzha, the ruler of Kashgar. The main hall has a ceiling with fine wooden carvings and precisely 100 carved wooden columns. If it is not prayer time, you can go into the mosque.

Wander up Jiefang Beilu, which intersects the square near the mosque. Here in the tangled lanes around the mosque are some of Kashgar's most intriguing **market stalls** and lively open-air markets. You'll find blacksmiths, coppersmiths, and other merchants selling jewelry, traditional Uighur instruments, knives, bright copper kettles, wedding chests, and brass sleigh bells for horses. Farther down, on Kumdarvaza Lu, is a row of traditional musical instrument stores and more outdoor craftsmen pounding out iron pots and brass bedposts, in cacaphonous syncopation. Up Jiefang Beilu, the road is lined with small restaurants that specialize in steamed dumplings (filled with lamb meat).

During the high season (May–October), you can follow Nuoerxi Lu on the right-hand side of the mosque past antiques shops, used-book stands, musical instrument shops, and curious locals to Seman Lu. Just outside the grounds of the Qiniwake Hotel you'll find **makeshift cafés** where the frenetic interaction of traders from all over the region, black-market money changers, and police (who seem to be involved in the commerce) is a show in itself. Tea, beer, fresh baked nan, and kebabs are for sale in small stands, and the tables are up for grabs. The **Caravan Café**, adjacent to the Qiniwake Hotel compound, is popular with the backpacker crowd; at dusk, a lively night market opposite the compound springs up on Nuoerxi Lu.

Take a taxi or bike to the **Xiangfei Mu** (Tomb of Abakh Hoja), 5 km (3 mi) northeast of the city, one of the most sacred sites in Xinjiang, where Muslims from all around the region come to pray and pay their respects. The ornate, sea green tiled hall that houses the tomb—actually about two dozen tombs—is part of a massive complex of sacred Islamic structures built around 1640, including a prayer hall. The Uighurs named the tomb and surrounding complex after Abakh Hoja, a 17th-century Islamic missionary who was believed to be a descendant of Mohammed and a powerful ruler of Kashgar and outlying regions in the 17th century. Excavations of the glazed-brick tombs indicate that the first occupant was Abakh Hoja's father, who is buried here along with Abakh Hoja and many of their descendants.

The Han, who prefer to emphasize the site's historical connection to their dynastic empire, call it the Tomb of the Fragrant Concubine. Iparkan, the grand-niece of Abakh Hoja, was chosen as concubine by the Qing emperor Qianlong in Beijing, to help maintain the stability of the border. One legend holds that Iparkan committed suicide rather than become the emperor's concubine, the other that she dutifully went to Beijing and spent 30 years in the emperor's palace, then asked to be buried in her homeland. Her alleged tomb was excavated in the 1980s—and found to be empty. Now the "fragrant concubine" is believed to be buried in Hebei province. Just outside the main gate, the adjoining lower and upper mosque are sometimes open to visitors. ⊠ *Izlati Lu; about 1 mi up hill from Sunday Bazaar district; look for sign on left, turn down dusty alley, go 500 yards.* ☏ *Y17,* ☎ *0998/282–2638.* ☉ *Summer, daily 9:30–8; winter, daily 10–7:30.*

In town, on Izlati Lu, turn left, going south, on Tauhuz Lu, then right on Renmin Donglu, and follow it about a mile to **Donghu Gongyuan** (East Lake Park). In this peaceful park you can rent paddleboats on the lake, and in summer, food vendors spread red carpets on the grass and serve drinks and refreshments. ⊠ *Renmin Donglu and Payinap Lu.* ☉ *Daily 10–8.*

The **Gong Anju Waishi Bangongshi** (Foreign Affairs Office of the Public Security Bureau) has a giant sculpture of Mao Zedong overlooking the city and the pool tables across the street—a stern reminder of what country this really is, although Kashgar looks little like China in any other way. ☒ *Renmin Donglu between Jiefang Lu and Tianman Lu.*

Dining and Lodging

In these small towns in western China, street numbers are not always used; the locals all know where certain hotels are. Reservations are not necessary or even possible to get in advance. If you want to be sure of having a room when you arrive in Kashgar or Turpan, ask CITS in Ürümqi (☞ Xinjiang A to Z) to phone and make a reservation for you. (Even so, you may get a puzzled look from the desk clerk when you say, "I have a reservation," and be asked the rote question: "You want a room?")

The best dining is at the major hotels, although the small family-owned restaurants around the Seman Hotel and near the Sunday Bazaar serve good Uighur fare, too: a delicious lamian, spicy kebabs, and nan. For vegetarians, the dining is a bit rougher, and the best option (if you're noodled out) is to head to the Chinese restaurants at the Seman or Qinibagh Hotels.

$–$$ ✕ **The Grapevine Restaurant.** Draped invitingly with grapevines, this outdoor café on the grounds of the Seman Hotel is a friendly place to come for very good Chinese food in sizable portions and for fresh leafy green vegetables—a scarcity in a town dominated by Muslim meat-based restaurants. At night, in season, you can hear the piercing, twanging sounds of Uighur music rise from the song and dance performance across the courtyard. ☒ *337 Seman Lu,* ☏ *no phone. No credit cards.*

$ ✕ **Chinese Restaurant.** This restaurant on the grounds of the Qiniwake Hotel serves good Chinese fare, with a regular Chinese-banquet style interior and some outdoor tables for summer months. ☒ *Qiniwake Hotel, 144 Seman Lu. No credit cards.*

$ ✕ **John's Information & Café.** Young Western travelers gravitate to John's for information and conviviality at comfy outdoor café tables, as Uighur locals shoot pool on adjacent billiard tables. Maps and postcards are for sale, and Internet services are also available. This is the original John's Café, which opened in 1990 and has since branched out to five other locations scattered across the Silk Road. The clientele seems oblivious to the cooking, which combines the worst of Western and Chinese. Even the tea is weak and lukewarm. ☒ *348 Renmin Xilu,* ☏ *0998/255–1186. No credit cards.*

$ ✕ **Kashgar Hotel Restaurant.** The cuisine here is a mix of Chinese and Uighur. You can order a barbecued sheep—the entire sheep, rolled out on a cart—a day in advance for special dinners. ☒ *Kashgar Hotel, 57 Tawaguzi Lu. No credit cards.*

$ ✕ **Muslim Restaurant.** The dark restaurant serves a set breakfast, lunch, and dinner with Uighur dishes that keep on coming. Excellent bread and fair coffee are available at breakfast, and a welcome variety of Chinese greens, eggplant, and other vegetables, as well as meat and chicken, for lunch and dinner. ☒ *Seman Hotel, 337 Seman Lu,* ☏ *0998/255–2001. No credit cards.*

$ ✕ **Norlook Kebab House.** You'll hear bursts of laughter and smell the scorched, smoky aroma of sizzling kebabs before you enter this lively outdoor café in a large gated garden. Here huge kebab platters, fresh seafood, and other local delicacies can be had for ultralow prices. Uighurs in the know congregate here at night in big groups for meals and stay playing cards and drinking beer till the wee hours. ☒ *285 Seman Lu,* ☏ *0998/283–4743. No credit cards. Closed Oct.–Apr.*

$–$$ 🏨 **Kashgar Hotel.** Formerly for government officials only, this sprawling hotel on the northeast edge of town opened to foreigners in 1976 and caters to large tour groups. The hotel has large quiet lush grounds and is close to the Sunday bazaar, but it's a bit far from the center of town. Renovations of two buildings in 1999 have spruced conditions up, and rooms are clean and fairly comfortable. ✉ *57 Tawuguzi Lu, 844000,* ☎ *0998/261–2991,* ℻ *0998/261–4679. 190 rooms, 22 suites. 3 restaurants, bar, hair salon, massage, shops, laundry service, business services, meeting room. No credit cards.*

$ 🏨 **Qiniwake Hotel** (Qinibagh Hotel, also called Chini Bagh). Once the British consulate, the Qiniwake has seen the end of its days of glory and intrigue, but the history remains. Famed European Silk Road travelers such as the explorer Sven Hedin, Sir Aurel Stein, Peter Fleming, and Ella Maillart stopped to rest here, after traveling for weary months in the dreaded Taklamakan Desert. British India's diplomat extraordinaire Sir George McCartney and his wife presided over the embassy (then called the Chini Bagh) for 26 years. The present hotel was built on the consulate's old gardens. It's large, relatively clean, and comfortable, if on the worn side, and is frequented by both backpackers and Pakistani travelers. Service can be slow, and any number of problems (from no phone service to no hot water) can suddenly emerge, but the staff is friendly and helpful. There's a branch of CITS on the grounds of the Qiniwake compound at the front gate. In 2001, the former Gilgit International Friendship Hotel, in the same compound, was converted into the Qiniwake Hotel's VIP building. Room prices here are 30% higher. ✉ *144 Seman Lu, 844000,* ☎ *0998/282–2291,* ℻ *0998/282–3842. 409 rooms, 14 suites. 4 restaurants, 2 bars, sauna, bikes, laundry service, business services, travel services. No credit cards.*

$ 🏨 **Seman Hotel.** This popular hotel, with its rambling, worn-down grounds and idiosyncratic Islamic-influenced architecture, was originally built in 1890 as the Russian consulate. Russia was Britain's chief rival then, and the consulate served as a center of political intrigue, spies, and secrets. In the oldest wing of the hotel, once the original consulate itself, you can stay in a suite decorated with luxurious rugs and old furniture. The newer rooms range from comfortable to dilapidated, no better and sometimes worse than those at the Qiniwake. Service is friendly, and showers work most of the time; and there is a clinic on the premises. The location is unbeatable, near a strip of sidewalk cafés. ✉ *337 Seman Lu, 844000,* ☎ *0998/255–2129,* ℻ *0998/255–2861. 131 rooms, 10 suites. 4 restaurants, hair salon, massage, shops, laundry service, business services, travel services. No credit cards.*

Nightlife and the Arts

In the courtyards of the **Seman Hotel** and **Qiniwake Hotel,** traditional Uighur music and dance are performed frequently at night from May through October. There is a cover charge of Y20–Y30 per person.

Cafés and pool halls, many scattered along Seman Lu between the Qiniwake and Seman Hotels, stay open past midnight Beijing time. There are also about two dozen outdoor pool tables, as well as some open-air cafés, on Renmin Donglu, at Renmin Square, across from the giant Mao statue.

Shopping

The **Sunday market** in the northwestern part of the city, is actually open every day, but the photo-opportunity-filled livestock market is here only on Sunday. Most of the activity takes place outside the bazaar, on Aizilati Lu. Farmers tug recalcitrant sheep through the streets, scarf-shrouded women dressed in garish colors preside over heaps of red eggs, and old Uighur men squat over baskets of chickens, haggling over the virtues and vices of each hapless hen. Farther up the hill away from the bazaar, look for a parking lot to the right, filled with the Kashgar vehicle of choice: rows of sleepy donkeys nodding off in the bright sunlight, their carts lined up neatly beside them. The main bazaar itself is in a large semi-Islamic structure with the bureaucratic name "Kashgar International Trade Market of Central and Western Asia." Here, under striped canopies with numerous stalls organized neatly in different sections, you can bargain for fabrics, lace scarves, *dopas* (embroidered hats), "handmade" knives, dried fruit, children's toys, and most other nonfood purchases. There's even a motorcycle section, where locals go to get their scooters tuned up. ⊠ *Aizilati Lu, about 2 km (1 mi) northwest of center of town; cab, Y10; bus, Y1.*

On the busy streets around the Id Kah Mosque, **outdoor vendors** sell brass bells for horse-drawn carriages, copper bowls and tea kettles, local gold jewelry, Chinese snuff bottles, ornamented wedding chests, and silver jewelry from Tibet and India.

The **Musical Instrument Shop** (⊠ 276 Kashgar Yusitang Buoyi Kasikhan Bazaar) has Kashgar's best selection of traditional Uighur string instruments, made in the workshop next door. At the **Uyghur Musical Instrument Shop** (⊠ 103 Nuoerxi Lu) you can watch the owner or his apprentice working on Uighur string instruments—stretching snakeskin to make a *ravap,* (a Uighur guitar) or inlaying the neck of a Uighur guitar with tiny bits of shell, then sanding them down.

Side Trips from Kashgar

Several kilometers northwest of Kashgar, you can visit the **Sanxian Dong** (Cave of the Three Immortals). According to legend, a Buddhist Kashgar king was told by a fortune teller that his three beloved daughters would all die, so he sequestered them in a cave to protect them. But the three princesses, fond of grapes, ordered their servants to bring great bunches. Bees followed the grapes inside, and sadly all three girls died of bee stings. Artists of the Buddhist period painted frescoes, now faded, inside the cave. You can climb in with a rope if you dare or view it from the outside, along with the surrounding desert and the snowcapped Tian Shan (Heavenly Mountains) in the distance. ⊠ *Hire taxi or go by bicycle (about 1½ hrs each way): follow Jiefang Beilu north from Seman Hotel to outskirts of town; about 3 km (2 mi) from town, road divides into two highways; take highway leading west, toward Turogart Pass and Kirgiziya, 1 mi farther; cave is on left.*

Pamir Mountains

305 km (189 mi) south of Kashgar (8 hrs by bus).

The **Karakorum Highway,** a spectacular pass winding across some of the most dramatic and inhospitable terrain in the world, traces one of the major ancient silk routes, starting in Kashgar and leading south for 2,100 km (1,302 mi) through three great mountain ranges over the **Khunjerab Pass** (Valley of Blood) into Pakistan. The story behind the highway is as remarkable as the scenery itself. Started in 1967 by the Chinese government, construction went on for 20 years during which more than 400 lives were lost. Workers blasted through hundreds of miles of sheer rock, even hanging by rope over deep gorges to drill holes for dynamite. The highway starts in the Pamir Plateau, following the gorge of the Gez River and passing the occasional goat-tending Tajik village as it winds through the foothills of the Kongurshan. About 200 km (124 mi) from Kashgar, the picturesque **Karakuli Lake** (at an elevation of 12,460 ft) comes into view, dominated on either side by stunning snowcapped mountains. Snowy white yurts stand by the river's edge and are rented out (Y40) by friendly nomads. Camel and yak rides are available here, too. Bring warm clothing even in summertime: the weather can be downright chilly. Going on, the road ascends to elevations of more than 15,000 ft, winding past the 25,600-ft-high **Muztagata Mountain,** or "father of the ice mountains"—a magnificent glacier-ridden giant in the Pamir range. Finally, the highway descends to 11,800 ft for the border check and the last stop before the land turns into Pakistan.

㊲ The border town of **Tashkurgan** (Tajik for "stone city") is nestled among the mountains and fields of rapeseed flowers. The town, composed of one poplar-lined main street, is dominated by Chinese soldiers, but the surrounding area is rustic and makes for a pleasant walk, with houses made of stone and wood inhabited by Tajiks, as well as some local cemeteries. On a little side alley north of the main street, marked by a tiny sign that says STONE CITY, look for the ruins of a 6th-century stone fort that gave the town its name. The dirt road at the base of the fort is reputedly the actual Silk Road itself. In the great Chinese classic *Journey to the West,* the monk Xuan Zang stopped to rest in Stone City after returning from a danger-filled journey to bring Buddhist sutras back to China.

Turpan

㊳ *184 km (114 mi) southeast of Ürümqi (2½–3 hrs by bus).*

Turpan lies in a desert basin at the southern foot of the Heavenly Mountains. Part of the basin, called the Turpan Depression, lies 505 ft below sea level, the hottest and lowest spot in China and the second-lowest point in the world, after the Dead Sea. Temperatures have been known to soar to more than 110°F, and the sunshine is relentless.

The oasis town of Turpan has a population of just under a quarter of a million people; 79% are minorities, mostly Uighur. It's surrounded by mountains and some of the richest farmland in Xinjiang; its fruit orchards and vineyards support a few small wineries. Late summer, when the grapes are ripe, is Turpan's busiest tourist season. Unfortunately, the city has been infected by the tourist bug of late; a 2001 city government poster proclaimed, "One hand grabs grapes, the other tourism." Accordingly, new roads to star attractions outside the city have been paved, cutting down on travel times, but new Disneyfied Buddhist caves and other simulacra are also popping up alongside ancient sites. Make a note of the sites you definitely want to visit before approaching taxi drivers, as they will attempt to bring you to some of the new attractions.

In the heat of summer you can stroll around if you start early in the morning and stop frequently at the outdoor stands for cold drinks. Grapevine-covered canopies provide welcome shade over many of the city sidewalks. You might also rent a bike or take a taxi, plenty of which cruise around town and many of which have air-conditioning.

Walk about 10 minutes west on Laocheng Zhonglu, which separates the two main hotels on the Qingnian Lu pedestrian walkway, to the **bazaar,** behind an ornate green gate. Some crafts are available here, as well as plenty of local fruit and nuts piled up in huge sacks. ✉ *Laocheng Xilu near Gao Jiang Nanlu, past Bank of China, opposite bus station.*

West on Laocheng stands the picturesque **Qingzhen Si** (City Mosque), the most active of the group of mosques in the district, about 3 km (2 mi) from the center of town. Out here in a predominantly Uighur neighborhood are sod huts and donkey carts, as well as family-run restaurants where cooks bake nan in deep, open well-sized ovens. ⌧ *Laocheng Lu.* ☉ *Nonprayer hrs.*

East on Laocheng Zhonglu, the side street Qiu Nian Zhonglu leads to **Emin Ta** (Tower for Showing Gratitude to Eminhoja, also called Sugong Tower), at the southeast end of town. The Emin Tower and adjoining **mosque** were built in 1777 in the Afghani style to commemorate a military commander who suppressed a rebellion by a group of aristocrats. The 141-ft tower is simple and elegantly spare, built in the shape of a cone, with bricks arranged in 15 patterns and a spiral staircase. The sun-baked roof of the mosque, which is cracking in places, can be scaled for a view of the surrounding lush vineyards. Renovations in 2001 added structural extensions and a large square at the entrance for "antiques" vendors. ⌧ *From east end of Laocheng Donglu, turn right on last paved road before farmland, walk south to tower,* ☎ *0995/856–7158.* ⌨ *Y20.* ☉ *Summer, daily 8–8; winter, daily 8–6.*

The remarkable 2,000-year-old **Kanerjing** (Karez Irrigation Tunnels) allowed the desert cities of the Silk Road to survive and even flourish despite an unrelentingly arid environment. In the oasis cities of Turpan and Hami, more than 1,000 wells linked to more than 1,600 km (1,000 mi) of underground tunnels brought water, moved only by gravity, from melting snow at the base of the Bogdashan Mountains to the cities. You can view the Karez Tunnels in Turpan from several sites, some without an admission fee. Most bus or cab drivers take visitors to the largely worthless Karez Irrigation Museum, opened in 2000 by a Sino-Japanese joint venture that also has a hotel next to the site. The admission fee here includes entry to the tunnel next to the museum, which been widened into a pleasant underground pathway that extends for a few hundred meters; bring good walking shoes, as you may need to pick your way over dead branches or dirt piles. ⌧ *888 Xincheng Lu, on the western outskirts of the city.* ⌨ *Y20.* ☉ *Summer, daily dawn–dusk; winter, daily 8–8.*

Dining and Lodging

Some of the best and safest dining, as in the rest of Xinjiang, is in the hotel restaurants, but a cluster of small cafés with outdoor seating and English-language menus offers cheap, filling meals along Laocheng Lu (between Qingnian Lu and Gaochang Lu). The lively night market, with rows of kebab and spicy hotpot stands, on Gaochang Lu just next to the huge public square, is also worth visiting.

$–$$ ✕ **Muslim Restaurant.** Like most hotel restaurants in the region, this one is dark and lacks ambience, but it does have a hearty variety of standard Uighur dishes—lamb, noodles, and vegetables. ⌧ *Turpan Guesthouse, 2 Qingnian Nanlu,* ☎ *0995/852–2301. No credit cards.*

$ ✕ **Chipu Café.** The most popular of the little cafés that cater to foreigners on a strip around the junction of Qingnian Lu and Laocheng Lu serves a variety of Chinese dishes, posted on the outdoor blackboard in English. ⌧ *Qingnian Lu above Laocheng Lu,* ☎ *no phone. No credit cards. No dinner.*

$ ✕ **Tian Shan Bai Huo Shang Chang.** It's easy to go numb on noodle dishes after you've been subject to a steady diet of Xinjiang fare, but this relatively clean hole-in-the-wall with pink tabletops creatively hammered out of linoleum serves up an especially tasty *lamian* (pulled noodles). ⌧ *21 Laocheng Lu, opposite bus station.* ☎ *0995/852–2313. No credit cards.*

$$ ⌂ **Oasis Hotel.** This hotel with a professional staff dolled up in traditional Uighur costume is one of the town's two main hotels. It has spacious, comfortable, and clean air-conditioned rooms, friendly service, and a pleasant grapevine-lined courtyard. The Turpan branch of CITS is on the grounds, next door to the hotel. The Oasis Café on the first floor has a good American-style breakfast. ✉ *41 Qingnian Beilu,* ☎ *0995/852–2491,* FAX *0995/852–3348. 180 rooms, 10 suites. 3 restaurants, bar, bicycles, laundry service, business services, travel services. No credit cards.*

$$ 🏨 **Turpan Binguan** (Turpan Guesthouse). In the grapevine-trellis-covered courtyard here, you can get fruit juices and beer during the summer. The rooms are nothing to write home about but are relatively clean and large, especially those in the newer wing. The Muslim restaurant is quite good, and the gift shop is one exception to Turpan's status as a shopping nonentity. ✉ *2 Qingnian Nanlu, off Laocheng Lu,* ☎ *0995/852–2301,* FAX *0995/852–3262. 200 rooms, 6 suites. 3 restaurants, shops, laundry service. V.*

Nightlife and the Arts

Every summer evening there are Uighur musical performances in the courtyards of both the Turpan Oasis Hotel and the Turpan Guesthouse.

The cafés in the center of town are open late, and much of the nightlife, Turpan-style, consists of drinking beer and kicking back at the outdoor tables. Many locals head to the night market on Gaochang Lu, at the west end of the public Tour and Culture (Luyou Wenhua Guangchang) square.

Side Trips from Turpan

About 47 km (29 mi) east of Turpan, in the middle of the Turpan Depression, the red clay **Huo Yan Shan** (Flaming Mountains), a branch range of the Heavenly Mountains, are named for the vibrant color and the way they seem to glow at sunset. The range is 100 km (62 mi) long and 10 km (6¼ mi) wide; the ground temperature here has been recorded at a scorching 110°F. In 1923 a scientific expedition unearthed the first dinosaur eggs discovered in modern times at the base of the cliffs, as well as a host of fossils and other Stone Age relics. Nowadays, the Flaming Mountains don't usually constitute a stop for most tours but can be seen en route as buses head for the Bezeklik Caves.

㊴ The **Bozikeli Qianfo Dong** (Bezeklik Thousand Buddha Caves), in a breathtaking valley nestled against the Flaming Mountains, are an ancient temple and monastery built between the 5th and 9th centuries AD by slaves whose entire lives went into the construction. Many of the fine examples of Buddhist sculpture and wall frescoes were destroyed after Islam came to the region in the 13th century. Other sculptures and fragments of frescoes, including several whole murals of Buddhist monks, all in excellent condition, were taken by 20th-century archaeologists like German Albert von Le Coq, who shipped his finds back to Berlin, where many of them were destroyed in World War II bombing. Though they remain a feat of early engineering, and some of the 77 grottoes have partially restored frescoes, the caves are really in atrocious condition. Go just to see the site itself, which is magnificent. A new Buddha Cave was constructed in 1980 by a local artist a few hundred meters in front of the Bozikeli Qianfo Dong. Cab drivers sometimes stop at this entrance, but the new site, with its garish colors and artificial atmosphere, isn't worth the separate Y20 ticket price. ✉ *Northwestern side of Huo Yan Shan.* 🎫 *Y20.* ☉ *Daily 9–6.*

㊵ The ancient **Atsana-Karakhoja Mu** (Atsana-Karakhoja Tombs) burial grounds southeast of Turpan are where the imperial dead of the city of Gaochang were once buried. Though the site was discovered by Western archaeologists in the early 1900s, extensive Chinese excavations were undertaken only in the early 1970s. These have unearthed more than 400 graves, which contain mummies and artifacts dating to the 3rd century AD. Many of the relics and mummies were relocated to the

Xinjiang Museum in Ürümqi. At present, three tombs here are now open to visitors. The tomb of Minister Feng Changqing, a Tang dynasty governor, contains a fresco depicting the governor's life stages, from innocent child to wise Buddha-like old age. Apart from the murals, the tombs contain three fairly well-preserved mummies. ⊠ *40 km (25 mi) southeast of Turpan,* ☎ *0995/869–2202.* ☞ *Y20.* ☉ *Summer, daily dawn–dusk; winter, daily 9–5:30.*

❹ The ruins of the **Gaochang Gucheng** (City of Gaochang) lie in the valley south of the Flaming Mountains. At the entrance to the ancient city are donkey-driven carts to take you around the ruins. Legend has it that a group of soldiers stopped here in the 1st century BC on their way to Afghanistan, found that water was plentiful, and decided to stay. By the 7th century the city was the flourishing capital of the Kingdom of Gaochang that ruled over 21 other towns, and by the 9th century the Uighurs had moved into the area from Mongolia, establishing the Kingdom of Kharakojam. In the 14th century Mongols conquered and destroyed the kingdom, leaving only the remains of walls and buildings that are here today. Despite repeated plundering of the site by local farmers and Muslim religious militants, in the early 1900s German archaeologists von Le Coq and Grunwedel were still able to unearth ancient manuscripts, statues, and frescoes in superb condition. Nowadays, only the city walls and a partially preserved monastery surrounded by muted, almost unrecognizable shapes remain, an eerie and haunting excursion into the pages of history. ⊠ *5 km (3 mi) southeast of Atsana-Karakhoja Tombs.* ☞ *Y20.* ☉ *Summer, daily dawn–dusk; winter, daily 9–5:30.*

❷ The impressive ruins of **Jiaohe Gucheng** (City of Jiaohe, also called Yarkhoto) lie in the Yarnaz Valley west of Turpan, on an island at the confluence of two rivers. The city, established as a garrison during the Han dynasty, was built on a high plateau, protected by the natural fortification of cliffs rising 98 ft above the rivers, rather than by walls. Jiaohe was governed from the 2nd century to the 7th century by the Kingdom of Gaochang and occupied later by Tibetans. Despite destruction in the 13th century by Mongol hordes, large fragments of actual streets and buildings remain, including a Buddhist monastery and Buddhist statues, a row of bleached pagodas, a 29-ft observation tower, government centers, and a prison. ⊠ *8 km (5 mi) west of Turpan.* ☞ *Y30.* ☉ *Summer, daily dawn–dusk; winter, daily 9–5:30.*

❸ **Putao Gou** (Grape Valley), at the western end of the Flaming Mountains, is lush and green in stark contrast to the blasted, gravel-strewn desert all around. Grapes were first introduced to the area more than 2,000 years ago. Pleasant pathways lead among trellises hanging with grapevines to a winery and to a restaurant. ⊠ *19 km (12 mi) northeast of Turpan.*

Xinjiang A to Z

To research prices, get advice from other travelers, and book travel arrangements, visit www.fodors.com.

AIR TRAVEL
Daily flights link Ürümqi with most major Chinese cities, including Beijing, Guangzhou, Shanghai, Xian, Lanzhou, and Chengdu. There are also weekly flights between Ürümqi and Hong Kong.

Flights from Ürümqi to Kashgar depart every evening but Friday. There are no flights to Turpan. Flights from Ürümqi to Yining run six days a week. As with the buses, return flights are frequently delayed or canceled.

BIKE TRAVEL

Few people ride bicycles in Ürümqi due to the heavy traffic and dusty roads. Bicycles can be rented (Y10–Y20 per day) at the entrance to the compound of the Qinibagh Hotel in Kashgar. The Oasis Hotel in Turpan has bike rentals, as does John's Information & Café. Present a photocopy of your passport to be held as identification.

BUSINESS HOURS

BANKS AND OFFICES

Government offices are open Monday through Saturday 9–noon and 4–8.

SHOPS

Uighur-run stores in Xinjiang generally operate on local time.

BUS TRAVEL

Buses (Y22 round-trip) leave for Tianchi (Heavenly Lake) at 9 AM and 9:15 AM from the north and south gates of Renmin Park and return at 4 PM or 4:30 PM.

City buses in Ürümqi (Y1–Y3) are generally crowded, and there have been reports of pickpocketing, and even some bombings.

FARES AND SCHEDULES

Daily buses link Ürümqi with Turpan (2½–3 hours) and Yining (1 day, with a stop at Sayram Lake). The return bus schedules for Kashgar and Yining are sporadic and unreliable.

For buses from Kashgar to Tashkurgan (Y62 one-way; 8 hours) you can get tickets at the bus depot. The buses continue from there onto Islamabad, Pakistan May–October.

Buses from Turpan go to Ürümqi (2½–3 hours) every two hours.
➤ BUS INFORMATION: **Kashgar bus depot** (✉ Qiniwake Hotel compound; 144 Seman Lu). **Turpan bus depot** (✉ 27 Laocheng Lu, ☎ 0995/852–2325).

CAR TRAVEL

Contact CITS in Ürümqi for round-trip car transportation to Yining and/or Sayram Lake (Y2,000 a day for two people to stop at both destinations).

DINING

MEALTIMES

Restaurants and Uighur-run stores in Xinjiang generally operate on local time. This means that meals are often served late; for instance, lunch is typically served from 1 to 3 Beijing time, and dinner starts at 7 Beijing time.

EMERGENCIES

➤ POLICE: **Kashgar PSB** (✉ 137 Yumulakexiehai Lu, 10-min walk down main road from Qiniwake Hotel, ☎ 0998/282–2030). **Ürümqi PSB** (✉ Guangmin Lu, just northeast of Renmin Square; ask hotel to phone PSB).
➤ HOSPITALS: **Chinese Medicine Hospital of Ürümqi** (✉ 60 Youhau Nanlu, Ürümqi, ☎ 0991/242–0963). **Er Yi Hospital** (✉ 1 Shagelamu Lu, Kashgar, ☎ 0998/252–2401). **People's Hospital** (✉ 4 Gaochang Lu, Turpan, ☎ 0995/852–2461).

INTERNET SERVICES

In Kashgar, CITS, John's Information Café, and New Century (☞ Tours, *below*) all provide Internet access for Y30–Y40. In Turpan, 168 Internet Bar opened by China Telecom, has Internet access for Y12 an hour. The bar is next to the 168 Binguan. Major hotels in Ürümqi usually have Internet access; for a lower rate, head to China Telecom, which charges Y10 per hour.

➤ CONTACTS: **168 Internet Bar** ✉ 32 Gaochang Lu, at Luzhou Lu, Turpan, ☎ 0995/853–5044). **China Telecom** (✉ 28 Huang He Lu, Ürümqi, ☎ 0991/231–2012).

TIME

Airline, train and bus schedules, banks, offices, government departments, museums, and police stations run on Beijing time. Many local residents, however, set their watches by local time, one hour behind Beijing time. When you make appointments, make sure to establish the designated hour as local time or Beijing time. In Kashgar there is the additional confusion of "Kashgar time" (one hour behind Xinjiang time and two hours behind Beijing time).

TOURS

In Kashgar, CITS (☞ Visitor Information), open March–November, arranges tours of the surrounding countryside. John's Information & Café provides similar services for a backpacker crowd; but check rates and itineraries first with the friendlier and more professional New Century across the street from John's.

CITS can arrange multiday large group tours in Turpan following the ancient silk routes.

The Ürümqi CITS offers a range of pricey but interesting tours, including horseback riding by Sayram Lake, adventure trekking into the Taklamakan Desert and Kunlun Mountains, and a 25-day tour to find the buried ruins of the kingdom of Loulan, located near Lop Nor Lake.

➤ TOUR-OPERATOR RECOMMENDATIONS: **John's Information & Café** (✉ Opposite Seman Hotel, ☎ 0998/282–4186). **New Century** (✉ 243 Seman Lu, ☎ FAX 0998/282–4500).

TRAIN TRAVEL
FARES AND SCHEDULES

Daily trains run between Ürümqi and Beijing (2 days), Shanghai (2¼ days), Chengdu (50 hrs), Xian (1½ days), and Lanzhou (1 day). A train departs Ürümqi for Kashgar (24 hrs) and Turpan (2 hrs) twice a day, though the rail station for Turpan is inconveniently located 58 km (36 mi) south of the city at Daheyan (making the bus quicker and more convenient). The new Kashgar rail station is at the eastern end of town on a street that turns into Renmin Donglu; a cab to the city center should cost Y10.

TRANSPORTATION AROUND XINJIANG
BY DONKEY CART

On the outskirts of Kashgar and Turpan you can hire a donkey cart (Y2 per ½ mi).

BY HIRED CAR

In Ürümqi and Kashgar, CITS (☞ see Tours, *above*) can provide a car with driver at about Y200 per day for driving within the city. Trips outside the city can be arranged for higher fees.

BY TAXI

The best way to get around Ürümqi, Kashgar, and Turpan is by taxi (seatbelts, though useful, tend to be very dusty and may leave marks on clothing). Ask your hotel desk attendant to write down your destination in Chinese for the driver, as well as the hotel's name for the return trip. For shorter distances, walking is fine, and the dry, sunny weather is almost always conducive to a stroll.

The best way to see the sights, which lie scattered all around Turpan, is to rent a taxi for the whole day (Y250–Y500). As an alternative, you can take a daily bus (Y36) that visits all the sights, departing from the bus station at 9 and returning at 6.

VISITOR INFORMATION

➤ TOURIST INFORMATION: **CITS** (✉ Qiniwake Hotel, Kashgar, first building to right in compound, ☎ 0998/282–5390); ✉ Turpan Oasis Hotel, 2nd floor, back entrance, Turpan, ☎ 0995/852–3215, FAX 0995/852–3706; ✉ Luyou Hotel, 51 Xinhua Beilu, 1st floor, Ürümqi, ☎ 0991/282–1428, FAX 0991/281–0689, WEB www.xinjiangtour.com; ✉ 88 Xin Hua Xilu, Yining, ☎ 0999/804–3722).

6 SHANGHAI

THE HEAD OF THE DRAGON

Shanghai, the most notorious of Chinese
cities, once known as the Paris of the East,
now calls itself the Pearl of the Orient. No
other city can better capture the urgency and
excitement of China's opening and reform.
Beauty and charm coexist with kitsch and
commercialism. From the colonial architecture
of the former French Concession to the neon-
lighted high-rises jutting above the city,
Shanghai is a city of paradox and change.

Updated by
Paul Davidson

SHANGHAI, literally, the "City on the Sea," in the 1990s became —and still is—the center of China's economic resurgence. Shanghai's allure begins with its glamorous past of sepia-lighted halls, opium dens, and French villas. A gathering of cultures, it once was a place where rich taipans walked the same streets as gamblers, prostitutes, and beggars, and Europeans fleeing the Holocaust lived alongside Chinese intellectuals and revolutionaries.

The Communist Party was born here, but its strict tenets could not stifle the city's unflagging internationalism, which was determined at its creation. Although the nation has a history thousands of years old, Shanghai itself could be called a new Chinese invention. Lying on the Yangzi River delta, it marks the point where Asia's longest and most important river completes its 5,500-km (3,400-mi) journey to the Pacific. Until 1842 Shanghai's location made it merely a small fishing village. After the first Opium War, the British named Shanghai a treaty port, forcing the city's opening to foreign involvement.

The village was soon turned into a city carved up into autonomous concessions administered by the British, French, and Americans, all independent of Chinese law. Each colonial presence brought with it its particular culture, architecture, and society. Although Shanghai had its own walled Chinese city, many native residents still chose to live in the foreign settlements. Thus began a mixing of cultures that shaped Shanghai's openness to Western influence. Shanghai became an important industrial center and trading port that attracted not only foreign businesspeople (60,000 by the 1930s) but also Chinese migrants from other parts of the country.

In its heyday, Shanghai was the place to be—it had the best art, the greatest architecture, and the strongest business in Asia. With dance halls, brothels, glitzy restaurants, international clubs, and even a foreign-run racetrack, Shanghai was a city that catered to every whim of the rich. But poverty ran alongside opulence, and many of the lower-class Chinese provided the cheap labor that kept the city running.

The Paris of the East became known as a place of vice and indulgence. Amid this glamour and degradation the Communist Party held its first meeting in 1921. The thirties and forties saw invasion and war. The city weathered Japanese raids and then the victory of the Communists in 1949 over the Nationalists, after which foreigners left the country. Closed off from the outside world with which it had become so comfortable, Shanghai fell into a deep sleep. Fashion, music, and romance gave way to uniformity and the stark reality of Communism.

Today Shanghai has once again become one of China's most open cities ideologically, socially, culturally, and economically, striving to return to the internationalism that defined it before the Revolution. Shanghai's path to this renewed prominence began in 1990 when China's leader, Deng Xiaoping, chose it as the engine of the country's commercial renaissance, aiming to rival Hong Kong by 2010. If China is a dragon, he said, Shanghai is its head. Today the city is all about business. Having embraced competition and a market-driven economy in just a few years, it now hosts the nation's stock market, accounts for one-sixth of the country's gross national product, and houses the most important industrial base in the nation.

Today Shanghai draws more parallels to New York City than Paris—a true city, it is laid out on a grid (unlike sprawling Beijing), and with a population of 16 million, it is one of the world's most crowded urban areas. Nowhere else in China can you feel the same pulse, dynamism, and enthusiasm.

The Shanghainese have a reputation for being sharp, open-minded, glamorous, sophisticated, and business-oriented, and they're convinced they have the motivation and attitude to achieve their place as China's powerhouse. Far away from Beijing's watchful political eyes, yet supported by state officials who call Shanghai their hometown, the people have a freedom to grow that their counterparts in the capital don't enjoy. That ambition can be witnessed firsthand across Shanghai's Huangpu River, which joins the Yangzi at the northern outskirts of the city. Here, Shanghai's most important project is being built—Pudong New Area, China's 21st-century financial, economic, and commercial center. "The east side of the river," is home to Shanghai's new stock market building, the tallest hotel in the world, the city's new international airport, and, soon, the world's tallest building. And rising from land that just a few years ago was dominated by rice paddies is the city's pride and joy, the Oriental Pearl Tower—a gaudy, flashing, spaceshiplike pillar, the tallest in Asia.

During the last decade, Puxi, (the west side of the river), has also gone through staggering change. Charming old houses are making way for shiny high-rises. The population is moving from alley housing in the city center to spanking-new apartments in the suburbs. Architecturally spectacular new museums and theaters are catching the world's attention. Foreign shopping centers and malls are popping up on every corner. Residents walk down to their favorite store only to find it's been torn down to make room for a new architectural wonder. In 1987 there were about 150 high-rise buildings in the city. Today there are more than 1,500, and the number continues to grow. Shanghai is reputed to be home to one-fifth of all the world's construction cranes.

Shanghai's open policy has also made the city the hot new attraction for foreign investors. As millions of dollars pour in, especially to Pudong, Shanghai has again become home to tens of thousands of expatriates. Foreign influence has made today's Shanghai a consumer heaven. Domestic stores rub shoulders with the boutiques of Louis Vuitton, Christian Dior, and Ralph Lauren. Newly made businessmen battle rush-hour traffic in their Mercedes and Lexus cars. Young people keep the city up till the wee hours as they dance the night away in clubs blasting the latest techno grooves. And everyone walks around with a de rigueur mobile phone or pager attached to his or her belt.

In Shanghai it's all about image; it's not surprising, then, that the Shanghainese enjoy one of the highest living standards in China. Higher salaries and higher buildings, more business and more entertainment— they all define the fast-paced lives of China's most cosmopolitan and open people.

Pleasures and Pastimes

Architecture

Shanghai's history is eclectic, and so is its architecture. Although significant portions of the city are making way for skyscrapers, some of what has defined its original charm still exists. From the neoclassicism of the Bund to the art deco of the French Concession to the quaint Chinese alleys of the old city, a walk through town can evoke memories of romantic old Shanghai. But hurry: as you read this, old buildings are being torn down.

The high points, literally, of new architecture are the skyscraping Jin-mao Tower and Oriental Pearl Tower in Pudong, both of which have opened sky-high observatories.

Dining

Shanghainese food is one of China's main regional cuisines, like Cantonese from the south and Sichuan from the west. Shanghai's restaurants tend to serve an amalgam of dishes from different regions, and it may be difficult to weed out a restaurant that serves true Shanghainese food. Typical Shanghainese fare includes *jiachang doufu* (home-style tofu, deep-fried), *pao fou* (a soupy rice concoction), and *su ban dou* (cold vegetables with bean mash). Shanghainese chefs like to use high doses of oil and sugar and oyster sauce. River fish is often the highlight of the meal, with hairy crab a specialty in winter. Shanghai is also known for its own style of dim sum, especially *xiaolong bao* (steamed pork dumplings). You can often find dumplings, wontons, *you tiao* ("grease sticks"—deep-fried unsweetened dough), Shanghainese fried noodles, and baked and fried breads being sold by street vendors throughout the city.

Western food is now readily available, with foreign establishments arriving on the scene monthly. In addition, China's reforms have allowed fast-food joints to flourish—KFC and McDonald's are popular with locals. You often see families taking their one child for a hamburger treat or couples sharing a pizza.

Although the younger generations can be found dining or snacking into the late hours, most Chinese people follow a very strict eating schedule, so if you're dining at a more traditional Chinese restaurant, you can expect larger crowds between 11:30 AM and 12:30 PM and between 5:30 PM and 6:30 PM. At some restaurants you must arrive early for dinner (at least by 6 PM), or you'll miss all the best food. Many restaurants also have English menus, and you may find it difficult to order at the ones that don't. If you can't find a server who can translate for you, pantomime and drawings usually work fairly well.

You're not obliged to tip, as it's not a custom in China. Actually, almost all of the fancier restaurants in Shanghai tack on a 10%–15% service charge, which technically takes care of the tip even though your server may not see any of it. If there is no mandatory service charge, tipping is still not required, although more and more people are doing so at Western restaurants.

CATEGORY	COST*	
$$$$	over Y165	over US$20
$$$	Y99–Y165	US$12–$20
$$	Y50–Y99	US$6–$12
$	under Y50	under US$6

Prices are for one entrée at dinner.

Lodging

Since the early 1990s the number of foreign hotels has exploded, pushing up the standards and quality of domestic-run hotels as well. Hotels here are now approaching Western standards, and there are some classy new establishments. Shanghai's hotels cater mostly to business travelers and can be divided into two categories: modern Western-style hotels that are elegant and nicely appointed or hotels built in the city's glory days that became state-run after 1949. The latter may lack great service, modern fixings, and convenient facilities, but they make up for it in charm, tradition, and history. All hotels have cashier counters where you can change foreign currency into yuan. Again, tipping is not mandatory.

CATEGORY	COST*	
$$$$	over Y1500	over US$180
$$$	Y1275–Y1500	US$150–$180
$$	Y650–Y1275	US$80–$150
$	under Y650	under US$80

Prices are for a standard double room with bath at peak season unless otherwise stated; 15% service charge is not included.

Nightlife

Other cities in China may close down after dinner, but Shanghai never sleeps. Whether playing pool at an American bar or dancing the night away at a chic club, young Shanghainese and expatriates alike have a fairly good selection of nighttime entertainment.

Most of the city's popular bars are in the center, concentrated in areas of the Luwan, Xuhui, and Jingan districts. And because Shanghai is small and traffic is light in the evenings, it's easy to bar-hop by cab. Karaoke is ubiquitous; KTV (Karaoke TV) establishments with private rooms complete with hostesses, XO cognac, and fruit platters are even more popular. Just beware of the prices.

Shopping and Markets

Because of Shanghai's commercial status as China's most open port city, it has the widest variety of goods to be found in the nation, with the exception of Hong Kong. Ritzy chrome shopping malls stand alongside the local dingy state-run stores, inundating the consumer with both foreign name brands and domestic goods. Two of Shanghai's main roads, Nanjing Lu and Huaihai Lu, have become the city's shopping meccas.

Traditional treasures, Chinese arts and crafts, and such special exports as silk and linen are available in stores as well as on the street. In the city's nooks and crannies, outdoor markets give a good view of Shanghai's bustling street life. Food markets are scattered in every neighborhood. Bird and flower markets offer everything from bonsai plants to songbirds. Most interesting, however, are the antiques markets, at which local hawkers sell their pieces of Chinese history—some real, some not.

EXPLORING SHANGHAI

Shanghai as a whole encompasses a huge area. However, the city center is a relatively small district in what is collectively called Puxi (west of the river). On the east side lies what many think is Shanghai's future—Pudong (east of the river). Shanghai's main east–west roads are named for Chinese cities, while some north–south streets are named for Chinese provinces.

The city was once delineated by its foreign concessions, and to some extent, the former borders still define the city. The old Chinese city is now surrounded by the Zhonghua Lu–Renmin Lu circle. North of the city, the International Settlement—run by the British, Americans, Europeans, and Japanese—was the area between the Huangpu River and Huashan Lu, and bordered by Suzhou Creek to the north and Yanan Lu to the south. The former French Concession lies south of Yanan Lu, north of Zhaojiabang Lu. The southwest corner of the Concession lies at Xujiahui, from which point it runs all the way east to the Bund, with the exception of the northern half of the old Chinese city.

Although technically most Shanghainese consider the city center to be whatever lies within the Ring Road, the heart of the city is found on its chief east–west streets—Nanjing Lu, Huaihai Lu, and Yanan Lu—

cut off in the west approximately at Wulumuqi Lu and in the east by the Bund. At one time, the closer you got to the Bund, the stronger the heartbeat became, but with the city's constant construction, demographics are also changing, and the heart of Shanghai seems to beat ever outward.

To the east and west of city center lie Shanghai's new development areas. In Hongqiao, the area outside the Ring Road to the west, are office and commercial buildings for foreign and domestic business and the residential area of Gubei. Rising from countryside across the Huangpu River to the east is Pudong, the new concrete behemoth that Deng Xiaoping designated as China's future financial, economic, and commercial center.

Shanghai is very much a walking city, so parts of it are easily explored on foot, and taxis are readily available. In compact central Shanghai, cab rides would be short if not for the outrageous traffic. Some spots outside Shanghai offer getaways from the city's urban chaos, and with ever-improving roads and public transportation, day trips to Suzhou and Hangzhou are possible.

Numbers in the text correspond to numbers in the margin and on the Shanghai map.

Great Itineraries

IF YOU HAVE 3 DAYS

Start with a trip to **Yuyuan** (Yu Garden), sip some tea, and take a walk around the surrounding old Chinese city and its old antiques markets. Afterward, work your way over to **Wai Tan** (the Bund) for a leisurely stroll, take a quick look at the historic **Heping Fandian** (Peace Hotel), and walk down **Nanjing Lu** to experience Shanghai's busiest street. For dinner the Peace Hotel Chinese restaurant offers good views of the river and the Bund lighted up at night. The next day take a cab north to **Yufo Si** (Jade Buddha Temple), head back to Nanjing Lu if you didn't finish its sights the day before, and then spend an afternoon at **Renmin Guang Chang** (People's Square), people-watching, taking in China's ancient treasures at **Shanghai Bowuguan** (Shanghai Museum), and swinging over to the nearby **Hua Niao Shichang** (Bird and Flower Market). Day three can be spent walking in the **French Concession,** particularly around Huaihai Lu, for a view of old Shanghai and the city's new chic stores. Here you can also tour **Sun Zhongshan Guju** (Sun Yat-sen's former residence) and the **Zhonggong Yidahuizhi** (Zhongguo Gongchangdang; First Chinese Communist Party Congress site). The evenings of day two and three can be spent catching a show of the Shanghai acrobats or relaxing on a night cruise of the Huangpu River. Afterward, experience Shanghai's happening nightlife.

IF YOU HAVE 5 DAYS

Follow the three-day itinerary and on the fourth day make a trip to **Pudong** and go to the top of the **Dongfang Mingzhu** (Oriental Pearl Tower) or the spectacular **Jinmao Dasha** (Jinmao Tower)—or both—for a bird's-eye view of the city. On day five go to the Hongkou District to stroll around the old houses and **Moxi Huitang** (Ohel Moshe Synagogue) and maybe take a peek at **Luxun Gongyan** (Lu Xun Park and Memorial). Fill any spare time with visits to Shanghai's antiques markets, antique-furniture warehouses, and arts and crafts stores.

IF YOU HAVE 7 DAYS

Start with the five-day itinerary. Then get away from it all with a day trip to the wonderful **Zhouzhuang,** the traditional canal city outside Shanghai. Or drive out to Songjiang County to see the **Fang Ta Yuan**

(Square Pagoda). If you're willing to take an hour train ride, **Suzhou** and **Lake Tai** are common day trips.

WHEN TO TOUR SHANGHAI

The best time to visit Shanghai is early fall. The weather is at its best in September and October, with a good chance of sunny days and mild temperatures. Winters are cold and rainy. In spring the days grow warmer, but the rain continues, sometimes unceasingly for weeks. The summers can be pleasant in June, but come July you can bet that the days will be hot and excruciatingly humid.

The Old City and the Bund

When Shanghai was carved up by foreign powers, one part of the central city remained under Chinese law and administration. These old winding back alleys eventually became notorious as a gangster- and opium-filled slum. Today the narrow meandering lanes, crowded but quaint neighborhoods, and tiny pre-1949 houses are still standing (though the vices have disappeared for the most part). A walk through the Old City gives an idea of how most Shanghainese once lived and many still do. The city's most important sightseeing spot, the Bund, on Shanghai's waterfront, showcases outstanding foreign buildings from pre-1949 times.

A Good Walk

Start at the **Yuyuan** ① (Yu Garden). Stroll through the garden, check out the bazaar surrounding it, and stop at the teahouse for a serene rest. You can also wander the small alleys of the Old City, which lies inside the Renmin Lu–Zhonghua Lu circle. Within these alleys is a bustle of activity. Meander through the **Fuyou Lu Gudai Chang** ② (Fuyou Lu Antiques Market), or even go farther west to the **Dongtai Lu Gudai Chang** ③ (Dongtai Lu Antiques Market); check out the wet market on tiny Dajing Lu, stop in at the **Chen Xiang Ge Temple** ④; or see the only remaining piece still standing of the Old City wall at **Dajing Ge** ⑤.

From the Old City you can walk or take a taxi or pedicab to the **Wai Tan** ⑥ (the Bund), which begins along the river. A raised concrete promenade borders the side of the street nearest the river. Walk north and mingle with the crowds of strolling families, lovers walking hand in hand and camera-snapping tourists. Continue to the intersection of Zhongshan Donglu and Jinling Lu, marked by a triangular commercial building on the water. If you're feeling adventurous, you can jump on a boat and start a tour of Pudong here. The Huangpu River Cruises dockis also nearby.

If you continue walking north, historic buildings begin appearing on the west side of the street facing the river. Just north of Yanan Donglu is the former **Shanghai Club** ⑦. Farther along is the **Pudong Fazhan Yinhang** (the former Hongkong & Shanghai Bank) ⑧ and the **Haiguan Lou** ⑨ (Customs House), which houses the Big Ching, or clock tower. At Shanghai's main thoroughfare, Nanjing Lu, you'll see one of the city's most famous monuments: the **Heping Fandian** ⑩ (Peace Hotel) consists of the two buildings on the corner of the Bund and Nanjing Lu. Just north of the Peace Hotel is the **Zhongguo Yinhang** ⑪ (Bank of China), the main bank in the city. You can spot it by all the black-market money changers loitering in front.

Across the street on the river lies **Huangpu Gongyuan** ⑫ (Huangpu Park), which has a statue of Chen Yi, Shanghai's first mayor after 1949. North of him is the obelisklike Memorial of the Heroes of the People. At this point you've come to the junction of the Bund and Beijing Donglu. Across the old Waibaidu Bridge on Suzhou Creek there are more pre-1949 buildings: the art deco Shanghai Dasha (Shanghai Mansions) is in front of you to the left, and the former Shanghai Stock Exchange and the Russian Consulate are to the right.

All these old buildings face the modern skyline of Pudong, which lies on the other side of the river, with the **Oriental Pearl Tower** and the **Jinmao Tower** rising above the water. The Bund provides a good vantage point for viewing both prerevolutionary and postopening and -reform Shanghai.

TIMING

It can take about two hours to stroll casually without stopping at any sights. Allow another two hours to wander through the Yuyuan Gardens, bazaar, and teahouse. Access to some of the Bund's old buildings is not allowed, but if you go inside the ones that are open to visitors, you should allow 15 minutes per building. For a cruise on the Huangpu River, count on one to three hours.

Yuyuan is almost always crowded but especially so on weekends and holidays. Shanghai's other popular tourist sights, including the Bund, are thronged with people on the weekends, but aren't too bad on weekdays.

On National Day, October 1, and Labor Day, May 1, the Bund is closed to bicycle and automobile traffic, and the roads are choked with people. On those days a fireworks show is usually put on over the water.

Sights to See

❹ Chen Xiang Ge Temple. If you find yourself passing by this tiny temple on your exploration of the Old City, you can make an offering to Buddha with the free incense sticks that accompany your admission. Built in 1600 by the same man who built Yuyuan, it was destroyed during the Cultural Revolution and rebuilt in the 1990s. ✉ *29 Chenxiangge Lu,* ☎ *021/6320–3431.* ▨ *Y4.* ☉ *Daily 7–4.*

❺ Dajing Ge (Old City Wall at Dajing Road). The Old City used to be completely surrounded by a wall, built in 1553 as a defense against Japanese pirates. Most of it was torn down in 1912, except for one 50-yard-long piece that still stands at Dajing Lu and Renmin Lu. You can walk through the remnant and check out the rather simple museum nearby, which is dedicated to the history of the old city (the captions are only in Chinese). Stroll through the tiny neighboring alley of Dajing Lu for a lively panorama of crowded market life in the Old City. ✉ *269 Dajing Lu, at Renmin Lu,* ☎ *021/6385–2443.* ▨ *Y2.* ☉ *Tues.– Sun. 9–4.*

❸ Dongtai Lu Gudai Chang (Dongtai Road Antiques Market). A few blocks west of the Old City, antiques dealers's stalls line the street. You'll find porcelain, Victrolas, jade, and anything else worth hawking or buying. Prices have shot up in the last few years, and fakes abound, so be careful what you buy. ✉ *Off Xizang Lu.* ☉ *Daily 9 AM–dusk.*

❷ Fuyou Lu Gudai Chang (Fuyou Road Antiques Market). When this well-known antiques market moved from the quaint alleys of the Old City to a nondescript warehouse, it lost some of its charm. Since then, however, hawkers have started setting up their wares outside the warehouse, and some of the hustle and bustle has returned. You'll find everything from old Mao paraphernalia to old Shanghai wicker baskets to real and fake antique porcelain. Back at Fuyou Lu, some antiques stores still line the narrow lane. ✉ *457 Fangbang Zhonglu.* ☉ *Daily 8–dusk.*

❾ Haiguan Lou (Customs House). Built in 1927, the Customs House still serves as the customs headquarters, although now in the service of a

Shanghai

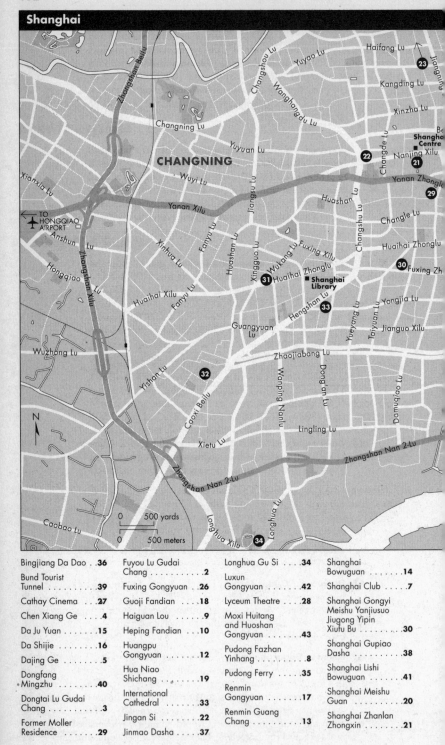

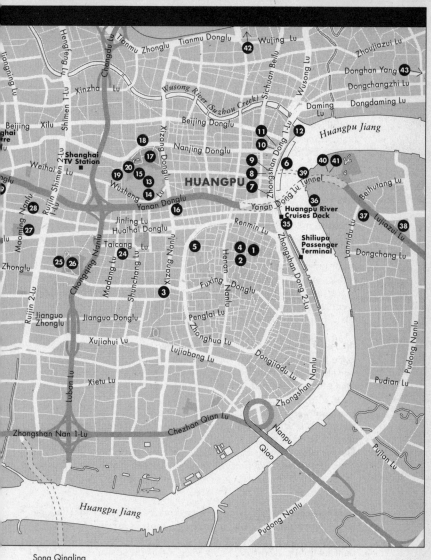

different government. The old clock tower is now called "Big Qing" by the Shanghainese. During the Cultural Revolution, the bells were taken down and replaced by speakers blaring out Mao Zedong's theme, "The East Is Red." Today the bells are back in the tower, but they can't be heard amid the cacophony of the city. ✉ *13 The Bund (Zhongshan Dong Yi Lu).*

★ ⑩ **Heping Fandian** (Peace Hotel). This hotel at the corner of the Bund and Nanjing Lu is among Shanghai's most treasured old buildings. If any establishment will give you a sense of Shanghai's past, it's this one. Its high ceilings, ornate woodwork, and art deco fixtures are still intact, and the ballroom evokes old Shanghai cabarets and gala parties.

The south building was formerly the Palace Hotel. Built in 1906 by the British, it is the oldest building on the Bund. The north building, formerly the Cathay Hotel, built in 1929, is more famous historically. It was known as the private playroom of its owner, Victor Sassoon, a wealthy landowner who invested in the opium trade. The Cathay was actually part of a complete office and hotel structure collectively called Sassoon House. Victor Sassoon himself lived and entertained his guests in the green penthouse. The hotel was rated on a par with the likes of Raffles in Singapore and the Peninsula in Hong Kong. It was *the* place to stay in old Shanghai; Noel Coward wrote *Private Lives* here. In the evenings, the famous Peace Hotel Old Jazz Band plays in the German-style pub on the first floor. ✉ *20 Nanjing Donglu,* ☎ *021/6321–6888.*

NEED A
BREAK?

The Peace Hotel Roof. For a memorable view, take the middle elevators to the top floor of the north building and then climb the last two flights of stairs to the roof. There's an outdoor café, from which you can see Sassoon's former penthouse and the action on the streets and river below.

⑫ **Huangpu Gongyuan** (Huangpu Park). The local government changed what once was a lovely green garden into this uninteresting concrete park. The park's only saving grace—besides the **Memorial of the Heroes of the People** obelisk—is the view it offers of both sides of the river. During colonial times Chinese could not enter the park; a sign at the entrance said, NO DOGS OR CHINESE ALLOWED. ✉ *North end of Bund, beside river,* ☎ *021/5308–2636.*

⑧ **Pudong Fazhan Yinhang** (former Hongkong & Shanghai Bank; Pudong Development Bank). One of the Bund's most impressive buildings—some say it's the area's pièce de résistance—the domed structure was built by the British in 1921–23, when it was the second-largest bank building in the world. After 1949 the building was turned into Communist Party offices and City Hall; now it is used by the Pudong Development Bank. In 1997 the bank made the news when it uncovered a beautiful 1920s Italian-tile mosaic in the building's dome. In the 1950s the mosaic was deemed too extravagant for a Communist government office, so it was covered by white paint, which, ironically, protected it from being found by the Red Guards during the Cultural Revolution. It was then forgotten until the Pudong Development Bank renovated the building. If you walk into the bank, look up, and you'll see the circular mosaic in the dome—an outer circle painted with scenes of the cities where the Hongkong & Shanghai Bank had branches at the time: London, Paris, New York, Bangkok, Tokyo, Calcutta, Hong Kong, and Shanghai; a middle circle made up of the 12 signs of the zodiac; and the center painted with a large sun and Ceres, the Roman goddess of abundance. ✉ *12 The Bund (Zhongshan Dong Yi Lu),* ☎ *021/6329–6188.* ☑ *Free.* ☉ *Weekdays 9–4:30, weekends 9–4.*

❼ Shanghai Club. Built in 1910, the Shanghai Club limited membership to wealthy British men. The first floor once contained the longest bar in the world; it has since been occupied by a fast-food chain restaurant and the rest of the building became the Dongfeng Fandian (Tung Feng Hotel). Much of the building retains its original glory: the lobby still showcases its marble floor, oak paneling, columns, barrel ceiling, and beautiful old cage elevator. You can go upstairs is the Seaman's Club, which houses the new Long Bar and is frequented by sailors passing through Shanghai's harbors. ⊠ *2 The Bund (Zhongshan Dong Yi Lu).*

★ **❻ Wai Tan** (the Bund). Shanghai's waterfront boulevard best shows both the city's pre-1949 past and its focus on the future. The district's name is derived from the Anglo-Indian and literally means "muddy embankment." In the early 1920s the Bund became the city's foreign street: Americans, British, Japanese, French, Russians, Germans, and other Europeans built banks, trading houses, clubs, consulates, and hotels in styles from neoclassical to art deco. As Shanghai grew to be a bustling trading center in the Yangzi Delta, the Bund's warehouses and ports became the heart of the action. With the Communist victory, the foreigners left Shanghai, and the Chinese government moved its own banks and offices here.

Today the municipal government has renovated the old buildings of this most foreign face of the city, highlighting them as tourist attractions, and even tried for a while to sell them back to the very owners it forced out after 1949.

On the riverfront side of the Bund, Shanghai's street life is in full force. The city rebuilt the promenade, making it an ideal gathering place for both tourists and residents. In the mornings just after dawn, the Bund is full of people ballroom dancing, doing aerobics, and practicing kung fu, *qi gong,* and tai chi. The rest of the day people walk the embankment, snapping photos of the Oriental Pearl Tower, the Huangpu River, and each other. In the evenings lovers come out for romantic walks amid the floodlit buildings and tower. ⊠ *5 blocks of Zhongshan Dong Yi Lu between Jinling Lu and Suzhou Creek.*

★ **❶ Yuyuan** (Yu Garden). Since the 18th century, this complex, with its traditional red walls and upturned tile roofs, has been a marketplace and social center where local residents gather, shop, and practice qi gong in the evenings. Although not as impressive as the ancient palace gardens of Beijing and accused of being overly touristed, Yu Garden is a piece of Shanghai's past, one of the few old sights left in the city.

Surrounding the garden is a touristy bazaar of stores that sell traditional Chinese arts and crafts, medicine, and souvenirs. In the last few years city renovations have turned the bazaar into a mall, complete with chrome and shiny glass—there is even a Starbucks across from the main gate to the garden. A basement antiques market with somewhat inflated prices is in the Haobao Building. On the west side of the central man-made lake is a great dumpling house famed for its xiaolong bao. You'll spot it by the long line of people outside.

To get to the garden, you must wind your way through the bazaar. The ticket booth is just north of the lake and the pleasant **Huxingting Chashi** (teahouse). The garden was commissioned by the Ming dynasty official Pan Chongtan in 1559 and built by the renowned architect, Zhang Nanyang, over 19 years. When it was finally finished it won international praise as "the best garden in southeastern China," an accolade that would be hard to defend today, especially when compared with the beautiful gardens of Suzhou. In the mid-1800s the Society of Small Swords used the garden as a gathering place for meetings. It was here that they planned their uprising with the Taiping rebels against the French colonialists. The French destroyed the garden during the first Opium War, but the area was later rebuilt and renovated.

Winding walkways and corridors bring you over stone bridges and carp-filled ponds and through bamboo forests and rock gardens. Within the park are an **old opera stage,** a **museum** dedicated to the Society of Small Swords rebellion, and the **Chenghuang Miao** (Temple of the City God). The temple was built during the early part of the Ming dynasty but was later destroyed. In 1926 the main hall was rebuilt and sometime after was renovated. The temple went through its most recent renovation in the early 1990s. One caveat: The park is almost always thronged with Chinese tour groups, especially on weekends. As with most sights in Shanghai, don't expect a tranquil time alone. ⊠ *Bordered by Fuyou Lu, Jiujiaochang Lu, Fangbang Lu, and Anren Lu, Old City,* ☎ *021/6328–3251.* ⊡ *Y25.* ☉ *Gardens, daily 8:30–5.*

NEED A   The **Huxingting Chashi** (Midlake Pavilion Teahouse; ⊠ 257 Yuyuan Lu,
BREAK?   ☎ 021/6373–6950 downstairs; 021/6373–0241 upstairs), Shang-
                hai's oldest, opened in 1856 and stands on a small man-made lake in
                the middle of the Yuyuan Gardens and Bazaar, at the center of the
                Bridge of the Nine Turnings. Although tea is cheaper on the first floor,
                be sure to sit on the top floor by a window overlooking the lake. Every
                night from 6:30 to 7:30 a traditional tea ceremony is performed, ac-
                companied by three musicians playing Chinese instruments. A bottom-
                less cup of tea comes with Chinese snacks.

⓫ **Zhongguo Yinhang** (Bank of China). Here, old Shanghai's Western architecture (British art deco in this case) mixes with Chinese elements. In 1937 it was designed to be the highest building in the city and surpassed the neighboring Cathay Hotel (now the Peace Hotel) by a hair, except for the green tower on the Cathay's roof. ⊠ *23 Zhongshan Dong Yi Lu,* ☎ *021/6329–1979.*

Nanjing Lu and the City Center

The city's *zhongxin,* or center, is primarily in the Huangpu and Jingan districts. These two areas make up most of what was known in imperial and republican times as the International Settlement. Nanjing Lu, Shanghai's main thoroughfare, crosses east–west through these two districts. You can spot it at night by its neon extravaganza and in daytime by the sheer volume of business going on. Hordes of pedestrians compete with bicycles and one another, and cars move at a snaillike pace in traffic jams.

A Good Walk (or Drive)

The following long walk can also become a series of cab rides. Go west on the shopping street Nanjing Lu from the Heping Fandian, meandering among the crowds and stores. The first blocks of Nanjing Donglu are shorter and still have some of Old Shanghai's architecture. On the blocks north and south of the street you can also sense the atmosphere of the place in the 1920s. The portion of Nanjing Lu between Henan Lu and Xizang Lu is a pedestrian walkway, so no need to worry about the road's infamous traffic here. At the start of Nanjing Xilu, turn left (south) on Xizang Lu, and in a block you'll arrive at the city's huge social and cultural center, **Renmin Guang Chang** ⓭, marked by an enormous TV screen on its eastern end. At the square you'll also find the wonderful **Shanghai Bowuguan** ⓮ (Shanghai Museum), the new municipal offices, and the spectacular **Da Ju Yuan** ⓯ (Grand Theater). The **Da Shijie** ⑯ (Great World) entertainment center lies southeast of the square, on the corner of Yanan Lu and Xizang Lu.

Just north of the square is **Renmin Gongyuan** ⑰, Shanghai's largest and most important park, though not necessarily the nicest. On the other side of the park is the historic **Guoji Fandian** ⑱ (Park Hotel).

On its western side, the People's Square is bordered by Huangpi Beilu. Turn right (north) on Huangpi Beilu, past the **Hua Niao Shichang** ⑲ (Bird and Flower Market), and to your right will be the **Shanghai Meishu Guan** ⑳ (Shanghai Art Museum), at the corner of Nanjing Lu. Turn left and continue on Nanjing Lu. Once you pass Chengdu Lu, the street of the overhead Ring Road, the Shanghai Television Station and Broadcasting Building is on the left, with a very large TV screen in front. About five blocks down, after the intersection of Xikang Lu, you'll see the huge hall built by the Russians that is now the **Shanghai Zhanlan Zhongxin** ㉑ (Shanghai Exhibition Center). It sits directly across from the convenient Shanghai Center. Two blocks farther west on Nanjing Lu, on the corner of Huashan Lu, is the **Jingan Si** ㉒ (Jingan Temple). From here or from the Shanghai Center, jump into a cab to the important **Yufo Si** ㉓ (Jade Buddha Temple), which lies several blocks north of Nanjing Lu.

TIMING
The above walk is fairly long and doesn't have to be done all at once. You can hop a cab between sights, especially to Yufo Si. The distance from the Bund to Jingan Temple is about 4 km (2½ mi). The whole walk without stopping will probably take you 1½–2 hours. Leave two to three hours for the Shanghai Museum. If you go to the Great World, Jingan Temple, the Bird and Flower Market, or Yufo Si, block off an hour for each of these sights. The rest you can walk through or by very quickly.

Nanjing Lu and the People's Square are both most crowded and most exciting on weekends. You may have to fight the hordes, but you'll get a good idea of what life is like in Shanghai.

Sights to See

⓯ **Da Ju Yuan** (Grand Theatre). This magnificent theater, along with the Shanghai Museum and the Shanghai Library, is part of the city's plan to remake itself as a cultural center. The theater, with its spectacular front wall of sparkling glass, has three stages, and hosts the best international and domestic performances. The dramatic curved roof atop a square base is meant to invoke the Chinese traditional saying, "The earth is square and the sky is round." See it at night. ⊠ *190 Huangpi Beilu,* ☏ *021/6387–5480.* ☎ *Tour Y50.* ☉ *Tours 9–4.*

⓰ **Da Shijie** (the Great World). A sanitized version of Old Shanghai's notorious gambling, cabaret, drug, and prostitution den has been restored. Today, the entertainment center, with its wedding cake–style tower, has turned wholesome with an eclectic set of performances—acrobatics, opera, magic, comedy, Chinese period films. Some take place in the outside courtyard. Other attractions include fortune-tellers, a Guinness Book of Records hall, fantasy rides, bumper cars, and a hall of mirrors. The center also houses fun-fair booths, a bowling alley, a dance hall, and food stalls. ⊠ *1 Xizang Nanlu,* ☏ *021/6326–3760.* ☎ *Y25.* ☉ *Daily 9 AM–9:30 PM.*

⓲ **Guoji Fandian** (Park Hotel). This art deco structure overlooking People's Park was originally the tallest hotel in Shanghai. Completed in 1934, it had luxury rooms, a nightclub, and chic restaurants; today it's more subdued. ⊠ *170 Nanjing Xilu,* ☏ *021/6327–5225.*

⑲ Hua Niao Shichang (Bird and Flower Market). At this colorful and busy market you'll find hawkers selling pets such as fish, birds, turtles, cats, and frogs; a whole range of plants, bonsai trees, orchids, and clay pots; and knickknacks and yummy snacks as well. ⊠ *Huangpi Beilu between Nanjing Lu and Weihai Lu.* ⊘ *Daily 9–dusk.*

㉒ Jingan Si (Jingan Temple). Originally built about AD 300, the Jingan Temple has been rebuilt and renovated numerous times. The temple would be wholly forgettable were it not for its bell, which was cast in 1183. The temple is now an active Buddhist center. ⊠ *1686 Nanjing Xilu, next to the Jingan Si subway entrance,* ☎ *021/6256–6366.* ☞ *Y5.* ⊘ *Daily 7:30–4:45.*

⑰ Renmin Gongyuan (People's Park). In colonial days it was the northern half of the city's racetrack. Today the 30 acres of flower beds, lotus ponds, trees, and fairground (which is rarely open) also contain a high percentage of concrete. The park is widely known for its English corner, where locals gather to practice their language skills. ⊠ *231 Nanjing Xilu,* ☎ *021/6327–1333.* ☞ *Y2.* ⊘ *Daily 6–6.*

⑬ Renmin Guang Chang (People's Square). Shanghai's main square, once the southern half of the city's racetrack, has become a social and cultural center. The Shanghai Museum, Municipal Offices, Telecommunications Building, and Grand Theater surround it. In the daytime, visitors and residents stroll, fly kites, and take their children to feed the pigeons. In the evening, kids roller-skate, people watch shows on the huge TV screen, ballroom dancers hold group lessons, and families relax together. Weekends here are especially busy. ⊠ *Bordered by Weihai Lu on south, Xizang Lu on east, Huangpi Beilu on west, and Fuzhou Lu on north.*

★ ⑭ Shanghai Bowuguan (Shanghai Museum). Truly one of Shanghai's treasures, this museum has the country's premier collection of relics and artifacts. Its 11 state-of-the-art galleries house China's first exhibitions of paintings, bronzes, sculpture, ceramics, calligraphy, jade, Ming and Qing dynasty furniture, coins, seals, and art made by indigenous populations. The bronze collection is among the best in the world. Three additional halls house rotating exhibitions. Information is well presented in English, and the acoustic guide is also excellent. You can relax in the museum's pleasant tearoom and the excellent shops offer antiques, crafts, and reproductions of the museum's works. ⊠ *201 Renmin Da Dao,* ☎ *021/6372–3500.* ☞ *Y20 (free after 4), Y60 with acoustic guide.* ⊘ *Sun.–Fri. 9–5, Sat. 9–8.*

NEED A BREAK?   **Espresso Americano** (⊠ Shanghai Center, 1376 Nanjing Xilu, ☎ 021/ 6247–9750) is a nice place to get a good cup of coffee. **Espresso Monica** (⊠ Nanjing Xilu at Tongren Lu, across from Shanghai Center) is one of the few places in the city to find a real latte or cappuccino.

---

⑳ Shanghai Meishu Guan (Shanghai Art Museum). At the northwest corner of People's Park, the former site of the Shanghai Library was once a clubhouse for old Shanghai's sports groups, including the Shanghai Race Club. The building has become the new home of the state-run Shanghai Art Museum. There are paintings, calligraphy, and sculpture in its permanent galleries and usually modern artwork exhibitions in its other gallery. ⊠ *325 Nanjing Xilu (at Huangpi Beilu),* ☎ *021/6327– 0557.* ☞ *Varies, depending on exhibition.* ⊘ *Daily 9–4.*

㉑ Shanghai Zhanlan Zhongxin (Shanghai Exhibition Center). This mammoth piece of Russian architecture was built as a sign of Sino-Soviet friendship after 1949. Special exhibitions are held here, and the complex has a shopping area, bowling alley, and restaurant. ☒ *1000 Yanan Zhonglu,* ☏ *021/6279–0279.* ☉ *Daily 9–4.*

★ ㉓ **Yufo Si** (Jade Buddha Temple). Completed in 1918, this temple is fairly new by Chinese standards. During the Cultural Revolution, in order to save the temple when the Red Guards came to destroy it, the monks pasted portraits of Mao Zedong on the outside walls so the Guards couldn't tear them down without destroying Mao's face as well. The temple is built in the style of the Song dynasty, with symmetrical halls and courtyards, upturned eaves, and bright yellow walls. The temple's great treasure is its 6½-ft-high, 455-pound seated Buddha made of white jade with a robe of precious gems, originally brought to Shanghai from Burma. Other Buddhas, statues, and frightening guardian gods of the temple populate the halls, as well as a collection of Buddhist scriptures and paintings. The 70 monks who live and work here can sometimes be seen worshiping. There's a vegetarian restaurant on the temple grounds. ☒ *170 Anyuan Lu,* ☏ *021/6266–3668.* ☒ *Y10.* ☉ *Daily 8–noon and 1–5.*

The Old French Concession

The former French Concession is in the Luwan and Xuhui districts. Once populated primarily by White Russians, the area is today a charming historic district known for its atmosphere and beautiful old architecture, as well as its shopping, and bars and cafés. Most of the action centers on the main east–west thoroughfare, the tree-lined Huaihai Lu, a relaxed, upscale, international shopping street. Many of the old consulates and French buildings still line it.

A Good Walk

You can start your walk at the **Zhonggong Yidahuizhi** ㉔ (Zhongguo Gongchangdang; First Chinese Communist Party Congress site), on Xingye Lu and Huangpi Lu. From here take a cab or walk 15–20 minutes to **Sun Zhongshan Guju** ㉕ (Sun Yat-sen's Former Residence). If you walk, go south on Huangpi Lu until you reach Fuxing Lu, where you turn right. On the corner of Chongqing Nanlu and Fuxing Lu is **Fuxing Gongyuan** ㉖ (Fuxing Park). Across the way, on the southeast corner of the intersection, is a beautiful old arrowhead-shape apartment building that was once American journalist and Communist sympathizer Agnes Smedley's residence. If you continue west on Fuxing Lu, turn right at the first corner (Sinan Lu); Sun Yat-sen's Former Residence is just ahead on your right, at Xiangshan Lu. From here turn right (north), back onto Sinan Lu. At Huaihai Lu, the main street of the old French Concession, take a left. This middle stretch of the shopping street Huaihai Zhonglu is the heart of the Concession. State-run and foreign shops, boutiques, and department stores dominate the area.

Continue down a couple of blocks on Huaihai and turn right on Maoming Lu at the old **Cathay Cinema** ㉗. At the intersection with Changle Lu stand the historic Jinjiang and Garden hotels. On the northeast corner is the old **Lyceum Theatre** ㉘. If you're really into looking at old architecture, you can walk one block west and one block north to the corner of Shaanxi Nanlu and Julu Lu. Here, you can view the dollhouselike **Former Moller Residence** ㉙. Another out-of-the-way old villa complex lies farther south on Maoming Lu, at what is now the Ruijin Guest House.

Back on Huaihai Lu, continue west. After another two blocks, turn left on Fenyang Lu. The **Shanghai Gongyi Meishu Yanjiusuo Jiugong Yipin Xiufu Bu** ㉚ (Shanghai Arts and Crafts Research Institute) is in an old French mansion on this street. If you return to Huaihai Lu and continue westward, the shopping district will give way to the consulate area. You can end your walk anywhere between Fenyang Lu and Wulumuqi Lu. If you decide to continue walking, eventually you'll pass the Shanghai Library, on your left (south) side past Wulumuqi Lu. Farther down the street at the corner of Xingguo Lu is **Song Qingling Guju** ③ (Soong Chingling's Former Residence). You can take a cab here.

Besides walking down Huaihai Lu, an excellent way of seeing the French part of town is to hop on the double-decker bus that runs up and down the thoroughfare. If you sit on the upper level, you can sneak a good view of the old homes that are otherwise hidden by compound walls.

Farther away in Xuhui District is the **Xujiahui Dajiaotang** ③ (Xujiahui Cathedral); from Huaihai Lu, go south on Hengshan Lu, which will end in Xujiahui. The church is on the west side of Caoxi Beilu. On the way you'll pass Shanghai's old **International Cathedral** ③, on Hengshan Lu near Wulumuqi Lu. You'll need to take a taxi to **Longhua Gu Si** ③ (Longhua Temple).

TIMING

Huaihai Lu, like Shanghai's other main thoroughfares, is most crowded on the weekends, when hordes of shoppers enjoy their weekly outings. Allow yourself at least 1–1½ hours just to walk the above itinerary without stopping at any shops or taking a look around at the old houses. Allow about a half hour to an hour for each of the more major sights, such as Sun Yat-sen's former residence, Soong Chingling's former residence, and the site of the First National Party Congress. You can walk through some of the historic buildings, while others involve only a short look from the outside.

Sights to See

㉙ **Former Moller Residence.** You can't go inside, but the facade of this old Shanghai mansion, which with its colorful details and pointy roofs can only be described as part dollhouse, part castle, is the main attraction anyway. According to one myth, its tycoon owner was told by a fortune-teller that if he finished the house he would die, so he kept adding wings to ward off the Grim Reaper. Another myth says he built the house in the likeness of a mansion that his little girl once envisioned in a dream. Whatever the case, the magical building now houses the offices of the Communist Youth League. ⊠ *Shaanxi Nanlu just north of Julu Lu, across from City Hotel.*

㉖ **Fuxing Gongyuan** (Fuxing Park). The grounds of this European-style park—known as French Park before 1949—provide a rare bit of greenery in crowded Shanghai. Here you'll find people practicing tai chi and lovers strolling hand in hand. ⊠ *2 Gaolan Lu,* ☎ *021/6372–0662.* ⊡ *Y1.* ⊙ *Daily 6–6.*

㉝ **International Cathedral.** This small ivy-covered cathedral dates to Shanghai's Concession days. Today it remains a Protestant church with regularly scheduled services. ⊠ *53 Hengshan Lu,* ☎ *021/6437–6576.*

NEED A
BREAK?

The **Promenade** (⊠ 4 Hengshan Lu) is across from the International Cathedral, in an area that has become a happening nightlife center. You'll find bars, clubs, and several restaurants. Just next door to the Promenade are the Orden Bowling Alley and Harn Sheh Teahouse.

㉞ **Longhua Gu Si** (Longhua Temple). Shanghai's tallest pagoda, at 131 ft, affords views of the city and surrounding countryside. The pagoda dates from the 10th century but has since been rebuilt. The temple's numerous halls have hexagonal windows, arched entryways, and roofs of curved eaves. The grounds contain a small traditional garden and a carp-filled pond. You might come upon Buddhist monks praying in the incense-filled courtyards. Attached is the Longhua Hotel and a vegetarian restaurant. ⊠ *2853 Longhua Lu,* ☏ *021/6456–6085.* 🎟 *Y5.* ⊙ *Daily 7–5.*

㉘ Lyceum Theatre. In the days of old Shanghai, the Lyceum was the home of the British Amateur Drama Club. The old stage is still in use—the theater now presents acrobatic shows. ⊠ *57 Maoming Nanlu,* ☏ *021/6217–8530.*

NEED A BREAK?

As the name **1931** (⊠ 112 Maoming Nanlu, ☏ 021/6472–5264) implies, this café exudes an old Shanghai atmosphere, down to the cute little tables, working Victrola and waitstaff clad in *qipao* (traditional Chinese dresses). The café serves simple drinks, coffee and tea, and excellent home-style Shanghainese cooking, with some Japanese selections, too.

One of the premier estates of old Shanghai, the **Morriss Estate,** now Ruijin Guesthouse, was built by a Western newspaper magnate. Today the estate's three huge houses, standing among green lawns and trees, have also become home to a few foreign restaurants and bars. Try the colorful restaurant/bar Zoobaa, or the Thai and Indian restaurants housed together with another bar, Face, in the north mansion, or the main mansion's lawn bar. Stroll around the estate to view its ornate details, including a stained-glass scene in the rear house.

㉚ Shanghai Gongyi Meishu Yanjiusuo Jiugong Yipin Xiufu Bu (Shanghai Arts and Crafts Research Institute). It's a little dusty, run down, and bare bones, but you can watch Shanghai's artisans as they create traditional Chinese arts and crafts. Works you can purchase include everything from paper cuts and engraved chopsticks to snuff bottles and lanterns, but prices can be a bit high compared to quality. Formerly, the old French mansion housed an official of the Concession's pre-1949 government. ⊠ *79 Fenyang Lu,* ☏ *021/6437–0509.* ⊙ *Daily 9–5.*

㉛ Song Qingling Guju (Soong Chingling's Former Residence). The residence from 1949 until 1963 of the wife of Dr. Sun Yat-sen has been partially preserved. The house itself is not very interesting, but the small museum next door has some nice displays from Madame Soong and Sun Yat-sen's life, including wedding pictures from their 1915 wedding in Tokyo. Madame Soong was sympathetic with the Communists, while her sister, Meiling, was married to Chiang Kai-shek. ⊠ *1843 Huaihai Zhonglu,* ☏ *021/6431–4965.* 🎟 *Y8.* ⊙ *Daily 9–11 and 1–4:30.*

㉕ Sun Zhongshan Guju (Sun Yat-sen's Former Residence). Dr. Sun Yat-sen, the father of the Chinese republic, lived in this two-story house for six years, from 1919 to 1924. His wife, Soong Chingling, continued to live here after his death until 1937. Today it's been turned into a museum, and you can tour the grounds. ⊠ *7 Xiangshan Lu,* ☏ *021/ 6437–2954.* 🎟 *Y8.* ⊙ *Daily 9–4:30.*

NEED A BREAK?

One example of Shanghai's cultural resurgence is the **Yandan Lu Pedestrian Street** (⊠ Yandan Lu between Huaihai Zhonglu and Nanchang Lu). Luwan District has repaved one block of Yandan Lu with tile, lined it with classic lampposts, thrown out all the traffic and run-down stores, and replaced them with pedestrians and quaint cafés.

㉜ Xujiahui Dajiaotang (Xujiahui Cathedral). Built by the Jesuits in 1848, this Gothic-style cathedral still holds regular masses in Chinese. ⊠ *158 Puxi Lu,* ☏ *021/6469–0930.*

㉔ **Zhonggong Yidahuizhi** (short for Zhongguo Gongchangdang Di Yi Ci Quanguo Daibiao Dahui Huizhi Jinian Guan; Site of the First National Congress of the Communist Party of China). The secret meeting on July 31, 1921, that marked the first National Congress was held at the Bo Wen Girls' School, where 13 delegates from Marxist, communist, and socialist groups gathered from around the country. Today you can enter the house, which was renovated in 1951, and view its relics, documents, and photos. Deep in the back is the very room where the first delegates worked. It remains in its original form, complete with a table set for tea for 13 people. ✉ *374 Huangpi Nanlu,* ☎ *021/6328–1177.* ☞ *Y3.* ☉ *Daily 8:30–11 and 1–4.*

Pudong New Area

East of the Huangpu River lies a constantly changing urban experiment that before 1990 was farmland and rice paddies. Here now, though, is what the city and the nation hope will be the financial, economic, and commercial center of Asia. Most of the big multinationals and international banks have their Shanghai factories or headquarters here. Although much of Pudong is still empty, and its sterility can't match the pockets of charm in Puxi, it does give an idea of where Shanghai is heading. Here you'll find the biggest of everything: the tallest tower in Asia, the largest department store on the continent, and the future tallest building in the world. Among the district's wonders are the Yangpu and Nanpu bridges (supposedly the second- and third longest in the world) connecting Pudong to Puxi, the architecturally absurd International Exhibition Center, the Jinmao Tower, and of course, the Oriental Pearl Tower.

A Good Walk

You can start by crossing the Huangpu River on the **Pudong Ferry** ㉟. Stand at the bow to get a good simultaneous view of the Bund and Pudong. The ferry drops you off at **Bingjiang Da Dao** ㊱ (Riverside Promenade). From here you can see the most beautiful views of the Bund. Standing above Bingjiang Da Dao is the Pudong Shangri-La Hotel, where you can get a drink and a somewhat higher vantage point over the Bund.

Bear right from the Shangri-La, and you'll eventually hit Lujiazui Lu. Keep to the right (heading southeast, away from the water), and you'll be facing the skyscrapers of Lujiazui, the central financial area, or Wall Street, of Pudong. Continue walking toward the tallest high-rise in front of you, the beautiful industrial pagoda **Jinmao Dasha** ㊲. Go up to the 88th-floor observation deck for a great view, and take a sky-high break at the Grand Hyatt.

From here you can head directly east to the **Shanghai Gupiao Dasha** ㊳ (Securities Exchange Building)—the building with the square hole in the middle—or back toward the water and the **Dongfang Mingzhu** ㊵ (Oriental Pearl Tower). You'll see it towering in its gargantuan grandeur at the northwest end of Lujiazui Lu. You can take a ride to the top for yet another 360-degree view of Shanghai. The **Shanghai Lishi Bowuguan** ㊶ (Shanghai History Museum) is in the bottom of the tower.

You can walk back to the ferry terminal to return to Puxi, or you can take a trip on the **Bund Tourist Tunnel** ㊴, which runs underneath the Huangpu River. Other options are to jump on the subway or take a taxi across the Nanpu Bridge or through the Yanan Lu Tunnel.

TIMING

The ferry ride takes just a few minutes. You can take a leisurely stroll at Bingjiang Dadao. Then allow about 15 minutes to walk to the Jinmao from the Shangri-La and another 15 to get to the Oriental Pearl from the Jinmao, or take a short taxi ride. You can spend a half hour to an hour at the observatory decks and at the Shanghai History Museum. If lines are long, you may have to wait a while to get to the top.

Sights to See

36 Binjiang Da Dao (Riverside Promenade). Although the park that runs 2,750 yards along the Huangpu River is sugary-sterile in its experimental suburbia, it still offers the most beautiful views of the Bund. You can stroll the grass and concrete and view a perspective of Puxi unavailable from the west side. If you're here in the summer, you can "enjoy wading," as a sign indicates, in the chocolate-color Huangpu River from the park's wave platform. ⊠ *Binjiang Dadao*. *Free*.

39 Bund Tourist Tunnel. For a look at Shanghai kitsch at its worst, you can take a trip across the Huangpu in plastic, capsular cars. The accompanying light show is part Disney, part psychedelia, complete with flashing strobes, blowing tinsel, and swirling hallucinogenic images projected on the concrete walls. The tackiest futuristic film of the 1960s couldn't have topped this. The five-minute ride will have your head spinning and you wondering if the Chinese central government isn't giving Shanghai just a little too much money. *Entrances are on the Bund at Nanjing Donglu and in Pudong near the Riverside Promenade.* *Y20 one-way, Y30 round-trip.*

40 Dongfang Mingzhu (Oriental Pearl Tower). The tallest tower in Asia (1,535 ft) has become the pride and joy of the city. It has become a symbol of the brashness and glitz of today's Shanghai. This UFO-like structure is especially kitschy at night, against the classic beauty of the Bund. Its several spheres are supposed to represent pearls (as in "Shanghai, Pearl of the Orient"). An elevator takes you to observation decks in each of the tower's four spheres. Go to the top sphere for a 360-degree bird's-eye view of the city or grab a bite in the Tower's revolving restaurant. On the bottom is the amusement center **Space City**, including laser tag and an arcade, as well as the **Shanghai History Museum.** ⊠ *No. 2, Lane 504, Lujiazui Lu, Pudong,* ☎ *021/5879–1888.* *Y20, first sphere; Y100, top sphere.* ⊙ *Daily 8 AM–9:30 PM.*

37 Jinmao Dasha (Jinmao Tower). This gorgeous 88-floor (8 being the Chinese number implying wealth and prosperity) industrial art deco pagoda is the third-tallest building in the world and the tallest in China. In it is also the highest hotel in the world—the Grand Hyatt Shanghai takes up the 53rd to 88th floors. The lower floors are taken up by office space, an entertainment center, and a neighboring exhibition center. The 88th-floor observation deck, reached in 45 seconds by two high-speed elevators, offers a 360-degree view of the city. The Jinmao, designed by Chicago's Skidmore Owings & Merrill, is both ancient and modern, Eastern and Western—the tapering tower combines the classic 13-tier Buddhist pagoda design with the postmodern steel and glass. Check out the Hyatt's dramatic 30-story atrium. ⊠ *2 Shiji Dadao,* ☎ *021/5049–1234 Grand Hyatt.* *Observation deck Y50.*

35 Pudong Ferry. The ferry between Pudong and Puxi, once more a necessity than a sight, is still fun to take on a nice day. The ferry labors carefully between the river's barges and boats; there are no seats, merely a lower deck entirely empty, wearily welcoming the masses. Stand at the bow for the best views of both the Pudong skyline and the Bund. ⊠ *Dock on Bund at Jinling Lu, dock in Pudong at Binjiang Da Dao.* *Eastbound Y1, westbound free.*

38 Shanghai Gupiao Dasha (Shanghai Securities Exchange Building). The Shanghai Stock Exchange shares its Lujiazui home with such foreign banks as the Bank of America, the Royal Bank of Canada, and the International Bank of Paris and Shanghai. The Stock Exchange Club is on the 27th floor, through which you can sometimes arrange free tours of the trading floor. ⊠ *Pudong Lu north of Lujiazui Lu,* ☎ *021/5840– 6101 Stock Exchange Club.*

❹ **Shanghai Lishi Bowuguan** (Shanghai History Museum). This small museum recalls Shanghai's pre-1949 heyday with the bronze lions that once ornamented the front of the former Hongkong & Shanghai Bank building, among other curiosities. It has relocated to the building that most represents Shanghai's motley modernism—the Oriental Pearl Tower. ⊠ *No. 2, Lane 504, Lujiazui Lu, Pudong,* ☎ *021/5879–1888.* 🎫 *Y25.* ☉ *Daily 9–5*

Hongkou District

On the west side of the river north of Suzhou Creek are the northeastern districts of Hongkou and Yangpu. At the turn of the 20th century Shanghai was not only an international port but also an open one, where anyone could enter regardless of nationality. As the century wore on and the world became riddled with war, Jews, first fleeing the Russian Revolution and then escaping Hitler, arrived in Shanghai from Germany, Austria, Poland, and Russia. From 1937 to 1941 Shanghai became a haven for tens of thousands of Jewish refugees. In 1943 invading Japanese troops forced all the city's Jews into the "Designated Area for Stateless Refugees" in Hongkou District, where they lived until the end of the war. Today you can still see evidence of their lives in the buildings and narrow streets of the area.

Sights to See

❷ **Luxun Gongyuan** (Lu Xun Park and Memorial). Lu Xun (1881– 1936)—scholar, novelist, and essayist—is considered the founder of modern Chinese literature. He is best known for his work *The True Story of Ah Q.* The park holds his tomb and a statue of the writer, as well as a **museum** of manuscripts, books, and photos related to his life and career. ⊠ *2288 Sichuan Beilu,* ☎ *021/5696–4208.* 🎫 *Park, Y1; memorial and museum, Y5.* ☉ *Park, daily 5:30 AM–6:30 PM; memorial and museum, daily 9–4:30.*

❸ **Moxi Huitang and Huoshan Gongyuan** (Ohel Moshe Synagogue and Huoshan Park). Built by Shanghai's Jewish residents in 1927, the Ohel Moshe Synagogue now has a small museum with photos and information about the Ashkenazi Jewish community of old Shanghai. Nearby Huoshan Park bears a memorial tablet erected in memory of the Jewish refugees who emigrated to the city.

Around the synagogue are lanes and old buildings that were once inhabited by Shanghai's Jewish residents. More than 20,000 Jewish refugees—engineers, lawyers, doctors, musicians, actors, writers, and academics—crowded into the district. They created their own community, with newspapers, magazines, cultural performances, and schools. Despite the crowded and unsanitary conditions, most of the Jews survived to see the end of the war, at which point the majority returned to Europe. ⊠ *62 Changyang Lu,* ☎ *021/6512–0229.*

Beyond the City

Apart from Yuyuan and a few temples, Shanghai really doesn't have much in the way of traditional Chinese culture. However, not far from the city are several wonderful spots, which can be easily reached as day trips.

Zhou Zhuang. During the 12th century, Shen Wanshan, a wealthy bureaucrat, diverted the water from the Baixian River to help create this quaint, little canal town. Ramshackle houses, many of which were once mansions of the rich now occupied by peasants, line the banks, and ancient stone bridges still cross the water. The best way to tour the town is by gondola, which is relatively inexpensive and surprisingly peaceful, especially for those coming from the chaos of Shanghai. Take a minibus from Zhujia Jiao Stop to Zhou Zhuang Zhen. Kunshan Shi, Zhou Zhuang Zhen, northwest of Shanghai. ✉ *Gondola rides Y30–Y70.*

Fang Ta Yuan (Square-Pagoda Garden). This relaxing, flower-filled garden is about 40 km (25 mi) outside the city center, in the small village of Songjiang (take a bus from Shanghai's main terminal to Songjiang and catch a bus to Fang ta Yuan from there). The most interesting feature of the garden is the brick wall on the north side with its depiction of a "Tan" monster. As legend has it, this creature—part deer, dragon, lion, and ox—tried to steal everything that existed in the whole world, but eventually died when he tried to swallow the sun. The view from the top floor of the pagoda is worth the seven flights of stairs. *Zhongshan Donglu, in Songjiang Village.* ✉ *Park admission Y5, Pagoda Y5.* ◷ *6–5.*

Zuibai Chi (Drunken Bai's Pond). One of the nicest and most peaceful gardens around Shanghai, Zuibai Chi was built by Gu Dajia in the 17th century, who named the garden in honor of the Tang Dynasty poet, Bai Juyi (772–846). Here, Gu followed the example of the great bard, and drank inordinate amounts of alcohol while composing verse and wandering through the garden's winding corridors. *64 Renmin Nanlu, in Songjiang Village.* ✉ *Y5.* ◷ *Daily 6–5.*

DINING

American

$–$$ ✗ **Johnny Moo.** As its name implies, this tiny, little-known malt shop, done in a cow motif, is all about burgers. It also has great twister fries and milkshakes. ✉ *Vanke Plaza, 101, No. 5, Lane 19, Ronghua Donglu,* ☎ *021/6219–7589. No credit cards.*

$–$$ ✗ **Malone's American Café.** This sports bar and grill serves American favorites such as Philly cheese steaks, buffalo wings, burgers, and pizza, as well as Asian specialties. The food isn't superb, but it's satisfying for a casual meal in a cheerful bar setting. ✉ *257 Tongren Lu,* ☎ *021/6247–2400. AE, DC, MC, V.*

Beijing

$$–$$$ ✗ **Quan Ju De.** Quan Ju De has been *the* place in Beijing to get Peking duck since 1864, but the first branch in Shanghai only opened in 1998. Expect a typical Chinese restaurant, big and noisy, complete with greasy food. The photos say U.S. president "Gorge" Bush enjoyed his duck at Quan Ju De, and you can, too. The restaurant's become so popular that a second branch has opened on Tianmu Xilu. ✉ *786 Huaihai Zhonglu, 4th fl.,* ☎ *021/6433–7286 or 021/6433–5799. 547 Tianmu Xilu,* ☎ *021/6353–8558. Reservations essential.*

$–$$ ✗ **Feng Zhe Lou.** People come here for the classic setting—in the Park, one of old Shanghai's premier hotels—and for the Peking duck, which is reputedly better than any to be found in Beijing. Served with pancakes, scallions, cucumbers, and duck sauce, it can be ordered whole or by the half. The *zuixia* ("drunken shrimp"—shrimp doused in rice

wine) makes a great appetizer. ⊠ *170 Nanjing Xilu,* ☎ *021/6327–5225.*
Reservations essential. AE, DC, MC, V.

Brazilian

$–$$ **Quilombo.** Of the several Brazilian-style *churrascarias,* or barbecue
restaurants, in Shanghai, this is best. The all-you-can-eat lunches and
dinners come at a reasonable price, and a delicious *feijoada* (traditional
Brazilian stew of pork, black beans, and rice) is served several times a
week. The downstairs salsa bar offers dance lessons several times a week
(admission and days vary). ⊠ *41 Huaihai Zhonglu, Lane 816,* ☎ *021/*
5467–0160. AE, DC, MC, V.

Cajun

$$$–$$$$ ✕ **Bourbon Street.** Not surprisingly, this is the only place in town to
get Cajun and Creole food. The three-story, upscale restaurant has a
relaxing patio and serves beautifully presented dishes like Louisiana
crab cakes, baked oysters, shrimp creole, and jambalaya. ⊠ *191 Heng-*
shan Lu, ☎ *021/6445–7556. Reservations essential. AE, DC, MC, V.*

Cantonese

$$$–$$$$ ✕ **Canton.** This exclusive restaurant in the Grand Hyatt serves formal
Cantonese food with precision. The atmosphere is slick modernity, with
an infusion of art deco. Try the soups: shark's fin or turtle. ⊠ *Grand*
Hyatt, Jinmao Bldg., 177 Lujiazui Lu, ☎ *021/5830–3338. Reserva-*
tions essential. AE, DC, MC, V.

$$$ ✕ **The Dynasty.** Although the food is mostly Cantonese, some other
cuisines have entered the picture, such as the first-rate Peking duck and
the Sichuan-influenced hot-and-sour soup. The Cantonese seafood
dishes, especially the prawns and lobster, are particularly good. The
shrimp *jiaozi* (dumplings) are delicious. ⊠ *Yangtze New World Hotel,*
2099 Yanan Xilu, ☎ *021/6275–0000. Reservations essential. AE, DC,*
MC, V.

$$ ✕ **Xian Yue Hien.** The dim sum is the big draw at Xian Yue Hien. The
restaurant's Cantonese-Shanghainese menu has a healthy slant, though
the amount of grease often counteracts these efforts. The original
branch is nestled in Dingxiang Garden, a verdant 35-acre playground
the late Qing dynasty Mandarin Li Hongzhang gave to his concubine
Ding Xiang. There's outdoor seating on a large terrace, and the sec-
ond floor overlooks the garden—book early if you want a table by the
window. A second location recently opened on Huaihai Zhonglu. ⊠
849 Huashan Lu, ☎ *021/6251–1166;* ⊠ *381 Huaihai Zhonglu,* ☎ *021/*
5382–2222. Reservations essential. No credit cards.

Chaozhou

$$–$$$ ✕ **Chaozhou Garden.** This restaurant's elegant setting and excellent
service complement its superb Chaozhou dishes. The core seafood of-
ferings are creatively prepared, the poultry dishes are hearty yet vir-
tually greaseless, and the vegetable and noodle selections are a sheer
delight. The soya goose with *doufu* (tofu) appetizer is a classic Chaozhou
dish. Try the crab claw with bamboo shoots and the braised shrimp
and turnip casserole. Chaozhou dim sum is served during lunch. ⊠
Yangtze New World Hotel, 2099 Yanan Xilu, ☎ *021/6275–0000.*
Reservations essential. AE, DC, MC, V.

Chinese

$$$ ✗ **Dragon and Phoenix Room.** It's a bit touristy, and the food isn't spec-
★ tacular, but the atmosphere—in particular the good views of the Bund
and Pudong—make the Dragon and Phoenix Room worth a stop. The
room's original art deco design carries a light-green tint. In one corner
a group of musicians plays traditional Chinese music at an unobtrusive
volume. The menu has a good variety of Chinese dishes, and the fried
noodles are some of the best in town. ✉ *Peace Hotel, 20 Nanjing
Donglu,* ☎ *021/6321–6888. Reservations essential. AE, DC, MC, V.*

$$–$$$ ✗ **Meilongzhen.** Probably Shanghai's most famous restaurant, the
★ Meilongzhen is one of the oldest establishments in town, dating from
1938. The traditional Chinese dining rooms have mahogany and mar-
ble furniture and intricate woodwork. Most of the dishes are Sichuan,
but are prepared with Shanghai cooking styles. In addition to the orig-
inal location on Nanjing Lu, the restaurant has two outlets nearby and
one in Pudong. ✉ *1081 Nanjing Xilu,* ☎ *021/6256–6688 or 021/6256–
2718;* ✉ *1455 Pudong Nanlu,* ☎ *021/5887–9698;* ✉ *77 Jiangning Lu,
Westgate Mall, 97 Jiangning Lu, 6/F. Reservations essential. AE, DC,
MC, V.*

$–$$ ✗ **The Grape.** During the mid-1980s, the Grape, a hole-in-the-wall with
eight tiny booths and dim lighting, became a haven for the small ex-
patriate community. Over the years the small Grape was torn down,
and two bigger outlets were built just across the street from one another. Today the two Grapes bustle with foreign and Chinese clientele,
friendly service, great food, and even better prices. Another outlet has
opened in Hongqiao, as well. The atmosphere is still simple, with
wooden tables and checkered tablecloths. Dishes that won't disappoint
are the garlic shrimp, *jiachang doufu* (home-style bean curd), *yuxiang
rouxi* (spicy pork and bamboo shoots), and fried chicken wings. ✉ *55
Xinle Lu,* ☎ *021/6472–0486;* ✉ *142 Xinle Lu,* ☎ *021/6472–0499;*
✉ *2600 Yanan Xilu,* ☎ *021/6295–2518. No credit cards.*

Chinese Hotpot

$–$$ ✗ **Tian Tian Wang.** *Huo guo,* or hotpot, is a popular Chinese ritual of
at-the-table-cooking, where you put fresh ingredients into a spicy red
soup or a white broth. Tian Tian Wang is the behemoth of hotpot eateries and can be considered somewhat of a *giant* hole-in-the-wall—three
stories, tattered and motley in decor, are dedicated to the dish. It is *the*
place for huo guo, and there's a huge variety of produce to throw into
the pot. Be forewarned: the place is so steamy that you'll leave with
your clothes smelling of the spicy soup. ✉ *975 Huaihai Zhonglu,* ☎
021/6415–7559. ✉ *19 Nanjing Xilu,* ☎ *021/6375–1590;* ✉ *2118
Sichuan Beilu,* ☎ *021/5671–3011. No credit cards.*

$–$$ ✗ **Tianfu Zhi Guo.** The ingredients at the crowded Tianfu Zhi Guo are
both plentiful and fresh. There's everything from fresh bay scallops to
a local type of frog, from spinach to tofu to glass noodles to add to
the concoction. ✉ *1164 Huashan Lu,* ☎ *021/6252–4862. Reservations essential. No credit cards.*

Chinese Vegetarian

$–$$ ✗ **Gongdelin.** Serving vegetarian specialties for more than 50 years,
Gongdelin combines cuisines from all over the country in its creations.
An outstanding dish is the mock duck made of tofu. Be sure to get here
early; if you arrive after 6 PM, when there is always a crowd, you may
not be able to get a table. ✉ *445 Nanjing Xilu,* ☎ *021/6327–0218.
No credit cards.*

Shanghai Dining and Lodging

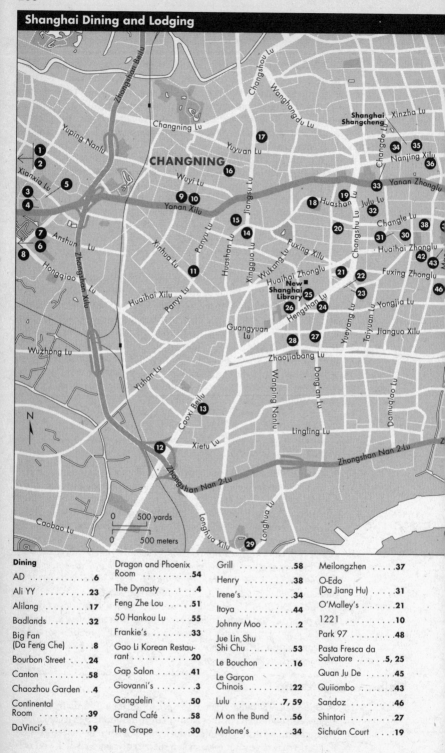

Dining

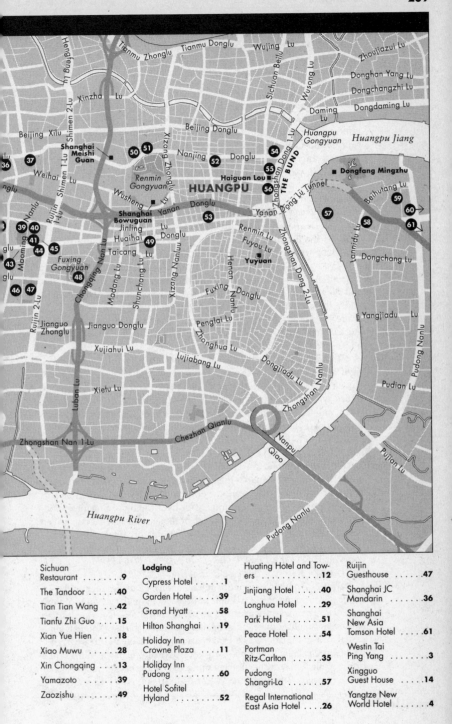

Sichuan Restaurant 9

The Tandoor 40

Tian Tian Wang ... 42

Tianfu Zhi Guo ... 15

Xian Yue Hien ... 18

Xiao Muwu 28

Xin Chongqing ... 13

Yamazoto 39

Zaozishu 49

Lodging

Cypress Hotel 1

Garden Hotel 39

Grand Hyatt 58

Hilton Shanghai ..19

Holiday Inn
Crowne Plaza 11

Holiday Inn
Pudong 60

Hotel Sofitel
Hyland 52

Huating Hotel and Towers 12

Jinjiang Hotel 40

Longhua Hotel ... 29

Park Hotel 51

Peace Hotel 54

Portman
Ritz-Carlton 35

Pudong
Shangri-La 57

Regal International
East Asia Hotel 26

Ruijin
Guesthouse 47

Shanghai JC
Mandarin 36

Shanghai
New Asia
Tomson Hotel 61

Westin Tai
Ping Yang 3

Xingguo
Guest House 14

Yangtze New
World Hotel 4

$ ✕ **Zaozishu.** It might be the only place in Shanghai where you can get real vegetarian food, without all the grease or imitation meats. The tofu dishes are particularly good. ☒ *77 Songshan Lu,* ☎ *021/5306–8001. No credit cards.*

Continental

$$$–$$$$ ✕ **Grand Hyatt.** Two of the Grand Hyatt's restaurants present Continental cuisine while offering absolutely spectacular views of Shanghai (unless the building is shrouded in fog). The sophisticated 24-hour restaurant **Grand Café** touts its "show kitchen"—a buffet that includes appetizers, daily specials, fresh seafood, and desserts. Up on the 56th floor is the **Grill**, part of the Hyatt's three-in-one open-kitchen restaurant concept (the connecting restaurants are Japanese and Italian), where you can feast on a great seafood platter or unbelievably tender steak. ☒ *Grand Hyatt, 177 Lujiazui Lu, Pudong,* ☎ *021/5830–3388. Reservations essential. AE, DC, MC, V.*

$$$–$$$$ ✕ **M on the Bund.** Espousing Shanghai's return to glamour, M does
★   everything with flair. Exquisite Mediterranean-influenced cuisine is served in a classy and inspired chic-modern-meets-retro interior, on the top floor of a 1920s building. Start with the crepe Parmentier with caviar, and then try the baked lamb, the roasted pigeon, or the Shanghainese goose for dinner. The tables with the most envied views of the Bund are reserved for the elite, but the elegant terrace overlooking the river is great alternative, especially for brunch. ☒ *20 Guangdong Lu,* ☎ *021/ 6350–9988. Reservations essential. AE, DC, MC, V.*

$$–$$$ ✕ **50 Hankou Lu.** This restaurant is in a beautiful old British building right off the Bund. The fare is a mix of East and West, and the decor is Southeast Asian, with primitive Indonesian and New Guinean full-figure wooden sculptures. The dishes—like baked escargot, grilled steak, and Caesar salad—are artfully presented, but they're fairly rich and heavy. The restaurant offers a daily set menu at lunch (Y80–Y90) and dinner (Y180–Y200). ☒ *50 Hankou Lu,* ☎ *021/6329–8999 or 021/6323–8383. AE, DC, MC, V.*

$$–$$$ ✕ **Le Garçon Chinois.** You'll feel like a guest in someone's home at this dimly lit restaurant in an old French villa. The walls are painted in warm hues, the art deco fittings are tasteful, and large windows frame surrounding trees and old mansions. Run by a Japanese-European couple, the restaurant presents a Continental menu: the carpaccio, grilled duck, and grilled cod fish are all sublime. For breakfast, flaky croissants and coffee are available from the café-bakery downstairs in the courtyard. ☒ *No. 3, Lane 9, Hengshan Lu,* ☎ *021/6431–3005 or 021/ 6431–1170. Reservations essential. AE, DC, MC, V.*

$$–$$$ ✕ **Park 97.** Another sign of Shanghai's return to its decadent past, attitude is everything at this très chic establishment on the grounds of Fuxing Park. The massive space has an art deco feel and is divided into a café, a late-night lounge, an art gallery, and a sushi bar. You can get a casual meal at the café, which serves pasta, meat dishes, and creative sandwiches and salads. At night the hip and stylish come to the lounge for a drink, while acid jazz and ambient music play in the background. ☒ *Fuxing Gongyuan, 2 Gaolan Lu,* ☎ *021/6318–0785. AE, DC, MC, V.*

French

$$$$ ✕ **Continental Room.** Perched at the top of the Garden Hotel, this very elegant restaurant offers fine French food and views of the surrounding former French Concession. Chic yet traditional and extremely quiet and subdued, it's a perfect setting if you want to impress business clients. ☒ *Garden Hotel, 58 Maoming Lu,* ☎ *021/6415–1111. Reservations essential. AE, DC, MC, V.*

$$–$$$ ✕ **Le Bouchon.** This charming French wine bar also serves up tasty French bistro fare—crepes, quiche, salads—in a relaxed and intimate setting, with greenhouse seating for cold days and an outdoor café for when spring arrives. The main draw is the extensive selection of good and affordable wines. ✉ *1455 Wuding Xilu,* ☎ *021/6225–7088. Reservations essential. AE, MC, V.*

Indian

$$–$$$ ✕ **The Tandoor.** Don't miss the unbelievable *murgh malai kebab* (tan-
★ doori chicken marinated in cheese and yogurt mixture) or try some vegetable curries—*palak aloo* (spinach with peas) or *dal makhani* (lentil). Decorated with mirrors, Indian artwork, and Chinese characters dangling from the ceiling, the restaurant is ingeniously designed to show the route of Buddhism from India to China. The management and staff, all from India, provide impeccable service. ✉ *Jinjiang Hotel, 59 Maoming Nanlu,* ☎ *021/6258–2582 ext. 9301 or 021/6472–5494. Reservations essential. AE, DC, MC, V.*

Irish

$–$$ ✕ **O'Malley's.** A real Irish pub, complete with the requisite super-friendly Irish staff, O'Malley's also has outdoor dining on a beautiful lawn in front of an old French mansion. The food is good and reasonably priced; the Guinness is equally good but not as kind to your wallet. ✉ *42 Taojiang Lu,* ☎ *021/6437–0667. AE, DC, MC, V.*

Italian

$$$–$$$$ ✕ **Giovanni's.** This upscale Italian trattoria has a good view of the Hongqiao area. The *zuppa di pesce alla Veneziana* (Venetian fish soup) is spectacular, as is the calamari, and the pastas are served perfectly al dente. Be sure to try the flat bread with aromatic olive oil—a treat in Shanghai. The crème brûlée is extraordinary. ✉ *Westin Tai Ping Yang, 27th floor, 5 Zunyi Nanlu,* ☎ *021/6275–8888. Reservations essential. AE, DC, MC, V.*

$$$ ✕ **AD.** Former head chef of Giovanni's, Antonio Donnaloia spared no expense in creating his own opera—marble, antique furniture, Gianni Versace uniforms, vaulted ceilings, a fireplace inside what looks like a plaster-of-Paris head of Zeus, and Italian fabric on the walls and furniture. With the exception of a few appetizers, the food is superb: the deep-fried calamari and prawns, the mixed seafood Amalfi soup, the hearty but delicious risotto, some of the best veal in Shanghai, and grilled portions of fresh, imported seafood. Don't miss the to-die-for desserts, such as the poached pear with cinnamon mousse and the *tartufo bianco.* ✉ *3896 Hongmei Beilu,* ☎ *021/6262–5620. Reservations essential. AE, DC, MC, V.*

$$$ ✕ **DaVinci's.** This chic establishment offers nouvelle Italian food. For starters, a colorful selection from the antipasto table can include carpaccio, eggplant salad, calamari, and Italian cold cuts. In addition to the excellent pastas and risotto, the meat dishes are outstanding, especially the lamb dusted with rosemary. ✉ *Shanghai Hilton, 250 Huashan Lu,* ☎ *021/6248–0000 ext. 8263. Reservations essential. AE, DC, MC, V. No lunch.*

$–$$ ✕ **Pasta Fresca da Salvatore.** The food isn't outstanding at this casual trattoria, but it's the only place to go for reasonably priced Italian food. The pizza here is better than the pasta. The set lunch menu costs Y68. ✉ *Friendship Shopping Centre, 6 Zunyi Nanlu,* ☎ *021/6270–4693 or 021/6270–0000 ext. 1211;* ✉ *4 Hengshan Lu,* ☎ *021/6473–0772. AE, DC, MC, V.*

Japanese

$$$$　✕ **Yamazoto.** The owners of this restaurant (and the pretentious hotel it is located in) seem to have forgotten that they are in China and not downtown Tokyo. The food is good, the sushi is fresh, but the prices are really outrageous. However, if you have a client whom you are trying to impress, this is a good place to blow some expense-account money. ✉ *Garden Hotel, 58 Maoming Nanlu,* ☎ *021/6415–1111. Reservations essential. AE, DC, MC, V.*

$$$–$$$$　✕ **Shintori.** With its characters etched in glass partitions and water and rock installations, this top-rate Japanese restaurant has chic post-modernism written all over it. The Taiwanese-owned establishment offers sublime and stylish dishes from excellent sushi to grilled cod to seafood steamed in sake. The nine-course set menu (Y395) is an experience. ✉ *288 Wulumuqi Nanlu,* ☎ *021/6467–1188. Reservations essential. AE, MC, V.*

$$–$$$　✕ **O-Edo (Da Jiang Hu).** This quaint Japanese restaurant is known for its all-you-can-eat-and-drink-for-Y200 offer. Expect an inordinate amount of sushi, sashimi, tempura, broiled cod, *agedashi* tofu, chicken yakitori, and so on—all washed down with a bottomless barrel of sake. The house specialty is the delicious raw beef *tataki* and *okoze* (stonefish). ✉ *30 Donghu Lu,* ☎ *021/6467–3332;* ✉ *2430 Xietu Lu,* ☎ *021/6468–5177. No credit cards.*

$$–$$$　✕ **Itoya.** The small, unassuming Itoya serves imposing portions of some of the freshest and tastiest fish in town. The menu is filled with a variety of satisfying traditional Japanese dishes like broiled cod, tempura, and reasonable lunch boxes, but the place to head for is the sushi bar. Itoya's other claim to fame is its 60 different kinds of sake. ✉ *24 Ruijin Er Lu,* ☎ *021/6467–0758;* ✉ *Ronghua Xidao, Lane 19, No. 6,* ☎ *021/6219–2286;* ✉ *381 Huaihai Zhonglu, 3F,* ☎ *021/5382–5777;* ✉ *1515 Nanjing Xilu,* ☎ *021/5298–5777. AE, DC, MC, V.*

Korean

$–$$　✕ **Alilang.** One of Shanghai's oldest Korean eateries, Alilang serves kimchi (pickled cabbage), unlimited cold appetizers, meat and seafood barbecued on smoky coals right before your eyes, and noodles. The meat dishes are the best choice here, although they fall a bit short of other Korean places in town. A specialty that is always delicious is the *congyoubing* (onion cake). ✉ *28 Jiangsu Beilu,* ☎ *021/6252–7146. AE, DC, MC, V.*

$–$$　✕ **Gao Li Korean Restaurant.** Hidden on a small lane, Gao Li is a bit of a hole in the wall, but it serves great, cheap food to crowds of diners until 2 AM, specializing in tender and delicious grilled meat. The noodle dishes are some of the best in town: try the cold vermicelli noodle appetizer. ✉ *No.1, Lane 181, Wuyuan Lu,* ☎ *021/6431–5236. No credit cards.*

Mexican

$–$$　✕ **Badlands.** This tiny restaurant draws foreign residents for quick and cheap Mexican food and the cheerful, friendly environment, which includes an outdoor deck and a bamboo bar. The favorites here are the burritos and tacos. On weekends Badlands also serves a Tex-Mex breakfast. ✉ *897 Julu Lu,* ☎ *021/6466–7788 ext. 8003. AE, DC, MC, V.*

Muslim/Uighur/Middle Eastern

$–$$$　✕ **Ali YY.** Ali YY's ground-floor Xinjiang restaurant serves good, wholesome Uighur food for bargain prices. Dishes are low on grease and high on flavor. Try the fried Xinjiang noodles and the lamb kebabs. Upstairs, proprietor Kenny Tang (owner of the nightclub YY) has opened an Arabic restaurant, where he has made eating a true event, complete with superstylish soft red-velvet cushions, and your own personal pair of Ali YY slippers. Upstairs Y200 will buy you great platters of hummus and falafel. ⊠ *5B Dongping Lu,* ☎ *021/6415–9448. Reservations essential. No credit cards.*

Portuguese

$$–$$$ **Sandoz.** This is Shanghai's first and only Portuguese restaurant. The chef, from Macau, cooks traditional Portuguese foods, such as *bacalhau* (codfish) and chorizo, as well as some famous Macanese dishes. Sandoz also has a great selection of wines and outdoor seating for when the weather is warm. *207 Maoming Nanlu,* ☎ *021/6466–0479. AE, DC, MC, V.*

Shanghainese

$$–$$$ ✗ **Big Fan (Da Feng Che).** The wood-paneled walls of this restaurant— in a 1930s apartment village—are decorated with framed colonial advertisements and banknotes, along with photos of street scenes, garden parties, and men's clubs from the 1930s. As you're seated, a waiter will pour you Sichuan tea in the traditional style from a pot with a foot-long spout. The cooking is home-style Shanghainese, with the seafood dishes standing out. ⊠ *1440 Hongqiao Lu,* ☎ *021/6275–9131 ext. 268. No credit cards.*

$$–$$$ ✗ **Henry.** Right in the heart of the former French Concession, Henry has a '20s retro feel, with huge French windows in the front, and jazz streaming quietly over the sound system. The atmosphere is very old Shanghai and classy, but the food—soup, noodles, lemon chicken, homestyle tofu—and service are sometimes hit or miss. ⊠ *8 Xinle Lu,* ☎ *021/6473–3448.*

$$–$$$ ✗ **1221.** This stylish but casual eatery has become a favorite of its hip
★ Chinese and expatriate regulars. Shanghainese food is the mainstay, but just about everthing is on the menu. The dishes are imaginative, the service attentive, and the atmosphere pleasing. From the extensive 11-page menu (in English, pinyin, and Chinese), you can order dishes like sliced *you tiao* (fried bread sticks) with shredded beef, a whole chicken in a green-onion soy sauce, delicious shredded pork with sweet bean sauce and small pancakes, and *shaguo shizi tou,* or "Lion's Head" meatballs. ⊠ *1221 Yanan Xilu,* ☎ *021/6213–6585 or 021/6213– 2441. Reservations essential. No credit cards.*

$–$$ ✗ **Gap Salon (Jinting Jiujia).** The Gap Salon, on Maoming Lu, is a spectacle you won't soon forget. This 20,500-square-ft establishment offers its mostly Chinese clientele just about everything—food, music, dancing, karaoke—with European decor (or at least what the Hong Kong–Chinese owners perceive as European). A genuine antique Red Flag— the car exclusively used by Shanghai officials of yesteryear—overhangs the entrance, hinting at the grandiosity to come. A huge central area evokes an outdoor courtyard. Filipino bands and Chinese dancers take the stage during your meal. Four other locations offer the same hearty Shanghainese food in somewhat more mellow environments. ⊠ *127 Maoming Nanlu,* ☎ *021/6433–9028;* ⊠ *8 Zunyi Lu,* ☎ *021/6278–2900;* ⊠ *Westgate Mall, 1038 Nanjing Xilu, 4/F,* ☎ *021/6218–6868;* ⊠ *960 Caoxi Beilu,* ☎ *021/6481–3249;* ⊠ *The Promenade, 8 Hengshan Lu,* ☎ *021/6473–4828. Reservations not accepted. AE, DC, MC, V.*

$–$$ ✗ **Lulu.** This small, crowded, smoke-filled restaurant is the hip late-night place for Shanghai's young fashionable crowd. Lulu is known for its fresh seafood; you'll be able to see what you're getting in the tanks lined up inside the entrance. The shredded pork and scallion wrapped in pancakes is also perfectly executed and *kofu* (cold braised tofu) doesn't get any better than this. Sometimes it's difficult to get a table, even at 3 in the morning, so be prepared to wait, especially on weekends. The Pudong branch is similarly crowded. ⊠ *336 Shuicheng Nanlu,* ☎ *021/6270–6679;* ⊠ *161 Lujiazui Lu, Pudong,* ☎ *021/ 5882–6679. Reservations essential. AE, DC, MC, V.*

Sichuanese

\$\$–\$\$\$ ✕ **Sichuan Court.** Get a sky-high view of the city at this sleek upscale eatery at the top of the Hilton. The Sichuan treasure box offers a good array of delicacies—cold sliced garlic pork, sliced suckling pig, sliced duck, some cold vegetables—to start off with. The tea-smoked duck (smoked on order in Chengdu), *mapo doufu* (spicy tofu), and *dan dan* (noodles) are typical of the Sichuan dishes served here. ⊠ *250 Huashan Lu,* ☎ *021/6248–0000. Reservations essential. AE, DC, MC, V.*

\$\$ ✕ **Sichuan Restaurant.** Here the most popular dish, which you'll see on almost every table, is the stewed beef. If you want something really spicy, typical of Sichuan food, try the crispy chicken. The restaurant also serves 14 varieties of Sichuan dim sum that come at a bargain. More daring choices such as fish maw, turtle, snake, pigeon, and frog are served up with unexpected flavors like almond bean curd, chili and peanuts, preserved eggs, and fried squid shreds with chili. ⊠ *739 Dingxi Lu,* ☎ *021/6281–0449. AE, DC, MC, V.*

\$ ✕ **Xin Chongqing.** This place is *hot* in the true Sichuan sense of the word—it's the local hangout for diehard chili fans. Try the *lazi ji* (chili chicken), *douhua* (tofu pudding), and the *nangua bing* (pumpkin cakes). The menu is in Chinese only, however, and there are no pictures to aid those who are not familiar with the language. ⊠ *98 Puhui Tang Lu,* ☎ *021/6428–6236. No credit cards.*

Singaporean

\$–\$\$ ✕ **Frankie's.** The bare decor and a-bit-too-bright lighting don't dis-
★ courage connoissieurs of Singaporean cuisine. The fried *kway teow* (an absolutely delicious version of the Singaporean noodle dish), the chicken curry, and the stir-fried broccoli with garlic are especially good, but the standout dish is the pepper crab. Don't miss the refreshing dessert made with coconut milk. ⊠ *118 Changde Lu,* ☎ *021/6247– 0886. No credit cards.*

Taiwanese

\$–\$\$ ✕ **Xiao Muwu.** When the weather's warm and it's not raining, this bamboo restaurant becomes an open-air eatery reminiscent of Thailand. The specialty of the house is barbecued meat and seafood marinated in Taiwanese hot spices. You order by the piece, and the chef cooks it on the spot. The best items are the barbecued squid, chicken, and tofu. ⊠ *825 Zhaojiabang Lu,* ☎ *021/6428–1402;* ⊠ *665 Shenxia Lu,* ☎ *021/6273–9337;* ⊠ *618 Beijing Xilu,* ☎ *021/6218–8078. No credit cards.*

Thai

\$\$–\$\$\$ ✕ **Irene's.** The Judy's Group, responsible for the nightclub Judy's Too, designed this restaurant to look like a traditional teak house complete with a few low tables and cushions on the floor, colorful Thai textiles, and wooden statues. The Thai food is good if not inspired, though the salads—especially the papaya salad—are wonderful. There is an all-you-can-eat buffet, with drinks included, every day except Saturday.

✉ *263 Tongren Lu,* ☎ *021/6247–3579. Reservations essential. AE, DC, MC, V.*

LODGING

Nanjing Lu and the Bund

$$$$ 🏨 **Shanghai JC Mandarin.** The 30-story blue glass towers of this hotel rise up east of the Shanghai Exhibition Center. In the lobby is a five-story-high hand-painted mural depicting the voyage of the Ming dynasty admiral Zheng Ho, as well as a coffee shop that serves great Southeast Asian food. Rooms are bright with earthy tones and natural wood. The Mandarin Club Lounge comprises the executive floors at the top of the hotel. The Cantonese restaurant has fine dim sum at affordable prices. ✉ *1225 Nanjing Xilu, 200040,* ☎ *021/6279–1888,* FAX *021/6279–1822,* WEB *www.jcmandarin.com. 564 rooms, 36 suites. 4 restaurants, bar, deli, pool, sauna, tennis court, gym, squash, dance club, billiards, shops, business services, meeting room. AE, DC, MC, V.*

$$$ 🏨 **Hotel Sofitel Hyland.** The only hotel directly on the Nanjing Lu pedestrian walkway, the Hyland is ideal for exploring the city center, shopping, and taking trips to the Bund. The 34-story Japanese-owned and French-managed hotel has eight floors of rooms designed specifically for business travelers. The top-floor Sky Lounge offers good views of downtown and a pleasant Sunday brunch. ✉ *505 Nanjing Donglu, 200001,* ☎ *021/6351–5888,* FAX *021/6351–4088,* WEB *www.cbw.com/hotel/sofitel/. 389 rooms and suites. 4 restaurants, bar, deli, beauty salon, gym, shops, business services, meeting room. AE, DC, MC, V.*

$$$ 🏨 **Portman Ritz-Carlton.** Its location in the Shanghai Center, along with
★   its outstanding facilities and furnishings, draws people to this 50-story luxury hotel. Rooms have a modern East-meets-West decor, with wooden Ming-influenced furniture. It's elegant if a bit impersonal. The health club is comprehensive. The hotel has four good food outlets, plus the Portman Deli in the supermarket. ✉ *1376 Nanjing Xilu, 200040,* ☎ *021/6279–8888,* FAX *021/6279–8887,* WEB *www.ritzcarlton.com. 492 rooms, 72 suites. 4 restaurants, 2 bars, indoor and outdoor pool, beauty salon, sauna, tennis court, gym, racquetball, squash, dance club, shops, business services, meeting room. AE, DC, MC, V.*

$$–$$$ 🏨 **Peace Hotel.** This romantic hotel is among Shanghai's most trea-
★   sured historic buildings. Its high ceilings, ornate woodwork, and art deco fixtures are intact, and the ballroom evokes old Shanghai cabarets and gala parties, though the rooms are no longer glamorous and even tend to be a bit stuffy. Built in 1906 by the British, the south building, formerly the Palace Hotel, is the oldest structure on the Bund. The more popular north building, formerly the Cathay Hotel, built in 1929, was known as the private playground of its owner, Victor Sassoon. The eighth-floor Dragon and Phoenix Room is a good choice for dinner, while the rooftop bar is one of the most romantic spots in Shanghai. ✉ *20 Nanjing Donglu, 200002,* ☎ *021/6321–6888,* FAX *021/6329–0300,* WEB *www.shanghaipeacehotel.com. 411 rooms and 9 suites. 3 restaurants, 2 bars, beauty salon, gym, shops, billiards, business services, meeting room. AE, DC, MC, V.*

$$ 🏨 **Park Hotel.** This historic 1934 art deco structure overlooking People's Park was once among Shanghai's more luxurious and fashionable hotels. It was completely renovated to recapture its pre-1949 glory, and it still has a musty charm, but the service and facilities are definitely second-rate. ✉ *170 Nanjing Xilu, 200003,* ☎ *021/6327–5225,* FAX *021/6327–6958. 215 rooms. 3 restaurants, beauty salon, dance club, shop, business services. AE, DC, MC, V.*

Old French Concession

$$$$ ☆ **Garden Hotel.** Managed by the Japanese Okura Group, this 33-story
★ hotel is beautifully appointed, presenting luxury with a cool Japanese
aesthetic. The first three floors, which were once old Shanghai's French
Club, have been renovated with many of the former art deco fixtures
and frescoes still intact. The third-floor terrace, overlooking the huge
garden, is a great place for a romantic drink. The hotel is also known
for its excellent—and high-priced—Japanese food. The rooms are spacious and tastefully decorated. ⊠ *58 Maoming Lu, 200020,* ☎ *021/
6415–1111,* FAX *021/6415–8866,* WEB *www.gardenhotelshanghai.com.
478 rooms, 22 suites. 4 restaurants, 3 bars, pool, beauty salon, sauna,
tennis, gym, shops, business services, meeting room. AE, DC, MC, V.*

$$$$ ☆ **Regal International East Asia Hotel.** This hotel is connected to the
exclusive Shanghai International Tennis Center and hotel guests can play
on one of ten tennis courts. The stout hotel has a large, rather austere
lobby. The rooms are large and modern, though a little bland. The main
attraction is the hotel's extravagant Club House—one of the best gyms
in town. ⊠ *516 Hengshan Lu, 200040,* ☎ *021/6415–5588,* FAX *021/
6445–8899,* WEB *www.regal-eastasia.com. 300 rooms. 3 restaurants, bakery, hair salon, sauna, pool, tennis court, squash, gym, bowling, billiards,
shops, business services, meeting room. AE, DC, MC, V.*

$$$–$$$$ ☆ **Holiday Inn Crowne Plaza.** This hotel on the western side of the French
Concession is known for its service. The staff here is among the friendli-
est in town and makes guests, mostly business travelers, feel right at
home. Although a bit outside the city center, the hotel is still close to
the Huaihai Lu shopping district and the Hongqiao area. The comfortable
guest rooms and suites are bright and homey. ⊠ *400 Panyu Lu, 200052,*
☎ *021/6280–8888,* FAX *021/6280–2788,* WEB *www.sixcontinentshotels.
com/holiday-inn. 467 rooms, 29 suites. 4 restaurants, bar, deli, pool,
hair salon, sauna, tennis court, gym, business services, meeting room.
AE, DC, MC, V.*

$$$ ☆ **Huating Hotel and Towers.** Just southwest of the old French Con-
cession, in the Xujiahui area, the first Western hotel to open in Shang-
hai is a former Sheraton property. Some of the interior is a bit kitschy,
while the exterior looks like an S-shape tiered wedding cake. Rooms
and suites are modern and comfortable. The Towers make up the
hotel's executive floors. ⊠ *1200 Caoxi Beilu, 200030,* ☎ *021/6439–
1000,* FAX *021/6255–0830,* WEB *www.huating.com/hotel. 1,008 rooms,
56 suites. 4 restaurants, bar, pool, tennis court, bowling, gym, squash,
shops, billiards, dance club, business services, meeting room. AE, DC,
MC, V.*

$$–$$$ ☆ **Hilton Shanghai.** The 43-story triangular building has some of the
★ best dining in town and top-rate accommodations. Rooms are modern and luxurious, with marble bathrooms. There are four executive
floors, as well as two floors decorated in a Japanese style. The hotel
coffee shop has a lovely sunlit atrium. The view from the top-floor Penthouse Bar and Sichuan Court is spectacular, a great place for watching fireworks on Chinese New Year. ⊠ *250 Huashan Lu, 200040,* ☎
021/6248–0000, FAX *021/6248–3848,* WEB *www.hilton.com. 754 rooms
and 21 suites. 7 restaurants, 2 bars, deli, pool, beauty salon, sauna,
tennis court, gym, squash, billiards, shops, business services, meeting
room. AE, DC, MC, V.*

$$–$$$ ☆ **Jinjiang Hotel.** The former Cathay Mansions, Grosvenor Gardens,
and Grosvenor House, now known collectively as the Jinjiang Hotel,
are among the few art deco buildings left standing in the city. The Cathay
was built as an apartment building in 1928 and the glamorous Grosvenor
House three years later. All rooms in the latter have been left in their
original design, with the beautiful art deco ornamentation intact. Stan-

dard rooms in the North Building—comfortable, traditionally furnished, and homey but not luxurious—also have an old-Shanghai feeling. The once-verdant central lawn has been replaced by a huge health center. ⊠ *59 Maoming Lu, 200020,* ☎ *021/6258–2582,* FAX *021/6472–5588,* WEB *www.jinjianghotelshanghai.com. 487 rooms, 28 suites. 5 restaurants, bar, beauty salon, health club, sauna, shops, dance club, business services, meeting room. AE, MC, V.*

$–$$ ☒ **Ruijin Guesthouse.** The Morriss Estate, now Ruijin Guesthouse, was built by a Western newspaper magnate. Today the estate's houses still stand amid huge green lawns and trees. Five old villas have rooms renovated in traditional Chinese style. You can have a cup of tea on the lawn on the south side of the main mansion or dine at one of the Western restaurants on the grounds. Stroll around the estate to view the ornate details, including a stained-glass window in the rear house. ⊠ *118 Ruijin Er Lu, 200020,* ☎ *021/6472–5222,* FAX *021/6473–2277,* WEB *www.shedi.net.cn/OUTEDI/Ruijin. 71 rooms. 5 restaurants, 3 bars, hair salon, business services. AE, DC, MC, V.*

$ ☒ **Longhua Hotel.** This hotel, within the walls of the Longhua Temple, caters to followers of Buddhism, but is open to everyone. Directed by the master abbot Ming Yang, the hotel is simply decorated in a Chinese style tinged with modern Western influences and post-1949 Communist starkness. The hotel's labyrinthine halls are fashioned according to traditional Chinese architecture and beliefs. Along with Chinese and Western cuisine, the hotel also serves Buddhist vegetarian dishes. ⊠ *2787 Longhua Lu, 200232,* ☎ *021/6457–0570,* FAX *021/6457–7621. 140 rooms and suites. 3 restaurants, hair salon, billiards. AE, DC, MC, V.*

$ ☒ **Xingguo Guest House.** This collection of old Shanghai villas, furnished in both traditional and western styles, sits around a huge green lawn. The service and food are not as good as at Western hotels, but the quaint atmosphere definitely has more charm. Both restaurants serve Chinese cuisine. ⊠ *72 Xingguo, 200052,* ☎ *021/6212–9998,* FAX *021/ 6251–2145. 2 restaurants, business services. AE, DC, MC, V.*

Hongqiao Development Zone

$$$ ☒ **Westin Tai Ping Yang.** This luxurious Japanese-managed high-rise hotel is extremely formal, and everything is done with a flourish. The hotel is within easy reach of the Shanghai International Exhibition Center and Shanghai Mart; Honqiao Airport is only a short ride away. Rooms are fresh and equipped with high-tech electronic amenities such as fax and data ports. Good Italian food can be found at Giovanni's, and the deli on the second floor offers a great selection of pastas, cold cuts, and breads. ⊠ *5 Zunyi Nanlu, 200335,* ☎ *021/6275–8888,* FAX *021/ 6275–5420,* WEB *www.westin-shanghai.com. 541 rooms, 39 suites. 5 restaurants, deli, pool, hair salon, sauna, tennis court, gym, shops, billiards, business services, meeting room. AE, DC, MC, V.*

$$–$$$ ☒ **Yangtze New World Hotel.** This hotel is adjacent to the International Trade and Exhibition Center and Shanghai Mart. It has an excellent Chinese restaurant and a New York–inspired bar, Graffiti's, with live music on the weekends. The spacious rooms all have data ports and modern amenities. ⊠ *2099 Yanan Xilu, 200335,* ☎ *021/6275–0000,* FAX *021/6275–0750,* WEB *www.newworldhotels.com/SHANW. 553 rooms and suites. 5 restaurants, deli, pool, beauty salon, sauna, gym, shops, dance club, business services, meeting room. AE, DC, MC, V.*

$$–$$$ ☒ **Cypress Hotel.** Once part of tycoon Victor Sassoon's estate, the beautiful, expansive grounds here are filled with trees, streams, bridges, and lawns. The recently renovated rooms are simple but comfortable, with modern and electronic amenities. ⊠ *2419 Hongqiao Lu, 200335,* ☎ *021/6268–8868,* FAX *021/6242–8178. 149 rooms. 5 restaurants, 2 bars,*

pool, sauna, tennis court, bowling, gym, squash, billiards, business services, meeting room. AE, DC, MC, V.

Pudong New Area

$$$$ ⊞ **Grand Hyatt.** Occupying floors 53 through 88 of the spectacular
★ Jinmao Tower, the Grand Hyatt is the world's highest hotel. A combination of traditional and postmodern design, the Hyatt's interior is defined by art deco lines juxtaposed with space-age grillwork and sleek furnishings and textures. The 30-story central atrium is a marvel in itself—a seemingly endless cylinder with an outer-space aura. Views from the rooms are spectacular; corner rooms have two walls of pure glass for endless panoramas of the city below, and from a marble bathtub you can look at the Oriental Pearl Tower. Amenities are space age as well: CAT 5 optical lines for laptop use, Internet connections on the TV through a cordless keyboard, and three high-pressure water heads in the shower. ⊠ *Jinmao Dasha, 2 Shiji Dadao, Pudong 200121,* ☎ *021/5049–1234,* FAX *021/5049–1111,* WEB *www.shanghai.hyatt.com. 511 rooms, 44 suites. 5 restaurants, 3 bars, pool, hair salon, sauna, gym, shops, billiards, business services, meeting room. AE, DC, MC, V.*

$$$$ ⊞ **Pudong Shangri-La.** One of the most finely appointed properties in
★ Shanghai, it overlooks the Huangpu River opposite the Bund, on the edge of Lujiazui. Next to the Pudong ferry terminal, the hotel also offers breathtaking, right-above-water-level views of the Bund, especially from its outdoor patio. The rooms have cream walls, marble bathrooms, and elm-colored furniture. The hotel has Chinese and Japanese restaurants, and a great bar-disco with rocking bands. ⊠ *33 Fucheng Lu, Pudong 200120,* ☎ *021/6882–8888,* FAX *021/6882–6688,* WEB *www.shangri-la.com/eng. 587 rooms and 25 suites. 5 restaurants, bar, pool, beauty salon, sauna, tennis, gym, squash, shops, billiards, nightclub, business services, meeting room. AE, DC, MC, V.*

$$$ **Holiday Inn Pudong.** The second Holiday Inn in Shanghai, in the commercial district of Pudong, is well situated for travelers with business in the area. The rooms are tidy and bright and all have data ports. The hotel's Irish pub Flanagan's serves Guinness and Kilkenny on tap. ⊠ *899 Dongfang Lu, Pudong 200120,* ☎ *021/5830–6666,* FAX *021/5830–5555,* WEB *www.sixcontinentshotels.com/holiday-inn. 320 rooms, 40 suites. 5 restaurants, bar, pool, health club, beauty salon, sauna, business services, meeting room. AE, DC, MC, V.*

$$$ ⊞ **Shanghai New Asia Tomson Hotel.** The first luxury hotel in Pudong is in the heart of the Lujiazui financial district. The *pièce de résistance* of the 24-story Shanghai-Taiwan joint venture is a nearly 200-ft-high Italian Renaissance–inspired atrium with an interior garden that brings in natural light to 18 floors of elegant and spacious guest rooms. There are three executive floors, and restaurants for every taste—Italian, Swiss, Cantonese, Shanghainese, Chaozhou, and Continental. Guests have access to the 18-hole course at the Tomson Golf Club in Pudong. ⊠ *777 Zhangyang Lu, Pudong 200120,* ☎ *021/5831–8888,* FAX *021/5831–7777,* WEB *www.shedi.net.cn/OUTEDI/NewAsia. 344 rooms, 78 suites. 7 restaurants, bar, indoor pool, hair salon, sauna, gym, shops, billiards, nightclub, business services, meeting room. AE, DC, MC, V.*

NIGHTLIFE AND THE ARTS

For up-to-date information about what's going on in the city, check out *Shanghai Talk* and *That's Shanghai*, the monthly expatriate magazines available at Western bars, restaurants, and hotels throughout town; the *Shanghai Star,* the English-language newspaper published by the *China Daily*; or *Shanghai Now*, available at most hotels and bookstores.

The Arts

Acrobatics

China's best, the **Shanghai Acrobatic Troupe** performs remarkable feats and stunts at the Shanghai Center Theater (✉ 1376 Nanjing Xilu, ☎ 021/6279–8663; ⊙ daily 7:15 PM).

Art and Architecture

In addition to the not-to-be-missed Shanghai Museum, a number of places exhibit Chinese art. For traditional Chinese art, check out the gallery of the **Guo Tai Auction House** (✉ 1298 Lujiabang Lu, ☎ 021/6210–1098), which holds auctions of traditional Chinese calligraphy and paintings by promising young artists on the eighth of every month at 2 PM. The **Liu Haisu Art Museum** (✉ 1660 Hongqiao Lu, ☎ 021/6270–1018), named after the famous Chinese traditional painter, holds regular exhibitions. If you really want to be where it's at, get familiar with Shanghai's young contemporary avant-garde artists, who are garnering increasing world attention, at **ShanghART** (✉ Park 97, 2 Gaolan Lu, ☎ 021/6359–3923 or 1391747857, FAX 021/5403–1602), the city's first modern art gallery. It's *the* place to check out the work of art-world movers and shakers such as Ding Yi, Xue Song, Zhou Tiehai, Wu Yiming, and Shen Fan.

If you want to learn more about all that old architecture you're seeing on the streets or maybe take home a photography book chronicling Shanghai's history, have a cup of coffee at the ever-so-charming **Old Chinahand Reading Room** (✉ 27 Shaoxing Lu, ☎ 021/6473–2526). This artistic café that looks like grandma's living room is run by Shanghainese photographer Erh Dongqiang, who has a library of history, architecture, art, literature, and coffee-table books.

Chinese Opera

Not only Beijing opera, but also China's other regional operas, such as Huju, Kunju, and Shaoxing, are performed regularly at the **Yifu Theatre** (✉ 701 Fuzhou Lu, ☎ 021/6351–4668). Call the box office for schedule and ticket information. On Sundays at 1:30 PM, students from the **Shanghai School of Music and Opera** perform a selection of acts from different operas at the Yifu Theatre. Ticket prices range from Y5 to Y20. The **Kunju Opera Troupe** (✉ 9 Shaoxing Lu, ☎ 021/6437–1012) holds matinee performances every Saturday at 1:30 PM.

Dance and Music

The modern **Shanghai Center Theater** (✉ 1376 Nanjing Xilu, ☎ 021/6279–8663) is one of the chief venues in town for quality performances. The spectacular **Grand Theatre** (✉ 300 Renmin Dadao, ☎ 021/6372–8701, 6372–8702, or 6372–3833) stages the greatest number of domestic and international classical music and ballet performances.

Asian and Western acts sporadically appear at the **Shanghai Gymnasium** (✉ 1111 Caoxi Beilu, ☎ 021/6473–0940). The **Majestic Theatre** (✉ 66 Jiangning Lu, ☎ 021/6217–4409) hosts both Asian and Western performances.

The **Jingan Hotel** (✉ 370 Huashan Lu, San Diego Hall, ☎ 021/6248–1888 ext. 687) has regular chamber music performances. The **Shanghai Concert Hall** (✉ 523 Yanan Donglu, ☎ 021/6386–9153) regularly presents classical ensembles and orchestras, mostly domestic. The **Shanghai Symphony Orchestra** performs here Saturday evening at 7:15.

Theater

Modern theater in China is primarily dominated by state-run companies. The **Shanghai People's Art Theatre** (⊠ 201 Anfu Lu, ☎ 021/6431–3523) presents regular performances of Chinese plays, as well as foreign plays in Chinese translation. The **Shanghai Theatre Academy** (⊠ 630 Huashan Lu, ☎ 021/6248–2920 ext. 3040) has three stages that periodically present student and professional works.

Nightlife

Bars

The **Cotton Club** (⊠ 1428 Huaihai Zhonglu, ☎ 021/6437–7110), a comfortable, unassuming, and relaxed lounge, is the place for live music, with blues and jazz by Chinese and foreign musicians. The historic and romantic **Peace Hotel** (⊠ 20 Nanjing Donglu, ☎ 021/6321–6888) has a German-style pub that has gained fame due to the nightly performances (Y50–Y80, depending on where you sit) of the Peace Hotel Old Jazz Band, whose members played jazz in dance halls in pre-1949 Shanghai.

If you're looking for the trendy, young Chinese hipsters and the more alternative local crowds, check out the Shanghai–cum–New York establishments. The minimalist **Bonne Sante** (⊠ Regency Shanghai, 8 Jinan Lu, ☎ 021/6384–2906) reads like a monochrome Manhattan apartment and draws in the sophisticated crowds for weekly wine tastings. **Goya** (⊠ 357 Xinhua Lu, ☎ 021/6280–1256) is a dark, cozy martini bar with couches, great drinks from an endless list, and acid jazz in the background. For glamour, go to **M on the Bund** (⊠ 20 Guangdong Lu, ☎ 021/6350–9988). The latenight lounge at **Park 97** (⊠ Fuxing Gongyuan, 2 Gaolan Lu, ☎ 021/6318–0785) is ever so chic.

Want to go American? Shanghai's **Hard Rock Café** (⊠ 1376 Nanjing Xilu, ☎ 021/6279–8133) has the latest loud DJs, live pop and rock music, and crowds of Chinese yuppies. **Jurassic Pub** (⊠ 8 Maoming Nanlu, ☎ 021/6253–4627 or 021/6258–3758) lives up to its Spielberg-inspired name with dinosaur skeletons wrapped around a central bar beneath a willow tree. In the Shanghai Center, the narrow, horseshoe-shape **Long Bar** (⊠ 1376 Nanjing Xilu, ☎ 021/6279–8268) has a loyal expat-businessman clientele and an eclectic jukebox. The sports bar **Malone's American Café** (⊠ 257 Tongren Lu, ☎ 021/6247–2400) has TVs broadcasting sports events, pool tables, darts, sports legend decor, and live Chinese bands covering rock 'n' roll.

If you find yourself across the river in Pudong, try the **Dublin Exchange** (⊠ Senmao Bldg., 101 Yincheng Donglu, Pudong, ☎ 021/6841–2052), with its upmarket Irish banker's club ambience, caters to the growing Wall Street that is Lujiazui. Locals love **O'Malley's** (⊠ 42 Taojiang Lu, ☎ 021/6474–4533), which has Guinness on tap, Irish music, and a great outdoor garden. The gigantic German beerhouse **Paulaner Brauhaus** (⊠ 150 Fengyang Lu, ☎ 021/6474–5700) and its Filipino band is a favorite among young Chinese white-collar types.

Clubs

Weekends at the casual **Judy's Too** (⊠ 176 Maoming Nanlu, ☎ 021/6473–1417), a beautiful two-level café with a strong old-Shanghai colonial theme, can get meat-markety as the dance floor fills up with a mix of Chinese and foreigners. Shanghai's new trendiness is represented to the extreme at **MGM** (⊠ 141 Shaanxi Nanlu, ☎ 021/6467–3353), where the dance floor is always full of beautiful and stylish young men and women. The vast **Real Love** (⊠ 10 Hengshan Lu, ☎ 021/6474–6830) is becoming *the* late-night spot, with its postmodern decor and young nouveau-riche Shanghainese clamoring to get to the dance floor. **Rojam**

Disco (✉ 4/F Hong Kong Plaza, 283 Huaihai Zhonglu, ☎ 021/6390–7181), a three-level techno behemoth, bulges with boogiers and underground lounge lizards. The small, mellow **Ying Yang (YY)** (✉ 125 Nanchang Lu, ☎ 021/6431–2668 or 021/6466–4098) club, lined with black velvet and illuminated with blue light, draws an eclectic crowd of foreign yuppies and Shanghai alternative types.

Hotel Bars

At the Pudong Shangri-La's **B.A.T.S.** (✉ 33 Fucheng Lu, ☎ 021/6882–8888), lively fun erupts around a central bar, with a great house band performing rhythm and blues, funk, or rock. When the weather's nice, you can get a cool drink at the **Garden Hotel** terrace (✉ 58 Maoming Nanlu, ☎ 021/6415–1111). The **Peace Hotel** rooftop (✉ 20 Nanjing Xilu, ☎ 021/6321–6888) is especially romantic. The Hilton's **Penthouse Bar** (✉ 250 Huashan Lu, ☎ 021/6248–0000) offers a quiet, elegant drink overlooking a great view of the city. The Grand Hyatt's luxurious and jazzy **Piano Bar** (✉ Jinmao Dasha, 177 Lujiazui Lu, Pudong, ☎ 021/5830–3338) has superb views. Cigar smoke and jazz cap the elite atmosphere at the Portman Ritz-Carlton's **Ritz-Carlton Bar** (✉ 1376 Nanjing Xilu, ☎ 021/6279–8888).

Karaoke

Karaoke TV (KTV) culture in China includes "KTV girls" who sing along with (male) guests and serve cognac and expensive snacks (at some establishments, KTV girls are also prostitutes). One of Shanghai's most popular KTV establishments is the giant **Cash Box** (✉ 457 Wulumuqi Lu, ☎ 021/6374–1111; ✉ 68 Zhejiang Nanlu, ☎ 021/6374–9909; ✉ 208 Chongqing Nanlu, inside Fuxing Park, ☎ 021/6358–3888). The **Golden Age** (✉ 918 Huaihai Zhonglu, ☎ 021/6415–8818) is a huge, mind-boggling operation with a wealthy clientele.

OUTDOOR ACTIVITIES AND SPORTS

Participant Sports

Golf

All clubs and driving ranges run on a membership basis, but most allow nonmembers to play when accompanied by a member. Some even welcome the public. Most clubs are outside the city, in the suburbs and outlying counties of Shanghai.

Grand Shanghai International Golf and Country Club (✉ Zhengyi Town, Kunshan City, Jiangsu Province 215347, ☎ 021/6210–3350) is an 18-hole championship course and driving range. **Shanghai Dianshan Lake Golf Club** (✉ Jiang Su, Kun Shan Shi, Ding Shan Hu Zen, ☎ 0520/748–1111), a 27-hole course on Dianshan Lake designed by Bobby J. Martin, includes a driving range. **Shanghai East Asia Golf Club** (✉ 135 Jianguo Xilu, ☎ 021/6433–1351) has a driving range. **Shanghai International Golf and Country Club** (✉ Zhu Jia Jiao, Qingpu County, ☎ 021/5972–8111), an 18-hole course, has a driving range and a three-hole practice course. **Shanghai Links Golf and Country Club** (✉ Tianxu Township, San Jia Bay, Pudong, ☎ 021/5882–2700), a Jack Nicklaus Signature–designed course, has nine holes so far. **Shanghai Riviera Golf Resort** (✉ Xiang Er, Nanxiang, Jiading County, ☎ 021/5912–8836) is an 18-hole course and driving range. **Sun Island International Club** (✉ Sun Island, Shenxiang, Qingpu County, ☎ 021/5983–0888), an 18-hole course designed by Nelson Wright Haworth, also has a driving range. **Tomson Pudong Golf Club** (✉ 1 Longdong Lu, Pudong, ☎ 021/5833–9999) is an 18-hole course with a driving range, designed by Shunsuke Kato.

Health Clubs, Swimming Pools, and Tennis Courts

Most of the best health clubs, gyms, and pools are at the Western hotels. Fees are charged for those who are not hotel guests. The **Garden Hotel** (✉ 58 Maoming Nanlu, ☎ 021/6415–1111) has an Olympic-size indoor pool. **Holiday Inn Crowne Plaza** (✉ 400 Panyu Lu, ☎ 021/6280–8888) has tennis and squash courts. The **Kerry Center** (✉ 1515 Nanjing Xilu, ☎ 021/6279–4625) has aerobics and weight rooms and a swimming pool. The **Portman Ritz-Carlton** (✉ 1376 Nanjing Xilu, ☎ 021/6279–8888) has a swimming pool and comprehensive aerobics and weight rooms, as well as tennis, squash, and racquetball courts. If you're not a hotel guest or a member, you can enter only with a member, at a fee of Y100. The impressive sports center and gym at the **Regal International East Asia Hotel** (✉ 516 Hengshan Lu, ☎ 021/6415–5588) has world-class tennis courts, a 25-meter indoor pool, squash courts, an aerobics room, a simulated golf-driving range, and a 12-lane bowling alley.

The **Shanghai Hilton** (✉ 250 Huashan Lu, ☎ 021/6248–0000) has a good health club. If you're looking for an outdoor pool, you can find a beautiful one at the **Shanghai International Convention Hotel** (✉ 2106 Hongqiao Lu, ☎ 021/6270–3388). The **Shanghai JC Mandarin** (✉ 1225 Nanjing Xilu, ☎ 021/6279–1888) has good tennis and squash courts. Some of the city's best tennis courts can be found at the **Xijiao Guest House** (✉ 1921 Hongqiao Lu, ☎ 021/6433–6643).

Outside the hotels, the American chain **Gold's Gym** (✉ 288 Tongren Lu, ☎ 021/6279–2000) has arrived in Shanghai, with comprehensive fitness classes and weight rooms, open 24 hours a day.

Yachting

Shanghai isn't known for its boating, but if you go out to Dianshan Lake, you can enjoy water sports in style at the **Regency International Yacht Club** (✉ 1860 Hongqiao Lu, ☎ 021/6242–3632), an elite, members-only club (that admits nonmembers for a fee) with a clubhouse, a pool, and food and beverage outlets. It provides boats, sailboats, jet skis, kayaks, surfboards, water skis, parasailing, and overnight accommodations in cabins right on the lake.

Spectator Sports

Professional league basketball is growing increasingly popular in Shanghai, with foreign-sponsored teams that include American professional players. The Hilton Basketball League plays an annual season from November through April at the **Luwan Gymnasium** (✉ 128 Jiaozhabang Lu; ☎ 021/6427–8673 IMG Sports Management). Games are occasionally played at the **Shanghai Gymnasium** (✉ 1111 Caoxi Beilu, ☎ 021/6473–0940).

The overwhelmingly grandiose, UFO-like **Shanghai Stadium** (✉ 666-800 Tianyaoqiao Lu, ☎ 021/6426–6888 ext. 8268) seats 80,000 spectators and holds athletic events regularly, especially soccer matches.

SHOPPING

Shanghai has more commercial goods available than any other place in China except Hong Kong. Shopping is an important part of the city's lifestyle, so most shops and department stores on the main shopping streets of Nanjing Lu and Huaihai Lu and in the Xujiahui area stay open from 10 until 10.

Antiques and Furniture

Antiques markets, shops, and furniture warehouses abound in Shanghai, as increasing numbers of foreigners, lured by news of great deals, flock to the city. Great deals, however, are gradually becoming only good deals. No matter what or where you buy, bargaining is an inescapable part of the sales ritual. Note that fake antiques are often hidden among real treasures. Also be aware of age: The majority of pieces date from the late Qing (1644–1911) dynasty; technically, only items dated after 1797 can be legally exported. When buying antique furniture, it helps to know age, of course, and also what kind of wood was used. Although the most commonly used was elm, a whole variety of wood can be found in Chinese antiques. All shops will renovate any pieces you buy.

The daily **Dongtai Lu Market** (⊠ Off Xizang Lu) offers goods in outside stalls lining the street. The **Fuyou Lu** (⊠ 457 Fangbang Zhonghu) Sunday market in the Old City, now open daily since it moved off the streets into a nondescript warehouse, still bustles as hawkers set up their goods in front of the warehouse. The **Haobao Building** (⊠ Yuyuan Garden, 265 Fangbang Lu, ☎ 021/6355–9999) houses a basement floor with 250 booths selling antiques. The government-owned **Shanghai Antique and Curio Store** (⊠ 218–226 Guangdong Lu, ☎ 021/6321–4697) has some good pieces; there's no bargaining, but you're sure not to get a fake, and the receipts are official.

Some **warehouses** to try are at 307 Shunchang Lu (☎ 021/6320–3812) and 1430 Hongqiao Lu and 1970 Hongqiao Lu, (☎ 021/6242–8734). The **Li Brothers** (⊠ 1220 Hongmei Lu, ☎ 021/6436–1500 ext. 195) run an antiques warehouse.

Arts and Crafts

Shanghai's artisans create pieces of traditional Chinese arts and crafts right before your eyes at the **Arts and Crafts Research Institute** (⊠ 79 Fenyang Lu, ☎ 021/6437–0509), where you can purchase everything from paper cuts to snuff bottles, from lanterns to engraved chopsticks. The state-owned **Friendship Store** (⊠ 40 Beijing Donglu, ☎ 021/6329–4600)—a chain for foreigners that started in major Chinese cities as a sign of friendship when China first opened to the outside world—has evolved into a six-story department store selling foreign and domestic goods; it welcomes everyone. It's touristy but a good quick source of Chinese arts and crafts (snuff bottles, jewelry, calligraphy, fans, vases, jade, lanterns, etc.) and silk. The state-owned **Shanghai Jingdezhen Porcelain Store** (⊠ 1175 Nanjing Xilu, ☎ 021/6253–3178) has a large selection of porcelain ware and other arts and crafts.

Carpets

Beijing has always been a better place to buy Chinese rugs, but Shanghai has a few shops that may give you a good deal. The **Carpet Factory** (⊠ 783 Honggu Lu, ☎ 021/6327–6539) has a wide selection of rugs. The **Shanghai Arts and Crafts Trading Company** (⊠ Shanghai Exhibition Centre, 1000 Yanan Xilu, ☎ 021/6279–0279 ext. 62222) has carpets as well as other handcrafts. You can watch artisans weave the carpets at **Shanghai Pine and Crane Carpet Store** (⊠ 410 Wukang Lu, ☎ 021/6431–7717). You can take a tour of the **Zhaohu Carpet Factory** (⊠ 98 Gubei Nanlu, ☎ 021/6436–1713) before you decide to buy.

Chinese Medicine

For Chinese medicines, try **Caitongde Drugstore** (✉ 320 Nanjing Donglu, ☎ 021/6350–4740). There are traditional cures and health products at **Jinsong Ginseng and Drug Store** (✉ 823 Huaihai Zhonglu, ☎ 021/6437–6700). For a selection of traditional as well as western medicines, go to **Shanghai No. 1 Dispensary** (✉ 616 Nanjing Donglu, ☎ 021/6473–9149).

Daily Necessities

Shanghai's modern supermarkets should be able to supply you with most personal-use and food products. **Watson's Drug Stores** (✉ Shanghai Center, 1376 Nanjing Xilu, ☎ 021/6279–8381; ✉ 789 Huaihai Zhonglu, ☎ 021/6474–4775) is the most reliable pharmacy. **The Market** (✉ Shanghai Center, 1376 Nanjing Xilu) can be counted on for products you can't find anywhere else in the city.

Fabrics and Tailors

For silk clothing, the **Friendship Store** (✉ 40 Beijing Donglu, ☎ 021/6329–4600) has a good selection. The **Golden Dragon Silk and Wool Company** (✉ 816 Huaihai Zhonglu, ☎ 021/6473–6691) has the best fabric selection in town. The **Jinling Silk Company** (✉ 363 Jinling Donglu, ☎ 021/6320–1449) has a wide choice. The **Shanghai Silk Commercial Company** (✉ 139 Tianping Lu, ☎ 021/6282– 5021) offers good quality.

Shanghai is home to many tailors who make clothing at reasonable prices. The most inexpensive are to be found at **Tailor Lane,** a small alley leading to Hunan Lodge on Wuyuan Lu (Nos. 52 and 72) near Maison Mode; bring in a garment to copy. **Ascot Chang** (✉ Dickson Center, 400 Chang Le Lu, Room 211, ☎ 021/6472–6888) makes quality suits, shirts, and other clothing. **Sakurai Yofuku** (✉ Friendship Shopping Center, 6 Zunyi Lu, ☎ 021/6270–0000) produces good clothing. The jovial and most reasonably priced **Taylor Lee** (✉ 2018 Huaihai Lu) specializes in men's and women's suits.

A few tailors specialize in making Chinese *qipaos* (cheongsams). The one at 258 Shimen Yi Lu does good work, as does the cute Shanghai Tang–like store on the west side of Maoming Lu south of Nanchang Lu. There are more cheongsam stores in a row on the south side of Changle Lu between Shaanxi Lu and Maoming Lu. **Long Feng** (✉ 942 Nanjing Xilu) makes cheongsams.

Outdoor Markets

Most of Shanghai's outdoor markets sell food and produce. The **Bird and Flower Market** (✉ Huangpi Lu between Nanjing Lu and Weihai Lu) gives a good slice of Shanghai life: you'll find hawkers selling pets such as fish, birds, turtles, cats, and frogs, and a whole range of plants, bonsai trees, orchids, and clay pots. You can find good, cheap Western clothing—seconds, irregulars, and knockoffs—at **Huating Market** (✉ Huating Lu between Changle Lu and Huaihai Zhonglu). The biggest market in Shanghai is the **Zhonghua Xin Lu Market** (✉ 100 Hengfeng Lu), which attracts private hawkers who sell everything under the sun.

Tea

The **Shanghai Huangshan Tea Company** (✉ 853 Huaihai Zhonglu, ☎ 021/6545–4919), with nine shops around Shanghai, sells a huge selection of China's best teas by weight; the higher the price, the better the tea. Beautiful Yixing pots are also for sale.

Western-Style Department Stores and Malls

In Shanghai, there are very few typical malls in the Western sense. At Isetan and the Orient, which are in large, department-store-like buildings, different brands are featured in different spaces. These places are organized like department stores, but the occupants are not all employed by one company. The 10-story **Babaiban Department Store** (⊠ 501 Zhangyang Lu, Pudong, ☎ 021/5830–1111) sells it all—clothes, household goods, shoes, accessories, cosmetics, sporting goods, arts and crafts, exercise equipment, stationery, audio/visual equipment, office equipment, even cars. The large, state-run **Hongqiao Friendship Shopping Centre** (⊠ 6 Zunyi Lu, ☎ 021/6270–0000) has everything, including Western finesse in merchandising—household items, gifts, cosmetics, clothing, furniture and audio/video equipment, and a grocery store and deli. The Japanese-run **Isetan** (⊠ 527 Huaihai Zhonglu, ☎ 021/6375–1111; ⊠ Westgate Mall, 1038 Nanjing Xilu, ☎ 021/6218–7878), one of the most fashionable in Shanghai, carries such brands as Lancôme, Clinique, Benetton, Esprit, and Episode.

The **Orient Shopping Center** (⊠ 8 Caoxi Beilu, ☎ 021/6407–1947) is the biggest and most comprehensive of three major department stores in Xujiahui. **Printemps** (⊠ 939–947 Huaihai Zhonglu, ☎ 021/6431–0118), the leader in French department stores, opened a beautiful branch, designed in the same style as the 130-year-old Printemps in Paris, in the center of Shanghai's old French Concession; most goods sold are at a price far too high for the ordinary Chinese person. The famous **Shanghai No. 1 Department Store** (⊠ 830 Nanjing Donglu, ☎ 021/6322–3344) is Shanghai's largest state-owned store and attracts masses of Chinese shoppers, especially on weekends; its seven floors have an amazing plethora of domestic items. **Westgate Mall** (⊠ 1039 Nanjing Xilu, ☎ 021/6218–6868) is a genuine mall in the Western sense.

SHANGHAI A TO Z

To research prices, get advice from other travelers, and book travel arrangements, visit www.fodors.com.

AIR TRAVEL
CARRIERS

Many offices of international carriers are represented in the Shanghai Center and Shanghai's western hotels. Major foreign airlines that serve Shanghai are: Air France, Asiana, British Airways, Dragon Airlines, Japan Airlines, Lufthansa, Malaysian Airlines, Northwest Airlines, Qantas, SAS, Singapore Airlines, Swiss Air, Thai Airlines, United Airlines, and Virgin Airlines.

Domestic carriers that connect international destinations to Shanghai include Air China and China Eastern Airlines.

A number of regional carriers serve Shanghai, but China Eastern Airlines is the main airline connecting it with other cities in China.

➤ AIRLINES AND CONTACTS: **Air France** (⊠ Shanghai Center, 1376 Nanjing Xilu, ☎ 021/6279–8600). **Air China** (⊠ 600 Huashan Lu, ☎ 021/6327–7888). **Asiana, British Airways, Dragon Airlines** (⊠ Shanghai Center, 1376 Nanjing Xilu, ☎ 021/6279–8099). **China Eastern Airlines** (⊠ 200 Yanan Xilu, ☎ 021/6247–5953 domestic; 021/6247–2255 international). **Japan Airlines** (⊠ Ruijin Dasha, 205 Maoming Nanlu, ☎ 021/6472–3000). **Lufthansa** (⊠ Shanghai Hilton, 250

Huashan Lu, ☎ 021/6248–1100). **Malaysian Airlines** (✉ Shanghai Center, 1376 Nanjing Xilu, ☎ 021/6279–8600). **Northwest Airlines** (✉ Shanghai Center, ☎ 021/6279–8088). **Qantas** (✉ Shanghai Center, ☎ 021/6279–8660). **SAS** (✉ Jin Jiang Hotel, 59 Maoming Nanlu, ☎ 021/6472–3131). **Singapore Airlines** (✉ Shanghai Center, ☎ 021/6279–8000). **Swiss Air** (✉ Shanghai Center, ☎ 021/6279–7381). **Thai Airlines** (✉ Shanghai Center, 1376 Nanjing Xilu, ☎ 021/6279–8600). **United Airlines** (✉ Shanghai Center, ☎ 021/6279–8009). **Virgin Airlines** (✉ 12 The Bund [Zhongshan Dong Yi Lu], ☎ 021/5353–4600).

AIRPORTS AND TRANSFERS

The ultramodern Pudong International Airport opened in 1999 across the river east of the city center. Many, though not all, international flights are routed through here. Hongqiao International Airport, in western Shanghai about 15 km (9 mi) from the city center, receives most domestic flights, especially those to smaller city airports. A taxi ride between the two airports will cost you about Y250 and take at least 45 minutes. Shuttle buses between the airports cost Y22 and take much longer.

➤ AIRPORT INFORMATION: **Hongqiao International Airport** (☎ 021/6268–8918 for 24-hr airport information). **Pudong International Airport** (☎ 021/3848–4500).

AIRPORT TRANSFERS

Depending on the traffic, the trip between Hongqiao International Airport and the city center can take anywhere from 30 minutes to an hour. Plenty of taxis are available at the lines right outside both the international and domestic terminals. Don't take a ride with drivers who tout their services at the terminal entrances; their cars don't have meters, and they'll try to charge you exorbitant rates. To get into the city, most drivers use the recently opened expressway that connects to the Ring Road. Expect to reimburse the driver for the toll.

Pudong Airport Shuttle Buses link the airport with a number of hotels and major sites in the city center; the trip takes about 1 hour and 20 minutes and costs about Y15–Y20, depending on the destination.

➤ TAXIS & SHUTTLES: **Pudong Airport Shuttle Buses** (☎ 021/6834–6912 or 021/6834–6645).

BOAT & FERRY TRAVEL

Boats running between Shanghai and Hong Kong (2½ days) and Shanghai and Osaka and Kobe in Japan dock at Waihongqiao Harbor. Tickets can be booked through CITS. The boat to Osaka leaves every Tuesday at noon arriving in Japan at noon on Thursday. The boat to Kobe leaves every Saturday at noon and arrives in Japan at 10 AM on Monday.

Most domestic boats leave from the Shiliupu Dock for such destinations on the Yangzi (Changjiang) River as Wuhan, Chongqing, Nanjing, Wuhu, and Jiujiang, as well as for such coastal cities as Guangzhou, Qingdao, Dalian, Ningbo, and Fuzhou. Boats for the outlying island of Putuoshan leave daily. All domestic tickets can be purchased at the foreigner ticket booth on the second floor of the Boat Ticket Booking Office, as well as at CITS. River passenger transport information can be obtained from the information line.

There's a wide range of boats, although most domestic boats are not luxurious. They do, however, offer different levels of berths, the most comfortable being first class.

➤ BOAT AND FERRY INFORMATION: **Boat Ticket Booking Office** (✉ 1 Jinling Donglu, ☎ 021/6328–0010). **CITS** (✉ Guangming Bldg., 2 Jinling Lu, ☎ 021/6321–7200). **Passenger information** (☎ 021/6326–1261). **Shiliupu Dock** (✉ Zhongshan Donglu just south of the Bund). **Waihongqiao Harbor** (✉ 1 Taiping Lu).

BUS TRAVEL TO AND FROM SHANGHAI

Getting to and from Shanghai by bus is usually less convenient than by train. A deluxe coach bus does run between Shanghai and Nanjing (3½ hours, Y60). Regular buses, most of which lack comfort, run from the long-distance bus station. These are acceptable for shorter distances, such as to Hangzhou and Suzhou. The ticket office for Suzhou tickets (Y50 round-trip) is at the eastern end of People's Square. Check out train fares and schedules before taking the bus.

➤ BUS INFORMATION: **Deluxe coach bus** (✉ 58 Laochongqing Nanlu, ☎ 021/6358–8089). **Long-distance bus station** (✉ Qiujiang Lu west of Henan Beilu).

BUS TRAVEL WITHIN SHANGHAI

Several Shanghai buses now have air-conditioning and plenty of seats. Most, though, are very old and uncomfortable, primarily standing-room only, and extremely inconvenient. Often you'll have to change buses several times to get where you're going. During busy traffic hours they're unbelievably crowded. On most buses the fare is Y1 for any stop on the line.

One exception to the above is the double-decker bus running down Huaihai Lu through the old French Concession. It's a pleasant ride, as these vehicles imported from Hong Kong and there are many seats. From the top deck, you have a great view over the compound walls of the beautiful old Shanghai buildings that line the thoroughfare. Fares on this bus line will run you a few yuan.

CAR TRAVEL

Although most travelers arrive in Shanghai by train or plane, the city is connected by some new highways to Suzhou and Nanjing, in the west, and Hangzhou, in the south. Travel by car is faster than ever before; you can hire a car and driver through your hotel's transportation service (due to government restrictions, it's virtually impossible for non-residents of China to drive).

CONSULATES

➤ AUSTRALIA: **Australian Consulate** (✉ 17 Fuxing Xilu, ☎ 021/6433–4604).

➤ CANADA: **Canadian Consulate** (✉ Shanghai Center, No. 604, 1376 Nanjing Xilu, ☎ 021/6279–8400).

➤ NEW ZEALAND: **New Zealand Consulate** (✉ Qihua Dasha, 15th floor, 1375 Huaihai Zhonglu, ☎ 021/6433–2230).

➤ UNITED KINGDOM: **British Consulate** (✉ Shanghai Center, No. 301, 1376 Nanjing Xilu, ☎ 021/6279–7650).

➤ UNITED STATES: **United States Consulate** (✉ 1469 Huaihai Zhonglu, ☎ 021/6433–6880 or 021/6433–3936; emergencies, ☎ 021/6433–6880 or 021/6433–3936).

EMERGENCIES

In a medical emergency don't call for an ambulance. The Shanghai Ambulance Service is merely a transport system. If possible, take a taxi; you'll get there faster.

AEA International 24-hour Alarm Center has information on emergency evacuations.

➤ EMERGENCY CONTACTS: **AEA International 24-hour Alarm Center** (☎ 021/6295–0099). **Ambulance Service** (☎ 120). **Fire** (☎ 119). **Police** (☎ 110).

➤ DENTISTS: **Shen Da Dental Clinic** (✉ 83–1 Taiyuan Lu, ☎ 021/6437–7987). **Sino-Canadian Shanghai Dental Center** (✉ 9th People's Hospital, 639 Zhizaoju Lu, 7th floor, ☎ 021/6313–3174).

➤ HOSPITALS: **Huadong Hospital** (✉ 221 Yanan Xilu, 2nd-floor Foreigners' Clinic, ☎ 021/6248–3180 ext. 6208). **Huashan Hospital** (✉ 12 Wulumuqi Lu, 19th-floor Foreigners' Clinic, ☎ 021/6248–3986). **New Pioneer Medical Center** (✉ 910 Hengshan Lu, 2nd floor, ☎ 6469–3898). **World Link Medical Center** (✉ Shanghai Center, 1376 Nanjing Xilu, ☎ 021/6279–7688).

ENGLISH-LANGUAGE MEDIA

Foreign Languages Bookstore carries maps, photography books, and nonfiction, literature, and poetry about China, as well as foreign periodicals and a good selection of English-language novels. Along Fuzhou Lu are spanking-new bookstores like Book City, which also have small selections of English books.

➤ BOOKSTORES: **Foreign Languages Bookstore** (✉ 390 Fuzhou Lu).

PASSPORTS AND VISAS

To extend your visa or ask for information about your status as an alien in China, stop by the Public Security Bureau Division for Aliens—it's open weekdays 9–11 and 2–5. The office is extremely bureaucratic, and the visa officers can be difficult. Most of them can speak English. It's usually no problem to get a month's extension on a tourist visa. You'll need to bring in your passport and your registration of temporary residency from the hotel at which you're staying. If you are trying to extend a business visa, you'll need the above items as well as a letter from the business that originally invited you to China saying it would like to extend your stay for work reasons. Rules are always changing, so you will probably need to go to the office at least twice to get all your papers in order.

➤ CONTACTS: **Public Security Bureau Division for Aliens** (✉ 333 Wusong Lu, ☎ 021/6357–6666).

SUBWAY TRAVEL

Still under construction, the Shanghai Metro is constantly being expanded. So far, two lines are functional, with a third in trial operation. Eight more lines are in the works, to be completed over the next two decades. With Shanghai's traffic-choked streets, it is by far the quickest way to get to most places. Line one travels between Xinzhuang and the Shanghai Railway Station, with stops in the French Concession at Changshu Lu, Shaanxi Lu, and Huangpi Lu. The second line, which will eventually link Hongqiao Airport with Pudong airport, currently runs from Zhongshan Gongyuan to Zhangjiang Station in Pudong.

The subway is not too crowded except at rush hour, and trains run regularly. Service begins just before 5 AM and ends at about 10:45, depending upon the line you are taking. Tickets cost Y2–Y5 with no charge for changing trains.

TAXIS

By far the most comfortable way to get around Shanghai, taxis are plentiful and easy to spot. Most are red Volkswagen Santanas, although they also come in white, green, yellow, and blue. They are all metered. You can spot the available ones by the red FOR HIRE sign in the window on the passenger side. The fare starts at Y12, with each km (½ mi) thereafter costing Y2. After 10 km (6 mi), the price per kilometer goes up to Y2.70. You also pay for waiting time in traffic.

Cabs can be hailed on the street or called for by phone. Most cab drivers don't speak English, so it's best to give them a piece of paper with your destination written in Chinese (keep a card or piece of paper with the name of your hotel on it handy for the return trip). Hotel doormen can also help you tell the driver where you're going. It's a good idea to study a map and have some idea where you are, as many drivers will take you for a ride—a much longer one—if they think they can get away with it.

➤ TAXI COMPANIES: **Dazhong Taxi Company** (☏ 021/6258–1688). **Friendship Taxi Company** (☏ 021/6258–3484). **Shanghai Taxi Company** (☏ 021/6258–0000).

TELEPHONES

Local directory assistance, ☏ 114 (Shanghai). Domestic directory assistance, ☏ 116 (other Chinese cities). Time, ☏ 117. Weather, ☏ 121.

TOURS

Guided bus tours of the city can be booked through CITS and are led in several languages.

Huangpu River Cruises 3½-hour trips (Y45–Y100) up and down the Huangpu River between Wusong and the Bund, include buffet and depart from the Bund at Jinling Lu at 2 PM and 3:30 PM. You'll see barges, bridges, and factories, but not much scenery; night-time cruises are better, as you get great views of the Bund beautifully floodlit. One-hour cruises (Y30) from the Bund between the Nanpu and Yangpu bridges leave at 10:45 AM and 4:15 PM. The evening cruise leaves at 7 PM. You can purchase all tickets at the dock.

Regal China Huangpu River Cruises, China's only foreign-owned and -managed cruise line, runs high-class dinner cruises (Y250) that blend views of the Bund and the Nanpu and Yangpu bridges with a comfortable sit-down buffet or Chinese à la carte dinner aboard a German-made 426-ft-long river liner. Boats leave at 7:30 PM and dock at 10:30 PM. The line also runs cruises (Y579–Y1240) to Wusong—the point where the Huangpu meets the Yangzi River—docking overnight before returning to Shanghai the next morning; dinner and breakfast are served.

For Yangzi River cruises to the Three Gorges from Shanghai, CITS handles bookings, as does Regal China Cruises.

➤ FEES AND SCHEDULES: **CITS** (✉ Guangming Bldg., 2 Jinling Lu, ☏ 021/6321–7200). **Huangpu River Cruises** (✉ 239 Zhongshan Dong Er Lu, ☏ 021/6374– 4461). **Regal China Huangpu River Cruises** (✉ 108 Huangpu Lu, ☏ 021/6306–9801, FAX 021/6306–9902).

TRAIN TRAVEL

Shanghai is connected to many destinations in China by direct train. The Shanghai Railway Station 24-hr train information) is in the northern part of the city. Several trains a day run to Suzhou, Hangzhou, Nanjing, and other nearby destinations. The best train to catch to Beijing is the overnight express that leaves around 7 PM and arrives in Beijing the next morning. An express train also runs to Hong Kong.

You can buy train tickets at CITS, but a service fee is charged. Same-day, next-day, and sometimes third-day tickets can also be easily purchased at the ticket office in the Longmen Hotel, on the western side of the train station.

➤ TRAIN INFORMATION: **Shanghai Railway Station** (✉ 303 Moling Lu, ☎ 021/6317–9090). **Ticket office** (✉ 777 Hengfeng Lu, ☎ 021/6317–0000).

TRAVEL AGENCIES

➤ LOCAL AGENT REFERRALS: **American Express** (✉ Shanghai Center, 1376 Nanjing Xilu, ☎ 021/6279–8600). **China International Travel Service (CITS;** ✉ Guangming Bldg., 2 Jinling Lu, ☎ 021/6321–7200). **Evrokantakt** (✉ 9T Tseng Chow Commercial Mansion, 1590 Yanan Xilu, ☎ 021/6280–9579). **Harvest Travel Services** (✉ 16–A6 Harvest Bldg., 585 Longhua Xilu, ☎ 021/6469–1860). **IRS International Travel Agency** (☎ 021/6486–0681 or 021/6486–0682). **Jebsen and Co. Ltd.** (✉ 16 Henan Lu, ☎ 021/6355–4001).

VISITOR INFORMATION

➤ COMMUNITY ORGANIZATIONS: **American Chamber of Commerce** (☎ 021/6279–7119). **Australia Chamber of Commerce** (☎ 021/6248–8301). **British Chamber of Commerce** (☎ 021/6218–5022). **Canadian Business Forum** (☎ 021/6279–8400). **Hong Kong Chamber of Commerce** (☎ 021/5306–9533). **Jewish Community of Shanghai** (☎ 021/6289–9903).

➤ TOURIST INFORMATION: **Shanghai Tourist Information Services** (✉ Hongqiao Airport, ☎ 021/6268–7788 ext. 6750; ✉ People's Square Metro Station, ☎ 021/6438–1693; ✉ Yuyuan Commercial Building, ☎ 021/6355–4909). **Spring Travel Service,** ☎ 021/6252–0000 ext. 0). **Tourist Hotline** (☎ 021/6439–0630).

7 EASTERN CHINA

WATERWAYS, GARDENS, WORKERS' MOVEMENTS, HIP CITIES

Imperial riches, peasant revolts, and some of China's first experiments with market economics—this heavily populated region has had intimate experience with the events that have shaped modern China. Rich in cultural capital, it is home to some of China's oldest and most renowned landmarks. The scenic mountain ranges that crisscross these provinces have inspired artists and provided refuge for revolutionaries.

By Anya
Bernstein and
Christopher
Knowles

Updated by
Paul Davidson

THE PROVINCES THAT MAKE UP the eastern section of the country present a microcosm of the forces at play in contemporary China. Here the rich legacy of the past and the challenges and aspirations for China's future combine in a present that is dizzying in its variation and speed of transformation. Jiangsu, Zhejiang, and Fujian—some of the most affluent provinces in China, well known for their fine silks, handicrafts, and teas—abut the poorer interior provinces of Anhui and Jiangxi, which are better known for natural beauty, material hardships, peasant revolts, and the birth of Mao's Communist forces. In the large cities of this region ancient temples are attracting new believers while new department stores stocked with the latest consumer goods vie with local markets for customers. China's nouveaux riches fill hip karaoke bars while migrant workers try to make ends meet in China's growing market economy.

In the northeast Jiangsu and Zhejiang harbor some of China's best-known landmarks. Described by Marco Polo as the finest and noblest city in the world, Hangzhou is famous for Xihu, or West Lake, which has inspired poets, painters, and other artists for more than 700 years. The largest artificial waterway in the world, the Grand Canal, extending from Beijing to Hangzhou, secured Hangzhou's importance as an early commercial and cultural center. Nearby Suzhou is famous for its many well-preserved gardens. Originally commissioned by wealthy intellectuals, these beautifully designed creations demonstrate a cultivated sense of artistic design as well as respect for sublime nature. Suzhou has easily accessible narrow streets and alleys—many retaining the flavor of an earlier China—ideal for afternoon strolls. Nanjing, an imperial capital during the Ming dynasty until 1421 and later twice the national capital of the Republic of China, is rich in cultural heritage and national monuments. On the slopes of Zijinshan (Purple and Gold Mountain) the tomb of the founder of the Ming dynasty is neighbor to the tomb of Sun Yat-sen, who led the revolution that toppled the dynastic system.

Since the Southern Song dynasty (1127–1279), numbers of Fujianese have emigrated around Southeast Asia; as a result Fujian province has strong historic ties with overseas Chinese. In 1979 Fujian was allowed to form the first special economic zone (SEZ)—a testing ground for capitalist market-economy ideas—at Xiamen. Today Xiamen is a pleasant city with a vibrant economy. Its numerous seafood restaurants appeal to both the palate and the pocketbook. The former colonial settlement on the peaceful, traffic-free island of Gulangyu is good for walking. The Wuyi Mountain Range, in the north of the province, has peaks that reach 6,000 ft. Protected as a nature preserve, these mountains are spectacular to look at and to hike.

Classic scenery can also be found at Huangshan, one of China's traditional Five Famous Mountains, in Anhui province. The mountain's peaks rising from the mist have inspired whole schools of Chinese painting. The rest of Anhui is better known for harshness—many of its streams and rivers flood seasonally, which in the past led to periodic peasant uprisings against unconcerned local governments. Although much of the flooding has been controlled by irrigation projects implemented since 1949, the province is still one of the least developed in all of China.

A reputation for hardship spills over into Jiangxi, the province rimmed by hills and mountains directly to the south. Here in the early 1930s Mao Zedong and Zhu De organized peasants, forming their own independent government. In 1933 Jiangxi witnessed violent struggles between the Nationalists and the Communists. The famous Long March began from the revolutionary stronghold at Jinggangshan. Jiangxi is also well known for its porcelain industry, which dates from the 11th century.

Pleasures and Pastimes

Cruises

You can travel on the Grand Canal between the old-style cities of Hangzhou and Suzhou. Shorter excursions down the Min River in Fuzhou and around West Lake offer a restful change of pace from these cities. Hotel travel desks and CITS, as well as other private travel agencies, can arrange tickets.

Dining

Jiangsu, Anhui, Zhejiang, Fujian, and Jiangxi cover a lot of ground, culinarily. Although the same basic dishes—cooked with greater or lesser success—can be found at cheap sit-down eateries pretty much everywhere in China, both the more serious specialty restaurants and the ubiquitous street foods here are different from those elsewhere in the country. The emphasis is on fish; the region is rich in water, with two major rivers and an ocean coast, as well as numerous lakes. Another tendency, especially in the easternmost cities, is a liberal use of oil.

The cuisine of Fujian is considered by some to have its own characteristics and by others to form part of the Eastern tradition, one of the four major styles of Chinese cooking. Spare ribs are a specialty, as are soups and stews using a soy and rice-wine stock. The coastal cities of Fujian offer a wonderful range of seafood, including shark's fin soup, a great delicacy usually served at the beginning of the meal rather than at the end, which otherwise is the usual custom with soups. Other dishes to look for are river eel with leeks, fried jumbo prawns, drunken chicken (chicken soused in Shaoxing wine), and steamed crab. Jiangxi, never noted for its cooking, has tended to absorb the traditions of the provinces that surround it. However, there are a few specialties to try— five-flower pork (slices of pork cooked in spice), sautéed frog, and soy-braised chicken. The cuisine of Jiangsu tends to be salty and sweet with specialties ranging from salty duck dishes to braised pork in a preserved bean-curd sauce. The cooking of Anhui is well-known for stewed or braised dishes that use thick sauces and heavy oils. Zhejiang dishes, in contrast, are more often steamed or roasted and have a more subtle salty flavor; specialties include yellow croaker with Chinese cabbage, sea eel, and stewed chicken.

Dress is usually casual by Western standards in even the more upscale places, but tends to be more formal in the hotel restaurants, especially the Western sections. Reservations are almost never necessary; in fact, many restaurants are loath to give out their phone numbers at all.

CATEGORY	COST*
$$$$	over Y200
$$$	Y125–Y200
$$	Y85–Y125
$	under Y85

*per person for a main course at dinner

Hiking

The mountain ranges of the region offer everything from leisurely one- or two-hour hikes to longer overnight excursions. Some mountains are sacred religious sites, while others are more historically significant or set aside as nature preserves. Depending on the day, time of year, and location, you may find yourself in the company of any number of Chinese tourists out in small groups. Most hikes are on well-worn paths. On all of them you are certain to happen upon temples, small shrines, or pavilions honoring famous individuals or beliefs. Lushan, in Jiangxi, Huangshan, in Anhui, and Gushan, in Fuzhou, are suitable for shorter hikes. Wuyishan Nature Preserve, in Fujian, and the area around Jing-gangshan, in Jiangxi, are excellent for longer excursions. Lodging and dining in these areas tend toward the simple and basic; the views, the fresh air, and the peaceful surroundings make up for that.

Lodging

The chief cities of the region have an impressive array of joint-venture or upscale domestic hotels. Many are comfortable, well-appointed, and well-managed establishments with facilities and staff training based on those of Western hotels of the same caliber. Other hotels are simpler, sometimes lagging in the customer service department. What's often missing in city hotels, though, is charm. Don't expect the decoration or the architecture to be enchanting in the metropolises. Reservations are strongly advised at major tourist spots like Huangshan at any time of year. Hangzhou and Suzhou are also popular tourist destinations in spring and autumn; you should make reservations in both cities during these seasons.

CATEGORY	COST*
$$$$	over Y1,200
$$$	Y700–Y1,200
$$	Y350–Y700
$	under Y350

*All prices are for a standard double room with bath, excluding service charge.

Nightlife

Every city in the region has begun to show indications of a budding nightlife. The mainstay in the local nightlife is the karaoke bar where, for a fee, groups of Chinese gather in small rooms to drink and sing pop songs. These karaoke centers range from the ultraexpensive to the cheap and sleazy—many have hostesses hanging around to accompany the would-be pop vocalists out on their one night of fame. Western-style bars, pubs, and dance clubs have started springing up, and nearly every large city has one or two that are frequented by young Chinese urban professionals and the occasional expatriate escaping his or her hotel. These bars tend to open and close down quite frequently, either due to lack of steady clientele or the arrival of the urban planners' wrecking ball.

Outdoor markets provide a more common form of nighttime entertainment for the majority of Chinese, for whom "nightlife" is still an unattainable extravagance. These markets provide an opportunity to gather for no other reason than to be social. The markets in Nanjing, Suzhou, and Hangzhou are well known for their variety of products, ranging from silk scarves and clothing to ceramic teapots to Cultural Revolution memorabilia. Xiamen, Jiangxi, and Hefei as well as smaller towns all have some version of the night market, especially in summer when urban residents take to the streets to escape their cramped, hot rooms. Street food, also a main part of these markets, is a cuisine unto itself.

Scenery

The provinces of eastern China afford some spectacular scenery. In Anhui is Huangshan, one of China's five most revered mountains. In northwest Fujian is Wuyishan, a land of 36 tree-clad mountains, skirted by the stream known as Nine Bend Creek. Jiangxi province has the Lushan

National Park, a historically important area designated as a World Heritage Site by UNESCO, as well as the relatively remote Jinggang Shan.

Shopping

In the east, silk rules. Suzhou and Nanjing, as well as Hangzhou, all have plentiful and well-priced silk products from scarves and skirts to Mao-style jackets and bolts of cloth that you can take to any number of tailors. Many of these wares are easily available at small shops around town and in the nightly markets. In the south and east the items of choice are porcelain and carvings. The kilns of Jingdezhen, in Jiangxi, have been churning out pottery since the 11th century; today these wares can be found stocking the shelves in Nanchang and other towns. In Fujian Shaoshan stone carvings and Huian carvings are the things to keep an eye out for. All over these areas tea and tea paraphernalia are good buys. Friendship stores sell local arts products as well as some antiques, and major tourist sites are surrounded by peddlers selling souvenirs. Small tradespeople occupying endless stands sell handmade trinkets that are sometimes quite precious. Bargaining is de rigueur in the outdoor markets, while prices are taken somewhat more seriously inside stores.

Exploring Eastern China

In the wealthy large cities of the coastal provinces of Jiangsu, Zhejiang, and Fujian, the dynamic economic growth of reform-era China is evident in both the vast amounts of consumer goods spilling out of stores and street stalls and in a growing cosmopolitan atmosphere. This growth has also led to unemployment and to pollution that occasionally lends the skies a gritty haze. The relatively underdeveloped inland provinces of Jiangxi and Anhui are much more rugged and rural. These are perhaps the best places to get a sense of what much of China was like during imperial—as well as revolutionary—China.

Great Itineraries

Given the vast geographical, cultural, and economic differences of this region, an ideal itinerary would mix visits to the famous tourist cities with one or two excursions to smaller inland or semirural areas. Transportation has improved in recent years and is becoming more and more dependable. It is, however, not always up to Western expectations of speed, cleanliness, or convenient access. In China getting there is definitely part of the tour; as you move from place to place, you get valuable glimpses into life off the beaten path. Too much concern with "getting there" will lead to unnecessary frustrations when the inevitable delay does occur.

Numbers in the text correspond to numbers in the margin and on the Eastern China, Nanjing, Suzhou, and Fuzhou maps.

IF YOU HAVE 3 DAYS

If you're flying into Shanghai or **Nanjing,** trains leave every couple of hours to take you into **Suzhou** for a day of wandering, exploring gardens, and shopping for silk, Suzhou's specialty. An overnight ferry down the Grand Canal gets into **Hangzhou** in the morning, and you can spend a day here exploring. You can take a sleeper train back up to Nanjing if you want a day on the town there, or stay another day in Hangzhou to walk in the outlying areas before returning to Shanghai.

IF YOU HAVE 5 DAYS

For a look at the scenery that has inspired Chinese art, follow first the three-day itinerary to **Hangzhou,** but catch a bus to **Huangshan** instead of returning eastward. The daylong trip passes through enthralling countryside as you wind around mountain curves past villages and farms.

After a day of mountain climbing, you can fly from Tunxi back to Shanghai. To journey farther off the beaten path, first follow the three-day itinerary to **Hangzhou,** then catch a plane to **Xiamen** and spend an afternoon wandering through the peaceful streets of Gulangyu as you enjoy the colonial architecture. If there is time, you should check out some other attractions on the mainland before settling down to a fresh seafood dinner either on Gulangyu or in town. The following day, arrange a day trip to either **Quanzhou, Chongwu,** or **Meizhou,** or simply continue on to **Fuzhou** in order to go to **Wuyishan.** Fly back to Shanghai either in the evening or the next morning.

IF YOU HAVE 8 OR MORE DAYS

Flying into **Nanjing,** spend a day exploring the city—Zijinshan is particularly pleasant, and Fuzimiao is a good evening hangout spot. Catch a morning train or bus into **Zhenjiang** the next day. The trip takes only an hour, so you will have plenty of time to stroll around this small city before heading off that evening or the next morning to **Wuxi.** Then go to **Suzhou** and the gardens, taking the overnight Grand Canal ferry down to **Hangzhou** before continuing on to **Huangshan** for a couple of days of climbing.

For a smorgasbord of ancient and revolutionary China, as well as a taste of the urban and the rural, start by spending a few days in **Xiamen,** followed by a side trip to spend an evening in **Chongwu.** Then catch an overnight train from Xiamen to **Nanchang** to check out the revolutionary sights and shop at the markets near Tengwang Pavilion. If you have time, you can easily take a day trip to **Lushan** or the kilns at **Jingdezhen.** From Nanchang fly or take a train to **Hangzhou** before returning to Shanghai.

When to Tour Eastern China

The most ideal time to travel around the region is in the spring, between April and late May, when the worst of winter is past and the heat is not yet unbearable. Nanjing is one of China's three summer furnaces; nevertheless, the region is surprisingly damp and cold in the winter. Spring is also ideal because the colors of the plants and flowers throughout the region are at their peak.

Mid-September to mid-October is also a comfortable time to travel. Unfortunately this is the peak of the tourist season, when cities such as Suzhou and Hangzhou experience their heaviest load of visitors.

Fujian has pleasant weather most of the year, though it is noted for its heavy rains that give the landscape its tropical flavor. To avoid most of the rains, visit in early spring or late autumn.

JIANGSU

One of China's richest provinces and home to some of its most arable land, Jiangsu has long been an economic and political center. It was raised to province status under the Ming dynasty (1368–1644), which brought the capital to Nanjing for a time before moving it back north to Beijing. Nanjing and Jiangsu retained their nationwide importance, owing partly to the Grand Canal, which cuts southward through the province. After the mid-19th-century Opium Wars, which saw British armies in the Yangzi Delta, the stretch between Nanjing and the sea was built up into the major metropolitan area of Shanghai and the smaller Wuxi. The Japanese occupation from 1937 to 1945 caused serious damage in the province, but restoration has taken place.

Jiangsu has a wealthy cultural heritage. The Sun Yat-sen Memorial in Nanjing is a national pilgrimage goal, while the gardens of Suzhou are

Eastern China

Bohai

Lianyungang

JIANGSU

Shangqiu

Xuzhou

HENAN

Huaiyin

Yancheng

Suzhou

Dongtai

Bengbu

Nanjing **1** **13**

Zhenjiang **14**

Nantong

Huai He

Hefei **26**

Wuxi **15**

Tai Hu

Shanghai

SHANGHAI SHI

Chang Jiang Yangzi R.

Suzhou **16**—**25**

Dabie Shan

A N H U I

Hangzhou **28**

Huangshan **27**

Lushan **45**

Jingdezhen

Poyang Hu

Nanchang **43**

Shangrao

ZHEJIANG

Gan Jiang

Yichun

Linchuan

38

Pinxiang

Wuyi Shan
Fengjinqu

Fuzhou **29**—**36**

JIANGXI

Nanping

Min Jiang

46 Jinggangshan

F U J I A N

Meizhou **37**

41 Chongwu

Longyang

40 Quanzhou

Yongding **42**

Xiamen **39**

Zhangzhou

Chinmen Tao
TAIWAN

T A I W A N

GUANGDONG

Han Jiang

Penghu Islands
(Pescadores)
TAIWAN

0   100 miles

0   150 km

Shantou

Chadyang

a showcase of Chinese artistry and tradition. Autumn tends to be warm and dry here, with ideal walking temperatures; spring can be rainy and windy, but it also brings the blooms to Nanjing's Plum Blossom Hill and Zhenjiang's Nanshan Park. Summers are oppressively hot and humid; winters are bearable though cold and damp.

Nanjing

2½ hours west of Shanghai by "tourist train," 4½ hours by normal trains.

The city's name, which means "southern capital," was originally used by the first Ming emperor, who relocated the imperial court here in 1356. Although his son returned the capital to Beijing, Nanjing has retained a special place in Chinese history. The Taiping Rebellion started here in 1851 and went on to conquer a large portion of southern China with its promises of egalitarianism, morality, and wealth— not to mention its significant armies. The Ming tombs on Zijinshan Hill are a reminder of the city's glorious dynastic past, as the Sun Yat- sen mausoleum, nearby, is a reminder of more recent honors. Sun Yat- sen harked back to the indigenous Ming dynasty in his determination that Nanjing should be the capital of the new Republic, not Beijing, which had housed the non-Chinese Qing dynasty until 1912. The city served as the republican capital from 1927 to 1937, a time known as the "Nanjing decade," and again as the Guomindang (GMD; Na- tionalist Party) capital during the civil war, from 1945 to 1949.

Nanjing was also the scene of some of the first unequal treaties, which forcibly opened Chinese ports to the West after the Opium Wars. The treaties and the European encroachment on Chinese sovereignty have been a sore point for more than 100 years. In the 1930s Japan occu- pied the area. The hundreds of thousands of civilians killed during the atrocities committed in what became known as the "Rape of Nanjing" in 1937, are commemorated at the Nanjing Massacre Memorial.

Sections and some gates of the 33-km (20-mi) Ming wall built around Nanjing in the 14th century still stand. The city is composed of a se- ries of small neighborhoods with winding streets, separated by major thoroughfares. You may want to explore one or two by simply taking a turn down an alleyway. However, be careful: although there's very little physical danger for foreigners walking around in daytime, it's quite easy to get lost on these small, twisting, unmarked lanes.

The rural areas under Nanjing's administrative control supply the city with most of its food. Vegetables, fresh meat, and fish fill huge, lively markets held daily in every neighborhood. Nanjing University, a quiet, green, tastefully constructed campus, now ranks as China's number- two educational institution, second only to Beijing University.

A Good Walk

The best place for a long stroll in Nanjing actually lies just outside the city proper, on **Zijinshan** (Purple Mountain). People come to this de- lightful area to escape the noise and traffic of the city, particularly in spring and autumn. A wealth of historic sites dots the mountain. Take a taxi to Mingling Lu, or take Bus 20 to its penultimate stop, ending up by **Meihuashan** and the **Zhongshan Zhiwuyuan** ① (Plum Blossom Hill and Middle Mountain Botanical Gardens), both just east of the road. After a stroll on the hill and in the gardens, head west again to the **Ming Xiaoling** ②, where the founder of the Ming dynasty is buried. Continue on uphill. In warm weather shuttle buses run to **Zhongshan Ling** ③, Sun Yat-sen's mausoleum. Also in warm weather, a cable car plies up the mountain. Otherwise, keep on going west to **Linggu Si** and **Linggu Ta** ④ (Spirit Valley Temple and Pagoda). Catch the shuttle back and walk or ride south along Lingyuan Lu to stop by the **Meiling Gong** ⑤, Chiang Kai-shek's weekend house.

A bit farther south, just outside the Zijinshan scenic area, you reach the city wall at the **Zhonghua Men** ⑥. Not far down the street is **Yuhua Tai Lieshi Lingyuan** ⑦ (The Rain Flower Terrace and Martyrs Memorial), a memorial dedicated to Communist martyrs. Backtrack on Zhongshan Nanlu and turn right on Jiankang Lu. A short way down the street is **Fuzimiao** ⑧, a Confucian temple sitting in the midst of a shopping and entertainment district. Northward just west of Zhongshan Lu is the **Gulou** ⑨ (Drum Tower). Farther north, east of Zhongshan Lu, you can take in the lakes of **Xuanwu Hu Gongyuan** ⑩. Grab the No. 8 bus and take it to it final stop, on the bank of the Yangzi, where the lovely **Yanzi Ji** ⑪ (Sparrow's Rock) overlooks the river. From Yanzi Ji, a taxi ride will take you across the **Changjiang Daqiao** ⑫ (Yangzi River Bridge), to the northwest of the city. Take a bus or cab across the Qinhuai River southwest of the city to visit the **Datusha Jinianguan** ⑬, commemorating those killed during the Japanese occupation of the city.

The above walk should be done over two days. An entire day alone is ideal for exploring the Purple Mountain Scenic Area.

Sights to See

⑫ **Changjiang Daqiao** (Yangzi River Bridge). The second bridge ever to span the Yangzi, it was the first built without foreign aid (after relations between China and the Soviet Union soured). Completed in 1968 at the height of the Cultural Revolution, the bridge provided the first direct rail link across the Yangzi. The Great Bridge Park lies on the south side—that is, the Nanjing side—and you can take an elevator from here up to a small museum. ✉ *Northwest side of city.* ✇ *Free; Y7 for elevator.*

⑬ **Datusha Jinianguan** (Nanjing Massacre Memorial). In the winter of 1937, Japanese forces occupied Nanjing and, in the space of a few days, thousands of Chinese were killed in the chaos, which became commonly known as the "Rape of Nanjing." This monument commemorates the victims, many of whom were buried in a mass grave on this site. Be advised, however: this is not for the squeamish. Skeletons have been exhumed from the "Grave of Ten Thousand" and are displayed with gruesomely detailed explanations as to how each victim lost his or her life. The memorial also displays artifacts from the Sino-Japanese reconciliation after World War II, which ended the conflict between the two countries on a less strident, more hopeful note. ✉ *195 Chating Dongjie (easily reached on the No. 7 bus),* ☎ *025/650–1033.* ✇ *Y8.* ☉ *Daily 8:30–5.*

⑧ **Fuzimiao** (Confucian Temple). The traditional-style temple on the banks of the Qin Huai, a tributary of the Yangzi, sits in the midst of the city's busiest shopping and entertainment district. A replica of the original statue of Confucius has been moved to the side of the temple. Here the master presides over children in bumper cars and arcades, and shopkeepers selling everything imaginable. The area becomes so crowded at night that it's difficult to move. ✉ *Zhongshan Lu and Jiankang Lu.* ✇ *Y6.*

⑨ **Gulou** (Drum Tower). The traditional center of ancient Chinese cities, the tower housed the drums used to signal events to the populace, from the changing of the guard to an enemy attack or a fire. Nanjing's tower, constructed in 1382, still has a certain centrality although it now holds only one drum. Its first floor is an exhibition hall for local art. ✉ *Dafang Kiang 1,* ☎ *025/663–1059.* ✇ *Y2.* ☉ *Daily 8 AM–11 PM.*

Nanjing

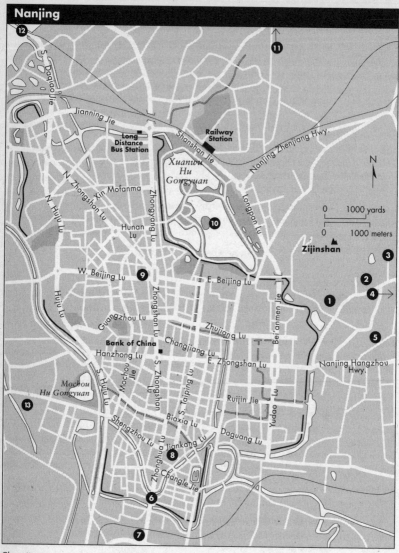

Long Distance Bus Station

Railway Station

Jianning Jie

S. Daqiao Jie

Shanshan Jie

Nanjing Zhenjiang Hwy.

Xuanwu Hu Gongyuan

Xin Mofanma

N. Zhongshan Lu

N. Huju Lu

Hunan Lu

Zhongyang Lu

Longpan Lu

N

Zijinshan

0   1000 yards

0   1000 meters

W. Beijing Lu

E. Beijing Lu

Huju Lu

Zhongshan Lu

Guangzhou Lu

Zhujiang Lu

Changjiang Lu

Bei'anmen Jie

Bank of China

Hanzhong Lu

Mochou Jie

S. Huju Lu

S. Zhongshan Lu

E. Zhongshan Lu

Mochou Hu Gongyuan

S. Taiping Lu

Ruijin Jie

Yudao Lu

Nanjing Hangzhou Hwy.

Shengzhou Lu

Biaxia Lu

Daguang Lu

Zhonghua Lu

Jiankang Lu

Changle Jie

★ ❹ **Linggu Si and Linggu Ta** (Spirit Valley Temple and Pagoda). Away from the hordes at Sun Yat-sen's mausoleum and set against forested hills, this is the best and most worthwhile sight in the Purple Mountain Scenic Area. The beautiful 14th-century Wuliang Dian (Beamless Hall)—made entirely of brick—leads you into the Linggu Temple, which has a hall with relics and altars dedicated to Xuan Zang, the monk who brought Buddhist scriptures back from India. (A piece of the monk's skull is on display as well.) At the rear of the park stands the 200-ft tall Linggu Pagoda, constructed in 1929. Climb the spiral staircase for spectacular views of Purple Mountain. ✉ *Ta Lu, eastern suburbs,* ☎ *025/444–6111.* 🚍 *Y10, Y3 more for the temple.* ☉ *Daily 8:30–5.*

❶ **Meihuashan and Zhongshan Zhiwuyuan** (Plum Blossom Hill and Middle Mountain [Sun Yat-sen] Botanical Gardens). Plum Hill is a favorite early spring outing for Nanjing residents, who delight in the myriad blossoms on the rolling hill. Several pavilions and running streams line the gardens' paths. Around the hill is the botanical garden, with more than 300 species of plants along the walkways. ✉ *Taiping Men Lu in the Zhongshan Scenic Area, eastern suburbs.* 🚍 *Y10 (Y20 in spring)).* ☉ *Daily 7:30–5.*

❺ **Meiling Gong** (Meiling Palace). Chiang Kai-shek built this house as a vacation and weekend retreat for himself and his wife, Song Meiling, who was a sister of Sun Yat-sen's wife, Song Ching-ling. The house, with its photographs, portraits, and historical blurbs, is mostly interesting as an artifact of modern Chinese views of this period's history. Although it is supposedly furnished with original furniture, it's well known that the place was looted several times over. ✉ *Lingyuan Lu, eastern suburbs.* 🚍 *Y6.* ☉ *Daily 8:30–5.*

❷ **Ming Xiaoling** (Ming Tomb). Zhu Yangzhang—the Emperor Hong Wu, founder of the Ming dynasty—ordered 100,000 men to construct this elaborate burial ground. When it was finally completed 30 years later in 1381 it was large enough to serve as the resting place for both the Emperor, who died in 1398, and the Empress, Ma Huanghou, who preceded him in death. The Emperor's tomb itself has been left unexcavated. Unfortunately, many of the buildings that once stood in the Ming Xiaoling environs were destroyed by fires. However, the highest edifice, the Ming Tower, survives mostly intact and open to visitors.

Down the road, about a quarter mile from the Ming Tomb ticket booth, lies **Shendao,** or the Divine Path. Animal figures—camels, lions, horses—carved out of huge stones line the path. The stones are real thing, dating from the Ming dynasty. Although a bus runs between the sights, walking from the Ming Tomb to the Divine Path (or the reverse) will give you idea of how big the place actually is. ✉ *Mingling Lu, eastern suburbs.* 🚍 *Y10 Ming Xiaoling; Y10 Shendao.* ☉ *Daily 8:30–5.*

❿ **Xuanwu Hu Gongyuan** (Xuanwu Lake Park). A favorite local getaway, this area offers more lake than park: the grounds are covered by three enormous bodies of water whose banks are set with benches along paths. There are better places in Nanjing to laze away the day, but for some reason the park remains a popular spot. Its outer rim goes along the old city wall on the south and west sides and it may be more interesting wandering through some of the old alleyways than the park itself. ✉ *Off Hunan Lu eastbound or north of Beijing Donglu.* 🚍 *Y10.* ☉ *Daily 8–8.*

⓫ **Yanzi Ji** (Sparrow's Rock). North of the city, overlooking the Yangzi, this small park is worth the extra effort it takes to get here. Paths wind up the hill to several lookout points for what may be Nanjing's best—and most pleasant—view of this great river. The park's name comes from the massive boulder that beetles over the water; it supposedly resembles a sparrow (you decide). A stone, appropriately named "Wine Barrel Rock," at the park's highest point, commemorates the visit of the Tang poet Li Bai who got drunk on the rock and wrote verse. *North of the city on the Yangzi; No. 8 bus to the last stop.* ✉ *Y6.* ⊙ *Daily 7:30–6.*

❼ Yuhua Tai Lieshi Lingyuan (The Rain Flower Terrace and Martyrs Memorial). The terrace gets its name from the legend of Yunzhang, a 15th-century Buddhist monk who supposedly pleased the gods so much with his recitation of a sutra that they rained flowers on this spot. Recent events on these grounds are not so charming: Chiang Kai-shek used the place as his execution fields, killing upwards of 100,000 Chinese Communists and anti-Nationalists. The park and memorial were completed in the 1980s. ✉ *215 Yuhua Lu, south of the city.* ✉ *Y10.* ⊙ *Daily 7 AM–10 PM (park), 8–5:30 (memorial).*

❻ Zhonghua Men (South Gate of City Wall). The gate dates from the early Ming dynasty. The caves built into the structure could hold 3,000 soldiers, and the gate was held to be absolutely impenetrable. It was in fact never taken or even attacked; aggressive armies wisely avoided it in favor of the less heavily fortified areas to the north. ✉ *South side of city wall.* ✉ *Y6.*

❸ Zhongshan Ling (Sun Yat-sen Memorial). Both the Communists and the GMD recognize Sun Yat-sen as the father of the Chinese revolution; he is widely admired and honored on the mainland today. Sun always insisted that the capital of China should lie in Nanjing, and after his death in 1925, this mausoleum was erected in his honor. The enormous stairway echoes the ascent to ancient emperors' tombs. Several bronzes stand in the middle and at the top of the stairway—some of these bear bullet marks incurred during the war with Japan. The ceiling of the first room of the mausoleum itself bears Sun's design for the flag; although it was used as the GMD flag, the Communist government has not covered it out of respect for the dead leader. The second room houses Dr. Sun's coffin with a marble sarcophagus carved in his likeness. On the ceiling is a beautiful blue-and-white-tile mosaic representing the sky and sun. Zhongshan Ling is one of China's most popular tourist spots and always crowded. Try to visit on a weekday. ✉ *Lingyuan Lu, eastern suburbs.* ✉ *Y25.* ⊙ *Daily 8:30–5.*

Dining and Lodging

$–$$$ ✕ Sichuan Restaurant. A Nanjing classic, this three-story restaurant increases in formality (and price) as you climb the stairs. Excellent Sichuan specialties mingle with more general Chinese cuisine here. It's also a great place to host banquets or formal dinners. ✉ *Taiping Nanlu 171,* ☎ *025/440–2038. No credit cards.*

$–$$ ✕ Dingshan Meishi Cheng. Run by the Dingshan hotel and in the Fuz-
★ imiao area, this is one of Nanjing's finest upscale restaurants. Built in traditional Chinese style, it has wooden latticework on the windows. The cuisine is the local Hauiyang—not as spicy as Sichuan (farther up the Yangzi River), not as sweet as Shanghai (farther down the Yangzi). ✉ *Zhangyuan Lu 5,* ☎ *025/662–7555. AE, MC, V.*

$ ✕ Dechangxing Jiaozi Restaurant. *Jiaozi* (boiled or steamed meat or vegetable dumplings) are a specialty throughout the east of China. The Dechangxing makes a special delight of this common fare, preparing dumplings in various shapes and sizes. While a bit over-priced, considering what jiaozi goes for elsewhere, the food is good enough and the variety large enough to overlook the extra cost. ✉ *Hunan Lu 38,* ☎ *025/361–9879. No credit cards.*

$ ✕ Jimingsi Vegetarian Restaurant. This establishment cooks up excellent Chinese fare with absolutely no meat, a rare occurrence in mainland

China. The food is not the only draw, however—the restaurant is near the Jiming Temple and provides a lovely view of the grounds as well as access to the Ming dynasty wall, which runs directly to the north of the park. The wall in this area has been restored, and from here you can climb up to get a closer look at the structure as well as the parks surrounding it. ☒ *Jiming Park, north side,* ☎ *025/771–3690. No credit cards. No dinner.*

$ ✕ **Tiandi Restaurant.** This charming restaurant standing on old temple grounds is surrounded by a small wood on a little hill off the road.
★ Seating is in pavilions. Outdoor seating near a stone wall with a stream and pond provides a quiet setting from which to view the pavilions. The staff speaks a little English and will be happy to guide you through the restaurant's Jiangsu specialties and other Chinese cuisine. ☒ *Huju Lu 179,* ☎ *025/372–0088. No credit cards.*

$$$$ ☷ **Jinling Hotel.** Nanjing's best-known hotel, the Jinling stands on the corner of Xinjiekou in the city's busy center. It's a huge, modern building with an excellent staff. The hotel is connected to a shopping center, and the travel agency on its first floor provides friendly and efficient service. On the second floor is the freshest and most authentic Japanese food in town. ☒ *2 Xinjiekou, 210005,* ☎ *025/471–1888 or 025/471–1999,* FAX *025/471–1666. 570 rooms, 30 suites. 7 restaurants, bar, 2 cafés, hair salon, gym, billiards, dance club, business services, meeting room. AE, MC, V.*

$$$–$$$$ ☷ **Grand Hotel.** This large, elliptical building in the center of town is a good base for seeing the sights around Nanjing. The Western restaurant on the 24th floor has a good circular view of the city. The health center has traditional Chinese medical services and massages, as well as acupuncture treatments. There's a nice roof garden atop the lower building. ☒ *Guangzhou Lu 208, 210024,* ☎ *025/331–1999,* FAX *025/331–9498. 294 rooms, 11 suites. Restaurant, bar, café, pool, hair salon, sauna, tennis court, health club, bookstore, meeting room, travel services. AE, DC, MC, V.*

$$$–$$$$ ☷ **Holiday Inn.** In a towering building that dominates most of the surrounding neighborhood, the Holiday Inn is just north of the Drum Tower and south of the bustling Shaanxi Lu night market. The standard rooms are on the small side, but they are spotlessly clean and comfortable. The hotel is well-known in Nanjing for its excellent Italian restaurant. ☒ *45 Zhongshan Beilu, 210008,* ☎ *025/330–8888,* FAX *025/330–9688,* WEB *www.holiday-inn.com. 214 rooms, 33 suites. 4 restaurants, hair salon, massage, sauna, gym, pool, business services, meeting room. AE, MC, V.*

$$$ ☷ **Mandarin Garden Hotel.** Contrary to the impersonal bent of most hotels of its caliber, this well-appointed establishment is warm and friendly, geared toward a quiet intimacy. Its setting on the north side of Fuzimiao lets you view the city center while keeping the noise out of your room. The excellent rooftop bar/lounge on the eighth floor affords a good view of the Fuzimiao District. The Huicui Ting (Galaxy Restaurant), on the second floor, serves Cantonese food. ☒ *Zhuang Yuan Jing 9, Fuzimiao, 210001,* ☎ *025/220–2555 or 025/220–2988,* FAX *025/220–1876,* WEB *www.mandaringarden-hotel.com. 500 rooms, 24 suites. 12 restaurants, bar, no-smoking floor, indoor pool, hair salon, sauna, miniature golf, health club, squash, business services, meeting room. AE, MC, V.*

$$–$$$ ☷ **Central Hotel.** Just off the Xinjiekou traffic circle, the Central caters to foreign guests. It arranges day tours of Nanjing and has 24-hour travel services. Fanciful touches, like double rooms in various international styles—Arabian, Japanese, French—accompany practical amenities. ☒ *Zhongshan Lu 75, 210005,* ☎ *025/473–3666,* FAX *025/473–3999. 354 rooms, 22 suites. 2 restaurants, bar, coffee shop, pool,*

sauna, health club, shops, dance club, business services, meeting room. AE, MC, V.

$$–$$$ ⊞ **Nanjing Hilton.** Everything here, from the glass-enclosed lobby to the
★ rooms, is spacious and comfortable. Rooms with northern exposure afford beautiful views of Zijinshan. Rental bicycles are available for afternoon rides up into the park. Be sure to ask about weekend rates. ⊠
Zhongshan Donglu 319, 210016, ☎ *025/480–8888,* FAX *025/480–9999,*
WEB *www.hilton.com. 490 rooms, 30 suites. 5 restaurants, hair salon, ten-*
nis court, gym, bicycles, business services, meeting room. AE, MC, V.

$$–$$$ **Sheraton Nanjing Kingsley Hotel and Towers.** This beautiful hotel has
a good location in the center of the city. The facilities here are some
of the best in town, and inside is Nanjing's only Irish Pub (Danny's).
Hanzhong Lu 169, 210029, ☎ *025/666–8888,* FAX *025/666–9999,*
WEB *www.sheraton.com. 350 rooms. 2 restaurants, 3 bars, no-smok-*
ing rooms, indoor pool, tennis courts, health club, business services,
meeting rooms. AE, DC, MC, V

$$–$$$ ⊞ **Xuanwu Hotel.** Just across the street from Xuanwu Park, the hotel
has a 20th-floor restaurant that affords an excellent view of Nanjing
and the park. The health club has an unusual feature: it offers lessons
in basic qi gong—a traditional Chinese healing movement practice related to tai chi—and examination by a trained specialist in traditional
Chinese medicine. ⊠ *Zhongyang Lu 193, 210009,* ☎ *025/335–8888,*
FAX *025/336–6777. 408 rooms, 161 suites. 6 restaurants, bar, massage,*
sauna, health club, business services, meeting room. AE, MC, V.

$–$$ ⊞ **Nanjing Hotel.** Originally built in 1936, the hotel is set back from
the road, surrounded by lawns and trees that seem pleasantly out of
place in such a busy area of town. The well-trained, friendly staff is
used to receiving tour groups and official visitors as well as individual travelers. A separate section has rooms that are older and mustier,
but they are half the standard rate. ⊠ *259 Zhongshan Beilu, 210003,*
☎ *025/341–1888,* FAX *025/342–2261. 307 rooms, 14 suites. 14 restau-*
rants, hair salon, massage, sauna, gym, business services, meeting
room. AE, MC, V.

Nightlife

COFFEE SHOPS/BARS

Since the late 1990s downtown Nanjing has been taken over by a vibrant late-night coffee culture. New coffee shops are being built almost
overnight and seem to be filled up just as quickly by Nanjing's well-
dressed nouveaux riches. **City Garden Coffee Shop** (⊠ Guanjiaqiao 87,
☎ 025/471–3515) draws a lively crowd that plays cards and chats while
fielding cell-phone calls and pagers. **Danfengyulu Coffee Shop** (⊠
Anren Jie 14-6, ☎ 025/335–6085) is usually packed at night with card-
players and people socializing.

A longtime favorite with the Chinese population, **Scarlet** (⊠ Gulou
Chezhan Dongxiang 29, off Zhongshan Beilu, ☎ 025/335–1916)—as
in O'Hara—has red-wood furnishings and two-story seating that re-
produce an authentic Western pub; the food could use a little work.
From classical guitar to Chinese punk, **The Answer** (⊠ Jinyin Jie, ☎
025/360–2486) is one of the only venues in Nanjing for live music.

DANCE CLUBS

The **Casablanca** (⊠ Xuanwu Hotel, ☎ 025/335–8888), the city's most
upscale dance club, draws a mostly over-30 crowd for dancing, drinking, and mingling. **Orgies** (⊠ Zhongshan Lu 202, ☎ 025/341–9991)
is actually quite prim by American big-city standards; the good bar and
small dance floor attract a mix of locals and expats.

Shopping

The main shopping districts center on the Zhongshan Beilu and Shaanxi Lu traffic circle in the northern section of town, the Xinjiekou traffic circle in midtown, and Fuzimiao, in the south.

The **Nanjing Arts & Crafts Company** (⊠ Beijing Donglu 31, ☎ 025/ 771–1193) has a great variety of items, from jade and lacquerware to silk *qipaos* (traditional Chinese dresses) and tapestries; they also will carve seals and draw calligraphy to order. The **Xinhua Bookstore** (⊠ Baiziting 34, ☎ 025/771–1793) has a good selection of calligraphy scrolls, along with brushes and other paraphernalia, as well as phrase books and dictionaries.

Your best bet for silks—both off the roll and ready-made—is the market areas; Fuzimiao has an excellent selection of shops and stalls. The **Shaanxi Lu night market** has a wide array of goods. A nameless new city **free market,** with everything from vegetables and clothes to live animals, has sprung up across from Gulou. The **Friendship Store** (⊠ Hanzhong Lu 16) here does not do so well in clothing, but it has a small selection of antique-style arts on the fourth floor. For the latest in fashion, try the **Golden Eagle department store** (⊠ Hanzhong Lu and Tieguan Xiang) or the **Xinjiekou department store** (⊠ Xinjiekou Traffic Circle).

Side Trip to Zhenjiang

⓮ *1-hr train ride from Nanjing on Shanghai–Nanjing rail line, 1 hr by long-distance bus.*

Zhenjiang was once a city of great administrative and economic importance, a vital grain shipping point as well as a tax collection center at the junction of the Grand Canal and the Yangzi River. By the 20th century the entrance to the canal had become heavily silted and virtually unusable. The city was damaged in the Opium Wars as well as during the Taiping Rebellion, when rebels used their base here to help defend Nanjing. Several old temples and pavilions are still standing, though. These and the parks make Zhenjiang a delightful day trip from Nanjing.

A little west of the city center is **Jinshan** (Gold Hill). The Tang dynasty Zen monk, Fa Hai, supposedly gave it its name when he dug up gold here. Inside the park are several temples and pavilions, most importantly **Jinshan Si** (Gold Hill Temple) and **Daxiong Baodian** (Heroes Palace), with its elaborate ornamentation. Also on the mountain are several interesting caves. Most notable of these is **Bailong Dong** (White Dragon Cave). According to legend, a huge venomous snake lived here, until Ling Tan, a Zen monk, came here and drove it out to sea with his magical powers. ⊠ *62 Jinshan Xilu.* ☜ *Y20.* ◷ *Daily 8–5:30.*

The **Zhenjiang Bowuguan** (Zhenjiang Museum), inside **Boxian Gongyuan** (Boxian Park), occupies what once was the British consulate building. The museum houses some artifacts and paintings dating from as far back as the Tang dynasty. North of the museum are a series of ancient alleyways—some dating more than a thousand years—undisturbed by the new and rapid development encroaching in on most other parts of Zhenjiang. *95 Boxian Lu (museum),* ☎ *0511/527–7143,* ☜ *Y5 (museum); Y5 (park).* ◷ *Daily 9–11 and 2–5 (museum); dawn–dusk (park).*

On the banks of the Yangzi, **Beigushan Gongyuan** (Beigushan Park) houses **Ganlu Si** (Temple of Sweet Dew) and its Tang dynasty pagoda. Views of the pagoda are more interesting than views from it. ⊠ *Dongwu Lu.* ☜ *Y8, Y1 more for the pagoda.*

In the middle of town, the restored **Mengxi Yuan** (Dream Spring Garden) provides pleasant walkways and rock formations in the Jiangsu garden style. It was originally the home of Chinese politician and writer Pan Kuo; today a large statue of him stands on the grounds. ⊠ *21 Mengxi Yuan Xiang, off of Huangcheng Lu,* ⊞ *Y5.* ☉ *Daily 8–5.*

To the south of the city, the **Nanshan Gongyuan** (South Mountain Scenic Park) affords good hiking and scenery. Partway up the mountain stands the **Zhulin Si** (Bamboo Forest Temple), worth a walk not only for itself but for the peaceful area around it. Buses stop near the mountain, but the park is accessible only by taxi or minivan.

East of the city, on a small island in the Yangzi, **Jiaoshan Gongyuan** (Jiao Hill Park) contains the **Dinghui Si** monastery. Artwork and miniature trees are on display inside. Nearby stand numerous pavilions as well as an 11th-century iron pagoda. From the top of the hill you get an excellent view of the river traffic. Take the ferry or cable car to get to the island. ⊠ *Southern end of Dongwu Lu.* ⊞ *Y10 (park), Y5 (ferry), Y20 (cable car).* ☉ *Daily 7–5:30.*

DINING AND LODGING

As Zhenjiang is best visited on a day trip from Nanjing or Suzhou, the few hotels here are most useful for their dining rooms.

$$–$$$ 🏨 **Zhenjiang International Hotel.** This is the best and biggest hotel in Zhenjiang. It caters mostly to businessmen and is located in the downtown area. The restaurant serves decent Jiangnan food. *218 Jiefang Lu, 212001.* ☎ *0511/502–1888,* 🖷 *0511/502–1777. 408 rooms. Restaurant, bar, health club, business services.*

$$ 🏨 **Zhenjiang Hotel.** Near the train station, this hotel is a convenient stop if you plan to stay the night. You can order Western food, but you might as well stick with the Chinese selections, which include regional specialties and river catches. ⊠ *Zhongshan Xilu 92, 212004,* ☎ *0511/523–3888,* 🖷 *0511/523–1055. 186 rooms, 10 suites. Restaurant, bar, hair salon, health club, business services. AE, MC, V.*

SHOPPING

Like the cities around it, Zhenjiang has a number of small roadside shops selling silks, and markets spring up around tourist sights and temples. The **Arts and Crafts Store** (⊠ Jiefang Lu 191) sells wares such as porcelain, jade, and chops (traditional stamps).

Wuxi

⑮ *2¾ hrs by train southeast of Nanjing; 1¼ hrs southeast of Zhenjiang; 40 mins northwest of Suzhou.*

To see it now, you'd never know Wuxi was once one of China's major grain markets, combining the harvests of its own fertile environs with those being transported on the Grand Canal. The canal once linked the city with other major economic and cultural centers. Shanghai industrialists, many of whom came from the Wuxi area, built up the city's textile works in the early part of the 20th century, making it China's largest silk-reeling center. Wuxi is best seen as a day trip from Suzhou or Shanghai.

The canal passes by the northeast edge of Wuxi's **Taihu** (Lake Tai). Taihu covers more than 2,200 square km (850 square mi) and is dotted with 48 islands; its fish provide much of the local cuisine.

Jutting into the southern part of the lake, **Yuantouzhu** (Turtle Head Beach) is a small peninsula set aside as a park that affords a great view of the lake. It also houses a few interesting old structures. **Guangfu Si**

(Broad Happiness Temple), originally built in the 6th century, stands on the site of a nunnery, and **Chenglan** (Clear Ripples Hall), a well-preserved prayer hall, now holds a teahouse. The park by the lake is laid out in four sections, each with its own pavilions and artistic remnants. ☒ *End of Hubin Lu, southeast of city.* ⊙ *Daily 7–5:30.*

A 20-minute ferry ride from Turtle Head Isle, **Sanshan Dao** (Three Hills Isles) offer more scenic spots, as well as a teahouse where you can sit and enjoy the view. ☜ *Ferry ticket Y35 (round-trip).*

★ Just outside the city, **Xihui Gongyuan** (Xihui Park) is home to the two hills that are Wuxi's symbols. The round Xishan (Tin Hill) is said to resemble a pearl. At its top, the **Longguang Ta** (Dragon's Light Pagoda) gives you a good view of the surrounding city and lake. Pavilions dot the paths, and there is a small zoo at the bottom of the hill. The coiling paths of Huishan (Generosity or Wisdom Hill), which rises to 1,077 ft above sea level, were laid out to suggest a dragon's tail. The hill also has scattered pavilions as well as the **Tianxia Dier Quan** (Second-Under-Heaven Spring), once thought to yield the second-best tea-brewing water in China (the First-Under-Heaven Spring is in Zhenjiang). At the eastern foot of Huishan, the Ming-style **Jichang Yuan** (Attachment to Freedom Garden) was the model for Beijing's Summer Palace Garden of Harmonious Interest. The garden's own landscape has been created to blend with the surrounding scenery. ☒ *Renmin Xilu and Hehui Lu, west side of city.* ☜ *Y8 (park); Y5 (zoo).*

The **Mei Yuan** (Plum Garden) is famed for its thousands of spring plum trees, which come in more than 30 varieties. Several pavilions provide views of the garden and the surrounding scenery. Early March, when the trees bloom, is the time to visit. ☒ *7 km (4 mi) west of city, near bus No. 2 terminal.* ☜ *Y10.* ⊙ *Daily 8:30–5:30.*

Dining and Lodging

$–$$$ ✕ **Wuxi Roast Duck Restaurant.** As its name implies, this restaurant
★ specializes in Wuxi-style roast duck (a sweeter, leaner cousin of Peking duck). Most nights diners pack its 28 banquet rooms. The restaurant's excellent English menu has a photo of every one of its many other delicious Chinese dishes, from dumplings to Lake Tai fish. ☒ *Zhongshan Lu 222,* ☎ *0510/270–8222. No credit cards.*

$–$$ ✕ **Lake Tai Jumbo Restaurant.** From the outside this restaurant looks like a smaller version of the Jumbo floating restaurant in Hong Kong. Inside, the dining rooms, with good views of Lake Tai, are clean and spacious. English menus list a wide variety of local fare. ☒ *Liyuan Garden, on shore of Lake Tai near Hubin Hotel,* ☎ *0510/510–1888. No credit cards.*

$ ✕ **Zuiyue Lou Restaurant.** The Drunken Moon has a selection of Wuxi specialties, snacks, and cold dishes. The furnishings are nothing special, and the place has perhaps seen better days, but it remains one of Wuxi's better-known venues. ☒ *Tongyun Lu 73,* ☎ *0510/272–0423. No credit cards.*

$$$ ⌂ **The Pan Pacific Wuxi.** Between the center of Wuxi and Lake Tai, this hotel is comfortable if fairly standard. ☒ *11 Liangqing Lu, 214000,* ☎ *0510/580–6789,* ⟨FAX⟩ *0510/270–0991,* ⟨WEB⟩ *www.panpac.com. 325 rooms, 36 suites. 4 restaurants, no-smoking floor. AE, MC, V.*

$$$ ⌂ **Sheraton Wuxi.** The first of three newly constructed Sheratons in Jiangsu province, the finest hotel in Wuxi provides the dependable service of the Sheraton chain. It stands in the downtown district and offers some of the finest food in Wuxi in its Western and Chinese restaurants. ☒ *Zhongshan Lu 443,* ☎ *0510/272–1888,* ⟨FAX⟩ *0510/275–2781,* ⟨WEB⟩ *www.sheraton.com. 396 rooms, 15 suites. 4 restaurants, pool, sauna, gym, travel services. AE, MC, V.*

$–$$　⊡ **Shuixiu Hotel and Hubin Hotel.** Next door and connected to one another, these hotels share management and service facilities; the Hubin is much more upscale than the economically priced Shuixiu. They lie close to the lake in a peaceful area next to the Liyuan Garden. Rooms in the hotels' three cozy lake villas are also available. ⊠ *Off Hubin Lu 214000,* ☎ *0510/510–1888,* ℻ *0510/510–2637. 202 rooms, 18 suites (Hubin); 106 rooms, 2 suites (Shuixiu). 4 restaurants, barber. AE, MC, V.*

Nightlife and the Arts

Wuxi has several song-and-dance ensembles, as well as its own style of Chinese opera. You can see these periodically at the **Renmin Theater** (⊠ Gongyuan Lu 134), the **Dazhong Theater** (⊠ Renmin Lu 90), or the **Jiefang Theater** (People's Bazaar No. 13, Beitang District).

Shopping

Wuxi is mostly famed for silk, as well as for more Western-style clothing and scarves. The city has a tradition of Huishan clay figurines, but they are not as attractive as the pottery brought in from Yixing County. In addition, you can find embroidery, carved seals, and jade carvings in many of the shops lining the streets near the city center at the intersection of Zhongshan Lu and Renmin Lu. Try the **Friendship Store** (⊠ Zhongshan Lu 297, ☎ 0510/286–8414). In these days of reform-era China, large stores like **Wuxi Shangye Dasha** (⊠ Junction Zhongshan Lu and Renmin Lu) have a wide selection and good service. The **Wuxi Arts and Crafts Store** (⊠ Renmin Lu 192, ☎ 0510/272–8783) is another major emporium.

Suzhou

On Nanjing–Shanghai rail line; approximately 3½ hrs by train southeast of Nanjing or 1 hr west of Shanghai.

If the renowned gardens of Suzhou form a thriving monument to the city's past, the passages leading up to them speak of a time of transition. Entire blocks of old-style houses still line some of the city's canals. Decorated gates and doorways from centuries ago catch the eye, but they now lead into shops selling silk and cashmere in Chinese and Western styles; the ramshackle houses from past eras border on tall office buildings and shiny new hotels; and the sloping, tiled roofs often sit atop structures built in the last few years. This mixture of old styles with new makes Suzhou's central districts a pleasure to explore.

Suzhou's many canals once formed the basis of its economy. Now falling into disuse, the waterways still line many a lamplighted street. These canals, however, are really only the younger cousins of the **Da Yunhe** (Grand Canal), which passes through the outskirts of town. Just 5 km (3 mi) south of the city is the Baodai Qiao (Precious Belt Bridge), one of the most famous and grandiose bridges on the canal. The canal used to be a main transportation route for eastern China but has been gradually replaced with newer, faster modes. The section south of Suzhou is still navigable and navigated; you can take an **overnight boat** (CITS; ⊠ Shiquan Lu 115, ☎ 0512/522–2401) to explore the canal more thoroughly.

Suzhou's main claim to fame is its fabulous array of gardens, which set a style and standard for gardens throughout the country. They were originally created by retired officials or unaffiliated literati as places in which to read and write poetry and philosophy, to stroll and drink with their friends, and to meditate and spend quiet hours. The attraction of these gardens goes beyond the mazes of bizarre rock formations or the thoughtfully arranged vegetation; rather, each garden is meant to be enjoyed for its overall atmosphere, as well as for its unique style and layout. Sit in a teahouse near the pond and feel the peaceful breeze as you watch it ruffle the water, carrying fragrances with it. Pathways lead to an artfully planted tree winding its way up the garden wall, a glimpse of lake from a small man-made cave, a pavilion displaying Qing dynasty tree-root furniture. Every plant, rock, bit of water, piece of furniture, wall, and even fish has been carefully created or chosen for its individual shape, color, shadow, and other characteristics and for the way each blends with the whole at different times of the day and year. Although spring is considered prime viewing time, each season works its own magic.

A Good Walk

Starting where Renmin Lu meets Xibei Jie in the northern section of town, check out the tall **Beisi Ta** ⑯ (North Temple Pagoda), with views of the city. Walk east along the restored street with its traditional-style fronts and shops until you come to the **Zhuo Zheng Yuan** ⑰ (Humble Administrator's Garden), Suzhou's largest garden. Then turn south along Yuan Lin Lu, checking out the silk shops that line the street. **Shizi Lin** ⑱ (Lion's Grove Garden), filled with caves, will be on your right about halfway down the short street. At the end of the street turn right and then left onto Lindun Lu; follow that south to Guanqian Lu and turn right to reach the **Xuanmiao Guan** ⑲ (Temple of Mystery), an ancient temple in a market square. Make your way down to Fenghuang Jie and head south to Shiquan Jie, turning left for the small, exquisite **Wangshi Yuan** ⑳ (Master of the Nets Garden). From here go left on Shiquan Jie to Renmin Lu, turn left again and follow it to **Canglang Ting** ㉑ (Blue Wave Pavilion), a large garden off the street to the left. Back up Renmin Lu, just north of Ganjiang Lu, stop to visit a newer garden, **Yi Yuan** ㉒ (Joyous Garden). Take a bus or taxi north and west across the city moat and a branch of the Grand Canal to the large, well-designed **Liu Yuan** ㉓ (Lingering Garden). Just to the west, at the end of Liuyuan Lu, is the Buddhist **Xi Yuan Si** ㉔ (West Garden Temple). From Xi Yuan Si, take another taxi or the No. 5 bus to **Huqiu** ㉕ (Tiger Hill), a large park north of the city with a leaning pagoda.

The most leisurely way to do this walk is to spread it out over two days.

Sights to See

⑯ **Beisi Ta** (North Temple Pagoda). A pagoda has stood on these grounds since the Three Kingdoms Period, though the existing pagoda dates from 1153. You can climb as high as the eighth floor of the nine-story structure to get what might be the best view (still) of Suzhou. There are large windows and balconies on each floor. The grounds form a garden of their own (though not a very good one), and there's an art gallery behind the pagoda. ⊠ *Xibei Jie and Renmin Lu.* ☞ *Y10; Y5 to climb the pagoda.* ☼ *Daily 7:45–6.*

㉑ **Canglang Ting** (Blue Wave Pavilion). In one of Suzhou's largest and oldest gardens you can thread your way through a maze of oddly shaped doorways, around an artificial pond, and into a large, man-made cave with a small stone picnic table. The garden was originally built in the 10th century and, although lovely in its own way, is not as delicately wrought as some of the smaller gardens. ⊠ *Off Renmin Lu between Shiquan Jie and Xinshi Lu.* ☞ *Y8.* ☼ *Daily 8–5.*

㉕ **Huqiu** (Tiger Hill). Five kilometers (three miles) northwest of the city center stands this park, home of the tomb of Helu, the supposed founder of the city. According to legend, a white tiger appeared here three days after he was interned, hence the name. Also here is **Xia Ta** (Leaning Pagoda), Suzhou's version of the Leaning Tower of Pisa, tilting at a 15° angle. ⊠ *Huqiu Lu, north of city.* ☞ *Y25.* ☼ *Daily 7:30–5:30.*

Suzhou

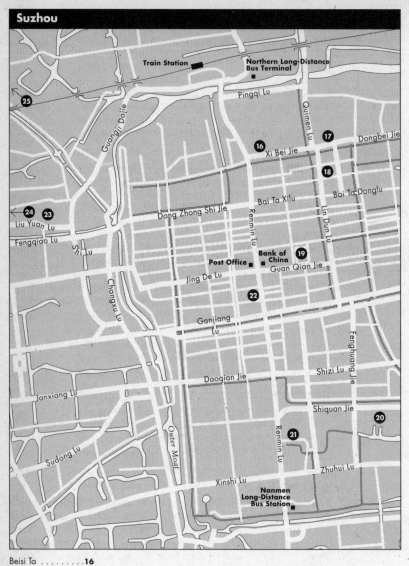

Train Station

Northern Long-Distance Bus Terminal

Pingqi Lu

Quimen Lu

Xi Bei Jie

Dongbei Jie

Bai Ta Xilu

Bai Ta Donglu

Dong Zhong Shi Jie

Liu Yuan Lu

Fengqiao Lu

Shi Lu

Renmin Lu

Lin Dun Lu

Post Office

Bank of China

Guan Qian Jie

Jing De Lu

Changxu Lu

Ganjiang Lu

Daoqian Jie

Janxiang Lu

Shizi Lu

Fenghuang Jie

Shiquan Jie

Sudong Lu

Outer Moat

Renmin Lu

Zhuhui Lu

Xinshi Lu

Nanmen Long-Distance Bus Station

㉓ **Liu Yuan** (Lingering Garden). In the western part of the city is another of Suzhou's larger gardens, originally installed during the Ming dynasty. Paths wind around a small pond area and through some impressive rock formations. Several pavilions are set around the park, inside of which are calligraphy expositions. Beyond the park's outer wall is a nursery with scores of carefully tended bonsai trees. ⊠ *Liuyuan Lu.* 🚊 *Y16.* ⊙ *Daily 8–5.*

⑱ **Shizi Lin** (Lion's Grove Garden). Here a labyrinth of man-made caves surrounds a small scenic lake. Its wall is divided and its pavilions are sited to make the garden seem more spacious than it really is. The illusions of space are expertly created here, and the bridges on the lake provide many a couple with a romantic photo op. You can get a wide view of the garden walking the paths around the lake, while the cave maze brings your attention to minute landscaping details. A tearoom on the second floor of the main pavilion overlooks the lake. At the garden's exit is a small marketplace with antique replicas and silks of all sorts. ⊠ *23 Yuan Lin Lu,* 🚊 *Y10.* ⊙ *Daily 7:30–5.*

★ ⑳ **Wangshi Yuan** (Master of the Nets Garden). Despite its comparatively small size, Wangshi Yuan, with its subdued beauty, is the most interesting garden in a city famous for its gardens. All of the elements of the Suzhou style are here—artificial rock hills, an abundance of flora, pavilions overlooking a central pond—in seemingly perfect balance, as if this were the culmination of the art of garden design. The park was originally constructed in the 12th century, and reworked in the 18th. The former living quarters now house exhibits of Qing dynasty tree-root furniture and some fine pieces of traditional ink painting and calligraphy. One placard announces that the **Dianchun Yi** (Spring Cottage) was reproduced for an exhibition in the Metropolitan Museum of Art in New York. ⊠ *Shiquan Jie,* ☎ *0512/520–3514.* 🚊 *Day, Y10; evening, Y60.* ⊙ *Daily 8–5 and 7:30–10.*

㉔ **Xi Yuan Si** (West Garden Temple). This Buddhist temple was originally constructed in the Yuan dynasty, although the current building dates from the 19th century (Qing dynasty). Behind the main temple is the Xihua garden, a large open area with several ponds. Of particular interest is the **Wubai Luohan Tang** (Hall of 500 Arhats), which houses 500 gold-painted statues of arhats, each with its own peculiar expression. ⊠ *8 Xiyuan Lu (down the street from Liu Yuan).* 🚊 *Y6.* ⊙ *Daily 7–5.*

⑲ **Xuanmiao Guan** (Temple of Mystery). One of the most well-preserved old-style temples, the Temple of Mystery backs a large market square, which used to be temple grounds. Founded in the 3rd century, the Taoist temple has undergone fewer restorations than most its age, still retaining parts from the 12th century. The main building, Sanqing Dian, is one of the largest wooden structures in China. Fortunately, it suffered very little damage in the Cultural Revolution. ⊠ *Guanqian Jie.* 🚊 *Y5; additional fees for different temples.* ⊙ *Daily 7:30–5.*

㉒ **Yi Yuan** (Joyous Garden). A more recent example of Suzhou style, this one also has a pleasant blending of pavilion and rockery, courtyard and pond. ⊠ *343 Renmin Lu.* 🚊 *Y4.* ⊙ *Daily 7:30–5.*

⑰ **Zhuo Zheng Yuan** (Humble Administrator's Garden). Suzhou's largest, this 10-acre garden is renowned for its its so-called high and low architecture and expansive pond area. It was built by Wang Xianjun, an unemployed official in the Ming dynasty, who drew its name from a line in a Tang dynasty rhapsody. The line of poetry, reading "humble people govern," seems like a clever bit of sarcasm when considered in conjunction with the grand scale of this private garden—perhaps explaining Wang's unsuitability for public life. The garden is separated into three parts—east, central, and west—each with its own pavilions and pond. Near the garden's entrance is a large display of bonsai trees. ⊠ *178 Dong Bei Jie.* ⊞ *Y20.* ⊙ *Daily 7:30–5:30.*

Dining and Lodging

$–$$$ ✕ **Deyuelou.** This restaurant which has served Suzhou-style food for more than 400 years has a wide array of fish dishes, local-style dim sum, and a particularly tasty *Deyue Tongji* (braised chicken). It also specializes in an attractive type of food presentation, the ancient art of "garden foods"—an assortment of dim sum specialties arranged to resemble various sorts of gardens, with foods portraying flowers, trees, and rocks. ⊠ *27 Taijian Nong,* ☎ *0512/523–8940, AE, MC, V.*

$–$$ ✕ **Huangtianyuan.** Here the specialty is the local favorite of *mifen* (rice gluten), made by pounding rice to a fine paste. In business since 1821, it has different seasonal menus, serving the foods traditionally considered most appropriate for specific times of year. Other house specialties include *babao fan* (syrupy rice with various sweets, nuts, and fruit bits) and *tang tuan* (a kind of dim sum whose skin is made of the thick dough of mifen). These come in a variety of sizes and with both meaty and sweet fillings. ⊠ *86 Guanqian Jie,* ☎ *0512/728–6933. No credit cards.*

$–$$ ✕ **Songhelou.** With almost 250 years of history, this is one of Suzhou's most famous restaurants. It serves Suzhou specialties and catches from the river that in the old days were actually eaten on riverboats during banquet cruises—hence their popular designation: "boat food." The recommended dish here is the *Songshu Guiyu,* or "squirrel-shaped Mandarin fish" (don't let the English translation turn you off). The restaurant has nine dining halls decorated with Suzhou regional arts and calligraphy. ⊠ *18 Taijian Nong,* ☎ *0512/523–7969. V.*

$$$ ⊞ **Nanlin Hotel.** This hotel has a quiet setting somewhat back from the road. Master of the Nets Garden and Blue Wave Pavilion are both within walking distance. ⊠ *20 Gunxiu Fang, Shiquan Jie, 215006,* ☎ *0512/519–4641,* ⅁⅄ *0512/519–1028,* ⍵⅁⅁ *www.nanlinhotel.com.cn.* *240 rooms, 12 suites. 2 restaurants, bar, hair salon, health club, business services, meeting room. AE, MC, V.*

$$–$$$ ⊞ **Nanyuan Hotel.** Priced just above the more budget-oriented accommodations, the Nanyuan relies on its excellent location to draw guests. It is west of Wangshi Yuan and near the most fashionable hotels in town. ⊠ *249 Shiquan Jie, 215006,* ☎ *0512/519–7661,* ⅁⅄ *0512/519–8806. 104 rooms, 10 suites. 2 restaurants, bar, hair salon, health club, business services, meeting room. AE, MC, V.*

$$–$$$ ⊞ **Suzhou Hotel.** The service and facilities here are excellent. It's a short walk down a popular street lined with silk and cashmere stores that leads to the Master of the Nets Garden. There is a post office conveniently located next to the lobby. ⊠ *115 Shiquan Jie, 215006,* ☎ *0512/520–4646,* ⅁⅄ *0512/520–4015,* ⍵⅁⅁ *www.suzhou-hotel.com. 280 rooms, 21 suites. 16 restaurants, 2 bars, hair salon, health club, business services, meeting room. AE, MC, V.*

$$ ⊞ **Bamboo Grove Hotel.** A modern facility, the Bamboo Grove caters to international business travelers and tourists. It is one of the city's choice establishments in terms of facilities and quality of service, though its location is somewhat out of the way. ⊠ *168 Zhuhui Lu, 215006,* ☎ *0512/520–5601,* ⅁⅄ *0512/520–8778. 356 rooms, 42 suites. 4 restaurants, bar, hair salon, health club, business services, meeting room. AE, MC, V.*

$–$$ ⊞ **Lexiang Hotel.** Catering mainly to Chinese guests, this budget option is more basic in its approach than the hotels on fashionable Shiquan Jie. It does have a fine location, just down the street from the Joyous Garden and a block from the beautiful Temple of Mystery. ⊠

18 Dajingxiang, ☎ 0512/522–2890, FAX 0512/524–4165. 38 rooms, 2 suites. 2 restaurants, bar, hair salon, health club, business services, meeting room. AE, MC, V.

Nightlife and the Arts

Wangshi Yuan (The Master of the Nets Garden) has nightly **traditional opera and music performances** throughout the year (Y60). The show presents a taste of various scenes from opera, as well as an opportunity to hear classical Chinese instruments. It can be a bit crowded during the peak of the tourist season. The beautiful location, however, makes the performance a uniquely enjoyable experience. Check at the entrance gate of the garden or with CITS about times and tickets.

Apart from the karaoke clubs, there really are no bars to speak of outside the few uninteresting ones in western hotels.

Shopping

Districts around the gardens and temples teem with silk shops and outdoor markets. The **Friendship Store** (✉ 504 Renmin Lu, ☎ 0512/523–6165) has a selection of local products in silk, wood, and jade. Since 1956 the **Suzhou Antiques Store** (✉ 328 Renmin Lu, near Leqiao Bridge, ☎ 0512/522–8368) has been selling antiques, calligraphy, jades, and other "cultural products." You can get jewelry and carvings at the **Suzhou Jade Carving Factory** (✉ 33 Baita Xilu, ☎ 0512/727–1224). The **Suzhou Silk Museum Shop** (✉ 661 Renmin Lu, ☎ 0512/753–4941) is really the reason to come to the Silk Museum in the first place. For local artworks and calligraphy, visit the **Wumen Artstore** (✉ 105 Liuyuan Lu, ☎ 0512/533–4808).

Jiangsu A to Z

To research prices, get advice from other travelers, and book travel arrangements, visit www.fodors.com.

AIR TRAVEL

International flights go through Shanghai or Beijing before continuing on to Nanjing. From Nanjing several flights leave daily for Shanghai, Beijing, Guangzhou, Xiamen, Wuhan, and Hong Kong; flights leave daily for Xian and Chengdu; and several flights leave weekly for Zhengzhou and Hangzhou.

CARRIERS

You can buy tickets at any travel agency, at major hotels like the Jinling, or at CITS. Dragonair, which also has a desk in the Grand Hotel, has daily flights to Hong Kong.

In Wuxi and Suzhou CITS can arrange plane tickets through the Shanghai or Nanjing airports for you, or you can get in touch with China Eastern Airlines in Suzhou.

➤ AIRLINES AND CONTACTS: **CAAC** (✉ 52 Ruijin Lu, Nanjing, ☎ 025/449–9378). **China Eastern Airlines** (✉ 192 Renmin Lu, Suzhou, ☎ 0512/522–2788). **CITS** (✉ 202/1 Zhongshan Beilu, Nanjing, ☎ 025/342–8999). **Dragonair** (✉ 208 Guangzhou Lu, Room 810, Nanjing, ☎ 025/331–1999 ext. 810). **Jinling** (✉ Xinjiekou, Nanjing, northwest corner, ☎ 025/471–1888).

AIRPORTS AND TRANSFERS

TRANSFERS

Taxis from Nanjing Airport to the center of town should take about 20 minutes and cost around Y170. There is also a bus from the airport to downtown Nanjing near the Sheraton for Y25.

BOAT AND FERRY TRAVEL

You can get to a great many places by boat from Nanjing, but for far-away destinations the prospect is risky: sanitary conditions are rarely good, and schedules are not convenient. A short trip down the Yangzi to Shanghai is a better idea; the trip is scenic enough, and boats leave every morning and three afternoons a week from the dock in the northwest side of town. You can get to Nanjing via boat by starting an eastbound Yangzi River cruise in Wuhan (☞ Chapter 10).

The overnight ride from Suzhou to Hangzhou along the Grand Canal takes you through some great countryside scenery between two of China's prettiest cities. Tickets can be purchased through your hotel or a travel agent. The Suzhou Ferry Terminal is on the south side of the city near the old city gate.

➤ BOAT AND FERRY INFORMATION: **Suzhou Ferry Terminal** (2 Renmin Lu, ☎ 0512/520–6681).

BUS TRAVEL

Frequent bus service runs between Nanjing, Zhenjiang, Wuxi, and Suzhou, with connections or direct lines to Shanghai as well. Some routes have modern tourist buses with air-conditioning. Nanjing's bus station lies west of the railway station. A new direct air-conditioned coach to Shanghai takes about 3½ hours.

In Zhenjiang the station is in the southeast corner of the city center. Direct buses run frequently to Nanjing, Suzhou, and Wuxi. In Wuxi the station is right across from the railway station. The Suzhou bus station offers trips to other Jiangsu destinations. For all of these, it's best to have the name of your destination written in Chinese to avoid misunderstanding. Buses are the most convenient choice for short trips like Nanjing–Zhenjiang and Wuxi–Suzhou. Otherwise, trains are more comfortable.

➤ BUS INFORMATION: **Nanjing bus station** (✉ Jianing Lu and Zhongyang Lu, ☎ 025/550–3672). **Suzhou bus station** (✉ Southern tip of Renmin Lu, ☎ 0512/520–4867). **Wuxi bus station** (✉ Tonghui Donglu, ☎ 0510/230–0751). **Zhenjiang bus station** (✉ Jiefang Lu, ☎ 0511/501–3270).

EMERGENCIES

All of the establishments below are open 24 hours.

➤ CONTACTS: **First Aid Station** (✉ 231 Zhongshan Lu, Nanjing, ☎ 025/330–4392; 025/663–3858; 110 for emergencies). **People's Hospital No. 1** (✉ 111 Renmin Zhonglu, Wuxi, ☎ 0510/270–0778). **People's Hospital No. 2** (✉ 26 Daoqian Jie, Suzhou, ☎ 0512/522–3691). **Wuxi People's Hospital No. 3** (✉ 320 Tonghui Donglu, Wuxi, ☎ 0510/270–7391).

TOURS

Major hotels will often arrange a tour guide for a group, as will CITS. Individuals may offer you day tours; just make sure the price is set and the guide's English is good enough to make it worthwhile. Because the major sights in Jiangsu lie inside the cities, they are generally quite accessible to individual travelers.

TRAIN TRAVEL

Nanjing, Zhenjiang, Wuxi, and Suzhou are all on the same rail line, which continues on to Shanghai. Two comfortable air-conditioned "tourist trains" run daily between Nanjing, Wuxi, Suzhou, and Shanghai, leaving Nanjing at 9 AM and 5 PM, reaching Wuxi in about an hour, Suzhou in about two hours, and Shanghai in about 2¾ hours. Other trains between all these destinations leave quite frequently. Several daily trains from Nanjing will take you on a day trip to Zhenjiang in about

On a little side street across a waterway from one of the city parks and set back from the road as it is, it promises a quiet stay. The rooms are a bit run down but still a value. ⊠ *Yi Huan Lu off Meishan Lu,* ☎ *0551/281–3355,* FAX *0551/281–6584. 149 rooms, 2 suites, 4 villas. 3 restaurants, health club, business services. AE, MC, V.*

Shopping

The **Anhui Antiques Shop** (⊠ 57 Renmin Lu, East Bldg., ☎ 0551/265–5989) has a limited selection. The local **department store** (⊠ 124 Changjiang Lu, ☎ 0551/265–3261) offers a small choice of paintings and other artworks. You can restock on English books at the **Foreign Languages Bookstore** (⊠ 29 Yimin Jie, ☎ 0551/265–8392).

Side Trips from Hefei

★ ㉗ By far the most important attraction in Anhui is **Huangshan** (Yellow Mountain), also known as Huangshan Fengjing Qu (Huangshan Scenic Area). A favorite retreat of emperors and poets of old, its peaks have inspired some of China's most outstanding artworks and literary endeavors. They were so beguiling, in fact, that years of labor went into their paths, which are actual stone steps rising up—sometimes gradually into the forest, sometimes sharply through a stone tunnel and into the mist above. The mountain is known particularly for three common sights: "grotesque pines" twisted by the winds, "unusual rock formations" coming in animal shapes, and the "sea of mist" that sweeps in and out of the upper reaches of the peaks. What you must see, though, is the sunrise from the top of the mountain. Hundreds of people gather to observe the stunning sight before walking sleepily back down for some breakfast.

The stone steps of the pathways can be wearying on the legs. The most common route leads from the Eastern Gate up the Eastern Steps, around the top of the range and down the Western Steps. The other way around, although equally and differently beautiful, is recommended only for the most stalwart and aerobically fit: the Western Steps are considerably longer and steeper than the Eastern. If you want the beauty without the pain, take the cable car (Y70) just past the Eastern Gate: it takes you almost all the way to the top of the mountain. Halfway down the Western Steps, another cable car (Y60) station allows you to ride down to the Western Gate. From either of these gates you can catch a minivan or bus down to the Main Gate. If you're planning to do the entire mountain in one day, it's best to take at least one cable car to make sure you have time. If you're staying at a hotel near the mountain top, you'll have time to walk both.

Getting to Huangshan takes a bit of planning. The town at the base of the mountain, Tangkou, is not on a rail line; the best you can do is either take a bus directly here or catch a train to Tunxi, from which you can get a local bus into town. Although Huangshan is in Anhui, it actually lies farther from Hefei than from Hangzhou in neighboring Zhejiang province. A bus route from Hangzhou to Tangkou follows mountain passes to reveal a patchwork of small, sloping, graded fields traversed by thin irrigation canals. You'll get a glimpse of peasant life in the hills as you pass small-time farmers dipping long-handled wooden ladles into the canals to water their crops, or working with sickles and other hand tools to set their lands in order. You could also go to Huangshan by bus from Wuhu or Guichi, towns on the Yangzi River at which the Wuhan–Shanghai ferry stops.

LODGING

Reservations are essential for any hotel in the Huangshan area, as this is one of China's major tourist spots. The mountaintop hotels tend to be overpriced; you pay more for Huangshan than for the facilities provided (Tunxi hotels are less expensive). Food in the area tends to be less than amazing, but after a day of hard climbing and breathtaking scenery, you probably won't care.

$$$ ⊞ **Xihai Hotel.** This joint venture is ideally situated at the top of the mountain, providing a convenient site for sunrise-watching as well as for comfortable living. It's not a luxury hotel (despite the price), but it is one of the best lodgings around. ⊠ *Huangshan Scenic Area, 242709,* ☎ *0559/556–2132,* FAX *0559/556–2988. 121 rooms, 5 suites. Restaurant, bar. AE, MC, V.*

$$–$$$ ⊞ **Beihai Hotel.** This is one of the three mountaintop hotels that accept foreigners. It really isn't worth the price, but it is clean and has a few extras—like a massage service and saunas—that might be a welcome end to a day of hiking. The hotel's rooms and villas are picturesquely sited. ⊠ *Huangshan Scenic Area, 242709,* ☎ *0559/556–2555,* FAX *0559/556–2996. 137 rooms, 2 suites. Restaurant, bar, massage, sauna. AE, MC, V.*

$$ ⊞ **Peach Blossom Hotel.** A winding road takes you over a bridge, past a waterfall to this enchanted-looking resort between the Main Gate of the mountain park and the beginning of the Western Steps. The Peach Blossom has the best food (both Chinese and Western) of the three mountain hotels. You'll have to hustle to catch the sunrise if you stay here, but the hot springs next door are great to come back to after a day of hiking. ⊠ *Huangshan Scenic Area, 242709,* ☎ *0559/556–2666,* FAX *0559/556–2888. 110 rooms, 4 suites. Restaurant, bar. AE, MC, V.*

Anhui A to Z

To research prices, get advice from other travelers, and book travel arrangements, visit www.fodors.com.

AIR TRAVEL
The Hefei airport has daily flights to major cities; it also has daily flights to Tunxi, from which you can catch a minibus to Huangshan. There are twice-weekly flights to Xian and Hong Kong. You can book flights at most major hotels or at China Eastern Airlines.

Huangshan's airport at Tunxi has daily flights to Hefei, as well as flights to Beijing and Guangzhou several times a week, Shanghai almost daily, Xian once a week, and Hong Kong twice a week. It's best to buy tickets at your hotel, or in advance at your starting point.

CARRIERS
➤ AIRLINES AND CONTACTS: **China Eastern Airlines** (⊠ 246 Jinzhai Lu, Hefei, ☎ 0559/282–2357).

BUS TRAVEL TO AND FROM ANHUI
Buses are the fastest way to get to Hefei from Nanjing. Coaches go between the cities about four times a day and take only 3½ hours; however, not all of these buses are air-conditioned, and they can be crowded and bumpy.

As the mountain town (Huangshanshi) of Huangshan itself has no railway station, you'll have to take a bus, either from Tunxi or from some point farther off. Although buses from Hangzhou (nine hours) and Hefei (11 hours) go through some gorgeous scenery, they often do not provide the most comfortable ride. You can try going to or from Hangzhou by bus and traveling the other direction by train or plane—the views from the bus really are worth the ride.

BUS TRAVEL WITHIN ANHUI

In Hefei the most useful buses are the No. 1, which passes through the center of town, and the No. 10, which travels just south of the southern parks and passes most of the foreign hotels. Both of these terminate at the train station.

EMERGENCIES

➤ CONTACTS: **Anhui Medical University Affiliated Hospital No. 1** (✉ 218 Jixi Lu, Hefei, ☎ 0559/363–6474).

TAXIS

Taxis are readily available in Hefei and easily flagged down on the streets or at the numerous taxi stops on each major road.

Minibuses and taxis from Tunxi to Tangkou congregate around the train station and will take you to the Huangshan main gates at the bottom of the mountain or up to the actual entrance to the climbing section for about Y20.

TOURS

At both the train station in Tuxi and at the main gates of Huangshan, street-side peddlers will offer you guided tours of the area, including transportation to various gates. These are usually reasonably priced; however, the guides' English tends to be minimal. You are usually better off just buying a map and hiring a taxi or taking a minibus up to the East Gate.

TRAIN TRAVEL

The train tracks between Nanjing and Hefei sweep through upper Anhui before descending south to Hefei, adding a good two hours onto what by highway is a 3½-hour ride. There is only one train a day from Nanjing to Hefei. Hefei is also connected to Beijing, Chengdu, and Xiamen; the direct connection to Zhengzhou passes through Kaifeng. There is also a direct line from Hefei to Jiujiang in Jiangxi. Sleeper tickets can be purchased in the ticket office east of the train station at window No. 2.

Trains to Huangshan stop in Tunxi, from where you can catch a minivan or cab to the Huangshan gates. The ride takes about an hour. It's best to arrive early in the day as many drivers are not eager to traverse the winding road in the dark, although they will for about Y100.

TRAVEL AGENCIES

Aside from hotel information desks, there are no travel agencies in Hefei or in Huangshan. It's best to plan from an agency in Nanjing or other major city.

VISITOR INFORMATION

The CITS is a small office and can assist with trips to Huangshan and ticket bookings. For other information it is easier to inquire at your hotel.
➤ TOURIST INFORMATION: **CITS** (✉ 153 Meishan Lu, ☎ 0551/281–2384).

ZHEJIANG

Zhejiang is a worthy province to house one of China's two "heavens on earth," the city of Hangzhou. Its scenery is known for lush beauty, and despite being one of China's smallest provinces, it is also one of the wealthiest. The river basin area to the north is countered by mountains in the south, and cultivated greenery is everywhere. The province was dynastically important starting in the 12th century, when Hangzhou was the capital of the Southern Song dynasty. It continued in importance even when the capital was moved away, largely because of its grain production and its scenic and cultural attractions. Zhejiang's farms are among the most prosperous in the country, producing tea, rice, wheat, barley, corn, and sweet potatoes. This province also provides one-third of China's silk. It's famous for its crafts and wares, including fine porcelain, silk products, embroideries, lace, wood and stone carvings, and sculptures. Zhejiang is also home to Putuoshan, a sacred Buddhist mountain.

Hangzhou

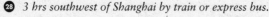

3 hrs southwest of Shanghai by train or express bus.

The southern terminus of the Grand Canal, Hangzhou was destined for greatness as an economic center from the canal's completion in AD 609. In 1126 the Song dynasty fled south from Kaifeng to Hangzhou to escape the Jurchen invaders. The era that ensued, later known as the Southern Song, witnessed the rise of Hangzhou's cultural and administrative importance. Its proximity not only to the canal but to river and ocean, as well as the unusual fertility of its environs, made Hangzhou the hub of southern Chinese culture. By the 13th century the city had a population of between 1 and 1.5 million people. From 1861 to 1863 it was occupied by the Taiping forces, and in the ensuing battles with the imperial forces, the city, along with its cultural artifacts and monuments, was largely destroyed.

As the center of so much traditional and imperial history, Hangzhou was also a natural target during the Cultural Revolution, when Red Guards smashed to bits much of what had survived the previous century's turmoil. However, many of the city's monuments have been repaired or reconstructed, and even the Red Guards couldn't destroy West Lake, which lends Hangzhou much of its romantic beauty. A little way outside the city, you can visit the plantations that produce the area's famous Long Jing tea, or stroll in forested hills to take in the views of the surrounding area. The lake provides a setting of serenity rarely seen in a Chinese city.

To explore Hangzhou's sights, you can start at the lake, which is the effective center of town. From the lake you can go on to visit the city proper and then move out to the less populous region to the southwest.

Hangzhou culture revolves around **Xihu** (West Lake). The lake was originally a lagoon, cut off from the nearby river, until the local government began taking steps to clear the lake's waters. A few years back they began pumping water from the nearby Qiantang River into the lake, and with the periodic dredgings of the lake floor and the daily skimmings of its surface, the lake is clearer and cleaner than it's been in centuries. The lake is crossed by two pedestrian causeways: the **Baidi** (named for the famed Tang dynasty poet, Bai Juyi) and the **Sudi** (named for the Song poet, Su Dongpo). Both walkways are lined with willow and peach trees, flowers and benches, and closed to automobiles, making them ideal for strolling or bicycle riding.

Officially run multiseat boats leave every half hour or so from near the **Hangzhou Overseas Chinese Hotel** (⊠ Hubin Lu 15) to the lake's islands, and a slew of smaller private boats are moored around the lake. If you want your own boat with no rower, you can rent a paddleboat, some of which look like science fiction inventions.

Gushan, in the middle of Baidi causeway, is the lake's largest island. Inside is **Zhongshan Gongyuan,** a small, but lovely park, centered on a pond and several pavilions. From here, you can follow the path up the hill to the **Xileng Yinshe** (Seal Engraver's Society). This was once the headquarters of a professional seal-carving operation. There are several small buildings with examples of carvings, including an engraved monument dating from nearly 2,000 years ago. The trip up the hill to the society is worth it, even for those who aren't interested in Chinese stamps. A beautiful garden in front of the society's buildings has the best views of Xihu in all of Hangzhou. Gushan Island is also home to the **Zhejiang Bowuguan** (Zhejiang Provincial Museum; ✉ Y8, ☉ weekdays 8:45–4:45). On display is an excellent collection of bronzes from the Shang and Zhou dynasties (1600 BC–221 BC); natural history and ceramics exhibits; and a section for locally made contemporary art. ✉ Y6. ☉ *Daily 8–dusk.*

NEED A
BREAK?

Adjacent to the Seal Engraver's Society is a small souvenir shop that serves tea. Order a cup and have a seat on the hilltop veranda. The view, especially at sunset, will explain why Chinese have loved this place for centuries.

Just off the banks of Gushan is the small man-made island of **Santan Yinyue** (Three Pools Reflecting the Moon). On the island are numerous ponds connected by small bridges and dotted with pavilions. Off the island's southern shore are three stone pagodas. During the autumn moon (August), fires are lit in the pagodas. The moonlight reflects three golden disks into the water, hence the name. Most boat rides include the Y10 admission in the fare. Be sure to check before boarding.

Parks and a paved waterfront-walkway ring most of West Lake. On the east shore is **Ertong Gongyuan** (Children's Park), a kitschy park with playgrounds and rides. More peaceful, and historic, is **Liulang Weny-ing** (Orioles Singing in the Willow Waves). This is a nice place to relax on a bench or in the grass and watch boats and windsurfers on the lake. Orioles still sing here, though not in the "willow waves." Rather, they cry from the large aviary that cages them near the water. On the southeastern shore rises a small hilltop park with nice views. **Leifeng Xizhao** (Evening Sunlight at Thunder Peak Pagoda) no longer has its pagoda, but the sunsets are still wonderful.

Baoshi Shan (Precious Stone Hill), with its famous pagoda, **Baochu Ta** (Protecting Chu Pagoda), can be seen on the north side of Xihu from just about anywhere on the lake. Numerous paths lead from the lakeside up to the hilltop, from where you can not only see all of West Lake, but also a good part of Hangzhou. The original pagoda was built about 970; the present structure dates from 1933. Both paved and unpaved paths cover the mountain; it's well worth your time to spend a morning or afternoon exploring. Baoshi Shan is dotted with Buddhist and Taoist shrines and temples—some impressive, others not so—as well as some mysterious caves. In the summer, locals often gather in the bigger caves for picnics or cards to escape the heat.

On the back side of Baoshi Shan is a well-kept park, also with a cave. **Huanglong Dong** (Yellow Dragon Cave) is famous for its (purportedly) never-ending stream of water spurting from the head of a yellow dragon into a pond several meters below. Above the fountain on the hillside is another yellow dragon's head, this time standing as the entrance to a fairly good-sized cave. Below, near the lower entrance, lies a stage, where several times a day Yue Opera performances are given. There is also a bamboo groove with rare "square bamboo." A bronze statue of two dragon angels stands before the grove. As the placard to the statue says, be sure to "touch the buttocks" of these cherublike imps for good luck. *Shiguang Lu.* ✉ *Y15; Y2 more for the opera performance.* ☉ *Daily 8–dusk.*

Near Gushan stands the **Yue Fei Mu** (Yue Fei Mausoleum), a temple built to honor the Song general Yue Fei (1103–42), a commander against the Jurchen invaders. A jealous courtier convinced the emperor that the loyal Yue Fei was a traitor, and the emperor ordered him executed. Before submitting himself to the emperor's will, Yue Fei had the words LOYAL TO THE LAST tattooed on his back. Twenty years later he was rehabilitated and deified and is now one of China's national heroes, a symbol of patriotic duty. The temple wall replicates the tattooed inscription, while a statue of the traitorous courtier kneels in shame nearby. Traditionally, you're supposed to spit on statues of traitors, but a recent sign near the statue asks visitors to refrain. ✉ *Beishan Lu, west of Gushan.* ✉ *Y15.* ☉ *Daily 7–6.*

A short ride southwest of the lake takes you to the **Longjing Wencha** (Dragon Well Tea Park), where you can buy the local Long Jing green tea from people who are serious about quality. This park, set in the middle of some tea plantations, is the site of the well from which water for the best tea comes. Tea sellers may invite prospective buyers to taste the tea, often at the seller's house. The prices seem ridiculous until you take a sip: there really is a difference. However, be sure to bargain for a good price. ✉ *South on Longjing Lu.*

Almost directly south of the lake, about 15 minutes by bus, the **Hupao Meng Quan** (Running Tiger Dream Spring) has a temple built on a dream. According to legend, Qi Gong, a traveling monk decided this setting would be perfect for a temple, but as there was no stream or other water in the place, he couldn't build one. Sleeping on the ground, he dreamed that two tigers came and ripped up the earth around him. When he awoke, he was lying next to the stream that they had dug for him. He duly built the temple. The grounds have a bamboo grove, a nondescript teahouse, a modern statue of the dreamer with his tigers, and an intriguing "dripping wall." This cutout part of the mountainside is so porous and moist that it exudes water from its surface. Locals always come here to fill their water jugs, believing the water has special qualities—and it does. If you don't believe it, ask one of the people working in the temple souvenir shop to float a coin on the surface of the water to prove it. ✉ *Hupao Lu, just south of lake.* ✉ *Y10.* ☉ *Daily 8:30–6.*

★ The **Lingyin Si** (Temple of the Soul's Retreat) was founded in 326 by Hui Li, a Buddhist monk from India (Hui Li was his Chinese name). Reportedly, he looked at the mountains surrounding the site of the current temple and exclaimed, "This is the place where the souls of immortals retreat," hence, the name. Perhaps even more than the temple itself, Lingyin Si is famous for the Buddhist iconographical figures carved into the limestone of the mountain, **Feilai Feng** (The Mountain that Flew Here), that faces the temple. From the 10th to the 14th centuries, monks and artists carved 338 stone iconographical images. Unfortunately, the destruction wrought by the Red Guards during the Cultural Revolution is nowhere in Hangzhou more evident than here, even though admirable attempts have been made to restore much than was damaged. The caves are interesting and full of carvings.

The temple itself is across from the Buddhist carvings. It is definitely worth visiting, being one of China's ten large Zen (Chan) Buddhist temples. However, beware: Lingyin Si is Hangzhou's most popular attraction, apart from Xihu, and is always crowded. Avoid the place on weekends and holidays if at all possible. ✉ *Lingyin Si Lu, west of the city.* ✉ *Y20 (park fee); Y15 (temple fee).* ☉ *Daily 5 AM–6 PM.*

A few miles outside the city, atop **Yuelin Shan** (Moon Mountain) and overlooking the banks of the Qiantang River, stands the impressive **Liuhe Ta** (The Pagoda of Six Harmonies). Looking from the outside, it seems as if this structure has more floors than it actually does, but you can climb to the top of the seven-story pagoda for great views of the river. On the 18th day of the eighth lunar month, the pagoda is packed with people, all wanting the best seat for "Qiantang Reversal." On this day the flow of the river reverses itself, creating large waves that for centuries have delighted observers. Behind the pagoda in an extensive park with a pagoda exhibition: expert re-creations of a hundred or so miniature pagodas, representing every Chinese style, are on permanent display here. ⊠ *Fuxing Jie, South of the city.* 🎫 *Y15.* 🕐 *Daily 6–6:30.*

Dining and Lodging

Hangzhou is one of China's most heavily visited cities; reservations for hotels are recommended any time of year but are absolutely essential on spring and autumn weekends, when crowds from outlying regions descend on the city.

$$–$$$$ ✕ **Louwailou Restaurant.** Founded in 1848, this restaurant on the
★ banks of West Lake is Hangzhou's most famous. Although a bit overrun with tourists during peak season, it serves festive afternoon teas as well as excellent meals. The fish dishes are made with fish raised in a small sectioned-off area of West Lake in front of the restaurant. The Hangzhou specialties include a shrimp dish made with Long Jing tea leaves and a cooked fish that comes to the table still smacking its lips. ⊠ *30 Gushan Lu,* ☎ *0571/796–9682. AE, MC, V.*

$–$$ ✕ **Zhiweiguan Restaurant.** The first floor here is a pay-as-you-go dim sum cafeteria. With no English menus you'll need to rely on body language to order a bamboo steamer of their famous dumplings. The second and fourth floors offer a much more pleasant dining experience (with English menus). The third floor hosts private parties. Try the peaceful dining room just off the banquet room on the fourth floor. ⊠ *83 Renhe Lu,* ☎ *0571/706–6933. No credit cards.*

$$$$ 🏨 **Shangri-La Hotel Hangzhou.** On the lakeside, the Shangri-La is the best-placed hotel in Hangzhou. The hotel's own gardens merge into the walkways around Xihu, and boat rides and parks are a few minutes' walk away. Suites face out onto the lake. ⊠ *78 Beishan Lu, 310007,* ☎ *0571/797–7951; 800/942–5050 from U.S.,* ℻ *0571/707–3545,* 🌐 *www.shangri-la.com. 341 rooms, 46 suites. 2 restaurants, meeting room. AE, MC, V.*

$$$ 🏨 **Dragon New World Hotel Hangzhou.** In the hilly area around Yellow Dragon Cave and Dragon Well, the Dragon New World stands in relatively peaceful and attractive surroundings. It makes a good starting point for walking tours of the city: you can reach the Baochu Ta and the lake on foot. ⊠ *7 Shuguang Lu, 310007,* ☎ *0571/799–8833,* ℻ *0571/799–8090. 476 rooms, 31 suites. 3 restaurants, pool, hair salon, massage, sauna, tennis court, health club, bicycles, baby-sitting, business services, meeting room, travel services. AE, MC, V.*

$$$ 🏨 **Wanghu Hotel.** A couple minutes' walk from the lake, the Wanghu is oriented toward business travelers. It offers a special "business club" service with a 24-hour business center and meeting rooms as well translation services and PCs. The hotel also serves complimentary breakfasts and teas to give business travelers a chance to meet. ⊠ *2 Huancheng Xilu, 310006,* ☎ *0571/707–1024,* ℻ *0571/707–1350,* 🌐 *www.wanghuhotel.com. 406 rooms, 14 suites. 2 restaurants, bar, pool, hair salon, sauna, health club, business services, meeting room. AE, MC, V.*

$$ 🏨 **Hangzhou Overseas Chinese Hotel.** In spite of the name, this hotel welcomes visitors of any origin. Rooms on upper floors offer good views of Xihu. The restaurant serves local specialties and traditional foods. You can also rent a car here to tour the area. ⊠ *15 Hubin Lu, 310006,* ☏ *0571/707–4401,* ℻ *0571/707–4978. 228 rooms, 2 suites. 2 restaurants, bar, hair salon, bicycles, business services, meeting room. AE, MC, V.*

$ 🏨 **Dong Po Hotel.** This budget business hotel is clean and comfortable. The smaller rooms are a bit spartan, but its prime location in the center of town—two blocks from the lake and two blocks from the night market—makes it a good pick. ⊠ *52 Renhe Lu, 310000,* ☏ *0571/702–4220. 80 rooms, 3 suites. Restaurant, business services. MC, V.*

Nightlife and the Arts

Yue Opera performances take place daily at the **Huanglong Dong Yuanyuan Mingshu Yuan theater** (⊠ 16 Shuguang Lu, ☏ 0571/798–5860, 🎫 Y2, plus Y15 park admission).

The nightlife in Hangzhou mostly consists of pleasant strolls along West Lake on balmy evenings. The lakeside portion of Hubin Lu south of the Wanghu Hotel has a number of small, cozy teahouses. A rarity for any city in China, a dark jazz-club atmosphere has been successfully reproduced at the **Golden Sax** (⊠ 1 Banqiao Lu, ☏ 0571/703–5542), a club run by the Hangzhou Musicians Cooperative. Bartenders in tux shirts and black bow ties add an air of sophistication to a nightly serving of live jazz and reasonably priced drinks. The muted brown-and-yellow interior of **Paradise Rock** (⊠ 15 Hubin Lu, next to Overseas Chinese Hotel, ☏ 0571/707–4401), a British-style pub, creates a warm atmosphere for light drinks and conversation. Live jazz and rock music is performed here weekends.

Shopping

The best things to buy in Hangzhou are green tea and silk, but all sorts of wooden crafts, silk fans and umbrellas, and antiques are available in a great variety of small shops sprinkled around town. The local **Friendship Store** (⊠ Hubin Lu and Qinchun Lu) sells crafts and silks. For the best Long Jing tea, you can go out to the tea plantations themselves (☞ Longjing Wencha, *above*). On a stretch of Yenan Lu in the center of town dotted with small tea shops, look for the large woklike tea roasters at each shop's entrance. The **Longjing Tea Shop** (⊠ 89 Yanan Lu, ☏ 0571/702–9605) has especially good selections.

Where Hubin Lu passes beside the lake, an informal shopping district stretches out to the east, culminating in the **night market** (⊠ Wushan Lu between Pinghai Lu and Youdian Lu); it's open 6 PM–10:30 PM. This is the best place in Hangzhou to find all the choice products of the region: silks—from dresses to boxers to straight off the reel—and artifacts from the Qing to the Cultural Revolution. Try the north end of the market for the clay teapots of Yixing County.

Zhejiang A to Z

To research prices, get advice from other travelers, and book travel arrangements, visit www.fodors.com.

AIR TRAVEL

CARRIERS

You can travel between Hong Kong and Hangzhou daily on Dragonair (Dragon New World Hotel Hangzhou). There are regular flights to all other major Chinese cities, often daily, depending on the season. ➤ AIRLINES AND CONTACTS: **CAAC** (⊠ 390 Tiyuchang Lu, ☏ 0571/515–4259). **Dragonair** (⊠ Shuguang Lu, ☏ 0571/799–8833 ext. 6061).

AIRPORTS AND TRANSFERS

TRANSFERS

Major hotels offer limo service to the airport. Taxis to the airport cost around Y80. A bus leaves from the Minhang Ticket Office (395 Tiyuchang Lu) every 40 minutes during the day for about Y25.

BIKE TRAVEL

Traffic makes biking a dodgy endeavor in Hangzhou. However, the two causeways, Baidi and Sudi, are closed to automobile traffic and perfect for cycling. Major hotels have bike rentals, as does the Liulang Wenying Park, south of the Children's Park (Ertong Gongyuan). The rental rate is usually about Y6 per hour, though a deposit of Y300 is usually required.

➤ BIKE RENTALS: **Liulang Wenying Park** (✉ Nanshan Lu, on east side of lake).

BOAT AND FERRY TRAVEL

You can travel overnight between Hangzhou and Suzhou by ferry up and down the Grand Canal. Tickets are available through CITS or at the dock. The boat leaves daily from Hangzhou at 5:30 PM and arrives in Suzhou the next morning at 7.

You can take a two- or four-seat paddleboat by yourself in Hangzhou's Xilu, but these can't be docked at the islands. Official boats run to Santanyinyue Island whenever they have enough passengers—usually about every 40 minutes. Walking around the lake, you'll be approached by vendors selling rides on private four-seaters. These are more expensive but quieter and will go wherever you want.

➤ BOAT AND FERRY INFORMATION: **CITS** (✉ Huancheng Beilu, ☎ 0571/ 515–3360).

BUS TRAVEL TO AND FROM ZHEJIANG

The bus hub of the province is Hangzhou, which has four stations in town. The West Bus Station has several buses daily to Huangshan, in Anhui. The East Bus Station is the town's biggest, with several hundred departures per day to destinations as far away as Beijing. Make sure you check with your hotel or travel agent which bus station you need to use.

➤ BUS INFORMATION: **East Bus Station** (✉ 215 Liangshan Xilu). **West Bus Station** (✉ 60 Tianmushan Lu).

BUS TRAVEL WITHIN ZHEJIANG

Nearly every street in Hangzhou except the causeways has bus stops; the buses come frequently and cost Y1. Unfortunately, you'd be lucky to find an uncrowded bus anytime before 9 PM. If you're willing to brave the crowds, though, ask at your hotel desk or the Xinhua Bookstore about English-language bus maps. Nos. 7 and 505 go to Lingyin Si (Temple of the Soul's Retreat); No. 514 goes to Hupao Meng Quan (Running Tiger Dream Spring); Nos. 16 and 28 take you to Huanglong Dong (Yellow Dragon Cave). Nos. 7, 27, and 507 all run along the north side of the lake. There is also a tourist bus (Y2) that stops at the major sightseeing spots.

EMERGENCIES

➤ CONTACTS: **Hangzhou Red Cross Hospital** (✉ 38 Huancheng Donglu, ☎ 0571/518–6042 or 0571/518–3137). **Zhejiang Medical University Affiliated Hospital No. 1** (✉ 261 Qingchun Lu, ☎ 0571/707–2524).

TAXIS

Red four-door cabs are in great supply in Hangzhou. Some larger taxis cost more. Beware of drivers who take the scenic route instead of the straight one.

TOURS

Hotels can set up tours for interested groups, and CITS will oblige for a fee. Hawkers or taxi drivers at the train station or in front of your hotel may offer tours; although these can be as good as the official ones, their English is often minimal.

TRAIN TRAVEL

Travel between Shanghai and Hangzhou is quick and convenient: normal trains take about three hours; the new "tourist train" takes only two. The train station is crowded and difficult to manage, but hotel travel desks can often book tickets for you for a small fee.

➤ TRAIN INFORMATION: **Hangzhou train station** (✉ Jiang Cheng Lu, in western part of city).

TRAVEL AGENCIES

Most hotels have their own agencies, as well as visitor information.

➤ LOCAL AGENT REFERRALS: **Zhejiang Comfort Travel** (✉ In Shangri-La Hotel, 78 Beishan Lu, ☎ 0571/796–5005). **Zhejiang Women's International Travel Service** (✉ 1 Huancheng Xilu, ☎ 0571/702–9348).

VISITOR INFORMATION

➤ TOURIST INFORMATION: **Hangzhou Travel and Tourism Bureau** (✉ 484 Yanan Lu, ☎ 0571/515–2645). **Zhejiang China International Travel Service** (CITS; ✉ 1 Shihan Lu, ☎ 0571/516–0877).

FUJIAN

Fujian has a long and distinctive recorded history, dating back at least as far as the Warring States period (475–221 BC). At that time the state of Yue—which ruled the area that covers today's provinces of Jiangsu and Zhejiang—moved southward to an area that included Fujian after being defeated by the neighboring state of Chu. Under the Qin dynasty, the first to rule over a united China, what is now Fujian became a prefecture known as Min, a name that even now is sometimes used as an abbreviation for Fujian.

Evidence of early civilizations that predated the Warring States period has been found in abundance. The strange so-called boat coffins from Wuyi almost certainly date from the mysterious Xia dynasty that, it is thought, flourished between 2100 and 1600 BC. Carved pictographs have also been discovered here from the earliest dynasty known to have existed, the Shang (about 1600–1100 BC).

Although very clearly part of mainstream—or Han—China, Fujian is home to a surprising number of non-Han ethnic groups. The Ding and the Guo, in the southern part of the province, are the descendants of Arabs and Persians who traded here in the Tang and Song dynasties, and the Dan people are thought to descend from the Mongols who settled here during the Yuan dynasty. Best known are the Hakka, with their distinctive fringed hats, who migrated to Fujian from Henan many centuries ago.

Hilly, rural Fujian is particularly associated with the massive waves of emigration that took place from China during the 19th century, when war and decadent government caused widespread poverty here. Its most famous agricultural product is tea, some of which is considered among the very best in China. (Wuyi Rock Tea is said to be an essential traditional drink for the British royal family.)

Fujian's main attractions are the principal cities of Fuzhou and Xiamen, which have become bustling paradigms of the new entrepreneurial China, and the scenic area of Wuyi Shan in the northeast. Food is distinctive and good in the coastal cities, and for the shopper Fujian is a famed provider of soapstone, much of which is used in the production of chops (traditional seals). Other crafts typical of the region include lacquerware, puppet heads from Quanzhou, and porcelain from Dehua.

Fuzhou

200 km (124 mi) northeast of Xiamen; 1,500 km (930 mi) southeast of Beijing; 700 km (434 mi) northeast of Hong Kong.

The capital of Fujian, lying about 40 km (25 mi) upstream from the Min River estuary, Fuzhou dates from the 3rd century BC, when it was well known as a center of ore smelting. Subsequently it became the capital of the independent and small kingdom of Minyue, when it was known as Minzhou. In the 8th century, when it was absorbed into the Chinese empire during the Tang dynasty, Fuzhou acquired its present name, which means "fortunate city." The name may derive from its splendid location close to the Fu Mountains on a green, subtropical plain. It became an important commercial port specializing in the export of tea, growing extremely wealthy in the process.

As a major port city, it was the home base for the voyages of the Ming eunuch admiral-explorer Zheng He. This status as a major port also attracted Western powers in the mid-19th century, making it one of the first ports opened to foreign traders and residents following the signing of the Treaty of Nanking in 1842.

Marco Polo is supposed to have passed through in the 13th century, referring to Fuzhou as a "veritable marvel." It cannot be described as such any longer; on the whole, despite its proliferation of banyan trees planted during the Song dynasty, it is a rather gray town in the modern Chinese idiom. It is, nevertheless, an important city—the home of Fujian University and several industries, including tea production and the making of stone handicrafts—with some sites of historical significance. It is also a good base for visits to other places of interest in the province. Getting around this sprawling city on foot is difficult—pedicabs or taxis are more efficient.

A Good Tour

Begin on Gutian Lu in the center of town. After returning a salute to the statue of Mao, head for the **Yushan Fengjing Qu** ㉙ (Yu Mountain Scenic Area) and its Baita (White Pagoda), a 16th-century brick-and-wood tower modeled on the 10th-century original. Walk up the paved path to the Fuzhou Shi Bowugaun (Fuzhou City Museum) and learn a bit about the city's history. Farther up, stop and have a cup of tea or soda in the relaxing Orchid Garden and take in the city views. **Wushan** ㉚ (Black Hill), another mountain park, is a ten-minute walk along Gutian Lu (though the name changes to Wushan Lu). Buy some incense and say a prayer in the Taoist temple at the top of the hill. From here walk or take a taxi to Aomen Lu, on the north side of Wushan, and the **Linzexu Jinianguan** ㉛ (Tomb of Lin Zexu) for a history lesson of the Opium War. Wander around the alleys of **San Fang Qi Xiang** ㉜ (Three Lanes and Seven Alleys) for a look at old Fuzhou. Another 15-minute walk up Bayiqi Lu will bring you to **Kaiyuan Si** ㉝ (Kaiyuan Temple), where you can check out the bronze Buddha. If you arrive at lunchtime

(11:30, sharp) the monks may invite you to eat a vegetarian meal with them. From here grab a taxi or the bus and head north to **Xihu** ㉞ (West Lake). Spend some time wandering around the lakeside park, perhaps visiting the zoo or prefectural museum. A taxi ride to the western suburbs will bring you to **Xichan Si** ㉟ (Western Chan Temple), Fuzhou's most important Chan (Zen) Buddhist temple. Finally, take a taxi east to the city's most famous sightseeing spot, **Gushan** ㊱ (Drum Mountain). The best time to visit Gushan is early in the morning, before the crowds and city smog from Fuzhou invade the place.

TIMING

You'll probably enjoy the sights more if you spread the tour across two days. It would be a shame to not spend at least a half day—an entire day would be ideal—exploring Gushan.

Sights to See

㊱ **Gushan** (Drum Mountain). Rising 3,200 ft, this beautiful park is only a 20-minute bus trip or a ten-minute taxi ride east of the city. A stone walkway goes up to the more important places on the mountain, but there are also dozens of unpaved trails leading off to more secluded spots: Near the top is **Yongquan Si** (Surging Spring Temple) (✉ Y6), a large, active temple founded in 908 by the Duke of Fujian to accommodate the monk Shen Yan. The temple is home to an outstanding library of more than 10,000 Buddhist sutras, some of which are said to have been written in the blood of disciples. Every afternoon at 4, the monks begin their chants, which you're welcome to listen to and watch. There are several paths that continue up to the top of Gushan and onto the surrounding mountains. Along the way are pavilions, stones, and grottoes with Buddhist inscriptions—many dating from the Song dynasty—waterfalls, and above all, marvelous views. *Fuma Lu, east of the city.* ⊙ *8–4:30.*

㉝ **Kaiyuan Si** (Kaiyuan Temple). Originally built in 548 during the Liang dynasty, the temple is known for its iron Buddha, weighing some 40 tons and thought to have been cast during the Tang dynasty. However, during the mid-16th century Qing-dynasty restorations, a silver pagoda was discovered under the Buddha that was dated to the Northern Song period, in the 11th century. ⊠ *17 Kaiyuan Lu, east of Jing Dalu.* ✉ *Free.* ⊙ *Daily 8–11:30, 3–5.*

㉛ **Linzexu Jinianguan** (Tomb of Lin Zexu). An enlightened imperial commissioner, Lin (1785–1850) confiscated 20,000 cases of opium from the British. This act led to the outbreak of the First Opium War, in 1840. The tomb, in the northern suburbs of the city, is lavish, with six chambers on four levels and a pair of guardian lions in front. ⊠ *16 Aomen Lu, on Jinshishan.* ✉ *Y3.* ⊙ *Daily 8–5:30.*

★ ㉜ **San Fang Qi Xiang** (Three Lanes and Seven Alleys). To get an idea of what much of Fuzhou looked like until the early 1980s, you can visit a number of small alleys and lanes that up to now have been protected from the wrecking ball of Chinese urban modernization. San Fang Qi Xiang refers to the streets that intersect with Bayiqi Lu between Gutian Lu and Dongda Jie just west of Yushan. On Bayiqi Lu look for the old stone archways—some with classical Chinese motifs and others with Communist hammer-and-sickle insignias. Although some of the lanes are gradually being squeezed out of existence by urban growth, others, with their whitewashed walls and peaceful courtyards of the Ming and Qing dynasties, are still home to old men playing *mah-jongg.* ⊠ *Guanglu, Wenru Lu, and Yijin Lu; Jibi Xiang, Gong Xiang, Ta Xiang, Anmin Xiang, Huang Xiang, Langguan Xiang, and Yangqiao Xiang; along Bayiqi Lu between Gutian Lu and Dongda Jie.*

Fuzhou

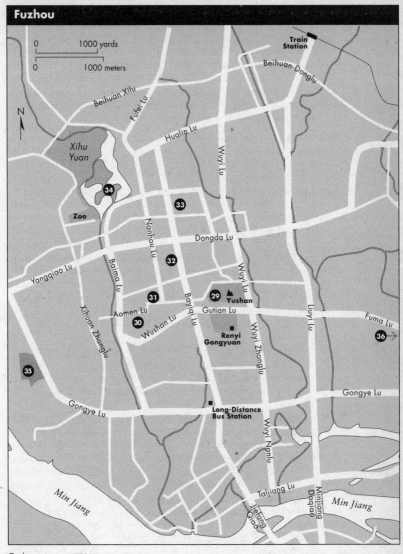

30 **Wushan** (Black Hill). In the center of the city, the slopes of Black Hill are covered in stone inscriptions, among them an example of the work of the famous Tang calligrapher Li Yangbing and records of the duties of Ming eunuchs, who were put to work in the shipyards. Historically, Wushan was known as a place for Taoists to gather for ascetic training. A small, active temple rests on the summit. At the bottom of the hill is the black granite **Wu Ta** (Black Pagoda). This 115-ft-high pagoda was originally built in 799 and is covered with fine carving work. ⊠ *Wushan Lu.*

35 **Xichan Si** (Western Chan Temple). Ancient Fuzhou had four Chan (Zen) Buddhist temples laid out along the four points of the compass—one each in the northern, southern, eastern, and western quarters of the city. Xichan Si is the only temple of the four to survive. It was originally built in the Sui dynasty, but most of the current buildings were constructed during the Qing. The incredible amount of recent construction financed by overseas donations is evidence of the growing vibrancy of Buddhism on the mainland. The beautiful giant multiton brass statue of Guanyin—the bodhisattva of mercy and compassion—in the **Guanyin Ge** was financed by a devout Singaporean businessman. It was cast in Shanghai and brought down by train in the early 1990s. The 15-story **Baoen Ta** (Pagoda of Declaring Grace), also built with foreign donations, affords a beautiful view of the temple. The spacious temple grounds are perfect for walking. ⊠ *45 Gongye Lu.* ☒ *Y3; additional Y1 for the pagoda.* ⊘ *Daily 7–7.*

NEED A BREAK? Near **Shuiyun Ting** (Water and Cloud Pavilion), next to a trickling waterfall and overlooking the valley and the Min River, is a small and inexpensive teahouse where for Y15–25 you can drink locally produced Wulong Tea and enjoy the pleasant scenery. The tearoom also serves snacks.

34 **Xihu** (West Lake). Dug in AD 282 to irrigate the surrounding countryside, Xihu has been used as a park ever since the Min kingdom (from the 8th century). On his return to Fuzhou toward the middle of the 19th century, after his time as an imperial official, Lin Zexu, a native of Fuzhou, had the lake cleared and some of the Tang pavilions restored. They eventually fell into disrepair but were restored in 1985 to commemorate the 200th anniversary of Lin's birth. A prefectural museum, with artifacts and art from Fuzhou, and the Fuzhou Zoo are also here. ⊠ *Xihu Yuan, east end of Hualin Lu, in northwest part of town.* ☒ *Y5 (park); Y10 (museum); Y10 (zoo).* ⊘ *Daily 7 AM–8 PM; zoo 7–6.*

29 **Yushan Fengjing Qu** (Yu Mountain Scenic Area). Downtown Fuzhou has two nice parks, both situated on small mountains, covered with banyan trees and flowers, and within walking distance of each other. Yushan Fengjing Qu is the larger and more central of the two, rising across the street from **Renyi Guangchang** (Renyi Square) and behind the large, alabaster statue of Chairman Mao. At the bottom of Yushan stands **Baita** (White Pagoda; ☒ Y10), an unspectacular pagoda, dating from 1548, whose main claim to fame are its inscriptions, some dating from the Song dynasty. For those interested in local history, check out the **Fuzhou Shi Bowugaun** (Fuzhou City Museum; ☒ Y5, ⊘ Daily 8:30–5), halfway up the Yushan. Closer to the top is an nice orchid garden with a tea patio. ⊠ *Gutian Lu.* ☒ Y3.

Dining and Lodging

For inexpensive food, the area around the train station abounds in street restaurants selling noodles and dumplings. The hotels in this area are also the some of the cheapest (and grimiest) in town. The better places are all closer to downtown.

$–$$$ ✕ **Beijing Restaurant.** Here crowds feast on Peking duck, beef kebabs, and Mongolian hotpot while the waitstaff and dishwashers rush to keep up. The decor is simple because the food is the main attraction. Come early or ask someone from your hotel staff to reserve a table for you. ⊠ *92 Dong Jie,* ☎ *0591/753–5922. No credit cards.*

$–$$$ ✕ **Fuzhou Restaurant.** At this comfortable restaurant you'll find local
★ dishes, especially fish and fried oysters. The master chef, Mr. Qiang Mugen, is famous for his *Fotiaoqiang,* which he prepared for Ronald Reagan during the president's visit to China in the 1980s. The dish arrives in a large pot sealed in a red ribbon. ⊠ *18 Dongda Lu, 5F,* ☎ *0591/753–5777. No credit cards.*

$–$$$ ✕ **Juchunyuan.** Founded in 1877, this esteemed restaurant has a very
★ cozy dining room and well-trained waitstaff. It specializes in seafood and *Fotiaoqiang* (Buddha Jumping Over the Wall), a dish made of shark's fin, fish heads, squid, sea cucumber, and pork tripe, among other things. ⊠ *2 Bayiqi Beilu, 3F,* ☎ *0591/753–3604. AE, MC, V.*

$–$$$ ✕ **Nantai Lezhuang.** The cuisine is local here, and although the atmosphere is unsophisticated, the dishes—which include fresh fish, when available, and subtly flavored soups such as shark's fin—are usually reliable. ⊠ *Guohuo Nanlu,* ☎ *0591/753–2034. No credit cards.*

$ ✕ **Xichan Si Sucai Guan.** On the grounds of Xichan Si, this restaurant cooks up excellent vegetarian fare. The menu is in Chinese, but fortunately most of the offerings are set meals. To order, simply select the number of people and the price range you would like. ⊠ *Xichan Si, Gongye Lu,* ☎ *no phone. No credit cards.*

$$$ ☷ **Hot Spring Hotel.** One of the first upscale hotels in Fuzhou, this one is still counted among the best. It's in the northern part of the city near the airport. ⊠ *218 Wusi Lu, 350003,* ☎ *0591/785–1818,* ℻ *0591/ 783–5150. 303 rooms. 2 restaurants, pool, hair salon, sauna, bowling, business services. AE, V.*

$$–$$$ ☷ **Foreign Trade Centre Hotel.** This hotel in the middle of the commercial
★ district is the spot for creature comforts. There are two wings; the newer, originally intended as office space, was recently turned into part of the hotel. Standard rooms are huge (and more costly). The hotel has an excellent Western restaurant. ⊠ *73 Wusi Lu, 350001,* ☎ *0591/752– 3388,* ℻ *0591/755–0358,* ⊞ *ftcfj.com. 343 rooms, 54 suites. 4 restaurants, pool, sauna, tennis court, gym, business services. AE, MC, V.*

$$ ☷ **Fuzhou Hotel.** This hotel is sparklingly clean, and the staff is eager to please. The location is ideal—in the center of town just south of Yushan. The complimentary breakfast buffet is enough to fuel you up for a day of excursions around Fuzhou. ⊠ *103 Bayiqi Lu, 350005,* ☎ *0591/333–3333,* ℻ *0591/332–9833. 255 rooms, 53 suites. 2 restaurants, hair salon, gym, nightclub, business services. AE, MC, V.*

$$ ☷ **Fuzhou Lakeside Hotel.** With simply but comfortably furnished standard rooms, this hotel is close to the West Lake and convenient for sightseeing. ⊠ *158 Hubin Lu, 350003,* ☎ *0591/783–9888,* ℻ *0591/ 783–9752,* ⊞ *www.lakeside-hotel.com. 423 rooms. 2 restaurants, pool, business services. AE, V.*

$ **Changcheng Duofu Hotel.** In the center of town near Yushan, this hotel is a good budget option. Price varies depending on which floor you choose. The rooms on the lower floors are a bit noisy. ⊠ *172 Wuyi Beilu, 350001.* ☎ *0591/752–0388,* ℻ *0591/752–1945. 143 rooms. Restaurant, bar. No credit cards.*

$ ☷ **Donghu Hotel.** Convenient to the railway station and reasonably central, this hotel has moderately priced rooms in its older building and more upscale rooms in its new building. It has Chinese and Western restaurants and hot springs. The rooms are well kept and a good value, though the hotel staff is a bit detached. ⊠ *73 Dongda Lu, 350001,* ☎

0591/755–7755, FAX 0591/555–5519. 255 rooms, 11 suites. 2 restaurants, pool, gym. AE, MC, V.

Nightlife and the Arts

There are no specific venues for the performing arts, but there are often concerts both of traditional music and of the local version of Chinese **opera.** Opera is often performed during the day in parks by local enthusiasts. Check with **CITS** (⊠ 107 Jing Da Lu, ☎ 0591/750–2794) for locations and times.

Bars in the Western sense do not exist outside the hotels. Those who can raise the money set up small establishments that serve snacks and beer, but they are usually singularly lacking in atmosphere. The best discos are in the expensive hotels. **Karaoke** parlors are all over the city—look for neon signs with the letters OK included in them.

Outdoor Activities and Sports

★ Through CITS you can arrange **boat trips** along the Min River, 40 km (25 mi) downstream to the sea. The scenery is attractive—you pass Drum Mountain as you go—and the various craft on the river make it an absorbing ride. Ticket prices start at around Y60.

You can rent a bicycle through CITS. The best swimming pools are in hotels, where nonresidents must pay a fee. There are also beaches at Meizhou. For hiking try the scenic area of Wuyishan or Gushan.

Shopping

Among the local specialties are Shoushan stone carving, made with a form of alabaster; porcelain from Dehua; lacquerware; and lacquer painting. Tea is also a good buy in this part of China. For arts and crafts try the **Fuzhou Cultural Products Center** and other stores along Gutian Lu just south of Yushan.

Among street markets, the most interesting is the **Flower and Bird Market** (⊠ Liuyi Zhonglu), which stocks ornamental fish, miniature trees, rock gardens, and exotic pets such as monkeys.

Meizhou

㊲ *2½ hrs by express bus from Fuzhou via Putian and Wenjia; 4 hrs by bus from Xiamen via Putian and Wenjia.*

A rocky offshore island ringed by beaches and small fishing villages, Meizhou is well known for its rugged beauty. According to Taoists it is the birthplace of Mazu, goddess of the sea. The **Meizhou Mazu Si** (Meizhou Mazu Temple), a short walk from the ferry pier, is the main center of activity on the island. The temple is actually a complex of dozens of structures filled with burning incense and hawkers selling cheap souvenirs. Stone paths lead up to a small peak where a huge statue of Mazu looks out over the ocean.

Mazu's original name was Lin Mo. She was born in AD 930 in Zhongmen to a prominent Fujian family. According to legend, as a child she never cried and was exceptionally intelligent. At the age of 13 she was adopted by a Taoist priest and devoted the rest of her life to scientific, spiritual, and charitable pursuits. In 987, deciding that she had had enough of temporal life, the legend goes, Lin Mo climbed Mt. Meifeng and sailed away on the clouds. Thereafter she was often sighted at sea at times of danger and acquired the name *Mazu* (ancestral mother).

Since numerous tour groups invade the island during the day, the temple is best visited in the morning before the people arrive or in the evening after they go. On the far side of the island are several nice fishing villages and secluded beaches worth exploring. The water is, however, a bit chilly.

The busiest days on the island are Mazu's birthday, on the 23rd day of the third lunar month, and the anniversary of her death, on the 9th day of the ninth lunar month. Puxian opera is performed on these days and all the halls are brightly illuminated.

You can reach the island by taking a bus from Fuzhou's main terminal to the city of Putian, and then a ferry from the pier at Wenjia. The fare is Y15 for a one-way ferry ride plus admission to the island.

Dining and Lodging

$ ⊞ **Meizhou Hotel.** This hotel is quiet and sleepy except in the peak of the tourist season. The rooms are clean and simple but small and a bit musty from the moist ocean air. ⊠ *Meizhou 351154,* ☏ *0594/669– 4600,* 𝔽𝔸𝕏 *0594/669–4602. 47 rooms, 3 suites. Restaurant, sauna, hair salon. No credit cards.*

Wuyi Shan Fengjingqu

★ ㊳   *½ hr by air from Fuzhou; 7 hrs by long-distance bus or train from Fuzhou.*

In the north of Fujian province, **Wuyi Shan Fengjingqu** (Wuyi Mountain Natural Reserve) is known for its spectacular scenery. Magnificent peaks covered in waterfalls (most notably the Shuilian), bamboo groves, and tea bushes rise from the banks of the Jiuqu Xi (Nine Meanders or Nine Bends Creek). You can enjoy the scenery on boats that wend their way up and down stream, or climb the mountains for the views or to visit the pavilions and temples that stand on the slopes of some—for example, Tianyou Feng.

The cliffs along the river were once used for "boat burials," in which wooden boat-shape coffins were placed in niches some 160 ft above the river. Some date as far back as 3,000 years but little is known about how and why these burials took place. From Fuzhou, you can fly or take a train to Nanping and then continue on by bus.

Lodging

$ ⊞ **Wuyi Shan Villa Hotel.** This is one of the nicer and more reasonably priced hotels in the area, and it's at the base of the mountain. Rooms are comfortable and have air-conditioning. ⊠ *Wuyi Shan, 354302,* ☏ *0599/525–1888,* 𝔽𝔸𝕏 *0599/525–2567. 203 rooms, 16 suites. 2 restaurants, bar, sauna, disco, business services.*

Xiamen

㊴   *3 hrs (200 km/124 mi) southwest of Fuzhou; 500 km (310 mi) northeast of Hong Kong.*

Known as Amoy to the foreign traders who made the town on these two islands their home from the middle of the 19th century on, Xiamen, with a total population of about 1 million, is an appealing place, with some interesting corners to explore. By Chinese standards Xiamen is a new town, founded only in 1394 during the Ming dynasty as a defense against pirate attacks. It has remained important ever since, with its well-located natural harbor, as a center of coastal trade.

At the end of the Ming era it became the stronghold of the Ming loyalist Zheng Chenggong, better known as Koxinga, who held out with some success against the Manchus. Born in Japan to a Chinese father and a Japanese mother, he went to China and became a favorite of the court during the final years of the Ming dynasty. When China was overrun by the Qing, he built up a fleet of more than 7,000 junks and a force of some three-quarters of a million men, including pirates. In 1661 he succeeded in driving the Dutch from Taiwan and went on to try to extend his power to the Philippines. He murdered both his cousin and his uncle for their ineptitude and killed himself in 1662 on Taiwan.

After 1842 Xiamen became one of the first treaty ports to be opened up to foreign trade, and by the 1950s it had become an important industrial center. Since Deng Xiaoping's open-door policy, it has been turned into one of the four Special Economic Zones (SEZs), where trade is practiced according to the laws of the free market. Only a few miles farther out to sea are other small islands that still belong to Taiwan.

The city consists of two islands: Xiamen, linked to the mainland by a causeway built in the 1950s, and Gulangyu. The main street on Xiamen, leading down to the port, is Zhongshan Lu.

★ The most interesting part of the city—and also the most attractive to the eye—is **Gulangyu** (Island of Drumming Waves), where foreign communities were established after 1842. The colonial buildings on Gulangyu, mostly dating from the late 19th and early 20th centuries, are surprisingly large, considering that in 1912 there were only 250 foreign residents. You can get to the island by the ferry that leaves every 15 minutes from Xiamen Island (✉ Y3 [return trip is free], ☉ daily 5:45 AM–12:30 AM).

Gulangyu is closed to automobile traffic, but the island is small enough that you can explore it on foot without exhausting yourself. Golf carts with drivers, which you can rent by the hour, are also available if you don't want to walk. Most of the interesting sights of Xiamen Island are along the No. 2 bus route passing by the ferry terminal. There are several nice parks here, all on the southern half of the island. From the ferry turn left and follow the oceanside street until you come to **Haoyue Yuan** (Bright Moon Garden; ☉ daily 8–7), with its large statue of Koxinga. On the way, you'll pass some quaint western villas. Continuing along Tianwei Lu, the waterfront road, you'll come to **Shuzhuang Huayuan** (Shuzhuang Garden; ✉ Y25). The grounds were originally private, before the owner donated them to the state in 1956. The garden is immaculately kept—something that cannot be said about too many parks in China—and dotted with pavilions and bridges, some extending out to rocks just off shore. The island's highest point is part of **Riguang Yan** (Sunlight Rock; ✉ Y40, Y20 after 5 PM, ☉ daily 8 AM–9 PM), which rises 300 ft. From its summit, you can get great views of not only Gulangyu and the Xiamen waterfront, but, on clear days, also the Taiwanese island, Jinmen, in the distance. Inside is a large aviary full of birds from around the world.

The Taiwanese island of **Jinmen** lies only a few miles off the coast of Xiamen. Chinese tourist boats leave regularly from the Xiamen quay, carrying mainlanders interested in seeing the land of their estranged countrymen. While the boats do not actually land on either Jinmen or any of the smaller rocks belonging Taiwan, you can get close enough to see the faces of the Taiwanese guards patrolling the shores or call out to the Taiwanese fisherman netting the waters. The boat leaves several times a day from the dock next to the Gulangyu ferry (✉ Y43, ☉ daily 8–5).

Nanputuo Si (Nanputuo Temple), on Xiamen Island in the southern suburbs of the city, dates from the Tang dynasty. It has been restored many times, most recently in the 1980s. The roofs of the halls are painted with a colorful array of flowers and traditional ornamentation; pavilions on either side of the main hall contain tablets commemorating suppression of secret societies by the Qing emperors. As the most important temple remaining in Xiamen, it is nearly always the center of a great deal of activity as monks and local believers mix with tour groups. Behind the temple a rocky path threads its way past a series of stone inscriptions. At the height of summer the lakes in front of the temple are covered with lotus flowers. Attached to the temple complex is an excellent vegetarian restaurant (☞ Dining, *below*). ✉ *Siming Nanlu, Xiamen; take No. 1 or 2 bus from port.* 🎫 *Y3.* ⊙ *Daily 7:30 AM–6:30 PM.*

Housed in a fascinating mix of local Minan-style and colonial-style buildings close to the Nanputuo Temple, **Xiamen Daxue** (Xiamen University) was founded in the 1920s with the help of overseas Chinese donations. The **Renlei Bowuguan** (Museum of Anthropology; 🎫 Y1, ⊙ daily 8:30–11 and 3–5), dedicated to the study of Neolithic southern China as well as local ethnology, is also here. It has a very good collection of fossils, ceramics, paintings, and ornaments. ✉ *Xiamen Daxue, Siming Nanlu.*

Southeast of the university at the end of the No. 2 bus line is the **Huli Cannon.** Made in Germany by the Krupp Company and placed here in 1891, at a cost of 60,000 silver taels, the cannon weighs 60 tons and measures 45 ft in length. It sits along with other smaller armaments on the bare bones of an old fortress, overlooking the sea. It is the only well-preserved coastal cannon left in China, a strange relic from the end of the declining Qing dynasty. A portion of the fortress has been converted into a museum that displays an exceptional collection of ancient weaponry, including swords, cannons, and 18th-century flintlocks. ✉ *Off Daxue Lu, in southeast of city, about 20-min walk from university.* 🎫 *Y25.* ⊙ *Daily 7:30–7:30.*

In the southern part of the city, the **Huaqiao Bowuguan** (Overseas Chinese Museum) is an institution founded by the wealthy industrialist Tan Kah-kee. Three halls illustrate, by means of pictures and documents, personal items and relics associated with the great waves of emigration from southeastern China during the 19th century. ✉ *Off Siming Nanlu, at foot of Fengzhao Shan.* 🎫 *Y5.* ⊙ *Tues.–Sun. 8:30–11:30 and 2–5:30.*

The undulating **Wanshi Zhiwuguan** (Wanshi Botanical Garden) has a fine collection of more than 4,000 species of tropical and subtropical flora, a pretty lake, strangely shaped rocks and caves, and several pavilions, of which the most interesting are those forming the **Tianjie Si** (Temple of the Kingdom of Heaven). Close to the lake is a large gray stone marking the spot where Koxinga killed his cousin and then took command of the troops to fight the Qing. The garden specializes in the flora of southern China and of Southeast Asia, including the varieties of eucalyptus that originated in Australia but have been widely planted throughout the south of China. ✉ *Huyuan Lu, off Wenyuan Lu, in eastern part of city.* 🎫 *Y10.* ⊙ *Daily 8–6.*

Dining and Lodging

Seafood is on the menu just about everywhere in Xiamen. The lanes of Gulanyu are lined with tanks, tubs, and buckets of just about anything that swims or crawls in the ocean—just point to what you want. One warning: make sure the price is established before you send your meal to the kitchen.

$$–$$$$ ✕ **Fuhao Seafood Restaurant.** You can eat plenty of excellent seafood here at good prices if you choose with care; make sure you know the price of what is on offer. ✉ *14 Huyuan Lu,* ☏ *0592/202–4127. No credit cards.*

$$–$$$$ ✕ **Jili Seafood Restaurant.** Tanks of fresh seafood line the walls of this restaurant, which serves southern-style dishes. Top-notch service, a beautiful skylighted dining room, and 19 private rooms decked out with silver means you can get dressed up for a meal here. There are English menus. ⊠ *819 Hubin Nanlu, 4F,* ☎ *0592/516–9999. AE, MC, V.*

$$–$$$$ ✕ **Shuyou Seafood Restaurant.** The name means "close friend," and that is how you're treated at this upscale dining establishment. Fresh seafood and a more friendly waitstaff than you know what to do with produce excellent dining. It may be the best-known restaurant in Xiamen. ⊠ *Hubin Beilu,* ☎ *0592/509–8888. AE, MC, V.*

$ ✕ **Puzhaolou Vegetarian Restaurant.** The comings and goings of monks add to the atmosphere of this Buddhist vegetarian restaurant adjacent to the Nanputuo Si. Two buildings offer different price ranges—the white building is the more expensive. There are no English menus; just point to the number of people and the price you are willing to pay. ⊠ *Nanputuo Si, Siming Nanlu, Xiamen,* ☎ *0592/208–5908. No credit cards.*

$$$$ ☷ **Holiday Inn Crowne Plaza Harbourview.** This modern hotel has an excellent location overlooking the harbor. Rooms are comfortable in the usual reliable Holiday Inn style. There is a medical clinic on the premises. ⊠ *12 Zhenhai Lu, 361001,* ☎ *0592/202–3333,* FAX *0592/203–6666,* WEB *www.holiday-inn.com. 334 rooms, 7 suites. 4 restaurants, pool, business services. AE, MC, V.*

$$$$ ☷ **Marco Polo Xiamen.** Situated between the older sections of town and the commercial district, the hotel is convenient to transportation if not to sights. The occasional barbecue is held for guests in summer at the beautiful swimming pool, which is surrounded with lush greenery. ⊠ *8 Jianye Lu, 361004,* ☎ *0592/509–1888,* FAX *0592/509–2888,* WEB *www.marcopolohotels.com. 246 rooms, 38 suites. 3 restaurants, pool, no-smoking rooms, sauna, gym, business services. AE, MC, V.*

$$–$$$ ☷ **Lujiang Hotel.** In a refurbished prerevolutionary building, this midrange hotel has an ideal location opposite the ferry pier and next to Zhongshan Lu. ⊠ *54 Lujiang Lu, 361001,* ☎ *0592/202–2922,* FAX *0592/202–4644. 107 rooms, 18 suites. 4 restaurants. AE, MC, V.*

$$–$$$ ☷ **Xiamen Hotel.** Fairly close to the center of town, this hotel has a good range of facilities. The rooms are comfortable and well appointed. ⊠ *16 Huyuan Lu, 361003,* ☎ *0592/202–2265,* FAX *0592/204–9960. 264 rooms, 22 suites. Pool, gym, business services. AE, MC, V.*

$$ ☷ **Gulangyu Villa Hotel.** On the west side of Gulangyu and near the Fujian Arts and Crafts School, this is about the most peaceful hotel you're going to find in Xiamen. The rooms are clean, but simple and the staff is friendly enough. There is a decent Chinese restaurant on the premises. *14 Gusheng Rd.,* ☎ *0592/206–0160 or 0592/206–3280,* FAX *0592/206–0165. 75 rooms. Restaurant, business services. No credit cards.*

$$ ☷ **Luzhou Hotel.** Near the ferry terminal on Gulangyu, this hotel is simple in its services, but its location, on an island with no automobiles, makes it very restful. Rooms with ocean views are available. ⊠ *Gulangyu, 361002,* ☎ *0592/206–5390,* FAX *0592/206–5390. 34 rooms, 5 suites. Restaurant. No credit cards.*

Nightlife and the Arts

Much of the nightlife in Xiamen centers on the strip of Zhongshan Lu that extends from the Gulangyu ferry pier to Siming Lu. Trawling this area and some of the side streets will turn up a vibrant mix of small tea shops, bars, fashionable stores, and locals out for evening strolls. There are some Western-style bars in **Bailu Zhou** off of Huzhong Lu. A particularly nice, and relatively inexpensive, one is the **Bailuzhou Yidian Yuan** (⊠ Hubin Zhonglu, ☎ 0592/889–8931), which is in a wooden lodge on the shore of the river that divides the city. Most Xiamenites in search of evening entertainment seek out one of the many karaoke parlors that dot the area (usually distinguished by the letters OK); they are of varying standard, with some offering "hostesses." One of the more outstanding discos in town is **XO-2** (⊠ Junction of Hubin Nanlu and Hubin Zhonglu.)

In spring and fall there are often performances of **traditional music, local opera, and acrobatics** by visiting troupes. CITS is likely to be the best source of information.

Outdoor Activities and Sports

Swimming is possible on the beaches of Gulangyu; otherwise, make use of hotel swimming pools, for which a fee will be charged for nonguests. The best place for **jogging** would also be on Gulangyu Island, where there is no traffic. On Xiamen Island the area around the university is reasonably quiet.

Shopping

Shops along Zhongshan Lu have squeezed out residential buildings. You can buy almost anything you want nowadays, but the local specialties are tea, Hui'an stone carving (of tablets and of products for ornamental and daily use), puppet heads, silk figurines, wood carving, and lacquerware. The **Friendship Store** (⊠ Si Ming Beilu) doesn't have as wide a selection as its counterparts in other cities. The widest selection and the best prices in Xiamen are definitely to be found in the narrow winding lanes of **Gulangyu.** There is a rather large **night market** that runs parallel to Zhongshan Lu near the ferry pier, but it is hit or miss, containing mostly clothing that is of questionable style by Western standards.

Quanzhou

❹ *1½ hrs by express bus (80 km/50 mi) north of Xiamen; 2½ hrs by express bus south of Fuzhou.*

Quanzhou is an ancient port on the Jin River. During the Song and Yuan dynasties it was the foremost port in China, sometimes described as the starting point of the Maritime Silk Road. As a result, it had a considerable Muslim population, which has bequeathed to the city what is probably the most interesting mosque in China. To Arabs, Quanzhou was called "Zaiton," from which the English word *satin* is derived.

The Quanzhou of reform-era China made a valiant effort to resist the shapeless, drab architectural malaise that has stricken most Chinese cities. The local answer was to combine selective demolition with renovation to re-create a Minan (southern Chinese)-style downtown area. Although it looks clean and colorful, the effect is closer to a suburban strip mall than to a classical Chinese architectural style. Although the downtown area has been artificially re-created, throughout Quanzhou, the growth of a number of temples indicates a revival of a more natural kind. Any visit to Quanzhou should include a visit to some or all these temples.

The mosque **Qingjing Si** was built in 1009, enlarged in 1309, and restored in 1350 and 1609. Unlike other ancient mosques in China, which were heavily influenced by Chinese styles, this one is mainly in the purely Islamic architectural idiom. Partially ruined, it still retains some impressive features, particularly the entrance, which is 66 ft high. ⊠ 174 *Tumen Jie.* ⌨ *Y3.* ☉ *Daily 8–5:30.*

★ The **Kaiyuan Si,** a temple founded in AD 686, is flanked by two pagodas that have some fine bas-relief carving on the niches of each story. The style is a Sino-Indian mix; following the death of the Chinese monk who had initiated the carving, an Indian monk was placed in charge of the work. In the temple's Mahavira Hall, among the roof timbers,

are some marvelous carvings of *apsaras* (Buddhist angels). ⌧ *Xi Jie.*
🎫 *Y6.* 🕐 *Daily 6:30–6.*

Two miles north of Quanzhou, the scenic **Qingyuanshan** area has a
huge 700-year-old **statue of Laotze,** the founder of Taoism. Also close
to the town are two stone bridges built in the Song dynasty to help
with the endless flow of goods into the port—the **Luoyang Qiao** (Luoyang Bridge) and the **Anping Qiao** (Anping Bridge), which is 2½ km
(1½ mi) long.

Dining and Lodging

$$ 🏨 **Quanzhou Hotel.** At the best hotel in Quanzhou the staff seems to
be concerned about things other than prompt service. The rooms are,
however, comfortable. Due to strict traffic rules city taxis are not al-
lowed to drive up to the hotel doors. For door-to-door service you'll
need to call ahead; the hotel will arrange a driver. ⌧ *22 Zhuangfu Lu,
362000,* 🕿 *0595/228–9958,* 🖷 *0595/218–2128. 271 rooms, 22 suites.
2 restaurants, pool, sauna, bowling, business services. AE, MC, V.*

$ 🏨 **Overseas Chinese Mansion.** The "mansion" in the name is surely
ironic. But what the hotel lacks in elegance it makes up in its price (which
often runs cheaper than quoted). The rooms are clean and fairly com-
fortable. ⌧ *362000, west of Baiyuan Pool,* 🕿 *0595/228–2192,* 🖷 *0595/
228-4612. 234 rooms, 13 suites. 3 restaurants, sauna, nightclub, busi-
ness services. AE, MC, V.*

Chongwu

④   *1½ hr by bus from Quanzhou.*

Chongwu is a bit off the beaten path (there are no direct buses from
Xiamen), but a journey out to this small fishing town at the end of a
peninsula jutting out into the Taiwan Strait is worth the extra effort.
Just past the county seat of Hui'an, on the final approach to Chongwu,
everything turns to granite; all the structures here are built from the
local ash-gray granite.

The **old town** of Chongwu, built in 1387 as a seaside fortress against
Japanese and local pirates, is protected by a 2½-km (1½-mi) granite wall
that has an average height of 22 ft. Squeezed within this wall are nar-
row lanes and alleys of markets, old men shuffling mah-jongg tiles, groups
of ancient grandmothers playing cards, and numerous little shrines and
temples.

Outside the city wall, along the coast, is the **Shidiao Bolanyuan** (Sea-
side Sculpture Garden), which contains hundreds of statues cut from
the local granite. The most impressive of the works are dozens of fish
carved into seaside rocks in 1992 by a contemporary sculptor, Hong
Shiqing, from Tianjin. These can only be seen when the tide is low. ⌧
Along coast outside east gate of city wall. 🎫 *Y10.* 🕐 *Daily.*

Local folk cultural artifacts hold center stage at the **Chongwu Wenwu
Guan** (Chongwu Town Museum). There's a room devoted to the local
Hui'an women. Their traditional way of dressing with butterfly scarf
and exposed navel ("feudal head, democratic belly") is unique to this
area. ⌧ *Across from harbor, near main gate of old town.* 🎫 *Y3.* 🕐
Daily 9–4:30.

Lodging

$$ 🏨 **Xin Hanghai Da Jiudian.** The fixtures are gaudy and the imitation
wood paneling is a bit excessive, but the staff of this hotel is eager to
be of service. The elaborate massage and sauna rooms seem, however,
to attract illicit local trade at night. ⌧ *362131, on main road from
Hui'an to Chongwu, just outside town from bus terminus,* 🕿 *0595/*

768–3132, FAX 0595/768–9691. 33 rooms, 7 suites. 2 restaurants, massage, sauna, business services. MC, V.

Yongding

 4 hrs by bus from Xiamen via Longyan.

This town in the rural, hilly southwest of Fujian is the site of the traditional fortresslike circular or square earthen houses of the Hakka, whose name means "guest peoples." These buildings are large, at least three stories high, and capacious enough to hold an entire clan. The **Zhencheng Building,** for example, consists of two circular sections big enough to hold dozens. The **Chengqi Building,** known as the "King of Round Buildings," consists of four circles, with 400 rooms and 57 households. The buildings stand amid rural greenery in the countryside, where old covered bridges made of wood still span rivers and where (at Liancheng) rice paper is still made in the ancient way.

Fujian A to Z

To research prices, get advice from other travelers, and book travel arrangements, visit www.fodors.com.

AIR TRAVEL
The local branch of CAAC is Xiamen Airlines. There are domestic flights all over China and international flights to Jakarta, Manila, Penang, and Singapore. Other airlines with offices in Xiamen include Dragonair and Philippine Airlines.

CARRIERS
➤ AIRLINES AND CONTACTS: **CAAC office** (⊠ Wuyi Lu, Fuzhou, ☎ 0591/334–5988). **Dragonair** (⊠ Seaside Bldg., Jiang Daolu, Xiamen, ☎ 0592/202–5433). **Philippine Airlines** (⊠ Holiday Inn, Xiamen, ☎ 0592/202–3333 ext. 6742). **Xiamen Airlines** (☎ 0592/602–2961).

AIRPORTS
Fuzhou airport is 12 km (7 mi) from the city center. It has flights to all the other major cities in China, including Hong Kong, as well as to Wuyi Shan. There are buses between the main CAAC office and the airport. Xiamen airport, one of the largest and busiest in China, lies about 12 km (7 mi) northeast of the city.
➤ AIRPORT INFORMATION: **Fuzhou airport** (☎ 0591/801–3249). **Xiamen airport** (☎ 0592/602–0017).

BOAT AND FERRY TRAVEL
Ferries for Meizhou leave from the pier at Wenjia, at the tip of a small peninsula along the coast between Fuzhou and Xiamen. Approaches to Wenjia are all made via Putian Shi a half hour away. Putian is about two hours south of Fuzhou and 3½ hours north of Xiamen by express bus. The Jimei Hao ferry travels once a week between Xiamen and Hong Kong. The trip is about 18 hours and costs around $45 dollars. To check times call the Jimei Hao information line.
➤ BOAT AND FERRY INFORMATION: **Jimei Hao information** (☎ 0592/202–2913).

BUS TRAVEL BETWEEN THE CITIES OF FUJIAN
There are three long-distance bus stations in Fuzhou, one in the north of the city near the train station, serving mostly destinations to the north, another in the south of the city, serving destinations to the south, and one next to the Minjiang Hotel, also serving southern destinations. From Fuzhou you can travel to most of the major coastal cities of the region, including Xiamen and Quanzhou and as far as Shanghai and Guangzhou.

There are also air-conditioned overnight buses to some more distant destinations.

Xiamen has service to Quanzhou and all the main cities along the coast as far as Guangzhou and Shanghai from the long-distance bus station. Private companies also run air-conditioned long-distance buses from offices around the town. Buses go to Yongding by way of Longyan.
➤ BUS INFORMATION: **Long-distance bus station** (✉ 56 Hubin Nanlu, Xiamen). **North Bus Station** (371 Hualin Lu, Fuzhou). **South Bus Station** (✉ 195 Wuyi Lu, Fuzhou).

BUS TRAVEL WITHIN THE CITIES OF FUJIAN

Like most cities in China, Fuzhou has a comprehensive and cheap public bus system. Buses can also be slow and very crowded. Route maps are available from hotels, from CITS, or from the railway station.

Maps for the comprehensive bus service around Xiamen are available from the railway station, CITS, and hotels. Much of interest in Xiamen (for example, the port area) can be explored on foot.

CAR RENTAL

There is no self-drive car rental in Fuzhou or Xiamen. Cars with drivers can be hired on a daily basis through CITS or through hotels.

EMERGENCIES

➤ CONTACTS: **PSB** (Gonganju; Public Security Bureau; ✉ Xian Ta Lu, Fuzhou; ✉ Off Zhongshan Lu, near Xinqiao Hotel, Xiamen).

MONEY MATTERS

Most major hotels in Fuzhou and Xiamen have foreign exchange counters that are open during the day (possibly closing for lunch).
➤ CONTACTS: **American Express** (✉ Holiday Inn, Xiamen, ☎ 0592/212–0268). **Bank of China** (✉ 10 Zhongshan Lu, Xiamen).

TAXIS

In Fuzhou, your best bets for getting around are taxis or pedicabs, which are comfortable and reasonably cheap. They are easily hailed in the street or from outside hotels. In Xiamen taxis can also be found around hotels or on the streets; they're good for visiting the sights on the edge of town.

TRAIN TRAVEL

The Fuzhou train station is on the northern edge of the city, about 6 km (4 mi) from the river. From Fuzhou there are direct trains to Guangzhou, Shanghai, and Beijing. Part of the journey to Wuyishan can also be undertaken by train as far as Nanping.

Rail travel to and from Xiamen is not very convenient. Many journeys will involve a change. There are, however, direct links to Shanghai and also to Fuzhou (a long journey better undertaken by bus). The railway station is about 3 km (2 mi) northeast of the port; bus service between the two is frequent.
➤ TRAIN INFORMATION: **Fuzhou train station** (✉ Liuyi Beilu). **Xiamen train station** (✉ Xiahe Lu).

VISITOR INFORMATION

➤ TOURIST INFORMATION: **CITS** (✉ 107 Jing Da Lu, Fuzhou, ☎ 0591/750–2794). **CITS** (✉ Hubin Bei Lu, Zhenxing Daxia 15F, Xiamen, ☎ 0592/505–1822).

JIANGXI

This inland province (the name means "west river") to the northwest of Fujian has been part of mainstream China since the Qin dynasty. It remained thinly populated until the 3rd century, when Han Chinese arrived, fleeing the steppe peoples beyond the Great Wall, who were threatening to invade. From the 7th century onward the construction of the Grand Canal channeled trade to the southeastern regions and brought more immigrants from the northern regions into what was still a sparsely populated area. At first most of those who came were poor peasants, but as silver mining and tea cultivation took hold, a wealthy merchant class developed. By the time of the Ming dynasty the province had acquired its present boundaries. After 19th-century coastal shipping ate into the canal trade, Jiangxi became one of the poorest Chinese provinces, which may explain why it was an important guerrilla stronghold for the Communists during the civil war.

Running south to north through the center of the 166,000-square-km (64,000-square-mi) province is a river known as the Ganjiang. One of the largest freshwater lakes in China, Poyang Hu, is also here. Much of Jiangxi is flat, but to the east, west, and south it is fringed by mountains that reach 6,500 ft.

Nanchang

🔹 *400 km (248 mi) northwest of Fuzhou; 750 km (465 mi) northeast of Hong Kong; 1,200 km (744 mi) south of Beijing.*

With its wide avenues and relative absence of tall buildings, Nanchang looks like much of China before the 1990s. The capital of Jiangxi is experiencing the changes of China's reform era but to a much lesser degree than China's wealthier coastal provinces. The city can be toured in an afternoon and is a useful stepping-off point for more interesting places in the region.

Nanchang has existed under a variety of names since the Han dynasty, when it became well known as a city of merchants and alchemists. Its current name means "to flourish from the south." It was often used as a transit point for the ceramics made in the imperial kilns at Jingdezhen; indeed, the son of the founder of the Ming dynasty was made ruler of the area. Matteo Ricci, the Jesuit missionary who was the first European to gain access to the Chinese court, reportedly visited Nanchang in the 16th century.

Nanchang is best known for events in the early part of the 20th century. On August 1, 1927, there was an uprising in the city, in protest of Chiang Kai-shek's attack on the Shanghai Commune in April of the same year. Several eminent Communists, officers in the Nationalist army—among them Zhou Enlai and Zhu De—were serving in the area of Nanchang. They decided to take the city, and with a force of 30,000 they succeeded in holding out for three days before the Nationalists retook it. The defeated soldiers fled to the mountains and later regrouped to form what was to become the Red Army. It was from this moment that Mao began to diverge from Soviet orthodoxy by concentrating on the rural peasantry instead of urban workers. The uprising is still celebrated nationally on August 1, known as Army Day. In 1986 the central government named Nanchang a national cultural heritage city.

The building housing the **Bayi Jinianguan** (Former Headquarters of the Nanchang Uprising and Revolutionary Museum; ✉ Zhongshan Lu, 🏷 Y10, 🕐 daily 8–5:30) was a hotel until it was taken over for use as the headquarters of the leaders of the Communist uprising of August 1, 1927. The somewhat esoteric exhibits consist of furniture of the period and photographs of the protagonists. The marble-and-granite **Bayi Jinianta** (Memorial to the Nanchang Uprising; ✉ Renmin Guangchang) was erected in 1977. The **Geming Lieshi Jinian Tang** (Memorial Hall to the Martyrs of the Revolution; ✉ 399 Bayi Dadao, 🕾 Y6, ☉ daily 8:30–11:30 and 2:30–5) details the lives of hundreds of local revolutionaries from the early part of the 20th century. The **Zhou En Lai, Zhu De Guju** (Residence of Zhou Enlai and Zhu De; ✉ Minde Lu) reveals how the leaders lived.

In the suburbs about 10 km (6 mi) south of the center is the country house Qingyun Pu (Blue Cloud Garden), where Zhu Da (sometimes known as Badashanren—"man of the eight great mountains") lived from 1626 to 1705. It's been preserved as **Badashanren Jinian Tang** (Memorial to Badashanren). The retreat has a long history; by the 4th century it had already found favor with Taoists. The rooms have been preserved, with reproductions of Master Zhu's works on the walls (the originals are mostly in the Shanghai Museum) and a number of items dating from the Ming dynasty. Zhu was a kinsman of the Ming imperial household, and when the Ming collapsed in 1637 he sequestered himself in a temple for the remainder of his life and devoted himself to painting. ✉ *Near Dingshan Qiao (Dingshan Bridge); best reached by taxi or bus from Bayi Da Dao near Renmin Guangchang,* 🕾 *0791/ 521–2565.* 🕾 *Y10.* ☉ *Daily 8:30–5.*

The huge **Tengwang Ge** (Tengwang Pavilion), on the banks of the Fu River, is the foremost sight in Nanchang. Reconstructed in 1989 on the site of a building that has known some 28 incarnations—the first during the Tang dynasty in AD 653—the pavilion is now part of a sprawling complex of shops, teahouses, and exhibits. Made of granite and nine stories high, it reflects the architectural styles of the Tang and Song dynasties. Performances of traditional Chinese music are given here throughout the day. ✉ *Yanjiang Lu.* 🕾 *Y30 for performances.* ☉ *Daily 7:30–5:45.*

Youmin Si (Youmin Temple), founded in the 6th century, is the largest and most active temple in Nanchang. It is notable for its 18-ton bell cast in 967 by order of a Tang dynasty general. There is also a large bronze Buddha in the rear hall and a bronze bell cast during the Ming period. ✉ *Huanhu Lu.* 🕾 *Y1.* ☉ *Daily 7–5:30.*

Dining and Lodging

Other than those in the hotels, there are very few restaurants of particular note in Nanchang. However, there is no shortage of choice along the main streets and around the railway station, where small, cheap restaurants sell dumplings and other sweetmeats.

$ ✕ **Far East Restaurant.** This is one of the best places to eat in Nanchang. The large dining room gets a little noisy, but the excellent selection of southern-style Chinese and Cantonese foods will satisfy. No need to worry about a menu; just walk into the small room near the entrance to peruse refrigerated sample dishes. Point at what looks good, and the chefs will prepare a dish like it for your table. ✉ *95 Fuzhou Lu,* 🕾 *0791/622–3688. No credit cards.*

$$$ 🏨 **Jiangxi Hotel.** The Jiangxi's exterior is vintage proletarian 1950s, but fortunately the interior has been completely renovated to a higher standard of bourgeois comfort. Some of the rooms are a bit dingy, but the hotel's location smack in the middle of town is perfect for walking. ✉ *368 Baiyi Dadao, 330006,* 🕾 *0791/622–1133,* FAX *0791/622– 4388. 243 rooms, 48 suites. 4 restaurants, bar. AE, MC, V.*

$$ ⊞ **Gloria Plaza Hotel.** This Hong Kong–managed hotel is next to Tengwang Ge. The entire hotel is done in a beautiful tropical forest motif, with imported furniture that has a 1960s retro feel to it. The rooms have river views. ⊠ *88 Yan Jiang Bei Lu, 330008,* ☎ *0791/673–8855,* FAX *0791/673–8533. 328 rooms, 30 suites. 2 restaurants, bar, pool, sauna, gym, shops, business services. AE, DC, MC, V.*

$ ⊞ **Nanchang Hotel.** This hotel convenient to the railway station is short on luxuries but very reasonably priced. ⊠ *16 Baiyi Dadao, 330006,* ☎ *0791/621–9698,* FAX *0791/622–3193. 265 rooms. Restaurant, shops. No credit cards.*

Nightlife and the Arts

Although there is the occasional opera or acrobatics performance, the odd bar or karaoke parlor, the main interest is ordinary Chinese life— **night markets,** where they exist, or perhaps a visit to the cinema. Ask at the CITS or your hotel about **performances.**

Outdoor Activities and Sports

Ask at your hotel for **bike** rentals. Renmin Park and Bayi Park are good for **jogging.** The best place for **hiking** in this area is at the hill resort of Lushan (☞ *below*).

Shopping

The chief item in this region is **porcelain.** Jingdezhen is the best place to buy, but it's also widely available in Nanchang and elsewhere. New shops, privately owned, are appearing all the time, and some are selling very good quality wares, especially reproductions of classical porcelain. Otherwise, try the **Nanchang Porcelain-ware Store** (⊠ Minde Lu). The area right around the entrance to Tengwang Ge is home to dozens of small privately owned shops that sell a smattering of everything: antiques, old coins, jade objects, and especially porcelain. Keep an eye out for porcelain statues from the Cultural Revolution, when the kilns of Jingdezhen churned out statues of Mao and members of the Red Guards. Bargaining is expected at these shops.

Jingdezhen

★ ➍➍ *4½ hours by train or long-distance bus from Nanchang.*

Artisans in the ancient town of Jingdezhen, on the banks of the Chang River, once created some of the finest imperial porcelain in China. The city is still a major manufacturer of ceramics, although the wares are mostly mass produced now.

There were kilns in operation here from as early as the Eastern Han dynasty. From the 4th century AD the local rulers in Nanking commissioned pottery wares for use in their palaces. At that time Jingdezhen produced mostly white ware with a transparent or pale blue glaze. As manufacturing methods were perfected, a finer porcelain, using kaolin, was created by firing at higher temperatures.

Beginning with the Song dynasty, the imperial court, compelled to move southward to Hangzhou, began to place orders on a serious scale, partly to satisfy the widespread demand for vessels from which to drink tea but also because metal was in shorter supply. In fact it is from this era that the town, formerly known as Xinping, acquired its current name: One period (1004–1007) of the Song was known as the Jingde, at which time all pieces of porcelain made for the court had to be marked accordingly. Both the custom and the name stuck.

In later centuries, during the Yuan and Ming dynasties, Jingdezhen became famous for its blue underglaze porcelain (the classic Ming blue and white), which was widely exported to the rest of Asia and to Europe. Much of the export material was fussy and overdecorated—classic porcelain was much simpler.

Although mass production is the norm now, this type of output is not an entirely modern phenomenon. Most of the finest artistic ware was made by special order, such as when the paintings of an artist favored at court were copied onto porcelain. But most production was on a considerable scale—certainly it was by the 18th century, when European travelers described the methods used. It is clear that much depended on organization, with certain workers responsible for certain roles in the creative process, just as in the modern-day assembly line.

The pottery ovens here are known as dragon kilns. They have several chambers and are fueled with wood. Many among the population of the town are involved in porcelain production, manufacturing some 400 million pieces each year. Although parts of Jingdezhen resemble a dreary Victorian manufacturing town that Charles Dickens would have relished describing, it is a fascinating place to visit.

Off the main streets, Zhushan Lu and Zhongshan Lu, older, narrower streets close to the river, have considerable character. Although it may be easy to walk into one of the innumerable pottery factories, you can get a more comprehensive tour of the porcelain works, including the **Yishu Taocichang** (Art Porcelain Factory) and the **Meidiao Taocichang** (Porcelain Sculpture Factory), by arrangement with CITS (⌕ *8 Lianhuating Lu,* ☎ *0798/822–2293).*

The **Gu Taoci Lishi Bowuguan** (Museum of Ceramic History) shows items found among the ancient kiln sites and has workshops demonstrating porcelain techniques of the Ming and Qing dynasties. ⌕ *Off Cidu Dadao.* ⌕ *Y10.* ⊙ *Daily 8:30–5.*

In the vicinity of Jingdezhen are a number of **ancient kilns: Liujia Wan** is 20 km (12 mi) outside the town, and **Baihu Wan** is 9 km (6 mi) out on the Jingwu road. Buses from downtown run to both places. A taxi ride to Liujia Wan will cost about Y40, to Baihu Wan, about Y25.

Lodging

$–$$ ⌕ **Jingdezhen Guesthouse.** The best lodgings Jingdezhen has to offer, this comfortable hotel stands next to the Lianhua Tang Park to the north of the city center. ⌕ *60 Fengjing Lu, 333000,* ☎ *0798/822–5010,* FAX *0798/822–6416. 150 rooms. Restaurant, bar, shops. No credit cards.*

$ ⌕ **Porcelain Capital Guesthouse.** Conveniently located near both the Jingdezhen train and bus stations, this budget hotel is rather spartan, but all right for a night or two. ⌕ *197 Ma'anshan Lu,* ☎ FAX *0798/ 821–1251. 95 rooms. No credit cards.*

Lushan

🐵 *1¼ hrs by bus from Jiujiang; 2½ hrs by bus direct return to Nanchang.*

Since 1949 Lushan has often been used for significant party conferences, notably the one in 1959 after the catastrophe of the Great Leap Forward, a meeting that attempted to sideline Mao and, some argue, indirectly led to the Cultural Revolution. In 1970 it was the scene of a bitter argument between Mao and his defense minister, Lin Biao, who died the following year in a plane that went down over Mongolia under mysterious circumstances.

This historically significant old mountain resort is a relaxing place to pass a couple of days if you can escape the crowds of Chinese tourists who flock here in summer. The whole area is a massif of 90 peaks, which reach a height of 1,475 meters (4,836 ft), liberally sprinkled with rocks, waterfalls, temples (mostly destroyed), and springs that have charmed visitors for more than 2,000 years. Entrance to the National Park Area is Y50; buses will stop at the main gate en route to allow all but locals to purchase admission tickets.

The lush vegetation and famous waterfalls and clouds, which often cover the mountain slopes in the mornings and evenings, have drawn painters and poets here for centuries. The natural beauty of the Lushan area, as well as its historical importance, led to its being designated a World Heritage Site by UNESCO in 1996.

The focal point of the Lushan region is the town of **Guling,** well known because eminent politicians, including Chiang Kai-shek, have had villas here and because it is home, in the Hanbokou Valley, to the Lushan Botanical Garden. Many villas here are European in style, having originally been built for Westerners working on the plains below. Like those in Shanghai, they are a fascinating mix of various styles of architecture from the early 20th century. Unfortunately, because of local regulations forbidding construction of any kind—including renovation—many houses, slouching with age in the moist mountain air, are making the transition from mature structures to run-down old buildings.

Guling is 3,838 ft above sea level; once you're here, most things of interest can be reached on foot. The **Meilu Bieshu** (Meilu Villa), built in 1903 by a British expatriate, was the summer home of Chiang Kai-shek from 1933 to 1948. Although the old wooden house has not weathered very well, there is an interesting photo exhibit here on Lushan in the 20th century. Tea and other drinks are served on the second-floor balcony. ⊠ *Hexi Lu.* 🎫 *Y15.* ☉ *Daily 7:30–6.*

About 4 km (2½ mi) south of the village is Lulin Hu (Lulin Lake), beside which is the **Mao Zedong Guju** (Former Residence of Mao Zedong), which also houses the **Lushan Bowuguan** (Lushan Museum). The building was used as a retreat for the late chairman and still contains his huge bed. Here you can also see an exhibition on local geology and natural history, as well as photographs commemorating important events in Lushan and items relating to the observations made about the area by various poets and scholars. ⊠ *Near Lulin Lu.* 🎫 *Y10.* ☉ *Daily 8–6.*

The **Zhiwuyuan** (Botanical Garden) lies about 2 km (1 mi) east of the lake and has a collection of alpine and tropical plants, as well as a cactus display. ⊠ *Southeast of Lulin Hu.* 🎫 *Y5.* ☉ *Daily 9–5.*

About 2½ km (1½ mi) west of Guling is **Ruqin Hu** (Ruqin Lake). You can take a walk beyond it to **Xianren Dong** (Xianren Cave) and **Longshouya** (Dragon Head Cliff).

Lodging

$–$$ 🏨 **Lushan Guest House.** This old hotel of some character is well managed. It has comfortable, modern rooms and an excellent restaurant. There are two sections, varying considerably in price. ⊠ *446 Hexi Lu, Guling, 332900,* ☎ *0792/828–2060,* 🖷 *792/828–2843. 56 rooms, 1 suite. Restaurant, bar, shops. AE, MC, V.*

$–$$ 🏨 **Lushan Villa Hotel.** This hotel actually consists of nearly two dozen villas of various sizes and comfort ranges nestled among picturesque pines and bamboo groves. Some of the villas here were once the country homes of political bigwigs. ⊠ *179 Zhihong Lu, Guling, 332900.* ☎ *0792/828–2525. 39 rooms, 8 suites. Restaurant. No credit cards.*

Jinggangshan

46 *7 hrs by long-distance bus from Nanchang.*

In the south of Jiangxi on the border with Hunan, this remote and mountainous area, with its picturesque villages, was the scene of Mao's first revolutionary activity in the 1920s. It became the base for the Red Army, which was founded as a result of the abortive uprising in Nanchang. The Long March started from here in 1934. There are some good opportunities for walking in the surrounding hills.

At the **Jinggangshan Geming Bowuguan** (Jinggang Mountain Revolutionary Museum) in the village of Ciping Zhen (on Jinggangshan, an eight-hour bus journey from Nanchang), you can visit the **Geming Jiujuqun** (Red Army Dormitory), which includes the old field hospital, and **Maozedong Guju** (Mao's House). ⊠ *Ciping Zhen.* 🚆 *Y3.* ⊙ *Daily.*

About 10 km (6 mi) northeast of Ciping Zhen is the **Shiyan Dong** (Grotto of the Stone Swallow), a 3,280-ft series of caves with stalagmites and stalactites.

Jiangxi A to Z

To research prices, get advice from other travelers, and book travel arrangements, visit www.fodors.com.

AIR TRAVEL
The airport lies 40 km (25 mi) south of Nanchang. There are flights to most of the main cities in China.

BOAT AND FERRY TRAVEL
Between Nanchang and Jingdezhen, you can take a ferry from Bayi Bridge in Nanchang across Lake Boyang to Boyang and then continue by bus.

BUS TRAVEL
From the Nanchang long-distance bus station, buses leave several times daily for Changsha, Jiujiang, and Jingdezhen. There is also regular service to Lushan and Jinggangshan.
➤ BUS INFORMATION: **Nancheng bus station** (⊠ Bayi Dadao, ☎ 0791/624–3217). **Jingdezhen bus station** (Tongzhan Lu, ☎ 0798/822–5159).

CAR RENTAL
Driving a rental car yourself is not possible, but cars with drivers can be arranged through CITS.

EMERGENCIES
➤ CONTACTS: **PSB** (⊠ Shengli Lu, Nanchang, ☎ 0791/677–2115).

MONEY MATTERS
➤ BANKS: **Bank of China** (⊠ Cidu Dadao, Jingdezhen). **Bank of China** (⊠ 1 Zhanqian Xilu, Nancheng).

TRAIN TRAVEL
Direct trains to Guangzhou, Fuzhou, Shanghai, Jiujiang, and Jingdezhen leave from the Nanchang train station.
➤ TRAIN INFORMATION: **Jingdezhen train station** (⊠ Tongzhan Lu, east of city center). **Nanchang train station** (⊠ end of Zhanqian Lu, in southeast part of city).

TRANSPORTATION AROUND THE CITIES OF JIANGXI

Nanchang has both buses and trolley buses. Maps for the system are sold at the train and bus stations. Pedicabs and taxis can be hailed on the streets or outside hotels and at the railway and bus stations.

Many, if not most, sights in Lushan, Jingdezhen, and Jiujiang can be visited on foot.

VISITOR INFORMATION

➤ TOURIST INFORMATION: **CITS** (✉ 8 Lianhuating Lu, Jingdezhen, ☎ 0798/822–2293; ✉ Jinggangshan Binguan Hotel, Jinggangshan; ✉ Nanhu Guest House, Jiujiang; ✉ Jiangxi Binguan Hotel, Nanchang, ☎ 0791/621–9711).

8 SOUTHEASTERN CHINA

FAR FROM THE EMPEROR

The Chinese have a saying: "Heaven is high, and the emperor is far away." Perhaps nowhere in China does this saying have more import than in the southeast, an area synonymous with distance from the political center and the excitement and uncertainty of contact with areas outside China.

By Shann
Davies

Updated by
Lara Wozniak

THE AREAS THAT COMPRISE SOUTHEASTERN CHINA—Guangdong and its vibrant port city Guangzhou (historically known as Canton), Macau, and Hainan—have been under the administration of Guangdong province for most of the past 700 years. With the exception of minor regional differences and the minority groups of Hainan, the entire area shares many cultural and linguistic similarities.

The region also shares the common distance from Beijing. Long ago, areas such as Hainan, on the edge of the empire, were seen as wild places on the frontier of civilization—destinations for exiles and political undesirables. Similarly, when foreigners began pushing into China, ports in these distant areas were ideal for engaging foreign influence. Both Macau and Hong Kong got their start as trading ports. Similarly, Shamian Island, in Guangzhou, was for foreigners only.

As the stereotype goes, people in this part of China are more concerned with economics than politics. This has not been entirely true, as contact with outside influences has also meant engagement with new ideas and ways of seeing the world. Sun Yat-sen, the father of the Chinese Revolution, was born in Guangdong.

Today Southeast China is at the center of many of the social and economic forces that are reshaping China. In reform-era China, the distance from the political center of Beijing makes this region ideal for experiments with capitalist market economics. The spectacular growth of the Shenzhen Special Economic Zone (SEZ), next to Hong Kong, and Zhuhai, next to Macau, exemplify these changes. In 1988 the entire island of Hainan, formerly under the control of Guangdong province, was turned into an SEZ.

All of this has led to dramatic change in the topography of the local urban, cultural, and social geography—rice paddies have sprouted skyscrapers, and older stone structures have been demolished to make way for new steel ones. Hainan, once a place of horrible imperial exile, is now a tropical vacation spot—a playland for China's new rich. With the 1997 return of Hong Kong and the 1999 return of Macau to Chinese control, these changes appear likely to continue.

Pleasures and Pastimes

Beaches

Although they're not up to the standards of many in Southeast Asia, the beaches outside Haikou and Sanya, on Hainan, are very good. The beaches of Sanya also offer scuba diving, Jet-Ski rental, and excellent sunbathing.

Cantonese Opera

There was a form of Chinese opera as early as the mid-16th century, as can be seen from the superb Wanfutai (Ten Thousand Blessings) stage in Foshan's Taoist temple. Built in 1658, it is the oldest surviving wooden stage in China. In the early 18th century one of the great men of Chinese theater, Master Zhang, moved to Foshan from the capital and set about establishing a distinctive Cantonese operatic tradition, which eventually led to the replacement of Mandarin by the local dialect.

In the north Peking opera was very much an aristocratic entertainment, but in the south opera became popular with everyone. The merchant class, which had grown rich from international trade, provided valuable patronage of the art. Operatic performances became an integral part of all major festivals, such as the Feast of the Hungry Ghosts and feasts honoring the seafarers' goddess, Tin Hau, and the Lunar New Year.

For these special occasions temporary stages were set up, with bamboo boards and roofs of rattan matting, in temple courtyards and village squares. Everybody came to watch and listen to stories based on well-known myths and legends. The troupes consisted of about 40 players, including six principals, acrobats, and martial arts experts. There were no scripts, only numbers to indicate the kind of action and music needed, and very little rehearsal for performances that typically consisted of 40 or 50 acts.

The performers belonged to acting families, learning from example and tradition the complex rules that governed everything that happened on stage. Each movement was prescribed: trembling arms indicated fear, an outstretched palm in front of the face meant tears. The music, often adapted from folk melodies, was sung according to the role—many tunes were used, with different words, for a wide variety of operas—with actors frequently using shrill falsetto to make themselves heard from stages in busy market squares.

Everyone in the audience knew the plots, which could be episodes from classics such as *Journey to the West, The Romance of Three Kingdoms, Dream of the Red Chamber,* or any of the action-packed epics of the Qing era. It wasn't *what* was being sung but *how* that mattered, so actors and actresses had to put all their energy and inspiration into a performance without breaking any traditional rules. This helped make Cantonese opera more exuberant and vital than the northern variety, a major reason why, unlike Peking opera, it continues to flourish in the modern age. It was also more flexible. In the latter part of the 19th century, for instance, writers would adapt plots to include subtle criticism of the Manchu government, and in the past decade there have been experiments using Western instruments to augment the traditional gongs, drums, clappers, fiddles, and various kinds of lutes.

Cantonese audiences remain dedicated, as can be seen at regular evening opera performances in Guangzhou's Culture Park. For the uninitiated, however, the art form needs some preparation. The music sounds cacophonous to Western ears, and the stylized movements are strange until you accept them as in a ballet. The costumes are brilliant, with silk robes embroidered, sequined, or covered with glittering beads, while headdresses have jeweled crowns, pompoms, or long feathers. Makeup is equally exotic, with colors to emphasize the character of the role. White means sinister, green is cruel, and black obedient; yellow stands for nobility and purple for royalty.

Sets are very basic and stage props simple: an actor striding behind two banners shows he's in a carriage, a player with a lantern indicates that it's night. Large fans are used to tell the audience that a character is commanding an army, inviting a lover, or hiding from an enemy. It's very much up to the players to hold the stage, especially as a Cantonese audience doesn't like to sit in rapt attention, preferring to stroll around, chat with friends, and take a snack. Visitors are welcome to do the same.

Dining

The incredibly diverse and ingenious Cantonese cuisine has developed from both abundance and scarcity. Guangdong province has some of the most fertile land in China, thanks to silt brought down by the Pearl River into its extensive delta. Here you have two crops of rice a year, vegetables of every kind—including European varieties introduced by the Portuguese from Macau—orchards of litchi, oranges, and other fruit;

chicken farms; duck ponds; and tropical waters rich in dozens of kinds of fish and seafood.

Cantonese chefs over the years learned to prepare these ingredients in the most satisfactory ways. Fresh fish needs steaming; meats are barbecued and roasted; vegetables are stir-fried; seafood is steamed or cooked in casseroles; suckling pigs are roasted on a spit with a glaze of honey, plum, and soy. Then to bring out the individual flavors, various sauces were devised, from black beans, garlic, oysters, and lobsters to lemon, plum, and soy. Meanwhile, another tradition grew up, in poverty-stricken regions where poor soil and rapacious landlords forced the people to eat whatever was edible. This included fungi and mushrooms, bamboo shoots and tree bark, seaweed and sea cucumbers, as well as any creature found in the forest.

With the most varied cuisine in the world, in Guangzhou eating is everyone's favorite activity, and restaurants are prime hubs of society. It is possible to have a Cantonese meal for two or four people, but ideally you need 12 or at least eight, so that everyone can share the traditional 8 to 10 courses. The table is never empty, from the beginning courses of pickles, peanuts, and cold cuts to the fresh fruit that signals the end of the meal. In between you'll have mounds of steamed green vegetables (known rather vaguely as Chinese cabbage, spinach, and kale), braised or minced pigeon, bean curd steamed or fried, luscious shrimp, mushrooms in countless forms, bird's nest or egg drop soup, fragrant pork or beef, and a large fish steamed in herbs, all accompanied by steamed rice, beer, soft drinks, and tea.

Although Cantonese restaurants predominate in Guangzhou, the city also offers excellent opportunities to enjoy the other great dining tradition from Guangdong province—**Chiu Chow cuisine**, better known as Chaozhou in China. It originated in the area around Shantou (formerly Swatow) on the coast east of Guangzhou and has been introduced to Chinatowns around the world by Chiu Chow people, who make up the largest number of overseas Chinese.

Like the Cantonese, Chiu Chow cooks can take advantage of bountiful supplies of fish and seafood but have far fewer resources on land, which is mostly arid. As a result farms are devoted to vegetables—which are served salted and pickled—and livestock, particularly chickens and lion-head geese, which average 26 pounds and stand 4 ft or more tall. These birds have been bred and treasured in the region for centuries, producing feathers, down, and a most delectable meat that is fried in goose blood and served cold with a sauce of vinegar and chopped garlic.

Many Chiu Chow dishes are fried, including such favorites as chicken wings stuffed with glutinous rice, shrimp, chopped mushrooms, and chestnuts, served with tangerine oil; *xinxing* beef balls, combining beef, shrimp, and fish; and milk mixed with corn flour and fruit. The Chiu Chow also like to combine sweet and salty tastes, for instance, wrapping the yolk of a salted duck egg with sweetened rice in thin sheets of bean curd; or cooking goose with pepper, aniseed, tangerine peel, licorice root, sugar, ginger, and mango and serving it with garlic and vinegar.

As tangerine bushes grow well here, the fruit is a staple for flavoring. The name was given to the little oranges after they were popularized in the West by the Portuguese in Macau and transplanted to Tangiers.

No account of Chiu Chow cuisine would be complete without a mention of Iron Buddha tea, also known as *kungfu* tea because of its strength. The oolong is brewed three times in an elaborate ceremony and served in tiny white bowls. It is tossed back in one gulp for the full mule-kick effect.

Least known of the cuisines found in Guangdong is Hakka, which was brought from the north in the 13th century by migrating Hakka people. They are of frugal peasant stock, and their cooking utilizes preserved vegetables and every part of an animal. Their most popular dish is salt-baked chicken. The bird, including all its insides, is wrapped in rice paper and cooked in rock salt to produce golden brown, tender meat, crunchy intestines, and moist liver. It is served with ginger and scallion or sesame sauce.

Other favorite dishes are stewed pork with preserved cabbage—a kind of Chinese sauerkraut—steamed bean curd with minced pork, deep-fried intestine stuffed with shrimp paste, pig's brain with wine sauce, and pig's tripe and bone marrow soup. To end the meal, Hakka fried noodles are served, dipped into a bowl of sugar before eating.

CATEGORY	COST*
$$$	over Y250
$$	Y150–Y250
$	under Y150

*per person for a main course at dinner

Golf

The development of first-class golf courses has given the Pearl River delta a new appeal as rapid industrialization has erased the area's more traditional attractions. The first clubs were built by and for golfers, but their success has given developers visions of big profits from corporate memberships. Famous as a vacation destination for Chinese businessmen, Hainan has also built a number of first-class courses, which in the off-season offer excellent rates.

Lodging

Superlatives are appropriate in describing the hotels of southeastern China. Here you'll find one of China's tallest hotels (Guangdong International in Guangzhou), the hotel that consistently tops the list of the most profitable business ventures in the country. The words *opulent, sumptuous,* and *no expense spared* apply equally to the White Swan and Garden hotels, also in Guangzhou. In Hainan lush tropical scenery outside enhances the effect of the beautiful interiors and excellent service of some world-class resort hotels. All hotels have business services and excellent telecommunications, and many have health clubs and evening entertainment. Unfortunately, the standard of English is not very high among hotel staff, although some are now employing native English speakers at their front desks.

As a result of the construction boom of the 1990s, much of southeastern China is overbuilt with hotels, so there are very substantial discounts on published rates, perhaps 30%–40%, especially on weekends, *except* during trade fairs, when prices are double or more the regular rates. Always ask the reservations or hotel desk staff for a discount.

CATEGORY	COST*
$$$	over Y1,150
$$	Y650–Y1,150
$	under Y650

*per standard double room, excluding tax

Exploring Southeastern China

While far from the geographical center of Southeastern China, Guangzhou is the transportation and communication hub for the entire region and should be the starting point for any journeys in this part of China. From here you can easily find tickets for comfortable express buses, planes, and boats to all of the destinations in Guangdong province. Guangzhou could be toured in a solid few days, but a better tactic might be to alternate explorations of Guangzhou with one-night excursions to other areas in the region.

Hainan's tropical geography and distance from the mainland lend it an atmosphere much different from Guangdong's. Transportation options to Hainan involve either a day by ship or bus/ferry combination or a flight from Guangzhou. You should set aside at least four free days. Although the accommodations are far from luxurious, the overnight boats to and from Hainan cruise past the beautiful coastline of the South China Sea. A one-way boat trip combined with a one-way flight to or from Hainan would give the best taste of the region. A return from Hainan can be easily booked to Chinese border towns for easy access to their former colonial cousins: Zhuhai (Macau) and Shenzhen (Hong Kong).

Great Itineraries

IF YOU HAVE 3 DAYS

Three days in southeastern China are best spent at the same hotel in Guangzhou. Mixing taxi trips with long leisurely walks adds optimal balance to a three-day stay here. If you are eager to get out of Guangzhou, a taxi ride to **Foshan** makes an excellent day trip. With Guangzhou's wealth of good restaurants, it's tempting to stop for leisurely lunches, but not advisable, as museums and temples close at 5. Save the big meal for dinnertime.

Start your exploration of Guangzhou by walking around **Shamian** (Shamian Island), with its restored colonial mansions. Cross the bridge to the **Qingping Shichang** (Qingping Market) and the antiques market, then stop for lunch at a restaurant with views of the Pearl River. In the afternoon take a taxi to the **Huaisheng Si Guang Ta** (Huaisheng Mosque) and stroll from there to the **Liu Rong Si Hua Ta** (Six Banyan Temple) and **Guangxiao Si** (Bright Filial Piety Temple). Take a taxi to the **Chen Jia Ci** (Chen Family Temple) and spend the evening in **Liuhua Gongyuan** (Liuhua Park), with dinner at a garden restaurant. The next day begin at **Yuexiu Gongyuan** (Yuexiu Park) and the **Guangzhou Bowuguan** (Guangzhou Museum). Have lunch in the park, then cross the street to the **Nan Yue Wang Mu** (Museum and Tomb of the Southern Yue Kings). Stroll to the **Lanpu** (Orchid Garden) and take traditional tea in one of the pavilions. On the third day begin at the **Sun Zhongshan Jinian Tang** (Sun Yat-sen Memorial Hall) and continue on to the **Nongmin Yundong Jiangxi Suo** (Peasant Movement Institute). After lunch proceed to the **Lieshi Lingyuan** (Memorial Garden for the Martyrs) and Revolutionary Museum. End the day at the **Huanghua Gang Qishi'er Lieshi Mu** (Mausoleum of the 72 Martyrs and Memorial of Yellow Flowers).

IF YOU HAVE 6 DAYS

Six days is a comfortable amount of time to really begin to soak up the excitement and energy of southeastern China. To see a lot with minimal traveling, follow the itinerary for the first three days and then stay in Guangzhou for three more; on day four take a taxi to the eastern suburbs, with their postmodern architecture and fine sports stadium. After lunch go by taxi to **Studio 2000,** Guangzhou's answer to Hollywood's Universal Studios. On day five take a bus or train to Foshan, where you can spend a day exploring the **Zu Miao** (Ancestral Temple) and shopping for paper cutouts and Shekwan pottery. On day six take a bus to the town of Cuiheng, in Zhongshan County, and see the **Sun Yat-sen Guju** (Sun Yat-sen's Birthplace). Have lunch at the Chung Shan Hot Springs Resort.

After three days in Guangzhou another option would be to take an air-conditioned express bus to **Shenzhen** and its wide variety of entertainment options: after checking into your hotel, go to **Jin Xiu Zhonghua** (Splendid China) to view the miniatures of Chinese historical sites. On the fifth day, you can spend the morning at the **Zhonghua Minzu Wenhua Cun** (Chinese Folk Culture Village) before returning to downtown Shenzhen for an afternoon of shopping. On day six you can either cross the border into Hong Kong or return to Guangzhou.

For a more travel-intensive six days, follow the first two days of the 3-day Guangzhou itinerary and then take a night ferry from Guangzhou to **Haikou.** (Purchase a first-class ticket. The travel conditions are not the best, but the sights range from fascinating to fantastic.) Sleep in on the morning of the third day, then spend the afternoon at the **Wugong Ci** (Temple of the Five Lords). Spend the evening walking through the streets and markets in the center of town. On the fourth day visit **Xiuying Paotai** (Xiuying Fort) in the morning and then take an air-conditioned express bus down the coast to **Sanya.** You should arrive just in time to enjoy sunset from the peak at **Luhuitou Park.** On the fifth day you can bake yourself on **Dadonghai Beach**, scuba dive, or hike in Luhuitou Park. On the sixth day either fly back to Guangzhou or return to Haikou and purchase a ferry ticket to Guangzhou, Shekou, or Hong Kong.

IF YOU HAVE 10 DAYS

If you have ten days, follow the second six-day itinerary, above, but fly to Hainan and depart from Haikou by ferry to Shekou. Upon arrival in **Shekou** on the morning of the seventh day, take a bus or taxi to your hotel in **Shenzhen.** Spend the next three days following the plan for days four, five, and six of the first six-day tour, above.

Numbers in the text correspond to numbers in the margin and on the Southeastern China, Guangzhou, and Guangdong maps.

GUANGZHOU

During the 19th century the only place foreigners were allowed to visit in China was Canton, now referred to as Guangzhou, where they traded for silk, tea, porcelain, lacquer screens, lace shawls, ivory fans, and other luxury goods. Since the late 1970s this port city has again become a gateway to areas outside China.

It all began with the Silk Road, when some merchants chose to take their caravans south and transport their silk and other luxuries by sea through the sheltered port of Guangzhou. From southeast Asia more merchants came to do business, selling pepper, nutmeg, and other spices, bird's nests for soup, and aromatic sandalwood for incense. Gradually they were joined by traders from farther afield. It is recorded that merchants from ancient Rome arrived to buy silk—at semiannual fairs that foreshadowed today's Canton Fair—during the Han dynasty (206 BC–AD 220), but it was the Arabs who came to dominate trade between East and West. In the 7th century they introduced Islam to Guangzhou, where they built China's first mosque.

The Cantonese talent and enthusiasm for business was as keen then as now, so the city's inhabitants welcomed the Portuguese explorer-merchants who arrived in the 16th century looking for a trading post. At the time the Ming court in Beijing banned all foreign trade, but, as the saying went, the emperor was far away. On their own initiative the local mandarins allowed the Portuguese to settle in Macau to act as middlemen for the Cantonese merchants' trade with Japan and the West.

Dominated by Japanese silver; Chinese silk, porcelain, and tea; Indian muslin; Persian damascene; African ivory; and European manufactured goods, this trade flourished for a century, until Japan closed its doors to the outside world. The Portuguese lost their sea lanes and cargoes to the newly mercantile nations of Europe, led by Britain, which used Macau as a base for doing business in Guangzhou. The British called Guangzhou "Canton," an anglicized version of the Portuguese *cantão*.

From the late 18th century Western merchants set up trading houses in Guangzhou where they negotiated the purchase of tea. The beverage became so important to Britain that the British East India Company had to find an import to match it in value. China didn't want more European manufactured goods or woolen cloth, but the British were able to create a market for opium. The British colonial government took control of the Bengal opium market, and private British companies were soon making fortunes from the opium trade.

The Chinese authorities tried to stop it, and in 1839 this resulted in the first of the Opium Wars, with naval battles in the Zhujiang (Pearl River) estuary. Defeated, the Chinese were forced to cede the island of Hong Kong to Britain and open treaty ports like Shanghai to foreign trade and influence.

Guangzhou lost its pivotal importance as an international trading hub and went into decline. Times were tough for many Cantonese, and in the 19th century tens of thousands of them left in search of a better life, often on coolie ships. Among the scholars who found an education overseas was Dr. Sun Yat-sen, who was born a few miles north of the Macau border. He led the movement to overthrow the Manchus that culminated in the 1911 Revolution.

Guangzhou next became a hotbed of revolutionary zeal and a battleground between Nationalists and Communists. Chiang Kai-shek founded the Whampoa Academy, and Mao Zedong taught at the Peasant Movement Institute, as did Zhou Enlai.

Following the 1949 Revolution, Guangzhou reinstituted its biannual trade fairs (April and September) and welcomed foreign business, but it wasn't until the open-door policy of Deng Xiaoping in 1979 that the port city was able to resume its role as a commercial gateway to China. Since then the city has become an economic dynamo; in 1999 it had a population of about 6.7 million.

Because of its rapid modernization during the 1980s and '90s, many parts of Guangzhou no longer evoke the original easygoing port city with its waterfront row of colonial mansions, streets lined with China coast shop-houses, verdant parks, and skyline dominated by a 7th-century minaret, a 10th-century pagoda, and a Ming dynasty tower. Today high-rise blocks and new highways dominate the old town, while new suburbs, bristling with skyscrapers and shopping malls, advance toward every horizon along new expressways—fed also by a new metro, a second railway terminal, and a modern sea terminal. Fortunately, the city has preserved some of its heritage in the splendid parks and busy temples, in some excellent museums, and, most of all, on Shamian Island.

Chongqing

Wulingyuan

Yuan Jiang

H U N A N

Xia

Zunyi

Wu Jiang

Shaoyan

G U I Z H O U

Liupanshui

Guiyang

Qingshui Jiang

Kaili

Anshun

Duyun

Guilin

Beipan Jiang

Nanpan Jiang

Hongshui

He

Liuzhou

Lijiang

Y U N N A N

Yu Jiang

G U A N G X I

G

Xi

Zha

Wuming

Xun Jiang

Yu Jiang

Nanning

VIETNAM

Huashan

Pinxiang

Maoming

Beihai

Zhanjiang

Hanoi

Gulf of Tonkin

LAOS

Haikou **30**

H A I N A N

Dongfang

△ Wuzhi Shan

32

Tongzha

31 Sanya

Exploring Guangzhou

Guangzhou can be roughly divided into six districts, each with unique sights to see and walks to take. Because of the logistics and time involved in moving from place to place around the city, it is best to concentrate on a neighborhood at a time. Colonial Canton consists of the area on and around Shamian Island and the Pearl River. The part of the city that was formerly encircled by the city wall comprises Ancestral Guangzhou. To the north of the former walled city is the Station District and even farther north, the airport area. On the eastern edge of the formerly walled city are sights related to Chinese revolutions, and farther east, the Eastern Suburbs and the Tianhe District.

Colonial Canton

To recapture the days of Canton as it looked to the foreign merchants in the latter half of the 19th century and first part of the 20th, stroll around Shamian Island and have lunch within sight and sound of the Pearl River traffic, which once included tea clippers and opium ships. Cross the small bridge to visit the antiques shops of Qingping.

A GOOD WALK

Start from the White Swan Hotel, leaving by the rear entrance. Follow the three streets that run parallel along the length of **Shamian** ① (Shamian Island). Here you can see restored buildings and watch the locals at leisure in the small central park. Then cross the north bridge to visit **Qingping Shichang** ② (Qingping Market).

Timing. This walk can be done in three hours, but lunch and shopping can add another two to three hours.

SIGHTS TO SEE

② **Qingping Shichang** (Qingping Market). Across the short bridge from the north shore of Shamian is the bustling, noisy complex of alleys packed with shops and market stalls. The Qingping Market caters to a wide variety of shoppers. The central alley contains herbalists, spice sellers, and fruit and vegetable stalls. To the left is the infamous meat market, with dogs, cats, and various endangered species on sale. If you have any qualms at all about seeing animals slaughtered, don't go here. Turn right on Dishipu Lu, and on the left is a collection of jade shops, along with stores selling reproduction antiques, old watches and jewelry, Mao memorabilia, and other collectibles. Farther north, on Daihe Lu, is the private **antiques market,** where you'll find plenty of old furniture, porcelain, jade, and bank notes. ⊠ *Dishipu Lu and Daihe Lu.*

① **Shamian** (Shamian Island). More than a century ago the mandarins of Guangzhou designated a 44-acre sandbank outside the city walls in the Pearl River as an enclave for foreign merchants. The foreigners had previously lived and done business in a row of houses known as the Thirteen Factories, near the present Shamian, but local resentment after the Opium Wars—sometimes leading to murderous attacks—made it prudent to confine them to a protected area, which was linked to the city by two bridges that were closed at 10 every night.

The island rapidly became a bustling township, as trading companies from Britain, the United States, France, Holland, Italy, Germany, Portugal, and Japan built stone mansions along the waterfront. With spacious gardens and private wharves, these served as homes, offices, and warehouses. There were churches for Catholics and Protestants, banks, a yacht club, football grounds, a cricket pitch, and the Victory Hotel.

Shamian was attacked in the 1920s but survived until the 1949 Revolution, when its mansions became government offices or apartment houses and the churches were turned into factories. In recent years, however, the island has resumed much of its old character. Many colonial buildings have been restored, and both churches have been beautifully renovated and reopened to worshipers. **Our Lady of Lourdes Catholic Church** (✉ Shamian Dajie at Yijie), with its cream-and-white neo-Gothic tower, is particularly attractive. A park with shady walks and benches has been created in the center of the island, where local residents come to chat with friends, walk their caged birds, or practice tai chi (shadow boxing).

The island has also resumed its role as a foreign enclave, with businesspeople at the deluxe White Swan Hotel and budget travelers at the reestablished and renovated Victory Hotel. Continental-style sidewalk cafés have opened, and the delightful Lucy's has become the only restaurant on the river's edge. In addition, Shamian has developed into a shopping district, with brand-name but bargain-priced boutiques in the White Swan and dozens of small shops selling Chinese paintings, pottery, minority handcrafts, and assorted souvenirs.

The biggest attractions, however, are the finely restored colonial buildings, now put to new uses. The old British consulate is now the Foreign Affairs Office of Guangdong province; the former U.S. consulate is now a restaurant, as is the stately, colonnaded Hongkong and Shanghai Bank; the Banque de l'Indochine and the offices of Butterfield & Swire house modern businesses; and the stuffy old Shamian Club is now the International Club Karaoke Lounge. ✉ *Shamian Island.*

Ancestral Guangzhou

To explore what used to be the walled city of Guangzhou takes a full day. The major attractions are scattered, and the narrow streets are invariably congested with human and vehicular traffic. Nevertheless, it's interesting to cover some of the itinerary on foot in order to experience the dynamism of Cantonese city life.

A GOOD WALK

It's best to start with a taxi ride to the **Huaisheng Si Guang Ta** ③ (Huaisheng Mosque), except on Friday, when it is closed to non-Muslims. You can walk from here to the **Liu Rong Si Hua Ta** ④ (Six Banyan Temple) and on to the nearby **Guangxiao Si** ⑤ (Bright Filial Piety Temple). After lunch take a taxi to the **Chen Jia Ci** ⑥ (Chen Family Temple) and end the day with a stroll in **Liuhua Gongyuan** ⑦ (Liuhua Park).

Timing. This itinerary should take six to seven hours, depending on how much walking you do and how long you take for lunch.

SIGHTS TO SEE

❻ **Chen Jia Ci** (Chen Family Temple). There are many brilliantly ornamented ridgepoles to be found in Guangdong and neighboring Fujian. Crafted by masters from local clay into birds, flowers, mythical beasts, sacred images, and historical tableaux, they usually crown a temple pavilion or study hall, representing one of the great folk art traditions of all China.

One of the most marvelous of these works of art can be found on the Chen Family Temple, where it stretches 90 ft along the main roof, depicting scenes from the epic *Romance of Three Kingdoms,* with thousands of figures against a backdrop of ornate houses, monumental gates, and lush scenery. This is the showpiece of the temple but only one of its treasures. Elsewhere in the huge compound of pavilions and courtyards are friezes of delicately carved stone and wood, as well as fine iron castings and a dazzling altar covered with gold leaf.

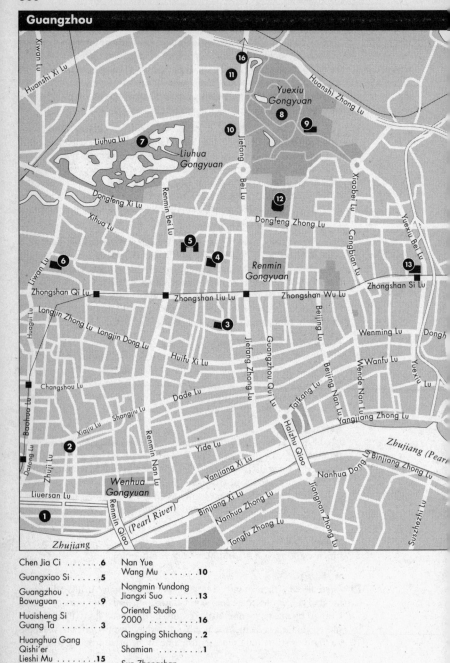

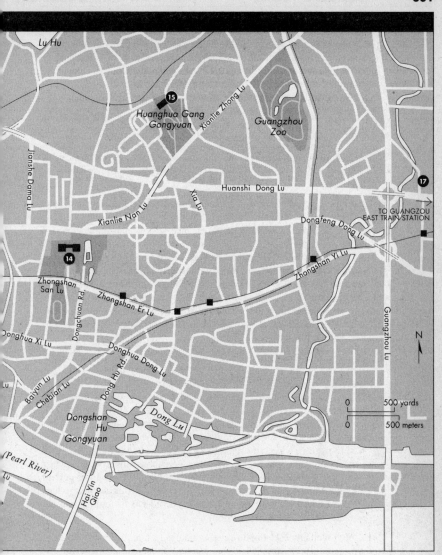

The Chen family is one of Guangdong's oldest and most numerous clans. In the late 19th century local members, who had prospered as merchants, decided to build a memorial temple. They invited contributions from the Chens—and kindred Chans—who had emigrated overseas. The money flowed in from 72 countries, and no expense was spared to make this a tribute to a successful family. The temple also houses a folk arts museum and shop. ⊠ *7 Zhongshan Qi Lu.* ☏ *Y4.* ☉ *Daily 8:30–5.*

❺ **Guangxiao Si** (Bright Filial Piety Temple). This Buddhist temple is the oldest in Guangzhou. It was originally the residence of the Nan Yue kings but became a temple in AD 401. During the Tang dynasty, Huineng, the monk who founded the southern sect of Buddhism, studied here. In 1629 it was rebuilt after a fire, with new prayer pavilions added.

Among the most charming of Guangzhou's temples, Guangxiao Si has a warm, welcoming atmosphere. A gilded wooden Laughing Buddha sits at the entrance, and a huge bronze incense burner, usually wreathed in joss-stick smoke, stands in the main courtyard. Beyond the main hall, noted for its ceiling of red-lacquer timbers, is another courtyard that contains several treasures, among them a small brick pagoda said to contain the tonsure of Huineng, and a couple of iron pagodas that are the oldest of their kind in China. Above them spread the leafy branches of a myrobalan plum tree and a banyan called Buddha's Tree because it is said Huineng was given his tonsure in its shade. ⊠ *Guangxiao Lu.* ☏ *Y2.* ☉ *Daily 6:30–5.*

❸ **Huaisheng Si Guang Ta** (Huaisheng Mosque). In the cosmopolitan era of the Tang dynasty (618–907) a Muslim missionary named Abu Wangus, said to be an uncle of the prophet Mohammed, came to southern China. He converted many Chinese to Islam and built this mosque in Guangzhou as their house of worship. Ever since he died here, his tomb in the northern part of the city has been a place of pilgrimage for visiting Muslims. The mosque, however, is his best-known memorial. The first mosque in China, it originally stood on the banks of the river and for 1,300 years provided a beacon for merchant ships from Southeast Asia, India, the Middle East, and Europe. Following progressive land reclamations, it is now almost downtown and surrounded by modern skyscrapers, yet it manages to retain an old-world dignity and an atmosphere of peaceful devotion.

A high wall encloses the mosque, which is dominated by the smooth, white minaret. Rising to 108 ft, it can be climbed using an interior spiral staircase, and the views from the top—where a muezzin calls the faithful to prayer—are still spectacular. Below is a gate-tower that was rebuilt in Tang style during the late 17th century, and the main prayer hall, which was refurbished in Ming dynasty style in 1936. Around the mosque are courtyards and gardens where local Muslims and visitors can rest and meditate. ⊠ *Guangta Lu.* ☏ *Free.* ☉ *Sat.–Thurs. 8–5, except special holy days.*

★ ❹ **Liu Rong Si Hua Ta** (Six Banyan Temple). Look at any ancient scroll painting or lithograph by early Western travelers, and you will see two landmarks rising above old Guangzhou. One is the minaret of the mosque; the other is the 184-ft pagoda of the Six Banyan Temple. Still providing an excellent lookout, the pagoda appears to have nine stories, each with doorways and encircling balconies. Inside, however, there are 17 levels. Thanks to its arrangement of colored, carved roofs, it is popularly known as the Flowery Pagoda.

The temple was founded in the 5th century, but following a series of fires, most of the existing buildings date from the 11th century. It was built by the Zen master Tanyu and is still a very active place of worship, with a community of monks and regular attendance by Zen Buddhists. It was originally called Purificatory Wisdom Temple but changed its name after a visit by the Song dynasty poet Su Dongpo, who was so delighted by six banyan trees growing in the courtyard that he left an inscription with the characters for six banyans.

The trees are no longer to be found, but the stone bearing his calligraphy can be seen in the temple, along with tablets telling the history of the place and a 1,000-year-old bronze statue of Zen master Huineng. In one prayer hall there are also three statues of Buddha—each weighing 5 tons—and one of the goddess of mercy, all made of brass and cast in 1663. ⊠ *Haizhu Beilu.* ☎ *Y6.* ☉ *Daily 8–5.*

❼ **Liuhua Gongyuan** (Liuhua Park). Next to the China and Dong Fang hotels, as well as the trade fair hall, this park is ideal for relaxation, people-watching, and dining. It has a serpentine lake, groves of trees, flower beds, and plenty of benches. You can sit and watch men gather to compare the talents of their pet songbirds, finches that are kept in exquisite bamboo cages fitted with porcelain feeding bowls and decorated with pieces of jade. In late afternoon the scene changes as young lovers come in search of secluded benches. As for dining, the glittering white palace in the lake is the Sun Kwong restaurant. ⊠ *Dongfeng Xi Lu and Renmin Bei Lu.* ☎ *Y3.* ☉ *Daily 11–6.*

Station District

The area around the main railroad station and exhibition hall offers an agreeable combination of ancient history and natural history. Dominated by the Zhenhai Tower, Yuexiu Park is Guangzhou's answer to New York's Central Park, while the Nan Yue Tomb Museum uncovers an extraordinary era in the city's past, and the Orchid Garden proves you can find peace and quiet in the busiest part of town.

A GOOD WALK

Begin at **Yuexiu Gongyuan** ⑧ (Yuexiu Park), strolling to pay respects to the Five Celestial Rams before visiting the **Guangzhou Bowuguan** ⑨ (Guangzhou Museum), housed in the 14th-century Zhenhai Tower. Have lunch in the park, then cross Jiefang Bei Lu to the **Nan Yue Wang Mu** ⑩ (Museum and Tomb of the Southern Yue Kings). End the day with a stroll through the **Lanpu** ⑪ (Orchid Garden), where you can stop for tea in a classic tea pavilion.

Timing. This walk, including lunch, should take about five and a half hours.

SIGHTS TO SEE

❾ **Guangzhou Bowuguan** (Guangzhou Museum). Dominating Yuexiu Park is the five-story, 92-ft **Zhenhai Lou** (Tower Controlling the Sea), which was first built in 1380. Three centuries later it was converted into a watchtower overlooking the old port. Today its entrance is still guarded by a dozen old cannons and three Krupp guns, but now it houses the municipal museum, whose displays outline the history of the city from prehistoric times to the present. On the first floor is a huge anchor from the Ming era, which was found in the river mud, and a bas relief model of Guangzhou as it was projected to look in the 21st century.

On the next floor are the remains of pottery from a Han dynasty (206 BC–AD 220) tomb; Han bronzes; and examples of early trade goods such as rhinoceros horns, hawksbill turtle shells, and precious stones. The third floor is devoted to Guangzhou's experience of the Western world. Here is the original clock face from the Roman Catholic cathedral, bibles, exportware porcelain, models of the first railway car and first plane used in Guangzhou, pictures of the foreign factories on Shamian, and a bas relief of the city in the 19th century.

Guangzhou after the Opium War is the focus of exhibits on the fourth floor. There are pictures of the first brewery, the first sugar refinery, and early sewing machines, along with displays of an old fire engine, telephone, radio, household implements, and a sedan chair. On the top floor are shops selling antiques, tea, jade, cheongsams (high-neck, split-skirt Chinese dresses), and such local specialties as snake wine. Tea, beer, soft drinks, and snacks are served at tables on the balcony, which affords marvelous views of the park. ⊠ *Yuexiu Gongyuan, Jiefang Bei Lu,* ☎ *020/8355–0627.* ⊡ *Y6.* ☉ *Daily 9–5.*

⓫ **Lanpu** (Orchid Garden). This garden offers a wonderfully convenient retreat from the noise and crowds of the city. It's spread over 20 acres, with paths that wind through groves of bamboo and tropical trees, beside carp-filled ponds, to a series of classic teahouses. Here you can sit and enjoy a wide variety of Chinese teas, brewed the traditional way. There are tables inside and on terraces that overlook the ponds. As for the orchids, there are 10,000 pots with more than 2,000 species of the flower, which present a magical sight when they bloom. ⊠ *Jiefang Bei Lu.* ⊡ *Y5.* ☉ *Daily 8:30 AM–11 PM.*

★ ⓾ **Nan Yue Wang Mu** (Museum and Tomb of the Southern Yue Kings). Until quite recently only specialist historians realized that Guangzhou had once been a royal capital. In 1983 bulldozers clearing ground to build the China Hotel uncovered the intact tomb of Emperor Wen Di, who ruled Nan Yue (southern China) from 137 to 122 BC. The tomb was faithfully restored and its treasures placed in the adjoining Nan Yue Museum.

The tomb contained the skeletons of the king and 15 courtiers—guards, cooks, concubines, and a musician—who were buried alive to attend him in death. Also buried were several thousand funerary objects, clearly designed to show off the extraordinary accomplishments of the southern empire. Now attractively displayed in the museum, with intelligent labeling in Chinese and English, they include jade armor, gem-encrusted swords and crossbows, gold jewelry, lacquer boxes, pearl pillows, 139 pottery pi-discs, 1,000 bronze and iron cooking pots, and an orchestra of bronze and stone chimes that are still in tune.

The tomb itself—built entirely of stone slabs—is behind the museum and is remarkable for its compact size. Divided into two parts, it is 66 ft deep, 40 ft wide, and 35 ft long. The emperor was buried in the central chamber, while six smaller adjoining rooms were packed from floor to ceiling with the funeral objects and the courtiers.

On the second floor an incomparable collection of 200 ceramic pillows—from the Tang, Song, Jin, and Yuan dynasties—was donated by Hong Kong industrialist Yeung Wing Tak and his wife. ⊠ *867 Jiefang Bei Lu.* ⊡ *Y12.* ☉ *Daily 9:30–5:30.*

❽ **Yuexiu Gongyuan** (Yuexiu Park). To take a break from business or get away from the bustle, residents and visitors alike adjourn to Yuexiu Park in the heart of town. The park's wide range of attractions and facilities cover 247 acres and include Yuexiu Hill and six hillocks, landscaped gardens, man-made lakes, theme parks, restaurants, and recreational areas.

The best-known sight in Yuexiu Park is the **Wuyang Suxiang** (Five Rams statue), which celebrates the legend of the five celestials who came to Guangzhou riding on goats to bring cereals to the people. Today Guangzhou families take each other's photo in front of the statue before setting off to enjoy the park. They hire boats on the three man-made lakes, which contain islands accessible by hump-backed bridges, or stroll along paths lined with flowering bushes, bamboo groves, and small forests of pine, cypress, and kapok.

For a different kind of enjoyment, the park has a stadium for soccer matches and other sports, a Journey to the West theme park—with a giant wooden cockerel that crows at the entrance—and a children's playground with fairground rides. ✉ *Jiefang Bei Lu.* 🎫 *Y3.* ⊘ *Daily 6 AM–9 PM.*

Revolutionary Guangzhou

In the center of the city are memorials to people who changed Chinese history in the 20th century, using Guangzhou as a base of operations. The most famous were local boy Dr. Sun Yat-sen, who led the over-throw of the Qing dynasty, and Communist Party founders Mao Ze-dong and Zhou Enlai. There were many others, among them thousands who died in the struggles. All are recalled in different ways.

A GOOD WALK

Start with a taxi ride to the **Sun Zhongshan Jinian Tang** ⑫ (Sun Yat-sen Memorial Hall), visit the hall and its grounds, then walk or take a taxi to the **Nongmin Yundong Jiangxi Suo** ⑬ (Peasant Movement In-stitute) to recapture the days when youthful revolutionaries Mao and Zhou taught their followers how to organize a peasant revolt. Walk on to the **Lieshi Lingyuan** ⑭ (Memorial Garden for the Martyrs) and Revolutionary Museum and finish with a cab ride to the **Huanghua Gang Qishi'er Lieshi Mu** ⑮ (Mausoleum of the 72 Martyrs).

Timing. This itinerary should take three to four hours.

SIGHTS TO SEE

⑮ **Huanghua Gang Qishi'er Lieshi Mu** (Mausoleum of the 72 Martyrs). In a prelude to the successful revolution of 1911 a group of 88 revo-lutionaries staged the Guangzhou armed uprising, only to be defeated and executed by the authorities. Of those killed, 72 were buried here. Their memorial, built in 1918, incorporates a mixture of international symbols of freedom and democracy, including replicas of the Statue of Liberty. ✉ *Xianlie Zhong Lu.* 🎫 *Y8.* ⊘ *Daily 6 AM–8:30 PM.*

⑭ **Lieshi Lingyuan** (Memorial Garden for the Martyrs). Built in 1957, this garden has been planted around a tumulus that contains the remains of 5,000 revolutionaries killed in the 1927 destruction of the Guangzhou Commune by the Nationalists. This was the execution site of many vic-tims. On the grounds is the **Revolutionary Museum,** which displays pictures and memorabilia of Guangdong's 20th-century rebellions. ✉ *Zhongshan San Lu.* 🎫 *Y3.* ⊘ *Daily 6 AM–9 PM.*

⑬ **Nongmin Yundong Jiangxi Suo** (Peasant Movement Institute). Today the atmosphere of the institute—with its quiet courtyards and empty cells—recalls its origin as a 14th-century Confucian temple, but it doesn't take long to detect the ghostly presence of the young idealists who came here in the early 1920s to learn how to create a new China based on equality and justice.

The institute was established in 1924 by some of the founders of the Chinese Communist Party, who had set up a Guangzhou Commune modeled on the 19th-century Parisian example. Young people came from all over the country to listen to party leaders. In 1926 Mao Zedong became director of the school, and Zhou Enlai was a staff member. They and their colleagues lectured on "the problem of the Chinese peasantry," "rural education," and geography to students who were then sent to the countryside to educate the peasants.

The venture proved short-lived, as it soon became obvious that the Nationalists under Chiang Kai-shek were planning to drive the Communists from the city. The institute was closed in late 1927, just before the Commune was crushed and 5,000 revolutionaries killed. In 1953 the Beijing government restored the buildings and made it into a museum. The result is very evocative. The main lecture hall, with desks arranged in front of a blackboard, looks as if the students might return any minute. Instead they can be seen in photographs displayed along the corridors: keen young men and women, bright-eyed with expectation, but in most cases doomed. As the captions reveal, a majority were captured and killed by the Nationalists. As for their leader, Mao is recalled in a re-creation of his room: a simple cell with a metal-frame bed, desk, and bookcase. ⊠ *42 Zhongshan Si Lu.* 🚍 *Y2.* ☉ *Daily 10–6.*

⑫ Sun Zhongshan Jinian Tang (Sun Yat-sen Memorial Hall). By the end of the 19th century the Qing dynasty was in its last throes. The moribund court and its corrupt mandarins were powerless to control the Westerners who had taken over much of China's trade or the warlords who kept the peasantry in feudal misery. Dissent was widespread, but it was Guangzhou that became a center for rebellion. The leader was Sun Yat-sen, a young doctor from a village in the Pearl Delta who had studied in Honolulu and graduated from Hong Kong's medical college. Inspired by democratic ideals, he set up the Revive China Society in Guangzhou in 1892 and petitioned the emperor, demanding equality and justice. In return, a price was put on his head, and he was forced to spend the next years as an exile in Japan, the United States, and Europe.

Everywhere he went he gathered supporters and funds for a revolution, which finally took place in 1911, when he returned to Guangzhou to be proclaimed "Father of the Revolution" and provisional president. However, Dr. Sun was no politician and soon lost Nationalist leadership to Chiang Kai-shek. He spent his last years in Shanghai and died in Beijing in 1925, but he remains a favorite son of Guangzhou.

Dr. Sun's Memorial Hall is a handsome pavilion that stands in an attractively landscaped garden behind a bronze statue of the leader. Built in 1929–31 with funds mostly from overseas Chinese, the building is a classic octagon, with sweeping roofs of blue tiles over carved wooden eaves and verandahs of red-lacquer columns. Inside is an auditorium with seating for 5,000 and a stage for plays, concerts, and ceremonial occasions. ⊠ *Dongfeng Zhong Lu.* 🚍 *Y10.* ☉ *Daily 8–5:30.*

Airport Area

One of the newest entertainments of Guangzhou is a reproduction film studio where you can get a close-up view of the action taken from kung fu and Shanghai gangster films. The studio is in the northern suburbs, next to Baiyun Airport. You can reach it by taxi in 10 minutes from the China Hotel.

🦢 ⑯ Oriental Studio 2000. Modeled on Hollywood's Universal Studios, this entertainment complex has two movie sets dedicated to the best-known genres of Chinese moviemaking: the kung fu epic and the movie about the good old bad days of Shanghai. The "Shanghai in the Roaring '30s" set has a chorus line of scantily clad girls, slick-haired gangsters, motorcycles, and machine guns. The "traditional Chinese courtyard" set, with stables and workshops, features a battle between "lion" armies whose warriors leap high into the air and perform breathtaking acrobatics.

The studio opened in 1996 in the **Dong Fang Leyuan** (Dongfang Amusement Park). The two shows utilize all the equipment to be found in local film studios, so there are overhead wires for "flying," facades that "collapse," mats that become springboards, and blowers to provide a snowfall or smoke. The introductions are in Chinese, and there's no program, but that does nothing to detract from this totally visual experience. The shows last 15 minutes, with three performances a day.

Along with the sets, the park has restaurants, some modeled on old films, serving Chinese and Western food; shopping arcades with souvenirs; staged folk dancing; acrobatics; and street performances by conjurers, magicians, and *qi gong* (traditional Chinese exercise said to release the inner power or *qi* of the spirit) experts. In the main part of the vast amusement park there's a huge Ferris wheel, a roller coaster, and other fairground rides, plus a lake with pleasure boats. ⊠ *Dajing Zhonglu in Dong Fang Leyuan,* ☎ *020/8662–8628 ext. 316.* ⊡ *Y80.* ☉ *Daily 9–5.*

Eastern Suburbs

Since 1980 Guangzhou has grown beyond all recognition, and the result is a city bursting at the seams. In response the local government decided to create a new downtown, to the east of the city, where there was space. The first move to lure residents from their traditional venues was the construction of a world-class sports stadium. The second was to invite Hong Kong's New World Company to build a brand-new suburb of apartments and offices. The third was the most drastic. The direct rail link between Guangzhou and Hong Kong is a vital artery, so the terminal for Hong Kong trains was moved to Tianhe, the new downtown.

A GOOD WALK

Take a taxi to the Guangzhou East train station, look inside, and from here stroll around **Tianhe** ⑰. See the handsome sports stadium and some attractive modern statuary, then take a look at the eclectic architecture of the city's newest skyscrapers, which combine Doric-column courtyards, neo-Gothic archways, colored glass–clad facades, and traditional Chinese roofs. Drop by the multistoried book shop and the newest shopping arcades of Teem Plaza.

Timing. An hour and a half is enough to see the highlights of Tianhe, unless there is a special event in the stadium.

SIGHTS TO SEE

⑰ **Tianhe.** There might be other contenders for the title of Asia's tallest building, but Guangzhou has a very prominent claimant, the **Guangdong Plaza,** which soars 1,300 ft with 80 stories of office space. It is already a city landmark, especially when viewed together with the neighboring **Metro Plaza**'s two gold-walled Romanesque towers. All three stand next to the **Guangzhou East station** (⊠ Linhe Lu), the new terminus for trains from Hong Kong. The station is light, airy, and very spacious, with a vast entrance hall and long distances to walk between trains and the immigration hall.

Tianhe is designed to be a hub of sports activity. The two outdoor and indoor arenas of the **Tianhe Stadium Complex** (⊠ Huanshi Donglu, East Guangzhou) appeal to the eye and are equipped for international soccer matches, track and field, and athletics competitions, as well as pop concerts and large-scale ceremonies. Around the stadiums is a pleasant landscaped park, with outdoor cafés and tree-shaded benches. The park surrounding the complex also contains a bowling center with 38 lanes and a floor of video games.

The area around the core of Tianhe is currently dotted with dozens of construction projects: offices, apartments, hotels, shops, and recreational facilities. Already the district is drawing shoppers. The **Guangzhou Book Center** (⊠ Huangshi Donglu, East Guangzhou, ☎ 020/8759–4208) has seven floors with space for books on every subject (including some bargain-priced art books in English), from software to literature. Across the street is **Teem Plaza,** a vast complex of shops and supermarkets.

Dining and Lodging

The only problem of dining in Guangzhou is choosing from the extraordinary range of restaurants (some 150,000 at last estimate). The following selection includes tried-and-true favorites for Chinese and Western meals. Unless specified otherwise, all restaurants are open daily for lunch and dinner, with most Chinese establishments also serving a traditional breakfast of rice porridge and dim sum snacks. Reservations are usually not necessary except in Western restaurants during the fair periods. Chinese banquets are part of all business deals here; you can organize a meal for local colleagues by contacting the restaurant at least a day in advance and either choosing the menu (if you're very familiar with banquet dishes) or specifying the number of guests—to fill each table with 12—and price range and leaving it in the restaurant's experienced hands.

The purpose of your visit to Guangzhou is likely to determine your choice of hotel, not least because heavy traffic on every road, exacerbated by encroaching construction sites, can make crosstown travel very time-consuming. Traditionally the hotels close to the main train station and trade fair headquarters were the choice of businesspeople, but since the terminal for Hong Kong train service has been moved to the eastern suburbs at Tianhe, where the local government is encouraging businesses to relocate, there has been a shift to hotels both in the east and on Huanshi Donglu, the major thoroughfare between the two business areas.

$$$ ✕ **Connoisseur.** You could almost be in Regency France in the Garden's premier restaurant. The arched columns with gilded capitals, gold-framed mirrors, lustrous drapes, and immaculate table settings are just right. And the food doesn't disappoint. A French chef is in charge, serving the finest Continental fare. ✉ *Garden Hotel, 368 Huanshi Dong Lu,* ☎ *020/8333–8989 ext. 3962. AE, DC, MC, V.*

$$$ ✕ **Guangzhou Restaurant.** Established in 1936, with branches in Hong Kong and Los Angeles, as well as two more in Guangzhou, this is probably the busiest Cantonese restaurant in town, serving 10,000 diners a day. The setting is classic, with courtyards of flowery bushes surrounded by dining rooms of various sizes ranged along arcaded corridors. The house specialties are abalone sprinkled with 24-carat gold flakes; Eight Treasures—game, chicken, ham, and mushrooms—served in winter melons carved to make a bowl; duck feet stuffed with shrimp; and roast sliced goose. ✉ *2 Wenchang Nanlu,* ☎ *020/8138–0439. AE, DC, MC, V.*

$$$ ✕ **Silk Road Grill Room.** As you'd expect from the superlative White Swan, the grill room is the ultimate in sophistication. It's furnished with brass fittings and big silver food covers, gleaming candlesticks, and crisp white linen. The service is impeccable and the menu a fine selection of Continental dishes. ✉ *White Swan, Shamian Yi, Shamian,* ☎ *020/8188–6968. AE, DC, MC, V. No lunch.*

$$ ✕ **Lai Wan Market.** This is a wonderful re-creation of the old Canton waterfront, with booths shaped like the flower boats that used to offer food, drink, opium, and girls; and small wooden stools at low counters. The Market is known for its dim sum and two kinds of rice, one made with pork, beef, fish, and seafood, the other with fish, beef, and pork liver. ⊠ *Garden Hotel, 368 Huanshi Donglu,* ☎ *020/8333–8989 ext. 3924. AE, DC, MC, V.*

$$ ✕ **The Roof.** China Hotel's fine-dining restaurant is tops in both senses: It sits in understated splendor on the 18th floor, with panoramic views of nighttime Guangzhou. The menu changes, offering seasonal food specialties, but such staples as saddle of lamb marinated in mint and yogurt, fettuccine, scallops in saffron sauce, and prime cuts of U.S. beef remain on offer. ⊠ *China Hotel, Liuhua Lu,* ☎ *020/8666–6888 ext. 71892. AE, DC, MC, V. Closed Sun. No lunch.*

$$ ✕ **Star Garden.** You'll find excellent Western fare here, including a rather tasty steak, as well as Asian dishes. The modern silver, white, and black decor and hip atmosphere make it a comfortable place to enjoy dinner and drinks. Daily happy hour, live music, and an outdoor bar top it all off. ⊠ *7 Shamian Nanjie, Shamian,* ☎ *020/8410–1819. MC, V.*

$–$$ ✕ **Chiu Chou City.** One of the best places for authentic food from the Shantou area is this restaurant in the Landmark Canton Hotel. It has a large main room and several private rooms, which are invariably packed for lunch and dinner. The house special is Chiu Chow goose, served as cold cuts or cooked in its own blood and dipped into a sauce of white vinegar and chopped garlic. ⊠ *Hotel Landmark Canton, Qiao Guang Lu,* ☎ *020/8335–5988. AE, DC, MC, V.*

$–$$ ✕ **Datong Restaurant.** Occupying all eight stories of an old building on the riverfront, with an open terrace on the top floor, this is one of the city's veteran dining places. It is famous for its morning dim sum and a 1,000-dish menu that includes peacock chicken—braised and cut in the shape of a peacock with its tail fanned—served with vegetables and ham; crisp-skin chicken; and roasted Xishi duck. ⊠ *Nanfang Dasha, 63 Yanjiang Xi Lu,* ☎ *020/8188–8988. AE, DC, MC, V.*

$–$$ ✕ **Dongjiang Restaurant.** This city-center stalwart has a simple setting but a brilliant menu. Among the favorites are braised duck stuffed with eight delicacies and glutinous rice, stuffed giant prawns, crab in black bean sauce, salt-roast chicken, stuffed bean curd, and steamed pork with salted, dried mustard cabbage. ⊠ *337 Zhongshan Wu Lu,* ☎ *020/ 8333–5568. MC, V.*

$ ✕ **Banqi Restaurant.** You feel like you're entering a Taoist temple or private estate, beautifully perched on the shore of Liwan Lake, but it's actually one of the city's most attractive traditional restaurants. Banqi consists of rooms of various sizes in rambling teahouses, one of them built on a floating houseboat. Between are landscaped gardens networked by zigzag paths over bridges across ornamental lakes and through bamboo groves. The food is just as good on the eye as the tongue, with dishes such as vegetables sculpted into birds for cold cuts, scallop and crab soup, and quail eggs cooked with shrimp roe on a bed of green vegetables among the huge selection. ⊠ *151 Longjin Xi Lu,* ☎ *020/ 8181–5955. AE, MC, V.*

$ ✕ **Black Swan Dumpling Restaurant.** A nationwide chain with five branches in Guangzhou, this place serves up 15 kinds of northern-style dumplings. The decor is basic Chinese family dining; the food is excellent. ⊠ *486 Huanshi Dong Lu, Gaoerfu Dasha 2F,* ☎ *020/8767–5687. No credit cards.*

$ ✕ **Caigenxiang Vegetarian Restaurant.** Established by Buddhists, this
★ is a joy for visiting vegetarians. Its menu lists 200 dishes and 100 snacks. Highlights are vegetables made with herbs to give the taste of duck, sausage, and meatballs. Such delicacies as Snow Mountain consommé are made from fungi. The restaurant's tables, chairs, and walls are made of bamboo. ⊠ *167 Zhongshan Lulu,* ☎ *020/8334–4363. No credit cards.*

Guangzhou Dining and Lodging

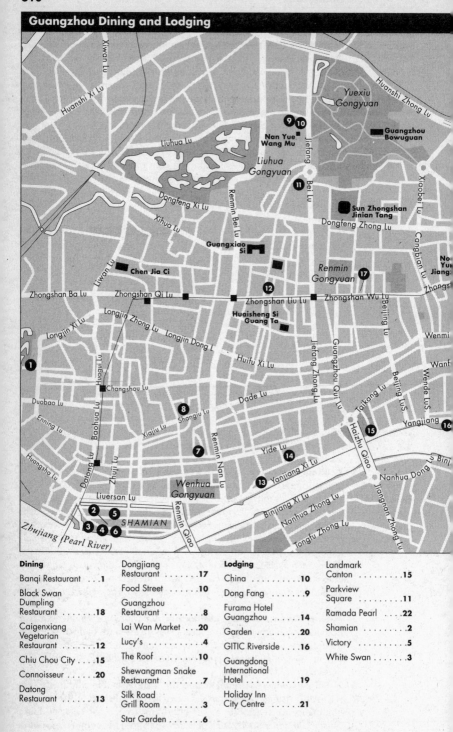

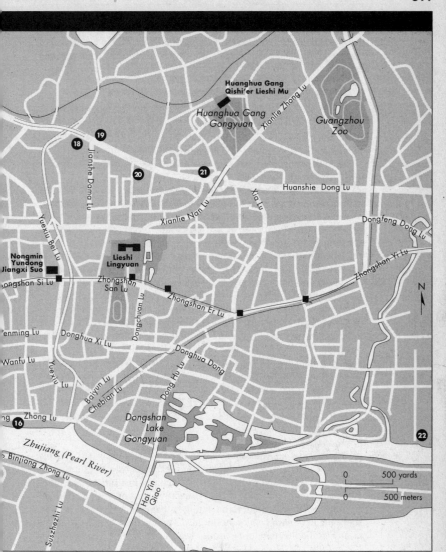

Huanghua Gang Qishi'er Lieshi Mu

Huanghua Gang Gongyuan

Guangzhou Zoo

Xianlie Zhong Lu

Huanshie Dong Lu

Xia Lu

Dongfeng Dong Lu

Jianshe Dama Lu

Xianlie Nan Lu

Zhongshan Yi Lu

Yuexu Bei Lu

Nongmin Yundong Jiangxi Suo

Lieshi Lingyuan

Zhongshan Si Lu

Zhongshan San Lu

Dongchuan Lu

Zhongshan Er Lu

enming Lu

Donghua Xi Lu

Donghua Dong

Wanfu Lu

Yuexiu Lu

Baiyun Lu

Chebian Lu

Dong Hu Lu

Dongshan Lake Gongyuan

Zhong Lu

Zhujiang (Pearl River)

Binjiang Zhong Lu

Suszhezhi Lu

Hai Yin Qiao

N

0   500 yards

0   500 meters

$ ✗ **Food Street.** The concept of a "food street," with a half-dozen open kitchens preparing food from different regions of China, was created here. Since then it has become a staple of all New World hotels and of plenty of other places. It is especially attractive for foreigners, who can see what's cooking before choosing from the menu. It's also ideal for casual meals at any time, and service is efficient and helpful. ✉ *China Hotel, 1/F, Liuhua Lu,* ☎ *020/8666–6888. AE, DC, MC, V.*

$ ✗ **Lucy's.** On Shamian, this restaurant has an eclectic mix of dishes at extremely reasonable prices. The main menu lists Asian curries, mixed grills, Tex-Mex dishes, fish-and-chips, noodles, burgers, sandwiches, and much more. It is one of the only places on Shamian where you can eat outside beside the river. ✉ *5–7 Shamian Nanjie, Shamian,* ☎ *020/ 2549–5599. No credit cards.*

$ ✗ **Shewangman Snake Restaurant.** This 80-year-old establishment specializes in snake meats. The living creatures fill tanks in the windows and are taken out as ordered. If you like, you can watch the waiters extract their bile to use in "healthy soup" or skin them. Otherwise it's done in the kitchen, which prepares dishes such as snake in mao-tai, chicken soup with three kinds of snake, and a clear broth with boa constrictor. ✉ *41 Jianglan Lu,* ☎ *020/8188–3811. No credit cards.*

$$$ ▦ **China.** This city within a city contains a hotel, office and apartment blocks, and shopping malls that include a supermarket, exhibition and banquet halls, and restaurants to suit all tastes. It stands opposite the Trade Fair Exhibition Hall—with bridge links over the road—and is a great favorite of fair regulars and year-round business visitors. The 66-room Executive Floor just below the Roof, possibly the best European restaurant in Guangzhou, has spacious private lounges. In the basement is the Hard Rock Café and Catwalk, an entertainment center with bar, disco, and karaoke areas. ✉ *Liuhua Lu, 510015,* ☎ *020/ 8666–6888; 852/2724–4622 in Hong Kong;* FAX *020/8667–7014; 852/ 2721–0741 in Hong Kong. 793 rooms, 124 suites. 6 restaurants, pool, tennis court, bowling, gym, shops, nightclub, business services, meeting room. AE, DC, MC, V.*

$$$ ▦ **Guangdong International Hotel.** The tallest hotel in China, this landmark is part of a spectacular complex, built as a flagship property by GITIC, China's second-largest financial institution. The hotel occupies the top floors of the 80-story tower, along with a complex containing 14 restaurants and lounges, banquet halls, and a large shopping mall with fashion boutiques. There are also extensive recreation facilities in an indoor-outdoor health spa. ✉ *339 Huanshi Dong Lu, 510098,* ☎ *020/8331–1888,* FAX *020/8331–1666. 402 rooms, 300 suites. 14 restaurants, bar, pool, 2 tennis courts, bowling, gym, shops, business services. AE, DC, MC, V.*

$$$ ▦ **White Swan.** The first international hotel in town, the White Swan occupies a marvelous site on historic Shamian Island beside the Pearl River. The huge luxury complex has landscaped gardens, two outdoor pools, a jogging track, and a separate health club and spa. Its restaurants are among the best in town; the windows of the elegant lobby bar and coffee shop frame the panorama of river traffic. Many rooms have replicas of Chinese antique furniture and porcelain. Even if you don't stay here, visit the lobby and take a look at the spectacular indoor waterfall. ✉ *Shamian Yi, Shamian, 510133,* ☎ *020/8188–6968; 852/2524–0192 in Hong Kong;* FAX *020/8186–1188; 852/2877–0811 in Hong Kong. 750 rooms, 150 suites. 12 restaurants, bar, 2 pools, gym, shops, business services, meeting room, travel services. AE, DC, MC, V.*

$$–$$$ ▦ **Dong Fang.** Across from Liuhua Park and the trade fair headquarters, this vast luxury complex is built around a 22½-acre garden with pavilions, carp-filled pools, rock gardens, trees, and assorted statuary. Amenities include a large fitness club for members and regular guests,

plus a complete spa. There are miles of arcaded corridors and numerous restaurants, plus scores of shops and service outlets. The shopping concourse holds an interesting selection of Chinese antiques and carpets, and the four-story Times Square, a block of shops and restaurants, includes branches of just about every big-name Hong Kong store. ⊠ *120 Liuhua Lu, 510016,* ☎ *020/8666–9900; 852/2528–0555 in Hong Kong;* ⅏ *020/8666–2775; 852/2520–0991 in Hong Kong. 1,060 rooms, 100 suites. 9 restaurants, hair salon, spa, gym, shops, recreation room, business services, meeting room. AE, DC, MC, V.*

$$–$$$ 🏨 **Garden.** In the northern business suburbs, this hotel, which is part of a huge complex that includes apartments and offices, lives up to its name with a spectacular garden that includes an artificial hill with a waterfall and pavilions. The extensive lobby, decorated with enormous murals, has a bar lounge set in an ornamental pool. Some great restaurants and cheerful pubs round out the offerings. Furnishings include genuine antiques, fine reproductions, and modern art. ⊠ *368 Huanshi Dong Lu, 510064,* ☎ *020/8333–8989,* ⅏ *020/8335–0467. 1,057 rooms, 63 suites. 7 restaurants, 2 pubs, pool, 2 tennis courts, bowling, gym, squash, shops, business services, convention center. AE, DC, MC, V.*

$$–$$$ 🏨 **GITIC Riverside.** Next to the river, this hotel really uses its location to advantage, with restaurants extending onto open terraces overlooking the water. Hong Kong and mainland groups bustle in the lobby, and children play around its fountain. ⊠ *298 Yanjiang Zhong Lu, 510100,* ☎ *020/8383–9888,* ⅏ *020/8381–4448. 305 rooms, 18 suites. 5 restaurants, bar, pool, gym, shops, dance club, business services, meeting room. AE, DC, MC, V.*

$$–$$$ 🏨 **Ramada Pearl.** In the eastern part of the city, this full-service hotel on the Pearl River has interesting views of the river traffic. Among its great assets are a two-story health club and a large garden with two swimming pools, tennis courts, and a children's playground. Its Canton 38 entertainment center has a pub, a disco, and a karaoke lounge. The Ramada benefits from being 10 minutes from the East Railway Station, the terminus for Hong Kong trains. ⊠ *9 Ming Yue Yilu, 510600,* ☎ *020/8737–2988,* ⅏ *020/8737–7486. 181 rooms, 26 suites. 5 restaurants, pub, 2 pools, 2 tennis courts, disco, gym, business services, meeting rooms. AE, DC, MC, V.*

$$ 🏨 **Furama Hotel Guangzhou.** This modest hotel stands beside the river downtown. Rooms are small but adequate, and the Gourmet Court restaurant serves excellent, reasonably priced Cantonese meals. ⊠ *316 Changdi Damalu, 510120,* ☎ *020/8186–3288,* ⅏ *020/8186–3388. 340 rooms, 20 suites. 3 restaurants, bar, dance club, business services. AE, DC, MC, V.*

$–$$ 🏨 **Holiday Inn City Centre.** Convenient to both train stations in the northern suburbs and next door to the Guangzhou World Trade Center, the hotel is a good, reliable place to stay with typically expert Holiday Inn management and superb restaurants for European and Cantonese food. An adjoining 800-seat cinema is sometimes used for film festivals. ⊠ *Huanshi Donglu, Overseas Chinese Village 28, Guangming Lu, 510060,* ☎ *020/8776–6999,* ⅏ *020/8775–3126. 354 rooms, 34 suites. 4 restaurants, lounge, pool, gym, business services, meeting rooms. AE, DC, MC, V.*

$–$$ 🏨 **Landmark Canton.** Towering above Haizhu Square and the main bridge across the river, this hotel is very much in the heart of central Guangzhou. It is managed by China Travel Service (Hong Kong) and gets much of its business from Hong Kong. Most of the guest rooms have great views of the river or city. The Chiu Chow restaurant is famous, as is the 39th-floor Continental restaurant and karaoke lounge. For a different kind of karaoke, go to the square in the morning, where locals practice their vocal skills with competing sound systems. ⊠ *8 Qiao Guang Lu, 510115,* ☎ *020/8335–5988,* FAX *020/8333–6197. 616 rooms, 48 suites. 3 restaurants, bar, pool, gym, shops, dance club, business services, meeting room. AE, DC, MC, V.*

$ 🏨 **Parkview Square.** On the edge of Yuexiu Park and close to the trade fair hall, this friendly little hotel is one of the most pleasant in town. It has spacious rooms and service apartments, half of which have wonderful park views. The dining rooms serve Chinese and Western food. ⊠ *960 Jiefang Beilu, 510040,* ☎ *020/8666–5666,* FAX *020/8667–1741. 207 rooms. 4 restaurants, bar, business services. AE, DC, MC, V.*

$ 🏨 **Shamian.** On Shamian Island this hotel is spartan with few amenities, but it is clean and a good value. ⊠ *52 Shamian Nanjie, Shamian, 510130,* ☎ *020/8188–8359,* FAX *020/8191–1628. 36 rooms, 11 suites. Air-conditioning. No credit cards.*

$ 🏨 **Victory.** This hotel on Shamian Island has two wings, both originally
★ colonial guest houses that have been superbly renovated. The main building has a pink-and-white facade, an imposing portico, and twin domes on the roof, where the pool is. Nevertheless, it is basically for budget travelers, with small rooms and inexpensive dining rooms. The setting among restored old mansions is priceless. ⊠ *53 Shamian Dajie, 510130,* ☎ *020/8186–2622,* FAX *020/8186–1062. 400 rooms. 4 restaurants, pool, gym, dance club, business services, meeting room. AE, DC, MC, V.*

Nightlife and the Arts

The Arts

Except for the survival of Cantonese opera, performed in temporary bamboo theaters in People's Park and at annual festivals, Guangzhou has little to offer in the way of performing arts.

Nightlife

Until recently Guangzhou's nightlife scene was the sole preserve of Chinese businessmen in search of relaxation and recreation at karaoke lounges staffed by hostess "singing companions." Recently the situation has improved with the opening of some agreeable pubs.

BARS

All the leading hotels have bars, where it's pleasant to relax after a hard day's work or sightseeing. The popular **Café Lounge** (⊠ Lobby, China Hotel, ☎ 020/8666–6888) has big, comfortable barstools, quiet tables for two, live music on weekends, and a fine selection of cigars. The big attraction of the **Hare & Moon** (⊠ White Swan Hotel, ☎ 020/8188–6968) is the panorama of the Pearl River as it flows past the picture windows.

DANCE CLUBS

For energetic dancing to the latest pop music, without the hassle of karaoke, a good place is **Catwalk** (⊠ Basement, China Hotel, ☎ 020/8666–6888). **Rock & Roll** (⊠ 101 Yanjiang Xi Lu, ☎ 020/8189–2995) features that music. The **Swan Club** (⊠ 68 Binjiang Xi Lu, ☎ 020/8435–7772) is home to the Go-Go disco, which has very sophisticated lighting and a huge dance floor.

PUBS

Café Elles (⊠ Huaxin Dasha 2F, 2 Shuiyin Lu, ☎ 020/8761–2939) caters to French expatriates and Francophiles with French music and food and a small dance floor. The **Hard Rock Café** (⊠ Basement, China Hotel, ☎ 020/8666–6888 ext. 2050) has Elton John's trousers, Tina Turner's black dress, and stained-glass pictures of rock icons such as John Lennon and Michael Jackson; there's live and taped rock music and a choice of hamburgers and Chinese dishes. Opened in 1996 by a Canadian-Chinese, **Kathleen's** (⊠ 60 Tao Jin Lu, ☎ 020/8359–8045) has become a popular meeting and drop-in place for many local expats and regular visitors from Hong Kong and overseas; it's where you find out what's going on in Guangzhou. **L'Africain** (⌧ 707 Dong Feng Zhong Lu, ☎ 020/8778–2433) is the place for late-night dancing, to African, reggae, Spanish, and American pop music.

Shopping

The city has long offered goods at prices well below those in Hong Kong, but only in the 1990s did the range grow to compare with that available in the former colony, with the addition of international name-brand boutiques and branches of Hong Kong department stores, such as Sincere and Jusco. Shops are usually open from 9 AM or 10 AM to late into the evening.

Antiques and Traditional Arts and Crafts

On Shamian Island, the area between the White Swan and Victory hotels has a number of small, family-owned shops that sell paintings, carvings, pottery, knickknacks, and antiques. **Guangzhou Arts Centre** (⌧ 698 Renmin Bei Lu, ☎ 020/8667–9898) has a fine selection of painted scrolls. **Guangzhou Ji Ya Zhai** (⌧ 7 Xinwen Lu, Zhongshan Wulu, ☎ 020/8333–0079) is a specialist in Chinese calligraphy and painting. The second and third floors of the **Shidai Guangchang** (Times Square; ⌧ next to Dong Fang Hotel) have a number of small shops selling the works of local painters and calligraphers. The **South Jade Carving Factory** (⌧ 15 Xia Jiu Lu, ☎ 020/8138–8040) offers a wide variety of jade and jadeite products at reasonable prices. On the second floor visitors can watch jade being carved.

Bookstores

Guangzhou Book Center (⌧ 123 Tianhe Lu, ☎ 020/8334–4762) is a chain with seven floors of books on every subject, including some bargain-priced art books in English. **Xinhua Bookstore** (⌧ 276 Beijing Lu, ☎ 020/8334–4762) sells an extensive catalog of books on a wide range of subjects at very affordable prices.

Department Stores

Friendship Store (⌧ 369 Huanshi Dong Lu) occupies a five-story building with departments selling a huge array of goods, including Western designer and other brands, and a wide range of children's wear, luggage, and household appliances. **Guangzhou Merchandising Building** (⌧ 295 Beijing Lu) has 11 departments on its six floors, selling watches, women's and men's garments, shoes and leather goods, children's wear, cosmetics, household appliances, and daily necessities.

Malls

GITIC Plaza Arcade (⌧ Huanshi Dong Lu) has stores in the mid- to upmarket range. Some are contained in the Monte Carlo Shopping Center, where women's and men's fashions, accessories, cosmetics, and stationery are sold. More clothing boutiques, jade shops, and Chinese arts and crafts are found here as well. The spacious arcade is particularly busy from 8 to 9 in the evening. The **Nanfang International Shopping Arcade** (⌧ Huanshi Dong Lu) is aimed at the top of the market, with Hong Kong–style boutiques selling name-brand products from Chanel, Christian Dior, and Pierre Cardin, plus Disney-licensed goods, Swatch watches, and Ulferts furniture. The **White Swan Arcade** (⌧ Shamian Island) has some of the city's finest upmarket specialty shops. They sell genuine Chinese antiques, traditional craft items, works of modern and classical art, Japanese kimonos and swords, jewelry, cameras, and books published in and about China. The fashion boutiques include China's first Benetton outlet and an Elizabeth Arden salon.

Outdoor Activities and Sports

Golf

The **Guangzhou Luhu Golf & Country Club** (☎ 020/8350–7777) has 18 holes spread over 180 acres of Luhu Park, 20 minutes from the Guangzhou train station and 30 minutes from Baiyun Airport. The 6,820-yard, par-72 course was designed by Dave Thomas. The club also offers a 75-bay driving range and a clubhouse with restaurants, a pro shop, and a health spa. Members' guests and those from affiliated clubs pay Y637 greens fees on weekdays, Y1,274 on weekends. Nonmembers pay Y849 and Y1,486, respectively. These prices include a caddie. Clubs can be rented for Y265. The club is a member of the International Associate Club network.

Guangzhou A to Z

To research prices, get advice from other travelers, and book travel arrangements, visit www.fodors.com.

AIR TRAVEL

Guangzhou's airport is an international gateway, served by direct flights from Los Angeles, Singapore, Bangkok, Sydney, and Phnom Penh, and from Amsterdam via Beijing. There are five flights daily from Hong Kong, a hop of 30 minutes. It is one of the busiest domestic airports, with at least seven flights a day from both Beijing and Shanghai, as well as services from virtually every other major city in China. Expect to pay about Y977 round-trip between Guangzhou and Hong Kong, plus Y106 departure tax from Hong Kong and Y90 from Guangzhou. The local China Southern Airlines is one of the big-three Chinese carriers.

➤ AIRLINES AND CONTACTS: **China Southern Airlines** (☎ 020/8666–2969).

BOAT AND FERRY TRAVEL

Turbo Cats (catamaran ferries) make the two-hour trip between Guangzhou's Pingzhou wharf and the China Hong Kong City (CHKC) ferry terminal in Hong Kong daily, departing at 7:30 AM and 2 PM, returning 10 AM and 4 PM. The trip costs Y311 first class, Y210 economy from Hong Kong, Y366 and Y239 from Guangzhou.

A ferry (from Y214 for a four-berth cabin) makes the journey from Hong Kong to Guangzhou's Zhoutouzui Pier every day, departing the CHKC terminal at 9 PM; it arrives at dawn, and passengers disembark at 7 AM. There are cabins of different classes as well as restaurants.

Tickets can be bought at Zhoutouzui Pier for ferries to Hainan. Boats depart every three days at 9 AM and make the journey to Haikou's Xiuying Pier in 24 hours. Ticket classes are based on the number of people per room.

➤ BOAT AND FERRY INFORMATION: **China Hong Kong City (CHKC) ferry terminal** (✉ Canton Rd., Kowloon). **Zhoutouzui Pier** (✉ Zhu Jiang, Guangzhou, ☎ 852/8444–8218).

BUS TRAVEL

Citybus, which charges Y143 from Hong Kong and Y160 from Guangzhou, has five round-trips a day between Hong Kong and Guangzhou using new vehicles that have toilets, drinks, snacks, reclining seats, and individual air-conditioning and lighting controls. The trip takes 3½ hours, and buses leave from CHKC and Shatin City One in Hong Kong and the Garden Hotel in Guangzhou. Among other bus services, China Travel Service (CTS; Y180) has 11 round-trips a day, with pickup and drop-off at major Guangzhou hotels. You can purchase your tickets at the concierge desks of these hotels.

Air-conditioned express buses link Guangzhou with Shenzhen (2½ hours), Zhuhai (1½ hours), and just about every other town in the region.
➤ BUS INFORMATION: **China Travel Service** (☎ 852/2853–3533).**Citybus** (☎ 852/2873–0818).

CONSULATES
➤ AUSTRALIA: **Australian Consulate** (✉ 1509 GITIC Plaza Offices, 339 Huanshi Dong Lu, ☎ 020/8335–0909).
➤ CANADA: **Canadian Consulate** (✉ Room 801, China Hotel, Liuhua Lu, ☎ 020/8666–0569).
➤ UNITED KINGDOM: **British Consulate** (✉ GITIC Plaza Offices, 339 Huanshi Dong Lu, 2nd Floor, ☎ 020/8335–1354).
➤ UNITED STATES: **U.S. Consulate** (✉ White Swan Hotel Annex, 1 Shamian Nan Jie, Shamian, ☎ 020/8188–8911).

EMERGENCIES
➤ CONTACTS: **Guangzhou Emergency Treatment Centre** (☎ 120). **Guangzhou Red Cross** (☎ 020/8444–6411). **Public Security Bureau** (☎ 110). **Tourist Hotline** (☎ 020/8668–7051).

MONEY MATTERS
You can easily change foreign currency at hotels and banks in Guangdong; the Hong Kong dollar is a very acceptable second currency here.

SUBWAY TRAVEL
Guangzhou is not an easy place to get around because of the vast amount of demolition and building going on. The first line of the Metro, opened in late 1997, connects Huangsha, close to the White Swan Hotel, with the southern suburbs. There are currently 16 stations open, and tickets range from Y2 to Y6. Future lines are planned to link the old and new railway stations and downtown areas.

TAXIS
Taxis provide the only viable means of city transport. There are plenty of them—at hotels, outside tourist sights, and on the roads. Some are obviously retired from Hong Kong service, with sagging suspension and inoperative air-conditioning. The large grille around the driver leaves little room in the back. Few drivers speak English, so you need your destination written in Chinese. At the flag's fall, it costs Y7 or Y9, with increments of 60 *fen* per 250 meters (about a sixth of a mile), and drivers will always give receipts.

TOURS
Four-day circular tours (Y2,675) of the region (departing Hong Kong Tuesday, Thursday, and Saturday), available through CITS and other agencies (☞ Travel Agencies, *below*), begin with a fast ferry to Macau (☞ Chapter 9). This is followed by a visit to Cuiheng, an overnight stay in Shiqi, a day in Foshan, a night in Zhaoqing, and a night and day in Guangzhou before a return by train to Hong Kong.

TRAIN TRAVEL
Five express trains (Y244 first class, Y202 second class) depart daily for Guangzhou's East Railway Station from Hong Kong's Kowloon Station. The trip takes about about 1¾ hours. The last train back to Hong Kong leaves at 5:25 PM.

The Guangzhou Railway Station, north of the city, is the terminus for daily express trains from Beijing.

➤ TRAIN INFORMATION: **East Railway Station** (☏ 020/8714–6222). **Guangzhou Railway Station** (☏ 020/8668–2043). **Kowloon Station** (✉ Hong Chong Rd., Tsim Sha Tsui East).

TRAVEL AGENCIES

If you're coming from Hong Kong, China Travel Service (CTS) is the most convenient place to book tickets to Guangzhou and the Pearl Delta area, although they add a service charge.

Travel agencies in Guangzhou can arrange tours of Foshan, Zhaoqing, and other nearby places of interest.

➤ LOCAL AGENT REFERRALS: **China Travel Service** (CTS; ☏ 852/2853–3533). **Guangdong CITS** (✉ 179 Huanshi Lu, ☏ 020/8666–6889 ext. 222, FAX 020/8667–8048). **Guangdong CTS** (✉ 10 Qiaoguang Lu, ☏ 020/8333–6888 ext. 5385, FAX 020/8333–2247). **Guangdong International Travel** (✉ 2/F Dong Fang Hotel, ☏ 020/8666–1646, FAX 020/8668–8921).

VISITOR INFORMATION

Obtaining information of any kind is extremely difficult in Guangzhou, even for the Chinese. The most valuable sources are the staff in hotel business centers, but even the best have limited knowledge of their city. Getting information over the phone is particularly frustrating. Don't try calling the railway station unless you have hours and patience to spare. Consulates are a good source of information. For business advice, call the Hong Kong Trade Development Council.

A few city magazines, published largely for expats, provide information about current events, art showings, and new openings. Look for *South China Citylife* and *Clueless in Guangzhou,* which are often found in better hotels and restaurants.

➤ TOURIST INFORMATION: **Hong Kong Trade Development Council** (✉ 23/F GITIC Plaza Offices, 339 Huanshi Dong Lu, ☏ 020/8331–2889). **Trade fair information** (☏ 020/8667–7000).

GUANGDONG

Far from the political center of Beijing and historically in close contact with areas outside China, Guangdong has found itself at the confluence of unique historical events. Next to the economic powerhouses of the Hong Kong Special Administrative Region (SAR) and Shenzhen Special Economic Zone (SEZ) as well as home to one of China's largest cities, Guangzhou, Guangdong is almost a kingdom unto itself. Indeed, since the mid-1980s scholars in the West have written about the possibility of Guangdong splitting from the rest of China. Although such a split is unlikely, it is clear that there is a strong regional culture in Guangdong.

The economic boom that in the space of 10 years transformed Shenzhen from rice paddies to a metropolis and Zhuhai from a village to a thriving city with one of China's highest standards of living has had a huge effect on the rest of Guangdong Province as well. Knit together by an expanding communication and transportation network, the Pearl River delta region has become wealthy, the destination for international businesses, upwardly mobile Chinese, as well as hundreds of thousands of migrant laborers from inland provinces.

Guangdong has few exotic sights, but the temples, shrines, and other markers of a more ancient China still exist in pockets. Most older structures have, however, been "developed" into high-rises or bulldozed for superhighways. Guangdong's phenomenal growth is itself a subject of interest.

Foshan

⑱ *1 hr by bus, 45 min by taxi northwest of Guangzhou.*

The history of Foshan (Buddha Mountain), a city on the main circuit of the delta region, goes back 1,200 years. At one time it was an important religious center with a population of a million. Today, after centuries of obscurity, it is again a prosperous town with numerous joint enterprises involving overseas cousins.

Happily, this prosperity has encouraged residents to maintain the legacy of their past, dramatically in the city's **Zu Miao** (Ancestral Temple). It dates from the building of a Taoist temple on this spot during the Song dynasty (960–1279). Rebuilt during the Ming dynasty, without the use of nails, the main prayer hall is a masterpiece of art and architecture. Its wooden roof with interlocking beams has a ridgepole crowded with porcelain figurines depicting the epic story of the *Romance of Three Kingdoms*. This is possibly the greatest example of porcelain tableaux art, which was developed by the potters of the nearby town of **Shiwan**, also known as Shekwan, where the art continues to flourish. You can visit workshops to see the artisans at work and buy their wares.

Inside the temple is a gilded altar table carved with scenes of Chinese defeating long-nosed foreign invaders. On the altar is a bronze statue of the Northern Emperor, cast in the Ming era and weighing 5,500 pounds. On either side are examples of old spears, swords, and other weapons, plus gongs and an Iron Cloud Board, which were carried by a mandarin's entourage.

In the courtyard outside is the **Wanfutai** (Wantu Stage); built in 1658, it's the oldest surviving wooden stage in China. A great roof sweeps over the large platform, and gilt carvings and colored glass decorate the walls. Behind the stage is a display of old theater masks. ✉ *Zumiao Lu.*

The vibrant artistic heritage of Foshan is not confined to historic buildings, however. At the **Renshou Si** (Renshou Temple) Folk Art Center craftsmen make intricate paper cutouts, huge paper lanterns, butterfly kites, and heads for lion dances. Shops display calligraphy, scroll paintings, and carvings of jade, wood, and bone. In addition, there are many examples of Shiwan pottery, including a set depicting Bruce Lee in different kung fu postures. All are for sale at very reasonable prices. ✉ *Renmin Lu at Aumiao Lu.* ☾ *Daily 8–6.*

Zhongshan

⑲ *2 hrs by long-distance bus southwest of Guangzhou.*

South of Foshan, Zhongshan is the county that abuts Macau. In the 16th century mandarins and merchants from here agreed to let the Portuguese settle on the tiny peninsula. Over the years it has become the source of vast numbers of emigrants leaving China for abroad and immigrants who came to trade and then remained. Formerly Heungshan (fragrant mountain), the area was renamed Zhongshan (central mountain) in honor of local hero Sun Yat-sen, who used the name as his nom-de-guerre. The county covers 690 square mi of the fertile Pearl River delta.

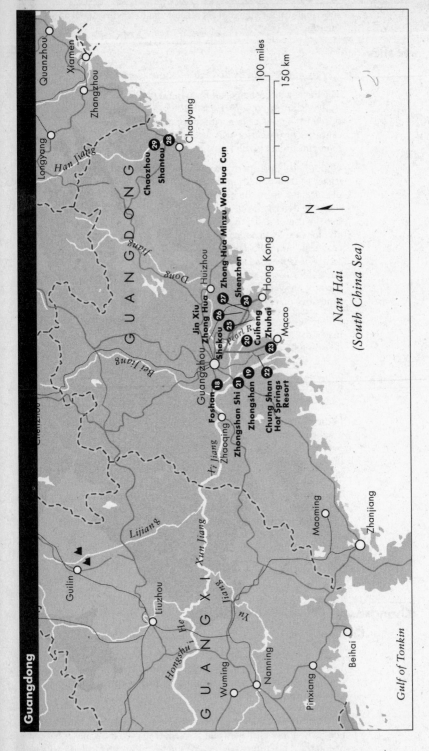

and Macau. ✉ *Shui Wanlu, Gongbei 519020,* ☎ *0756/887–7998,* FAX *0756/887–8998. 218 rooms, 21 suites. 4 restaurants, bar, pool, gym, billiards, nightclub. AE, DC, MC, V.*

Outdoor Activities and Sports

In Zhuhai, next to a Formula-1 racing circuit, the **Lakewood Golf Club** is about a half hour by car from Macau, 20 minutes from the Zhuhai Ferry terminal. It opened its Mountain Course and clubhouse at the end of 1995 and the Lake Course in 1997. The club is a joint venture of Zhuhai and Malaysian companies. Greens fees for visitors are Y637 weekdays and Y1,274 weekends, while caddies are Y127 and golf carts Y255. ✉ *Jinding, Zhuhai,* ☎ *0756/335–2502,* FAX *0756/338–0452.*

Shenzhen/Shekou

1 hr by express train, 2½ hrs by express bus from Guangzhou.

㉔ **Shenzhen** was just a farming village across the border from Hong Kong until it was designated a Special Economic Zone in the late 1970s and became the first "instant China" excursion for foreign tourists. Since then it has been transformed into a bustling industrial center, complete with one of the highest gross domestic products in China and the attendant pollution, crowding, and sleaze. Today most visitors to Shenzhen are Chinese from Hong Kong, engaged in business or on family holidays, golfing, and relaxing in lavish but moderately priced resorts. Foreign tourists are drawn to Shenzhen's series of theme parks.

㉕ **Shekou** came into being in 1978 as the company town of China Merchants, a mainland shipping and trading conglomerate with headquarters in Hong Kong. The company recognized the potential of Shekou's location, at the entrance to the Pearl River estuary and next door to Hong Kong, not only as a new port but as a base for oil exploration firms. Since then all the big oil companies have made their regional headquarters here, and it shows. There are spacious California-style suburbs, with balconied villas, swimming pools, and garages (a rarity in China). Nearby are supermarkets, high-rise office blocks, and a row of trendy bars and Western restaurants. The streets are clean and the beach immaculate. There's virtually no crime and certainly no unemployment, as everyone has to be cleared by China Merchants to live here.

Most foreign visitors come to Shekou by sleek, Norwegian-made catamaran ferries, which commute in 50 minutes from Hong Kong, but the opening of new expressways has made the port city readily accessible from Shenzhen City, a half hour's drive away, and Guangzhou, less than two hours away. There is also good ferry service between Shekou and Macau and Guangzhou, which is important for the planned development of Shekou into a convention venue.

㉖ **Jin Xiu Zhong Hua** (Splendid China) draws crowds of Chinese visitors— Deng Xiaoping joined them on a journey south—because of the way it presents their historical and geographic heritage. It also appeals to Western visitors, who are equally impressed by the park as a masterpiece of folk art, where 74 of China's best-known attractions are shown in brilliant replicas on a scale of 1:15.

Each exhibit in the 74-acre site illustrates the ingenious craftsmanship of the Chinese. There is the incredible, waist-high Great Wall winding over the park's central hillock, and the Forbidden City looking like a celestial emperor's dollhouse. Nearby are Tibet's Potala Palace and the Buddhist sculptures of the Magao Grottoes, while around the corner is a water village from Jiangsu and the Ming Tombs.

Cleverly arranged between paths for pedestrians and electric hire cars, the exhibits are well labeled in both English and Chinese. By some magic they offer individual worlds in spite of their often illogical proximity. For instance, the mausoleum of Genghis Khan, surrounded by a Mongol horde that seems to shimmer in the desert heat, is just a short stroll from the Ice Lantern Show of Harbin— with tinted glass for ice. Best of all is the population of this miniworld. Thousands of tiny porcelain people, each one different, come to life in a triumph of folk art. ⊠ *Shenzhen Bay, Shenzhen,* ☎ *0755/660–2111.* ⊠ *Y70 (Y80 on weekends).* ⊙ *Daily 8:30–5:30.*

㉗ Zhong Hua Minzu Wen Hua Cun (China Folk Culture Villages), the theme park CTS built next to Splendid China, is a collection of faithfully reproduced buildings from different ethnic areas of China, along with some typical scenery. What was a small spit of flat land on the bay side now has soaring concrete peaks of the Stone Forest with life-size houses of some of Yunnan's many minority peoples nearby: a stone Bouyei house, a bamboo-and-thatch Yao residence, and a Miao compound. Nearby is the monumental Wind and Rain Bridge and Drum Tower from Guizhou, together with traditional houses. Elsewhere there's a Tibetan house and lamasery, a Muslim mosque beside a Uighur house, and a Beijing quadrangle.

Among the many attractions of the park are the craft workshops set up in some of the houses, where native experts produce local specialties, such as embroidery, weaving, carving, painting, and jewelry, while you watch. The finished articles are for sale. Another popular activity is a dine-around-China tour, on which you can sample regional dishes made by locals using ingredients from back home.

Performances of songs, dances, and acrobatics from diverse parts of the country take place throughout the day. They are held in the relevant villages, on small stages in front of benches for the audience. ⊠ *Shenzhen Bay, Shenzhen,* ☎ *0755/660–0626.* ⊠ *Y85.* ⊙ *Daily 10–10.*

Dining and Lodging

$$–$$$ ✕🏨 **Landmark Shenzhen.** This handsome hotel in downtown Shenzhen looks and feels European. Its lobby is like a foyer, with informal check-in counters, and the central Piazza Café is really like an Italian square, with a skylight roof, overhanging balconies, striped canopies, and tables set out as in a sidewalk café. The Landmark is also popular for its Chinese abalone restaurant and 27th-floor Hollywood entertainment center featuring movies and video games. ⊠ *3018 Nanhu Lu, Shenzhen 518001,* ☎ *0755/217–2288,* FAX *0755/229–0473. 72 rooms, 33 suites. 3 restaurants, bar, pool, gym, shops, dance club, business services, meeting room. AE, DC, MC, V.*

$$$ 🏨 **Shangri-La Shenzhen.** Opposite the stations for trains from Guangzhou and Hong Kong and alongside the bus station, this hotel nevertheless has the characteristic Shangri-La class. The top-floor revolving restaurant is furnished like a country house lounge, and the health club has an outdoor pool terrace and marbled spa facilities. The hotel has a grand ballroom that can accommodate 1,500 people. It is also home to Henry J. Bean's American Grill. ⊠ *1002 Jianshe Lu, Shenzhen, 518001,* ☎ *0755/233–0888,* FAX *0755/233–9878. 256 rooms, 30 suites. 6 restaurants, bar, pool, hair salon, gym, shops, business services, meeting room. AE, DC, MC, V.*

$$ 🏨 **Marina Ming Wah Convention Center Hotel.** Adjoining a 25-story multipurpose high-tech commercial complex that opened in 1997, the older hotel has large, irregularly shaped rooms, many with private terraces. The complex has Cantonese and Western restaurants, as well as the popular Marina Tavern and the top-floor Crow's Nest tea lounge, complete with a dance floor, which is served by the city's first scenic elevators. The floor below is devoted to the Asian buffet Spice Market. ✉ *8 Gui Shan Lu, Shenzhen, 518067,* ☎ *0755/668–9968,* FAX *0755/ 668–6668. 85 rooms, 35 suites, 28 service apartments. 8 restaurants, bar, pool, bowling, gym, dance club, business services, convention center. AE, DC, MC, V.*

$$ ⊡ **Sunshine.** Although it looks like an average Shenzhen multipurpose building from the outside, this is one of the most attractive hotels in the region. The grand lobby flows from the entrance through the lounge and bar, past the white-marble staircase to the executive wing. Here you find the Sunshine City Health Club, with a vast indoor pool, a golf putting green and simulator, a fully equipped gym, and a TV-aerobics room. ✉ *1 Jiabin Lu, Shenzhen, 518005,* ☎ *0755/223–3888,* FAX *0755/222– 6719. 283 rooms, 24 suites. 7 restaurants, bar, lounge, pool, hair salon, putting green, tennis court, gym, squash, shops, dance club, business services, conference center, meeting room. AE, DC, MC, V.*

$$ ⊡ **Nan Hai.** This was the first luxury hotel in Shenzhen, designed for international oil company demands. The rooms are large and expensively furnished, and all have terraces. The hotel has its own beach and extensive resort facilities. ✉ *1 Gongye Yilu, Shekou, 518069,* ☎ *0755/ 669–2888,* FAX *0755/669–2440. 131 rooms, 85 suites. 7 restaurants, bar, pool, hair salon, miniature golf, 2 tennis courts, jogging, shops, billiards, dance club, meeting room. AE, DC, MC, V.*

$ ⊡ **Overseas Chinese Hotel.** Near the Shenzhen train station, this comfortable hotel is as close to the border with Hong Kong as a hotel can get. Completely refurbished in 1998, it is clean and has great service—a no-frills establishment and the best deal in town. ✉ *1043 Heping Lu, Shenzhen, 518010,* ☎ *0755/557–3811,* FAX *0755/557–2243. 190 rooms, 4 suites. 2 restaurants, hair salon, shop, business services. AE, MC, V.*

Outdoor Activities and Sports

Mission Hills Golf Club (✉ Guanlan Zhen, Gaoerfu Dadao, Shenzhen, ☎ 0755/802–2931) hosted the World Cup of Golf in 1995. In addition to four 18-hole courses, it has a spectacular clubhouse and an adjoining 228-room resort, courts for basketball tournaments, tennis and squash courts, a variety of restaurants, and an indoor/outdoor pool around a stage for concerts or fashion shows. The courses are not open to nonmembers except for resort guests, for whom greens fees are Y1,284 weekdays and Y1,927 weekends; caddies are Y117 and caddy carts Y234.

Just inside the border of Hong Kong and Shenzhen, the **Sand River Golf Club** (✉ Baishi Lu, Shenzhen Bay, Shenzhen, ☎ 0755/690–0111) offers two courses—one is nine holes and floodlighted—designed by Gary Player. Other facilities include a large driving range, a fishing lake, and various resort amenities. Greens fees for visitors are Y425 weekdays and Y637 weekends for 9 holes, Y849 weekdays and Y1,274 weekends for 18 holes. Caddies are Y191.

Shantou/Chaozhou

㉘ *5 hrs by express bus or 45 mins by air northeast of Guangzhou; 6 hrs by long-distance bus or overnight by ferry north of Hong Kong.*

The ancestral homeland of the Chaozhou people—better known outside China by the Cantonese pronunciation *Chiu Chow*—is the region on the east coast of Guangdong province between the port of Shantou (formerly written Swatow) and the historic capital of Chaozhou.

Although there was a settlement here from the 2nd century BC, the original Chiu Chow arrived in the 4th century, fleeing war-torn central China. They developed a distinctive dialect, cuisine, and operatic style, as well as a talent for business, which was conducted through Chaozhou. Silt-ing of the Han River forced business downstream to Shantou, locally known as Swatow, which in 1858 became one of the ports opened up to foreigners by the Treaty of Tianjin.

Companies like Jardine Matheson and British American Tobacco set up shop, but Swatow remained a minor-league treaty port compared with Shanghai. Nevertheless, the local lace and porcelain became world famous. Meanwhile, droughts and warlords spurred the Chiu Chow people to emigrate on a mass scale to Southeast Asia and beyond.

Today there are an estimated 6 million overseas Chiu Chow, half of them in Thailand, 1.2 million in Hong Kong, and large numbers in Tai-wan, Malaysia, and North America. An amazing number have made their fortunes in their new homes, but they don't forget their roots, which is why Shantou was chosen in 1980 as a Special Economic Zone for investment from abroad.

The results have exceeded every expectation, with vast sums flowing in to build a new port and new highways, hospitals, and schools, as well as office buildings and homes. Today the picturesque port of old Swatow lies on 30 international and domestic shipping routes; mod-ern vessels far outnumber the traditional fishing boats. Gleaming high-rises have replaced all but a handful of the Victorian houses and offices, with their neoclassical facades and colonnaded verandas. The best of the survivors is the former British consulate in Jiaoshi Scenic Park, which now houses government offices.

The waterfront **Xidi Gongyuan** (Xidi Park), with its parade of beauti-fully sculpted stone animals and people alongside tree-shaded benches and open-sided pavilions, is where locals play Chinese chess and read newspapers. From here you have intimate views of the busy harbor with its fleets of fishing boats, ferries, and freighters, which somehow steer clear of oyster farms that produce the key ingredient for delicious oys-ter pancakes.

Dining and Lodging

Although Chiu Chow food ranks as one of China's great cuisines, it is not easy to sample it in its homeland unless you have local contacts. There are, of course, plenty of restaurants around Shantou and Chaozhou, but virtually none has an English menu or English-speak-ing staff, and in most cases even the name is in Chinese only. Happily, restaurants in the major hotels serve Chiu Chow meals and have En-glish menus and at least one English-speaking staff member.

$$–$$$ ✕🖪 **Golden Gulf Hotel.** Sophisticated elegance aptly describes this, the only luxury hotel in the region. Guest rooms occupy a white, semicir-cular tower. The pool terrace and tennis courts are laid out on an open podium, and the lobby is a circular courtyard with a globe-shape foun-tain as a centerpiece and a glass-domed ceiling. Restaurants and shops are arranged around the colonnaded gallery. The decor is stylish through-out; the Magnificent Palace Chiu Chow restaurant is suitably lavish and the City Bar a cozy retreat with Tiffany lamps, marble-top tables, and a newspaper rack. The food served at both is as good as the setting, with fresh, beautifully prepared Chiu Chow and Cantonese dishes, plus Japanese and Chinese hot pots and good Western food. ⊠ 96 Jinshan Lu, Shantou, 515041, ☎ 0754/826–3263, ☒ 0754/826–5162. 230 rooms, 23 suites. 4 restaurants, bar, pool, tennis court, gym, dance club, business services, meeting room. AE, DC, MC, V.

$–$$ ✕🖪 **Shantou Harbour View.** Overlooking the harborside park, a block or so from the International Ferry Terminal, this smartly modern hotel has marvelous views of the busy port. It has a nautical theme, with a blue-and-white color scheme and a tower of rooms that suggests a giant sail. Rooms are attractively decorated; each garden suite has a private terrace. The Harbor View Restaurant is a superior coffee shop, serving Western and Chinese food against a backdrop panorama of the port. For fine dining Chiu Chow and Cantonese style there's the Palace Restaurant. The Paradise Disco and an extensive sauna provide recreation and relaxation. ⊠ *Haibin Lu, Zhongduan, Shantou, 515041,* ☎ *0754/854– 3838,* FAX *0754/855–0280. 65 rooms, 17 suites. 2 restaurants, bar, gym, dance club, business services, meeting room. AE, DC, MC, V.*

$–$$ ✕▥ **Shantou International Hotel.** Opened in 1988, this was the first international-class hotel in East Guangdong, and it remains a major landmark with its zigzag facade and revolving restaurant. It is a few blocks from the Special Economic Zone and close to the shops. The 26th-floor Palace Revolve is where guests and locals come for a comprehensive Western and Chinese buffet breakfast. For the rest of the day, it's a Western restaurant and bar. The Han Jiang Chun, a banquet hall, serves some of the best Chiu Chow food in the region. You can also find the local cuisine, along with dim sum, noodles, and Cantonese, Sichuan, and Beijing dishes, in the casual Fragrant Court food street. In the elaborately traditional Tea House, you prepare your own kung fu tea around a carved wooden cabinet that opens up to reveal a small sink, where the first infusions of tea are poured before the powerful brew is ready to drink. The hotel's guest rooms are large and comfortably furnished. ⊠ *Jinsha Lu, Shantou, 515041,* ☎ *0754/825–1212,* FAX *0754/825–2250. 273 rooms, 16 suites. 3 restaurants, bar, gym, dance club, business services, meeting room. AE, DC, MC, V.*

Shopping

All kinds of locally made porcelain are available in Shantou shops and roadside stores in **Fungxi,** a village on the outskirts of Chaozhou, where family factories produce customized dinnerware and commemorative mugs, openwork Chinese stools, and waist-high jars encrusted with brightly colored and gilded figures. Most are for export around the world but are sold here for the best prices. Most shops pack and ship overseas. Lace is very cheap and abundant in shops in Shantou and Chaozhou. If you're lucky, you also might find some of the local three-dimensional wood carvings.

Side Trip from Shantou

The best reason for visiting Shantou is to make the 50-minute drive inland to **Chaozhou.** During the Tang and Song dynasties, it thrived as an inland port with its own sophisticated cultural style. The port succumbed to river silt, but Chaozhou preserved much of its heritage. Thanks to the fine local clay and traditional craftsmen, it continues to produce all kinds of Chinese porcelain in workshops that welcome visitors. One company still makes Chaozhou wood carvings, and there are factories producing lace, but the distinctive sculpted embroidery is no longer made, for lack of skilled needleworkers.

The **Kaiyuan Si** (Kaiyuan Temple), built in AD 738 as one of the 10 major temples in China, is a Chaozhou treasury that contains three huge gilt statues of Buddha, a 3,300-pound Song dynasty bronze bell, and a stone incense burner said to have been carved from a meteorite. Its prayer pavilions have ridgepole decorations of multicolor porcelain birds and flowers in exuberant swirling patterns.

Not much is left of the old **Ming dynasty wall,** except for two carved wooden gates that have been attractively restored. There were also plans to restore the original bridge built over the Han in the 12th century. It once rested on 18 wooden boats in a traditional "floating gate," which swung with the tide, a device to overcome the problem of building foundations in the then-swiftly flowing river; they have since been replaced by concrete piers.

Guangdong A to Z

To research prices, get advice from other travelers, and book travel arrangements, visit www.fodors.com.

AIR TRAVEL
Shenzhen Airport is very busy, with flights to 50 cities. There is commuter service by catamaran ferries and buses between the airport and Hong Kong. Bus service links the Shenzhen railway station, via Huaren Dasha, direct to Shenzhen Airport for Y25 (one-way). Zhuhai International Airport, the largest in size in China, despite its name operates only domestically, to 24 cities.
➤ AIRPORT INFORMATION: **Shenzhen Airport** (☎ 0755/777–6789). **Zhuhai International Airport** (☎ 0756/889–5494).

BOAT AND FERRY TRAVEL
Fast, modern catamaran ferries (Y251 first class, Y224 second, Y208 third) make eight round-trips daily to the pier at Jiuzhou (on the coast of Zhuhai, just north of Macau), with five departures from CHKC and three from the Macau Ferry terminal. The trip takes 90 minutes.

Catamarans (Y266 first class, Y245 second, Y235 third) make six round-trips daily between Hong Kong and Zhongshan Harbor, close to Zhongshan, with five departures from the CHKC Terminal and one from Shun Tak Centre on Hong Kong Island. The trip takes approximately 80 minutes.

Comfortable double-deck catamaran ferries (Y154 first class, Y117 economy) make the pleasant 50-minute trip between Macau and Shekou (passing under the new Tsing Ma Bridge), with five departures daily from the Macau Ferry terminal.

Tickets for an overnight ferry to Hainan can also be purchased at the Shekou pier.
➤ BOAT AND FERRY INFORMATION: **Jiuzhou CHKC** (✉ Canton Rd., Kowloon). **Macau Ferry terminal** (✉ Shun Tak Centre, Connaught Rd., Central, ☎ 853/2546–3528).

BUS TRAVEL
Citybus buses make eight round-trips daily between Hong Kong and Shenzhen, with six continuing on to Shenzhen Bay theme parks. Buses depart from Hong Kong's Admiralty Station and CHKC Terminal (Shenzhen City Y69 one-way weekdays, Y90 weekends; Shenzhen Bay Y80 one-way weekdays, Y101 weekends).

Air-conditioned express buses crisscross most of the Pearl River delta region. These buses are reasonably priced and have many departures each day. Most areas can be reached in only a few hours. Ask at your hotel for the closest bus station.
➤ BUS INFORMATION: **Citybus** (☎ 852/2873–0818).

TOURS
By far the most popular tour is from Hong Kong to Zhongshan via Macau, which provides a full and interestingly diverse, if rather tiring, daylong outing. All one-day Zhongshan tours include a bus transfer from Macau to the border at Gongbei in the Zhuhai Special Economic Zone, a trip to Cuiheng Village for Sun Yat-sen sites, a six-course lunch, a visit to a "typical" farming village kept traditional for tourists, and return to Hong Kong via Zhongshan Harbor.

The other established one-day China trip takes in the Shenzhen Special Economic Zone, immediately across the border from Hong Kong, to visit either Splendid China or the adjoining theme park, China Folk Culture Village, as well as a Hakka village, a kindergarten, and a market. Purchase tickets for either tour from any travel agent in Hong Kong.

TRAIN TRAVEL
There is a rail route from Beijing to Hong Kong via Shenzhen, and Shenzhen can easily be reached from Hong Kong by taking the KCR railway to Lo Wu Station and then crossing over to Shenzhen on foot.

VISITOR INFORMATION
Most travel can be easily arranged in Guangzhou. In other areas CITS may be of assistance.
➤ TOURIST INFORMATION: **CITS** (⊠ 8 Jinling Lu, Shantou, ☎ 0754/824–0557, FAX 0754/862–5653; ⊠ 6 Yenhe Nan Lu, near East exit of Shenzhen Station, Shenzhen, ☎ 0755/233–8822, FAX 0755/232–9832; ⊠ 142 Zhongshan Yilu, Zhongshan, ☎ 0760/861–1888, FAX 0760/861–7064; ⊠ Next to Zhuhai Hotel, Zhuhai, ☎ 0756/333–3859, FAX 0756/333–6718).

HAINAN

Just off the southern coast of China in the South China Sea, large, tropical Hainan island is generally mountainous, with large portions covered by dense tropical rain forests. Most of the population inhabits the coastal plain that rings the island.

Hainan has been under Chinese control since the end of the 2nd century BC. For most of this time it has been under the administration of either Guangxi or Guangdong province. Hainan's distance from the mainland, coastal piracy, disease, and the dissatisfaction of the indigenous Li peoples have kept large numbers of Han from settling on the island. Until the 19th century Hainan was seen by the Chinese as a disagreeable backwater. For the official who fell into disfavor with the Chinese court, Hainan was "the gate of hell"—a place of banishment.

Since the 1980s Hainan's reputation has changed greatly. In 1988 Hainan was removed from the administration of Guangdong province and established as an independent province. Moreover, the entire island was granted the status of Special Economic Zone (SEZ), a place where capitalist markets were allowed to flourish. In the early 1990s Hainan was China's Wild West, where its distance from Beijing led to a market free-for-all; rumors spread of boundless opportunity as well as local corruption. Those days saw double-digit economic growth and a real-estate boom. This bubble burst in the mid-1990s, leaving the skeletal remains of hundreds of unfinished construction projects scattered throughout the larger cities—especially in Haikou. The world's eyes turned to Hainan briefly in 2001 when a U.S. Navy plane made an emergency landing there and China refused to return the "spy plane" or release its crew.

Hainan's economy is now growing at a more natural pace. The island is working on its image as a place where tourists can come to see *da ziran* (great nature) and enjoy the customs of the local minorities, though the locals seem ambivalent about all this.

Haikou

30 *520 km (322 mi) southwest of Guangzhou, 480 km (298 mi) southwest of Hong Kong.*

The capital of the province and its largest city, Haikou stands on the northern coast of the island directly across the Hainan Strait from the southern coast of Guangdong province. It is the commercial and transportation hub of the island—nearly everything coming in and out of Hainan makes its way through Haikou—but the moist tropical breezes, palm tree–lined streets, and sunlight make even afternoon traffic in Haikou seem somehow less irritating. Chinese settlements in and around the Haikou area since at least the Tang Dynasty (618–907) have left behind some interesting sites.

The **Wugong Ci** (Temple of the Five Lords), in the southeastern part of the city, is a complex of buildings devoted to five officials who were exiled to Hainan during the Tang and Song (960–1279) dynasties. The first building was constructed by a local official in 1889 on the site of two ancient springs dug in 1097 during the Song. These springs, called **Fu Su Quan** (Fu Su Springs), have been flowing for more than 1,000 years. Outside the complex, across a small, arched bridge, is the **Wugong Ci Zhanlan Guan** (Five Lords Exhibition Hall), which has a number of good exhibits on the history of the Chinese in Hainan. ⊠ *169 Haifu Lu,* ☏ *no phone.* ☞ *Y10.* ⊗ *Daily 7–6.*

Hai Rui Mu (Hai Rui's Tomb) was built in 1589 to honor Hai Rui (1514–1587), a prominent Ming dynasty official who gave up his post for the good of the empire. Criticism, written in the spring of 1966, of a play about this prominent historical figure was one of the opening salvos in the Cultural Revolution. The walkway of stone figures near the grave exhibits a heavy Southeast Asian influence. ⊠ *Sugang Lu,* ☏ *no phone.* ☞ *Y5.* ⊗ *Daily 8–6.*

In the northern part of the city near the coast is the well-preserved **Xiuying Paotai** (Xiuying Fort), one of a number of coastal forts that once ringed Hainan. Built in 1891 at the end of the Qing dynasty by the Krupp Company, the fort is one of five still in existence in China. Inside are a network of underground passages and a museum of weaponry. ⊠ *Off Jingmao Dong Lu,* ☏ *no phone.* ☞ *Y15.* ⊗ *Daily 7:30–6:30.*

For a fine walk, stroll Haikou's **old town.** Meander the narrow streets, which, happily, are less jam-packed than in larger cities. Here you'll find a number of beautiful older buildings in the Portuguese-Chinese style so common in Southeast Asia. You'll often see curving arches and tiles from Portugal with red Chinese script written on the signs hanging out front. ⊠ *Xinhua Lu and Zhongshan Lu.*

Wanluyuan (Wanlu Park), a vast expanse of green in the northeast part of the city near the shore, would be a great place to let children run, play games, or jog.

The most famous of Haikou's parks is **Jinniuling Gongyuan** (Golden Ox Park). The park is named after a legendary golden ox that was sent to Hainan by the Jade Emperor to aid the people of Hainan after a volcanic eruption devastated the land. When the ox landed, four streams sprung from its hooves and brought water to the island's impoverished inhabitants. A statue of the ox stands near the entrance to the park. The park also has the **Jinniuling Dongwuyuan** (Golden Ox Zoo). The zoo's fascinating exhibits of local animal life, including macaques, would be more enjoyable if the animals had better living conditions. ⊠ *Western part of city.* ☞ *Y2 park, Y15 park and zoo.* ⊗ *Park, daily 6:30 AM–7:30 PM; zoo, daily 8–5.*

Lending some credence to legends of Golden Oxen and volcanic eruptions, **Huoshankou Gongyuan** (Volcano Mouth Park), 15 km (9 mi) inland southwest of Haikou, is an ancient volcanic cone encrusted with tropical growth. The volcano is the highest point in the northern maritime plain and affords fantastic views of Haikou, the Hainan Strait, and far-off Guangdong province. At the edge of the crater is the **San-shen Bei** (Tablet of the Three Gods), which honors the gods who have the responsibility for putting out mountain fires, ensuring abundant crops, and protecting the indigenous Li people. ⊠ *Qiongshan City.* ▧ *Y15.* ☉ *24 hrs.*

Along the coast to the west of Haikou, about 25 minutes by taxi, is **Jiari Haitan** (Holiday Beach). The place is packed on weekends, when hordes of people from the city descend on it. During the week, however, the beach is a fine place to sunbathe or walk and enjoy the scenery of the Hainan Strait. You don't want to go swimming here, however, unless you don't mind pollution and sharks.

Dining and Lodging
Besides hotel dining, the best bet for good food is along Jinlong Lu, Haikou's **Zhonghua Fengwei Meishi Jie** (Street of Beautiful Chinese Flavors), which is lined with restaurants that offer various regional styles of Chinese cooking.

$$$ ✗ **Aiwanting Restaurant.** Serving well-known dishes from all over China and seafood as well, this restaurant is one of the key draws on Haikou's Street of Beautiful Chinese Flavors. ⊠ *61 Jinlong Lu,* ☎ *0898/ 853–8699. No credit cards.*

$$$ ✗ **Heyou Seafood Restaurant.** This well-known restaurant earned its reputation for serving the freshest seafood to military officials. Now, however, it is open to the general public with only the red star in the middle of the dining room ceiling as a token of its former status. There are no English menus, so you'll have to point. ⊠ *28 Haixiu Lu,* ☎ *0898/671–1002. No credit cards.*

$$$ ▥ **Golden Coast Lawton.** A grand hotel in a less-than-desirable location: It stands in the middle of a district of unfinished buildings in the north of town. The hotel has a number of beautiful architectural flourishes, such as trim around the windows and brass fixtures in the more expensive rooms. The lobby is a vast open space tastefully decorated with dark wood and Chinese antiques. ⊠ *68 Renmin Dadao, 570208,* ☎ *0898/625–9888,* ℻ *0898/625–8889. 285 rooms, 62 suites. 3 restaurants, pool, beauty salon, 2 tennis courts, gym, dance club, shops, business services, meeting room. AE, MC, V.*

$$–$$$ ▥ **Baohua Harbourview.** This huge complex on the shore directly across from the vast green expanse of Wanlu Park affords beautiful views of the Straits. The smallish rooms, clean and comfortable, are given a feeling of space by large windows overlooking the Straits. A shopping arcade fills the first floor. ⊠ *69 Binhai Dadao, 570105,* ☎ *0898/853– 6699,* ℻ *0898/853–5358. 390 rooms, 36 suites. Restaurant, bar, pool, hair salon, gym, dance club, shops, business services. AE, MC, V.*

$$ ▥ **Haikou Mandarin.** The clean lines and fine design of this Meritus hotel are further enhanced by the excellent service. One of the most comfortable establishments in Hainan, it is in the financial district. ⊠ *18 Wenhua Lu, Binhai Dadeo, 570105,* ☎ *0898/854–8888,* ℻ *0898/ 854–0453. 298 rooms, 20 suites. 3 restaurants, pool, hair salon, gym, shops, business services. AE, MC, V.*

$ ▥ **Binhai.** In this hotel near the shore, wooden floors and floral prints lend the small, somewhat worn rooms an airy feeling. The hotel can arrange golf trips. ⊠ *1 Longkun Beilu, 570105,* ☎ *0898/679–5033,* ℻ *0898/679–7632. 156 rooms, 10 suites. Restaurant, gym, business services. AE, MC, V.*

$ ▥ **Haikou.** Although it's showing its age, this hotel in the center of town makes an excellent base for exploring Haikou on foot. ⊠ *4 Haifu Lu, Haifu Dadao, 570203,* ☎ *0898/535–0221,* ℻ *0898/535–0232. 202 rooms, 8 suites. 2 restaurants, hair salon, gym, dance club, shops, business services, meeting room. AE, MC, V.*

Nightlife and the Arts

Haikou is infamous as a place where Chinese businessmen go to "get away" to do business. As a result, most of the nightlife in Haikou is of the red-light kind; the ubiquitous karaoke center doubles as a den of iniquity. Although it might pay to check with CITS for local **dance performances** or **ethnic performances** of various kinds, the best bet for evening entertainment is to grab a coconut and stroll the streets. There are two interesting night markets just off of Jichang Lu south of Haixiu Lu.

Shopping

The area around the intersection of Haixiu Lu and Jichang Lu has a large number of small shops selling everything from coconut carvings to pearls to minority costumes. The main shopping complex in Haikou, **DC Department Store** (⊠ Haixiu Lu at Jichang Lu, ☎ 0898/677–4312), has a wide assortment of sundries as well as local art. This is also a good place to buy suntan lotion; ask for *fangsai lu*. **Hongsheng Jewelry** (⊠ 6 Wahai Lu, ☎ 0898/672–2091) has a wide assortment of fine pearls, silver, and jade.

Sanya

🕮 *3 hrs by air-conditioned express bus from Haikou.*

Near the southernmost tip of Hainan, Sanya is synonymous in China with sunshine, fresh air, and white-sand beaches. As a result, the economy of the entire city is geared toward the throngs of tourists that descend here, especially in winter when the rest of China is cold and unfriendly. January and February, around Chinese New Year, are the peak months.

Sanya itself is a fairly bland Chinese city; it's no tropical paradise. The area around the fishing harbor is colorful, however, especially in the early evening when boats of various shapes and sizes are all lashed together and filled with people cooking, fishermen dealing cards, and children playing.

Dadonghai Haitan (Dadonghai Beach; northeast edge of town along Haikou–Sanya highway) is the center of most of the tourist activity in town. The beach is a great place to swim or tan, but it is often crowded. For relaxing walks and beautiful scenery, the Luhuitou Peninsula has much more to offer. **Luhuitou Gongyuan** (Luhuitou Park) has lush tropical flora, and from the peak there are fabulous views of the city and the ocean. ⊠ *On rise just east of downtown Sanya.* 🎫 *Y20.* ☉ *Daily 7 AM–11:30 PM.*

The major attraction for Chinese tourists is **Tianya Haijiao** (literally, "edge of the sky and rim of the sea"), a beach famous for its rock formations and Chinese calligraphy. The location is beautiful: The site is portrayed on the back of the Chinese two-yuan bill. Swimming is not allowed. ⊠ *45-min drive along coast west of Sanya.*

Dining and Lodging

$$–$$$ 🏨 **Sanya Shanhaitian.** This hotel's name literally means "mountain–sea–sky." Nestled up against a mountain overlooking Dadonghai Beach and the blue skies of southern Hainan, it is aptly named. The hotel, opened in 1998, is by far the most luxurious in the area. Many rooms, decorated in peaceful pastels, have sunrise views. ⊠ *Luling Lu, 572021,* ☎ *0899/821–1688,* 🖷 *0899/821–1988. 180 rooms, 21 suites. 3 restaurants, bar, grill, pool, hair salon, sauna, bowling, nightclub, business services. AE, MC, V.*

$ 🏨 **Jinling Holiday Resort.** Every room in this hotel on Dadong Beach faces the sea. Built in the early 1990s, the hotel is already beginning to show signs of wear, but the rooms are clean and comfortable, and the staff is very friendly. ✉ *Luling Lu, 572021,* ☎ *0899/821–4081,* FAX *0899/821–4088. 120 rooms, 6 suites. Restaurant, bar, hair salon, beach, business services. AE, MC, V.*

$ 🖭 **Sanya Maintint.** This hotel in downtown Sanya is geared toward budget business travelers. Standard rooms are larger than average, and the staff is very friendly. ✉ *Xinfeng Lu, 572000,* ☎ *0899/825–9888,* FAX *0899/825–9666. 187 rooms, 13 suites. Restaurant, hair salon, bowling, gym, business services. AE, MC, V.*

$ 🖭 **Yù Lin Bay Holiday Resort.** One of the older hotels on Dadonghai, it shows the wear. The rooms, however, are clean and of good value. ✉ *Luling Lu, 572021,* ☎ *0899/821–3698,* FAX *0899/821–2536. 33 rooms, 27 suites. Restaurant, hair salon. AE, MC, V.*

Nightlife and the Arts

Nightlife, such as it exists in Sanya, is centered along **Dadonghai Beach.** Most of the action is on **Yuhai Lu** near the Dadonghai Hotel, where there are rows of seafood restaurants and beachside bars. Some of the beachside hotels have barbecues and various types of musical performances (both Western and Chinese).

Outdoor Activities and Sports

Other than **swimming,** there are also **Jet-Ski rentals** at Dadonghai Beach. On the beach, near the Yu Lin Bay Holiday Resort, there are two dive operations that take groups and individuals out **scuba diving** to nearby reefs. The shore on the south side of Luhuitou Park, which is relatively empty of people, affords beautiful views and is ideal for **walking** or **jogging.** Trips to local **golf** clubs can be arranged through the Sanya Shanhaitian hotel.

Shopping

Sanya does not offer much shopping. The stores along Dadonghai sell kitschy coconut carvings, small trinkets, and shells. Your best bet is to head into town to the night market on **Xinmin Lu,** where the local scene is full of energy.

Side Trips from Sanya

1 hr north of Sanya or 5 hrs south of Haikou by bus on Central Cross-Island Hwy.

㉜ **Tongzha** is Hainan's third-largest city and the former administrative center for the island's Li and Miao (Hmong) autonomous prefecture. In a valley at the foot of Hainan's highest peak, Wuzhishan (Five-Finger Mountain), Tongzha is reached by way of the narrow, two-lane, Central Cross-Island Highway from Haikou to Sanya. It passes through a richly textured green tropical landscape, where small farms have been cut from the forests.

Tongzha is home to one of Hainan's finest museums. The **Hainan Sheng Minzu Bowuguan** (Hainan Provincial Ethnology Museum), on a hill overlooking the city, is spacious and well laid out, displaying artifacts from the Neolithic period to the present. It contains a rich collection of objects from the Li and Miao (Hmong) minority groups, as well as some interesting relics of the Japanese occupation. English notations make the exhibit easily accessible to visitors. ✉ *Haiyu Beilu,* ☎ *0899/862–2336.* 🎟 *Y15.* ⊘ *Daily 8–5:30.*

For a live, if a bit touristy, exhibit of local minority customs, visit the **Hainan Zhonghua Minzu Wenhua Cun** (Hainan Chinese Folk Culture Village), just outside town. Costumed performers from all of China's officially recognized ethnic minority groups display their talents, and some excellent stores sell batiks, carvings, baskets, and other ethnic products. ⊠ *Haiyu Lu,* ☎ *0899/662–8429.* ⊒ *Y40.* ☉ *Daily 9:30–5.*

DINING AND LODGING

Tongzha does not offer much in the way of fine dining. As in the rest of China, small restaurants line the streets. If you want to play it safe, eat at your hotel.

$ ⌂ **Tongzha Tourist Mountain Villa.** Nestled against a mountain at the top edge of the city, this hotel provides good views of the urban scene below. Though not a luxury hotel, it is comfortable, with very friendly staff all dressed in minority costume. ⊠ *38 Shanzhuang Lu, 572200,* ☎ *0899/662–3188,* ℻ *0899/662–2201. 103 rooms, 3 suites. Restaurant, bar, hair salon, business services. AE, MC, V.*

Hainan A to Z

To research prices, get advice from other travelers, and book travel arrangements, visit www.fodors.com.

AIR TRAVEL

Haikou's Meilan Airport has daily flights to major cities; it has two daily flights to Sanya and Hong Kong and four daily fights to Beijing. You can book flights at most major hotels, through CITS, or at China Eastern Airlines.

Sanya's Phoenix Airport has daily flights to Guangzhou and Haikou as well as four flights a week to Shenzhen, Shanghai, and Beijing.
➤ AIRLINES AND CONTACTS: **China Eastern Airlines** (⊠ 22 Nanhang Dong Lu, Haikou, ☎ 0898/671–4467).
➤ AIRPORT INFORMATION: **Meilan Airport** (☎ 0898/671–4467). **Phoenix Airport** (☎ 0899/677–2167).

BOAT AND FERRY TRAVEL

Haikou has two ports. Xingang Matou (New Harbor Port) handles ferries across the strait to Hai'an, in Guangdong, where there are bus connections with Zhanjiang. Tickets range from Y30 to Y50 for the three-hour trip. Combination ferry and bus trips depart five times daily for Shenzhen, Shantou, Zhuhai, and Guangzhou. Tickets range from Y100 to Y220 for the trip that lasts 13 hours if you go as far as Guangzhou. Xiuying Matou (Xiuying Port) has overnight ferries direct to Guangzhou and Shekou (Shenzhen). The Guangzhou trip takes a full day (25 hours) and costs as little as Y140 for the third class, which lumps six to eight passengers per cabin. Or you can spend up to Y350 per ticket for second-class, two-passenger berths and up to Y400 for first-class berths. The boats are comfortable, but they are not cruise ships. The trip to Shenzhen takes 18 hours and costs Y120 to Y450.

BUS TRAVEL

Buses are the fastest way to get anywhere in Hainan. Comfortable express buses with air-conditioning and toilets run regularly between Haikou and Sanya (three hours; Y70) on the Eastern Highway. Buses depart Haikou from the east bus station. Buses depart Sanya from the bus station in town, but tickets can also be purchased from nearly every small shop along the highway near Dadonghai.

Buses to Tongzha can be picked up in Sanya at either the long-distance bus station downtown or at the Dadonghai bus station.
➤ BUS INFORMATION: **East bus station** (⊠ Haifu Lu near Fucheng, ☎ 0898/537–4547).

CAR RENTAL

There is no self-drive car rental anywhere in Hainan. Cars with drivers can be hired through CITS.

➤ CONTACTS: **CITS** (✉ 8 Haifu Dadao, ☎ 0898/237–1097, FAX 0898/537–3997).

EMERGENCIES

In an emergency, dial ☎ 110 for police or call the Haikou People's Hospital for medical emergencies.

➤ CONTACTS: **Haikou People's Hospital** (✉ 68 Deshengsha Lu, Haikou, ☎ 0898/6222–2412).

TRAIN TRAVEL

The Xingang Matou (New Harbor Port) ticket office in Haikou sells combination tickets for ferries that leave from the port and then hook up with trains either in Zhanjiang or Guangzhou.

TRANSPORTATION AROUND HAINAN

In Haikou and Sanya, taxis are your best bet for getting around. The most convenient mode of transportation is to get a ride from one of the many motorcycles that drive around and often wait in front of hotels. Just look for a motorcycle driver with an extra helmet on the back of his bike. Make sure to set the price in advance; Y5–Y8 should get you just about anywhere in either city.

TRAVEL AGENCIES

In Haikou, CITS can assist with booking air tickets as well as arranging other transportation. They also have a number of package tours and diving tours available.

➤ LOCAL AGENCY REFERRALS: **CITS** (✉ 8 Haifu Dadao, ☎ 0898/237–1097, FAX 0898/537–3997).

VISITOR INFORMATION

In Haikou or Sanya, inquire at your hotel. The Hainan Tourism Administration has set up Tourist Complaint Hotlines in Haikou and Sanya.

➤ TOURIST INFORMATION: **Haikou** (☎ 0898/625–0780). **Sanya** (☎ 0899/827–1737).

9 HONG KONG

FINANCE, COMMERCE, AND HIGH STYLE

Much has changed for Hong Kong in recent years, from the handover to China in July 1997 to the region-wide economic crisis that hit soon after, yet it is still the sheer audacity of the place that inspires. One of the world's premier business centers has been crafted out of barren rock and political turmoil, and a walk through its surging, swirling streets is like a shot of adrenaline to the system.

TO STAND ON THE TIP OF the Kowloon peninsula and look out across the harbor to the full expanse of the Hong Kong Island skyline—as imposing in height as Manhattan but only a few blocks deep and strung along the entire north coast—is to witness the triumph of ambition over fate. Whereas it took Paris and London 10 or 20 generations to build the spectacular cities we know today and it took New York six, Hong Kong has built almost everything you see before you in the time since today's young investment bankers were born.

Updated by
Denise
Cheung, Eva
Chui, Tobias
Parker, Lara
Wozniak

Hong Kong's current prosperity was not inevitable. When the 30-square-mi island of Hong Kong was ceded to the British after the Opium War of 1841, it consisted, in the infamous words of the British minister at the time, of "barren rock." Its primary value was its control of access to Guangzhou (Canton) and thus China's trade with the outside world. It was a juggernaut that proved highly profitable.

If that were all Hong Kong had going for it, however, its prosperity would have faded with the British empire. No, the real story of Hong Kong begins in the 1920s and continues through the Communist revolution in China in 1949, when wave after wave of refugees from Guangdong, Fujian, Shanghai, and elsewhere settled in the territory to avoid the civil unrest on the mainland. Many of these new arrivals came from humble farming backgrounds, but many others had been rich not long before and had seen their wealth and businesses stripped away from them by the revolutionaries. They arrived in Hong Kong poorer than they'd been in generations, yet by virtue of their labor, their descendants are the wealthiest generation ever.

Because Hong Kong has always lived and breathed commerce, the various shrines to mammon are likely to make the strongest impression when you first arrive. Hong Kong Island itself has been thick with skyscrapers bearing the names of banks and conglomerates for years, yet it continues to build more, squeezing them in on irregular plots of land that would seem insufficient for buildings half the size. Kowloon, too, is a dense urban jungle. In fact, parts of Kowloon boast the highest population density in the world. Originally the height of the buildings was held back by the proximity of the old Kai Tak Airport. But now, with height restrictions lifted, new sky-high skyscrapers are starting to poke into the heavens, à la Hong Kong Island. In the New Territories, once Hong Kong's farmland, the new towns (where once small villages of the same name stood) are connected by great expanses of highway cutting a swath through the land. These new towns now have their own columns of concrete reaching upward, putting an end forever to Hong Kong's rural heritage.

Amid all the change it can be easy, even for residents, to forget that most of Hong Kong has nothing to do with business or skyscrapers: 40% of it is rural wilderness. In addition, there are 235 lesser-known islands, most of which are little more than jagged peaks and tropical scrub, home to a few small fishing villages. Even Hong Kong Island, so relentlessly urban along its north coast, consists mostly of rolling green hills and sheltered bays on its south side. Whether you are looking for the hectic Hong Kong or the relaxed one, both are easy enough to find—indeed, may only be a few minutes apart.

Pleasures and Pastimes

Dining

Anywhere you go in Hong Kong, in any direction you'd care to look, you're bound to see a restaurant sign. Nowhere in the world is cook-

Hong Kong

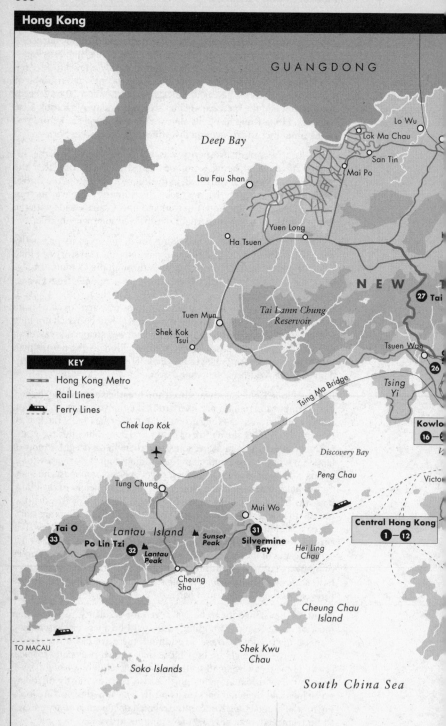

GUANGDONG

Deep Bay

Lo Wu

Lok Ma Chau

San Tin

Mai Po

Lau Fau Shan

Yuen Long

Ha Tsuen

N E W

27 Tai

Tai Lamn Chung
Reservoir

Tuen Mun

Shek Kok
Tsui

Tsuen Wan

26

*Tsing
Yi*

Tsing Ma Bridge

KEY

Hong Kong Metro

Rail Lines

Ferry Lines

Chek Lap Kok

Discovery Bay

Kowlo

16

Tung Chung

Peng Chau

Victor

Lantau Island

Mui Wo

31

*Sunset
Peak*

Central Hong Kong

1 12

Tai O

33

Po Lin Tzi

32

*Lantau
Peak*

**Silvermine
Bay**

*Hei Ling
Chau*

Cheung
Sha

*Cheung Chau
Island*

TO MACAU

*Shek Kwu
Chau*

Soko Islands

South China Sea

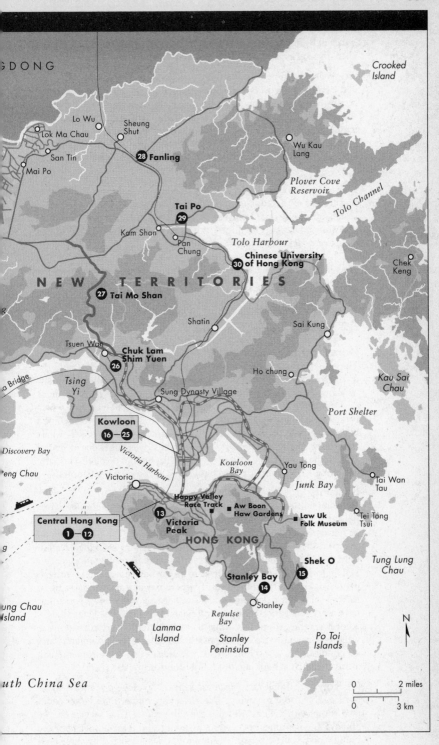

ing more varied than in this city, where Cantonese cuisine (long regarded by Chinese gourmands as the most intricate and sophisticated in Asia) is joined by delights not only from other parts of China, but also from virtually every other culinary region on earth.

Five styles of Chinese cooking are prominent in Hong Kong. As 94% of the population comes from Guangdong (Canton) province, **Cantonese** is considered the indigenous style. The Cantonese ideal is to bring out the natural taste of ingredients by cooking them quickly at very high temperatures. This creates *wok chi,* a fleeting energy that requires food to be served immediately. There are also many restaurants in Hong Kong serving **Chiu Chow, Shanghai, Peking,** and **Sichuan** food.

Tips are expected at most restaurants, even if there is already a service charge on the bill. In more traditional Chinese restaurants, however, tips are not expected, although it is customary to leave small change. Unless otherwise noted, the restaurants listed are open daily for lunch and dinner. Dress is mentioned only when men are required to wear a jacket or a jacket and tie.

CATEGORY	COST*
$$$$	over HK$280
$$$	HK$180–HK$280
$$	HK$80–HK$180
$	under HK$80

per person for a main course at dinner.

Horseracing

The only legal gambling in Hong Kong is betting on horses, and the track rivals business as the city's main obsession. The amount of money bet can be staggering; indeed, more is wagered on an average Wednesday or Saturday in Hong Kong than during all of Ascot weekend, which is the United Kingdom's biggest racing event. But even if you're not a big gambler yourself, the excitement of the track (whether it is the older, more distinctive track in Happy Valley or the newer, larger one in Shatin) is not to be missed. The season runs from September through May, and the Hong Kong Tourist Board has copies of the racing schedules.

Lodging

Accommodations are very expensive in Hong Kong. But almost no one pays the full rate quoted, as travel agents often offer huge discounts or packages. It is essential to check for bargains. The hotels also do their bit, such as offering discounts and credits for use in their restaurants and bars. Most hotels provide such amenities as magnificent views and high-tech facilities—and strive to please business clientele with expense accounts at their disposal. Expect to pay at least US$150 a night for a room of normal international standards. For that price you won't have a prime location, but you will have basic and reliable facilities—color TV, radio, telephone, same-day valet laundry service, room service, secretarial service, safe deposit box, refrigerator and minibar, and air-conditioning. Most hotels also have at least one restaurant and bar, a travel and tour-booking desk, and limousine or car rental.

Categories for hotel rates are based on the average price for a standard double room for two people. Prices are higher for a larger room or a room with a view. All rates are subject to a 10% service charge and a 3% government tax, which is used to fund the activities of the Hong Kong Tourist Board. Accommodations are listed by three geographical areas—Hong Kong Island, Kowloon, and New Territories and the Outer Islands—alphabetized within each price category.

CATEGORY	COST*
$$$$	over HK$3,000
$$$	HK$2,000–HK$3,000
$$	HK$1,200–HK$2,000
$	under HK$1,200

*All prices are for a standard double room, excluding 10% service charge and 3% tax.

Shopping

Hong Kong has long been famous as a world-class shopping destination, but rising rents in most of the 1990s threatened its reputation for low prices. Since the economic crisis began in 1997, however, rents have fallen sharply, and deep discounts have prevailed at many stores, once again putting Hong Kong on any global shopper's map. Local tastes have moved decidedly upmarket over the years, so you'll see a staggering range of luxury goods and clothing boutiques, but many of the city's traditional offerings—inexpensive clothing, Chinese antiques, consumer electronics—remain good bargains. The most rewarding spoils are the Chinese clothes, fabrics, antiques, jewelry, tea, and collectibles that you can find on Hollywood Road, in outdoor markets, and even tucked away in high-tech shopping malls.

Water Trips

The favored ship in Hong Kong is a modern version of the traditional Chinese junk, usually running on a motor rather than sails but retaining the distinctive elevated stern of old. They can be easily rented for jaunts to one of the smaller outer islands for a fresh seafood lunch or to a nature park like Sai Kung for an afternoon of sunbathing and water sports. If that sounds too elaborate, you can always take the Star Ferry between Kowloon and Hong Kong Island and enjoy, for a moment, the pleasures of life on the waters.

EXPLORING HONG KONG

Just 77 square km (30 square mi) in size, **Hong Kong Island** is where the territory's action is, from high finance to hip nightlife to luxury shopping. There are few historical landmarks on the island and no more than a handful of cultural sights, but it boasts an extraordinarily dynamic and exhilarating contemporary life. In general, the commercial and shopping districts are along the island's north coast, interspersed with the ubiquitous apartment blocks, while the towns on the rest of the island tend to be quieter and more residential. The island's districts, each with a slightly different character, have straightforward names like Central, Western, or Causeway Bay (usually the same as the MTR stop in the area), but the borders tend to blur together. One of Hong Kong Island's surprises is that despite its sometimes unrelentingly urban feel, property development has been restricted to a few small areas; a 20-minute taxi ride from downtown Central can have you breathing fresh air and seeing only lush green vegetation on the horizon.

The **Kowloon** peninsula lies just across the harbor from Central and is bounded in the north by the string of mountains that give Kowloon—a word derived from *gau lung,* or "nine dragons"—its poetic name. Kowloon is closer to China than Hong Kong in more ways than just geography: although the island is home to international finance and glittering modern skyscrapers, Kowloon's urban fabric is more densely woven. Nevertheless, Kowloon has many of the territory's best hotels as well as a mind-boggling range of shopping options, and no visit is complete without taking on the commercial chaos of Nathan Road.

The expansive **New Territories** lies between Kowloon and the Chinese border and feels far removed from the congestion and urban rigors of the rest of the region. Lush parks and therapeutic nature walks are spread out across its 200 square mi. You can also get a glimpse of the pre-colonial culture of ethnic groups like the Hakka by visiting some of the temples and villages that preserve a traditional way of life—or at least as close as you can get to it in this modern age. But the New Territories is not all ancient: over the last few decades public housing projects throughout the area have led to the creation of new towns like Sha Tin and Tsuen Mun, some of which are now home to a half million people. They may lack the sights of interest to visitors, but they represent real life for a large percentage of Hong Kong's residents.

Great Itineraries

Numbers in the text correspond to numbers in the margin and on the Hong Kong map.

IF YOU HAVE 3 DAYS

Spend the first day exploring Hong Kong Island, starting with a ride on the **Star Ferry.** Walk through the territory's Central business district, which includes the headquarters of **Hongkong & Shanghai Bank** and the **Bank of China,** then on to the antiques stores along **Wyndham Street** and **Hollywood Road.** Proceed on to **Man Mo Temple** and then take a taxi to the **Peak Tram,** which runs up a near-vertical cliff to **Victoria Peak,** where there are views of the harbor. Late afternoon and evening is a good time to spend on the south side of the island shopping in **Stanley Village** or strolling around **Shek O.**

On day two you can discover Kowloon, starting with the **Space Museum** and **Museum of Art** along the waterfront near the Star Ferry pier. Stop at the colonial-style **Peninsula Hotel** for tea, then wander up **Nathan Road,** one of the most densely packed shopping streets on earth. Proceed to the **Jade Market** or the **Bird Market,** then end the day with the **Temple Street night market.**

The final day should be spent on one of the outer islands like **Lantau,** where you can take a bus to the **Po Lin Monastery** and visit the **Giant Buddha.** Also on the island are the fishing villages of **Tai O** and **Mui Wo,** now somewhat modernized but still sedate compared to Central.

IF YOU HAVE 6 DAYS

With more time you can add a second day for exploring Hong Kong Island, visiting the bustling department store district of **Causeway Bay** and, farther afield, the fantastical sculptures of the **Aw Boon Haw** (Tiger Balm Gardens) or the historic remains in the **Law Uk Folk Museum.** Spend the afternoon in the dried foods and traditional herbal medicine shops in the **Western district,** and come nightfall, you can meander through the back alleys of **Wanchai** looking for the dens of iniquity that were once so legendary among sailors of the Pacific.

Your last two days provide an opportunity to visit the old Chinese villages of the **New Territories** (best done on a tour as the sights are so spread out) and the charming East/West hybrid of neighboring **Macau,** the former Portuguese colony just an hour away by boat.

IF YOU HAVE 8 DAYS

Follow the six-day itinerary above, then stay overnight in Macau and give yourself time to discover a hidden gem of a town, one underrated even by many in Hong Kong. Best known for its casinos and fantastic food, Macau also has pastel-color baroque churches, traditional Chinese gardens, and even a black-sand beach. You can also take a day to visit either **Lamma** or **Cheung Chau Island** to see a slower-paced side of Hong Kong life and try fresh-caught seafood cooked Cantonese style.

Hong Kong Island

Most districts on the island are best explored on foot, but taxis are so plentiful (except during typhoons, when you really need them) that it is easy to get a ride farther afield. The best strolling weather is in the dry season from late September to mid-December; the rest of the year you should carry a folding umbrella.

A Good Tour

For more than a century, the natural starting point for any walk through this area has been the Star Ferry terminal in Central. Follow the awnings to the right of the terminal and go straight through the underground walkway to come to Statue Square. The intriguing Victorian/Chinese hybrid building on the east side of the square is the **Legislative Council Building** ①. Along the southern end of the square are the buildings of the three note-issuing banks in Hong Kong: the art deco former headquarters of the **Bank of China** ②, the spectacular strut-and-ladder facade of the **Hongkong & Shanghai Bank (HSBC)** ③, and, pressing up against it, the rose-color wedge of Standard Chartered Bank. You can walk under the HSBC building, looking up into the atrium through a curved glass floor, and then exit on the south side. Turn right (that is, west) on Queen's Road Central, and you'll see the glass arcs of the Henley Building, which houses the **Tsui Museum of Art** ④.

A little farther ahead on the right, at the intersection of Queen's Road Central and Pedder Street, lies the **Landmark** ⑤, the mother of all luxury shopping centers, but by turning left and heading up the hill, you will run into **Wyndham Street** ⑥, which is lined with Chinese art and antiques stores. Wyndham eventually turns into **Hollywood Road** ⑦, which leads to the colorful **Man Mo Temple** ⑧. To reach the curios and trinkets shops of **Upper Lascar Row** ⑨, also known as **Cat Street,** walk down the steps of Ladder Street, just across from Man Mo Temple. By walking straight down the hill and continuing toward the waterfront, you'll run into **Bonham Strand East and West** ⑩, which has many traditional shops selling dried seafood. When you're just about ready to turn back, head toward the harbor and follow Connaught Road east until you come to the cream-and-brown **Western Market** ⑪, which dates from 1906 and has been lovingly restored. From there it's an easy tram ride back to Central, or you can take a taxi to the **Peak Tram** ⑫ terminal and ride up to **Victoria Peak** ⑬. From the peak you can take a taxi to the south side of the island to visit **Stanley Bay** ⑭ or the seaside village of **Shek O** ⑮.

TIMING
This is a difficult tour to complete in a day; two would be ideal. The Central and Western districts walk will take about four hours, and it's worth leaving time at the Peak for coffee or a meal. The trip to the south side can make for a day's outing on its own.

Sights to See

❷ **Bank of China.** In the politics of Hong Kong architecture, the stylish art deco building of the old Bank of China headquarters was the first trump. Constructed after World War II, it was a symbolically important 20 ft higher than the adjacent Hongkong & Shanghai Banking Corporation (HSBC) building. It is now one of the smallest buildings in Central, utterly dwarfed by the imposing new structure HSBC built in the mid-1980s. The Bank of China refused to take this challenge lying down, however, and commissioned the Chinese-American architect I.

344

Central Hong Kong

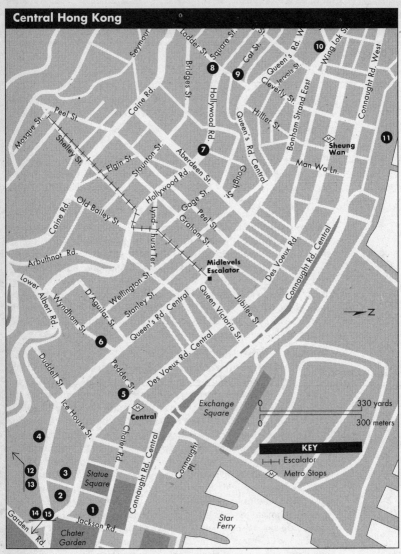

M. Pei to build a new headquarters nearby. The result, the **Bank of China Tower** (✉ 1 Garden Rd.) completed in 1990, is a masterful twisting spire of replicating triangles that was the first to break the ridge line of Victoria Peak. It may not be as innovative as the new HSBC building, but it dominates Hong Kong's urban landscape and embodies the new balance of power after the handover. The old building now houses Sin Hua Bank and, on the top floor, David Tang's exclusive China Club, which manages to be both postmodern and nostalgic for pre-Communist Shanghai. ✉ *4 Queen's Rd., Central.*

★ ⑩ **Bonham Strand East and West.** A major thoroughfare in one of Hong Kong's most charmingly traditional areas, Bonham Strand is lined with shops selling goods that evoke the old China Coast trade merchants. A few shops sell live snakes, the meat of which is used in winter soups to ward off colds, while the gall bladder reputedly improves vigor and virility. Bonham Strand West, in particular, is known for its Chinese medicines and herbal remedies; many old shops have their original facades. Inside, walls are lined with drawers and shelves of jars filled with hundreds of strange-smelling ingredients, such as wood barks and insects, which are consumed dried and ground up, infused in hot water or tea, or taken as powders or pills. ✉ *Parallel to Queen's Rd. in Sheung Wan (Western) District.*

❼ **Hollywood Road.** At this road's eastern end, where it joins Wyndham Street, are many of the city's best antique, furniture, and traditional arts galleries. As it heads west, the shops move down-market, selling mostly porcelain, curios, and not-very-old trinkets labeled antiques. Look to the left for a sign saying POSSESSION STREET, where Captain Charles Elliott of the British Royal Navy stepped ashore in 1841 and claimed Hong Kong for the British empire. It is interesting to note how far today's harbor is from this earlier shoreline—the result of a century of aggressive land reclamation. ✉ *Between Wyndham St. and Queen's Rd. W.*

❸ **Hongkong & Shanghai Bank.** This striking building with its distinctive ladder facade is a landmark in modern architecture. Designed by Sir Norman Foster as the headquarters of Hong Kong's premier bank (you'll see it depicted on most of the paper money) and completed in 1985, the building sits on four props, which make it possible to walk under it and look up through its glass belly into the soaring atrium within. Imposing as that may be, it is the sensitive use of high-tech details that is most interesting. The mechanics of everything from the gears and pulleys of the elevators to the circuit boards of the electric signs have been left visible. In addition to its architectural triumph, however, the building served a symbolic function as well: built at a cost of almost US$1 billion at a time of insecurity vis-à-vis China, it was a powerful statement of the bank's intention not to take its money out of the territory. ✉ *1 Queen's Rd. Central, across from Statue Sq.*

❺ **The Landmark.** There are few world-class fashion designers, luggage makers, watch craftsmen, or luxury-goods makers who do not have (or wouldn't love to get) a boutique in the Landmark. The building is no longer the city's most opulent, but its location on Pedder Street is still priceless. There is an MTR entrance in the building, and concerts and fashion shows are occasionally held near the fountain in the glass-covered atrium. ✉ *Des Voeux Rd. between Ice House St. and Pedder St.,* ☎ *no phone.* ☉ *Building, 9* AM–*midnight; most shops, 10–6.*

❶ **Legislative Council Building.** Built for the Supreme Court in 1912 and now home to the Legislative Council (or LegCo, as it is called), this is one of the few remaining grand Victorian structures left in the area. Note the Chinese-style eaved roof, however, which offers a hint of British concession to local culture. For most of Hong Kong's history as a British colony, the council had no real power, but starting in 1991 it had a majority of elected members who challenged the administration at sessions held every Wednesday. After the handover in 1997, mainland attempts to muzzle the pro-democracy members of LegCo were only moderately successful, and it continues to serve as a forum for debate. In front of the council building is the **Cenotaph,** a monument to all who lost their lives in the two world wars. ✉ *Statue Sq. at Jackson Rd.*

★ ❽ **Man Mo Temple.** Built in 1847 and dedicated to the gods of literature and of war—Man and Mo, respectively—this is Hong Kong Island's oldest temple. It now serves primarily as a smoke-filled haven for elderly women paying their respects, in which ashes flutter down on to your clothes from the enormous spirals of incense that hang from the roof beams. The statue of Man is dressed in green and holds a writing brush, while Mo is dressed in red and holds a sword. To their left is a shrine to Pao Kung, god of justice, whose face is painted black. To the right is Shing Wong, god of the city. The temple bell, cast in Canton in 1847, and the drum next to it are sounded to attract the gods' attention when a prayer is offered. ✉ *Hollywood Rd. at Ladder St.,* ☎ *no phone.* ☾ *Daily 8–6.*

⓬ **Peak Tram.** Starting from the Lower Peak Tram Terminus is the world's steepest funicular railway. It passes five intermediate stations en route to the upper terminal, 1,800 ft above sea level. The railway was opened in 1880 to transport people to the top of **Victoria Peak,** the highest hill overlooking Hong Kong Harbour. Before the tram, the only way to get to the top was to walk or take a bumpy ride up the steep steps in a sedan chair. The tram has two 72-seat cars, which are hauled up the hill by cables attached to electric motors. A shuttle bus to and from the Peak Tram leaves from Edinburgh Place, next to City Hall. ✉ *Between Garden Rd. and Cotton Tree Dr.,* ☎ *852/2522–0922.* ▣ *HK$20 one-way, HK$30 round-trip.* ☾ *Daily 7 AM–midnight, every 10–15 mins.*

⓯ **Shek O.** The easternmost village on the south side of the island is a popular weekend retreat for residents trying to escape the rigors of the city. The village is filled with old houses, great mansions, a superb golf course and club, a few simple restaurants, a pretty beach, and fine views that are intruded on by some ugly new housing developments. Leave the town square, full of small shops selling inflatable toys and other beach essentials, and take the curving path across a footbridge to the "island" of **Tai Tau Chau,** really a large rock with a lookout for scanning the South China Sea. Little more than a century ago this open water was ruled by pirates. You can hike through **Shek O Country Park** (✉ Southeast side of Hong Kong Island) in less than two hours. Look here for birds that are hard to find in Hong Kong, such as Kentish plovers, reef egrets, and black-headed gulls, as well as the colorful rufus-backed shrike and the ubiquitous, chatty bulbul.

⓮ **Stanley Bay.** The town became notorious as the home of the largest World War II prisoner-of-war camps that the Japanese ran in Hong Kong. Today Stanley is known for its picturesque beaches and its market, where casual clothing and tourist knickknacks are sold at wholesale prices. You can also visit the old police station, which was built in 1859 and now houses a restaurant. Past the market, on Stanley Main Street, a strip of restaurants and pubs faces the bay. On the other side of the bay is a Tin Hau Temple, wedged in among giant new housing estates. ✉ *Southern tip of Hong Kong Island.*

④ Tsui Museum of Art. On the fourth floor of the Henley Building, this often overlooked treasure houses the private collection of local *taipan* and renowned Chinese art connoisseur, T. T. Tsui. The more than 3,000 pieces include ceramics, bronze, carved wood, ivory, even a recreation of a Ming dynasty scholar's study. ⊠ *5 Queen's Rd., Central,* ☎ *852/2868–2688.* ⌺ *HK$30.* ⊙ *Weekdays 10–6, Sat. 10–2.*

⑨ Upper Lascar Row. Cat Street, as Upper Lascar Row is often called, is a vast flea market. You won't find Ming vases here, but you may come across an old Mao badge or an antique pot or teakettle. It's marvelous to wander here and watch the bargaining going on, but be careful if you venture into the negotiating game: these vendors wrote the book.

★ ⑬ Victoria Peak. Known in Chinese as Tai Ping Shan, or Mountain of Great Peace, the Peak is Hong Kong's one must-see sight. On a clear day there is nothing to rival the view from 1,805 ft up of the dense, glittering string of skyscrapers that runs along the north coast of Hong Kong and the carpet of buildings that extends to the nine mountains of Kowloon. It is well worth timing a visit to see the view both by day and by night, perhaps by taking in a meal at one of the restaurants near the upper terminus. The Peak is more than just a view. It also offers extensive parkland that is perfect for a picnic or long walks in a residential neighborhood that is the city's—indeed, perhaps all of Asia's—most prestigious address. ⊠ *Mountain rising just south of Central.*

⑪ Western Market. Erected in 1906 as the north block of a market building dating from 1858, this is the only part that has survived. It functioned as a produce market for 83 years and included living quarters for coolies and inspectors in the four corner towers. Threatened with demolition, it was instead exquisitely restored and turned into a unique shopping outlet. Unfortunately, the developers have never gotten the retail mix quite right, filling the place with souvenir and trinket shops on the ground floor, fabrics on the first floor, and a Chinese restaurant on the top floor. The building, however, is worth the trip, gorgeously decorated with Chinese bunting. ⊠ *323 Connaught Rd. W.* ⊙ *10 AM–11:45 PM.*

★ ⑥ Wyndham Street. The galleries that pack the single curving block of Wyndham Street from the Fringe Club to where it turns into Hollywood Road should be thought of more as a collection of miniature museums than as mere shops. Within their showrooms you can find some spectacular antique furniture, art, and artifacts at prices that, although not cheap by any means, are a fraction of what they would cost at home. Note that most shops are open 10–7 or so every day, although some have abbreviated hours or close altogether on Sunday. ⊠ *Wyndham St. at Glenealy and Lower Albert Rds.*

Kowloon

The southernmost part of Kowloon, Tsim Sha Tsui, harbors such landmarks as the Star Ferry terminal and the elegant Peninsula Hotel. North of Tsim Sha Tsui you'll find the market districts of Jordan and Mong Kok, where everything from pirated videos to electronics to name-brand clothes can be purchased at fire-sale prices. Tsim Sha Tsui is best reached by the Star Ferry, while the rest of Kowloon is easily accessible by foot or via MTR or taxi.

A Good Walk

The Star Ferry pier on the Kowloon side is a 10-minute ferry ride from the pier on the Hong Kong side; the ferry ride is the most romantic way to see the harbor, day or night. East of the pier is a long promenade along Salisbury Road, where you can visit the **Hong Kong Cul-**

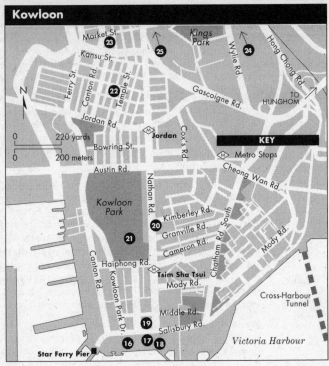

tural Centre ⑯, **Hong Kong Space Museum** ⑰, and the **Hong Kong Museum of Art** ⑱. The luxurious **Peninsula Hotel** ⑲ is across the street, on the corner of Salisbury and Nathan Road. Walk north on **Nathan Road** ⑳ to experience one of the territory's most famous (and congested) shopping districts, then on to Haiphong Road to get to **Kowloon Park** ㉑. Continue north on Nathan Road three blocks to Jordan Road; make a left and then a right onto **Temple Street** ㉒. Follow Temple Street north to the **Kansu Street Jade Market** ㉓, to the west. From here take a taxi to **Wong Tai Sin Temple** ㉔ or the newly relocated and renamed **Bird Garden** ㉕.

Sights to See

㉕ **Bird Garden.** Built in 1997, this garden replaces the narrow streets of bird shops of the old Bird Market, which has been redeveloped. What the garden lacks in terms of the spontaneous tumult of the original market, it makes up for with an attractive outdoor location in the shadow of the Kowloon-Canton Railway (KCR) tracks, where the rumble of each passing train sends the birds into a frenzy. The garden is composed of various courtyards filled with trees and 70 stalls selling birds, cages, and such accoutrements as tiny porcelain feeders and fresh grasshoppers. There are plenty of free birds as well who swoop in to gorge on spilled food and commiserate with their imprisoned kin. The street leading here from the MTR is aromatic with flower shops. ⊠ *Yuen Po St., near Prince Edward MTR station.* ⊙ *Daily 7 AM–8 PM.*

⑯ **Hong Kong Cultural Centre.** This stark, architecturally controversial building has tiled walls inside and out, sloped roofs, and no windows—an irony, as the view is superb. It houses a concert hall and two theaters. ⊠ *10 Salisbury Rd.,* ☎ *852/2734–2010.*

⑱ **Hong Kong Museum of Art.** The exterior is unexciting, but inside are five floors of well-designed galleries. One is devoted to historic photographs, prints, and artifacts of Hong Kong, Macau, and other parts of the Pearl River delta. Other galleries display Chinese antiquities and fine art and visiting exhibitions. ⊠ *10 Salisbury Rd.,* ☎ *852/2721–0116.* ⊠ *HK$20 for adults; HK$10 students and seniors; half price Wed.* ☉ *Fri.–Wed. 10–6.*

🕙 **⑰ Hong Kong Space Museum.** Across from the Peninsula Hotel, this dome-shape museum houses one of the most advanced planetariums in Asia. The museum has interactive models explaining basic aspects of space exploration (although some of these confuse nearly as much as they clarify) as well as flywires to let you feel weightlessness and other phenomena. It also contains the **Hall of Solar Science,** whose solar telescope permits visitors a close look at the sun, and the **Space The-atre** (☉ seven shows daily, 2:30–8:30, ⊠ HK$24–HK$32), with Omnimax movies on space travel, sports, and natural wonders. Children under 3 are not admitted. ⊠ *10 Salisbury Rd.,* ☎ *852/2734–2722.* ⊠ *HK$10.* ☉ *Mon. and Wed.–Fri. 1–9, weekends 10–9.*

㉓ Kansu Street Jade Market. The daily jade market carries everything from fake jade pendants to precious carvings. If you don't know much about jade, take along someone who does, or you may pay a lot more than you should. The best time to visit is from 10 to noon. ⊠ *Kansu St. off Nathan Rd.* ☉ *10–6.*

🕙 **㉑ Kowloon Park.** The former site of the Whitfield Military Barracks is today a restful, green oasis. Signs point the way to gardens with different landscaping themes. One of its most popular sections is the sculpture garden; the Chinese Garden has a lotus pond, streams, and a lake, and there's an aviary nearby with a colorful collection of rare birds. The **Jamia Masjid and Islamic Centre** is in the south end of the park, near the Haiphong Road entrance. This is Hong Kong's principal mosque, albeit not its most graceful. Built in 1984, it has four minarets, decorative arches, and a marble dome. At the northern end of the park sits an extraordinary public swimming complex built, like so much else in the city, by the Hong Kong Jockey Club with revenues from the horse races. ⊠ *Haiphong Rd. off Nathan Rd.* ☉ *6 AM–midnight.*

⑳ Nathan Road. The spine of Kowloon, the so-called Golden Mile runs for several miles both north and south. The most densely packed shopping street in town is filled with hotels, restaurants, and shops of every description. To the left and right are mazes of narrow streets lined with even more shops crammed with every possible type of merchandise—jewelry, electronics, clothes, souvenirs, and more. ⊠ *North from Kowloon waterfront.*

⑲ Peninsula Hotel. The grande dame of Hong Kong hotels, The Peninsula is a local institution. The exterior of this sumptuous hotel draws attention with a fleet of Rolls Royce taxis and doormen in white uniforms, while the huge colonnaded lobby has charm, grandeur, string quartets, and the sedate air of excessive wealth being tastefully enjoyed. ⊠ *Salisbury Rd.,* ☎ *852/2366–6251.*

NEED A BREAK?   Tsim Sha Tsui is short on quiet cafés, but the **Peninsula Hotel** offers high tea—frankly, the perfect way to rest your shopping feet in style. You even have options: dine on a majestic array of scones and pastries in the lobby (daily 2–7 for HK$165 per person) or settle down for tea in the Verandah Restaurant (Fri–Sun. 3–5).

㉒ Temple Street. The heart of a busy shopping area, Temple Street is ideal for wandering and people-watching. By day you'll find market stalls with plenty of kitsch and a few worthwhile clothing bargains, but the best time to visit is after 8 PM, when the streets become an open-air market filled with street doctors offering cures for almost any complaint, fortune-tellers, and, on most nights, Cantonese opera.

Such nearby lanes as **Shanghai Street** and **Canton Road** are also worth a visit for their colorful shops and stalls selling everything from herbal remedies to jade and ivory. **Ning Po Street** is known for its shops selling paper kites and the colorful paper and bamboo models of worldly possessions that are burned at Chinese funerals. ✉ *North from Austin Rd. to Kansu St.*

㉔ Wong Tai Sin Temple. Have your fortune told at this large, colorful compound with a Buddhist shrine dedicated to a shepherd boy who was said to have had magic healing powers. In addition to the main altar, the pavilions, and the arcade—where you'll find soothsayers and palm readers happy to interpret Wong Tai Sin's predictions for a small fee— there are two lovely Chinese gardens and a Confucian Hall. ✉ *Wong Tai Sin Rd. and Nga Chuk St.,* ☎ *852/2327–8141.* 💰 *Small donation expected.* 🕑 *Daily 7–5.*

New Territories

Because of its size, the New Territories can be difficult to explore without a car, although between the bus, MTR, and the Kowloon–Canton Railway you can get close to many sights by relying on public transport. Perhaps the best way to see smaller villages is on one of the **Hong Kong Tourist Board**'s organized tours—even if you don't think you're a tour kind of person—which do a loop through the region. Book through your hotel tour desk or an **HKTB Visitor Information Centre** (✉ Ground floor, The Center, 99 Queen's Rd. Central, Hong Kong; ✉ Star Ferry Concourse, Kowloon).

A Good Drive

A typical HKTB package tour takes you to **Chuk Lam Shim Yuen** ㉖, a monastery; **Tai Mo Shan** ㉗, Hong Kong's tallest mountain; **Fanling** ㉘, a local market; a country park, **Tai Po** ㉙; and the **Chinese University of Hong Kong** ㉚.

TIMING
Set aside a full day for the tour.

Sights to See

㉚ Chinese University of Hong Kong. The modern university's **Art Gallery**, in the Institute of Chinese Studies building, is well worth a visit. It has large exhibits of paintings and calligraphy from periods ranging from the Ming to modern times. There are also important collections of bronze seals, carved jade flowers, and ceramics from South China. ✉ *12 Miles Tai Po Rd., Shatin, KCR to University Station and then campus bus or taxi,* ☎ *852/2609–7416.* 💰 *Free.* 🕑 *Mon.–Sat. 10–4:30, Sun. 12:30–4:30.*

㉖ Chuk Lam Shim Yuen (Bamboo Forest Monastery). One of Hong Kong's most impressive monasteries, it has three large statues of Buddha. Crowds of worshipers on festival days demonstrate its continuing importance to the Chinese. ✉ *Castle Peak Rd., Tsuen Wan.* 💰 *Free.* 🕑 *Daily 7–4.*

㉘ Fanling. This town combines the serene atmosphere of the Hong Kong Golf Club with the chaos of rapid growth. The nearby **Luen Wo Market** is a traditional Chinese market, well worth visiting. You might find snakes for sale here in the winter months, and you're sure to see whole dried chickens prominently displayed. ✉ *North-central part of New Territories, 2 towns below Chinese border on KCR line.*

㉗ Tai Mo Shan. In the south-central portion of the New Territories is Hong Kong's highest peak, rising 3,230 ft above sea level. A trail through the bush allows you to climb to the top if you're fit enough, but even from halfway up you'll have a nice view of the surrounding country park area. Unfortunately the summit is fenced off, serving as a government communications post.

㉙ Tai Po (Shopping Place). In the heart of the region's breadbasket, Tai Po has long been a trading and meeting place for farmers and fishermen. It is now being developed as an industrial center, with new housing and highways everywhere you look. A fine traditional **market** (⊠ Tat Wan Rd.) stretches several blocks alongside the Tai Po Market KCR station, with most of the action taking place outdoors; it's open daily 9–6. Adjacent to it is the 100-year-old **Man Mo Temple.**

OFF THE
BEATEN PATH

SAI KUNG PENINSULA – To the east of Shatin, the **Sai Kung Peninsula** is regarded by most residents as one of Hong Kong's greatest blessings: beaches, nature walks, and tranquillity lying in close proximity to the city. Take the MTR to Choi Hung and then Bus 92, Bus 96R, or Minibus 1 to Sai Kung Town. You can also take a taxi along **Clearwater Bay Road**, which will take you into forested areas and land that is only partially developed, with Spanish-style villas overlooking the sea. Stroll along the waterfront, and you'll see some of the most unusual marine life ever—in tanks that are sitting outside restaurants. (If you choose to eat in a seafood restaurant, note that physicians caution against eating raw shellfish here because of hepatitis outbreaks.) To cruise around the harbor, rent a *kaido* (pronounced guy-doe; one of the small boats run by private operators) for about HK$130 round-trip, stopping at tiny **Yim Tin Tsai Island**, which has a rustic Catholic mission church built in 1890. In **Sai Kung Country Park** one of Hong Kong's most spectacular hiking trails passes through majestic hills overlooking the water. This excursion will take one day, and you should go only in sunny weather.

The Outer Islands

It is easy to forget that there are hundreds of islands in the territory, not just one: Hong Kong. For residents the Outer Islands have become a favorite way of escaping the city and enjoying some of life's smaller pleasures: the waterfront, good seafood, and a little peace and quiet. The four that are most readily accessible by ferry are Lantau, Lamma, Cheung Chau, and Peng Chau. The villages on the islands are definitely part of the modern world, but they run at a more humane pace. For maximum relaxation, try to come on a weekday, as the Hong Kong weekenders often bring their stresses and crowds with them.

The island of **Lantau** lies due west of Hong Kong. At 143 square km (55 square mi), it is almost twice the size of Hong Kong Island. Hong Kong's new airport, at Chek Lap Kok, and Walt Disney World, currently under construction at Penny's Bay and due for completion in 2005, may eventually change the face of Lantau, but for the time being it's sparsely populated and makes a nice getaway from the city.

A Good Tour

The ferry will take you to the town of Mui Wo on **Silvermine Bay** ㉛, which is being developed as a commuter suburb of Hong Kong Island. The island is very mountainous, so for a tour of the outlying villages, plan to hike or take a bus. From Mui Wo, the island's private bus services head out to **Po Lin Tzi** ㉜ (Precious Lotus Monastery), home of a giant Buddha; and **Tai O** ㉝, an ancient fishing village.

The New Territories and the Outer Islands

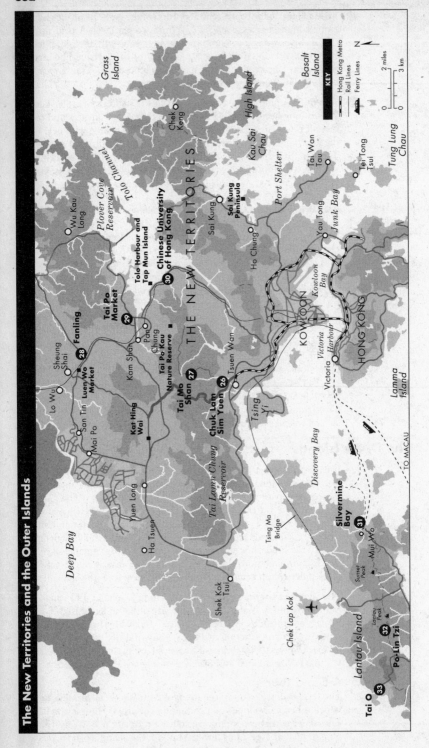

Grass Island

Basalt Island

Plover Cove Reservoir

Tolo Channel

High Island

Chek Keng

Kau Sai Chau

Port Shelter

Tung Lung Chau

Tai Wan Tau

Tei Tong Tsui

Wu Kau Long

Sai Kung Peninsula

Sai Kung

Ho Chung

Yau Tong

Junk Bay

Kowloon Bay

KOWLOON

THE NEW TERRITORIES

Tolo Harbour and Tap Mun Island

Chinese University of Hong Kong 30

Tai Po Market 29

Tai Po Kau Nature Reserve

Pan Chung

Fanling 28

Sheung Shui

Luen Wo Market

Kam Shan

Tsuen Wan

Tsing Yi

Victoria Harbour

Victoria

HONG KONG

Lamma Island

Lo Wu

San Tin

Kat Hing Wai

Mai Po

Tai Mo Shan 27

Chuk Lam Sim Yuen 26

Tai Lam Chung Reservoir

Discovery Bay

TO MACAU

Yuen Long

Ho Tsuen

Tsing Ma Bridge

Silvermine Bay 31

Mui Wo

Sunset Peak

Shek Kok Tsui

Chek Lap Kok

Lantau Island

Lantau Peak

Po Lin Tsi 32

Tai O 33

Deep Bay

KEY

Hong Kong Metro

Rail Lines

Ferry Lines

N

2 miles

3 km

TIMING
Take an entire day to tour the island.

Sights to See

③② **Po Lin Tzi** (Precious Lotus Monastery). In the mountainous interior of Lantau towers the world's tallest outdoor bronze statue of Buddha, the **Tin Tan Buddha.** At more than 100 ft high and weighing 275½ tons, it is all the more impressive for being situated at the peak of a hill, forcing pilgrims to stare up at it as they ascend. The adjacent monastery, gaudy and exuberantly commercial, is also famous for the vegetarian meals served in the temple refectory. ⊠ *Look for signs at bus stands or ask dispatcher at Silvermine Bay bus depot.* ☉ *Daily dawn–dusk.*

③① **Silvermine Bay.** This busy fishing bay is the point of entry from the Lantau Ferry, with some pleasant little seaside cafés. The village of **Mui Wo,** which lies along the bay, has a few hotels where you can stay overnight or rent bicycles to ride through the side streets and along the rice fields.

③③ **Tai O.** Divided into two parts connected by a rope-drawn ferry, the village still has many stilt houses and fishing shanties along the water. However, part of the old village was devastated by a fire in 2000, which subsequently raised concerns about the safety of the traditional stilt houses. There are plans to build new homes under modern safety guidelines, while the dwellings that were spared from the fire are a reminder of earlier village life. Visit the local temple, dedicated to Kuanti, the god of war, and taste local catches at the seafood restaurants. ⊠ *Take bus marked* TAI O *at Silvermine Bay.*

DINING

Hong Kong Island

Central

ASIAN

$$ ✕ **Indochine 1929.** Colonialism in Asia may be history, but many in Hong Kong retain romantic memories thereof. That may help explain the smashing success of Indochine 1929, which looks like a French plantation verandah at the height of the colonial era. The food is equally tasty; most of the ingredients used are imported twice a week from Vietnam. Highlights include salt-and-pepper soft-shell crab, fried beef and tomato, stir-fried fillet of pork with shallot and lemongrass, and fried fish Hanoi style. This is not the cheapest Vietnamese food in town, but it's arguably the best. The staff's traditional costumes—*ao dais,* straight, elegant silk gowns worn over flowing pants—and the surrounding old maps and antique fans and lamps add to the authentic atmosphere. ⊠ *California Tower, Lan Kwai Fong, 2nd floor,* ☎ *852/2869–7399. AE, DC, MC, V. No lunch Sun.*

$$ ✕ **Yung Kee.** For more than a half century, this massive eatery has served
★ Cantonese food amid riotous decor featuring writhing gold dragons. Convenient to both hotels and businesses, Yung Kee attracts a varied clientele—from office workers to visiting celebrities—all of whom receive the same cheerful, high-energy service. Roast goose is a specialty, its skin beautifully crisp. Adventurous palates must check out Yung Kee's famous thousand-year-old eggs with ginger. The preserved blackish eggs literally melt in your mouth. Seafood fanciers should try sautéed fillet of pomfret with chili and black-bean sauce or braised *garoupa* (grouper). ⊠ *32–40 Wellington St.,* ☎ *852/2522–1624. AE, DC, MC, V.*

Hong Kong Dining and Lodging

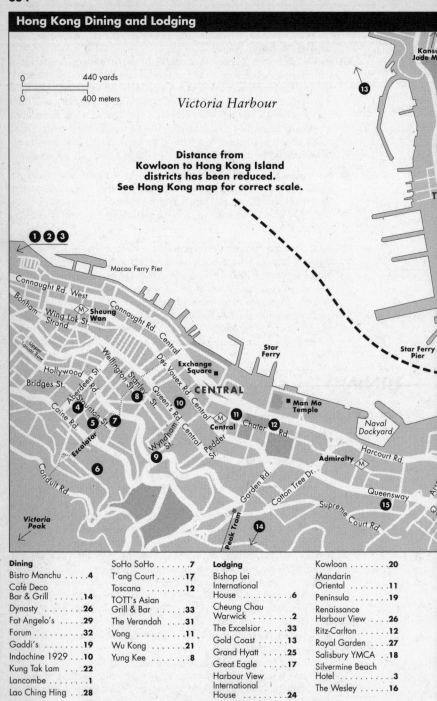

Victoria Harbour

Distance from
Kowloon to Hong Kong Island
districts has been reduced.
See Hong Kong map for correct scale.

Macau Ferry Pier

Connaught Rd. West

Bonham Strand

Wing Lok St.

Sheung Wan

Connaught Rd. Central

Upper Lascar Row

Hollywood

Bridges St.

Caine Rd.

Aberdeen St.

Staunton St.

Wellington St.

Stanley St.

Des Voeux Rd. Central

Exchange Square

Queen's Rd.

Star Ferry

CENTRAL

Central

Chater Rd.

Man Mo Temple

Wyndham St.

Central Rd.

Pedder St.

Naval Dockyard

Escalator

Conduit Rd.

Victoria Peak

Admiralty

Harcourt Rd.

Garden Rd.

Cotton Tree Dr.

Queensway

Supreme Court Rd.

Peak Tram

Star Ferry Pier

Kansu Jade M.

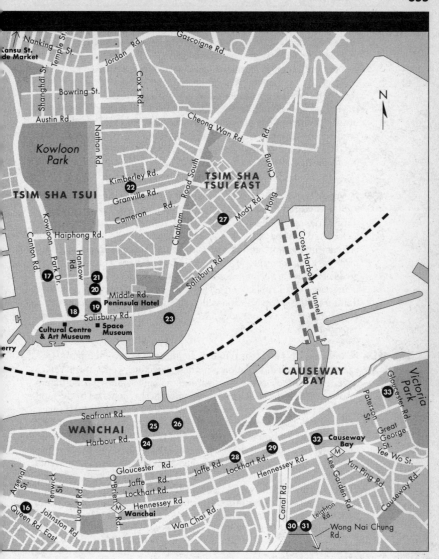

EUROPEAN

$$$ ✕ **M at the Fringe.** Set above the Fringe Club, M sets itself apart with
★ quirky yet classy decor and a seasonal menu that mixes Continental
with Middle Eastern cuisine. Both vegetarians and carnivores are well
served, and it can be hard to choose from the long list of intriguing
descriptions on the handwritten menu. Highly recommended are the
soft-shell crabs on cucumber salad, the Turkish vegetable platter, and
the house-smoked salmon with a potato-and-leek pancake and green
beans. The seasonally changing menu always lives up to high expec-
tations. The set lunch is a good value. ✉ *South Block, 2 Lower Albert
Rd., 1st floor,* ☎ *852/2877–4000. Reservations essential. AE, MC, V.
No lunch Sun.*

FRENCH

$$$ ✕ **Vong.** This is designer dining. With sister establishments in London
and New York, Hong Kong's glamorous version sits atop the Man-
darin Oriental Hotel looking down on Central and across the harbor.
Celebrated chef patron Jean-Georges Vongerichten is an advocate of
culinary innovation, and this is reflected in the menu. Billed as Asian-
inspired French cuisine, it combines herbs and spices with other ingredients to create a genuine fusion. Foie gras with ginger and caramelized
mango and quail rubbed with Thai spices are good examples. Lastly,
don't miss the warm Valrhona chocolate cake. ✉ *Mandarin Oriental
Hotel, 25th floor, 5 Connaught Rd.,* ☎ *852/2825–4028. Reservations
essential. AE, DC, MC, V.*

ITALIAN

$$$–$$$$ ✕ **Toscana.** This is classical Italian dining at its finest—sumptuous, el-
★ egant, and relaxed. Huge oil paintings depicting scenes from Venice
cover the walls, elegant drapes shroud the high windows, and Italian
opera softly fills the air. The opulent atmosphere is matched by the food
and smooth, friendly service. The lobster and *rucola* (arugula) salad,
with salty bursts of caviar mixing with fresh angel hair, is heavenly.
Dishes such as venison saddle with walnut tagliatelle and chocolate sauce,
and coral trout in herb dressing, fennel, and black olive puree exem-
plify Chef Umberto Bombana's thoughtful culinary creations. Match
these with a wine from the well-selected list, and you'll know why reg-
ulars from around the world visit whenever in town. The roast mango,
banana, and wild-berry tart with vanilla ice cream is a perfect finale.
✉ *Ritz-Carlton, 3 Connaught Rd.,* ☎ *852/2532–2062. Reservations
recommended. AE, DC, MC, V. Closed Sun.*

Midlevels

ASIAN

$$ ✕ **Bistro Manchu.** This smart bistro serves up heartwarming, soul-
soothing, and stomach-filling Manchurian dishes. Noodles, dumplings,
vegetables, meat—you won't be disappointed by this rarely encountered cuisine. The vegetable stew is a large bowl full of beautifully cooked
eggplant, potato, cabbage, and green beans in a clear broth. The north-
eastern-style smoked chicken surprises with its delicate texture and subtle smoky flavor. Meat lovers shouldn't miss the stir-fried lamb with
scallions. To complement the hearty dishes try a selection from the vast
array of Chinese teas or a light, sweet Harbin beer. Take the time to
read the introduction to Manchurian cuisine on your menu. ✉ *33 Elgin
St.,* ☎ *852/2536–9218 or 852/2536–9996. AE, DC, MC, V.*

$$ ✕ **Nepal.** If you're feeling adventurous, but not quite up to an assault
on Everest, you can stimulate your imagination with a Yaktail or Yeti
Foot cocktail in this tiny Nepalese restaurant. Take a look at the wood-
carving, *manne* (praying tools), and musical instruments as you enjoy
the Indian and Nepalese background music. The menu has simple ex-
planations of the Royal Nepalese cuisine. For a main course, the royal

chicken, a light curry, is highly recommended. End the meal with the Nepalese ice cream. ⊠ *14 Staunton St.,* ☎ *852/2521–9108. Reservations essential. AE, DC, MC, V.*

BRITISH

$$ ✕ **SoHo SoHo.** This smart little restaurant is doing its best to uphold
★ Britain's new reputation for fine food. Calling its cuisine "Modern British," SoHo SoHo takes traditional dishes, combines them with eclectic ingredients, and transforms them into modern classics. Panfried duck liver with egg served with balsamic vinegar surprises with its outrageously creative presentation and is utterly delicious. The roast cod with mashed potatoes, white beans, chorizo, and garlic aioli delivers a pleasant Mediterranean flavor, while the lamb shank shepherd's pie brings the traditional dish to a new height. The restaurant's crowds are a testament to its winning formula of high-quality, delicious food; helpful service; and good value. ⊠ *9 Old Bailey St.,* ☎ *852/2147–2618. AE, DC, MC, V. Closed Sun.*

Admiralty

FRENCH

$$$$ ✕ **Petrus.** Fine modern French dining with Mediterranean accents matched with glittering views sums up Petrus. From the 56th floor of this five-star hotel, Petrus literally looks down on nearly all other Hong Kong restaurants in location and culinary standards. Artichoke-and-truffle terrine with chives and olive oil dressing simply melts in your mouth and makes a beautiful kickoff for a luxurious evening. The flavorsome seared North Sea scallops go perfectly with the distinct texture and aromatic taste of salsify, baby spinach, and truffle butter. If you're looking for something rich and satisfying, the sweetbread, pig trotters, and morels crepinette don't disappoint. Naturally enough, the extensive wine list is largely French. ⊠ *Island Shangri-La, Pacific Place, Supreme Court Rd., 56th floor,* ☎ *852/2820–8590. Reservations essential. Jacket required. AE, D, MC, V.*

The Peak

PAN-ASIAN

$$–$$$ ✕ **Cafe Deco Bar and Grill.** If you're in Hong Kong on a clear day, take
★ the Peak tram to the top and dine at this spiffy double-decker restaurant overlooking the city. The views are stunning, and the decor is art deco to the hilt—you can spend an age looking at original period fittings. The menu is international, with Chinese, Indian (the kitchen has a proper tandoor), Italian, Mexican, and Thai dishes. The appetizer selection features some of the must-try dishes here, including crab cakes and barbecue-duck salad. Pizza and pasta choices are always popular, and the tandoori Himalayan kebab makes you feel as if you're up in the Nepalese mountains. The reasonably priced wine list features an extensive selection from around the world. Eat in the dining room, at the oyster bar, or in the ice-cream parlor. ⊠ *Peak Galleria, 118 Peak Rd., 1st level,* ☎ *852/2849–5111. AE, DC, MC, V.*

Wanchai

ASIAN

$$ ✕ **Dynasty.** Palm trees and live traditional Chinese music provide a total contrast to the modernity on display outside the windows. The menu is extensive, comprising luxurious abalone and bird's nest along with a variety of elegantly presented high-quality meat, seafood, and vegetable dishes (which can drive the dinner price for one up to HK$400). ⊠ *Renaissance Harbour View, 1 Harbour Rd.,* ☎ *852/2802–8888. AE, DC, MC, V.*

SHANGHAINESE

$$ ✕ **Lao Ching Hing.** One of the oldest Shanghainese restaurants in Hong Kong, Lao Ching Hing has been serving a variety of northern dishes since its opening in 1955. From simple offerings such as Shanghainese buns and dumplings to deluxe abalone, the range of choices is bound to include something that tickles your taste buds. Chicken in wine sauce and sautéed shrimps are among the favorites here. Try the freshwater crab if you're visiting in September and October—it's a seasonal specialty. ⊠ *Century Hong Kong Hotel, Basement, 283 Jaffe Rd.,* ☎ *852/2598–6080. AE, MC, V.*

Causeway Bay

ASIAN

$$ ✕ **Forum.** There are two elements that can't be detached from this prestigious restaurant—chef Yeung Koon-yat and his abalone. Yeung has made his name known from China to Europe with his special Ah Yat abalone, braised and served with a dense brown sauce. At a few hundred dollars, the price is steep, but if you want to truly experience this luxurious Asian ingredient, there's no better place than this comfortable restaurant. ⊠ *485 Lockhart Rd.,* ☎ *852/2891–2516. AE, DC, MC, V.*

CONTEMPORARY

$$$ ✕ **TOTT's Asian Grill & Bar.** Talk-of-the-Town sits atop the Excelsior Hotel looking down on Causeway Bay and the marina. The funky decor, including zebra-stripe chairs, a central oval bar, and designer tableware, is matched by the East-meets-West cuisine. Sushi and sashimi, tandoori dishes and pizzas, you name it—this restaurant has it all. Grilled rare tuna steak and roasted duck breast with Thai curry sauce are long-standing favorites. Live music kicks in later in the evening, offering a chance to burn off a few calories on the dance floor. ⊠ *Excelsior Hotel, 34th floor, 281 Gloucester Rd.,* ☎ *852/2837–6786. AE, DC, MC, V.*

ITALIAN

$$ ✕ **Fat Angelo's.** If you get pangs for some good, down-to-earth pasta, this is the place to get it. Fat Angelo's is an Italian American–style eatery that genuinely lets you enjoy a happy, hearty, and unpretentious meal. It gets packed, due in part to the lively atmosphere, but mostly because of the huge piles of pasta that load down the tables. Portions come in two sizes—"big" (serving five to eight) and "not-so-big" (serving two to four). Mains come with salad and bread basket included, and wine is served in water glasses. ⊠ *414 Jaffe Rd.,* ☎ *852/2574–6263. Reservations essential. AE, DC, MC, V.*

Stanley

EUROPEAN

$$ ✕ **Lucy's.** There's something incredibly comforting about Lucy's: Light-
★ ing is low, decor is warm, waiters are friendly and casual. A colorful chalkboard displays the chef's recommendations for the day as well as a list of wines from around the globe. The flavorful Stilton cheese, spinach, and walnut in phyllo pastry is the perfect way to warm·up your taste buds. The veal fillet with polenta and crispy Parma ham is delicate in texture and powerful in taste, while the sea bass with pumpkin mash is delightfully light and clear. ⊠ *64 Stanley's Main St.,* ☎ *852/2813–9055. Reservations essential. MC, V.*

Repulse Bay

EUROPEAN

$$$–$$$$ ✕ **The Verandah.** Step into another era at the Verandah. Walls are white,
★ doors are dark wood, fans turn silently high overhead, palm trees wave through the arched teak windows, and white-tuxedoed waiters attend to your every whim. A pianist plays tunes while budding Bog-

arts and Bergmans take in the romance. This is an unashamed celebration of the halcyon days of colonial rule. The chef artistically makes
use of ingredients from all fronts, and comes up with unique and impressive takes on such traditional dishes as lobster and rack of lamb.
⊠ *109 Repulse Bay Rd.,* ☎ *852/2812–2722. AE, DC, MC, V.*

Kowloon

Tsim Sha Tsui

ASIAN

$$ ✕ **T'ang Court.** Adorned with golden silk drapes and contemporary sculp-
tures, T'ang Court is one of the most elegant Chinese dining spots on
the Kowloon peninsula. Spread over two floors connected by a spiral
staircase, the restaurant delivers a distinctively modern, classy feel. Baked
Blue Point oysters with port wine is an unfamiliar yet beautiful appe-
tizer. The baked salty chicken, ordered half or whole, has the most del-
icately flavored meat and a gorgeous crisp skin. Lunchtime dim sum
are real delicacies. ⊠ *Great Eagle Hotel, 8 Peking Rd.,* ☎ *852/2375–*
1133 ext. 2250. Reservations essential. AE, DC, MC, V.

$$ ✕ **Wu Kong.** You won't miss the big sign hanging out in the air just
at the corner of Nathan Road and Peking Road, but you can easily
miss the tiny entrance that leads down to this unpretentious restaurant. The pigeon in wine sauce is an excellent appetizer to share. Vegetarian goose with vegetables wrapped in crisp bean-curd skin is
delicious. A whole fish smothered in a piquant sweet and vinegary sauce
makes you want more, but leave some space for the deep-fried sweet
ball whipped up with fluffy egg white stuffed with red bean and banana. ⊠ *Alpha House, basement, 23–33 Nathan Rd.,* ☎ *852/2366–*
7244. AE, DC, MC, V.

$ ✕ **Kung Tak Lam.** Health-conscious palates appreciate the simple
Shanghainese vegetarian food here. Don't turn your back when you
see the no-frills decor—it's the food that makes this joint so popular.
Try the cold noodle plates, which come with an array of sauces to mix
and make as sweet or as sour as you want. The bean-curd ravioli also
rates a rave. The mock meat is so tasty that it almost makes you forget you're in a vegetarian restaurant. ⊠ *45–47 Carnarvon Rd., 1st floor,*
☎ *852/2367–7881. AE, DC, V.*

EUROPEAN

$$$$ ✕ **Gaddi's.** A world unto itself, this is one of the few traditional French
★ fine-dining restaurants left in Hong Kong. It manages to remain a success by staying true to form. The cut-crystal chandeliers, sparkling silverware, and ornaments give a classical look. Seemingly psychic waiters
appear at all the right moments and not before, and the food is authentic fine dining at its best. Poached salmon ravioli with Osetra
caviar has a delicate flavor; the Barbary duck in a five-spice sauce set
on a puree of haricots verts demonstrates the chef's creative fusion of
French style and local ingredients—and it works remarkably well. End
with the cheese board or Gaddi's famous soufflé. ⊠ *Peninsula Hotel,*
Salisbury Rd., ☎ *852/2366–6251 ext. 3989. Reservations essential.*
Jacket and tie required for dinner. AE, DC, MC, V.

Outer Islands

Lamma Island

ASIAN

$$ ✕ **Lancombe.** This Cantonese seafood restaurant is Lamma's best
source for no-nonsense food at no-nonsense prices. The huge En-
glish/Cantonese menu offers seafood, seafood, and more seafood. Try
deep-fried squid, *garoupa* in sweet-corn sauce, broccoli in garlic, and

beef with black beans. Dishes come in three sizes; the small is suffi-
cient for most. Go through the front of the restaurant via the kitchen
(don't loiter, they're busy in there) to the terrace out back, where you'll
have a view of the sea and distant Peng Chau Island. ⊠ *47 Main St.,
Yung Shue Wan,* ☎ *852/2982–0881. AE, MC, V.*

LODGING

Hong Kong Island

Admiralty and Central

$$$$ 🏨 **Island Shangri-La.** From the moment you walk into the spacious lobby,
★ this deluxe hotel sparkles. With more than 780 Austrian crystal chandeliers, high ceilings, and huge windows allowing the sun in, there is a
sense of space and light. A 16-story glass-topped atrium houses the world's
largest Chinese landscape painting, *The Great Motherland of China,*
hanging from the 39th through 55th floors. Take the elevator from the
39th floor and watch the mainland's misty mountains drift by. Priding
itself on Asian hospitality, the staff is friendly and efficient. Extra-large
desks in each room are handy for business travelers, who can also plug
in laptop computers readily, while suites have in-room DVD players and
a host of movies. You can eat very well at the renowned French eatery
Petrus, the classy Lobster Bar, and the imperial Chinese outlet Summer
Palace. The tranquil outdoor pool and health club overlook Hong
Kong Park. ⊠ *Supreme Court Rd., 2 Pacific Pl., 88 Queensway,* ☎ *852/
2877–3838; 800/942–5050 in the U.S.,* 🖷 *852/2521–8742,* 🌐
*www.shangri-la.com. 531 rooms, 34 suites. 4 restaurants, bar, in-room
data ports, in-room safes, minibars, no-smoking floors, room service,
pool, barbershop, hair salon, gym, dry cleaning, laundry service, concierge, business services. AE, DC, MC, V.*

$$$$ 🏨 **Ritz-Carlton.** A rare gem of a hotel, the Ritz-Carlton couples an air
★ of refinement with superb hospitality. European antiques and reproductions mix with Asian accents, and everything from the Chippen-
dale-style furniture to the gilt-frame mirrors is spotless and shining.
Complimentary homemade cookies and mineral water in the reception
area hint at the level of customer care, and twin bathroom sinks, shoe
polish, a beautiful tea and coffee cabinet, and fresh flowers help make
you feel welcome in your own quarters. Rooms overlook either Victoria Harbour or Chater Garden. The main restaurant, Toscana, serves
northern Italian cuisine, and you can order from a special bath menu
from room service while soaking in your tub. The Executive Business
Center has Internet and E-mail access as well as computer worksta-
tions and color printers. ⊠ *3 Connaught Rd.,* ☎ *852/2877–6666; 800/
241–3333 in the U.S.,* 🖷 *852/2877–6778,* 🌐 *www.ritzcarlton.com.
187 rooms, 29 suites. 5 restaurants, bar, lounge, in-room data ports,
in-room safes, minibars, 13 no-smoking floors, room service, pool, gym,
shop, dry cleaning, laundry service, concierge, business services. AE,
DC, MC, V.*

$$$ 🏨 **Mandarin Oriental.** Long acclaimed as one of the world's great ho-
★ tels, the Mandarin Oriental represents Hong Kong high style. Other
luxury hotels in the city may be more modern, but the highly profes-
sional level of service here sets the Mandarin Oriental apart. The hotel
has a distinctly timeless elegance: the vast lobby is decorated with Asian
antiques, and the ample guest rooms have antique maps and prints,
traditional wooden furnishings, Eastern knickknacks, and glamorous
black-and-gold accents. Bucking the current trend, the rooms are de-
signed for luxury rather than mere efficiency. The top floor houses Vong,
a restaurant run by world-renowned chef Jean-Georges Vongerichten,
serving French-Asian fusion cuisine and overlooking the harbor. Man

Wah, on the 25th floor, serves Cantonese cuisine in a genteel atmosphere. A live band performs in the mezzanine Clipper Lounge early in the evening. Centrally located beside the Star Ferry concourse, the Mandarin is the lodging of choice for many a celebrity and VIP. ⊠ *5 Connaught Rd.,* ☎ *852/2522–0111,* FAX *852/2810–6190,* WEB *www.mandarin-oriental.com. 502 rooms, 40 suites. 4 restaurants, 3 bars, in-room data ports, in-room safes, minibars, room service, indoor pool, barbershop, hair salon, gym, dry cleaning, laundry service, concierge, business services. AE, DC, MC, V.*

Midlevels

$$ ⊞ **Bishop Lei International House.** Owned and operated by the Catholic diocese, this guest house is in a residential area of the Midlevels. Rooms are clean and functional, and half have harbor views. It's one of the few places on Hong Kong Island that combines a great view and proximity to the nightlife of Lan Kwai Fong and SoHo with an affordable price tag. ⊠ *4 Robinson Rd.,* ☎ *852/2868–0828,* FAX *852/2868–1551. 122 rooms, 81 suites. Restaurant, in-room data ports, minibars, pool, gym, laundry service, business services. AE, DC, MC, V.*

Wanchai

$$$$ ⊞ **Grand Hyatt.** "Grand" is the key word here. The Hyatt's art deco–
★ style lobby is topped by a ceiling painted by Italian artist Paola Dindo, while artful black-and-white photographs of classic Chinese scenes lend interest to the modern backdrop. A black-and-tan color scheme and light-wood paneling in the rooms and suites resemble the airy modern apartments you might see featured in an interior-design magazine. Work space has been subtly maximized, with twin phone lines and hidden fax machines in every room. A huge Internet TV on a rotating plinth with a cordless keyboard provides entertainment. The business center features an IBM room with IBM's latest technology and software, and access to Reuters Business Briefing. The Italian Grissini restaurant and the Cantonese One Harbour Road are notable—as is JJ's nightclub— and the ground-floor breakfast buffet is a decadent feast. The Grand Hyatt is close to the Wanchai Star Ferry, yet its slight removal from the main walkways assures less foot traffic than other high-profile hotels. Perhaps that's why Sir Andrew Lloyd Webber stayed here when *Cats* came to town, and why such celebrities as Luciano Pavarotti, Cindy Crawford, Sylvester Stallone, and Bruce Willis have also signed the guest list. ⊠ *1 Harbour Rd.,* ☎ *852/2588–1234, 866/333–8880 in the U.S.,* FAX *852/2802–0677,* WEB *www.hongkong.hyatt.com/hkggh. 519 rooms, 51 suites. 4 restaurants, bar, in-room data ports, in-room safes, minibars, room service, pool, hair salon, driving range, 2 tennis courts, gym, nightclub, dry cleaning, laundry service, concierge. AE, DC, MC, V.*

$$$ ⊞ **Renaissance Harbour View.** Sharing the Hong Kong Convention & Exhibition Centre complex with the Grand Hyatt is this more modest but equally attractive hotel. Guest rooms are medium-size and modern, with plenty of beveled-glass mirrors. Rooms on the executive floors are done in sophisticated dark colors and have large desks. More than half of the rooms have superb views overlooking the harbor. Amenities include the Dynasty and Scala restaurants, a cozy bar, one of the largest hotel outdoor pools in town, gardens, jogging trails, tennis courts, and health-club facilities on the recreation deck between the two hotels. The lobby lounge has one of the best easy-listening jazz bands in town, and is a popular rendezvous spot for local and visiting businesspeople. ⊠ *1 Harbour Rd.,* ☎ *852/2802–8888,* FAX *852/2802–8833,* WEB *www.re-naissancehotels.com/hkghv. 807 rooms, 53 suites. 4 restaurants, 2 bars, in-room data ports, in-room safes, minibars, no-smoking floors, room service, pool, barbershop, hair salon, gym, 4 tennis courts, dry cleaning, laundry service, concierge, business services. AE, DC, MC, V.*

$ ▦ **Harbour View International House.** This waterfront YMCA property offers small but clean and relatively inexpensive accommodations near the Wanchai Star Ferry pier. The best rooms face the harbor. It's well placed for travelers who want to attend cultural events in the evening: both the Arts Centre and Academy for Performing Arts are next door. Opposite Harbour View is the Hong Kong Convention & Exhibition Centre. The 16-story hostel provides free shuttle service to Causeway Bay and the Central Star Ferry. ⊠ *4 Harbour Rd.,* ☎ *852/2802–0111,* FAX *852/2802–9063. 320 rooms. Restaurant, no-smoking floor, laundry service. AE, DC, MC, V.*

$ ▦ **The Wesley.** This 21-story, moderately priced (for Hong Kong) hotel is a short walk from the Hong Kong Convention & Exhibition Centre, the Academy for Performing Arts, and the MTR. Rooms are small but pleasantly furnished, and the more spacious corner "suites" have alcove work areas. No health center or pool is on the premises, but you can use the facilities in Wesley's sister Grand Plaza Hotel, in Quarry Bay, for a discounted fee. A tram stop is right outside the door, and Pacific Place and the bars of Wanchai are close by. ⊠ *22 Hennessy Rd.,* ☎ *852/2866–6688,* FAX *852/2866–6613,* WEB *www.grandhotel.com. hk/wesley. 251 rooms. Restaurant, no-smoking floor, laundry service, business services. AE, DC, MC, V.*

Causeway Bay

$$ ▦ **The Excelsior.** The Excelsior opened in 1974 and remains one of Hong
★ Kong's most popular hotels. Though a veteran, it readily adapts to the changing demands of visitors. Eighty percent of the rooms enjoy splendid sea views, including the Hong Kong Yacht Club's neatly aligned yachts and boats. The spacious and clean rooms have large beds, long desks, and—according to the hotel—the cheapest minibars in town. The location is ideal for shopping and dining. At Talk of the Town (TOTT's), the top-floor restaurant-bar-nightclub, you can sample creative East-meets-West cuisine while listening to live music. The fitness-minded will appreciate the rooftop tennis courts, the well-equipped gym, and the jogging track in adjacent Victoria Park. A business center provides fax machines, computer terminals, and Internet access. ⊠ *281 Gloucester Rd.,* ☎ *852/2894–8888,* FAX *852/2895–6459,* WEB *www. mandarin-oriental.com/excelsior. 866 rooms, 21 suites. 6 restaurants, 2 bars, in-room data ports, in-room safes, minibars, no-smoking floor, room service, hair salon, 2 tennis courts, gym, shop, dry cleaning, laundry service, concierge, business services. AE, DC, MC, V.*

Kowloon

Tsim Sha Tsui

$$$$ ▦ **Inter-Continental Hong Kong.** The Inter-Continental is modern lux-
★ ury at its most opulent. Its world-class style and innovation are coupled with what may well be the best views in Hong Kong. All this has a price, but management is constantly coming up with packages that allow you to stay here without first having to rob a bank. The spacious, bright, and sophisticated rooms all have huge desks. Browse the Web through the TV, or plug in your own laptop and get a local high-speed connection. All rooms have sunken baths in Italian marble, and most suites have a separate steam shower. The health spa, also open to the public, is highly recommended for those who wouldn't mind feeling five years younger. The hotel's five restaurants include the high-profile Yü, serving spectacular seafood; Plume, with contemporary European cuisine; and The Steak House. ⊠ *18 Salisbury Rd.,* ☎ *852/2721–1211; 800/545–4000 in the U.S.,* FAX *852/2739–4546,* WEB *www.hongkong-ic.interconti.com. 510 rooms, 92 suites. 5 restaurants, pool, spa, gym, shop, dry cleaning, laundry service, concierge, business services. AE, DC, MC, V.*

$$$$ ⊞ **Peninsula.** Established in 1928, the Pen is a legend worldwide. Its
★ old-world style and impeccable details are evident throughout: colonial architecture, a columned and gilt-corniced lobby where high tea
is served, a fleet of Rolls-Royces, attentive room valets, luxurious bath
accessories. Classically European deep blue, gold, and ivory fabrics adorn
the spacious guest rooms and decadent suites; Chinese prints and furniture lend a subtle Eastern accent. Service is marvelously professional
and always discreet. All rooms have silent fax machines, deluxe bed-
side remotes that operate everything from the overhead lights to the
curtains on the windows, and the Pen's famous shoe box (staff retrieve
your shoes through an opening in the corridor). Huge corner suites allow
you to wallow in your private hot tub while you look out over the glorious city skyline. The superb spa treats you like royalty, with a pool,
sundeck, hot tub, sauna, and steam room. For some retail therapy head
to the swanky shops—including a branch of Shanghai Tang—located
in the Pen's exclusive shopping arcade or stop off at the in-house
Clarin's beauty spa, where you'll be buffed and polished into a blissful state. Restaurants include Gaddi's, one of the finest eateries in
town; Chinese Spring Moon; and the hippest of the hip rooftop restaurants, Felix. ✉ *Salisbury Rd.,* ☎ *852/2366–6251,* FAX *852/2722–4170,*
WEB *www.peninsula.com. 246 rooms, 54 suites. 7 restaurants, bar, in-
room data ports, in-room safes, minibars, room service, pool, hair salon,
spa, gym, shops, dry cleaning, laundry service, concierge, business services, helipad. AE, DC, MC, V.*

$$$ ⊞ **Great Eagle.** What Great Eagle lacks in exterior presence it makes
up for in understated comfort. The lobby ceiling is painted with beau-
tiful murals, and glowing backlit onyx pillars create a comfortable yet
sophisticated atmosphere. Guest rooms are comfortable yet elegant,
and all rooms on the Renaissance Club executive floors have fax ma-
chines and modem lines. The Bostonian restaurant offers a great va-
riety of seafood dishes, meats, and wines; Asian-attuned palates will
love the innovative and delicately presented Chinese dishes at T'ang
Court. ✉ *8 Peking Rd.,* ☎ *852/2375–1133,* FAX *852/2375–6611,* WEB
*www.gehotel.com. 473 rooms, 27 suites. 3 restaurants, 2 bars, lounge,
in-room data ports, in-room safes, minibars, no-smoking floors, room
service, pool, gym, shop, dry cleaning, laundry service, concierge, busi-
ness services. AE, DC, MC, V.*

$$$ ⊞ **Royal Garden.** A garden atrium with lush greenery and whispering
running water rises from the ground floor to the Royal Garden's
rooftop. Glass elevators, live classical music, trailing greenery, and trickling streams create a sense of serenity. All the soft, spacious, and comfortable rooms surround the atrium. Guests and locals alike appreciate
Sabatini, sister to the famous Roman restaurant, and the state-of-the-
art rooftop health club complete with tennis court, indoor-outdoor pool,
and spa services. Fashioned after an ancient Roman bath with fountains, a colorful sun mosaic, and underwater music, the pool is heated
and covered in winter by a huge bubble top. ✉ *69 Mody Rd.,* ☎ *852/
2721–5215,* FAX *852/2369–9976,* WEB *www.theroyalgardenhotel.com.hk.
374 rooms, 48 suites. 4 restaurants, bar, in-room data ports, in-room
safes, minibars, no-smoking floor, room service, indoor-outdoor pool,
hair salon, spa, tennis court, gym, shop, dance club, dry cleaning,
laundry service, concierge, business services. AE, DC, MC, V.*

$$ ⊞ **Kowloon.** A shimmering, mirrored exterior and a chrome, glass, and
★ marble lobby reflect the Kowloon's efficient, high-tech orientation.
Kowloon—Chinese for "nine dragons"—is the design theme here. The
triangular windows and pointed lobby ceiling, made from hundreds
of hand-blown Venetian-glass pyramids, represent dragons' teeth.
Lesser sibling to the adjacent Peninsula hotel, the Kowloon allows guests
to charge services at the Pen to their room account. Although the clean

and functional guest rooms are small, each is equipped with a "work and entertainment center" that includes Web and E-mail access, on-line news, and a CD-ROM drive, as well as a fax machine. On the southern tip of Nathan Road's Golden Mile, the Kowloon is next door to the Tsim Sha Tsui MTR and minutes from the Star Ferry. ✉ *19–21 Nathan Rd.,* ☎ *852/2929–2888,* ⛕ *852/2739–9811,* 🌐 *www.peninsula.com. 719 rooms, 17 suites. 3 restaurants, in-room data ports, minibars, no-smoking floors, room service, hair salon, shop, dry cleaning, laundry service, business services. AE, DC, MC, V.*

$ 🛏 **Salisbury YMCA.** If you can't afford the Pen, settle at this five-star
★ Y, where you can enjoy the same magnificent harbor view at a fraction of the price. You can't compare the YMCAs in Hong Kong with the Ys in other parts of the world in terms of either price tag or amenities. The Salisbury YMCA, Hong Kong's most popular, sits on a huge, sterile-looking block opposite the Cultural Centre, Space Museum, and Art Museum—an excellent location for theater, art, and concert crawls. Thanks to an upgrade in mid-2000, the clean rooms are now polished up in pastels and equipped with modem lines. The superb health facilities include a fitness center, sauna, hot tub, dance studio, and even an indoor climbing wall. The Y also has a beautiful garden, lecture rooms, a conference room with a built-in stage, and a children's library. The restaurants serve good, cheap food, and the shops are very affordable. ✉ *41 Salisbury Rd.,* ☎ *852/2369–2211,* ⛕ *852/2739–9315,* 🌐 *www.ymcahk.org.hk. 303 rooms, 62 suites. 2 restaurants, lounge, in-room data ports, in-room safes, room service, indoor pool, hair salon, gym, squash, shop, coin laundry, meeting room. AE, DC, MC, V.*

New Territories and the Outer Islands

New Territories

$ 🛏 **Gold Coast.** Opened in 1994, the Gold Coast is Hong Kong's first conference resort. Its vast complex on Kowloon's western harbor front is well connected to the city center by public bus, and the hotel runs shuttle buses to the MTR and the airport. Inside, the decor is extravagant, with acres of marble, miles of wrought-iron balustrades, a grand ballroom, and palm-court atriums. Facilities include a large marina, a water-sports area, tennis courts, volleyball and soccer fields, pitch-and-putt golf, a full-service spa, and even an archery range. All guest rooms face the sea over a beautiful beach. Last, but not necessarily least, this is the only hotel in Hong Kong with equipment for Outward Bound courses. ✉ *1 Castle Peak Rd., Tuen Mun, New Territories,* ☎ *852/ 2452–8888,* ⛕ *852/2440–7368,* 🌐 *www.goldcoasthotel.com.hk. 440 rooms, 10 suites. 4 restaurants, bar, in-room data ports, minibars, room service, pool, hair salon, spa, putting green, 2 tennis courts, archery, gym, soccer, volleyball, boating, laundry service, business services. AE, DC, MC, V.*

Cheung Chau Island

$ 🛏 **Cheung Chau Warwick.** Miles from the fast-paced city, this six-story beachfront nook aims to assure you a carefree and relaxed stay—a nice pool and a sandy beach take the place of business services and executive floors. An hour by ferry from Hong Kong Island, it's a popular getaway for Hong Kong families. There are no cars on the leisurely island, but the hotel is just a 10-minute walk from the pier. ✉ *East Bay, Cheung Chau,* ☎ *852/2981–0081,* ⛕ *852/2981–9174. 71 rooms. 2 restaurants, pool, beach. AE, DC, MC, V.*

Lantau Island

$ 🛏 **Silvermine Beach Hotel.** This bayside resort in Mui Wo steers entirely clear of Hong Kong's sound and fury. It's an hour by ferry from

Hong Kong Island, then a five-minute walk from the pier. A pool is open in summer, and a tennis court, exercise room, and sauna are open year-round. The island of Lantau has plenty of sights of its own, including the bronze statue Tin Tan Buddha, the Po Lin Monastery, and Tai O fishing village; and you'll thank yourself for hiking a section of the Lantau Island trail—the scenery is unexpectedly beautiful. ✉ *D.D. 2, Lot 648 Silvermine Bay, Mui Wo, Lantau Island*, ☎ *852/2984–8295*, FAX *852/2984–1907. 128 rooms, 2 suites. 2 restaurants, pool, gym. AE, DC, MC, V.*

NIGHTLIFE AND THE ARTS

The Arts

The most comprehensive calendar of cultural events is *HK Magazine,* a free weekly newspaper distributed each Friday to many restaurants, stores, and bars. You can read daily reviews in the Features section of the *South China Morning Post*, which also has an entertainment pull-out every Friday called *24/7.* The free monthly *City News* newspaper also lists events and is available at City Hall. **City Hall** (✉ By Star Ferry, Hong Kong Island, ☎ 852/2921–2840) has posters and huge bulletin boards listing events and ticket availability. Tickets for cultural events held in government centers can be purchased in booths on the ground floor by the main entrance. **URBTIX** (☎ 852/2734–9009) outlets are the easiest place to purchase tickets for most general performances; there are branches at City Hall and the Hong Kong Arts Centre.

Chinese Opera

Cantonese Opera. There are 10 Cantonese opera troupes in Hong Kong, as well as many amateur singing groups. These groups perform so-called street opera in venues such as the Temple Street Night Market (almost every night), at temple fairs, in City Hall, or in playgrounds under the auspices of the Urban Council (☎ 852/2922–8008). Visitors unfamiliar with the form are sometimes alienated by the strange sounds of this highly complex and extremely sophisticated art form. Every gesture has its own meaning; in fact, there are 50 different gestures for the hand alone. It is best to have a local friend translate the gestures, as the stories are so complex that they make Wagner or Verdi librettos seem almost simplistic.

Peking Opera. A highly stylized musical performance, this type of opera employs higher-pitched voices than Cantonese opera. It is an older opera form and more respected for its classical traditions. Several highly regarded troupes visit Hong Kong from the mainland each year. They perform in City Hall or at special temple ceremonies. Call the Urban Council (☎ 852/2922–8008) for information.

Dance

Hong Kong Dance Company (☎ 852/2853–2642). This company has been promoting the art of Chinese dance and choreographing new work with Chinese historical themes since 1981. The 30-odd members are experts in folk and classical dance. Sponsored by the Urban Council, they perform about three times a month throughout the territory.

Performance Halls

HONG KONG ISLAND

City Hall (✉ Edinburgh Pl., by Star Ferry, Central, ☎ 852/2921–2840). Classical music, theatrical performances, films, and art exhibitions are presented at this complex's large auditorium, recital hall, and theater. **Hong Kong Academy for Performing Arts** (✉ 1 Gloucester Rd., Wanchai, ☎ 852/2584–8500). This arts school has two major theaters, each seating 1,600 people, plus a 200-seat studio theater and a 500-seat outdoor theater. Performances include local and international drama, modern and classical dance, and music concerts.

Hong Kong Arts Centre (⊠ 2 Harbour Rd., Wanchai, ☎ 852/2582–0232). Several floors of auditoriums, rehearsal halls, and recital rooms welcome local and visiting performers. Some of the best independent, classic, and documentary films are shown, often with themes that focus on a particular country, period, or well-known director.

Hong Kong Fringe Club (⊠ 2 Lower Albert Rd., Central, ☎ 852/2521–7251). This club hosts some of Hong Kong's most innovative visiting and local entertainment and art exhibitions. Shows range from the blatantly amateur to the dazzlingly professional. It also has good jazz, avant-garde drama, and many other events.

Queen Elizabeth Stadium (⊠ 18 Oi Kwan Rd., Wanchai, ☎ 852/2591–1346). Although basically a sports stadium, this 3,500-seat venue frequently presents ballet and orchestral and pop concerts.

KOWLOON

Broadway Cinemathèque (⊠ Prosperous Garden, 3 Public Square St., Yau Ma Tei, ☎ 852/2388–3188). The train station–like design of this art-house cinema is award winning; foreign and independent films are announced on a departure board (local films are rare). Here you can read the latest reel-world magazines from around the globe in a minilibrary. A shop sells new and vintage film posters, and there's a coffee bar as well. Use the Temple Street exit at the Yau Ma Tei MTR to get here.

Hong Kong Coliseum (⊠ 9 Cheong Wan Rd., Hunghom Railway Station, Hunghom, ☎ 852/2355–7234). This 12,000-plus seat stadium presents everything from basketball to ballet, from skating polar bears to local and international pop stars.

Hong Kong Cultural Centre (⊠ 10 Salisbury Rd., ☎ 852/2734–2009). This venue for shows and conferences contains the Grand Theatre, which seats 1,750, and a concert hall, which accommodates 2,100. The center is used by visiting and local artists, whose performances range from opera to ballet to orchestral music.

NEW TERRITORIES

Tsuen Wan Town Hall (⊠ 72 Tai Ho Rd., Tsuen Wan, ☎ 852/2414–0144; MTR to Tsuen Wan Station). Although it's off the beaten track, this auditorium has a constant stream of local and international performers. Groups include everything from the Warsaw Philharmonic to troupes of Chinese acrobats. It has a seating capacity of 1,400 and probably the best acoustics of all the performance halls in Hong Kong.

Shatin Town Hall (⊠ 1 Yuen Wo Rd., Shatin, ☎ 852/2694–2511). This impressive building, attached to New Town Plaza, an enormous shopping arcade, is a five-minute walk from the KCR station at Shatin. It hosts cultural events including dance, drama, and concert performances.

Performing-Arts Ensembles

Hong Kong Philharmonic Orchestra (☎ 852/2721–2320; 852/2721–2030 for ticket information). Almost 100 musicians from Hong Kong, the United States, Australia, and Europe perform everything from classical to avant-garde to contemporary music by Chinese composers. World-class soloists join the ensemble regularly. Performances are usually held Friday and Saturday at 8 PM in City Hall or in recital halls in the New Territories.

Hong Kong Chinese Orchestra (☎ 852/2853–2622). Created in 1977 by the Urban Council, this group performs only Chinese works. The orchestra consists of strings, plucked instruments, wind, and percussion.

Nightlife

Hong Kong's nightlife districts—Lan Kwai Fong and Wanchai are two of the best known—announce themselves with a riot of neon, heralding frenetic after-hours action. Hectic workdays make way for an even busier night scene. Clubs and bars fill to capacity nightly, evening markets pack in shoppers looking for bargains, cinemas pop corn as fast as they can, and theaters and concert halls prepare for full houses. Hong Kong has sophisticated piano bars, elegant lounges, superstrobe discos, rowdy pubs, smoky jazz dens, hostess clubs, and classy bars.

Think twice before succumbing to the city's raunchier hideaways. If you stumble into one, check out cover and hostess charges *before* you get too comfortable. Pay for each round of drinks as it's served (by cash rather than credit card), and never sign any blank checks. Hong Kong is a surprisingly safe place, but as in every tourist destination, the art of the tourist rip-off is well practiced to some degree. If you're unsure, visit spots that are sign-carrying members of the Hong Kong Tourist Board (HKTB). You can pick up its free membership listing (including approved restaurants and nightspots) at any HKTB Visitor Information Centre.

Nightclubs

C Club (⊠ Basement, California Tower, 32–34 D'Aguilar St., Lan Kwai Fong, Central, ☎ 852/2526–1139) is the latest to open in the popular Lan Kwai Fong area. Star sightings among the upscale, wall-to-wall crowd are common. **Club 97** (⊠ 9 Lan Kwai Fong, Central, ☎ 852/2810–9333 or 852/2186–1819), which charges a HK$97 admission, is a small, glitzy, often crowded gathering spot for the "beautiful people." The crowds don't arrive until well after midnight at **Propaganda** (⊠ 1 Hollywood Rd., lower ground floor, Central, ☎ 852/2868–1316), off a quaint but steep cobblestone street. It's one of the most popular gay clubs in the territory, with a stylish art deco bar area and a dance floor with pseudo go-go boys.

Cocktail and Piano Bars

High-altitude harbor gazing is the main attraction at the Island Shangri-La's 56th-floor music lounge, **Cyrano** (⊠ 2 Pacific Pl., Supreme Court Rd., 88 Queensway, ☎ 852/2820–8591). The Peninsula's **Felix Bar** (⊠ Salisbury Rd., Tsim Sha Tsui, ☎ 852/2366–6251) not only has a brilliant view of the harbor, but the impressive bar and disco were designed by the visionary Philippe Starck. At the Excelsior's **Talk of the Town** (⊠ 281 Gloucester Rd., Causeway Bay, ☎ 852/2837–6786), or TOTT's, you're greeted by a 270-degree vista of Hong Kong Harbour.

Discos

As its name suggests, **Club Ing** (⊠ 4/F, Renaissance Harbour View, 1 Harbour Rd., Wanchai, ☎ 852/2824–0523) is about slipping into a pair of dancing shoes and hitting the floor. The perennial favorite nightspot is **JJ's** (⊠ Grand Hyatt, 1 Harbour Rd., Wanchai, ☎ 852/2588–1234), which contains a disco and a pizza lounge with a dart board and a bar screening major sporting events, but is best remembered for its flashy disco lights, good house band, and the wall-to-wall suits and their escorts. The **Lost City** (⊠ Chinachem Golden Plaza, 77 Mody Rd., Tsim Sha Tsui East, ☎ 852/2311–1111) is undoubtedly the most popular and thriving disco for young Chinese. A cross between a cheesy B-grade film set, Las Vegas camp glamour, and an over-the-top Broadway production, it contains a massive 100,000 square ft of disco areas, karaoke rooms, a kitschy café, and plenty of zebra-stripe sofas and chairs.

Hostess Clubs

Club BBoss (✉ Mandarin Plaza, Tsim Sha Tsui East, Kowloon, ☎ 852/2369–2883) is the grandest and most boisterous of the hostess clubs. Executives, mostly locals, entertain in this oddly named club, tended by a staff of more than 1,000. If your VIP room is too far from the entrance, you can rent an electrified vintage Rolls Royce and purr around an indoor roadway. Be warned that this is tycoon territory, where a bottle of brandy can cost HK$18,000. Along the harbor in Kowloon is **Club Deluxe** (2/F, New World Centre, Salisbury Rd., Kowloon, ☎ 852/2721–0277), a large, luxurious dance lounge that caters to the karaoke crowd.

Jazz and Folk Clubs

The Jazz Club (✉ 2/F, California Entertainment Bldg., 34–36 D'Aguilar St., Central, ☎ 852/2845–8477) presents a wide selection of local jazz, R&B, and soul talent as well as top-notch international acts every month. **Ned Kelly's Last Stand** (✉ 11A Ashley Rd., Tsim Sha Tsui, ☎ 852/2376–0562) is an Aussie-managed home for pub meals and Dixieland, courtesy of Ken Bennett's Kowloon Honkers. Get here early, before 10 PM, to get a comfortable seat. Wanchai's unpretentious alternative to the topless bar scene is the **Wanch** (✉ 54 Jaffe Rd., Wanchai, ☎ 852/2861–1621), providing live local folk and rock performances.

Pubs

Trendy Knutsford Terrace is an out-of-the-way strip in Tsim Sha Tsui, where a new breed of bars and restaurants has made its home. Tropical rhythms bathe the Caribbean-inspired **Bahama Mama's** (✉ 4–5 Knutsford Terr., ☎ 852/2368–2121). In Central the business folk flock to the British-managed, oak-beamed **Bull & Bear** (✉ 10 Harcourt Rd., Central, ☎ 852/2526–1953). This place draws all types—a large share of whom are English expats—serves standard pub fare, and is known to get a little rowdy on weekends. Both branches of the Irish pub **Delaney's** (✉ Basement, 71–77 Peking Rd., Tsim Sha Tsui, ☎ 852/2301–3980; ✉ 2/F 1 Capital Pl., 18 Luard Rd., Wanchai, ☎ 852/2804–2880) have interiors that were "made in Ireland" and shipped to Hong Kong. There's Guinness and Delaney's ale (a specialty microbrew) on tap, private corner "snugs," and a menu of Irish specialties.

Café Bars

Sophisticated guys and dolls flock to **Alibi** (✉ 73 Wyndham St., Central, ☎ 852/2167–1676), a cool bar (with fine dining upstairs) that's wall to wall with bodies most nights. The arts-minded mingle at the **Hong Kong Fringe Club** (✉ 2 Lower Albert Rd., Central, ☎ 852/2521–7251), in a historic redbrick building that also houses the members-only Foreign Correspondents Club. The tiny bar of **La Dolce Vita** (✉ G/F, 9 Lan Kwai Fong, Central, ☎ 852/2810–9333), underneath its sister restaurant, Post 97, and next to its other sibling, Club 97, often spills out onto the pavement. With sleek decor, this is a place to be seen. Just on the outskirts of the Fong, as the area is known, is the fashionable **Petticoat Lane** (✉ 2 Tun Wo La., Central, ☎ 852/2973–0642)—a little difficult to find but definitely worth the wandering (it's near the Midlevels escalator between Lyndhurst Terrace and Hollywood Road). It opened as a gay bar, but individuals of all preferences lounge in its opulent, plush pink setting and quaint outdoor area. Hotel bars are frequented by both locals and expats. For the more laid-back set, the tiny **Phibi** (✉ Basement, 79 Wyndham St., Central, entrance off Pottinger St., ☎ 852/2869–4469), which really gets going around 11 PM, plays dance music. The **Hyatt Regency**'s **Chin Chin** or **Nathan's** (✉ 67 Nathan Rd., Tsim Sha Tsui, ☎ 852/2311–1234) are likely

from September through June. Some 65 races are held at two race tracks—**Happy Valley,** on Hong Kong Island, and **Shatin,** in the New Territories. Shatin's racecourse is one of the most modern in the world. Both courses have huge video screens at the finish line so that gamblers can see what is happening each foot of the way. The **Hong Kong Tourist Board** (☏ 852/2566–3995) organizes tours to the club and track from HK$245 to HK$490. Or as an alternative, you can view races from the public stands, where the atmosphere is lively and loud. The cost is only HK$10; it provides a truly local experience.

Rugby

One weekend every spring, usually in March, the whole town goes rugby mad when Hong Kong hosts the international tournament of Sevens-a-Side teams, otherwise known as the Rugby Sevens or just the Sevens, at the Hong Kong Stadium. To avoid camping outside the stadium all night to buy tickets, you can purchase them in advance from an overseas agent. For a list of agents contact the **Hong Kong Rugby Football Union** (✉ *Sports House, 1 Stadium Path, Room 2003, So Kon Po, Causeway Bay,* ☏ *852/2504–8300,* ℻ *852/2576–7237).*

SHOPPING

Although Hong Kong is no longer the mercantile paradise it once was, many shopping aficionados still swear by it, returning year after year for such items as Chinese antiques, art from China and Southeast Asia, porcelain, tea and tea ware, pearls, watches, cameras, computers and peripherals, eyeglasses, silk sheets and kimonos, tailor-made suits, and designer clothes found in off-the-beaten-path outlets. The Hong Kong Tourist Board publishes two comprehensive guides, *The Official Dining, Entertainment & Shopping Directory* and *Factory Outlets for Locally Made Fashion and Jewellery,* both of which list stores approved by the HKTB for their merchandise and service policies. The guides can be obtained free at the HKTB **Visitor Information Centres.**

If you are short on time, visiting one of Hong Kong's many malls might be the answer. On Hong Kong Island, in Central District, the main ones are Landmark, Prince's Building, Shun Tak Centre, Admiralty Centre, and Pacific Place. Times Square is in Causeway Bay and Cityplaza in Quarry Bay. In Kowloon, just next to the Star Ferry, is Harbour City, encompassing the Ocean Terminal and Ocean Centre. Up the street a bit is the New World Centre and Palace Mall. In Kowloon Tong is Festival Walk.

For expert guidance try **Asian Cajun Ltd.** (✉ 12 Scenic Villa Dr., 4th floor, Pokfulam, ☏ 852/2817–3687, ℻ 852/2855–9571), which offers customized shopping tours at US$100 per hour.

Hong Kong Island

Art and Antiques

Hollywood Road is the place to look for Chinese antiques and collectibles. **Altfield Gallery** (✉ Prince's Bldg., Central, ☏ 852/2537–6370) carries furniture, fabrics, and collectibles from all over Asia. **C. L. Ma Antiques** (✉ 43–55 Wyndham St., Central, ☏ 852/2525–4369) has Ming dynasty–style reproductions, especially large carved chests and tables made of unlacquered wood. **Eastern Dreams** (✉ 47A Hollywood Rd., Central, ☏ 852/2544–2804; ✉ 4 Shelley St., Central, ☏ 852/2524–4787) has antique and reproduction furniture, screens, and curios. **Galerie La Vong** (✉ 1 Lan Kwai Fong, 13th floor, Central, ☏ 852/2869–6863) is the place to see the works of today's leading Vietnamese artists, whose creations reveal a combination of French and Chinese influences, as well as purely contemporary styles. **Honeychurch Antiques** (✉ 29 Hollywood Rd., Central, ☎ 852/2543–2433) is known especially for antique silver jewelry from Southeast Asia, China, and England. **Schoeni Fine Arts** (✉ 27 Hollywood Rd., Central, ☎ 852/2542–3143) sells Japanese, Chinese, and Thai antiques; Chinese silverware, such as opium boxes; and rare Chinese pottery. **Teresa Coleman** (✉ 79 Wyndham St., Central, ☎ 852/2526–2450) carries antique embroidered pieces and unusual Chinese collectibles.

Department Stores

Blanc de Chine (✉ 12 Pedder St., Central, ☎ 852/2524–7875) has beautiful Chinese clothes, in styles similar to those at the more famous Shanghai Tang, but in subtler colors, plus reproductions of antique snuffboxes and silver mirrors and picture frames. **Shanghai Tang Department Store** (✉ 12 Pedder St., Central, ☎ 852/2525–7333), on the ground floor of the Pedder Building, is the current retro rage in Hong Kong, selling old-fashioned Mandarin suits for men and women, either custom-made or ready-to-wear, and Chinese memorabilia, including novelty watches depicting Mao Zedong and Deng Xiaoping.

CHINESE DEPARTMENT STORES

Traditionally, Chinese department stores specialize in merchandise from the People's Republic of China, everything from fine silk and hand-stitched, embroidered tablecloths to porcelain and jade. Many also carry everyday goods ranging from pots and pans to school stationery.

China Resources Centre (✉ Yee Wo St., Causeway Bay, ☎ 852/2890–8321; Argyle Centre, Tower I, 65 Argyle St., Mongkok, Kowloon, ☎ 852/2391–3191) is particularly good for fabrics, white porcelain, silk-embroidered clothing, jewelry, and carpets. **Chinese Arts & Crafts** (✉ 3 Salisbury Rd., Tsim Sha Tsui, Kowloon, ☎ 852/2735–4061; China Resources Bldg., 26 Harbour Rd., Wanchai, ☎ 852/2839–1888; Shop 230, Pacific Place, 88 Queensway, Central, ☎ 852/2523–3933) has a number of branches. **Yue Hwa Chinese Products Emporium** (✉ Pearl City Plaza, 24-36 Paterson St., Causeway Bay, ☎ 852/2808–1363; Basement, Mirador Mansion, 54-64 Nathan Rd., Tsim Sha Tsui, Kowloon, ☎ 852/2368–9165; Park Lane Shopping Blvd., 143-161 Nathan Rd., Tsim Sha Tsui, Kowloon, ☎ 852/2739–3888) sells a wide selection of Chinese goods.

Factory Outlets

The Joyce Warehouse (✉ 34 Horizon Plaza, 2 Lee Wing St., Ap Lei Chau, ☎ 852/2814–8313) has taken shopaholic locals by storm. This is the outlet for women's and men's fashions that are sold in the ritzy Joyce Boutiques in Central and Pacific Place, with labels by major designers. The **Pedder Building** (✉ 12 Pedder St., Central), just a few feet from a Central MTR exit, contains five floors of small shops, most offering discounts of around 30% off retail. **Cascal** (☎ 852/2523–4999) has Celine, Dior, and Prada bags at about 20% off retail. **Ça Va** (☎ 852/2537–7174) has fabulous knitwear, along with suits and designer casual wear. **Shopper's World–Safari** (☎ 852/2523–1950) has more variety than most outlets and a small upstairs department with men's fashions. **Stanley Village Market** (Stanley Village; take Bus 6, 6A, or 260 from the Central Bus Terminus) is a popular haunt for designer sportswear, washable silk, and cashmere sweaters at factory outlet prices and in Western sizes. **China Town** (✉ 39 Stanley Main St., ☎ 852/2798–2489) has bargains on cashmere sweaters. **Sun and Moon Fashion Shop** (✉ 18A–B Stanley Main St., ☎ no phone) sells casual wear, with good bargains on such familiar names as L. L. Bean, Yves St. Laurent, and Talbot's. The market is at its most enjoyable on weekdays, when it's less crowded.

Clothing—Tailor Made

A-Man Hing Cheong Co., Ltd. (✉ Mandarin Oriental Hotel, Central, ☎ 852/2522–3336) is known for European-cut men's suits and custom shirts and has its own list of distinguished clients. **Ascot Chang** (✉ Prince's Bldg., Central, ☎ 852/2523–3663; ✉ Peninsula Hotel, Tsim Sha Tsui, ☎ 852/2366–2398; ✉ Regent Hotel, Tsim Sha Tsui, ☎ 852/2367–8319) has specialized in making shirts for men since 1949.

Jewelry

Kai-Yin Lo (✉ Pacific Place, Admiralty, ☎ 852/2840–0066; ✉ Mandarin Hotel, Central, ☎ 852/2524–8238; ✉ Peninsula Hotel, Tsim Sha Tsui, ☎ 852/2721–9623) has fabulous modern jewelry with an Asian influence. **K. S. Sze & Sons** (✉ Mandarin Oriental Hotel, ☎ 852/2524–2803) is known for its fair prices on one-of-a-kind pearl and gemstone creations. **Po Kwong** (✉ 82 Queen's Rd., Central, ☎ 852/2521–4686) is a good place to shop for South Sea Island pearls and other varieties. **The Showroom** (✉ Room 1203, 12th floor, Central Bldg., Pedder St., Central, ☎ 852/2525–7085) specializes in creative pieces using diamonds and other gems.

JEWELRY FACTORY OUTLETS

TSL Jewellery Showroom (✉ Wah Ming Bldg., 34 Wong Chuk Hang Rd., Aberdeen, ☎ 852/2873–2618; ✉ Summit Bldg., 30 Man Yue St., Hung Hom, ☎ 852/2764–4109) has fairly good prices on diamonds and other precious stones in unique settings, and each location has an on-premises workshop where you can watch the jewelry being made.

Kung Fu Supplies

Kung Fu Supplies Co. (✉ 188 Johnston Rd., Wanchai, ☎ 852/2891–1912) is the most convenient place to buy your drum cymbal, leather boots, sword, whip, double dagger, studded wrist bracelet, Bruce Lee kempo gloves, and other kung fu exotica.

Photographic Equipment

Photo Scientific Appliances (✉ 6 Stanley St., Central, ☎ 852/2522–1903) has excellent prices on a wide variety of cameras and other photographic equipment.

Tea

Fook Ming Tong Tea Shop (✉ Prince's Bldg., Central, ☎ 852/2521–0337; other branches at Mitsukoshi and Sogo department stores in Causeway Bay and Ocean Terminal, Harbour Centre, Tsim Sha Tsui) is a mecca for the sophisticated tea shopper. You can get superb teas in beautifully designed tins or invest in some antique clay tea ware.

Outdoor Markets

Hong Kong's best-known market is **Stanley Village Market** (✉ south side of Hong Kong Island; Bus 6, 6A, 6X or 260 from terminus under Exchange Square in Central), a crowded haunt popular with Western residents and tourists looking for designer sportswear, washable silk, and cashmere sweaters at factory outlet prices and in Western sizes. Dozens and dozens of shops line a main street so narrow that awnings from each side meet in the middle. The stores open at about 10 and close between 5 and 6.

Kowloon

Art and Antiques

Charlotte Horstmann and Gerald Godfrey (✉ Ocean Terminal, Tsim Sha Tsui, ☎ 852/2735–7167) is good for wood carvings, bronze ware, and antique furniture. **Eileen Kershaw** (✉ Peninsula Hotel, Tsim Sha Tsui, ☎ 852/2366–4083) has fine Chinese porcelain and jade carvings.

Clothing—Tailor Made

Jimmy Chen (✉ Hongkong Hotel, Tsim Sha Tsui, ☎ 852/2730–5045; ✉ Peninsula Hotel, Tsim Sha Tsui, ☎ 852/2722–1888) can make everything from a suit to a shirt for a man or woman. **Sam's Tailor** (✉ Shop K, Burlington Arcade, 94 Nathan Rd., Tsim Sha Tsui, ☎ 852/2721–8375) is one of the most famous of all Hong Kong's men's and women's custom tailors, having outfitted everyone from the royal families of Europe to American and British politicians. **W. W. Chan & Sons** (✉ Burlington House, 92–94 Nathan Rd., Tsim Sha Tsui, ☎ 852/2366–9738) is known for top-quality classic cuts and has bolts and bolts of fine European fabrics from which to choose. **Irene Fashions** (✉ Burlington House, 92–94 Nathan Rd., Tsim Sha Tsui, ☎ 852/2367–5588) is the women's division of W. W. Chan.

Jewelry

China Handicrafts & Gem House ✉ 25A Mody Rd., Tsim Sha Tsui East, Kowloon, ☎ 852/2311–9703) sells loose gemstones. **Chow Sang Sang** (✉ 74 Queen's Rd., Central, ☎ 852/2526–2009; Tung Hing Bldg., Nathan Rd., Mongkok, Kowloon, ☎ 852/2782–3633) has shops all over. **Chow Tai Fook** (✉ 29 Queen's Rd., Central, ☎ 852/2523–7128; Shop 14, Park Lane Blvd., 143–161 Nathan Rd., Tsim Sha Tsui, Kowloon, ☎ 852/2735–7966) is one of the biggest jewelry chains. The **Hongkong Jade House** (✉ 162 Ocean Terminal, Tsim Sha Tsui, Kowloon, ☎ 852/2736–1232) is a good place to shop for Hong Kong's most famous stone. The jade here, which comes both loose and in settings, ranges in color from green to shades of purple, orange, yellow, brown, white, and violet. **Tse Sui Luen** (✉ 35 Queen's Rd., Central, ☎ 852/2921–8800; 190 Nathan Rd., Tsim Sha Tsui, Kowloon, ☎ 852/2926–3210) specializes in gold and jade.

Outdoor Markets

The **Flower Market** (✉ Flower St., near Prince Edward MTR station) is a collection of street stalls offering cut flowers and potted plants, with a few outlets specializing in plastic plants and silk flowers. The **Jade Market** (✉ Kansu St. off Nathan Rd., Yau Ma Tei) displays jade in every form, color, shape, and size. Some trinkets are reasonably priced, but unless you know a lot about jade, don't be tempted into buying expensive items. The **Ladies Market,** outside the Mong Kok MTR subway station along Mong Kok Road, has outdoor stalls full of women's clothes. If you rummage around enough, you might find a designer item or two at rock-bottom prices. **Temple Street** (✉ Near Jordan MTR station) becomes an open-air market at night, filled with a colorful collection of clothes, handbags, electrical goods, gadgets, and all sorts of household items. The market, stretching for almost a mile, is one of Hong Kong's liveliest nighttime shopping experiences.

SIDE TRIP TO MACAU

In Chinese hands since 1999 after almost 450 years of Portuguese rule, Macau is one of the few places in the world that can legitimately lay claim to being a hybrid of East and West. It had a brief period of prosperity in the 16th century but then entered a long decline made worse by the rise of nearby Hong Kong. It is now in the midst of something like a rebirth, although it is still poorer and more traditional than its brash neighbor, and it is known within the region primarily for its good food, graceful colonial buildings, and bustling casinos. Macau's 450,000 people live squeezed into its 9-square-mi peninsula and two outlying islands, Taipa and Coloane; while most of them speak Cantonese, English is widely used in tourist areas.

Exploring Macau

★ **Largo do Senado** is the heart of the old city and perhaps the most charming square in Asia, surrounded by an exquisite collection of brilliantly colored colonial buildings. It was renovated in 1994 with black-and-white stone tiles, benches, plants, and a fountain. It is occupied day and night by old women chatting and children playing. At night the buildings are lighted up by spotlights, and the square takes on an even more alluring atmosphere. ✉ *Av. Almeida Ribeiro.*

The **Leal Senado,** which anchors the southern end of Largo do Senado, is a magnificent example of late-18th-century colonial architecture. The Senate serves as a municipal government and, in addition to its political functions, the building houses a gallery and library, along with a charming garden hidden away in back. ✉ *Largo do Senado, 2nd floor, at Rua Dr. Soares.* ☉ *Mon.–Sat. 1–7.*

Macau Forum. This multipurpose facility has two interesting museums. The **Grand Prix Museum** (☎ 853/798–4126; 🎫 10 patacas, simulator 20 patacas; ☉ daily 10–6) is a required stop for all racing fans, with an exquisite collection of winners' cars. There are two simulators—one of which is interactive—in which you can experience the sensation of driving in the Grand Prix. The **Wine Museum** (🎫 15 patacas, ☉ daily 10–6), where you're greeted with a glass of wine, lovingly illustrates the history of wine making and features antique wine presses, Portuguese wine fraternity costumes, and 750 different Portuguese wines. ✉ *Rua Luís Gonzaga Gomes,* ☎ *853/798–4188.*

Maritime Museum. This gem of a museum is ideally situated on the waterfront in **Barra Square,** at the southern tip of the peninsula. The four-story building resembles a sailing ship; its collection includes a breathtaking series of detailed models of local and foreign ships, with visual explanations of how each one catches fish or captures the wind. The museum also operates a 30-minute pleasure junk (🎫 10 patacas per person, ☉ daily except Tues. and first Sun. of the month) around the Inner and Outer Harbours. ✉ *Largo do Pagode da Barra, opposite A-Ma Temple,* ☎ *853/ 307–161.* 🎫 *10 patacas.* ☉ *Wed.–Mon. 10–5:30.*

São Domingos. Following late-1990s restoration, this is once again the most beautiful church in Macau. Originally a convent founded by Spanish Dominican friars in 1587, it was rebuilt as a church in the 17th century. When convents were banned in Portugal in 1834, this church became a repository for a great deal of sacred art, which forms the basis of the collection on display in the **Museum of Sacred Art** on the upper floors, accessible via a small staircase to the right of the altar. ✉ *Rua de São Domingos at Largo do Senado.* 🎫 *Museum, free.* ☉ *Museum, daily 10–6.*

São Paulo. Adopted as the official symbol of Macau, the only thing that remains of the once-spectacular Church of St. Paul is its facade; the rest was destroyed in a disastrous fire in 1835. The story of the church is told on its carved stone facade and in the excavated crypt, which contains the tomb of the church's founder, Alessandro Valignano, and the bones of Japanese and Indochinese martyrs. Built between 1602 and 1627 under the direction of the Jesuits, it has always been tied to the struggle to preserve a Christian presence in Asia and was also part of the first Western-style university on the continent. ✉ *Rua de São Paulo at Largo da Companhia.* 🎫 *Free.* ☉ *Daily 9–6.*

Dining

CATEGORY	COST*
$$$	over 200 patacas
$$	100 patacas–200 patacas
$	under 100 patacas

per person for a main course at dinner.

$$$ ✕ **A Galera.** Among the city's most expensive restaurants, this fine-
★   dining treasure has the atmosphere of an elegant men's club. The wine
menu alone is 25 pages long, while the food ranges from seafood to
grill to distinctive Macanese dishes. The specialties include crisp-fried
Kobe beef, which is a rare delicacy, as well as such local favorites as
bacalhau (codfish). ⊠ *Hotel Lisboa, 3rd floor, new wing, 2–4 Av. de
Lisboa,* ☎ *853/577–666 ext. 3151. AE, MC, V.*

$–$$ ✕ **A Lorcha.** Locals say this restaurant near the Maritime Museum serves
★   the best Portuguese food in town. It is also one of the most attractive
places to dine, with stone archways, white stucco, and terra-cotta tile
floors. Popular dishes include seafood rice, bread-based *açorda* casseroles,
kidney beans, and codfish. Service is first-rate. ⊠ *289 Rua do Almirante
Sergio,* ☎ *853/313–195. Reservations essential. MC, V. Closed Tues.*

$–$$ ✕ **Litoral.** This fabulous restaurant serves Portuguese and Macanese
★   dishes that may not be flashy but are undeniably delicious. Be prepared,
though, as the Portuguese favor cuts of meat that are an acquired taste
for most others: things like pig's ear and ox tripe, to name just two.
The owner, Manuela Ferreira, produces near-perfection with such
dishes as braised duck served in a complex sweet-soy sauce. For dessert
try a classic: *bebinca de leite* (coconut milk custard) or the traditional
egg pudding, *pudim abade de priscos.* ⊠ *261 Rua Almirante Sergio,*
☎ *853/967–878. AE, MC, V.*

$ ✕ **Pizzeria Toscana.** Owned by a Macanese family of long standing,
★   with roots in Pisa, the restaurant serves consistently good Italian food,
from such appetizers as air-cured beef topped with shaved fontina or
salmon carpaccio to pastas, entrées—such as king prawns in spicy garlic sauce or tender roasted chicken with rosemary—and pizzas, to
dessert. The owner is a major wine importer, so the wine list is superb
and the prices very reasonable. ⊠ *Av. da Amizade, opposite ferry terminal,* ☎ *853/726–637. MC, V.*

$ ✕ **Praia Grande.** Wonderfully situated on the Praia Grande, this clas-
★   sic Portuguese restaurant was cleverly created from a prefab corner building. The decor is simple, and the menu presents such imaginative fare
as Portuguese dim sum, African chicken, mussels in white wine, and
clams *cataplana* (in a stew of pork, onions, tomatoes, and wine). The
esplanade, with a serving kiosk and umbrella-shaded tables, is ideal
for drinks and snacks. ⊠ *10A Lobo d'Avila, Praia Grande,* ☎ *853/
973–022. AE, MC, V.*

Lodging

CATEGORY	COST*
$$$	over 1,200 patacas
$$	600 patacas–1,200 patacas
$	under 600 patacas

*Prices are for a standard double room on the weekend, not including 10%
service charge and 5% tax.*

$$$ ▣ **Pousada de São Tiago.** This small inn was ingeniously built into a
★   17th-century Portuguese fortress that once guarded the southern tip
of the peninsula. The entrance alone is worth a visit, with a staircase
that runs through an old lichen-covered tunnel where water seeps in
soothing trickles. In the hallways the bedrock has been allowed to pro-

trude through the floor tiles, while the rooms have been decorated with unusual mahogany furnishings and blue-and-white tiles that enhance the general old-world atmosphere. Book well in advance for weekends and holidays. ⊠ *Av. da República,* ☎ *853/378–111; 852/2739–1216 in Hong Kong,* FAX *853/552–170. 23 rooms. Restaurant, bar, pool, chapel. AE, DC, MC, V.*

$$ 🏨 **Hyatt Regency and Taipa Island Resort.** The Hyatt's rooms have a
★ sleek, contemporary look. The extensive facilities of its attached Taipa Resort make it especially attractive: a complete health spa, with various baths and massage and beauty treatments, a running track, a botanical garden, and a huge outdoor pool. The hotel is close to the racetrack and operates a shuttle-bus service to the wharf and to the Lisboa. ⊠ *Taipa,* ☎ *853/831–234; 852/2559–0168 in Hong Kong; 800/ 233–1234 in U.S.,* FAX *853/830–195. 326 rooms. 3 restaurants, 2 bars, pool, barbershop, hair salon, 4 tennis courts, gym, squash, casino. AE, DC, MC, V.*

$$ 🏨 **Lisboa.** Rising above a two-story casino, this utterly bizarre building has, for better or worse, become one of the popular symbols of Macau. It is the flagship hotel in local *taipan* Stanley Ho's empire; parts of his art collection—including an intricately carved 2-ton piece of jade— are scattered throughout the lobby. Surprisingly, the rooms are tastefully decorated. In Macau, all roads lead to the Lisboa, making it an exceptionally convenient place to stay. ⊠ *Av. da Amizade,* ☎ *853/377– 666; 852/2546–6944 in Hong Kong,* FAX *853/567–193. 1,050 rooms. 12 restaurants, 3 bars, coffee shop, pizzeria, in-room data ports (some), minibars, pool, sauna, bowling, casino, dance club, theater, video games. AE, DC, MC, V.*

$$ 🏨 **Westin Resort.** Although it is only 15 minutes by taxi from the city
★ center, from the moment you enter the lobby the pace slows to tropical-island speed, where a day spent by the pool or out on the golf course counts as ambitious. The resort occupies a magnificent headland overlooking the black-sand beach of Hac Sa and is surrounded by open water and total silence. The luxuriously appointed rooms are large and the terraces even larger, while the list of sports and recreational facilities is endless. The Macau Golf and Country Club has a clubhouse in the building; the 18-hole championship course is laid out behind it. ⊠ *Hac Sa Beach, Coloane Island,* ☎ *853/871–111; 852/2803–2015 in Hong Kong; 800/228–3000 in U.S.,* FAX *853/871–122. 208 rooms. 4 restaurants, 2 bars, 2 pools, golf course, 8 tennis courts, gym, jogging, squash, shops. AE, DC, MC, V.*

$ 🏨 **Sintra.** The Sintra, although affiliated with the Lisboa, has a completely different character: quiet where the Lisboa is brash, understated where the Lisboa is gaudy. It is one of the best-value hotels in the city and couldn't have a more convenient location, within easy walking distance of both the old quarter and the new districts. It has few facilities apart from a sauna and a modest European restaurant with picture windows and Mediterranean decor. ⊠ *Av. Dom João IV,* ☎ *853/710– 111; 852/2546–6944 in Hong Kong,* FAX *853/566–7749. 236 rooms. 2 restaurants, sauna. AE, DC, MC, V.*

Nightlife

Though the city has tried to develop the waterfront along the Outer Harbour into a bar and nightclub area—dubbing it the "Lan Kwai Fong of Macau"—the strip lacks energy and seems more like the Fong's poor cousin. Another option is the Embassy bar at the Mandarin Oriental hotel. Unequivocally, gambling is the main form of nightlife entertainment. The casinos are not glamorous affairs and appeal mostly to the hard-core bettor. There are 24-hour money exchanges and automatic teller machines for drawing cash from Hong Kong banks. Bets are almost always in Hong Kong dollars.

Of the six hotel casinos, the one in the **Lisboa** (⊠ Av. da Amizade, ☎ 853/377–666) is the busiest, in a two-story operation where the games are roulette, blackjack, baccarat, pacapio, and the Chinese games fantan and "big and small"; there are also hundreds of slot machines, which the Chinese call "hungry tigers." The other five hotel casinos are in the **Holiday Inn** (⊠ Rua de Pequim, ☎ 853/783–333); **Hyatt Regency** (⊠ Taipa, ☎ 853/831–234); **Kingsway** (⊠ Rua Luis Gonzaga Gomes, ☎ 853/702–888); **Mandarin Oriental** (⊠ Av. da Amizade, ☎ 853/567–888); and the **New Century** (⊠ Est. Almirante Marques Esparteiro, Taipa Island, ☎ 853/831–111). The nonhotel casinos are at the **Jai Alai Stadium** (⊠ Terminal Maritimo do Porto Exterior, off Av. da Amizade, ☎ 853/726–086); the **Kam Pek** (⊠ Almeida Ribeiro, ☎ 853/780–168), and the **Palacio de Macau,** (⊠ end of Av. Almirante Sergio, ☎ 853/346–701), usually known as the floating casino.

Macau A to Z

To research prices, get advice from other travelers, and book travel arrangements, visit www.fodors.com.

BOAT AND FERRY TRAVEL

Most ships to Macau leave Hong Kong from the Macau Terminal in the Shun Tak Centre. A fleet of Boeing jetfoils operated by the Far East Jetfoil Company provides the most popular service between Hong Kong and Macau. In Macau ships use the modern three-story ferry terminal, which opened in 1994.

FARES AND SCHEDULES

There are three classes of tickets: super, first, and economy. Depending on class, the prices (including departure tax) are HK$232/144/130 weekdays, HK$247/154/141 weekends and public holidays, and HK$260/175/161 nights. The return trip from Macau is HK$7 extra per ticket. Boats are so frequent you don't have to reserve in advance unless you want to go to Hong Kong late Saturday night.

➤ BOAT AND FERRY INFORMATION: **Far East Jetfoil Company** (⊠ Shun Tak Centre, Hong Kong, ☎ 852/2516–1268). **Ferry Terminal** (⊠ Av. da Amizade, Macau, ☎ 853/790–7039). **Shun Tak Centre** (⊠ 200 Connaught Rd., Hong Kong).

CAR RENTAL

Avis rents cars for use in Macau only. You can rent mokes, little Jeep-like vehicles that are fun and ideal for touring, from Happy Mokes.

➤ MAJOR AGENCIES: **Avis** (Mandarin Oriental Hotel, 956–1110 Avenida da Amizade, ☎ 853/336–789).

➤ LOCAL AGENCIES: **Happy Mokes** (Ferry Terminal, Level 1, Counter 1025; New Century Hotel, Taipa Island, ☎ 853/831–212).

HELICOPTER TO AND FROM MACAU

Helicopter service run by East Asia Airlines is available from the Macau Terminal in Hong Kong, with departures daily every 30 minutes 9:30–5:30. The helicopter rides are mostly free perks to big gamblers, as traveling by helicopter doesn't save all that much time relative to the jetfoils.

FARES AND SCHEDULES

The 20-minute flight costs HK$1,206 weekdays, HK$1,310 weekends from Hong Kong, and HK$1,205 and HK$1,309, respectively, from Macau, including taxes.

RESERVATIONS

Book through the Shun Tak Centre or the terminal in Macau.

➤ CONTACTS: **Macau Terminal** (☎ 852/2559–9800). **Shun Tak Centre** (☎ 852/2859–3359).

MONEY MATTERS

CURRENCY

Macau's currency, the pataca, is pegged at near parity with the HK dollar, but although the HK dollar can be used as a second currency in Macau, the pataca is not accepted in Hong Kong. Pataca conversion rates at press time were 8.03 to the U.S. dollar, 11.19 to the pound sterling, 5.27 to the Canadian dollar, and 4.15 to the Australian dollar.

PASSPORTS AND VISAS

Passports are required for everyone. As of August 2001, travelers from the United States, Australia, Canada, the European Union, New Zealand, and South Africa, among other countries, were permitted to stay in Macau for 20 days without a visa, and Hong Kong ID-holders could stay for 90 days without a visa.

TAXIS

Metered taxis (flag fare, 10 patacas; surcharge to other islands) cruise the streets and wait outside hotels.

TOURS

There are a number of licensed tour operators in Macau that specialize in English-speaking visitors: Able Tours, International Tourism, Macau Tours, and Sintra Tours.

➤ TOUR OPERATORS: **Able Tours** (☎ 853/566–939 or 852/2368–7111). **International Tourism** (☎ 853/975–183 or 852/2541–2011). **Macau Tours** (☎ 853/710–003 or 852/2542–2338). **Sintra Tours** (☎ 853/710–361 or 852/2540–8028).

TRANSPORTATION AROUND MACAU

Walking is the best method of getting around in the old parts of town and in shopping areas—the streets are narrow and crowded. You can rent a bicycle for about 10 patacas an hour at shops near the Taipa bus station. Public buses (2.50 patacas–5 patacas) are convenient. Tricycle-drawn two-seater pedicabs cluster at the ferry terminal and near hotels; be sure to bargain with the driver.

VISITOR INFORMATION

➤ TOURIST INFORMATION: **Macau Government Tourism Office** (✉ Largo do Senado, ☎ 853/315–566). **Macau Tourist Bureau** (✉ Shun Tak Centre, 200 Connaught Rd., Central, Hong Kong, ☎ 852/2540–8180; ✉ Hong Kong International Airport, ☎ 852/2769–7970). **Macau Trade and Investment Promotion Institute** (✉ World Trade Centre, 5/F, Av. da Amizade, Macau, ☎ 853/712–660).

HONG KONG A TO Z

By Lara Wozniak

To research prices, get advice from other travelers, and book travel arrangements, visit www.fodors.com.

AIR TRAVEL TO AND FROM HONG KONG

CARRIERS

Major international carriers between Hong Kong and North America are Canadian Airlines International, Cathay Pacific Airways, China Airlines, Northwest, Singapore Airlines, and United Airlines.

From the U.K., British Airways, Cathay Pacific Airways, and Virgin Atlantic have daily flights from London's Heathrow Airport to Hong Kong. From Australia, Qantas, Ansett Australia, and Cathay Pacific fly out of all major cities. From New Zealand, Air New Zealand and Cathay Pacific fly out of Wellington. From South Africa, South African Airways and Cathay Pacific Airways fly out of Johannesburg.

➤ AIRLINES AND CONTACTS: **Ansett Australia** (☎ 852/2527–7833). **Air New Zealand** (☎ 852/2524–9041). **British Airways** (☎ 852/2868–0303). **Canadian Airlines International** (☎ 852/2867–8111). **Cathay Pacific Airways** (☎ 852/2747–1577, 852/2747–1888). **China Airlines** (☎ 852/2868–2299). **Northwest** (☎ 852/2810–4288). **Qantas** (☎ 852/2842–1438). **Singapore Airlines** (☎ 852/2520–2233). **South African Airways** (☎ 852/2877–3277). **United Airlines** (☎ 852/2810–4888). **Virgin Atlantic** (☎ 852/2532–3533).

AIRPORTS AND TRANSFERS

The gateway to Hong Kong is the mammoth Hong Kong International Airport (universally referred to as Chek Lap Kok), off Lantau. Be warned: because the arrivals hall is so vast, arriving passengers often have trouble finding those meeting them. This vastness also translates into long, long walks to or from the plane, made worse by the lack of baggage carts on the airplane side, which can mean dragging your hand luggage more than a mile in some cases. Two Hong Kong Hotels Association counters take reservations, and two Hong Kong Tourist Board counters offer assistance.

➤ AIRPORT INFORMATION: **Hong Kong International Airport (Chek Lap Kok)** (☎ 852/2181–0000).

AIRPORT TRANSFER

The high-speed, high-frequency Airport Express Railway whisks you via the spectacular Tsing Ma Bridge from the airport to Kowloon in 19 minutes and to Hong Kong Station in Central, Hong Kong Island, in 23 minutes. You arrive directly across from the Departure Hall. (If you're arriving, the Airport Express is directly across from the arrival gates.) *Note:* For in-town check-in—including bags, boarding passes, and taxes—you must first purchase a ticket on the Airport Express. Airlines recommend in-town check-in three hours before your flight and will not accept passengers whose flights are departing in under two hours. Hong Kong Station connects to Mass Transit Railway's Central Station, but be prepared for a long underground walk with no carts. The one-way fare on the Airport Express to or from Hong Kong Station in Central is HK$70, to or from Kowloon is HK$60.

Airbus offers service on eight routes that stop at just about all the hotels and hostels in Hong Kong, Kowloon, and the New Territories. Prices range from HK$20 to HK$45 for the one-hour trip. Airport Express runs a free shuttle bus service between major hotels and the Hong Kong or Kowloon stations. To board, you must show your ticket, boarding pass, or Air Express ticket. A 24-hour Airport Shuttle bus runs from all hotels every 30 minutes, 24 hours a day for HK$120. A number of regular public bus routes to and from the airport are cheaper (HK$23 and under) and take longer.

For DCH Limo Service, prices range from HK$450 to HK$600. A pickup service is also available, as is a car-hire service from HK$300 to HK$360 per hour, minimum two hours.

In taxis, expect to pay up to HK$320 for Kowloon destinations and up to HK$400 for Hong Kong Island destinations. The fees include the two-way bridge and tunnel tolls. There is a luggage-handling charge of HK$5 per piece.

Useful publications: The HKTB's *Public Transport from Hong Kong International Airport*, the Airport Express's *Tourist Information Guide*, and the Airport Authority's *Hong Kong International Airport Transport* are all free and contain information on the various ways to get to and from the airport.

➤ TAXIS AND SHUTTLES: **Airbus** (☎ 852/2745–4466). **Airport Express Railway** (☎ 852/2881–8888 for hot line). **Airport Express Shuttle Bus** (☎ 852/2508–1234). **Airport Shuttle** (☎ 852/2377–0733). **DCH Limo Service** (✉ Kiosk 4, Arrivals Hall, ☎ 852/2262–1888). **Public bus lines** (☎ 852/2873–0818 Citybus's Cityflyer; 852/2745–4466 Kowloon Motor Bus; 852/2786–6036 Long Wing Bus Company).

BOAT AND FERRY TRAVEL
FARES AND SCHEDULES
The quickest and most romantic way to get between Central and Tsim Sha Tsui is by the Star Ferry. Fares are HK$2.20 for first class, HK$1.90 for second class. The ferry runs from 6:30 AM to midnight daily.

Ferries (including the high-speed ones) to the islands of Lantau (excluding Discovery Bay resort), Cheung Chau, Lamma, and Ping Chau— the Outlying Islands as they are called in Hong Kong—leave from the Central District Ferry Piers. Prices range from HK$15 to HK$50, depending on class and day. The Discovery Bay (known fondly by one and all as Disco Bay) high-speed ferries leave from the east side of the Star Ferry Concourse, Hong Kong side. Single class price is HK$25 one way.

The simplest way to find out the schedules is to telephone the HKTB Visitor Hotline or visit one of the HKTB Visitor Information and Service Centres.
➤ BOAT & FERRY INFORMATION: **Central District Ferry Piers** (✉ just west of Star Ferry and GPO, north of Airport Express Station on Hong Kong Island).**HKTB Visitor Hotline** (☎ 852/2508–1234). **HKTB Visitor Information and Service Centres** (✉ Star Ferry Concourse, Kowloon; ✉ ground floor, The Center, 99 Queen's Rd. Central, Hong Kong, ☎ 852/2508–1234 for both offices).

BUS TRAVEL WITHIN HONG KONG
Double-decker buses have extensive routes with fixed bus stops; you can pick up a route map at any HKTB Visitor Information Centre.

Sixteen-seat maxicabs have scheduled departures from their terminals. They have green roofs with cream-color bodies, a route number, and a prominently displayed fixed price. Minibuses, also 16-seaters, are unscheduled and have red roofs and a cream body color. Destinations and prices are displayed (the English words are very small) and changed depending on the length of the journey, but routes and prices can be altered quickly to take advantage of demand. Both are waved down, and both require exact fares. Minibuses can be more difficult if you don't know where you are going.

FARES AND SCHEDULES
Double-decker bus fares range from HK$2.70 to HK$32 in exact change. Pay as you enter.

Maxicab rates run from HK$1.50 to HK$18; pay as you enter. Minibus fares range from HK$2 to HK$20; pay as you exit.

CAR RENTAL
Renting a self-drive car in Hong Kong is not worth it. The roads are tricky, traffic jams are common, and parking spaces are in short supply. Steering wheels are on the right-hand side, and driving is on the left. It's easiest just to get a chauffeured car from your hotel or from

DCH Limo Service or Fung Hing Hire Co., but both Avis and Hertz are here.

➤ Major Agencies: **Avis** (☎ 852/2890–6988). **Hertz** (☎ 852/2525 – 2838).

➤ Car Rental Alternatives: **DCH Limo Service** (☎ 852/2262–1888). **Fung Hing Hire Co.** (☎ 852/2572–0333).

CONSULATES AND COMMISSIONS

➤ Australia: **Australian Consulate** (✉ 21st–24th floors, Harbour Centre, 25 Harbour Rd., Wanchai, ☎ 852/2827–8881).

➤ Canada: **Canadian Commission** (✉ Tower 1, Exchange Sq., 11th–14th floors, 8 Connaught Pl., Central, ☎ 852/2810–4321, FAX 852/2810–8736).

➤ Ireland: **Irish Consulate** (✉ 6th floor, Chung Nam Bldg., 1 Lockhart Rd., Wanchai, ☎ 852/2527–4897).

➤ New Zealand: **New Zealand Consulate** (✉ 6508 Central Plaza, 18 Harbour Rd., Wanchai, ☎ 852/2525–5044).

➤ South Africa: **South African Consulate** (✉ 2706–2710, 27th floor, Great Eagle Centre, 23 Harbour Rd., Wanchai, ☎ 852/2577–3279).

➤ United Kingdom: **British Trade Commission** (✉ Visa Section, 3rd floor, 1 Supreme Court Rd., Central, ☎ 852/2901–3111).

➤ United States: **United States Consulate** (✉ 26 Garden Rd., Central, ☎ 852/2523–9011, FAX 852/2845–0735).

EMERGENCIES

➤ Emergency Services: Dial ☎ 999 for police, fire, or ambulance services.

➤ Hospitals: **Pamela Youde Nethersole Eastern Hospital, Hong Kong East Cluster** (3 Lok Man Rd., Chai Wan, ☎ 852/2595 6111). **Prince of Wales Hospital** (✉ 30–32 Ngan Shing St., Shatin, New Territories, ☎ 852/2636–2211). **Princess Margaret Hospital** (✉ 2–10 Princess Margaret Hospital Rd., Laichikok, Kowloon, ☎ 852/2990–1111). **Queen Elizabeth Hospital** (✉ 30 Gascoigne Rd., Kowloon, ☎ 852/2958–8888). **Queen Mary Hospital** (✉ 102 Pok Fu Lam Rd., Hong Kong, ☎ 852/2855–5311). **Tang Shiu Kin Hospital** (✉ 284 Queen's Rd. E, Hong Kong, ☎ 852/2831–6800).

➤ Hot Lines: **AIDS Hotline** (☎ 852/2780–2211). **Hong Kong Police Visitor Hot Line** (☎ 852/2527–7177).

MAIL AND SHIPPING

➤ Post Offices: **General Post Office** (GPO; ✉ Next to Star Ferry Concourse, Central, ☎ 852/2921–2222).

MONEY MATTERS

CREDIT CARDS

➤ Reporting Lost Cards: **American Express** (☎ 852/2811–1200 customer service; cardholders or traveler's check holders only).

CURRENCY

Hong Kong continues to mint its own currency, apart from China. The units of currency in Hong Kong are the Hong Kong dollar (HK$) and the cent.

CURRENCY EXCHANGE

For the most favorable exchange rate, go to a bank. Most banks have foreign exchange counters and charge a commission of 5% to 10% for the transaction. There are 24-hour automated teller machines (ATMs) in banks all over Hong Kong, with Cirrus or Plus systems.

PASSPORTS AND VISAS

ENTERING HONG KONG

Hong Kong's immigration laws function under the jurisdiction of the Special Administrative Region and are not the same as those in the rest of China. U.S., Canadian, and U.K. citizens need only a valid passport to enter and do not have to obtain a visa before entering. U.S. and EU (including U.K.) passport holders visiting Hong Kong as tourists may stay for up to 30 days, Canadians for up to 90 days. No visas are necessary for Australians, New Zealanders, or South Africans.

➤ CONTACTS: **Hong Kong Immigration** (☎ 852/2824–6111, FAX 852/ 2877–7711).

SUBWAY TRAVEL

The Mass Transit Railway (MTR) links Hong Kong Island to most of Kowloon and to parts of the New Territories. Color-coded maps of the system are on display in all stations. Station entrances are marked with a simple line symbol resembling a man with arms and legs outstretched.

FARES AND SCHEDULES

Clearly marked ticket machines are inside the station; change is available at the Hang Seng Bank counters inside the stations. Fares range from HK$4 to HK$26.

The special Tourist Ticket (HK$30) is worthwhile if you plan to use the MTR frequently. The magnetic Octopus Card is valid on the MTR, buses, and the Kowloon–Canton Railway (KCR). The minimum for the Octopus Card is HK$100 (plus HK$50 deposit). It is sold at Customer Service booths in the MTR and the KCR. For information and schedules contact the Mass Transit Railway.

➤ SUBWAY INFORMATION: **Mass Transit Railway** (MTR, ☎ 852/2881– 8888).

TAXIS

Taxis are plentiful except in rain and rush-hour traffic—and a bargain. As many taxi drivers do not speak English, it is wise to get someone at your hotel to write out your destination in Chinese. Taxis in Hong Kong and Kowloon are red and have a roof sign that lights up when the taxi is available. Fares in the urban areas are HK$15 for the first 2 km (1.2 mi) and HK$1.20 for each additional .2 km (.12 mi). There is a surcharge of HK$5 per large piece of baggage plus surcharges of HK$20 for the Cross-Harbour Tunnel, HK$30 for the Eastern Harbour Tunnel, HK$45 for the Western Harbour Tunnel, HK$5 for the Aberdeen Tunnel, HK$8 for the Lion Rock Tunnel, HK$3 for the Junk Bay Tunnel, and HK$30 for the Tsing Ma Bridge. Taxis cannot pick up passengers where there are double yellow lines. Urban taxis may travel into rural zones, but rural taxis must not cross into the urban zones. There are no interchange facilities for these taxis, so do not try to reach the urban area using a green or blue nonurban taxi.

TELEPHONES

COUNTRY AND AREA CODES

The code for Hong Kong is 852.

DIRECTORY AND OPERATOR ASSISTANCE

Dial ☎ 1081 for directory assistance from English-speaking operators.

INTERNATIONAL CALLS

You can make overseas phone calls from your hotel room, but it is cheaper to make calls on your phone card or credit card outside the hotel on a public phone (most take cards). If you want to pay cash, go direct to an office of Cable & Wireless HKT.

➤ INTERNATIONAL CALL SERVICES: **Cable & Wireless HKT** (⊠ Shop 116, Prince's Bldg., Des Voeux Rd., Central, ☎ 852/2810–0660; ⊠ TST Hermes House, 100 Middle Rd., Kowloon, ☎ 852/2724–8322).
➤ INTERNATIONAL OPERATOR ASSISTANCE: Call ☎ 10013 for international inquiries and for assistance with direct dialing.

LOCAL CALLS

To make a local call from a pay phone, use the HK$1 coin.

PHONE CARDS

You can dial direct from specially marked silver-color phone booths that take phone cards (HK$25, HK$50, and HK$100), available from the Hong Kong Telephone Companies retail shops and 7-Eleven convenience stores throughout the island. Multilingual instructions are posted in the phone booths.

TIPPING

Hotels and major restaurants add a 10% service charge. It is customary to leave an additional 10% tip in all restaurants, as well as in taxis and beauty salons.

TOURS

HKTB (☞ Visitor Information, *below*) offers a variety of tours, from horse racing to a four-hour Heritage Tour.

BOAT TOURS

For a variety of tours that cover the Inner Harbour and outer islands aboard junks and cruisers, contact Harbour and Islands, Watertours of Hong Kong Ltd. or the Seaview Harbour Tour Co. Ltd.
➤ FEES AND SCHEDULES: **Harbour and Islands, Watertours of Hong Kong Ltd.** (☎ 852/2739–3302 or 852/2724–2856). **Seaview Harbour Tour Co. Ltd.** (☎ 852/2561–5033).

TRAIN TRAVEL

As Hong Kong consists mostly of islands, the only surface transportation in and out is by train to and from mainland China across the Kowloon Peninsula.

FARES AND SCHEDULES

The Kowloon–Canton Railway (KCR) has 13 commuter stops on its 34-km (21-mi) journey through urban Kowloon to Lo Wu, at the former Chinese border. The main station is at Kowloon. Fares range from HK$7.50 to HK$40. The trip takes about 40 minutes. The crossover point with the MTR is at Kowloon Tong Station.

Four express trains, called through trains, (HK$230 premium class, HK$190 first class) depart daily to Guangzhou from Kowloon Station. The trip takes about two hours. The last train back to Hong Kong leaves at 5:25 PM. There are also direct trains (30 hours) to Beijing. In Hong Kong contact China Travel Service (CTS) for reservations and information.
➤ TRAIN INFORMATION: **China Travel Service** (☎ 852/2853–3888). **Kowloon–Canton Railway (KCR) main station** (⊠ Hong Chong Rd., Tsim Sha Tsui East, Kowloon). **Kowloon Tong Station** (⊠ Suffolk Rd., Kowloon Tong).

TRAM TRAVEL

Trams run along Hong Kong Island's north shore from Kennedy Town in the west through Central, Wanchai, Causeway Bay, North Point, and Quarry Bay, ending in Shaukiwan. A branch line turns off in Wanchai toward Happy Valley.

When you pack your MCI Calling Card, it's like packing your loved ones along too.

Your MCI Calling Card is the easy way to stay in touch when you travel. Use it to call to and from over 125 countries. Plus, every time you call, you can earn frequent flier miles. So wherever your travels take you, call home with your MCI Calling Card. It's even easy to get one. Just visit **www.mci.com/worldphone.**

EASY TO CALL WORLDWIDE

1. Just enter the WorldPhone® access number of the country you're calling from.
2. Enter or give the operator your MCI Calling Card number.
3. Enter or give the number you're calling.

Australia ◆	1-800-881-100
China	108-12
Hong Kong	800-96-1121
India	000-127
Japan ◆	00539-121▶
Kenya	080011
Morocco	00-211-0012
South Africa	0800-99-0011

◆ Public phones may require deposit of coin or phone card for dial tone.
▶ Regulation does not permit intra-Japan calls.

EARN FREQUENT FLIER MILES

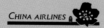

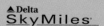

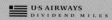

SEE THE WORLD IN FULL COLOR

Fodor's Exploring Guides bring all the great sights vividly to life with hundreds of photographs, fascinating historical background, and colorful anecdotes. Detailed maps and practical information keep you headed in the right direction.

Pair a **Fodor's** Exploring Guide with your trusted Gold Guide for a complete planning package.

Fodor's EXPLORING GUIDES

At bookstores everywhere.

Destinations are marked on the front; the fare is HK$2. Avoid trams at rush hours (weekdays 7:30 AM–9 AM and 5 PM–7 PM).

VISITOR INFORMATION

➤ TOURIST INFORMATION: **Hong Kong Tourist Bureau** (HKTB; Visitor Information Service Centres, ✉ Citicorp Centre, Central, Hong Kong, ☎ 852/2508–1234 multilingual Visitor Hotline; ✉ ground floor, The Center, Star Ferry Concourse, Kowloon, ☎ 852/2508–1234 multilingual Visitor Hotline, FAX 852/9006077–1128 24-hour facsimile information service: HK$2 per minute 8 AM to 9 PM/HK$1 after, WEB www.discoverhongkong.com).

10 SOUTH CENTRAL CHINA

RURAL CHINA AND THE LIMESTONE VALLEY

China's south central region attracts visitors with its natural scenery, from the magnificent limestone peaks of Guilin to the Wuling Mountains in Hunan to the white-sand beaches of Beihai. Guiyang is a good base from which to explore surrounding villages, while Wuhan, Changsha, and the pilgrimage site of Shaoshan attempt to maintain the intrigue surrounding the long-departed Chairman Mao.

By Anya
Bernstein and
Christopher
Knowles

Updated by
Keming Liu

SOUTH CENTRAL CHINA—the provinces of Hubei, Hunan, Guangxi, and Guizhou—is a region as varied as it is large, from the river towns of Hubei to the tropical coastline of Guangxi; from the lofty mountains of Hunan to the lush scenery of Guizhou.

Hubei and Hunan are known for their historical significance as much as for their natural beauty. It was in this region that the modern revolutionary spirit first took hold, during the Taiping Rebellion in Hubei from 1850 to 1860 and later as the site of major Communist uprisings in the 1920s. Wuhan was the base for a time of the left-leaning faction of the Nationalist Guomindang party. Today it's an important port of departure for boats taking the Three Gorges river cruise. Hunan, although primarily known as the province where Mao Zedong was born, is also the site of Hengshang Shan, one of China's Five Holy Mountains, and the magnificent nature reserve of Zhangjiajie.

In Guangxi you'll find the sublime karst and river scenery of Guilin. This is one of the great natural sites of the world. It has been commercialized to exploit its beauty, and there is an atmosphere of gold fever about this town that can be disconcerting. The scenery, however, is typical of central Guangxi and can still be appreciated in smaller towns across the province. At Guangxi's southern tip lies the peaceful coastal city of Beihai.

Guizhou is the site of China's mightiest waterfall and home to a large number of colorful non-Han peoples. Many small minority villages are scattered about the province and can be visited by tour or on your own from the metropolitan city of Guiyang.

Pleasures and Pastimes

Dining

The cuisine of **Hunan** tends to be spicy, not unlike Sichuanese food. Although it lacks Sichuan's variety, it produces some fine dishes, such as hot bean curd, spicy noodles, chicken with peanut sauce, and dishes cooked in a sauce heavily spiced with ginger, garlic, and chili. In **Hubei** you can sample fish from the Yangzi River at Wuhan's restaurants.

The cooking of **Guangxi** and **Guizhou** tends to have strong influences from both Guangdong and the spicy dishes of Hunan and Sichuan. There is a wide range of vegetables and fruit, and a love of dishes that may seem at best exotic and at worst repellent—snake, dog, and—illegally—rare animals such as the pangolin. Both snake and dog are said to have warming effects and are therefore winter specialties. Guizhou in particular has a wide variety of traditional dishes, as the province is home to so many ethnic groups; bean curd is again a specialty, most famously *Lian'ai Doufu,* or "fall in love bean curd," which is mixed with chili sauce, wild garlic shoots, vinegar, and soy sauce. An unexpected specialty of Guizhou is beef kebab, introduced by Uighur immigrants from Xinjiang and adapted to local produce. Look also for hotpot (*Huo Guo* or "fire pot" in Chinese), a specialty dish that involves dipping meat into a pot fondu-style, and for ginkgo fruit served in beaten egg white.

CATEGORY	COST*
$$$$	over Y225
$$$	Y175–Y225
$$	Y100–Y175
$	under Y100

Prices are per person for a five-course meal, excluding drinks, taxes, and tip.

Lodging

The following chart gives an approximate idea of the cost of lodging in the region. Note that in China, price may have but a superficial bearing on quality.

The $$$$ category generally refers to the new generation of Chinese hotels, often built with foreign money and with facilities associated with foreign standards. The $$$ category refers to hotels with good facilities but where service and comfort have been compromised in some way. The $$ category refers to generally older hotels that have been modernized. In the final, $, category, facilities may be simple or offer dormitory accommodations.

CATEGORY	COST*
$$$$	over Y850
$$$	Y650–Y850
$$	Y450–Y650
$	under Y450

Prices are for a standard double room in high season, including taxes.

Scenery

The greatest highlight of a visit to this part of China is the breathtaking scenery. Most famous, of course, is the fairy-tale landscape of **Guilin,** in Guangxi province, with its hundreds of karst-formation mountains rising sheer out of a vast plain of streams and paddy fields; the Tang dynasty poet Han Yu likened them to "kingfisher jade hairpins." But Guilin is far from the only possibility for lovers of natural beauty. Guizhou is home to China's highest waterfall, at **Huangguoshu Pubu.** In Hunan, **Wulingyuan Fengjingqu** (Wulingyuan Scenic Reserve), among the Wuling Mountains, is home to several minority peoples and the largest cave in Asia. Hunan and Hubei both have green rice-paddy fields and mountains, including **Hengshang Shan** in Hunan.

Exploring South Central China

To travel here, you need to be well organized. Unless you have limitless patience and time on your hands, set your priorities in advance. Hunan is rugged and deeply rural, and perhaps the best place in the region to get a sense of both imperial China (the museum at Changsha) and revolutionary China (Mao's birthplace at Shaoshan). Most of Hubei's cities of interest lie along or near the Yangzi River and can easily be reached by train or a cruise down the river. Guilin is in the heart of the tropical province of Guangxi, which borders Vietnam to the west and the South China Sea to the south. Lush and green most of the year round, Guangxi unfolds south from the highlands it shares with Guizhou to a tropical coast. In Guizhou, a territory of high valleys and low mountains, you can visit the villages of the province's indigenous peoples, composed of at least nine non-Han ethnic groups, of whom 82% are farmers.

Great Itineraries

To get the most out of this large area, a minimum stay of two weeks is recommended, three to explore it properly. However, with good planning, it would be possible to extract some of its flavor within a week or 10 days. For shorter stays you'll be limited to one or two destinations in the region.

Numbers in the margin correspond to points of interest on the South Central China, Changsha, Guilin, and Nanning maps.

IF YOU HAVE 2 DAYS

Fly directly to **Guilin** and book a place on the cruise along the Li River to Yangshuo. This effectively takes up a whole day but is one of the

highlights of any visit to China. On the second day either explore the town on foot or, better still, rent a bicycle and spend the day cycling around the countryside through the mountains and tropical-fruit farms, perhaps including a visit to the gaudy attractions of the Reed Flute Cave. At night there may be an acrobatic display, or you might join a party following a cormorant fisherman on the river.

IF YOU HAVE 7 DAYS

Start with Guilin, as above; then fly north to **Guiyang** and find your way to **Huangguoshu Pubu.** From there arrange a tour to Kaili or surrounding minority villages or take a cruise down the Wuyang River. Next fly to **Zhangjiajie** and observe the spectacular peaks and waterfalls.

IF YOU HAVE 10 DAYS

Stay in **Guilin** for three nights. Next fly to **Guiyang** and see the waterfall and minority villages. Fly to **Zhangjiajie.** Depending on your tastes, you can then either relax on the beaches in the south of Guangxi at **Beihai** or go see the sacred mountain **Hengshang Shan** in Hunan.

IF YOU HAVE AT LEAST 12 DAYS

After visiting **Guilin, Guiyang, Zhangjiajie,** and **Beihai** or **Hengshang Shan,** visit the rural countryside of Mao's birthplace at **Shaoshan.**

When to Tour South Central China

The best time of year is in the spring, in April or early May. The winter months can be surprisingly cold (except on the south coast of Guangxi), and the heat in the summer months is stifling. Mid-September can also be a comfortable time to travel here. The falls at Huangguoshu are at their best in the rainy season from May through October. Inhabitants of coastal areas celebrate the birthday of Mazu or Tianhou, goddess of the sea, on the 23rd day of the third lunar month (May/June). The minority peoples of Guizhou hold frequent festivals, particularly during the first, fourth, and sixth lunar months. For example, the *lusheng* festivals, celebrated by the Miao people, take place in January or February, when mothers trying to find a partner for their daughters present them to local boys, who play their *lusheng* pipes. To obtain a festival schedule, contact local CITS or travel agencies.

Hubei

The Yangzi River cuts lengthwise from west to east through Hubei, giving the province an age-old edge on transportation and a whole stretch of densely foliated land. Centrally located, Hubei, with more than 56.5 million people and a host of waterways, has long been one of China's most important provinces. In the mid-19th century it suffered through battles between the Taiping rebels and imperial troops. Shortly afterward, several of its cities were opened to European trade, which spread some Western influence through parts of the province. The 1911 revolution started here, toppling the already unsteady Qing dynasty. Over the next 38 years the province hosted some of the country's leading politicians and military leaders as they vied for control of China's future. Known for both its scenery and its history, the province offers water travel, hiking, mysterious wildlife—and Mao Zedong, who lived in the city of Wuhan for a time before and during the Cultural Revolution.

Wuhan is the port for river cruises through the Three Gorges, which range from western Hubei to eastern Sichuan province. The Three Gorges, where China's longest river, the Yangzi, passes between soaring cliffs, has become a point of contention both domestically and internationally. The Yangzi, which runs 3,900 km (2,418 mi) from Tibet

South Central China

to the Pacific Ocean, has long been one of the most heavily populated regions in China. In summer, when torrential rain falls in this region, the Yangzi unleashes its massive current and floods the plain. The worst flooding occurred in the summer of 1998 when 3,656 lives were lost. To control flooding and increase power supply, the Chinese government has embarked on what is arguably the biggest hydroelectric facility in the world: the Three Gorges Dam. The project will involve not only the forced relocation of 1 million people, but also—scientists predict—a major disaster for the ecosystem. Before the natural scenery changes forever, Chinese and foreign tourists rush to see the Yangzi River and the ancient temples, rocks shaped like mythical figures, and dramatic landscapes that line its shores.

In the west of the province, the Wudangshan Mountain range holds several important Taoist temples, while the Shennongjia region, in the northwest, is China's cross between the Bermuda Triangle and the abode of Bigfoot: travelers are warned of ghostly beasts of unknown origin and purpose, and rumors persist of visitors who penetrate the Shennongjia never to return. Nevertheless, the number of people around to testify to the existence of the unidentifiable animals seems surprisingly high. As long as you aren't too overwhelmed by the beauty of the place, you'll probably make it back, too.

Wuhan

❶ *13 hrs (1,225 km/760 mi) by train south of Beijing; 6 hrs (536 km/332 mi) by train south of Zhengzhou.*

Whether you're coming into town on a train or in a shuttle from the airport, you can't miss the water. The land around Wuhan seems permanently half-submerged, a swampy marsh traversed by tributaries of the Yangzi River. This impression does not stop when you get to the city. Various lakes, large and small, appear all around town, among which Donghu (East Lake) is often named as a sort of little sister counterpart to Hangzhou's famous Xihu (West Lake). (That the East Lake actually lies far to the west of West Lake does not faze anybody.)

Wuhan is actually a conglomerate of what used to be, until 1949, when New China was established by Mao, Wuchang, Hankou, and Hanyang—three distinct towns. Wuhan is the only city in China to lie on both sides of the Yangzi River, which separates Hankou and Hanyang, in the west, from Wuchang, in the east. The smaller Hanshui River separates Hankou from its southern partner, Hanyang. All these waterways make Wuhan a little cumbersome to traverse. Taxi rides are long, bus rides almost always require at least one transfer, and ferry rides across the river, although fun, take a bit of planning. A two-day layover here can be broadly divided along the river: one day for the east and one for the west. Be sure to visit during the pleasant seasons of early spring and autumn: Wuhan is one of China's summer "furnaces."

The area has historically been a hotbed of revolutionary activity of one sort or another. It was a center of anti-Qing unrest during the Taiping Rebellion of 1850–1864 and the cradle of the 1911 Republican revolution. During the uneasy 1920s it was the site of one of the decade's most prominent and most brutally put-down railway strikes. In 1926 it hosted an unlikely and short-lived coalition government of Guomindang (a.k.a. the Nationalist Party which overthrew the Chinese monarchy and established the Chinese Republic in 1912) and Communist forces; an even shorter-lived right-wing Guomindang faction ran the city after the coalition with the Communists, against the wishes of Chiang Kai-shek, whose headquarters were in Nanjing. Mao Ze-

dong ran the Peasant Movement Institute here until the city was taken by the Guomindang in 1928. During the civil war in the late '40s, the uprisings and strikes led by students and workers in the city helped to bring on the Communist victory in the area in 1949. Nowadays it is home to major iron and steel complexes, as well as such other industries as textiles, heavy machinery, glass, railroad cars, and trucks.

Wuhan was one of the Great Helmsman's favorite getaways. **Maozedong Bieshu** (Mao Zedong's Villa), near East Lake and now open for viewing, takes on some of the cult aspects that come with his presence. The villa has guided tours and lots of photos. ⊠ *Zhongnan Lu.* 🚅 *Y20.* ☉ *Daily 9–noon and 2–5.*

★ The **Hubei Sheng Bowuguan** (Hubei Provincial Museum), west of East Lake, has Mao memorabilia—from photos of Mao lounging by the river to more unusual relics, such as the playing card he chose when asked by schoolchildren to pick a card. The rest of the museum, although it has no English captions, holds a magnificent collection of ancient artifacts: the entire contents of a 5th-century BC tomb are housed here, including thousands of ceremonial objects, decorations, and, most impressively, a set of 65 bronze bells that are still taken out and played on special occasions. ⊠ *Just south of Donghu Lu and Huangli Lu.* 🚅 *Y10.* ☉ *Tues.–Sun. 8:30–noon and 2–4.*

Dong Hu Gongyuan (East Lake Park) covers 87 square km (34 square mi) divided into six "districts" that surround the lake on three sides. Various pavilions—the **Huguang Ge** and the **Xingyin Ge** are the most famous—are scattered about. Some have been recast as teashops with great views. You can cross the lake eastward along a narrow land bridge or hire a boat to end up at Moshan, a lakeside hill, and visit its **Tangshan Zhiwuyuan** (botanical garden). ⊠ *Off Donghu Lu, Wuchang, east side of city.*

On the way back from Wuchang to Hankou, **Hongshan,** a hill lying southeast of the lake, is a pretty place to wander around. At the top stands a small pagoda. ⊠ *Off Wulou Lu.*

The **Changchun Si** (Changchun Taoist Temple) has a few monks in residence. Worshipers come and go at all hours of the day. The temple also hosts a small market on the surrounding grounds where you can get sweets and souvenirs. ⊠ *West of junction of Wulou Lu and Zhongshan Lu.*

Sheshan (Snake Mountain) holds the **Baiyun Ge** (White Cloud Pavilion). The park leads almost to the Yangzi River Bridge. Near Sheshan, the gorgeous pagoda **Huanghe Lou** (Yellow Crane Tower) retains the aged elegance of its original AD 223 form, despite numerous restorations since. The combination of the tower and the pavilion behind it architecturally embodies Wuhan's more literary name: *Huanghe Baiyun,* or Yellow Crane White Cloud. ⊠ *Wulou Lu and Jiefang Lu.*

The **Wuhan Changjiang Da Qiao** (Yangzi River Bridge) links Snake Mountain in Wuchang with Turtle Hill in Hanyang. The bridge and its approaches are 1.7 km (1 mi) long and comprise a six-lane highway and a two-track railway running along its eight piers and nine arches. Vehicles on the motorway travel 80 meters (262 ft) above the river. It is the first steel modern bridge completed after the founding of the People's Republic of China and appear frequently in government propoganda as a symbol of Socialist achievement. ⊠ *From Wuchang, take Minzhu Lu; from Hanyang, take Lanjiang Lu.*

South of the Hanyang end of Wuhan Changjiang Da Qiao lies the ★ **Guiyuan Si** (Temple of Return to First Principle), one of Hubei's four

largest and oldest. First built in 1658, the Buddhist temple has more than 200 rooms and pavilions. The hall of arhats contains some 500 19th-century statues—displays of Buddhism's fashionable status at the time, more than of its historical importance in China. ⊠ *Cuiwei-heng Lu at Cuiwei Lu, Hanyang.* ☜ *Y10.* ☼ *Daily 8:30–5.*

Near the bridge up to Hankou you can stop in at the **Guqin Tai** (Platform of the Ancient Lute), built in honor of Yu Boya, an ancient lute player, and his friend and avid listener, Zhong Ziqi. Constructed during the Northern Song dynasty (AD 960–1126), the building has retained that dynasty's style through subsequent restorations. ⊠ *Eastern end of Qinhe Lu.* ☜ *Y5.* ☼ *Daily 8:30–5.*

Guishan (Tortoise Mountain) lies across the road from the Yangzi and holds an object of Wuhan pride: the **Dianshi Ta** (Hubei TV Tower), completed in 1986—the first in China to be built without foreign aid. It stands in the park as a symbol of China's modernizing drive.

Wuhan's main hotels and restaurants are in **Hankou,** but that section of the city also holds the fewest places of interest. The stretch of Hankou that runs along the river between the two bridges—Yanjiang Dadao as well as the street directly west of it, Shengli Jie—retains some pretty buildings from the late 19th century. The city was open then to European concessions; Chinese architects eagerly accepted the foreign influence but with their own interpretations. Several parks here make good places for a walk. **Zhongshan Gongyuan** (Sun Yat-sen Park; ⊠ Jiefang Dadao, 2 blocks east of Qingnian Lu, ☜ Y5, ☼ daily 7 AM– 10 PM) has some rather intricate waterways and paths. **Jiefang Gongyuan** (Jiefang Park; ⊠ Jiefang Dadao at Jiefang Gongyuan Lu, ☜ Y5, ☼ daily 8 AM–10 PM) has a small lake with a historic preservation center on its island.

Dining and Lodging

$$ ✕ **Da Zhonghua Fandian** (Da Zhonghua Restaurant). Once Mao's favorite, this restaurant serves Hubei "small eats" such as roast squab as well as regional seafood specialties. Visitors go for the history, but locals go for the food. ⊠ *198 Peng Liu Zhou Lu, Wuchan,* ☏ *027/ 8887–3775. No credit cards.*

$$ ✕ **Kanglong Taizi Jiuxuan** (Crown Prince Wineshop). This busy restaurant serves good traditional and contemporary Sichuan, Hunan, and Cantonese specialties, from snake to fish from the Yangzi River. Despite the crowds and flashy neon exterior, prices are very reasonable, and the service is excellent. ⊠ *226 Yanjiang Dadao, Hankou,* ☏ *027/ 8271–1778. MC, V.*

$ ✕ **Sili Meitang Fandian** (Sili Meitang Dumpling Restaurant). This restaurant, named for the brothers who founded it, has a rather basic setting and decor. But its dumplings—a specialty throughout east central China—are well known in Wuhan for their juicy fillings. ⊠ *898 Zhongshan Dadao, Hankou,* ☏ *027/8283–2842. No credit cards.*

$$$$ ⊞ **Tian'an Jiari Jiudian** (Tian'an Holiday Inn). This is Wuhan's most
★ upscale hotel, carefully decorated and amply staffed. Near the Hankou city center, it has a variety of eating options, satellite TV and IDD telephones in every room, and the staff provides sound travel advice. ⊠ *868 Jiefang Dadao, Hankou 430022,* ☏ *027/8568–7888,* 🖷 *027/ 8584–5353,* WEB *www.holiday-inn.com. 394 rooms. 2 restaurants, bar, beauty salon, pool, gym, dance club, business services, meeting room, travel services. AE, MC, V.*

$$$$ ⊞ **Xi Shujie Fangyi Dian** (Marriott New World Inn Courtyard). On a
★ small, quiet street a short walk from two city parks, the inn is known for its excellent service. The accommodations are comfortable without being imposing, and the Western restaurant and the coffee shop

are serious about quality. It's also directly across the street from the CITS office. ✉ *9 Taibei Yi Lu, 430015 Hankou,* ☎ *027/8578–7968,* FAX *027/8578–9171,* WEB *www.marriott.com. 138 rooms. 2 restaurants, bar, beauty salon, sauna, gym, business services, meeting room. AE, MC, V.*

$$$$
★ 🏨 **Yazhou Dajiudian** (Asia Hotel). The Asia vies with the Tian'an Jiari Jiudian for pride of place as Wuhan's most favored business-traveler enclave. The hotel interior is elegant and the rooms are spacious, many with views of the city. The staff is professional and attentive. ✉ *616 Jiefang Dadao, 430030 Hankou,* ☎ *027/8380–7777,* FAX *0278/8380–8080. 350 rooms. 2 restaurants, bar, beauty salon, gym, business services, meeting room, travel services. AE, MC, V.*

$ 🏨 **Shengli Fandian** (Victory Hotel). The Victory is on a quiet street in Hankou's pretty riverside district, where colonial-style houses are scattered alongside more modern Chinese structures. The hotel provides excellent, friendly service, and the rooms, although not luxurious, are decent. Its Chinese restaurant is one of Wuhan's very best. ✉ *11 Siwei Lu,* ☎ *027/8283–1241,* FAX *027/8283–2604. 130 rooms. 3 restaurants, beauty salon, shops, business services. AE, MC, V.*

Nightlife

In Wuhan, as in many large Chinese cities, favorite local hangouts include the bars, discos, and, especially, karaoke rooms of the major joint-venture hotels. The **Tian'an Jiari Jiudian** (Holiday Inn) and its surroundings have quite a few foreigner-friendly bars.

Shopping

Impromptu markets surround every temple and pagoda, and the **train station area** also hosts stands catering to tourists. The **Gongyi Dalou** (✉ Zhongshan Dadao and Minsheng Lu) carries antiques and local artifacts. The **Wuhan Antiques Store** (✉ Zhongshan Dadao 169, ☎ 027/8585–6538) sells local antiques and replicas. **Wuhan Friendship Company** (✉ Zhongshan Dadao 263, ☎ 027/586–4814) offers typical Friendship Store artifacts and prints. The **Xinhua Bookstore** (✉ Hankou, Jianghan Lu 87, ☎ 027/382–4040) carries a limited selection of English-language books, as well as useful maps. **Yuehan Matou** (✉ Yanjiang Dadao at Huanliao Shichang shopping center) has a wide selection of goods ranging from everyday to artistic and antique.

Side Trips from Wuhan

The real reason to come to Hubei is not for the capital but for the scenery in the west and northwest of the province. Wuhan is the stopover on the way to wilder places, and many Yangzi River tours start or end here. You can buy tickets at your hotel travel desk or book them through CITS (☞ Visitor Information, *below*), which will also be able to arrange unusual, tailor-made packages.

EASTWARD

A two-day trip down the scenic river ends at what is arguably China's most cosmopolitan city: Shanghai. The trip downriver also provides side-trip possibilities of its own. The boat stops at Jiujiang in Jiangxi province. From here Jiangxi's Lu Shan Mountains are easily accessible. Guichi and Wuhu in Anhui province are both excellent places to start a trip to one of China's most famous, and most beautiful, mountain ranges: Huangshan. Because the mountains are not well served by railroad lines, a combined river-land approach—traveling inland by bus—is the best way to go. You can stay overnight and explore Huangshan before boarding the boat again for other cities on the river. Boats also pass the major metropolis of Nanjing and the small but attractive city of Zhenjiang, in Jiangsu province, both worth exploring if you have the time.

WESTWARD

The trip upriver is slower because of the current, but it also has some of China's most fabulous scenery. A four-day trip northwest to Chongqing in Sichuan province will take you through a variety of sights.

② You'll first pass **Jingzhou,** in the southern part of Hubei province. This city, which still retains part of its ancient wall, was a major center during the Spring and Autumn and Warring States periods (770 BC–221 BC) and has been the site of several archaeological digs (the museum contains a 2,000-year-old preserved male body). The boat also passes the Shennong River, which flows into the Yangzi from **Shennong**

③ **Mountain.** Nanjin Pass in **Yichang,** western Hubei, marks the easternmost entrance point of the Three Gorges: Qutang, Wu, and Xiling.

④ **Shennongjia** is the wildest part of Hubei and one of the strangest in the country. The area, thought to hold more than 1,000 types of trees, is named for the legendary peasant Shennong, who discovered and collected medicinal herbs here. Possessed of amazing natural beauty, Shennongjia also carries an aura of magic and mystery. With enough time and the help of a travel agent or CITS, you may find this one of the most interesting trip possibilities in China.

⑤ **Wudang Shan** is a sacred mountain area in northwest Hubei. The range of 72 peaks stretches for 400 km (248 mi). At 1,600 meters (5,250 ft), Tianzhu Feng, whose name means pillar to the sky, is the highest of Wudang Shan's peaks. Many of Wudang Shan's hills have Taoist temples scattered on their slopes, which date back to the Ming dynasty (1368–1644); the area is one of the most sacred for Taoists. The Ming emperor Zhen Whu, who became a Taoist deity, lived here during the 15th century; there's a statue of him in the impressive Taihe Temple, which is about halfway up Tianzhu Feng. Jinding (Golden Summit) is at the top of Tianzhu Feng Peak. The climb takes about three hours. There are numerous other temples to visit in this scenic area, including the 1413 Zixiao Gong (Purple Cloud), which is northeast of Tianzhu Feng.

It's said that tai chi has its origins in Wudang Shan, based on a style of boxing developed by Zhang Sanfeng, a Taoist monk who lived in the 14th century and created a martial art from his observations of birds and animals in Wudang Shan. Monks reside here and practice martial arts at what is considered to be the highest level of the world. You've probably seen it before: it was the setting for the final scene in the 2000 Academy Award–winner, *Crouching Tiger, Hidden Dragon*.

Trains and buses from Yichang can take you to the Wudangshan village.

Hubei A to Z

To research prices, get advice from other travelers, and book travel arrangements, visit www.fodors.com.

AIR TRAVEL

Wuhan has daily flights to Beijing, Kunming, Shanghai, Guangzhou, and Shenzhen; and service four times a week to Fuzhou, Xian, and Nanjing. Due to airline deregulation and the breakup of the government monopoly through CAAC, the domestic airline travel situation is a bit fragmented. To get from Wuhan to other major cities in China, contact your hotel or the Hubei CITS (☞ Travel Agencies) for information.

➤ CONTACTS: **Wuhan Tianhe International Airport Arrivals** (☎ 027/8581–8305). **Wuhan Tianhe International Airport Departures** (☎ 027/8581–8494).

BOAT AND FERRY TRAVEL

Boats run in either direction from Wuhan along the Yangzi River, going to Chongqing in the west and Shanghai in the east. A few private ferries offer first-class accommodations; these are definitely advisable for sanitation and service, but cost more. Tickets can be purchased at your hotel travel desk; check also with CITS.

Ferries cross the Yangzi between Hankou and Wuchang frequently. This is faster and more enjoyable than the bus.

BUS TRAVEL

Buses run daily from Wuhan to Xiamen and Nanchang, northern Hubei, northern Anhui, and Yichang. Planes are preferable if you are going between Wuhan and Hangzhou, Nanjing, or Xian.

Buses traverse Wuhan, but the system is a little unwieldy. You can expect to switch buses one or two times if you're crossing the river between city sections. Taxis, which are easy to flag down on any major street, and the ferry are more convenient.

EMERGENCIES

➤ CONTACTS: **Fire** (☎ 119). **First-Aid Center** (☎ 120). **Police** (☎ 110). **Traffic Accident** (☎ 122). **Wuhan Public Security Bureau** (☎ 027/8271–2355).
➤ HOSPITALS: **Hubei Medical University Affiliated Hospital No. 1** (✉ Jiefang Lu, Wuchang, ☎ 027/8884–4437). **Tongji Hospital** (☎ 027/8363–4585 or 027/8363–4605). **Wuhan Hospital No. 1** (✉ Zhongshan Dadao, Hankou, ☎ 027/8585–5900).

TOURS

CITS has the latest information on tours of northern Hubei and of the Three Gorges area. Look into tours for seeing the northwest—the region can be difficult going without a working knowledge of Chinese.

TRAIN TRAVEL

Train service to and from this region is excellent. There are varying levels of comfort depending on how much you want to pay, from "hard seat" for budget travelers to first-class sleepers. Trains from Beijing, Guangzhou, Shanghai, Guilin, and Xian arrive in the region several times a day. For information, contact the Hubei CITS.

TRAVEL AGENCIES

➤ LOCAL AGENT REFERRALS: **Hubei CITS** (✉ 26 Taibei Rd., Wuhan 430015, ☎ 027/8578–4117, FAX 027/8578–4096). **Wuhan Overseas Tourism Corp.** (✉ 48 Baofeng Rd., Hankou 430030, ☎ 027/8362–6473, FAX 027/8362–6601).

VISITOR INFORMATION

CITS is a good source of tourist information.
➤ TOURIST INFORMATION: **Hubei Tourism Administration Foreign Affairs Office** (☎ 027/8271–2355). **Hubei Tourist Complaint Line** (☎ 027/8481–8760). **Directory Assistance** (☎ 114). **Time Inquiry** (☎ 117). **Weather Forecasting** (☎ 121). **Wuhan CTS** (✉ Bldg 3, 2 Railway Rd., Hankou 430014, ☎ 027/8280–0940).

HUNAN

This large inland province of rural communities and thinly populated mountainous regions is particularly associated with Mao Zedong, who was born and educated here. It was his upbringing and experiences in rural Hunan that provided the impetus for his revolutionary activities.

Hunan was part of the Kingdom of Chu during the era before the unification of China, known as the Warring States period (475–221 BC). In several waves of migration starting in the 3rd century AD, the northern Han people moved to avoid the constant threat of invasion from the steppe lands of Manchuria and Mongolia. But only in the 8th century, after heavier migrations from the north, did Hunan begin to develop. Its population increased many times over up to the 11th century, the rich agricultural land proving a great attraction for settlers. During the Yuan and Ming dynasties, Hunan and its neighbor to the north, Hubei, were united to form the province of Huguang, becoming the principal source of grain and rice for the Chinese empire. In 1664 Hunan became an independent province.

In the 19th century the population outgrew its resources, a problem aggravated by constant war and corrupt government, so that the Communists found a ready supply of converts here in the early 20th century. Mao was not the only influential revolutionary from Hunan—Liu Shaoqi, China's Vice Chairman before the Cultural Revolution, was born here, and so was Hu Yaobang, a Mao-installed Chairman who was stripped of power soon after Mao's death. Hunan is essentially Han China but is also home to a few non-Han minority peoples, the Miao and Yao (the original natives of the area), the Dong, and the Tujia.

Hunan (literally, "south of the lake") occupies an area of 210,000 square km (81,000 square mi) and has a population of 65 million. The flat northern part of the province falls within the catchment area of the Dongting Hu (Dongting Lake); the remaining regions are hilly or mountainous. The climate is sharply continental with short, cold, and wet winters and long, very hot summers. It is still an important agricultural region; half of the cultivated land is devoted to the production of rice.

The capital, Changsha, is a good place to visit not only for its excellent museum but also for its revolutionary sites. Mao's birthplace is in rural Hunan at Shaoshan, and Wulingyuan is beautiful.

Changsha

300 km (186 mi) west of Nanchang; 675 km (419 mi) northwest of Hong Kong; 1,300 km (806 mi) southwest of Beijing.

The capital of Hunan province, with a total population of just over 1.3 million, stands on the shore of the Xiangjiang, a tributary of the Yangzi. Built on a fertile plain, it has been an important settlement for well over 2,000 years. Known as Qinyang, it was famous for its textiles and handicrafts during the tumultuous Spring and Autumn period. In the Warring Kingdoms period it was in fact the capital of the Chu, whose state, while it lasted, was certainly innovative for its time, introducing measures to prevent corruption among officials and paring down the number of hereditary offices. The Chu were ultimately subjugated by the Qin (221 BC–206 BC), who made Changsha one of the most important cities of the recently united China. It was then that it acquired its present name. During later dynasties, it was well known as an educational center and became the provincial capital in 1664.

At the beginning of the 20th century it was opened up to foreign trade, attracting a small number of American and European residents; but it is best known as the home of Mao Zedong between 1911 and 1923. He studied here and then taught at the College of Education. Since 1949 much of the town has been rebuilt, and it has become a port and commercial center of some importance.

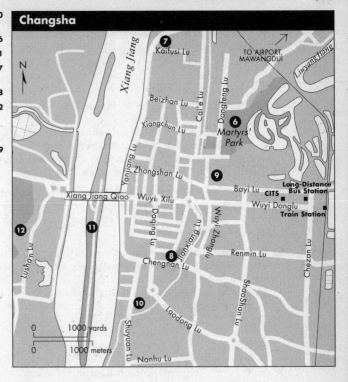

Changsha

★ **6** The **Hunan Bowuguan** (Hunan Provincial Museum), on the banks of Lake Nianjia, contains some interesting exhibits, most notably those from the royal graves at Mawangdui. These were the family graves of the Marquis of Dai, who died in 186 BC. The bodies were in extremely good condition upon discovery, especially that of the Marquis's wife, whose body had been wrapped in 20 layers of silk and whose coffin was sealed in charcoal and white peat, which excludes moisture and air. The beautiful coffins are on display, as are many of the funerary objects, including illustrated books and documents and a silk banner depicting Han afterlife beliefs. Also exhibited here are Shang bronzes and illustrated items from the Warring States period. ☒ *3 Dongfeng Lu.* ☒ *Y15.* ☉ *Daily 9–noon and 2:30–5:30.*

7 The **Kaifu Si** (Temple of Blissful Happiness) was founded in the 10th century AD, during the Five Kingdoms Period, when the Kingdom of Chu made a brief reappearance. Much added to and altered over the succeeding centuries, it received its last extension in 1923. Very much in the southern style in its rich decoration, it consists of a *pailou* (decorative, ceremonial gate) and several temple halls. ☒ *Kaifusi Lu.* ☉ *Daily 8:30–5.*

8 **Tianxin Gongyuan** (Heart of Heaven Park), at what was the southeast corner of the old city wall, was occupied by a rebel leader during the 19th-century Taiping Rebellion. The **Tian Xin Dian** (Pavilion of the Heart of Heaven), was restored in 1759. ☒ *Jianxiang Lu.* ☉ *Daily 9–5.*

9 The **Zhonggong Xiangqu Weiyuanhui Jiuzhi** (Headquarters of the local Communist Party) is sometimes known as the Qing Shui (Clearwater Pool). It was here that the first meeting of the local Communist Party was held, under the auspices of Mao Zedong, in July 1921. Mao and his first wife, Yang Kaihui, the daughter of one of his teachers at Changsha, lived here between 1921 and 1923. It was also home to Yang's mother. On display are a conference room and the room where Mao

and his wife lived, with furniture in the traditional Hunan style. ⊠ *Qing-shui Tang.* 🎫 *Y10.* 🕑 *8:30–5.*

⑩ Mao studied at the **Diyi Shifan** (Hunan No. 1 Teacher Training College) between 1913 and 1918, becoming "student of the year" in 1917 (though presumably not for his various political activities, which were already in full swing by this time). The original school was destroyed in 1938 during the war with the Japanese, but the buildings associated with Mao were later meticulously reconstructed, and some parts of them have been turned into a small museum. On view here are photographs, documents, and schoolbooks associated with his time here, as well as period newspaper clippings relating to revolutionary events around the world. ⊠ *Shuyuan Lu.* 🎫 *Y5.* 🕑 *Daily 8:30–5.*

⑪ The narrow 5-km (3-mi) **Juzi Zhou** (Island of Oranges), in the Xiangjiang (Xiang River), is known for its orange orchards. A park at its southern tip affords some fine views. On a tablet here is inscribed a poem written by Mao in praise of the town.

⑫ **Yuelu Shan** (Yuelu Hill) supports the lush grounds and bamboo thickets of Hunan University. Other educational establishments preceded this one, notably the 10th-century Yuelu Academy, one of the most celebrated of the Song dynasty. Several illustrious figures, including the philosopher Zhu Xi, whose texts became the basis for the imperial examinations, studied there. Nothing is left of the academy, except a single stela, but there are still some beautiful pagodas from the Qing dynasty, including the **Aiwan Ting**, with its severe eaves, built in 1792, and at the summit, the **Yunlu Gong**, a pavilion built in 1863. The **Lushan Si**, on the lower slopes, was originally built in AD 268 and is one of the oldest temples in the province. The doorway and a pavilion remain. ⊠ *Lushan Lu, west bank of river; Bus 12.* 🕑 *Daily 8–5.*

Just outside Changsha lie the **Han Mu** (Han graves), discovered in 1972. The contents of these three graves, more than 2,000 years old, have provided much of the interest of Changsha's Provincial Museum. They belonged to the Marquis of Dai, Li Cang (Tomb 2), who was prime minister to the king of Changsha between 193 BC and 186 BC; his wife, To Hou (Tomb 1); and their son (Tomb 3), who died in 168. To Hou's tomb was in a pounded earth mound 65 ft high and up to 200 ft in diameter, lying about 50 ft from the top; her body lay in the innermost of several coffins, the outer ones highly decorated and covered in bamboo mats. It seems that Tomb 1, the last to be built, completely escaped the depredations of tomb robbers (the other two were less fortunate); bamboo slips listing everything that was placed in the tomb to help To Hou on her way to the underworld showed that nothing had been removed for 2,100 years. ⊠ *Mawangdui, 4 km (2½ mi) northeast of Changsha.* 🎫 *Y10.* 🕑 *Daily 8:30–5.*

Dining and Lodging

$$–$$$ ✕ **Changdao Fandian** (Changdao Restaurant). Centrally located, this bustling restaurant, popular with locals, serves a wide variety of Chinese dishes, from *gongpao* chicken to meat- and vegetable-filled dumplings. ⊠ *Wuyi Xilu,* ☎ *no phone. No credit cards.*

$$–$$$ ✕ **Changsha Canting** (Changsha Restaurant). One of the original restaurants in Changsha before private restaurants were permitted, this large, upscale establishment serves good Hunanese food, such as *gualieng fen* (cold rice noodles in a hot and spicy sauce). ⊠ *116 Wuyi Donglu,* ☎ *no phone. No credit cards.*

$$–$$$ ✕ **Youyicun.** At this pleasant, conveniently located restaurant, with a traditionally decorated interior, you can choose from a wide variety of dishes from all over China. Try the *hongshao rou* (red cooked pork)

or *mapo doufu* (mapo tofu). ✉ *225 Zhongshan Lu,* ☎ *no phone. No credit cards.*

$–$$ ✕ **Kaiyulou.** In this simple restaurant the fare is snack foods such as jiaozi (pork and cabbage dumplings) and soups, including *niuroumian* (beef noodle soup). ✉ *Wuyi Donglu,* ☎ *no phone. No credit cards.*

$$$$ ⌂ **Huatian Dajiudian** (Hunan Huatian Hotel). This luxury hotel in the center of town is well maintained, provides good service, and is much frequented by the business community. ✉ *380 Jiefang Lu, 410001,* ☎ *0731/444–2888,* ℻ *0731/444–2270. 205 rooms. 2 restaurants, bar, air-conditioning, shops, business services. AE, V.*

$$$ ⌂ **Xiao Tian'e Jiudian** (Cygnet Hotel). In the heart of the city, this hotel, of a reasonably high standard, has both new and old wings. The rooms are simply equipped with basics, including a TV and a minibar. ✉ *176 Wuyi Zhonglu, 410001,* ☎ *0731/441–0400,* ℻ *0731/442–3698. 215 rooms. 3 restaurants, air-conditioning, pool, gym, nightclub. AE, MC, V.*

$$$ ✕⌂ **Bucheng Jianshen Huisuo** (Dolton Hotel Changsha). Striving to be one of the nicest hotels in the city, this sprawling hotel and health club works hard to please. Rooms are comfortable, and the staff is friendly and professional. ✉ *149 Shaoshan Lu, 410001,* ☎ *0731/444–8888,* ℻ *0731/416–0900. 432 rooms. 3 restaurants, bar, air-conditioning, shops, travel services, business services. MC, V.*

Nightlife and the Arts

Besides local opera and acrobatics, Hunan's specialty is **shadow puppets,** and the province has its own troupe. For information ask CITS or at your hotel.

Karaoke is popular here; the best bars are in the hotels.

Outdoor Activities

For **bicycle** rentals see CITS on Wuli Donglu. For **jogging** the best place is Lie Shi Gongyuan (Martyrs' Park; ✉ off Dongfeng Lu, near museum). The best places for **walking and hiking** are in nearby Wulingyuan; maps with trails are for sale in the area.

Shopping

Tea is a good buy in Hunan, and Changsha embroidery is some of the best known in China. The main shopping district of Changsha is Zhongshan Lu; there is also an antiques shop in the Provincial Museum.

Shaoshan

★ ⑬ *130 km (81 mi) southwest of Changsha.*

The small town of Shaoshan, within fairly easy driving distance of Changsha, is in many ways indistinguishable from thousands of similar towns all over China. For many years, however, pilgrims came to this town every day, pouring out of the trains that arrived regularly on the railway line especially built for the purpose, eager to see Mao Zedong's birthplace. At the height of his cult, in the mid-'60s, particularly during the Cultural Revolution, some 3 million visitors came here every year—that's 8,000 a day. The numbers declined, of course, as the terrible consequences of the period became clear, but as time has passed, those consequences have come to be placed in the context of Mao's overall achievements, and a train to Shaoshan still leaves Changsha daily at 7 AM.

The older part of Shaoshan and its surrounding countryside are quite charming. The original town—about 4 km (2½ mi) away from the newer, uninspired buildings by the train station—is a farming community. It stands among reflective paddy fields and is cradled by lush green hills

covered in tea plantations, orange orchards, and bamboo groves. Apart
from the Mao industry, Shaoshan offers an opportunity to enjoy one
of China's greatest attributes—its countryside.

Mao appeared at the **Mao Zedong Guju** (House Where Mao Was
Born) in 1893. The son of a farmer (who was better-off than the poor
peasant of Communist mythology), Mao lived here until 1910 when
he moved to Changsha to begin college. The house, which became a
museum in 1964, is surprisingly large, with a thatched roof and mud
walls. It is, of course, in a better state of repair than most of its neighbors. Nonetheless, the spirit of simplicity has been retained, and it has
an air of formal homeyness. From the courtyard you enter a room originally devoted to the ancestral altar. Then come a kitchen, a dining room,
three family bedrooms, and a guest room, all within close proximity
to the livestock pens. Personal items belonging to Mao and his family
are on display here, as well as photos of his parents and of him from
his revolutionary days. ✉ *Northeastern outskirts of village.* 🎫 *Y5.*
🕐 *Daily 8:30–5.*

The **Mao Zedong Tongzhi Jinianguan** (Museum of Comrade Mao), which
opened during the Cultural Revolution, is devoted to Mao's life in its
revolutionary context. The museum is filled with photographs and items
relating to Mao's revolutionary career. Unfortunately, the exhibition
has few English captions. ✉ *Village square.* 🎫 *Y5.* 🕐 *Daily 8:30–5.*

When you have had enough of Mao, you may wish to simply explore
the countryside around the town. A path leads up **Shaofeng,** the hill that
dominates the town, meandering among trees and bamboo groves past
inscribed tablets up to the Taoist pavilion at the top. **Dishuidong** (Dripping Water Cave) is about 3 km (2 mi) from the village, close to the Mao
family tombs where Mao apparently retired for 11 days of contempla-
tion in 1966 just as the Cultural Revolution was getting under way.

Dining and Lodging
Simple dining is available all over Shaoshan.

$$ ✕🏨 **Shaoshan Binguan** (Shaoshan Guesthouse). The rooms here are
comfortable, though far from luxurious. You can find something a lit-
tle more sophisticated in the way of dining options at the restaurant
next door, which serves tasty Hunanese specialties. ✉ *Village Square,
behind statue of Mao,* ☎ *0731/682127. 50 rooms. Restaurant, shop.
No credit cards.*

Nightlife and the Arts
Occasional performances of traditional **opera** or of one of the more mod-
ern versions permissible during the Cultural Revolution, which are
revived from time to time, take place here. Inquire with the CITS
(☞ Visitor Information *in* Hunan A to Z) in Changsha for information.

Outdoor Activities and Sports
Walking on the hills around Shaoshan is enjoyable—there are paths
that can be followed across and alongside fields.

Hengyang

⑭ *140 km (87 mi) south of Changsha.*

The second-largest city in Hunan has a few points of interest—**Shigushan**
(Stone Drum Mountain) and the **Huiyanfeng** (Mountain of the Wild
Geese), with its temple remains. But the main reason for visiting
★ Hengyang is to go on to the beautiful 4,234-ft **Hengshang Shan** (also
known as Nanyue; ✉ 1 hr by road northeast of Hengyang), one of
China's Five Holy Mountains. At the foot of the massif is the large

Nanyue Damiao (Nanyue Grand Temple), originally built in AD 725. Covering a considerable area, it consists of an array of halls and pavilions dedicated to various aspects of Buddhism and, about 4 km (2½ mi) from the main monastery, the tomb of the monk Xi Qian, who founded the Japanese sect of Buddhism in the 8th century.

Wulingyuan

⑮ *350 km (217 mi) northwest of Changsha.*

★ This nature reserve in northwest Hunan comprises three areas— Suoxiyu, Tianzishan, and **Zhangjiajie**, among which the latter is the best known. A spectacular area of peaks eroded into dramatic shapes, waterfalls, and caves, including the largest cavern in Asia, Zhangjiajie is a splendid place for relaxing and for walking along trails (maps are available). The natural scenery speaks for itself, but many of the rocks, pools, and caves have been given names in accordance with their perceived resemblance to buildings, animals, and so on.

Dining and Lodging

$$–$$$ ☷ **Zhangjiajie Binguan** (Zhangjiajie Hotel). This, the best option in town, has a wing with quite clean, well-appointed rooms and an older part where the rooms are damp and rather shabby. ⊠ *Off the main street,* ☎ *0744/857–2388. Restaurant, shop, travel services. No credit cards.*

Yueyang

⑯ *150 km (93 mi) north of Changsha.*

This small town on the Yangzi has a lively port atmosphere. The **Yueyang Lou** (Yueyang Pavilion), one of the best known south of the Yangzi, is a temple set above the river that dates from the Tang dynasty, famous as a meeting place for such great classical poets as Du Fu and Li Bai. The main tower is surrounded by pavilions, including the **Sancui Ting** (Pavilion of the Three Drinking Sprees), named in honor of the Taoist Lu Dongbin, who became drunk here on three occasions. The brick **Cishi Ta** (Cishi Pagoda) dates from 1242. Both are on the shoreline of Dongting Hu, the second-largest freshwater lake in China, with an area of 3,900 square km (1,500 square mi). On one of the islands of the lake, Junshan Dao, silver needle tea, one of the most famous and expensive teas in China, is grown. The island can be easily reached on one of the boats that regularly depart from the town.

You can board a steamer in Yueyan for the journey up or down the Yangzi.

Dining and Lodging

$$ ✕ **Yueyang Binguan** (Yueyang Hotel). The best hotel in town (given that the other possibilities are not very appealing) has comfortable rooms. ⊠ *26 Dongting Beilu,* ☎ *0730/832–0011,* ℻ *0730/832–0235. Restaurant, air-conditioning, shop. No credit cards.*

Hunan A to Z

To research prices, get advice from other travelers, and book travel arrangements, visit www.fodors.com.

AIR TRAVEL

The Changsha airport is 15 km (9 mi) east of the city. For bus or train services to the airport, contact the Changsha CITS. Flights go to all major cities in China, including a handful every week to Hong Kong.

You can fly to Zhangjiajie from Changsha, Beijing, Guangzhou, Shanghai, and Chongqing.

➤ CONTACTS: **Changsha CITS** (✉ 38 Zhanlanguanlu Rd., ☎ 0731/443–3943).

BUS TRAVEL

Changsha's long-distance bus station is in the eastern part of the city, close to the train station. There is daily service to major cities across the country, such as Guangzhou (18 hours), Nanchang, and Nanking (30 hours), as well as frequent departures to Hengyang, Shaoshan, Yueyang, and Zhangjiajie (10 hours).

Shaoshan's bus station is in the new town close to the railway station.

CAR RENTAL

Self-drive cars are out of the question, but cars with drivers can be hired through CITS.

EMERGENCIES

➤ CONTACTS: **PSB** (✉ Huangxing Lu, western part of Changsha).

MONEY MATTERS

The Huatian and the Dolton have hotel exchange counters in Changsha. The Bank of China also exchanges currency.
➤ BANKS: **Bank of China** (✉ Wuyi Donglu, Changsha).

TRAIN TRAVEL

The Changsha railway station is in the eastern part of the city. Changsha is linked by direct services to Guangzhou, Guilin, Beijing, Kunming, Lanzhou, Shanghai, and Xian, as well as to Hengyang, Yueyang, and Zhangjiajie (15 hours), and to the Mao shrine at Shaoshan.
➤ TRAIN INFORMATION: **Changsha railway station** (✉ Wuyi Donglu, ☎ 0731/229–6421).

TRANSPORTATION AROUND HUNAN

Changsha has comprehensive bus service (maps are available from the railway station and from book shops). Taxis and pedicabs can be hailed or found at hotels and at the railway station.

Everything in Shaoshan village can be reached on foot. Pedicabs and taxis are available around the railway and bus stations to take you to the village.

VISITOR INFORMATION

➤ TOURIST INFORMATION: **CITS** (✉ 38 Zhanlanguanlu Rd., ☎ 0731/443–3943).

GUANGXI

The Autonomous Region of Guangxi is famous above all for the scenery of Guilin, an oasis of fairy-tale stone peaks rising from valleys and rivers that has been celebrated by painters and poets for centuries.

Guangxi has a population of a mere 46 million, occupying an area of 236,000 square km (91,000 square mi). It has often been the object of struggle between its indigenous peoples and the Han, who established suzerainty only in the 19th century. At the same time, it drew the attentions of the French and British, who were competing for trade advantages in the region. Several towns and cities were compelled eventually to open themselves up to trade with the Western powers of the era. During World War II Guangxi was occupied at various times by the Japanese. In 1958, at last, as a sop to the indigenous peoples of the region—the Dong, Gelao, Hui, Jing, Maonan, Miao, Shui, Yao, Yi, and, in particular, the Zhuang people, who constitute about a third

of the Guangxi's population—the government in Beijing turned Guangxi into one of five autonomous regions, which, in theory alone, have an element of self-government.

Although thoroughly assimilated into Chinese life today, there's enough archaeological evidence—including a fantastic series of prehistoric rock friezes along the Zuo River near the Vietnam border—to link the Zhuang with a Bronze Age culture of Southeast Asia. The Zhuang language is unusual in that, instead of using pinyin, it follows its own method of rendering Chinese characters into roman text. This accounts for the novel spellings you'll encounter on street signs and elsewhere: "Minzu Dadao" (Nationality Avenue), for example, becomes "Minzcuzdadau." Other areas of Guangxi, such as the northeastern hills around Sanjiang, are home to less integrated groups, such as the Dong, whose more actively traditional way of life makes for a fascinating trip (you can hop between villages on public buses). The attraction of Guangxi's cities is more ephemeral, as their characters are vanishing along with traces of their colonial heritage. Liuzhou is at the heart of Guangxi's rail network, while plenty of people pass through easterly Wuzhou, terminus for the journey up the Xi River from Guangzhou. Far fewer manage to reach the south and the tropically languid capital, Nanning, or the coastal port of Beihai. Those who do, cross a central region whose history touches on the origins of the Taiping Uprising, 19th-century China's most widespread rebellion against the rotting Qing empire.

Guangxi is an essentially mountainous region, 85% of which is composed of the distinctive karst rock formations that have made Guilin so famous. They rise from the coastal plain in the south, by the Gulf of Tonkin, and reach a height of 7,030 ft. The climate is subtropical, affected by seasonal monsoons, with long, hot, humid, and frequently wet summers and mild winters.

Guilin

500 km (310 mi) northwest of Hong Kong; 1,675 km (1,039 mi) southwest of Beijing; 400 km (248 mi) southwest of Changsha.

By Chinese standards Guilin is a small town and architecturally not very distinguished at that, mostly because of the amount of bombing it suffered during the Sino-Japanese War. Yet it is plumb in the middle of some of the most beautiful scenery in the world. This landscape of limestone karst hills and mountains, rising almost sheer from the earth and clustered closely together over hundreds of square kilometers of orchards, paddy fields, and shallow streams, has a dreamy quality that is hypnotic.

The town itself has a surprisingly long history. Its current name dates only from the Ming dynasty; before that it was Shian. The first emperor of a united China, Qin Shihuang, established a garrison here when he made a military expedition to the south in 214 BC. He later built the Lingqu Canal to link the Lijiang (Li River), which flows through Guilin, with the Xiangjiang (Xiang River) to create what was for centuries the most important traffic route between central and south China and between the Zhu (Pearl) and Chang (Yangzi) rivers.

During the early years of the Ming dynasty Guilin was the capital of a small kingdom ruled by Zhu Shouqian, a nephew of the dynasty's founder. The last of the Ming royal house took refuge here in the mid-17th century as the Manchurians seized power in the country to begin the last imperial dynasty, the Qing. The town's population grew quickly during the Sino-Japanese War, when refugees fled here from the north. Nowadays the population is swollen, indeed saturated, by a constant

Guilin

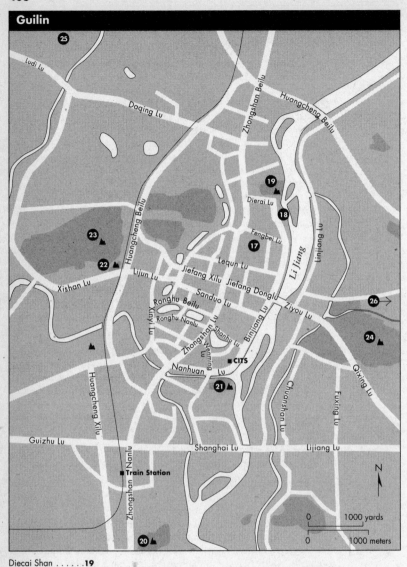

flow of visitors, a challenge to which local entrepreneurs have risen with alacrity.

Formation of the hills dates back about 200 million years, to when the area was under the sea. As the land beneath began to push up, the sea receded, and the effects of the ensuing erosion over thousands of years produced this sublime scenery.

Although the real beauty of the countryside lies outside the town and is best enjoyed by boat, there are several hills in the town itself. By means of the stairways that have been cut into their flanks, it is possible to climb them without too much trouble and enjoy wonderful views **(17)** across the town to the sea of misty hills beyond. **Duxiu Feng** (Peak of Solitary Beauty) is about 492 ft high, the summit reached by just over 300 steps. It is within the precincts of the old Ming palace, which was built in 1393 and of which little remains. The peak is also inside Guangxi Shifan Xueyuan (Guangxi Teachers College) and is accessible only after 2 PM, when classes end. Caves along the way are decorated with inscriptions, some dating to the Tang dynasty; many are in fact important historical records or, in some cases, literary masterpieces.

(18) **Fubo Shan** (Whirlpool Hill) offers views, and at its base is a huge bell and the **Qian Ren Gang** (Vessel of a Thousand Men) from the Qing dynasty. Here, too, is the **Huanzhu Dong** (Cave of the Returned Pearl), containing a 10-ft stalactite.

(19) **Diecai Shan** (Mountain of Piled Brocades) stands, at 732 ft, on the banks of the Li River and was for centuries a famous retreat for literary and philosophical figures, who built pavilions and halls here. None survive, but in the past their fame attracted visitors from all over China, long before the idea of modern tourism was even considered. In several grottoes there remain inscriptions and Buddhist statues from the Tang and Song periods, not to mention the poem "Ascending to gaze upon the magical birds amongst the clustered peaks by the light of the brilliant moon," by Yuan Mei, the Qing dynasty poet.

(20) **Nanxi Shan** (South Creek Hill), to the south of the town, has two almost identical peaks and is rich in geological formations and inscrip- **(21)** tions from the Tang and Song dynasties. An image of **Xiangbi Shan** (Elephant Trunk Hill) at one time appeared on Chinese currency bills. On the banks of the river in the south of the town, it takes its name from a branch of rock extending from the hill and arching into the river like the trunk of an elephant. There is also a legend attached to this phenomenon: An elephant descended from paradise to help the citizens of Guilin in their toil. The King of Heaven, disgusted at this display of charity, turned the elephant to stone as he drank at the river's edge. As with many Chinese legends, you almost feel that something crucial has been omitted from the story, but nobody seems to know what it is. Behind the trunk is a grotto covered in poetic inscriptions inspired by the beauty of the place, some by the greatest poets of the Song dynasty.

(22) On the western fringes of the town are other hills of interest. **Yin Shan** has some fine carvings from the Tang dynasty and by a Five Dynasties **(23)** monk. At **Xi Shan** the Buddhist carvings are considered among the finest Tang dynasty works in China.

(24) The arrangement of the hills in **Qixing Gongyuan** (Seven Star Park) is said to resemble the Great Bear constellation. The park is an extremely pleasant place in which to get a feeling for the hills. It is dominated by **Putuoshan**, where there are some famous examples of Tang calligraphy, protected by a pavilion. There is also calligraphy on the hillside by the Taoist philosopher of the Ming dynasty, Pan Changjing, while below is an array of interestingly shaped rocks.

Just by Putuoshan is the **Qixing Dong** (Seven Star Cliff) with several large caves. The largest contains rock formations that are thought to resemble a lion with a ball, an elephant, and other figures. An inscription in the cave dates from AD 590.

South of Putuoshan is **Yueya Shan** (Crescent Moon Hill). At its foot is **Longyin Dong** (Dragon Lair Cave), rich in carved inscriptions, some of which are said to date back 1,600 years. With imagination, you can see the imprint of a recently departed dragon in the roof of the cave. ⊠ *Jiefang Donglu, east of Li River; take taxi or pedicab from station.* ☉ *Daily 8–5.*

㉕ In the countryside on the northwest fringes of Guilin, **Ludi Yan** (Reed Flute Cave) is an underground extravaganza—curious rock formations gaudily illuminated to emphasize their coincidental similarity with birds, plants, and animals—that you either love or hate. A path, a third of a mile long, threads through what is in many ways quite an entertaining and sometimes dramatic underground palace. Some of the formations are remarkable, but perhaps the most impressive item is the Crystal Palace of the Dragon King, where there is an area of pools and small mounds that resemble a miniature Guilin. Although the cave is illuminated, a flashlight is useful. The hawkers outside the cave can be particularly aggressive and dishonest. ⊠ *Northwest edge of town; take bicycle, taxi, or pedicab from station.* 🎟 *Y50.* ☉ *Daily 8:30–11 and 12:30–3:30.*

㉖ A few miles east of the town is the **Zhu Shouqian Ling** (Ming Tomb), the tomb of Zhu Shouqian, the nephew of the first Ming emperor, who founded a principality here. The tomb is complete with a sacred way and makes a pleasant excursion by bicycle. ⊠ *Take Jiefang Donglu to Jiefang Bridge and Ziyou Lu. Take second left, and follow road about 9 km (5 mi).* 🎟 *Free.* ☉ *Daily.*

Dining and Lodging

The main streets of Guilin are lined at night with tables serving simple, flavorsome, and cheap dishes (always check on the price in advance). Other restaurants serve exotic dishes like snake soup—these are easily spotted because of the snakes coiled up in cages outside.

$$ ✕ **Tailian Fandian** (Tailian Hotel). At this restaurant, well known to locals, you'll find a tasty array of Cantonese dim sum. ⊠ *102 Zhongshan Lu,* ☎ *0773/282–2888. V.*

$$ ✕ **Yueyalo.** This pleasant restaurant, surrounded by a park dominated by its karst rocks and hills, serves local and regional dishes. Specialty dishes feature a combination of Southern Guangdong flavor with local indigenous recipes, such as noodles with scallions, kale, and peanuts in a hot sauce. Sweating, red-faced locals sit together gossiping and challenging each other to hotter and hotter chili peppers. ⊠ *Seven Star Park,* ☎ *no phone. AE, V.*

$–$$ ✕ **Yiyuan Fandian** (Yiyuan Restaurant). At this friendly restaurant, with its all-wood exterior, the specialty is Sichuanese cooking. ⊠ *Nanhuan Lu,* ☎ *no phone. No credit cards.*

$$$$ 🏨 **Guilin Dayu Dafandian.** (Sheraton Guilin). This modern, comfortable, well-managed hotel overlooking the river has good facilities and rooms that are smart, clean, and spacious. The formal restaurant serves excellent Chinese cuisine. A small café attracts homesick Westerners and stylish locals with a '50s rock 'n' roll motif and eclectic snacks such as pizza, steak sandwiches, and pumpkin soup. ⊠ *Binjiang Lu, 541001,* ☎ *0773/282–5588,* FAX *0773/282–5598,* WEB *www.sheraton.com. 411 rooms, 19 suites. 3 restaurants, bar, air-conditioning, room service, shops, nightclub, meeting rooms, travel services. AE, MC, V.*

$$$–$$$$ ☎ **Guilin Diyuan Jiudian** (Guilin Royal Garden Hotel). Located directly on the east bank of the tranquil Lijiang River, the Guilin Royal Garden Hotel now offers both an unparalleled setting, and service and facilities meeting with internationally recognized 5-Star standards. Overlooking the east bank of the Li River, this luxury hotel offers spacious, airy rooms with views of some of Guilin's famous peaks. ⊠ *Linjiang Lu, 541004,* ☎ *0662/913–6030,* 𝐅𝐀𝐗 *0662/587–8657. 335 rooms. 3 restaurants, bar, pool, beauty salon, exercise room, shops, meeting room, travel services, business services.*

$$$–$$$$ ☎ **Jiari Guilin Binguan** (Holiday Inn Guilin). Here you'll find the
★ chain's standard comfort and value, in a pleasant location by the bamboo-lined Banyan Lake, in the older part of town. ⊠ *14 Ronghu Beilu, 541002,* ☎ *0773/282–3950,* 𝐅𝐀𝐗 *0773/282–2101. 259 rooms. 2 restaurants, health club, shops, nightclub, pool. AE, MC, V.*

$–$$ ☎ **Dangui Dajiudian** (Osmanthus Hotel). This midrange hotel in a
★ pleasant location has good facilities, though the rooms, which are modern and basically comfortable, could use a face-lift. Some have riverside views. The service of this hotel is superior thanks to its bilingual staff. ⊠ *451 Zhongshan Nanlu, 541002,* ☎ *0773/383–4300,* 𝐅𝐀𝐗 *0773/ 383–5316. 400 rooms. 2 restaurants, bar, air-conditioning, pool, shops, nightclub. AE, MC, V.*

$–$$ ☎ **Lijiang Fandian** (Lijiang Hotel). For many years the main tourist hotel, it still has one of the best locations in town, right next to the Li River. It is fairly well appointed, though it has been surpassed in quality by newer hotels in town. ⊠ *1 Shanhu Lu, 541001,* ☎ *0773/282–2881,* 𝐅𝐀𝐗 *0773/282–2891. 388 rooms. 2 restaurants, bar, shops, nightclub, travel services. AE, MC, V.*

Nightlife and the Arts

Performances of **opera** or acrobatics frequently take place; to find out what's on, ask CITS or at your hotel.

There are plenty of popular **karaoke bars** near the hotels. The best **bars** are in the hotels.

Outdoor Activities and Sports

Taking a night excursion on the river in order to follow a cormorant fisherman at work can be an unusual diversion. Inquire with CITS, or simply head toward the congregation of boats along the Li riverbank at dusk. Watch as the slender birds plunge into the river and retrieve fish. They can't swallow the fish because their throats are bound by metal collars, and the fishermen sit in the stern of their boats to collect the catch.

Guilin is an excellent place for **bicycling,** which is the best way to appreciate the countryside. The areas between the hills are almost dead flat, and bicycles can readily be hired from around the town. You can go **jogging** around Banyan Lake, along the Li River, or in the country.

Shopping

A few items of local interest—jewelry, bamboo products, indigenous peoples' woven clothes, and handwoven linen and tablecloths and crochet work—are available. Be aware that tourists in Guilin are frequently seen as potential victims: a favorite technique at stalls is for the seller to bend down to place the chosen item in the bag and switch it for something cheaper. To browse, head toward the Li River, where many merchants display their wares, especially in the evening.

Side Trip from Guilin

The best way of absorbing the beauties of Guilin's landscape is to spend a long time in the area and explore the countryside on foot. The next
★ best thing is the **Li River Cruise,** which operates most days between Guilin and Yangshuo. The shallow and limpid Li River, overhung in many

places by bamboo fronds and disturbed only by the splashing of children and water buffalo cooling themselves in the shallows, takes you through breathtaking scenery, threading its way between the mountains. Narrow, flat rafts made of bamboo skim by, perhaps with cormorants, used for fishing, tethered to the prow. So, although you are likely to be on one of a fleet of boats, you will hardly know it. Where the route begins will depend on the level of the water. Sometimes it's not possible to start from Guilin, in which case a transfer by bus is made about 40 minutes downstream. The cruise lasts about four hours (lunch is served on board, and delights caught en route are often offered as extras), terminating in the small market town of Yangshuo, from which it's a 2-hour bus journey back. The peaks that you pass en route have all acquired fantastic names—Dou Ji Shan (Cockfighting Hill), Si Hua Shan (Embroidery Hill)—conjuring something familiar out of nature. ⊠ *Boat leaves from docks on Binjiang Lu.* ☎ *Approximately Y450, includes lunch and return by bus.*

Yangshuo

★ ㉗ *60 mi south of Guilin.*

The boat cruise from Guilin ends at the small market town of **Yangshuo.** Most days the whole town seems to be one giant market. If you watch out for pickpockets, you'll enjoy the experience. In the immediate vicinity are a number of interesting sights, including **Bilian Feng** (Green Lotus Peak) and **Long Tou Shan** (Dragon Head Hill). A short bike ride away are **Heifo Dong** (Black Buddha Cave), **Yueliang Shan** (Moon Hill), a number of other caves, and an underground river. Yueliang Shan has breathtaking views of the surrounding countryside.

A pleasant place to relax, it's also a good base from which to explore the surrounding countryside. You can also go by boat farther down river to the village of Fuli, where indigenous people farm and live in centuries-old style.

Dining and Lodging

Outside the hotels are a number of small, informal restaurants serving good coffee and Western and Chinese food. Prices are low, and there's a wide selection of dishes. Street stands sell noodles, won ton soup, and other delicious fare.

$$$–$$$$ 🏨 **Yangshuo Dujia Fandian** (Yangshuo Paradise Resort). On a quiet patch of land away from the main road, this resort has amenities you won't find in other parts of Yangshuo, in addition to a superior bilingual staff, proximity to local markets, and authentic local food. Rooms are comfortable, and some have nice views of the surrounding karst peaks. ⊠ *102 Xilu, 541900,* ☎ *0773/882–2109,* 𝐅𝐀𝐗 *0773/882–2106. 112 rooms. 2 restaurants, pool, health club, shops, business services. AE, MC, V.*

Nightlife

Many restaurants double as bars in the evenings, catering to young individual travelers. Karaoke is popular here.

Outdoor Activities and Sports

You can hike in the countryside or rent canoes to explore the river and its creeks. Hiking and biking, especially to the surrounding peaks, is popular; bikes can be rented from most of the small hotels on Xilu. In warmer months you can go swimming in the river. As in Guilin, you can also hire boats to follow the cormorant fishers along the Li River at night. For information on rentals, contact the local CITS or the Guilin Overseas Tourist Corporation (☎ 0773/383–4116).

Shopping

There is plenty to buy in the market—Mao paraphernalia, batiks, T-shirts, and antiques. Prices in Yangshuo are more reasonable than those in Guilin.

Longsheng

28 *120 km (74 mi) northwest of Guilin.*

A small town near the northern border of Guizhou, Longsheng is in the middle of a mountain area populated by several indigenous peoples, notably the Dong, Miao, Yao, and Zhuang. The countryside around the town, made up of steeply terraced hills and bamboo forests, is particularly beautiful. North of Longsheng, the town of **Sanjiang** is close to several Dong villages. It is reached via a very bad gravel road. The Dong villages, crowded with beautifully built brown wooden houses, are extraordinary. One impressive spot, about 20 km (12 mi) west of Longsheng, is the **Longji Titian** (Dragon's Backbone Rice Terraces)—a mesmerizing pattern of undulating fields that have been cut into the hills up to a height of 2,625 ft and are reachable by bus.

Liuzhou

29 *130 km (81 mi) southwest of Guilin; 250 km (155 mi) northeast of Nanning.*

Liuzhou is a major railway junction on the Liujiang (Liu River). It first attained importance at the time of the unification of China under the first emperor, Qin Shihuang. But it's primarily associated with the Tang dynasty scholar and minister of rites, Liu Zongyuan (AD 773–819), who was exiled here in 815 after trying unsuccessfully to have government reforms enacted. Notwithstanding his banishment, in Liuzhou he rose to an eminent position and was widely respected for his good works.

Since 1949 Liuzhou has become an industrial town of considerable importance. There is little left of the handsome town described by Liu Zongyuan. The surrounding scenery is a somewhat paler version of that at Guilin, but you are unlikely to find many other foreigners in the neighborhood.

Named for the Tang dynasty man of letters, who was dubbed a prince during the Song dynasty, **Liuzhou Gongyuan** (Prince Liu Park), in the city center, contains his tomb and his ancestral temple, originally built in 821 and rebuilt in 1729. Inside is a stela with Liu's portrait inscribed upon it, as well as a number of others from various dynasties. The park also has caves and hills that you can climb for a panoramic view of the city. ⊠ *East of Liuzhou Guangchang.* 🎫 *Y2.* ⊙ *Daily 8:30 AM–10 PM.*

Yufeng Shan (Fishpeak Hill) is in a park of the same name. The name comes from the reflection of its summit in the **Xiaolong Tang** (Little Dragon Pool) below, which resembles a fish jumping out of the water. The hill is also tied up with a legend, in which a girl named Liu Sanjie sang songs on the mountain complaining of the oppressive rule of the local despots. Finally she threw herself into the pool, whereupon a fish sprang out and bore her up to heaven. To commemorate this, a song festival is held every year on the 15th day of the eighth lunar month. The summit of the hill is reachable by chairlift. ⊠ *Longcheng Lu, in Yufeng Gongyuan, south of river.* 🎫 *Y2.* ⊙ *Daily.*

In the south of the city, **Maan Shan** (Horse-Saddle Mountain) reaches almost 500 ft. So named because of its shape, it bears inscriptions in

its praise and has a cave with interesting geological features. ☒ *Next to Yufengshan.*

Dining and Lodging

$$–$$$ ✕⊞ **Liuzhou Hotel** (Liuzhou Fandian). The best hotel in town is not wonderful, but it does have air-conditioned rooms and is reasonably well located near Liuzhou Park. In a city not known for its cooking, the Liuzhou's restaurant is an oasis; it serves varied regional food. ☒ *1 Youyi Lu, 545001,* ☏ *0772/282–4921,* ℻ *0772/282–1443. 120 rooms. Restaurant, bar, shops, business services. AE, MC, V.*

Nightlife and the Arts

Check with CITS for performances, such as the traditional **Zhuang People's Singing Festival,** at which young men court young women by singing love songs to them from opposite mountain tops. When a young woman is interested in one of the men's singing, she responds with her own song; the exchange is known as *duige* (paired singing).

Apart from karaoke parlors, there are a couple of entertaining bars on **Liuzhou Guangchang.**

Outdoor Activities and Sports

The chief option is to get out into the countryside and **walk.** Try Liuzhou Park for **jogging.**

Nanning

350 km (217 mi) southwest of Guilin; 440 km (273 mi) southeast of Guiyang; 600 km (372 mi) west of Hong Kong.

In the south of Guangxi, Nanning, with a population of about 900,000, is built on the banks of the Yongjiang (Yong River), about 200 km (124 mi) north of the border with Vietnam. Now an important industrial city, 1,600 years ago it was the political and military center of the Jin Dynasty (AD 265–420), outside the rule of the Chinese emperors. Nanning, called Yong at the time, was subjugated only during the Mongolian Yuan dynasty (1271–1368), when it received its present name.

Nanning became capital of Guangxi province in 1912, and then capital of the Zhuang National Autonomous Region of Guangxi in 1958, when Guangxi became one of five autonomous regions. Like Chengdu and Kunming (although it lacks their charm), Nanning has become a busy exponent of economic policies that bear more resemblance to those of the Western democracies than to those normally associated with communism. It is not a beautiful town but has some interesting sites and lies amid attractive countryside. It has also become a transit point for travelers continuing to Vietnam. Visas can be obtained here, and although it may be necessary to change trains at the border, you should be able to reach Hanoi by rail. The link that was built after World War II was severed in 1979, but in recent years, as relations between China and Vietnam have thawed, the journey has become much easier, to the extent that Chinese travel agents host trips to Vietnam.

㉚ Renminyuan/Bailong Gongyuan (People's, or White Dragon, Park) is a picturesque, comparatively tranquil area of flowers and greenery, with some 200 species of rare trees and flowers. The **Bailong Hu** (White Dragon Lake) and some pagodas can be found here, as well as the remains of fortifications built by a warlord in the early part of the 20th century. Within the **old fort,** which offers attractive views of the area, is a cannon built by the German Krupp firm, placed here in 1908 as part of a defensive line against a possible French invasion from Vietnam. The lake is traversed by an attractive zigzag bridge, a traditional design intended to throw evil spirits, who evidently thrive only on a

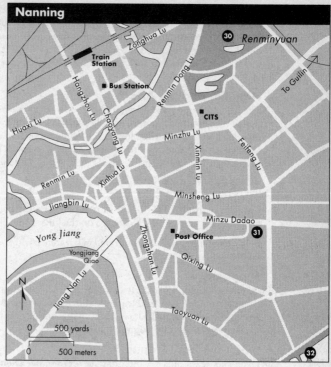

straight line, off the scent. For a relaxing afternoon you can rent a boat and float along the lake, passing by several other bridges and pagodas. ✉ *Renmin Donglu.* 🎫 *Y2.* ⊙ *Daily 8:30–6.*

㉛ The **Guangxi Sheng Bowuguan** (Guangxi Provincial Museum) is a history museum with an emphasis on the numerous indigenous peoples who live here. You can see examples of traditional costumes, pots, and tools. In the back is a magnificent life-size reconstruction of houses, pagodas, and drum towers, set among attractive pools and bridges. A collection of more than 300 bronze drums made by local peoples is also on display. ✉ *Minzu Dadao.* 🎫 *Y5.* ⊙ *Daily 8:30–11:30 and 2:30–5.*

㉜ In the southeast part of the city, **Nanhu** (South Lake) covers 230 acres and has a good fish restaurant, as well as a bonsai exhibition and an orchid garden in the surrounding park. Close by is a botanical garden specializing in herbs. ✉ *Gucheng Lu.* 🎫 *Y2.* ⊙ *Daily.*

Dining and Lodging

$$ ✕ **Nan Hu Yu Fandian** (Nanhu Fish Restaurant). In an ugly concrete building by the pretty lake, the restaurant serves some excellent fish dishes, as well as other Chinese food. ✉ *Nanhuyuan,* ☎ *no phone. No credit cards.*

$–$$ ✕ **American Fried Chicken Restaurant.** Close to the railway station, it serves Western, Chinese, and Vietnamese snacks, including soup and noodles. ✉ *Chaoyang Lu,* ☎ *no phone. No credit cards.*

$$ ▥ **Mingyuan Xindu Jiudian** (Majestic Hotel). This older luxury hotel,
★ close to the main square and department stores, has been refurbished reasonably well and is efficiently run by its overseas Chinese management. ✉ *38 Xinmin Lu, 530012,* ☎ *0771/283–0808,* 🖷 *0771/283–0811. 302 rooms. 3 restaurants, bar, air-conditioning, pool, health club, shops. AE, MC, V.*

$–$$ ⊡ **Yongjiang Binguan** (Yongjiang Hotel). Fairly centrally located, this is a comfortable hotel on the riverside, with well-decorated rooms and an older part where the rooms are considerably cheaper and rather worn. ⊠ *41 Binjiang Donglu, 530012,* ☎ *0771/280–8123,* ℻ *0771/280– 0535. 6 restaurants, bar, air-conditioning, shops, dance club. AE, MC, V.*

Nightlife and the Arts

The colorful **Duanwujie** (Dragon Boat Festival) takes place on the fifth day of the fifth lunar month, usually sometime in June. Oarsmen row long, narrow boats, sitting low in the water, on the river, urged on by a coxswain at the back who screams encouragement as he beats out a rhythm on a drum. Other festivals include the **Zhuang Zou Ge Hui** (Zhuang People's Song Festival), on the third day of the third lunar month.

Theaters (consult CITS for information) often host performances of local opera, some of which is based on the lore of the Zhuang people.

In Nanning nightlife is concentrated in karaoke parlors and bars in the hotels.

Shopping

Nanning is a good place for crafts by the local minority peoples, including bamboo ware and traditional clothes. Try the **Arts and Crafts Store** (⊠ Xinhua Lu). There is a reasonable antiques store attached to the **Guangxi Sheng Bowuguan** (Guangxi Provincial Museum).

Side Trips from Nanning

㉝ Over 700 years old, the little hamlet of **Yangmei Zhen** has the best-preserved Qing Dynasty architecture in Guangxi Province. At the heart of it is the alley, with its distinctive Qing-style carved eaves. Inside, the walls are covered with frescoes of landscapes, portraits, and still-lifes, all in remarkably good condition. The outside lane is paved with ancient slates that remain cool on sweltering hot summer days.

Long favored by artists and poets, Yangmei Zhen inspired Wang Wei, one of the Tang dynasty's greatest poets and painters, to write a quatrain, the traditional four-line lyric that is memorized by scholars and schoolchildren alike: "Indigenous are the red beans to the southern atmosphere/ Sprouting at the first sign of spring./ Come, passionate young gentlemen,/ Pick a few for your beloved." It is believed that, once showered by the red beans, beautiful young women become intoxicated with love. More recently, Yangmei Zhen has become a favorite location for contemporary Chinese filmmakers. For a day trip to the village, contact the regional tour agency: Nanning Tourist Office (⊠ 71 Chaoyang Lu, Yangmei Zhen, ☎ 0772/242–0371) or the Nanning CITS (⊠ 14 Jiaoyu Lu, ☎ 0772/532–0165). ⊠ *30 km (19 mi) west of Nanning.*

㉞ Among the Nanning Hills, the **Yiling Dong** (Yiling Cave) is noted for its exotic and colorful arrangement of illuminated stalactites and stalagmites, through which a path threads for about 1 km (⅔ mi). It is said to have been the refuge of a Taoist hermit who lived here 1,500 years ago and a retreat for people in difficult times. *30 km (19 mi) northwest of Nanning* ⊡ *Y10.* ☉ *Daily 9–5.*

㉟ **Ling Shui** (Waters of the Soul), is a 1-km-long (½-mi-long) lake close to Wuming, with clear spring-fed waters that have a temperature of 18–22°C (64–72°F) year-round. There are bathing pools and pavilions on its shores. ⊠ *42 km (26 mi) north of Nanning.* ⊡ *Y10.* ☉ *Daily 8:30–5.*

Huashan and the Zuo River

㊱ *200 km (124 mi) southeast of Nanning.*

★ In the **Huashan** (Hua Mountain) vicinity is spectacular scenery, much like the karst formations more famously found around Guilin. Nearby are several examples of **Zhuang rock paintings,** depicting very primitive sketches of hunters, animals, and local scenes, sometimes on a gigantic scale (almost 150 ft high). Several dozen sites all told, in varying states of repair, lie within a rough triangle formed by the towns of **Chongzuo, Longzhou,** and **Ningming.** They have yet to be precisely dated, though they are believed to be at least 2,000 years old. CITS runs excursions to the area from Nanning.

Beihai

㊲ *175 km (109 mi) southeast of Nanning.*

With its tree-lined streets and wide boulevards, tropical Beihai has managed to retain the peaceful and relaxing demeanor so often associated with coastal towns. The beaches here, in particular **Yin Tan** (Silver Beach), named after its white sands, are good by Chinese standards. Many Chinese tourists also pass through Beihai en route to the neighboring island of Hainan, which is accessible by overnight ferry from Beihai.

Guangxi A to Z

To research prices, get advice from other travelers, and book travel arrangements, visit www.fodors.com.

AIR TRAVEL

There are flights to Beihai from Guangzhou, Changsha, Guiyang, Guilin, Beijing, and Hong Kong. The Guilin airport, amid splendid scenery, is about a half-hour ride outside the town. Information concerning flights to and from Guilin can be obtained from the ticket office of the **Guilin Aviation Tourism Company** (Zhongshan Lu, Guilin, ☎ 0773/383–5789). Flights go to all main destinations in China.

Liuzhou has several flights a week to Guangzhou, Guiyang, Beijing, and Shanghai. Nanning has direct flights daily to Guangzhou and Beijing, regular flights to Kunming and Shanghai, and a weekly flight to Guilin, as well as flights to Hanoi and Hong Kong.
➤ CONTACTS: **Guangxi Airlines** (✉ 1 Huaqiao Lu, Guilin; ✉ Chaoyang Lu, Nanning, ☎ 0771/243–1459).

BOAT AND FERRY TRAVEL

There is boat service between Hong Kong and Wuzhou. Nightly river service operates from Liuzhou to Guangzhou (12 hours); accommodation is dormitory-style.

BUS TRAVEL

From Guilin's long-distance bus station on Zhongshan Lu, you can get regular buses to Liuzhou and Nanning. There are also various types of buses (sleepers, with or without air-conditioning) to Guangzhou (16 hours) and Wuzhou (9 hours). Buses and minibuses leave regularly from the Guilin railway station for Yangshuo.

Daily buses link Beihai with Nanning, Guilin, and Liuzhou. From Liuzhou buses run frequently direct to Guilin (6 hours) and once a day to Yangshuo. There is also direct service to Beihai, Guangzhou, and Nanning. Longsheng is about four hours by bus from Guilin.

From Nanning's long-distance bus station (⊠ Corner Chaoyang Lu and Huaxi Lu, close to railway station) buses run to Beihai (5 hours), Guangzhou (19 hours), Liuzhou (5 hours), and Wuzhou (9 hours); minibuses go to the Yiling Caves.

CAR RENTAL

A car with driver can be arranged through CITS in any of the cities.

CONSULATES

The nearest consulates are in Guangzhou or Hong Kong. In Nanning, visas for Vietnam can be arranged through CITS.

EMERGENCIES

➤ CONTACTS: **PSB** (⊠ Sanduo Lu, near Banyan Lake, Guilin, ☎ 0771/282–4290).

MONEY MATTERS

Money can be changed in the major hotels or at the Bank of China.
➤ BANKS: **Bank of China** (⊠ Shanhu Beilu, just east of Zhongshan Lu, Guilin; ⊠ Feie Lu, south of Liu River, Liuzhou; ⊠ Binjiang Lu, close to river, Yangshuo).

TRAIN TRAVEL

Guilin's railway station (⊠ Just off Zhongshan Nanlu) is in the center of the city. There is direct service to most major Chinese cities, but journey times are long; for example, to Beijing and Kunming, it's 30 hours; to Shanghai and Xian, 35 hours. Guangzhou is a bit better at 15 hours.

Liuzhou has direct service to Guangzhou, Changsha, Guilin (4 hours), Guiyang, Nanning, Kunming, Beijing, Shanghai, and Xian. Nanning's station is at the northwest edge of town; there are direct trains to Beihai, Guilin, Chongqing, Liuzhou, Beijing, Shanghai, Wuhan, Guiyang, and Xian.
➤ TRAIN INFORMATION: **Guilin railway station** (⊠ Off Zhongshan Nanlu). **Liuzhou Railway Tourist Information** (⊠ Fei'e Lu, ☎ 0772/361–8201). **Nanning station** (⊠ Off Zhonghua Lu).

TRANSPORTATION AROUND GUANGXI

In Guilin the best way to get around, even in the heat, is by bicycle; these can be hired from several places around town. Nanning has motorbike taxis, which means riding pillion or in a sidecar. Bicycles can be rented in Yangshuo.

All cities have comprehensive public bus service, with maps available from CITS and the railway station. Otherwise, pedicabs and taxis gather at hotels and at the railway and bus stations.

VISITOR INFORMATION

➤ TOURIST INFORMATION: **CITS** (⊠ 41 Binjiang Lu, Guilin, ☎ 0773/282–3518; ⊠ 33-1 Dongsi St., Yaru Rd., Liuzhou, ☎ 0772/281–7294, FAX 0772/282–1407; ⊠ 40 Xinmin Lu, Nanning, ☎ 0771/532–0165; ⊠ Xi Jie, near junction with Pantao Lu, Yangshuo).

GUIZHOU

With its green terraced paddy fields, undulating mountains, and traditional villages, Guizhou is among China's most attractive provinces. Because it is also one of the least developed, however, few people pass through the region. Guizhou remains poor partly because of the unpredictable weather (often cloudy and rainy) and partly because of the difficult terrain, with its thin limestone soil.

Guizhou's ethnic groups include the Dong, Hui, Yao, Zhuang, and Miao, among whom the latter are in the majority. The history of Guizhou has been marked by the constant struggle of the native population, now dominated by the Miao, for independence from Chinese subjugation. Chinese influence was established here around 100 BC, when farms and garrisoned towns were spread along the relatively accessible and fertile Wu River, a tributary of the Yangzi which settlers followed down from southern Sichuan. Beyond the river valley, however, the Han Chinese encountered fierce opposition from the indigenous peoples they were displacing, and the empire eventually contented itself less with occupying the province than with extracting an honorary recognition from local chieftains. This did not prevent uprisings: one Miao uprising in the 16th century, near Zunyi, lasted more than two years. Full subjugation didn't come until the Qing era, after war and population growth in central China sent waves of immigrants flooding into Guizhou's northeast. The tribes rose in rebellion but were overwhelmed, and finally retreated into remote mountain areas.

Consisting of about 30 ethnic groups and forming a quarter of Guizhou's population, they remain there today as farmers and woodworkers: principally the Miao and Dong in the eastern highlands; the Bouyei, a Thai people, in the humid south; and the Yi and Muslim Hui over on western Guizhou's high, cool plateaus. Currently Guizhou is increasingly influenced by Beijing, and occasional conflicts between the Han and the Hui do ensue over religious beliefs and practices. The most recent incident occurred in January 2001 when six Hui people were killed by armed police officers in Luoyang, Henan Province; the incident touched off a nationwide protest by the Hui people.

Guizhou's capital, Guiyang, has a few sites of interest, but the province's main attraction is Huangguoshu Pubu. The countryside surrounding Guiyang and Kaili is sprinkled with fascinating villages whose impressive wind and drum towers can be visited by tour or boat. Guizhou is one of the few provinces that has managed to preserve traditions that are rapidly disappearing throughout the rest of China.

About 85% of the province is high plateau intersected by mountains, which reach a height of 9,520 ft. It has warm, reasonably comfortable summers and fairly mild winters, the main disadvantage of which is the high volume of rain brought by monsoons.

Guiyang

③⑧ *350 km (217 mi) northwest of Guilin; 425 km (264 mi) northwest of Nanning; 850 km (527 mi) northwest of Hong Kong; 1,650 km (1,023 mi) southwest of Beijing.*

The provincial capital of Guizhou, with a population of about 3 million, is noted for its mild climate and its convenience as a starting point for a visit to Huangguoshu Pubu. In the center of the province on a high plateau surrounded by mountains, the city stands on the banks of the Nanminghe (Nanming River). The town's historical name is Zhu, but not a lot is known about its history. There was a settlement here during the Han dynasty (206 BC–AD 220), and it became a military base during the Yuan (Mongol) dynasty in the 13th century. It was only during the following dynasty, the Ming, that the town rose to prominence. Then it acquired its city walls (parts of which still stand). It became known as Xingui and only acquired its current name in 1913.

Guiyang, with its large boulevards and metropolitan atmosphere, is a pleasant city. Although like most cities in China it is fast losing its older quarters, enough still remains to render a short stay here worthwhile.

The main streets of the sprawling town are Zhonghua Lu and Yan'an Lu.

The **Jiaxiu Lou** (Pavilion of the Erudite Man) is a collection of wood-shingled pagodas attractively located on the Zhu River in the center of the city. Built during the Ming and Qing dynasties, one pagoda has a handsome triple roof 65 ft in height. Two 18th-century iron pillars stand in the forecourt. ⊠ *East of Fushui Lu and south of river.*

In the old quarter of the city, the **Hua Jia Lou** (Hua Jia Pavilion), an attractive Ming dynasty pagoda, is brightly painted with dragons and phoenixes. ⊠ *Huancheng Donglu, off Minsheng Lu.* 🎫 *Free.* ☉ *Daily 9–5.*

The colorful Ming Dynasty **Wen Chang Lou** (Wen Chang Pavilion) is surrounded with buildings that house a collection of ancient coins and tools. ⊠ *Huangcheng Donglu, off Minsheng Lu.* 🎫 *Y2.* ☉ *Daily 9–5.*

Hebin Gongyuan (Riverbank Park), a pleasant spot of green on the banks of the Nanning River, is most noted for its Ferris wheel. The park has attractions for children in addition to its bamboo groves and ascending walkways. ⊠ *Huangcheng Donglu, off Minsheng Lu.* 🎫 *Y2.* ☉ *Daily 6:30 AM–10:30 PM.*

Qianlingshan Gongyuan (Qianlingshan Park) lies just outside the city. Covering an area of about 740 acres, it has a bit of everything—thousands of different species of plants and trees, medicinal herbs, a lake and hills, and a collection of birds and monkeys. The park is dominated by 4,265-ft-high Qianlingshan (Mt. Qianling), which has fine views of the town from its western peak. The **Hongfu Si** (Temple of Great Fortune), on the higher slopes of the mountain, was built in 1672. The **obelisk** on the wooded slopes behind the mountain, erected in 1949, is dedicated to those who fell in the 1946–1949 Civil War and in the Sino-Japanese War.

The **Qiling Dong** (Cave of the Unicorn), discovered in 1531, was used as a prison for the two Nationalist generals Yang Hucheng and Chang Hsueliang, who were accused by the Guomindang of collaborating with the Communists when Chiang Kai-shek was captured at Xian in 1937. ⊠ *Zhaoshan Lu, 1½ km (1 mi) northwest of city.* 🎫 *Y2.* ☉ *Daily 8 AM–10 PM.*

Huaxi Gongyuan (Huaxi Park) is a scenic enclave about 18 km (11 mi) south of Guiyang on the banks of the Huaxi, the River of Flowers. The Huaxi Waterfall is nearby; the park itself is filled with teahouses, pavilions, and ornamental scenery. ☉ *Daily 8–6.*

Dixia Gongyuan (Underground Gardens) is the poetic name for a cave about 25 km (15 mi) south of the city. In the cave, at a depth of 1,925 ft, a path weaves its way through the various rock formations, which are illuminated to emphasize their similarity with animals, fruit, and other living things. 🎫 *Y15.* ☉ *Daily 8:30–11:30 and 2:30–5.*

Dining and Lodging

$$ ✕ **Jinqiao Fandian** (Jinqiao Restaurant). Although the decor is rather plain, the menu at this good restaurant offers regional food from Beijing and Canton. ⊠ *34 Ruijin Zhong Lu,* ☎ *0851/582–5310. MC, V.*

$$ ✕ **Jue Yuan Sucaiguan** (Jue Yuan Vegetarian Restaurant). Excellent vegetarian food, featuring many tofu and eggplant dishes, is the draw here. ⊠ *51 Fu Shui Beilu,* ☎ *0851/582–9609. No credit cards.*

$-$$ ✕ **Hongfu Si Sucaiguan** (Hongfu Temple Vegetarian Restaurant). You'll
★ find good vegetarian food here at very reasonable prices in appealing
surroundings. ⊠ *Qianling Park,* ☎ *0851/682–5606. No credit cards.
No dinner.*

$-$$ 🏨 **Guizhou Fandian** (Guizhou Park Hotel). The most luxurious hotel
★ in town is a high-rise standing in the north close to Qianling Park.
⊠ *66 Beijing Lu, 550004,* ☎ *0851/682–2888,* 🖷 *0851/682–4397. 410
rooms. 2 restaurants, bar, dance club, shops, travel services, business
services. MC, V.*

Nightlife and the Arts
Ask CITS (☞ Guizhou A to Z, *below*) or at your hotel about the occasional performance of **opera** or local song and dance, particularly
in the village of Caiguan, near Anshun.

Nightlife is generally limited to karaoke and hotel bars.

Shopping
Crafts to buy in Guiyang and surroundings include batik, Miao and
Bouyei embroidery and jewelry, Yuping flutes, lacquerware, opera
masks, tea, and Jinzhu glazed pottery.

Anshun

㊴ *80 km (50 mi) southwest of Guiyang.*

The most important town in western Guizhou, with some nice old streets
and wooden houses, Anshun lies in an attractive area of karst rock formations. Its Ming dynasty **Wen Si** (Wen Temple), 30 minutes northeast of town off Hongshan Donglu, was built in the Ming Dynasty at
the end of the 14th century and later refurbished. Inside the temple are
four 15-ft-high exquisitely carved stone columns; the carved dragons
that wind their way up the columns are considered the acme of Chinese stone carving. Anshun is also a good base for visiting the Huangguoshu Pubu, 45 km (28 mi) to the southwest, and the **Longgong
Dong** (Dragon Palace Caves), 32 km (20 mi) to the south. The caves,
parts of which are adorned with spectacular rock formations, meander for some 30 km (19 mi) through a chain of mountains; part of them
are visible from tin boats that can be hired here (Y35).

Huangguoshu Pubu

★ **㊵** *60 km (37 mi) south of Anshun; about 160 km (99 mi) southwest of
Guiyang.*

Here the Baishuio River streams over nine sets of rocks, creating nine
waterfalls over a course of 2 km (1 mi). At their highest, **Huangguoshu Pubu** (Yellow Fruit Trees Falls; Y30) drop 230 ft and are 263 ft
wide. The largest in China, they're set in lush countryside that is home
to a number of minority peoples. You can enjoy the falls from afar or
by wading across the **Xiniu Jian** (Rhinoceros Pool) to the **Shui Lian
Dong** (Water Curtain Cave) behind the main fall. Seven kilometers (4½
miles) downstream are the **Xing Qiao Pu** (Star Bridge Falls). The falls
are at their best from May through October.

The most populous group at Huangguoshu are the Bouyei, a Thai people who have a festival in the village at the lunar new year. Their specialty is the production of batik cloth, which you can buy at a very
comfortable price.

Xingyi

㊶ *160 km (99 mi) southwest of Huangguoshu Pubu; 320 km (198 mi)
southwest of Guiyang.*

This small town in the southwest of Guizhou has a minorities museum but is mainly notable for the **Maling Hexiagu** (Maling Gorge), which cuts deeply and impressively into the mountains for 15 km (9 mi), with a path running alongside it. The gorge lies close to the town and is best reached by taxi.

Kaili

42 *About 200 km (124 mi) east of Guiyang.*

Kaili is in the middle of some of the most interesting countryside in Guizhou, occupied by a number of minority peoples (mostly Miao and Dong). In the town itself are a few sights: the **Gu Lou** (Drum Tower) in Jinquanhu Park, the Dong people's gathering place for entertainment and holiday celebrations; the **Zhou Minzu Bowuguan** (Minorities Museum; ✆ Y10, ☺ closed Sun.), which displays arts, crafts, and relics of the local indigenous peoples; and the **pagoda** in Dage Park.

Outside town the local villages are of great interest. To the north is the Wuyang River, which passes by many mountains, caves, and Miao villages. At **Shibing**, you can take boat rides (contact CITS) through spectacular limestone gorges and arrange stops at these towns. South of Kaili are the Dong villages of **Leishan, Rongjiang,** and **Zhaoxing.**

Zunyi

43 *160 km (99 mi) north of Guiyang.*

The small town of Zunyi has associations with the Communists' Long March of 1934. Having set out from Jiangxi in October, the party members reached Zunyi in December. In January they held a conference here to analyze their position, a conference at which Mao distinguished himself, establishing a reputation that would ultimately lead him to power. In the west of town, the **Zunyi Huiyi Zhi** (Zunyi Conference Center, open daily), is a Western-style house built in the 1920s for a wealthy landowner. It's furnished as it would have been in the 1930s when the party members held their conference here. The **Changzheng Bowuguan** (Long March Museum) is in an old house and church built by the French in the 19th century. A huge Soviet-inspired monument to the Red Army Martyrs stands in **Fenghuang Shan Gongyuan** (Phoenix Hill Park).

Northwest of Zunyi is the town of **Maotai,** home to the distilleries that produce the liquor of the same name, considered the best in China. ✉ *100 km (62 mi) northwest of Zunyi.*

Guizhou A to Z

To research prices, get advice from other travelers, and book travel arrangements, visit www.fodors.com.

AIR TRAVEL
The Guiyang airport lies to the southwest of the city. There are direct flights between Guiyang and most of the main cities in China, including Beijing, Chengdu, Guangzhou, Guilin, Hong Kong, Shanghai, Xiamen, and Xian. The Guizhou Overseas Travel Service, a branch of CITS, can help with arrangements.
➤ CONTACTS: **Guizhou Overseas Travel Service** (✉ 20 Yan'an Zhonglu, Guiyang, ☎ 0851/586–4678).

BUS TRAVEL
From Guiyang's station there is regular bus service to Anshun (2 hours), Kaili (5 hours), Xingyi (12 hours approximately over very bad roads), and Zunyi (5 hours). There are also special tour buses to

Huangguoshu Pubu from the Guiyang railway station. From Anshun the journey to Xingyi is eight hours.

➤ BUS INFORMATION: **Guiyang station** (✉ Yan'an Xilu, ☎ 0851/685–5336).

CAR RENTAL
Cars with drivers can be hired through the CITS in Guiyang.

EMERGENCIES
➤ CONTACTS: **PSB** (✉ Zhongshan Xilu, Guiyang).

MONEY MATTERS
Change money at your hotel or at the Bank of China.
➤ BANKS: **Bank of China** (✉ Ruijin Lu, Guiyang).

TRAIN TRAVEL
Direct trains link Guiyang with Chongqing, Guilin, Kunming, Liuzhou, Nanning, and Shanghai. The railway station is at the southern edge of the city. There is train service from Guiyang to Kaili (three hours) and Zunyi (about three hours).
➤ TRAIN INFORMATION: **Guiyang railway station** (✉ Zunyi Lu).

TRANSPORTATION AROUND GUIZHOU
Maps for the comprehensive public and minibus network around Guiyang can be obtained from book shops, stations, or CITS.

VISITOR INFORMATION
➤ TOURIST INFORMATION: **CITS** (✉ 20 Yan'an Zhonglu, Guiyang, ☎ 0851/582–5873).

11 SOUTHWESTERN CHINA

THE YANGZI RIVER
AND THE BORDERLANDS

Southwestern China, encompassing
Yunnan, Sichuan, and the Yangzi River,
promises a journey to an altogether
different China, where minority cultures
and unique geographical phenomena offer
glimpses into a colorful and significant
past. A cruise down the Yangzi River
offers the opportunity to explore ancient
cities and view the beautiful scenery of the
Three Gorges, whose future appearance
may be altered by the completion of the
huge dam, Gezhouba.

By Christopher
Knowles

Revised and
updated by
Paul Davidson

Southwestern China includes cities of several million inhabitants and destinations that are among the most beautiful in the country. Sharing borders with Tibet, Burma, Laos, and Vietnam, Yunnan and Sichuan have each integrated influences from their neighbors in a way that has enhanced and enriched their original characters and landscapes. The Yangzi River, and especially its Three Gorges, has recently become the worldwide focus of this region as China proceeds at full throttle with its plans to complete a huge dam across the river by 2009.

Sichuan is famous for its delicious, spicy cooking, its mountain landscapes, and the Yangzi River, as well as for being the principal home of the panda. In and near the province are the cities of Chengdu, the capital and these days known as the modern gateway to Tibet, and Chongqing, the Yangzi River port where most boats embark on the Three Gorges river cruise. Natural and religious sites are also significant here: Jiuzhaigou, a wonderland of waterfalls and pools that is a home to the Tibetan people; Emeishan, a sacred mountain to Buddhists; and Leshan, site of the largest Buddha in the world. A predominantly rural province whose beauty has attracted the likes of poets Li Bai and Du Fu, Sichuan has often been noted for its distinctive character and people. Beyond the modernization progressing in the cities lies a countryside of paddy fields and serene mountains.

Much of Yunnan is subtropical China, a diverse land of tepid rain forests, the colorful non-Han minority peoples, and the natural wonders of the Stone Forest and the spectacular Tiger Leaping Gorge. A bit more slowly paced than Sichuan, Yunnan brims with the influences of its 26 minority peoples, and every city, from Dali to Xishuangbanna, brings an encounter with some new minority culture. Of all regions, Yunnan seems the most unlike the rest of the China, with its distinctive Burmese, Thai, and minority influences and geographical features. Its capital, Kunming, is a big, but more relaxed city. The hot and humid southwest exudes a languor and a cheerful charm that harks back to a simpler past, far from the formal complexities of mainstream Han China.

Pleasures and Pastimes

Dining

In Yunnan and, above all, in Sichuan, the food is excellent. Sichuanese-style cooking is hot, spicy, and strongly flavored, a more hearty version of traditional Chinese cooking. It is said that the use of peppers and spices, which abound in the province, came about to make people sweat in summer (in order to cool the eater in the great summer heat) and to warm them in winter. The adaptable Sichuan peppercorn, when mixed with other ingredients, produces a whole range of flavors, from the fish-based soya and garlic sauce to the tangy vinegar, pepper, and ginger sauce, which has a hint of sweetness.

A famous Sichuanese dish is *mapo doufu* (bean curd with minced pork, chili sauce, and hot peppers); its name comes from its supposed inventor, a certain Pockmarked Granny Chen, who owned a restaurant in Chengdu. Dumplings are very good in Sichuan, too—for example, *tangyuan*, which might consist of four separate dumplings, each stuffed with a different honeyed filling. Chongqing's specialty is the Sichuanese *huoguo* (hotpot), a simmering broth flavored with hot bean paste and fermented soya beans into which raw meat, vegetables, and noodles are dipped to cook. And then there is *gongbao jiding* or Viceroy's Chicken, a stir-fried dish of diced chicken, peanuts, and green chilies.

Lijiang, in Yunnan, is famous for its *baba* (pancakes), while the minority peoples in the subtropical part of the province are liberal with coconut, fish, lemongrass, bamboo, and peanuts. Fried river moss and Burmese-style food are delicacies in the border areas. In Kunming, try *guoqiao mixiang* (literally, "across-the-bridge-noodles"), a bowl of hot soup with a film of oil, into which raw pork or chicken, vegetables, and noodles are added to cook. The Muslim quarter also has good food, particularly the noodles and pastries.

CATEGORY	COST*
$$$$	over Y100
$$$	Y70–Y100
$$	Y40–Y70
$	under Y40

per person for a main course at dinner.

Festivals

This is festival country. The most famous is probably the mid-April **Water Splashing Festival,** in the rain forests of Xishuangbanna, the purpose of which is to wash away the sorrow of the old year and refresh you for the new. At Hidden Lake, in the area of the Stone Forest near Kunming, the Sani people hold the June 24 **Torch Festival,** which includes, apart from singing and dancing, bullfighting and wrestling. Dali has two festivals of note—the **Third Moon Fair,** from the 15th day to the 21st day of the third lunar month, in honor of Guanyin, the bodhisattva of mercy; and the **Three Temples Festival,** from the 23rd to the 25th day of the fourth lunar month. Lijiang has a **fertility festival** on the 13th day of the third lunar month.

Hot Springs

Outside Chongqing are two—the **Northern and Southern hot springs.** Outside Kunming, Yunnan, are the **Anning Hot Springs,** where natural hot water is piped into rooms at hotels and guest houses. At Tengchong, in the mountainous west of Yunnan, is a region of volcanoes and hot springs with both indoor and outdoor facilities. In China mixed bathing is usually not encouraged.

Lodging

Kunming is the only city in the region with first-class hotels. Most smaller cities have at least a few comfortable hotels and many smaller and cheaper guest houses.

CATEGORY	COST*
$$$$	over Y800
$$$	Y550–Y800
$$	Y200–Y550
$	under Y200

Prices are for a standard double room with bath at peak season, unless otherwise stated.

Scenery

Eastern Sichuan and northern Yunnan are dominated by the majestic beginnings of the high Tibetan Plateau. If the mountains are high, the gorges are deep, including the Tiger Leaping Gorge in northern Yunnan, which is among the deepest in the world. The Yangzi, the world's third-longest river, cuts across both Yunnan and Sichuan as well as five other provinces before merging with the East China Sea. The land of the Three Gorges, which slice between Chongqing and Yichang in Hubei (☞ Chapter 10), looms high above some of the Yangzi's most turbulent waters before flattening out into a gently sloping countryside of rice paddies and rocky shorelines. In Yunnan green hills dotted with

villages that have remained unchanged for centuries stretch to the farthest horizon beyond Lijiang, while Xishuangbanna's palm trees sway over the placid Mekong River. In central Sichuan, scalloped terraces rise up hills that give way in the north to crystalline pools and daunting mountains.

Walking, Hiking, and Trekking

In Yunnan you can spend a couple of days walking along the side of Tiger Leaping Gorge, three hours to the north of Lijiang. In the southwest of Yunnan, Xishuangbanna offers numerous opportunities to explore the subtropical forest (CITS should be able to provide a guide). In Sichuan you can try the three-day pilgrimage up Emeishan, or hike around Qingcheng Shan, near Chengdu. In the north of the province, in the Aba Autonomous Region, you can go horse trekking in the mountains around Songpan. Beautiful Jiuzhaigou, also in the north of Sichuan, has excellent hiking trails.

Exploring Southwestern China

Sichuan is one of the largest provinces in the country and has the densest population. In the eastern part of the province is the rural Chuanxi plain; to the west is its mountainous border with Tibet. In the north and south are less populated areas; the north is noted particularly for its high mountain landscapes, which are still inhabited by the Tibetan people. Watered by the Yangzi, Sichuan is rich in natural resources.

Yunnan, bordering Burma, Laos, and Vietnam, is the most southwesterly of the Chinese provinces. Home to about a third of China's ethnic minorities, it is also an area of considerable physical variety, from the rain forests of the deep southwest and the mountains in the north on the border with Tibet to the alpine plateaus around Kunming.

You can begin your exploration of southwestern China on a four-day cruise up the Yangzi River before disembarking at Chongqing or flying to Kunming from Chonqing to explore the rest of the region. To cover the most territory, you can start in Chongqing, Sichuan, with a one-day excursion to Dazu; move on to Yunnan's Kunming, with its year-round comfortable temperatures, and take a day trip to the Stone Forest and, if time allows, a few days in the remoter areas, such as Tiger Laeping Gorge and Xishuangbanna. Another alternative is to choose a particular area and go into it in as much depth as time, money, and tolerance allow.

From Chengdu you can easily plan a tour by bus to the sacred mountain Emeishan or to Leshan. Beyond these sites, still comparatively difficult to get to, are the Tibetan villages and magnificent scenery of northern Sichuan. From Kunming you can fly to Dali, Lijiang, Zhongdian, or Xishuangbanna, until recently accessible only by long road journeys.

Great Itineraries

As distances are vast, reaching many of these places can be time-consuming. When you plan a trip to this region, give yourself generous time allowances and leave as little as possible to chance.

Numbers in the margin correspond to points of interest on the Southwestern China, Kunming, Chengdu, and Chongqing maps.

IF YOU HAVE 4 DAYS

Fly to Wuhan in Hubei (☞ Chapter 10) and cruise up the **Yangzi River** to Chongqing. The cruise will take you through the magnificent scenery of the Three Gorges, in addition to providing you with ample opportunities to stop at ancient towns and small villages, many quite typi-

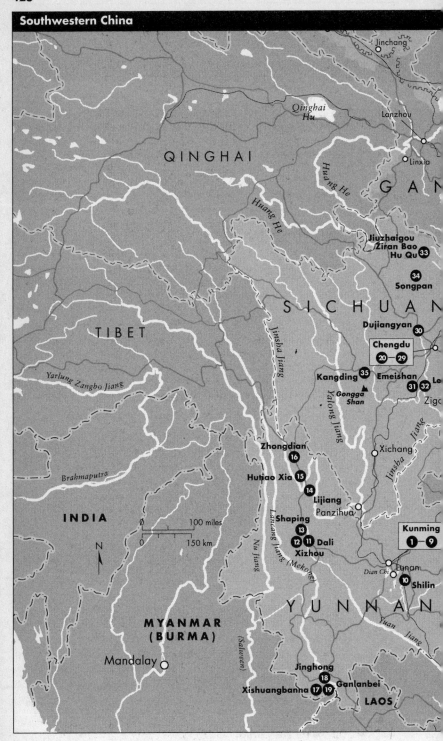

Jinchang

Lanzhou

Qinghai Hu

Linxia

QINGHAI

G A N

Huang He

Jiuzhaigou Ziran Bao Hu Qu 33

34 Songpan

Huang He

S I C H U A N

TIBET

Dujiangyan 30

Chengdu
20 — 29

Kangding 35 Emeishan Le

Jinsha Jiang

Gongga Shan 31 32

Zig

Yarlung Zangbo Jiang

Yalong Jiang

Xichang

Zhongdian 16

Brahmaputra

Jinsha Jiang

Hutiao Xia 15

14

INDIA

Lijiang
Panzihua

0 100 miles

N

0 150 km

Shaping 13

12 11 Dali

Xizhou

Kunming
1 — 9

Nu Jiang

Lancang Jiang (Mekong)

Dian Chi Lunan

10 Shilin

Y U N N A N

Yuan Jiang

MYANMAR
(BURMA)

(Salween)

Mandalay

Jinghong 18

Xishuangbanna 17 19 Ganlanbei

LAOS

cal of rural China, along the way. In **Chongqing** you can take a brief look at the city and enjoy the local spicy food. You can also plan a day trip to **Dazu** if time permits.

IF YOU HAVE 6 DAYS

After following the four-day itinerary above, fly to ☷ **Kunming** and plan a one-day excursion to the remarkable **Stone Forest.** Spend an additional day visiting the areas around Kunming, especially the Yunnan Nationalities Village, which will give you a chance to witness the richness and diversity of Yunnan's minority cultures.

IF YOU HAVE 10 DAYS

After following the four-day itinerary above, go to ☷ **Chengdu** in Sichuan and stay long enough to visit both **Emeishan Sacred Mountain** and **Leshan,** where the largest Buddha in the world overlooks the river. Go by train or fly to ☷ **Kunming** in Yunnan, from where you can visit ☷ **Dali** and ☷ **Lijiang.** If time permits, fly to ☷ **Xishuangbanna** for a couple of days to see the minority peoples in a tropical setting.

When to Tour Southwestern China

In general, high summer is not the best time (the heat is intense and unrelenting, and the humidity is high)—unless you are visiting the mountainous areas, in which case the summer is the best time. Lowland Yunnan is at its best in winter; the rest of the region is most comfortable during either spring or autumn. A number of festivals take place throughout the year (☞ Pleasures and Pastimes, *above*).

YUNNAN

Bordering Burma, Laos, Vietnam and Tibet, as well as the Chinese provinces of Sichuan, Guizhou and Guangxi, Yunnan is a rich and picturesque province that has absorbed influences from many of its neighbors. Dali, Lijiang, and Xishuangbanna immerse you in an astounding environment of cultural and geographical diversity in a region that is both traditionally and untraditionally Chinese.

Yunnan has always been an unwilling member of the Chinese empire. Originally the home of peoples that now form ethnic minority groups, Yunnan was first absorbed into China during the Qin dynasty, but long managed to maintain a determined, if uneasy, independence. By the 7th century, for example, the Bai people had established a considerable kingdom, Nanzhao, which by the 8th century had become sufficiently powerful to defeat the Tang armies. In the 10th century the Nanzhao was succeeded by the Dali kingdom; it was only during the Mongol Yuan dynasty that this area finally submitted directly to Beijing. Nonetheless, separatist movements persisted into the 20th century.

Yunnan has an area of 394,000 square km (152,000 square mi) and a population of approximately 38 million, including the Bai, Dai, Hani, Naxi, and Yi peoples. Geographically, it is characterized by high plateaus, with an average altitude of some 8,250 ft, which are part of the foothills of the Tibetan Plateau. In the northwest the average altitude reaches 16,500 ft. The climate is varied throughout the province—harsh and wintry in the north, subtropical in the south and southwest, and mild and vernal all year round in the area of Kunming. About one-third of China's minorities live here, while half of the country's plant and animal species originated here.

Kunming

11 hrs (400 km/248 mi) by train southwest of Guiyang; 21 hrs (650 km/403 mi) by train southwest of Chengdu; 1,200 km (744 mi) north-

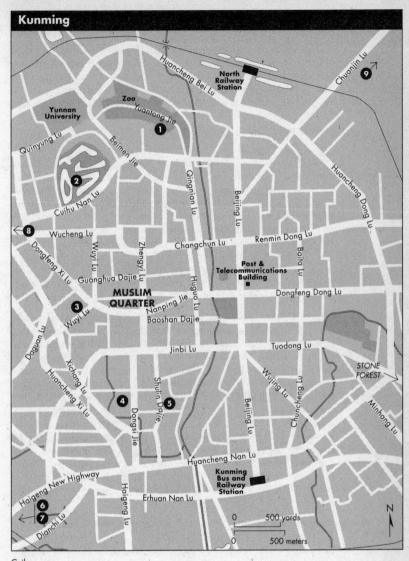

west of Hong Kong; 45 hrs (2,000 km/1,240 mi) by train southwest of Beijing.

Kunming, the capital of Yunnan, with a population of 3.5 million, is one of the more relaxed and pleasant of China's major cities. Like most cities in China, Kunming has lost much of its heritage, but here and there pockets remain. The mild climate has caused Kunming to be known as "the city of eternal spring." Both the city and the immediate area harbor places of interest. Kunming is also the jumping-off point for visits to other sites in the region.

Although there is archaeological evidence of peoples inhabiting this area as early as 30,000 years ago, the city of Kunming is relatively young by Chinese standards. During the 3rd century BC, the Eastern Zhou Period, General Zhuang Qiao was forced to retreat to the shores of Lake Dian Chi, where he founded Kunming. It became an important military base for subsequent dynasties and eventually became a capital of the Nanshao kingdom and a focal point of trade with India, Burma, Indochina, and central China. Later it briefly became the capital of the final vestige of the Ming empire when the last prince of the house of Ming took refuge here to rule over the Southern Ming kingdom, destroyed after 11 years in about 1660 by the invading Qing. The last prince was strangled here in 1662.

Kunming did not, however, lose its antipathy to subjugation; in 1855 the local Muslims (a couple of whose mosques still exist in the city), descended from the 13th-century Mongol conquerors, staged an uprising against the Manchurian rulers, a rebellion that was brutally put down. In 1863 a Muslim leader, Du Wenxiu, took the city and proclaimed a new kingdom. It lasted for a decade before the Qing reasserted themselves. The advent of the railways at the beginning of the 20th century turned Kunming into a modern city. Built by the French to link Kunming with Hanoi, the railway made possible the export of the region's copper and forestry resources. The process of modernization continued during the Second World War, when a number of industries were transferred here to protect them from the invading Japanese. The recent growth of Kunming gradually pushed many industries to the gray outskirts of town, leaving the city center relatively open, with large parks and plazas.

★ ❶ **Yuantong Si** (Yuantong Temple), the largest temple in the city, dates back some 1,200 years to the Tang Dynasty. It is composed of a series of pavilions and temples partially surrounded by water. There are plenty of vantage points from which to enjoy the busy and colorful comings and goings of worshipers and pilgrims, and there are frequently displays of flowers and miniature plants here. Among the temples is a recent addition housing a statue of Sakyamuni, a gift from the king of Thailand. ✉ *30 Yuantong Jie.* 🎟 *Y10.* ☉ *Daily 8:30–5.*

❷ **Cuihu Gongyuan** (Emerald Lake Park), in the northwest part of the city next to Yunnan University, is one of the better big-city parks in China. Trees and flowers line the paths, and carp and goldfish fill the large pond surrounding the park—as in most traditionally styled Chinese parks. The grounds are immaculately kept and the crowds are at a minimum. Several nice tearooms serving various Yunnan teas are in and just outside the park. ✉ *Cuihu Nan-Lu.* 🎟 *Y3.* ☉ *Daily 7 AM–10 PM.*

❸ The **Yunnansheng Bowuguan** (Yunnan Provincial Museum) is mostly devoted to the ethnic minorities that live in the province. Although few exhibits have English captions, to a certain extent they speak for themselves, consisting of traditional costumes, photographs of people in their native environment, and the tools and artifacts they made and used.

More than anything else it gives you an idea of the extraordinary ethnic diversity that thrives in this region. ✉ *118 Wuyi Lu,* ☎ *871/361–1548.* 🎫 *Y10.* ☉ *Mon.–Thurs. 9–5, Fri. 9–2.*

④ ⑤ Both **Xisi Ta** (Western Temple Pagoda) and **Dongsi Ta** (Eastern Temple Pagoda), a short distance from each other in the city center, were originally constructed during the Tang dynasty, when Kunming was still part of the Nanshao Kingdom. While neither is that impressive, as far as pagodas go, they do give a sense of the city's history. ✉ *Both off Dongsi Jie, south of Jinbi Lu.* 🎫 *Y5 for Xisi Ta; Y7 for Dongsi Ta.* ☉ *Daily 8–5.*

Dining and Lodging

Bad restaurants don't survive long in Kunming, so just about any established place in the city is going to have good food. Below are some of the best places serving cuisines hard to come by outside the province.

$$–$$$ ✕ **Cheng Bian Xiang Restaurant.** This popular restaurant specializes in Yunnan dishes. The waiters will point out the boiled chicken with lotus seeds as the place's specialty. It is excellent, but so is everything else on the menu. Go with an empty stomach so you can sample several dishes. ✉ *82 Huancheng Dong Lu,* ☎ *0871/331–1323. No credit cards.*

$ ✕ **Baitadaiwei Canting.** This is the place for Dai minority–style food—
★ including fried pork in banana leaf and black rice in pineapple—at very reasonable prices. Also consider the deep-fried goat cheese, sweetened with *rushan* (sugar). The restaurant is typically Chinese: large and noisy. ✉ *23 Shanyi Lu,* ☎ *0871/317–2932. No credit cards.*

$ ✕ **Guoqiao Mixianguan** (Across-the-Bridge Noodles Restaurant). This restaurant, simple to beyond minimalism in terms of decor, specializes, of course, in cook-it-yourself "across-the-bridge noodles." ✉ *148 Xichang Lu,* ☎ *871/414–4976. No credit cards.*

$$$$ 🏨 **Jinlong Fandian** (Golden Dragon). A joint venture with Hong Kong, this was the best in town before the appearance of the international chain hotels. It is still comfortable, if overpriced, and offers reasonable service. The location is very convenient to the railway and bus stations. ✉ *575 Beijing Lu, 650011,* ☎ *0871/313–3015,* 📠 *0871/313–1082. 150 rooms. 2 restaurants, bar, pool, beauty salon, shops, business services. AE, D, MC, V.*

$$$$ 🏨 **Kunming Fandian.** The oldest of the luxury hotels in town is centrally located and has reasonably comfortable, if overpriced, rooms. There is a pool and a practice range for golfers on the premises. ✉ *52 Dongfeng Dong Lu, 650051,* ☎ *0871/316–2063,* 📠 *0871/316–3784. 320 rooms. 3 restaurants, 2 bars, air-conditioning, pool, driving range, gym, business services. AE, D, MC, V.*

$$–$$$$ 🏨 **Cuihu Binguan** (Green Lake Hotel/Kunming Hilton). In a pleasant part of town near the university and Cuihu Park, just outside the center, the hotel has old and new sections. The lobby and coffee shop are restful, and the rooms are comfortable. The Chinese restaurant hosts performances of traditional music. ✉ *6 Cuihu Nan Lu, 650031,* ☎ *0871/515–8888,* 📠 *0871/515–3286. 307 rooms. 4 restaurants, bar, shops, business services.*

$$$ 🏨 **Yonghua Jiari Jiudian** (Holiday Inn Kunming). Close to the city mu-
★ seum, this hotel has an inner courtyard with attractive Chinese architectural accents. The live music on the weekends and Thai/Western food attract Kunming's community of expatriates. The rooms are standard. ✉ *25 Dongfeng Dong Lu, 650011,* ☎ *0871/316–5888,* 📠 *0871/313–5189,* 🌐 *www.sixcontinentshotels.com/holiday-inn. 237 rooms. 4 restaurants, bar, pool, dance club, shops, baby-sitting, laundry service, business services. AE, D, MC, V.*

Nightlife and the Arts

The main arts possibilities are minority dance performances or acrobatic displays. The **Yunnan Xiu** troupe gives performances Monday through Saturday evenings at 6:30. Tickets can be purchased at the **Kunming Art Theatre** (Nianqing Lu, ☎ 0871/316–5583).

In addition to the numerous karaoke bars, several Western-style bars have popped up around town. Many of these, as well as Chinese teahouses, cluster outside Cuihu Gongyuan and near Yunnan University. These tend to fill up with rowdy students in the evening. The **Bluebird** (✉ Dongfeng Dong Lu, ☎ 871/531–4071) is a comfortable and relaxed café-bar that attracts mostly locals. The **Holiday Inn** (✉ 25 Dongfeng Dong Lu, ☎ 0871/316–5888) has a good bar and disco. **The Hump** (✉ Jinbi Lu at Shulin Jie, ☎ 0871/364–4197), with its several bars and both Western and Chinese bartenders, is popular especially among the younger expatriate crowd.

Outdoor Activities and Sports

Bicycles can be rented at the **Kunming Fandian** (✉ 52 Dongfeng Dong Lu, ☎ 0871/316–2063). You can jog in Cuihu Gongyuan or, even better, jog or hike around **Lake Dian**, near Kunming.

Shopping

Yunnan specialties include jade, batiks and other ethnic clothes and fabrics, embroidery, musical instruments, jewelry, marble, pottery, tea, and medicinal herbs. The main shopping streets are Zhengyi Lu, Dongfeng Dong Lu, Beijing Lu, and Jinbi Lu. The **Kunming Wenwu Shangdian** (Kunming Antiques and Handicrafts Shop; ✉ Next to Holiday Inn) has items of interest. The **Flower and Bird Market** (✉ Tongdao Jie) is worth a visit for the atmosphere and for the array of antiques, fake and otherwise, and crafts on sale. The **Yunnan Wenwu Shangdian** (Yunnan Antiques Store; ✉ Qingnian Lu) has objects from the region.

Side Trips from Kunming

Most of the reasons for coming to Kunming lie outside the city. The strangest and most compelling of the famous tourist sites is the Stone Forest (Shilin), a minimum of two hours by train from Kunming.

⑥ **Dian Chi** (Lake Dian), with a shoreline of about 150 km (93 mi), lies just south of Kunming. As it is still exploited for fishing, junks with their traditional sail and rigging can be spotted at work here (it was the model for the Kunming Lake in the Summer Palace in Beijing). Away from the industrial areas, it is a pleasant place for its scenery, sites, and general rural atmosphere.

At the lake's northern tip **Daguan Gongyuan** (Daguan Park), which was first landscaped in 1682 for a Buddhist temple, offers rowboats, pavilions, and the 1690 Daguan Tower, inscribed with a rhapsody on the lake's beauty by the Qing poet Sun Ranweng. Boats can be taken from the park's dock to **Shan Yi village** at the foot of the Western Hills.

Zheng He Gongyuan (Zheng He Park) lies near the southeastern point of the lake. It is dedicated to the admiral of the same name, a Muslim eunuch, who between 1405 and 1433 made a series of extraordinary sea voyages throughout Asia and Africa, leading to the establishment of trading links between China and large parts of the world. In a mausoleum here tablets record his life and achievements.

Near the lake's northeast end is another park, Haigeng Gongyuan, which features the **Yunnan Minzu Cun** (Yunnan Minorities Village), a sort of living ethnographic display of the architecture and ways of life of the province's various minority peoples. It has life-size replicas of the

towers at Dali and Xishuangbanna—worthwhile if you don't have the chance to visit other parts of Yunnan. ⊠ *Buses from West bus station serve road around lake.*

★ ❼ **Xishan Senlin Gongyuan** (Western Hills Forested Park) stretches more than 40 km (25 mi) along the western shores of Lake Dian Chi. As its name implies, it is a mostly wooded, nature park, ideal for hiking or strolling. Footpaths begin at both Gaoyao and Shan Yi, and it's also possible to drive to the places of interest in the park. Several temples of average interest are scattered throughout the area, mostly on mountaintops, situated for the best views of the lake.

The verdant grounds of **Huating Si** (Huating Temple; 🕿 Y3), a relic from the Nanxia Kingdom dating from the 11th century, lie at the foot of the hills. Rebuilt in the 14th century, it was further embellished in the final two dynasties. Farther up is the pretty **Taihua Si** (Taihua Temple; 🕿 Y3), from the Ming dynasty. Next to the temple is the **Tomb of Nie Er** (🕿 Y3), who was the composer of the Chinese national anthem. Behind it, a chairlift (Y10, Y15 on weekends) rises to the top of the mountain. Close to the top is the Taoist **Sanqing Ge** (Sanqing Temple), formerly the residence of a Yuan (Mongol) dynasty prince. Finally you reach the **Long Men** (Dragon Gate; 🕿 Y10), a network of narrow corridors, shrines, and grottoes dug out of the hillside by Taoist monks between 1781 and 1835. Tremendous views open out across the lake from up here, but the rock corridors are narrow and become crowded.

❽ Northwest of Kunming is the much-restored Tang-dynasty **Qiongzhu Si** (Bamboo Temple), the birthplace of Zen Buddhism in Yunnan. It is said that as two princes of the Kingdom of Dali were hunting, they came across a horned bull, which they pursued to the hill on which the temple stands. It disappeared in a cloud of smoke, through which the princes espied a monk whose staff sprouted to become a grove of bamboo. During its last major reconstruction, between 1883 and 1890, the abbot of the day employed a lay Buddhist, a master sculptor from Sichuan, to fashion 500 *arhats* or *lohans* (life-size statues of those freed from the material shackles of earthly existence) of particular vividness. ⊠ *In hills, about 10 km (6 mi) northwest of city; minibus from West bus station.* 🕿 *Y10.* ⊗ *Daily 8–5.*

❾ The Taoist **Jindian Si** (Golden Temple) sits on a forested hill northeast of Kunming. Its current incarnation dates from the Ming dynasty, after which, during the early Qing, it was enlarged when it became the residence of Wu Sangui, a general sent here to deal with the recalcitrant locals. The most interesting construction is a pavilion, built on a vast slab of Dali marble and surrounded by a crenellated wall that is much decorated with cast bronze, from which the temple acquired its name. The bronze work, which is used in many parts of the pavilion's construction, is meant to resemble timber work; the use of real timber has been kept to a minimum. Among the many trees in the temple are two camellias thought to date from the Ming period. There is also a large bronze bell cast in 1423. ⊠ *About 10 km (6 mi) northeast of town; Bus 10 from North train station.* 🕿 *Y15.* ⊗ *Daily 8–5.*

One of the most important sites near Kunming is a geological phe-
★ ❿ nomenon known as the **Shilin** (Stone Forest). It is composed of closely knit outcrops of dark gray limestone karst that have weathered into interesting shapes since their formation beneath a sea some 270 million years ago. Many have been given names to describe their resemblances to animals (phoenixes, elephants, and turtles) and people. The journey here takes you through hilly countryside dotted with the timber-frame architecture typical of the area.

You can take walks through the forest, which is watered with small lakes and pools; you'll find plenty of Sani tribeswomen eager to act as guides and sell you their handicrafts. The area that most tourists go to has, inevitably, become rather commercialized, but there are plenty of similar formations in other parts of the park if you wander off the main trail.

There are several ways to get to Shilin from downtown Kunming. The best is the new train, which leaves once a day at 8:30 AM on the two-hour trip; a return train leaves Shilin in the afternoon (Y30 round-trip). Many people opt for one of the cheap bus tours (Y20 round-trip), which leave each morning from the area around the train station. However, the bus trip takes twice as long as the train ride—at least four hours— as the driver makes numerous "rest" stops at souvenir stands and junk stores along the way. ⊠ *Lunan, 125 km (78 mi) southeast of Kunming.* ☎ *Y80.* ☺ *Open 24 hrs.*

Dali

★ ⑪ *5 hrs (250 km/155 mi) northwest of Kunming; 4 hrs (140 km/87 mi) south of Lijiang.*

The charming town of Dali, at the edge of the Erhai Hu (Ear Sea Lake), has become something of a cult destination for independent travelers, like a miniature Katmandu. The old gate towers stand intact at either end of the town, and between them stretches a long, single main street (Fuxing Lu) intersected by smaller streets leading to the lake on one side and up to the hills behind. The most heavily frequented street, Huguo Lu, known to locals as the Yangrenjie (Westerner Street), is lined with a whole variety of quaintly named cafés and restaurants that are largely aimed at the young foreigners passing through. Nearby, street markets and food stands abound among shops selling jade, clothing, and batik.

Dali is now the capital of the Bai Autonomous Region, a sop by the Beijing government to the independence aspirations of minority peoples. The Bai, a branch of the Yi people, first settled this area some 4,000 years ago. During the Tang dynasty, with the support of the Chinese, the Nanzhao Kingdom (AD 738–902) exerted considerable influence over large parts of Yunnan Province and even Burma. Dali, called Taihe at the time, was the kingdom's capital. During the Song dynasty the independent Dali kingdom grew up before the region finally came under the heavy hand of Beijing in the Mongol period.

It is worth noting that there are actually *two* Dalis. One is the charming, old city of Dali, Dali Gucheng; the other is an ugly, gray model of Chinese sprawl called Dali Xiaguan. Unfortunately, most bus traffic is routed through the latter. If you find yourself Dali Xiaguan, jump in a taxi or on the No. 4 bus, which will take you to the interesting part of town.

Walking down almost any street from Fuxing Lu will bring you, after about a half hour, to the shore of **Erhai Hu.** Here, apart from the scenery, you may catch a glimpse of fishermen with their teams of cormorants tied to their boats awaiting the chance to go fishing. The birds are used in much the same way as they are in Guangxi province—with a sort of noose about their necks that prevents them from swallowing the fish once they have caught them. There is also a temple on **Xia Putuo Dao** (Putuo Island).

Regular ferry crossings around various parts of the lake offer, in good weather, wonderful views of the lake, distant pagodas, and the surrounding mountains. The ferries usually cost between Y30 and Y70

CAR RENTAL
Self-drive cars cannot be rented in Kunming or Dali, but cars with drivers can be hired through CITS.

CONSULATES
➤ BURMA: **Burma** (Myanmar; ✉ Camellia Hotel, Kunming, ☎ 0871/312–6309).
➤ LAOS: **Laos** (✉ Camellia Hotel, Kunming, ☎ 0871/317–6623).
➤ THAILAND: **Thailand** (✉ Golden Dragon Hotel, Kunming, ☎ 0871/396–8916).

EMERGENCIES
➤ CONTACTS: **PSB** (✉ Beijing Lu, Kunming; ✉ Huguo Lu, Dali).

MONEY MATTERS
In Kunming money can be changed in most of the hotels or at the Bank of China. In Dali, change money at the Bank of China or the Industrial and Commercial Bank.
➤ BANKS: **Bank of China** (✉ Fuxing Lu, Dali; ✉ Renmin Dong Lu, Kunming). **Industrial and Commercial Bank** (✉ Huguo Lu, Dali).

TRAIN TRAVEL
Direct service links Kunming with Guangzhou, Chengdu (24 hours), Chongqing, Emeishan (21 hours), Guilin, Guiyang, Beijing, and Shanghai (60 hours). The station is on the southern edge of the city.

TRANSPORTATION AROUND YUNNAN
Kunming has no shortage of taxis, and the public bus system is comprehensive and cheap. To see things outside town, you can rent a bicycle or take a minibus from the Yunnan Hotel or one of the railway stations. The town of Dali can easily be explored on foot. You can go farther afield by bicycle or ferry; both are available locally.

VISITOR INFORMATION
➤ TOURIST INFORMATION: **CITS** (✉ 1–8 Wuyi Lu, 220 Huancheng Nan Lu, Kunming, ☎ 0871/313–2332; ✉ Galan Zhong Lu, Jinghong, ☎ 0691/213–1165).

SICHUAN

This beautiful province (known to the Chinese as *tian fu zhi guo*, or "heaven on earth"), with an area of 567,000 square km (219,000 square mi), is larger than France (though it forms only one-seventeenth of the whole country) and is the most populous (109 million people) in China. Essentially Han, it is also home to a number of ethnic minorities—the Hui, Qiang, Miao, Tibetans, and Yi.

Geographically it is dominated by the Sichuan Basin, or Red Basin (because of the red sandstone that predominates here), in the east of the province, which accounts for almost half its area. On all sides it is surrounded by mountains: the Dabashan in the northeast, the Wushan in the east, the Qinghai Massif in the west, beneath which extends the fertile Chengdu Plain, and the Yunnan and Guizhou plateaus in the south. Sichuan's natural beauty is augmented by its cultural and agricultural wealth. It is home to several minority groups, and the Sichuan valley (Sichuan Pendi) is one of China's more fertile regions.

Sichuan has a variable climate, influenced by the annual monsoons. The plains areas enjoy mild winters and long, hot summers. The mountain areas of the northwest are subject to harsh conditions year-round,

while the highlands of the southwest have moderately severe winters and temperate summers.

Although the civilization of northern China reached Sichuan about 2500 BC, the province has always exhibited a character of its own, perhaps due to its strongly rural nature. Kingdoms with a distinct culture ruled the area from 1600 BC to 300 BC approximately, but by 221 BC Sichuan had become part of a united China.

After the founding of the first Republic of China in 1911, Sichuan fragmented into territories controlled by warlords and petty fiefdoms. Until the 1930s the province degenerated into poverty, massive debt, and corruption. The civil war and the threat of Japanese invasion threw the situation into relief. Many warlords sided with the Nationalists, although a large part of the Long March undertaken by the Communist troops passed through Sichuan. Then, when the Japanese took Nanking, Chongqing unexpectedly became the temporary capital of China.

Since Mao's death in 1976, Sichuan has gone from strength to strength, making the most of the economic reforms introduced by Deng Xiaoping, who came from Sichuan. Even now rumblings are to be heard on the subject of an independent Sichuan, but that seems remote. The vibrant city of Chengdu, the holy mountain of Emeishan, the giant Buddha at Leshan, and the river port of Chongqing on the Yangzi are among the region's attractions.

Chengdu

4 hrs (240 km/149 mi) by bus northwest of Chongqing; 32 hrs (1,450 km/900 mi) by train southwest of Beijing; 1,300 km (806 mi) northwest of Hong Kong.

Chengdu (Perfect Metropolis) has long been recognized as a significant city on the Chinese agricultural and cultural landscape. With a population of more than 9 million (including the suburbs), it has been progressive since its founding as the capital of the province of Sichuan in 1368. More recent ventures by westward-bound travelers have given Chengdu another title as the "Gateway to Tibet."

Chengdu has more than 2,500 years of recorded history. Until 316 BC it was capital of the Zhou Shu Kingdom, before the first unification of China under the short-lived Qin dynasty. In the centuries that followed, it never lost its importance, becoming the chief political, cultural, and economic center of southwest China. Indeed, because of its growing importance at the center of the silk industry, it quickly became known as Brocade City (Jin Cheng, by which it is still sometimes known today).

Its importance as a center of the arts was enhanced during the period known as the Three Kingdoms (AD 220–280), when it became capital of the state of Shu Han, its reputation for the production of brocade reaching its peak at this time. In the 8th century, during the Tang dynasty, perhaps the greatest period of Chinese history from the point of view of culture, the arts of lacquerware and silver filigree were cultivated here as the city became a major center of trade and commerce. At the same time, it developed a reputation as a place outside the mainstream of Chinese life (partly, no doubt, due to its position in the far west of Han China), a refuge for poets and artists. Its reputation as a cultural center, in the academic sense, persists to this day—there are 14 colleges in Chengdu, including Sichuan University.

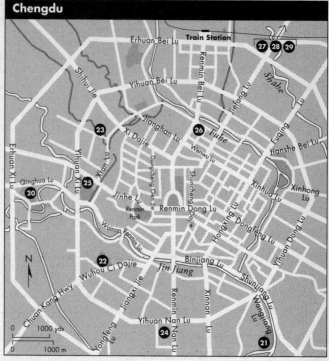

Like many large cities, Chengdu is still negotiating its role in China's rapid economic development. As in other parts of this region, merchants toting baskets of cabbage and well-dressed bicyclists chatting on cell phones somehow manage to coexist, despite the statue of the Great Helmsman that still stands in the main square, gazing portentously along Renmin Dong Lu. Beyond the circuits of furious traffic, however, lies a city of tree-lined boulevards from which here and there radiate streets lined with traditional Chinese architecture.

It is perhaps especially interesting as an example of a great city, obscurely located as far as the rest of the world is concerned, that reflects the pace of change—and the tensions that go with it—of modern China. It is also a great center for Sichuan cooking, which many believe to be the best in China, and is one of the last bastions in China of the art of tea drinking. The places of interest for most visitors are scattered about the town at inconvenient distances. To see the city well, at least three days are necessary. Within a reasonable distance from Chengdu are Emeishan, one of China's sacred mountains; Leshan, home of the world's largest Buddha; and the beautiful landscape of the mountainous Jiuzhaigou.

20 **Du Fu Caotang** (Du Fu's Cottage) belonged to the famous poet Du Fu (712–770) of the Tang dynasty, whose poetry continues to be read today. A Manchurian, he came to Chengdu from Xian and built a cottage or hut overlooking the bamboo and plum tree–lined Huanhua River in 759, spending four years here and writing well over 240 poems. After his death the area became a garden; a temple was added during the Northern Song dynasty (960–1126). A replica of his cottage now stands among several other structures, all built during the Qing dynasty. Some of Du Fu's calligraphy and poems are on display here. ✉ *Caotang Lu, off Yihuan Xi Lu,* ☎ *028/731–9258.* ⊡ *Y30.* ☯ *Daily 7-7.*

㉑ The four-story wooden pavilion in **Wangjiang Lou Gongyuan** (Riverview Pavilion Park), dating from the Qing dynasty, offers splendid views of the river and the surrounding countryside. The poet Xue Tao, who lived in Chengdu during the Tang dynasty, was said to have spent time on this site by the Fuhe (Fu River), from which she apparently drew water to make paper for her poems. The pavilion stands amid more than 120 species of bamboo, a plant particularly revered by the poet. There are also several other pavilions to enjoy in the park. ⊠ *Wangjiang Lu.* 🎫 *Y15.* ☉ *Daily 9–5.*

㉒ The **Wuhou Ci** (Memorial of the Marquis of Wu), in Nanjiao Park in the southwest of the city, was built in the 6th century to commemorate the achievements of one Zhuge Liang (AD 181–234), a prime minister and military strategist of the Three Kingdoms era. Of the two pavilions here, one is dedicated to Zhuge, the other to Liu Bei of the Kingdom of Shu, emperor at the time of Zhuge Liang, whose tomb is close to the Liu temple. The pleasant grounds also have a museum and tea garden. ⊠ *231 Wuhou Ci Dajie.* 🎫 *Y20.* ☉ *Daily 8–6.*

㉓ In the northwest section of Chengdu stands the 49-ft-high, 262-ft-in-diameter **Wang Jian Mu** (Tomb of Emperor Wang Jian), which honors the ruler of the Kingdom of Shu from AD 847 to 918. Made of red sandstone, it is distinguished by the male figures that support the platform for the coffin and the carvings of musicians, thought to be the best surviving record of a Tang dynasty musical troupe. There is a lovely park and teahouse on the grounds, both quite popular among locals. ⊠ *Off Fuqin Dong Lu.* 🎫 *Y20.* ☉ *Daily 7–5:30.*

㉔ The **Sichuan Sheng Bowuguan** (Sichuan Provincial Museum), in the far south of the city, has two sections—historical on the ground floor and revolutionary (from the end of the Qing Dynasty to the establishment of the PRC) on the upper floor. You can see pottery from the early Daxi settlements, bronzes from the Ba and Shu kingdoms, and some exceptionally interesting stone decoration and earthenware figures from Han tombs discovered around Chengdu. Also on display are Tang and Song porcelain and a magnificent 19th-century loom with examples of the brocade that would have been woven on it. ⊠ *Renmin Nan Lu, just south of Yihuan Nan Lu (Ring Rd.),* ☎ *028/522–2907.* 🎫 *Y15.* ☉ *Tues.–Sun. 9–5.*

㉕ First built during the Tang dynasty, **Qingyang Gong** (Qingyang Palace) is the oldest Taoist temple in the city and one of the most famous in the country. Six courtyards open out onto each other before arriving at the sculptures of two goats, which represent one of the earthly incarnations of Lao Tzu. If you arrive mid-morning, you will be able to watch the day's first worshippers before the stampede of afternoon pilgrims arrives. ⊠ *Yihuan Xi Lu at Xi Erduan,* ☎ *028/776–6584.* 🎫 *Y2.* ☉ *Daily 6 AM–8 PM.*

★ ㉖ **Wenshu Yuan** (Wenshu Monastery), the largest in Chengdu, is in the northern suburbs of the city. It dates from the Tang dynasty, though the current incarnation was constructed in the Qing dynasty. Besides the small museum of calligraphy and paintings, the monastery has exquisite carving on some of the buildings. Worshipers come here in great numbers, creating the restful atmosphere special to Buddhist temples. The streets in the immediate vicinity are interesting, too, as much of the commerce is related to worship at the temple. ⊠ *Wenshu Yuan Jie, off Renmin Zhong Lu.* 🎫 *Y15.* ☉ *Daily 8:30–5.*

㉗ The **Chengdu Dongwuyuan** (Chengdu Zoo) wouldn't be worth mentioning were it not for the number of giant pandas (10 at last count)

in captivity here. However, like nearly every zoo in the Far East, the place is mostly depressing and very crowded. As well as the other animals you'd expect to find in zoos, Chengdu also exhibits some rare animals native to China, including the eccentric-looking golden-hair monkey and the red panda. The best time to view is in the early morning. ⊠ *Northeastern suburbs; Bus No. 302 or No. 9 from near train station on Erhuan Bei Lu.* ☎ *Y15.* ☉ *Daily 8–6.*

28 Founded in the Tang dynasty, **Zhaojue Si** (Zhaojue Temple) became an important place of instruction for both Chinese and foreign (mostly Japanese) Zen (Chan) Buddhists. It has been rebuilt several times over the centuries, most recently in 1985. ⊠ *Northeastern suburbs, next to zoo.* ☎ *Y5.* ☉ *Daily 8–5.*

★ **29** For those only interested in pandas, the **Daxiongmao Bowuguan** (Giant Panda Breeding Research Base) is perhaps a better choice than the Chengdu Zoo. Recently opened to the public, here about a dozen giant pandas live in luxurious conditions. There is a special breeding area and a small museum that explains the evolution and habits of pandas. As with the zoo, the best time to see the pandas in action is in the early morning. ⊠ *Jiefang Lu,* ☎ *028/351–6748.* ☎ *Y30.* ☉ *Daily 8–6.*

Dining and Lodging

Chengdu is one of the few places in China where restaurants exist that have established reputations reaching back, in some cases, hundreds of years.

$$ ✕ **Shizi Lou Dajiudian.** The specialty here is Sichuan-style hotpot—very spicy, and delicious. It's more expensive than your run-of-the-mill places, but worth it. If you're lucky, your visit might coincide with evening entertainment, most often music. ⊠ *2 Mannian Lu, off Er Xi Lu at Dong Sanduan,* ☎ *028/431–4732. No credit cards.*

$–$$ ✕ **Banna.** At this casual restaurant, decorated with minority wall hangings and trinkets, the food is Dai, so if you are not going to the Dai minority areas, this is your chance to at least sample their cooking. Specialties include rice cooked in pineapple and deep-fried fish stuffed with chives. ⊠ *Hongxing Lu,* ☎ *no phone. No credit cards.*

$–$$ ✕ **Shufengyuan.** At this restaurant, where the dining rooms are arranged around a courtyard, the decor is handsome and the food excellent. For a set price you can choose from a wide variety of Sichuan specialties. ⊠ *153 Dong Dajie,* ☎ *028/665–7629. No credit cards.*

$ ✕ **Chengdu Canting.** This unobtrusive restaurant is known for serv-
★ ing a good range of Sichuan food. It has two sections, one with simpler food (for a fixed fee you can sample a number of specialties, such as marinated squid and sweet-and-savory dumplings), the other with full meals. ⊠ *134 Shandong Dajie,* ☎ *no phone. No credit cards.*

$ ✕ **Chen Mapo Doufu.** This chain of restaurants has been famous for
★ more than 100 years because of the consistently high quality of its cooking, particularly the hot bean-curd dish *mapo doufu,* named after the original proprietor. ⊠ *197 Xi Yulong Jie,* ☎ *028/675–4512;* ⊠ *145 Qingyang Zhengjie,* ☎ *028/776–9737. No credit cards.*

$$$ 🏨 **Jinjiang Binguan.** This giant, the original major hotel in Chengdu, displays Soviet architecture in a good location. The rooms are little more than standard. A bank and a clinic are on site. ⊠ *80 Erduan, Renmin Nan Lu, 610012,* ☎ *028/558–2222,* FAX *028/558–1849. 523 rooms. 5 restaurants, bar, air-conditioning, shops, dance club. AE, MC, V.*

$$$ 🏨 **Minshan Fandian.** In a good location, this modern hotel with a grand lobby has comfortable but overpriced rooms. The Taibai Lou Restaurant inside is one of Chengdu's popular places for Sichuan cooking. ⊠ *55 Erduan, Renmin Nan Lu, 610016,* ☎ *028/558–3333,* FAX *028/*

558–2154. 422 rooms. 2 restaurants, bar, air-conditioning, shops, business services. AE, D, MC, V.

$$ ⊞ **Xizang Fandian.** Near the train station, this hotel built by the Tibet Autonomous Region Government is a good option for those planning trips to Tibet. There is a tourist office in the hotel lobby specializing in travel to Tibet and a good Tibetan restaurant. ⊠ *10 Renmin Bei Lu, 610081.* ☎ *028/318–3388,* FAX *028/318–5678. 360 rooms. 3 restaurants, business services, travel services. AE, D, MC, V.*

$–$$ ⊞ **Chengdu Dajiudian.** Close to the railway station in the north of the city, this old standby, although a tad tired, has reasonably commodious if overpriced rooms. ⊠ *29 Erduan, Renmin Bei Lu, 610041,* ☎ *028/317–3888,* FAX *028/317–6818. 468 rooms. 2 restaurants, shops, business services. AE, D, MC, V.*

Nightlife and the Arts

Chengdu normally has something going on somewhere. Find out about local opera performances, visiting acrobatic troupes, art exhibitions, shadow puppet shows, and other events from CITS or from your hotel. Check the **Jinjiang Theater** (⊠ Huaxingzheng Jie) for performances. Tea drinking in teahouses is a traditional pastime in Chengdu, and sometimes amateur opera performances take place in them. The best time to go is in the afternoon. Many parks have teahouses; try the **Renmin Chaguan** (Renmin Park) or the teahouse at the **Qingyong Palace.** On the nightlife scene, as well as the usual karaoke parlors, there are private bars around Renmin Nan Lu in the area of the Jinjiang Hotel. The major hotels have bars, and the Jinjiang has a disco as well.

Outdoor Activities and Sports

Rent **bicycles** at the Traffic Hotel (⊠ Just off Renmin Nan Lu south of river). For **jogging** try the riverbank, Renmin Park, or perhaps the park of Du Fu's Cottage. There is a **swimming** pool at Mengzhuiwan (⊠ Off Xinhua Dong Lu, in east of city).

Shopping

The main street for shopping is Chunxi Lu, to the east of the People's Square, where there are a number of shops selling interesting items, including the **Arts & Crafts Service Department Store.**

Dujiangyan

🟠 *1 hr (55 km/34 mi) northwest of Chengdu.*

The **Dujiangyan** (Du River Canal Irrigation System) has been in place for 2,200 years. In 256 BC the local governor, Li Bing, tired of seeing maidens sacrificed to placate the river gods, decided to harness the power of the Minjiang (Min River) to irrigate the Chengdu Plain. The river was divided in two and then further divided to feed 6,500 square km (2,500 square mi) of canal. If you cross the Inner and Outer rivers via the **Anlan Cable Bridge,** you will reach the **Erwang Miao** (Two Princes Temple), dedicated to Li Bing and his son, who saw his father's plan to fruition. Buses (Y5–Y10) leave the Chengdu terminal about every 15 minutes for Dujiangyan. ⊠ *Lidui Park.* 🎫 *Y5.* ⊙ *Daily 8–6.*

Emeishan

★ 🟠 *3 hrs (100 km/62 mi) by train southwest of Chengdu.*

One of China's holy mountains, the dwelling place of the Samantabhadra, the Buddhist Bodhisattva of Pervading Goodness, 10,000-ft-high Emeishan (Lofty Eyebrow Mountain) is in the south of Sichuan. On

it are some 50 km (31 mi) of paths leading to the summit; the climb can be accomplished in two or three days. No mountaineering skills are required, but be prepared for sudden weather changes, which can produce mist or rain at a moment's notice. There are several temples (with simple accommodations) and places of interest en route. You can spend the night at the summit to see the sea of clouds and the sometimes spectacular sunrise. Solid footwear with a good grip is required, and a staff could be useful. The mountain is known for its wily golden monkeys, who have been known to steal items (such as cameras) and hang them in trees. Too much attention has made them rather spoiled and audacious, and they should not be approached.

For an easier pilgrimage, use the minibus service up to **Jieyin Dian** at 7,800 ft, from where the climb to the top will take about two hours. To avoid climbing altogether, ride the cable car (Y40 round-trip) to the summit from Jieyin Dian (though long queues can form for this). At the top of the mountain is the **Jinding Si** (Golden Summit Temple).

Direct bus (4 hrs) service links Chengdu with Baoguo, at the foot of the mountain and about 6 km (4 mi) from the town of Emei, where trains from Chengdu stop.

$$ ⊞ **Emeishan Dajiudian.** This three-star "luxury" hotel is at the foot of the mountain, offering good access for those going on early hikes. The place is a bit worn, but this is about the best in Emei. ⊠ *Baoguo Si, 614201,* ☎ *0833/552–6888,* 𝔽𝔸𝕏 *0833/552–2061. 200 rooms. Restaurant, bar, business services. No credit cards.*

$ ⊞ **Baoguo Monastery.** This monastery, at the foot of the mountain, is one of the better among those offering accommodation. The monks here kindly keep all vermin that sneak inside away from the guests' belongings. ⊠ *Baogu Si,* ☎ *No phone. No credit cards.*

Leshan

★ ㉜ *3 hrs (165 km/102 mi) by bus south of Chengdu.*

In the small, swiftly changing town of Leshan a towering Buddha, carved from the rock face, sits inscrutably at the confluence of the Dadu and Min rivers. The Leshan **Da Fo** (Grand Buddha), at 233 ft, is the tallest stone Buddha and among the tallest sculptures in the world. The big toes are each 28 ft in length. The construction of the Grand Buddha was started in AD 713 by a monk who wished to placate the river waters that habitually took local fishermen's lives. Although the project took more than 90 years to complete, it had no noticeable effect on the river waters. It is possible to clamber down, by means of a cliff-hewn stairway, from the head to the platform where the feet rest; or you can take a boat ride (about Y30) to see it in all its grandeur from the river. ▦ *Y50.*

There are also several temples or pagodas in the vicinity, including **Wuyou Si** on Wuyou Shan (Wuyou Mountain), with its hall of recently restored statues of arhats. Right next to the Buddha on Lingyun Shan is the **Lingyun Si,** more interesting for the expansive view it offers of the Min River. ⊠ *To get to Wuyou Si, take the boat from Leshan jetty and climb staircase.* ▦ *Y2 each.* ⊘ *Daily 8–5.*

The town of Leshan is quite a lively place, with some interesting old streets—Dong Dajie and Xian Jie—and a good market.

Jiuzhaigou

8–10 hrs (350 km/217 mi) by bus north of Leshan; 4–6 hrs (225 km/140 mi) by bus northwest of Chengdu.

㉝ High among the snowcapped peaks of the Aba Autonomous Prefecture of northern Sichuan lies the **Jiuzhaigou Ziran Bao Hu Qu** (Jiuzhaigou Natural Preserve), a wonderland of turquoise pools and interwoven waterfalls that has long been home to the Qiang and Tibetan peoples. Jiuzhaigou provides an invaluable opportunity to observe the customs and lifestyles of people still living as they did hundreds of years ago. Although reaching these places is a matter of long bus journeys on potentially treacherous roads, the opening of a new airport in 2002 should make the trip much easier.

㉞ **Songpan** (two hours south of Jiuzhaigou by bus) is a lively market town in the midst of beautiful scenery where horse trekking is popular. Both Jiuzhaigou and Songpan have fine hiking trails.

Kangding

㉟ *8 hrs (215km/133 mi) by bus southwest of Chengdu.*

Western Sichuan, toward Tibet, has tougher terrain than other parts of the region. The scenery at Kanding is magnificent, its enormous mountains snowcapped year-round. Just south of here, **Hailuogou Bingchuan** (Hailougou Glacier), part of 24,790-ft Gongga Shan (Mt. Gongga), is at the lowest altitude of any glacier in Asia. There are several Buddhist monasteries in the region, and you can go hiking and pony trekking.

Chongqing

4 hrs (240 km/149 mi) by bus southeast of Chengdu; 3 hrs (1,800 km/1,116 mi) by plane southwest of Beijing; 1,025 km (636 mi) northwest of Hong Kong.

In 1997, the Chinese separated Chongqing from Sichuan, making it one of China's four municipalities (the other three are Beijing, Tianjin, and Shanghai). Though Chongqing is technically no longer part of Sichuan, Sichuan still survives in the city's food, dialect, and culture. Built on undulating hills at the point of confluence of the Yangzi with the Jialing River, it is one of the few cities in China where the bicycle is all but useless (in fact it is sometimes referred to as Mountain City). Chongqing is a major point of embarkation or disembarkation for the Yangzi cruise. Although gray, the city is animated and industrious. The vicinity affords fine scenery and numerous day trips.

The recorded history of Chongqing (which means "Constant Celebrations," a name conferred by the first Song emperor to celebrate his conquest of the area) goes back some 3,000 years. During the 13th century BC, before the unification of China, it was the capital of the Kingdom of Ba. Its importance has always depended on trade, which in turn has depended on the city's position on the river at the head of the Yangzi Gorges, through which the river flows to the ports of Wuhan and Shanghai. Before the arrival of the train and the airplane, nearly all of Sichuan's trade flowed through Chongqing, and yet it received the status of "city" only in 1927.

Once the Western powers established permanent footholds in China, from the mid- to the late 19th century, they showed interest in exploiting the markets of Sichuan. The first westerners reached Chongqing by river in 1898, after the Chefoo Agreement of 1876 was amended in 1890 to allow the city to be opened to foreign trade. A regular steamer ser-

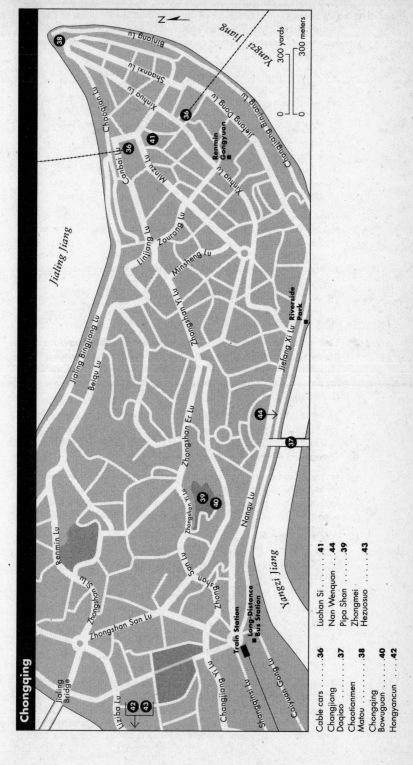

Chongqing

Cable cars **36**
Changjiang **37**
Daqiao **37**
Chaotianmen . . . **38**
Matou **38**
Chongqing
Bowuguan **40**
Hongyancun . . . **42**

Luohan Si **41**
Nan Wenquan . . **44**
Pipa Shan **39**
Zhongmei
Hezuosuo **43**

vice began to ply the length of the river. By the first years of the 20th century a substantial foreign community had established itself, with offices of all the great trading companies of the day and with consulates to serve the residents.

When the Japanese took the Nationalist capital of Nanjing in 1938, the Chinese government moved to Chongqing, regarded as an impregnable fortress because of its location. The population grew quickly, particularly as it became home to the so-called united front, the temporary alliance between the Communists and the Nationalists against the Japanese. Chongqing's population swelled to 2 million, and it became a place of intrigue and desperation, where the misery of overcrowding and squalor was exacerbated by endless air raids by the Japanese, who were able to identify the city easily by following the Yangzi on moonlit nights.

What had been at the turn of the century an attractive town of temples within a city wall was largely destroyed by the end of the war. And yet the city still has something—there are sections where it is possible to grasp some idea of how it must once have been. It has not lost that air of activity, of arrival and departure, that characterizes any port. The spicy cooking of Sichuan is recognized by the Chinese themselves as the best in the country. It is an interesting city to stroll around—but not in high summer when it becomes unbearably hot, fully deserving of its reputation as one of the furnaces of China.

★ 36 Two items almost unique to Chongqing are its **cable cars.** One links the north and south shores of the Jialing River, from Canbai Lu to the Jinsha Jie station. It is a worthwhile experience for the view of the docks, the city, and the confluence of the Jialing and Yangzi rivers. The other crosses the Yangzi itself and starts close to Xinhua Lu.

There are also three bridges across the rivers—the oldest, built between 1963 and 1966, crosses the Jialing while the two newer bridges, built in 1981 and 1989, cross the Yangzi. The biggest of these is the 37 **Changjiang Daqiao** (Great Changjiang Bridge).

38 Perhaps not as busy and bustling as once upon a time, **Chaotianmen Matou** (Chaotianmen Docks) still offer an opportunity to glimpse something of China at work. From here you can see the various boats departing for the Three Gorges river cruise. ⊠ *Shaanxi Lu.*

39 At 804 ft, **Pipa Shan** (Loquat Hill), until 1950 a private garden, is the highest point in the city. It is a good place from which to see the layout of the city and the activity on the river below or, at night, the city lights. ⊠ *Zhongshan Er Lu.* 🚋 *Y10.*

40 At the foot of the hill is the **Chongqing Bowuguan** (Chongqing Museum), in which the main items of interest are dinosaur remains discovered in the mid-1970s in different parts of Sichuan. Here, too, are some fine illustrated Han dynasty tomb bricks and exhibits of ethnographic interest, such as local puppets and woodblock prints. ⊠ *Foot of Pipa Shan.* 🚋 *Y10.* ☉ *Daily 9–5.*

Originally built about 1,000 years ago (Song dynasty) and rebuilt in 41 1752 and again in 1945, the **Luohan Si** (Luohan Temple) is a popular and atmospheric place of worship. A small community of monks is still active here. The main attraction is the hall of 500 lifelike painted clay arhats, Buddhist disciples who have succeeded in freeing themselves from the earthly chains of delusion and material greed. ⊠ *Minzu Lu.* 🚋 *Y2.* ☉ *Daily 8:30–5:30.*

④ **Hongyancun** (Red Crag Village) is where Zhou Enlai, among other luminaries of the Chinese Communist Party, lived between 1938 and 1945 and where the Chongqing office of the Chinese Eighth Route Army was situated. A **geming bowuguan** (revolutionary history museum) has some interesting photographs of the personalities who played a significant role in the events of the time. There is, however, nothing written in English; you may perhaps find an English-speaking guide on the site. ☒ *Hongyan Bus Terminus.* 🚍 *Y6.* ⊘ *Daily 8:30–5.*

④ In the name **Zhongmei Hezuosuo** (U.S.-Chiang Kai-shek Criminal Acts Exhibition Hall & SACO Prison), SACO stands for the Sino-American Cooperation Organization, a group developed through collaboration between Chiang Kai-shek and the U.S. government dedicated to the training and supervision of agents for the Guomindang. It was jointly run by the Chinese and the Americans, who built prisons outside Chongqing where sympathizers of the Communist Party were imprisoned and tortured. The exhibition hall houses a few photographs and examples of the hardware used on the prisoners but has nothing in English. The prisons are a considerable walk from the exhibition hall. ☒ *Foot of Gele Hill, northwest suburbs.* 🚍 *Y5.* ⊘ *Daily 8:30–5.*

④ To the south of the city is a set of hot springs set amid attractive scenery in **Nan Wenquan** (Southern Hot Springs). The springs produce sulfurous water at 38°C (100°F). Catch the bus on Changjiang Daqiao to Wenquan. ☒ *20 km (12 mi) south of city.* 🚍 *Y15.* ⊘ *Daily 8:30–5.*

Dining and Lodging

$$$–$$$$ ✕ **Lao Sichuan.** The best-known restaurant in Chongqing because it has been in existence for as long as anyone can remember, the Old Sichuan has traditional and exotic food (for example, chili-braised frogs) at reasonable prices. The hot pepper dishes are as spicy as you'll get in Sichuan. ☒ *15 Bayi Lu,* ☎ *023/6384–1957. AE, MC, V.*

$$–$$$ ✕ **Yizhishi Fandian.** This is one of Sichuan's most famous eateries. The upper floors are upscale and can be pricy; head upstairs for full-scale local meals with specials like tea-smoked duck. You can eat local snacks such as pastries and *jiaozi* (dumplings) during the morning downstairs. ☒ *114 Zourong Lu,* ☎ *023/6384–2429. No credit cards.*

$$ ✕🏨 **Chongqing Fandian.** This hotel's location in the center of town ★ in an art deco–style building, low price, and relatively well-equipped rooms (each has a television and a minibar) make it a good value. The restaurant—one of the city's older, more famous eateries—serves generally very good local and regional food in pleasantly modernized surroundings. ☒ *41–43 Xinhua Lu, 630011,* ☎ *023/6383–8888,* ℻ *023/ 6384–3085. 197 rooms. 2 restaurants, bar, air-conditioning, minibars, shops. MC, V.*

$$$$ 🏨 **Yangzijiang Jiari Fandian** (Holiday Inn Yangzi Chongqing). This international standard hotel is just outside the city center. The rooms on the hotel's north side offer full views of the Yangzi River. ☒ *15 Nanping Bei Lu, 400060,* ☎ *023/6280–3380,* ℻ *023/6280–0884. 365 rooms, 5 restaurants, bar, pool, gym, dance club, business services. AE, MC, V.*

$$$ 🏨 **Renmin Binguan.** This grand and opulent structure, originally built in the 1950s to resemble the Temple of Heaven in Beijing, is where Jiang Zemin stays when he's in town. Although the building is impressive, rooms in the hotel are just standard. ☒ *173 Renmin Lu, 400015,* ☎ *023/6385–1421,* ℻ *023/6385–2076. 227 rooms. 2 restaurants, bar, shops, dance club. AE, MC, V.*

Nightlife and the Arts

There are often performances of Sichuan opera and acrobatics—ask CITS or at your hotel for information. The square in front of the **Ren-**

min Binguan also usually hosts free public performances. It is worth trying to visit the **Huajia Zhi Cun** (Painters Village) at Hualongqiao. Established as a sort of collective in the 1950s, it has produced some good work.

Despite Chongqing's being a port, it has even less in the way of nightlife than most other cities in China; beyond the karaoke parlors there is little besides a few **bars** along Chaotianmen Dock.

Shopping

The principal shopping area is in the vicinity of the Liberation Monument in the center of town. It is a lively district of shops and restaurants where you might pick up examples of lacquerware, embroidery, and bamboo ware, as well as teas and local produce.

Side Trip from Chongqing

North of the city on **Jinyun Shan** (Jinyun Mountain) are some pretty views and a smattering of pavilions from the Ming and Qing periods. Three house imposing statues of the Giant Buddha, the Amitabha Buddha, and the famous general of the Three Kingdoms Period, Guan Yu, respectively. The park also has a set of **hot springs**, where it is possible to bathe in the 30°C (86°F) water, either in a swimming pool or in the privacy of cubicles with their own baths. ⊠ *Jinyun Shan, 2 hrs (50 km/30 mi) by bus north of city.* ⊡ *Y15.* ⊘ *Daily 8:30–6.*

Dazu

★ ⓸⓺ *3 hrs (160 km/99 mi) by bus northwest of Chongqing.*

At Dazu, a group of Buddhist cave sculptures that rival those at Datong, Dunhuang, and Luoyang is worth the effort to reach if you have the opportunity. The impressive sculptures, ranging from tiny to gigantic, contain unusual domestic detail in addition to the purely religious work. There are two major sites at Dazu—Bei Shan and Baoding Shan. Work at the caves began in the 9th century AD (during the Song and Tang dynasties) and continued for more than 250 years.

Located 14 km (9 mi) outside Dazu, **Baoding Shan,** where the carvings were completed according to a plan, is the more interesting site. Here you will find visions of hell reminiscent of similar scenes from medieval Europe; the Wheel of Life; a magnificent 100-ft reclining Buddha; and a gold, thousand-armed statue of the goddess of mercy. ⊠ *16 km [10 mi] east of Dazu town; take minibus.* ⊡ *Y85.* ⊘ *Daily 8–5.*

Lodging

$$ ⊡ **Dazu Binguan.** Most foreign guests end up staying in this comparatively nice hotel, where each room is equipped with a television and air-conditioning. The on-site travel agency can help you buy bus or train tickets. ⊠ *47 Gongnong Jie,* ☎ *023/4372–1888,* 𝖥𝖠𝖷 *023/4372–1443. 132 rooms. Restaurant, business services. D, MC, V.*

Sichuan A to Z

To research prices, get advice from other travelers, and book travel arrangements, visit www.fodors.com.

AIR TRAVEL

Chengdu has flights to and from all the major cities of China, including Beijing, Guangzhou, Chongqing, Guilin, Guiyang, Hong Kong, Kunming, Lhasa (if you can get a visa), Nanking, and Shanghai. A bus service links the CAAC office (Renmin Lu) and the airport, which is 20 km (12 mi) west of the city.

There are daily or regular flights between Chongqing and all the major cities in China. The airport lies 25 km (16 mi) north of the city, and CAAC runs shuttle buses between it and their office.

➤ AIRLINES AND CONTACTS: **CAAC** (✉ 161 Zhongshan Sanlu, Chongqing, ☎ 023/6360–3223).

BOAT AND FERRY TRAVEL

Boats go on the Yangzi from Chongqing all the way to Shanghai (7 days), but the most popular route is the cruise downstream from Chongqing to Yichang or Wuhan (3–4 days) or upstream from Wuhan to Chongqing. Most major sights, including the Three Gorges and Three Little Gorges, lie between Chongqing and Yichang. Tourist boats offer air-conditioned cabins with television and private bath; the ordinary passenger steamers used by most Chinese offer minimal comforts. Tickets can be arranged through CITS or your travel agent.

It is possible to get to Leshan by boat from Chongqing.

BUS TRAVEL

There are three bus stations in Chengdu. Buses leave frequently for Emeishan, Leshan, and Chongqing. There is also service to Dazu and Kangding.

With one or two exceptions, arriving and departing Chongqing by bus is the least practical method because of its hilly location. The bus station offers regular departures for Chengdu (4 hours), Dazu (3 hours), Yibin (5½ hours), and Zigong (3½ hours). The Kangfulai Passenger Transport Company runs air-conditioned buses to Chengdu, Dazu, Yibin, and Zigong.

Buses link Leshan with Chengdu (5 hours) and Emeishan, only 31 km (19 mi) away.

➤ BUS INFORMATION: **Chengdu bus stations** (✉ off Xinnan Lu south of river; ✉ near railway station in north of city; ✉ Ximen, off Shihui Jie in western part of city—serves Jiuzhaigou). **Chongqing bus station** (✉ Off Nanqu Lu in southwest of city, close to railway station). **Kangfulai Passenger Transport Company** (✉ 223 Renmin Lu).

CAR RENTAL

Self-drive cars cannot be hired in either Chengdu or Chongqing, but cars with drivers can be hired through CITS.

CONSULATE

➤ UNITED STATES: **United States** (✉ 4 Lingshiguan Lu, Chengdu, ☎ 028/558–3992).

EMERGENCIES

➤ CONTACTS: **PSB** (✉ Wenwu Lu, part of Xinhua Dong Lu; 40 Wenmiaohou Jie, Chengdu, ☎ 028/630–1454; ✉ Linjiang Lu, Chongqing, ☎ 028/383–1830).

MONEY MATTERS

In Chengdu money can be exchanged in the major hotels and at the Bank of China. You can change money in Chongqing in the hotels or at the Bank of China.

➤ CONTACTS: **Bank of China** (✉ Renmin Nan Lu, Chengdu; ✉ Minzu Lu, Chongqing).

TRAIN TRAVEL

There are services from Chengdu to Chongqing (12 hours), Dazu (7 hours—trains stop at Youtingpu, about 30 km [19 mi] from Dazu),

Emeishan, Kunming (23 hours), and Xian. It is also possible to get to Guangzhou, Lanzhou, Beijing, Shanghai, and Ürümqi.

The train station in Chongqing is in the southwest of the city. Direct trains serve Guangzhou (39 hours), Chengdu (11 hours), Kunming (23 hours), Nanning (35 hours), Beijing (32 hours), Shanghai (2 days), and Xi'an (30 hours).

➤ TRAIN INFORMATION: **Chengdu Train Station** (☎ 028/333–2633). **Chongqing Train Station** (✉ Off Nanqu Lu, ☎ 023/6386–2607).

VISITOR INFORMATION

The chief way to visit the Three Gorges is by arranging a package tour through a travel agent in the United States or through any of the CITS offices in Chongqing, Wuhan, Chengdu, or Kunming. Depending on the itinerary, boats may stop at all or a select number of sights—ask your travel agent in advance about which destinations you will be visiting; you may be able to request some. In the United States, many travel agents offer one- to two-week tours that may also include visits to Beijing, Hong Kong, Lhasa, Xian, and Guilin. These tours, although more expensive, provide English-speaking guides, first-class living quarters, and prearranged lodging, meals, and flights to all destinations; they tend to be more reliable. Tickets bought through CITS may involve taking a smaller, less well-equipped boat suited to Chinese standards with meals arranged by your guide or yourself.

➤ TOURIST INFORMATION: **CITS** (✉ Renmin Nan Lu, Chengdu, ☎ 028/ 667–4986 or 028/667–8369; ✉ Renmin Hotel, Renmin Lu, Chongqing, ☎ 028/385–0589). **Tibet Tourism Office** (✉ 10 Renmin Bei Lu, Chengdu, ☎ 028/667–5578).

CHANGJIANG (YANGZI RIVER)

The third-longest river in the world after the Amazon and the Nile, the Yangzi cuts across 6,380 km (3,956 mi) and seven provinces before flowing out into the East China Sea. After descending from the mountain ranges of Qinghai and Tibet, the Yangzi crosses through Yunnan to Sichuan, winding its way through the lush countryside between Sichuan and Hubei before flowing northward toward Anhui and Jiangsu. Like other civilizations that have flourished around great waterways, the Chinese are fond of calling the Yangzi, or Changjiang (Long River), the "cradle of ancient Chinese civilization." The river has long been a source of food and transport, as well an inspiration to painters and poets. Before the 20th century plenty of brave boatmen lost their lives trying to pass through the fearsome stretch of water running through what is known as the Three Gorges—the complicated system of narrow cliffs between Fengjie, in Sichuan, and Yichang, in Hubei.

In 1992 the Chinese government recognized the value of harnessing the power of the river and decided to begin the construction of a huge dam, or *gezhouba*. When completed in 2009, the dam is intended to supply one-third of the nation's electrical power output, control flooding, and improve overall navigation along the river. On the downside, flooding from the construction will prompt the relocation of 1.2 million riverside residents, mostly to the already burgeoning Chongqing Municipality. More than 1,000 important cultural and archaeological sites are expected to be submerged and lost forever. Ecologists and scientists also predict dire effects from pollution and temperature changes on the river wildlife when the dam opens. Even more frightening is the location of this massive project: right on top of an earthquake fault line. Disaster scenarios abound with what may befall those living

downstream should a dam of this size break during an earthquake. The official view is that the spectacular scenery of the Three Gorges—Qutang, Wu, and Xiling—will not be submerged once the dam is completed. There is some concern, though, that the sheer cliffs and rapids may be compromised, as flooding may create a much shallower and altogether less impressive landscape. Currently, a trip through the Three Gorges offers a view of the old China that no longer exists in cities on the path to modernization. Panoramas of hills covered with rice fields; fishermen scooping the waters with large nets from the shores; cliffs and clouds parting to reveal narrow passages of water barely wide enough for two boats—these are the images that have persisted for centuries.

The cities and sights you see on a cruise on the Yangzi River depend on what type of cruise you select and the tour operator you use.

Fengdu

❹❼ *193 km (120 mi) northeast of Chongqing, 1,055 km (654 mi) southwest of Wuhan.*

On the banks of the Yangzi, Fengdu, also known as Guicheng or the "city of devils," is filled with temples, buildings, and statues depicting demons and devils. During the Tang Dynasty, the names of two local princely families, Yin (meaning "hell") and Wang (meaning "king"), were linked through marriage, making them known as Yinwang, or the "king of hell." Ever since, people have believed that the town is populated by ghosts. You can take a series of staircases or a cable car to the top of the mountain. The bamboo-covered **Mingshan** (Ming Hill) has a Buddhist temple, a pavilion, and pagodas with brightly painted dragons and swans emanating from the eaves. The hill has a nice view of the Yangzi River.

Shibaozhai

❹❽ *6 hrs (290 km/180 mi) by bus northeast of Chongqing, 10 hrs (945 km/586 mi) by bus southwest of Wuhan.*

Shibaozhai (Stone Treasure Stronghold) is actually a rectangular rock with sheer cliffs, into one face of which is built an impressive 12-story pagoda, constructed by Emperor Qianlong (1736–96) during the Qing dynasty. Wall carvings and historical inscriptions describing the construction of the building can be seen along the circuitous stairway that leads from the center of the pagoda to the top.

San Xia (Three Gorges)

★ *475 km (295 mi) northeast of Chongqing, 655 km (406 mi) west of Wuhan.*

❹❾ Between the cities of Fengjie, in Sichuan, and Yichang, in Hubei, lie the Three Gorges. The westernmost gorge, **Qutang Xia** (Qutang Gorge) is the shortest, at 8 km (5 mi). Although the currents are strong here, the surrounding cliffs are not very high. At the top of some of the cliffs are caves that once held coffins of officers from the Warring States Period.

❺⓿ Near **Wushan,** at the entrance to Wu Xia, you can change to a smaller boat navigated by local boatmen to the **Xiao San Xia** (Little Three Gorges). Here there are cliff formations similar, on a smaller scale, to those of the Three Gorges. Sometimes you can hear monkeys and other wildlife from your boat.

⑤ The impressive **Wu Xia** (Wu Gorge) is 33 km (20 mi) long. Its cliffs are so sheer and narrow that they seem to be closing in upon each other as you approach in the boat. Some of the cliff formations are noted for their resemblances to people and animals.

⑤ At the city of **Badong** in Hubei, just outside the eastern end of Wu Gorge, boats leave for Shennongjia (☞ Chapter 10) on the Shennong River, one of the wildest and strangest parts of the country.

⑤ **Xiling Xia** (Xiling Gorge), 66 km (41 mi) long, is the longest and deepest of all the gorges, with cliffs that rise up to 4,000 ft. At the eastern

⑤ end of the gorge is the **Gezhouba** (Gezhou Dam), sometimes simply referred to as **Da Ba** (Big Dam). When completed, the 607-ft-high dam will be a total of 2 km (1¼ mi) long.

12 INNER MONGOLIA AND THE REPUBLIC OF MONGOLIA

The Mongolias are a land of horses, sheep, and vast grasslands. Nights in yurts and days on horseback are part of the romance of the traditional nomadic culture. Many areas of the two Mongolias are sparsely populated and maintain their traditional way of life. From Hohhot and Ulaan Baatar you can explore the legacy of Genghis Khan and the spiritual influence of Lamaism, a Tibetan branch of Buddhism with shamanist elements.

T HE MONGOL EMPIRE once covered most of the Eurasian landmass, stretching from the Yellow Sea in the east to Budapest in the west and from Lake Baikal in the north to Myanmar (Burma) in the south. Genghis Khan united the fierce tribes of the Mongolian steppes in the early 13th century. In Mongolia, Karakorum—the site of Genghis Khan's capital—attracts many visitors, though little remains of the original city.

By Bill Smith

Updated by
Grace Fan

Under Kublai Khan, Genghis Khan's grandson, the Mongols conquered most of China, establishing their Yuan dynasty capital in present-day Beijing in 1272. The Great Mongol Empire disintegrated after the Yuan dynasty collapsed in 1368. In the 17th century the Chinese Qing (Manchu) dynasty took control of Mongolia, separating it into Inner Mongolia and Outer Mongolia. The overthrow of the Qing in 1911 brought independence to Outer Mongolia, which became first a theocracy under a Living Buddha; then, from 1921, a Communist state under strong Soviet influence. Inner Mongolia was occupied by the Japanese from 1931 to 1945. It became the Inner Mongolia Autonomous Region of China in 1947.

Both Mongolias were closed to the outside world for many years, and today, huge areas of countryside remain largely untouched by Western culture. Soviet and Chinese communism increased the differences between the two areas.

There are 2.2 million ethnic Mongolians in Mongolia—comprising 85% of the population (the rest are Turkic, Tungusic, Chinese, and Russian)—and over 4 million in Inner Mongolia. In its cities and southern farming areas, Inner Mongolia is dominated by Han Chinese, who constitute 80% of the region's overall population of 23.7 million. Mongolia has more wildlife and is less developed, and the grasslands are generally less populated than those of Inner Mongolia. Its residents have a more traditional lifestyle. Wool, leather, meat, and dairy industries continue to form the mainstay of the rural economies. Inner Mongolia has large agriculture, coal, iron, and steel industries; Mongolia has some copper and coal. The influx of Han Chinese has made Mandarin the main language of Inner Mongolia, although Mongolian and Chinese characters are found together on all official notices and street signs. In Mongolia, on the other hand, Cyrillic (Russian) script has largely replaced Mongolian characters, but everyone speaks Mongolian.

In both Mongolias you can stay in yurts (circular felt tents called *gers* in Mongolian—the word *yurt* is of Turkic origin), eat mutton, drink *airag* (fermented mare's milk), and watch riders use *urgas* (pole-mounted lassos) to round up horses, sheep, goats, cows, and camels. Midsummer Naadam fairs feature spectacular competitions in archery, Mongolian wrestling, and horseracing.

Pleasures and Pastimes

Dining
Mongolians traditionally subsist on mutton, beef, noodles, and dairy products. The main specialties are "finger" mutton (hunks of boiled or roast mutton eaten from the bone), milk tea, cheese, and airag. Less common in the cities, this fare is usually served at grassland yurt sites. Mutton hotpot, thin slivers of meat plunged fondue style into a circular trough of boiling water surrounding a miniature stove, is popular in Inner Mongolia. Served with bean curd, noodles, vegetables, and chili and sesame sauces, a hotpot is perfect for a group. Two of Ulaan Baatar's most popular snacks are *buuz* (mutton-filled dumplings like

Chinese *baozi*) and *horshoo* (mutton fritters). Hohhot and Ulaan Baatar have restaurants serving good Chinese, Korean, Muslim, and Russian-style dishes.

CATEGORY	INNER MONGOLIA*	REPUBLIC OF MONGOLIA*
$$$$	over Y150	over T20,000
$$$	Y100–Y150	T13,000–T20,000
$$	Y50–Y100	T5,000–T13,000
$	under Y50	under T5,000

per person for a main course at dinner

Grassland Tours

The spectacle of a Mongolian rider chasing galloping horses across a lush green plain or steppe is something most visitors to the Mongolias want to see. Because of the great distances involved and lack of settlements and public transport, it is best to travel by minibus, Jeep, horse, or plane. Unless you are competent in Chinese or Mongolian, an English-speaking guide is essential. Before you book a tour, ensure that both the booking office and the tour guides are licensed, check the itinerary carefully, and make sure the price is agreed upon in advance. There's no better way to see the grasslands than by horse; the small, sturdy Mongolian horse is amazingly well-suited to the high plains—though long rides can be hard for novices. On some tours yurts are carried with the group, providing a taste of real nomadic life. All tours of more than one day need to be booked in advance. Camel tours of desert areas can also be arranged. Many different tours are possible in both Mongolias, incorporating varied terrains—steppes, mountains, deserts, forests—ancient ruins, temples, traditional crafts, animal husbandry, and wildlife.

Lodging

Retiring to the comfort of a yurt after watching a vivid sunset over boundless grassland, you can open the roof flap to reveal the clear, starry night sky. Yurts are warm but do not have toilets or showers; the latter are usually provided in separate blocks of circular wood, concrete, or tin buildings styled to blend with the yurts. Hohhot and Ulaan Baatar both have high-quality hotels. Rural hotels can be very basic, with few facilities in the rooms other than TV sets, so yurt accommodation is generally more enjoyable. Some tourist yurts in Inner Mongolia have smaller tin "yurts" attached, which house en suite toilets and washbasins. When entering a yurt, especially one belonging to a Mongolian family, avoid treading on the wooden threshold; many local people believe this represents stepping on the neck of the yurt's owner.

CATEGORY	INNER MONGOLIA*	REPUBLIC OF MONGOLIA*
$$$$	over Y830	over T100,000
$$$	Y400–Y830	T55,000–T100,000
$$	Y200–Y400	T27,000–T55,000
$	under Y200	under T27,000

Prices are for a double room in high season.

Naadam Fairs

Naadams are annual gatherings of nomadic Mongol tribes for shamanist worship, trade, and courtship, along with archery, wrestling, equestrian, and drinking competitions. Although a few fairs are now staged mainly for tourists, the games and pageants are taken seriously by local people. Events, including evening song and dance performances, usually take place in a wide arena encircled by yurts, market stalls, and food tents. Naadam fairs normally last three days and start around July

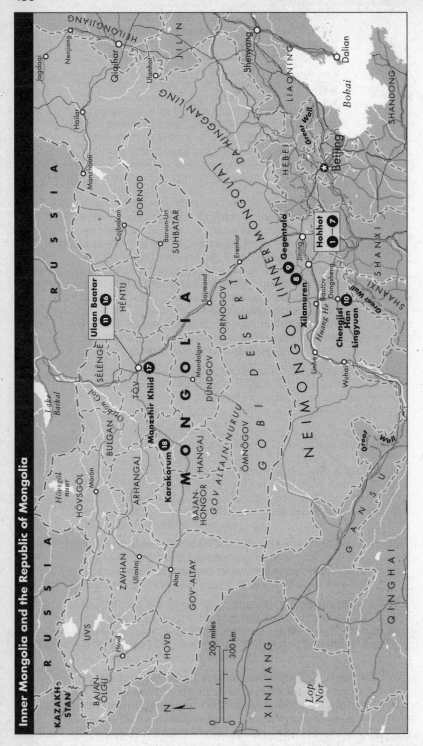

458

Inner Mongolia and the Republic of Mongolia

11 in Mongolia and in late July or mid-August in Inner Mongolia. Exact dates vary each year.

Temples

With greater religious freedom in China and Mongolia, many Buddhist temples have been revived. During the Stalinist purges of the 1930s, more than 500 monasteries and temples were destroyed in Mongolia alone. Only a few have been rebuilt. Temples in the Mongolias follow Lamaism, a Tibetan branch of Buddhist beliefs. Two of the best temples for Lamaist art, music, monks, and local devotees are Gandan Khiid, in Ulaan Baatar, and Xiletuzhao, in Hohhot.

Exploring the Mongolias

Inner Mongolia is a crescent-shape region that stretches 2,400 km (1,500 mi) along China's northern and northeastern borders. The Gobi Desert straddles much of Inner Mongolia's long border with Mongolia to the north. Both Mongolias are landlocked, with Siberia to the north and east and China's Xinjiang province and Kazakhstan to the west.

Visiting the Republic of Mongolia has become much less difficult as government restrictions have been relaxed in the past few years. Letters of invitation and tour bookings are no longer required in order to obtain a Mongolian visa. Visas are issued from Mongolian embassies and at the Mongolian consulate office in the border town of Erenhot. Depending on where you apply, tourist visas are issued for either 14 or 30 days and can be extended once you are in the country. Border and visa regulations require foreign tourists to travel in both directions between Mongolia and China, including Inner Mongolia, by rail or air. So travel back and forth between rural areas of the two Mongolias is not possible. Customs and immigration formalities are conducted on the train, and there is a two-hour wait at the border while the bogies on the carriages are changed.

Touring the Mongolian countryside is nothing less than spectacular. The difficulty is deciding where to go and how to get there. As distances are great and public transportation either slow or unavailable, you may be best off taking a tour, which can be easily arranged in both Hohhot and Ulaan Baatar. If you're traveling alone, you can cut down on costs by attaching yourself to a tour that has already been booked. Otherwise, try to meet other travelers and form your own group.

In Ulaan Baatar travel agencies will design tours to meet your specifications in terms of both duration and destination. A good method for traveling across Mongolia's varied terrain is to hire a Russian-made four-wheel-drive van or Jeep. Prices vary considerably between agencies, so shop around. The no-frills companies charge a minimum of $90 a day for a van (and driver) regardless of the number of tourists piled in the back. This price includes all necessary transportation expenses (gasoline and road tolls), camping and cooking equipment, and food. A guide costs an additional $10 per day for someone who just speaks English and more for one who has a bit of historical knowledge. The cooking, cleaning, and tent setup is usually performed by the driver and guide no matter how often you ask to help. Hotels, if necessary, are not included.

Great Itineraries

Numbers in the margin correspond to points of interest on the Mongolias, Hohhot, and Ulaan Baatar maps.

IF YOU HAVE 2–3 DAYS

Go to **Hohhot** to explore its temples, mosque, and old town. The next day travel 87 km (54 mi) to **Xilamuren** to tour the grassland, visit *aobaos* (hilltop shrines) and local people, and try horse riding and Mongolian wrestling. Stay one or two nights in a yurt. Return to **Hohhot.**

IF YOU HAVE 5–6 DAYS

Take the train from Beijing to **Ulaan Baatar.** Spend the first day visiting the city, temples, and museums. Travel 360 km (223 mi) west across the grasslands by four-wheel-drive vehicle to **Karakorum.** Stay two or three nights in a yurt, spending the days touring the grassland, horseback riding, visiting historic sites and Mongolian families, and watching horses, sheep, camels, and wildlife. Drive back to **Ulaan Baatar,** stopping to climb sand dunes. If time permits, add a day trip from **Ulaan Baatar** to **Manzshir Monastery.** Fly back to Beijing.

IF YOU HAVE 10 DAYS

Starting from **Hohhot,** drive 250 km (155 mi) to **Ejin Horo Qi,** site of the **Genghis Khan Mausoleum.** Stay in a yurt and return the next day to **Hohhot.** Spend a day visiting Hohhot's temples and old town. Drive 170 km (105 mi) to **Gegentala** for a taste of life in the grasslands; spend two nights in a yurt. Return to **Hohhot** before flying direct or via Beijing to **Ulaan Baatar.** Then visit **Karakorum** and the **Manzshir Monastery** as above. Return from **Ulaan Baatar** to Beijing by train.

When to Tour the Mongolias

The dry, continental climate makes May to September the best time for temperatures and for greenery. Because most of the Mongolias occupy a plateau at an altitude of 3,250–4,900 ft, even summer evenings can be cool. Severe cold and wind make winter touring impractical.

Naadam fairs take place from mid-July to mid-August. As a result, this is peak tourist season when some tours and hotels may be fully booked. For photographing temples or grassland scenery, early mornings and late afternoons give the best light. Ulaan Baatar's Gandan Khiid Temple is especially interesting to visit when the monks and local worshipers arrive for early morning prayers.

INNER MONGOLIA

Inner Mongolia (Nei Menggu) is a vast, crescent-shape area across northern China. Its borders with Soviet-influenced Mongolia and eastern Siberia made it a sensitive region during the Sino-Soviet Cold War. Around 70% of Inner Mongolia is arid grassland sparsely occupied by herds of sheep, horses, goats, cattle, and camels. Open steppe land with yurts, horses, and sheep can be found in most parts of the region. Short trips, even day trips, are possible from Hohhot.

Hohhot

10 hrs by train (410 km/254 mi) west of Beijing.

In Chinese-dominated Hohhot the only yurts you see are in restaurants and entertainment centers, though some of the modern white-tile office blocks are topped by yurt-style domes. Hohhot, pronounced "hu-he-hao-te" and Mongolian for "blue city," is the capital of the Inner Mongolia Autonomous Region. Hui Muslims are the most prominent minority in a population of 1 million. Mongolian, Ewenki, Daur, and other minorities live in the city but rarely wear traditional dress and are relatively invisible among the large Han Chinese majority.

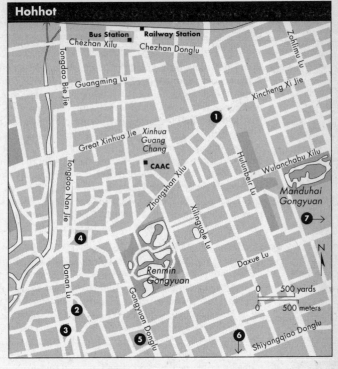

A trip to Inner Mongolia must include a visit to the grassland, and Hohhot is the region's main base for grassland tours. The city itself has several interesting diversions, notably the Inner Mongolia Museum, Baita, and the old city section next to Dazhao Si.

Despite the rarity of real horses and camels, other than those used as photographers' props in Xinhua Square, the city's equine symbols are outlasting newer icons. Hohhot's Mao statue, which stood outside the railway station as many others still do across China, was felled in 1987 and replaced by a rearing silver horse. Another sign of China's reforms are the thriving mosques and Lamaist temples of Hohhot's old town.

Xinhua Square is fascinating in the early morning, when it is full of people practicing *qi gong* (breathing exercise), playing badminton, basketball, volleyball, or soccer, or just promenading. In the evening, children's rides and trampolines, food stalls, an English-language corner, photographers, and skateboarders take over. On the streets are kebab sellers, cigarette and yogurt stands, cyclists, yellow taxis, and tricycle carts carrying wardrobes and refrigerators. Restaurants are busy every evening and, as in Ulaan Baatar, many men drink heavily.

★ ❶ Visit the **Nei Mengu Bowuguan** (Inner Mongolia Museum) to find out how to build a yurt or a birch-bark teepee, or to learn how Mongolians once used boomerangs to hunt hares, marmots, and other small animals from horseback. The museum has a section devoted to fossilized remains of dinosaurs and other ancient animals and houses Asia's largest dinosaur skeleton, as well as a giant brontosaurus skeleton in its own room. On the other side of the museum are exhibitions of minority cultures, with items such as Mongolian bows and saddles and a yurt, a Daur shaman's costume, and an Oroqen teepee. The second floor's focus is on the history of Inner Mongolia: one wing is devoted to Stone Age artifacts; another section, with photographs and war mem-

orabilia, offers a glimpse of the region's 20th-century history—as seen through the eyes of the Chinese Communist Party. Most captions have English translations. ✉ *2 Xinhua Dajie*, ☎ *0471/696–5892*, 💰 *Y6.* 🕐 *Summer, Wed.–Mon. 9–5; winter, Wed.–Mon. 10–4.*

★ **❷** Bare wood and subtle, faded shades of green and red make **Xiletuzhao Si** (Xiletuzhao Temple) more of a genuine throwback to the past than many of China's more garishly renovated temples, though the plain, unadorned facade may leave some visitors disappointed. Although the temple boasts a 400-year history, the current buildings date from the 19th century, after the original structure burned down; the ruined annex opposite the temple's main entrance was being renovated at press time. Duck into caverns under the temple to visit the Tibetan Buddhist vision of hell, with graphic depictions of the various tortures awaiting sinners. If you go on weekdays, you may meet the 11th Grand Living Buddha (now in his 60s), who runs the temple. Monks still come to pray in the mornings from 8 to 10. ✉ *Off Da Nan Jie, 5 minutes north of Dazhao Temple, on the east side of the street.* 💰 *Y5.* 🕐 *Daily 8–6.*

❸ First built in the Ming dynasty, **Dazhao Si** (Dazhao Temple) is also known as Silver Buddha Temple, for its statue of the Sakyamuni Buddha cast mainly from silver. The temple was rebuilt in 1640, and many of the existing structures and artifacts date from then, though the result isn't awe-inspiring if you've been to other Chinese temples. Still, the temple is an active one, with several young monks in brown robes who wander hourly around the pavilions chanting. The 400-year-old Silver Buddha is housed in one of China's best-preserved Ming dynasty wooden halls. Close to the altar is an exquisite pair of carved dragon pillars, and by the door to the hall are two cast-iron lions, with cast-iron incense burners in the courtyard outside. To the west of the temple, a street market and the cobblestone lanes of the old city section may prove more fascinating to wander through; under the sloping eaves of old wooden roofs, an older generation of Chinese live out their days as they've done for years. ✉ *Da Zhao Qian Jie (off Da Nan Jie, on the west side),* ☎ *0471/630–3154.* 💰 *Y10.* 🕐 *Daily 8–7.*

❹ A gray medieval fortress set amidst the green-trimmed walls of a Chinese courtyard, the **Qingzhen Dasi** (Great Mosque) is readily identified by its crescent-top minaret and Arabic script, and by the bearded Muslim men who congregate outside. The mosque dates mainly from the Qing dynasty and is surrounded by *hutongs* (alleys) of Hui Muslim houses, shops, and restaurants. A lively street market has sprung up just outside the mosque. ✉ *28 Tongdao Lu (at Zhongshan Xilu).* 🕐 *Daily 10–4, except during prayer.*

❺ The Indian-style **Wuta Si** (Five Pagoda Temple) was built in 1733 as a stupa. In the Qing dynasty the temple was part of a larger complex, but little else remains. Its square base tapers upward to five glazed pagodas decorated with Buddhas and Mongolian, Tibetan, and Sanskrit script. Behind the pagoda is a carved screen that includes a Mongolian astronomical chart, purportedly the only one of its kind ever discovered. Climb the narrow stairwell up to the pagodas for a view of the surrounding neighborhoods of tile-roof adobe houses. ✉ *Wuta Si Hou Jie (off Gongyuan Dong Dajie).* 💰 *Y10.* 🕐 *Daily 8–6:30.*

❻ The **Zhaojun Mu** (Tomb of Wang Zhaojun) is one of nine such tombs spread across Inner Mongolia. Many variants of Wang Zhaojun's story are floating around, but the most intriguing one goes something like this: One of China's four historical beauties, Wang Zhaojun was a ravishing imperial concubine who lived during the Han Dynasty. Despite her beauty, she was never called by Emperor Yuandi to serve him, for the

ruler used portraits of the women to decide his bed partner for the night, never realizing that his crafty court painter was beautifying the portraits of the concubines who bribed him. When Emperor Yuandi decided to appease the chief of the warring Southern Hun tribes with a bride, he chose the ugliest of the concubine pictures; and discovered his mistake too late. Wang Zhaojun's "sacrifice" in 33 BC, which led to 60 years of peace, is still celebrated throughout the region. A pyramid-shape burial mound 98 ft high is topped by a small pavilion. There are good views of the surrounding park and farmland. One story says that only a pair of Wang Zhaojun's shoes was buried here. To get here, hire a taxi for about Y50–60 (all cabbies know the way), or hire a care through CITS. ⊠ 9 km (6 mi) south of Hohhot. 🎫 Y10. ☉ Daily 8–6.

❼ Few tourists visit the **Baita** (White Pagoda), but it is one of the finest brick pagodas in northern China. The 138-ft-high octagonal structure has seven stories coated in chalk. Restored in the 1990s, the pagoda was first constructed in the Liao dynasty (916–1125) and was once a destination for pilgrims from all over Asia. Easy to get to by taxi or by a bicycle ride through flat farmland, the pagoda grounds make a good picnic spot. Note that no buses run here; a hired car with driver will run Y60–70. ⊠ *16 km (10 mi) east of Hohhot.* 🎫 *Y10.* ☉ *Summer, daily 8–6; winter, daily 9:30–5.*

Dining and Lodging

Hohhot's main specialty, Mongolian hotpot, is traditionally a group meal eaten from a large communal pot. The city's best restaurants are in the best hotels; eateries outside the hotels don't usually have English-speaking staff or English menus. Casual, neat dress is acceptable.

$–$$ ✕ **Min Shu Cun.** At the end of a long, dark alleyway, this rustic white double-decker warehouse of a Chinese eatery rises into view, replete with folk touches like red lanterns, hewn wooden furniture, and banquet rooms ornamentally trimmed with tiled eaves. Popular with locals, this hotel restaurant is touted for its hotpot as well as good traditional Chinese fare served up in a cheerful atmosphere: servers in red-flowered overalls bring prompt service with a smile. ⊠ *Xincheng Hotel, 40 Hulunbei'er Nanlu (the entrance is off Wulanchabu Lu, just west of the Inner Mongolia Hotel; look for the red Fu Li Hua sign),* ☎ *0471/629–2534 or 0471/629–2533. No credit cards.*

$ ✕ **Malaqin Fandian.** In a sunny, spacious dining room an army of waiters wearing bright pink-and-green vests serves up excellent southern Chinese cuisine with friendly aplomb, starting with a silver cart laden with a selection of cold dishes, followed by tea shooting out from a long-necked Dai brass teapot. Succulent meat, vegetable, and seafood entries are available—try the *xiangpu daieu liu* (tender deep-fried carp cutlets cooked with chili peppers, onions, and other spices)—but save room for the house specialty: a delicious *yindu shoupao bing* (Indian-styled nan), served in a variety of salty and sweet flavors from curried beef to apple. No English menu is available. ⊠ *122 Xincheng Xi Jie,* ☎ *0471/692–6685. No credit cards.*

$$–$$$ 🏨 **Xincheng Binguan** (Xincheng Hotel). The only luxury hotel in Inner **★** Mongolia, this former 1950s Soviet-style sanitarium is now a vast hotel complex surrounded by evergreens and lush gardens, and crowned by an indoor 25-m swimming pool. A 1998 high-rise set amid various one-story buildings has modern, standard rooms that have some of the prettiest views in town. An older building, to the side, offers shabbier accommodation, with similar views, for much lower rates. The complex houses the three-story Xincheng Club, a conference and entertainment center that has a variety of activities from bowling to minigolf to karaoke. It's popular with locals. ⊠ *40 Hulunbei'er Nanlu, 010010,*

☎ *0471/629–2288,* FAX *0471/693–1141,* WEB *www.xincheng-hotel. com.cn. 313 rooms, 45 suites. 9 restaurants, pool, hair salon, massage, tennis court, bowling, gym, bicycles, business services, travel services. AE, MC, V.*

\$\$–\$\$\$ ✕🏨 **Zhaojun Dajiudian** (Zhaojun Hotel). Beyond the sand-color tiles
★   of the exterior, a garish gold mural depicting Wang Zhaojun and grassland scenes rise above the reception area of this sleek but aging Hong
Kong joint venture. While the rooms are comfortable and spacious,
with touches like gold-striped comforters and pine wooden panels, the
bathrooms are tiny, the reception desk downstairs is often chaotic, and
the elevators are slow. From the reception area, a corridor leads to a
large shopping arcade, with a bank, travel center, and a bowling alley.
The hotel's main restaurant, popular with locals for a delicious seafood
hotpot, also serves Cantonese dishes, such as sizzling "iron plate" beef
and Singapore rice noodles, vegetable hotpot, and snake, frog, and crab
dishes. ✉ *53 Xinhua Dajie, 010050,* ☎ *0471/696–2211,* FAX *0471/696–
8825. 247 rooms, 18 suites. 3 restaurants, bar, hair salon, bowling,
gym, dance club, travel services, business services. AE, MC, V.*

\$\$ 🏨 **Bayantala Hotel.** The Bayantala is surprisingly modern, from its sloping entranceway to the bar in the brightly lit reception area: only the
pink cement floor betrays the Socialist origins. Wood and amber tones
dominate the clean, standard rooms in the VIP building. Popular with
Chinese travelers and conveniently located, one of the hotel's few
drawbacks is that not much English is spoken here. On the first floor
is a branch of Beijing's famed roast duck restaurant, Quanjude. ✉ *42
Xilin (Guo Le) Beilu, 010020,* ☎ *0471/696–3344,* FAX *0471/696–
7390. 122 rooms, 4 suites. 6 restaurants, bar, hair salon, billiards, business services, travel services. No credit cards.*

\$\$ 🏨 **Jin Hui Hotel.** This distinctive glass-and-steel high-rise would look
more at home in modern Shanghai than in dilapidated Hohhot. A high-
ceilinged lobby with a glittering ballroom chandelier and white marble columns has a restaurant and money-exchange services. Although
the hallways and lobby appear strangely narrow, the large-windowed
rooms are spacious and have bright carpeting, wooden furniture, and
floral bedspreads. The hotel is close to the railway station, restaurants,
and shopping. The entrance is hidden to the left of the large Industrial
and Commercial Bank of China in the same building. ✉ *105 Xilin (Guo
Le) Beilu, 010050,* ☎ *0471/694–0099 or 0471/694–0214,* FAX *0471/
694–0088,* WEB *www.jh-hotel.com.cn. 73 rooms, 30 suites. Restaurant, bar, food court, massage, gym, shops, billiards, nightclub, business services, travel services. AE, MC, V.*

\$\$ 🏨 **Nei Menggu Fandian** (Inner Mongolia Hotel). Set to be completely
renovated with a smart new look, Inner Mongolia's first hotel for foreign tourists is slated to have a 20-m swimming pool, the province's
first McDonald's, and Chinese five-star status. The hotel has always
been a favorite with tour groups. *Wulan Chabu Lu, 010010,* ☎ *0471/
696–4233,* FAX *0471/696–1479. 370 rooms, 30 suites. 4 restaurants,
bar, pool, massage, sauna, dance club, business services, travel services.
AE, MC, V.*

\$ 🏨 **San Yuan Da Jiu Dian.** A block away from the train station amidst
a strip of small noodle shops, the San Yuan may have worn red rugs
in its corridors, but it also has spacious, clean rooms with 24-hour hot
water, modern bathrooms, and friendly service. ✉ *188 Che Zhan
Dong Jie, 010050,* ☎ *0471/628–0423 ext. 8666,* FAX *0471/628–0426.
47 rooms, 3 suites. Restaurant, sauna. No credit cards.*

Nightlife

All the major hotels have discos and/or karaoke bars. The Xincheng
Club at the Xincheng Hotel has the widest range of evening activities.

Many smaller hotels and restaurants offer similar but less grandly presented options.

Shopping

The **Minzu Shangchang** (Minorities' Department Store; ⊠ 69 Zhongshan Xilu) is the best place for cashmere clothing and souvenirs such as Mongolian robes and hats, hotpots, ornamented teapots, knives, and bowls, though you may have to hunt amongst the tourist kitsch. The large hotels sell similar items, but choice is more limited and prices higher. The Dazhao and Xiletuzhao temples both have shops selling Buddhist and other souvenirs.

Side Trips to the Grassland

In Hohhot tour companies compete fiercely for independent travelers to the grassland. Tourists are often assailed as soon as they arrive at the railway station. Some companies even have stands at the Beijing station. Most tours will give you a wonderful experience of the grassland, but don't be rushed into booking. Check the itinerary and price carefully first, especially if you want to do some serious horseback riding. Standard packages usually allow little more than a few minutes on a horse. Major operators all offer the following destinations.

⑧ At **Xilamuren** you can spend your days roaming across the carpet of green on foot or on horseback, trying Mongolian wrestling, and visiting local families, a temple, and aobaos. Nights involve folk songs and dancing, listening to the *matouqin* (horse-head fiddle), and eating roast mutton. Some people criticize tourist sites like Xilamuren as not being genuine, but the rolling grassland scenery, horses, sheep, temples, and aobaos are all authentic. Local people in this area mainly live in villages or isolated farmhouses, so yurts are restricted to seasonal use by herdspeople. Visitors can sleep in a traditionally constructed yurt with some modern facilities. If you're a first-time visitor to the grassland, you're likely to enjoy it, but return visitors may be disappointed. A Naadam fair is held for tourists in the second half of August. ⊠ *Road to Bayan Aobao, 87 km (54 mi) northwest of Hohhot; book a tour, or take a bus to Zhaohe, Xilamuren (2–3 hrs, about Y10).*

⑨ **Gegentala** has scenery and activities similar to those at Xilamuren but is better during the Naadam fair. Events at the tourist site merge with those of a larger fair nearby, and wrestling, archery, horse-racing, and rodeo competitions at the tourist site are all attended enthusiastically by the locals. The men and women of the region are known for their wrestling skills; the Inner Mongolia regional team usually takes part in the local Naadam wrestling competitions. Over the hill to the south of the tourist camp, a tent-encircled Naadam arena is set up with food stalls, circus tents, and a stage for Mongolian song and dance. The lively fair lasts for about a week, immediately following the events at the tourist site. Book a tour, as Gegentala is difficult to get to independently. ⊠ *Siziwang Qi, 170 km (105 mi) northeast of Hohhot.*

⑩ A journey to the **Chengjisi Han Lingyuan** (Genghis Khan Mausoleum) involves crossing the Yellow River to the desert and grassland of the Ordos Highland, where eventually the imposing navy-and-tan ceramic domes of the mausoleum come into view. The tomb was built in 1954 and refurbished after the Cultural Revolution. In front of the central chamber stands a large golden censer between gigantic pikes topped with the nine-yak-tail banner of the Mongol armies. At the entrance a white-marble effigy of the all-conquering warrior greets visitors with a steely gaze. Rich murals decorate the interior walls, portraying the life story of Genghis Khan with details such as a depiction of the traditional Mongolian method of skinning a sheep. Mongolians place of-

ferings of incense, liquor, cigarettes, sweets, and trinkets in front of a yellow-silk yurt purported to contain the great khan's funeral bier. Near the mausoleum are reconstructions of a Yuan dynasty village and Genghis Khan's summer palace, built for a film set. From the buildings you can see open grassland grazed by sheep, horses, goats, and camels. A trip to the Resonant Sand Gorge and Wudang Lamasery (Lamaist Monastery), near Baotou, can be combined with a visit to the mausoleum; expect to book a two-day tour, minimum, if you're visiting from Hohhot. ⊠ *25 km (15 mi) from Ejin Horo Qi. From Hohhot, take a 3-hr bus ride (Y35) to Dongsheng and then a 1½-hr bus ride from there.* ☎ *Y10.* ⊘ *Daily 9–5.*

DINING AND LODGING

Xilamuren, Gegentala, and the Genghis Khan Mausoleum have yurt camps for tourists. All camps have dining halls where mutton dominates the set menus, accompanied by seasonal Chinese standards such as stir-fried chicken and chili, green beans, and egg-fried rice. Vegetarian and other special meals also can be ordered. All camps have bathroom facilities, including basic showers that do not always have hot water, in communal blocks outside the yurts. Xilamuren and Gegentala also offer individual tourist yurts, which have a tiny hut attached containing a toilet and washbasin. At all sites yurts are spaced out on concrete bases. They have traditional latticed frames with birch roof struts, wool felt walls covered with canvas, and thick rugs and low beds on the floor. Quilts, pillows, hot water flasks, and electric lights are standard. In summer you are unlikely to be cold in a yurt, but at other times you should take warm clothes to sleep in.

Inner Mongolia A to Z

To research prices, get advice from other travelers, and book travel arrangements, visit www.fodors.com.

AIR TRAVEL TO AND FROM INNER MONGOLIA

Regular flights connect Hohhot with Beijing, Guangzhou, Shenzhen, Shanghai, Xian, and Wuhan. There are flights between Ulaan Baatar and Hohhot every Monday and Thursday.

CARRIERS

The Mongolian airline, MIAT, runs flights twice a week from Hohhot to Ulaan Baatar.

➤ AIRLINES AND CONTACTS: **MIAT** (⊠ 5 Wu Lan Xiao Qu, Xin Cheng Qu (same building as the Mongolian embassy), ☎ 0471/430–3590, FAX 0471/430–2015).

AIRPORTS AND TRANSFERS

Hohhot Airport is 35 km (22 mi) east of the city center. Airport buses leave from the CAAC office.

➤ AIRPORT INFORMATION: **Hohhot Airport** (☎ 0471/696–6768).
➤ TAXIS AND SHUTTLES: **CAAC Office** (⊠ 33 Xilin Beilu, ☎ 0471/693–3637 or 0471/693–4005).

BIKE TRAVEL

Hohhot is flat, and cycling is the best way to get around. Bicycles can be rented outside the Xincheng Hotel. You will normally be asked to deposit some form of identification. If you're fit, you can ride to the White Pagoda or the Tomb of Wang Zhaojun. Traffic is much lighter than in Beijing and other larger cities, but take care. Watch the locals, then copy their moves.

BUS TRAVEL TO AND FROM INNER MONGOLIA

Modern buses, many equipped with video, run daily to Datong and Beijing. These buses, some with sleepers, are quicker and cheaper than the train, but less comfortable. The Hohhot bus station is right outside the railway station, to the west of the station square.

➤ Bus Information: **Hohhot bus station** (✉ Chezhan Xilu).

BUS TRAVEL WITHIN INNER MONGOLIA

City buses in Hohhot are crowded and relatively slow, though the fare is less than Y2. They can be useful if you're just exploring the downtown shopping area.

EMERGENCIES

There are no hospitals or clinics with English-speaking staff. If you need medical help, ask your hotel to assist. The large hotels have competent security staff and sometimes police officers on site.

INTERNET SERVICES

Several Internet bars have sprung up around Hohhot, most of them small, functional, and crowded with teens playing video games. The privately run Dian Xin Wang Ba, inside a small long-distance telephone branch of the main branch of China Telecom, has on-line services for Y3 an hour. Zhong Yu Diannao Gong Se Wang Ba has 24-hour cyberaccess for Y2.5 an hour. It's a block away from the train station, across the street from the Zhonghui Hotel.

➤ Contacts: **Dian Xin Wang Ba** (✉ Zhongshan Donglu, 150 ft east of China Telecom, ☎ 0471/691–4553, ◷ 1–11 PM). **Zhong Yu Diannao Gong Se Wang Ba** (✉ across the street from the Zhonghui Hotel).

MAIL AND SHIPPING

The central post office is on Zhongshan Donglu, at Renmin Lu.

MONEY MATTERS

ATMS

There are no ATMs in Hohhot.

CURRENCY EXCHANGE

The main branch of the Bank of China, opposite the Zhaojun Hotel, changes all major foreign-currency traveler's checks and cash. Smaller branch banks and larger hotels have foreign exchange services.

➤ Exchange Services: **Bank of China** (✉ Xinhua Dajie).

TAXIS

Taxis are plentiful and cheap in Hohhot. Metered fares begin at Y6, and most destinations within the city will cost no more than Y15.

TRAIN TRAVEL

Daily trains run from Hohhot's train station to Datong (4½ hours), Yinchuan (10 hours), Zhongwei (12 hours), Lanzhou (17½ hours), Tianjin (11 hours), and Beijing (10 hours). If you're traveling on to Mongolia, you can reach Ulaan Baatar by direct train that runs Wednesday and Sunday night (roughly 36 hours, Y500 hard sleeper, Y800 soft sleeper), or via the border town of Erlian.

To save Y150–200 on the trip, budget travelers can first buy a ticket from Hohhot to Erlian (or to the Mongolian border town of Zamin Uud), and then purchase the rest of the ticket to Ulaan Baatar from a train official, once customs inspections are complete. Train tickets, especially sleepers, are hard to obtain during holidays and high season; book through CITS, CTS, or hotel travel services at these times.

➤ Train Information: **Hohhot Train Station** (✉ Chezhan Jie, ☎ 0471/692–4004).

TRAVEL AGENCIES
➤ LOCAL AGENT REFERRALS: **CITS** (main office: ⊠ Nei Menggu Lu You Ju [Inner Mongolia Tourism Bureau], Xincheng Qu, 3rd floor, 95 Wulan Chabu Lu, Hohhot, ☎ 0471/620–1791 or 0471/629–7046; ⊠ Lu You Da Sha [Tourism Building], 28 Jianguomenwai Dajie, Beijing, ☎ 010/6515–8844 ext. 2110). **CTS** (⊠ 69 Wulan Chabu Lu, Hohhot, ☎ 0471/620–1770). **Inner Mongolia Grassland Tour Travel Service** (⊠ Dongfeng Dajie, Hohhot, ☎ FAX 0471/492–4633). **Railway International Travel Service** (⊠ 112 Xilin Beilu, Hohhot, ☎ FAX 0471/624–3942).

VISITOR INFORMATION
Little information is available other than tour-company leaflets. Hotels and bookstores sell city maps in English and Chinese. The Foreign Languages Bookstore stocks an English-language guide to Inner Mongolia. In summer CITS and CTS have stands inside the soft-seat waiting room of the Beijing railway station. Other tour companies also have representatives at the station and most of the larger hotels offer package tour deals as well.
➤ TOURIST INFORMATION: **Foreign Languages Bookstore** (⊠ Xinhua Dajie).

SIDE TRIP TO THE REPUBLIC OF MONGOLIA

The Republic of Mongolia, once known as Outer Mongolia, was a Soviet satellite state from the 1920s until the late 1980s. In the post-Communist era, Genghis Khan is once more a national hero. Mongolia is one of the world's least developed countries but is a paradise for wildlife enthusiasts, refugees from consumerism, and anyone who likes open spaces. The country is home to snow leopards, Gobi bears, wild camels, giant sheep, wolves, falcons, golden eagles, buzzards, marmots, deer, and gazelles. The horse and the yurt remain the mainstays of life on the steppes and even on the outskirts of the capital, Ulaan Baatar. Lamaism, a Tibetan form of Buddhism that incorporates many shamanistic elements, has resumed its position as the main religion.

Ulaan Baatar

36 hrs by train (850 km/527 mi) north of Hohhot; 30 hrs by train (1,120 km/694 mi) northwest of Beijing.

Grassland and forested hills surround the Russian-style capital of Ulaan Baatar, creating a frontierlike atmosphere completely different from that of any Chinese city. Alongside ice-cream-color baroque buildings, dilapidated wooden shacks, empty run-down lots, and vast Soviet-style apartment blocks, people occasionally ride horses along the quiet streets, and cows graze outside the Mongolian parliament. Trendy Western fashions—blue jeans, tight turtlenecks, and leather jackets—are in vogue among the city's youth, but *dhels* (long robes tied at the waist and designed for horseback riding), knee-length boots, and felt or fur hats are common, too. Yurt neighborhoods on the outskirts of the capital still house up to a third of the city's population.

In old Mongolia even the capital was nomadic. It moved more than 20 times along the Orkhon, Selenge, and Tuul River valleys before an encampment was established in 1639 at Urga, now Ulaan Baatar. After several more moves and three name changes, modern Ulaan Baatar was founded in 1924 and named after the hero of the Mongolian Communist revolution, Sukhbaatar, after whom the city's central square is

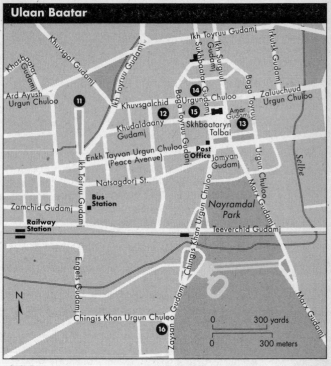

also named. Today the city has a population of more than 700,000. As a result of the Communist government's promotion of population growth, more than 60% of Ulaan Baatar's—and the rest of the country's—residents are under 30, making Mongolia arguably the youngest nation in the world.

Once drab under Soviet control, Ulaan Baatar is home to a growing international development community. An influx of loans from institutions such as the World Bank, combined with the needs of an ever-increasing expatriate community, has led to the development of new housing complexes, stylish Western restaurants, Korean cosmetics boutiques, and improved facilities within the city limits. Though UB, as the city is known to its foreign community, is rapidly modernizing (with all the concomitant pollution, which at times casts a haze over the surrounding mountains), the metropolis continues to have a laid-back small-town atmosphere that makes it an exciting and pleasant place to while away a week.

Richly adorned museums, traditional Mongolian culture, and the Gandan Khiid monastery are the prime attractions. The Naadam Fair, which begins around July 11, has horse racing, archery, and Mongolian wrestling. The city's main east–west boulevard is Enkh Tayvan Urgan Chuloo, also known as Peace Avenue, which runs past the city's center—Sukhbaatar Square—on the south side.

★ ⓫ At **Gandan Khiid** (Gandan Monastery), golden roofs and Tibetan script, brilliant white walls, and red-, green-, and yellow-painted woodwork provide a colorful backdrop to morning worshipers who gather outside the temples. Monks dressed in red, gold, burgundy, violet, chocolate, and amber robes mingle with local people in suits, miniskirts, or traditional dhels. Built in 1840, Gandan Khiid is one of Mongolia's most important Lamaist monasteries (lamaseries). Most of the temple

buildings were destroyed or ransacked in Mongolia's Stalinist purges and have been rebuilt.

Sometimes shaven-headed young monks will offer to show visitors the prayer circuit around the temples, where Buddhists turn copper- and brass-covered prayer wheels, prostrate themselves on prayer stands in front of the monastery's central white stupa, and touch the sacred temple walls, prayer flag mast, and bronze censers. The current Dalai Lama, head of the Yellow Hat sect of Lamaism, to which the monastery belongs, has visited several times. His picture is displayed in front of the altars. Photographs are not allowed inside the temples. ⊠ *Zanabazar Gudamj*, ☎ *01/360–023*. ▣ *Free.* ☉ *Mon.–Sat. 9–11, Sun. 9–1.*

⑫ Beautifully presented Buddhist art is the main treasure of the small **Orligiin Muzei** (Zanabazar Museum of Fine Arts). In this green two-story building, scowling Tsam dancing masks, delicately brushed landscape paintings, and gorgeous Tibetan-Mongolian *thangkhas* (embroidered silk scroll pictures of Buddhist deities) are the pick of the collection. The first floor houses a small collection of Stone Age petroglyphs and Bronze Age knives and pottery. ⊠ *East side of Barylgachidyin Square, off Khudaldaany Gudamj*, ☎ *01/323–986, 01/326–837.* ▣ *T2,400.* ☉ *Daily 9–6.*

⑬ From naturalistic paintings of herdsmen to violent cubist and batik-inspired fantasies, the **Oorun Ehoorgiin Oodzehstehpen** (Mongolian National Art Gallery) gives an intriguing overview of the country's modern and contemporary art scene. The second floor houses rotating exhibitions, of varying quality, with occasional works by distinguished contemporary artists. The sprawling and poorly lit third floor showcases state-honored paintings from 1950 to the present, as well as a hodgepodge of glass cases filled with ceramic figurines, chess sets, and silver bowls, among other esoterica. ⊠ *3 Sukhbaatar Sq., Central Cultural Palace*, ☎ *01/313–191.* ▣ *T1,500.* ☉ *Summer, daily 10–6; winter, Wed.–Sun. 9–5.*

⑭ Two complete Dinosaur skeletons, several nests of cracked dinosaur eggs, and fossilized footprints enliven the musty and packed **Baigaliin Muzei** (Museum of Natural History). In one of the world's richest countries for dinosaur fossils, many of them from the Gobi Desert area, the museum displays some of the best finds. Three floors of exhibits also show Mongolian steppe culture, wildlife, flora, and geology: you'll pass several rooms of stuffed animals as you wind your way through colorful hallways crowned by antelope heads. ⊠ *Khuvsgalchid Urgun Chuloo and Sukhbaatar Gudamj*, ☎ *01/318–179 or 01/315–679.* ▣ *T1,700.* ☉ *Wed.–Sun. 10–4:30.*

⑮ Traditional decorations, ethnic clothing, jewelry, and handicrafts fill the white-pillared **Tub Muzei** (Museum of Mongolian National History), which houses more than 40,000 artifacts dating from the Stone Age to the present day. The first floor exhibition—prehistoric stone axes, bronze arrowheads, and ceramic shards—may be of interest to history buffs, but the real attraction is the sumptuous third-floor exhibition, which gives a peek at the riches of the Mongol Empire in all its glory—from carved wooden bank notes to princely gold-threaded headdresses to the implements of war with which the Mongols once wreaked havoc on Europe and Asia, including gold crossbows, bronze drums, a saddle-mounted cannon, and a trunk-size wooden jail cell with a tiny hole for air. ⊠ *Khudaldaany Gudamj*, ☎ *01/325–656.* ▣ *T2,000.* ☉ *Summer, daily 10–4; winter, Thurs.–Mon. 10–4.*

★ ⑯ The **Bogd Khanny Vliin Ordon** (Winter Palace Museum of Bogd Khan) is the splendid European-style residence of the debauched and pow-

erful Bogd Khan, a Living Buddha who governed Ulaan Baatar's districts of monks, nobles, merchants, artisans, and Russians and Chinese until 1924 as a god-king. The museum is worth visiting just to walk around the courtyards and admire the faded glory of the architecture, but the real strength of the museum lies in its resplendent collection of the Khan's innumerable possessions, from the silver knives that he used to cut off people's fingers to precious Buddhist artifacts and jeweled ceremonial robes, including his winter coat made from 130 minks, a lavish ger (yurt) decorated with 150 leopard skins, and a stuffed zoo of exotic animals. Wind past the Khan's Western luxuries, crowned by a 19th-century London carriage, to find his bizarre collection of curios, capped off by a nobleman's dried brain, a Buddha's tooth, and two eggs hatched from a male hen. In other courtyards, divided by Chinese-style archways, there are six more halls of intricate Buddhist embroideries, paintings, and sculptures. Be sure to request an English-language tour if one isn't offered to you. ⊠ *Chingis Khan Urgun Chuloo, south of Peace Bridge,* ☎ *01/342–195.* ☎ *T2,200, photo permit T5,000.* ☉ *Fri.–Tues. 9:30–4:30.*

Dining and Lodging

The variety and quality of restaurants available in Ulaan Baatar improved considerably in the late 1990s. Outside the capital there may only be mutton, but within the city limits you can find Italian, French, Korean, Japanese, Czech, and an assortment of fast-food establishments. Many restaurants in Ulaan Baatar double as bars or discos, so they stop serving food between 6 PM and 9 PM. It is best to dine early, like the locals, as restaurants sometimes run out of food well before they close. Casual, neat dress is acceptable. Shorts and vest tops are rarely worn in Mongolia and are not advised.

$$–$$$$ ✕ **Sekitei Restaurant.** From the patterned-mosaic stone floor to white paper screens and a rock pool with lazy goldfish, Sekitei has an atmosphere of quiet tranquility more reminiscent of Tokyo than Ulaan Baatar; expect to pay through the nose for the superb Japanese sushi, udon, tempura, teppanyaki, and other traditional fare, however, as virtually all ingredients are imported from other parts of Asia. Private dining rooms are available. The Japanese-run restaurant is diagonally opposite the Flower Hotel, at the north end of the minimall. ⊠ *Sansar Service Center, Bayanzurkh District,* ☎ *01/458–723 or 01/451–361. AE, MC, V.*

$–$$$ ✕ **Seoul Restaurant.** In a white-planked whale of a building in a park,
★ on the second floor of the gold-lettered Seoul Club, is this South Korean joint venture. Downstairs is a bakery and karaoke bar and restaurant; walk up to the second floor for the cafeteria-style Asian eatery, which has red-backed chairs, plaid tablecloths, and a central counter topped by dozens of futuristic chrome-plated serving pots. Korean chefs are on hand to panfry delicious marinated beef and potatoes; choose from a wide variety of set-price buffets of Korean, Japanese, Chinese, and Western food. ⊠ *Nayramdal Children's Park, across from Bayan Gol Hotel,* ☎ *01/329–709. AE, MC, V.*

$$ ✕ **Hazara.** Quality Indian food has made its way to Ulaan Baatar with this chain, which has restaurants in Shanghai, Jakarta, and Singapore as well. Tandoori ovens bake delectable breads and a variety of meat and poultry dishes. Delicately spiced basmati rice, curries, fruit *lassis* (yogurt drinks), and a wide assortment of vegetarian dishes are also served proudly by an attentive staff. Each of the wooden tables is draped by a brightly colored cloth tent, and pleasant Indian music plays softly in the background. ⊠ *16 Enkh Tayvan Urgun Chuloo, next to Negdelchin Hotel,* ☎ *01/455–071. Reservations essential. AE, MC, V.*

$–$$ ✕ **Ding Chen Hotpot Restaurant.** Spicy and flavorful Chinese hotpot is the mainstay of this small, no-frills establishment. Sit at one of the three tables, underneath a poster of a turquoise sea, and cook to your liking a choice of meats, sprouts, tofus, noodles, and an assortment of seasonal vegetables. The divided hotpot allows for two levels of spiciness, and the selection of sauces provides a wide variety of flavorings. A range of other northern Chinese dishes can be ordered, though vegetable selections are limited. ⊠ *Baga Toiruu, 100 yards north of Enkh Tayvan Urgun Chuloo, across the street and south of People's Movie Theater,* ☎ *01/317–172. No credit cards.*

$–$$ ✕ **Ikh Khuraidai.** A spacious pale yellow ger, decorated with sculpted figures on the outside and a silver tree of dragons' heads sprouting from the circular bar on the inside, Ikh Khuraidai is a meat-lover's delight, serving everything from pork schnitzel and real T-bone steaks to Mongolian roast sausages. Soups, salads, sandwiches, and other classic Western entrées are also served. The sophisticated eatery is the latest and most upscale venue by the Chinggis Beer Brewery Company, a Mongolian-Swiss joint venture that makes a beer of the same name and has a string of popular bars in Ulaan Baatar. There's music on the weekends, as well as Formula 1 racing nights, and a beer garden opens in the summer months. The restaurant is just next to the Palace Hotel, a stone's throw west from the Winter Palace Museum of Bogd Khan. ⊠ *2 Chinggis Ave.,* ☎ *01/342–511 or 01/9919–7525. AE, MC, V.*

$–$$ ✕ **Los Banditos.** Vibrant colors light up the city's first Mexican restaurant, from the Crayola-colored chairs to the blue-striped cloth laid over long wooden tables to the white wolf's pelt hanging by the bar. Generous portions of Mexican fare—cooked up by an Indian chef—are heaped on orange-rimmed plates, from nachos and chicken wings to fajitas, enchiladas, and burritos, as well as a creative sampling of Indian fare. The restaurant may be hard to find: look for the log-cabin of an exterior, surrounded by a log-stump of a fence, just south of Peace Avenue opposite Pizza della Casa. The eatery is on a little alleyway behind the post office. ⊠ *Namnansvren St., south of Enkh Tayvan Urgun Chuloo,* ☎ *01/9515–6322, 01/9919–4618. AE, MC, V.*

$–$$ ✕ **Taj Mahal.** The city's second Indian restaurant, opened by the former manager of Hazara, radiates a quiet sophistication with its polished pine-wood floors, lime-green and beige tablecloths, and Indian-style window facades. The eclectic menu has a dizzying array of tandoori, curries, vegetarian selections, and breads prepared by the Taj's two Indian chefs—don't miss the succulent naan. The wine list has imported French and German labels. There are also good-value lunch specials here, with a choice of one main dish served with nan, rice, salad, and pickles. The restaraunt is across the road from the Ulaan Baatar Hotel; the entrance is in an interior courtyard through the archway connecting the Sports Palace and Teacher's College on Baga Toiruu. ⊠ *Baga Toiruu,* ☎ *01/311–002, 01/9919–5062. AE, MC, V.*

$ ✕ **Chez Bernard Café.** Up a flight of russet-color stairs, this quaint backpacker's café lined with wooden tables is a homey place to stop for coffee and desserts—brownies, cheesecake, vegetable quiche, loaves of peasant bread, and other homemade goods. The message board by the door lists art events about town, and a small outdoor patio completes the set-up. The café is on Peace Avenue, just west of the State Department Store and east of the Central Post Office. ⊠ *Enkh Tayvan Urghan Chuloo,* ☎ *01/324–622. No credit cards.*

$ ✕ **Khan Brau.** The Khan Brau has a formal dining area, a relaxed bar/restaurant, and an ice-cream parlor, plus an outdoor patio in summer. Roast pork, pizza, schnitzel, and a plethora of pastas are served in your choice of dining areas. The bar/restaurant has a small dance floor in the middle and hosts live music on weekends. The locally mi-

crobrewed Khan Brau is proudly served on tap. ⊠ *Tamian Junii Gudamj, across from Bayan Gol Hotel, catercorner to the Central Post Office,* ☎ *01/324–064. No credit cards.*

$ ✕ **Millie's Espresso.** This checkerboard-floored coffee shop with superb cappuccinos and friendly service will satisfy your cravings for Western food. Spinach lasagna, chicken tacos, huevos rancheros, Cuban pork sandwiches, fruit smoothies, and lemon pie often appear on the menu board. Tables at this popular expat hangout can be hard to come by at lunch hours. ⊠ *Khudaldaany Gudamj, south side of Barylgachidyin Sq., 2nd floor of Aero Voyage Building/Center Hotel,* ☎ *01/328–721. No credit cards.*

$ ✕ **Pizza della Casa.** Favorites with the expat crowd, both locations of this bistro have good, moderately priced salads, pastas, and pizzas served on blue peasant plates. The original Pizza della Casa is just east of Centrepoint on Peace Avenue; the stylish Ristorante della Casa, with flowing white curtains, large windows, and light-color tiles, is opposite the restaurant of the Ulaan Baatar Hotel in an oval redbrick building fronted with windows. ⊠ *Enkh Tayvan Urgun Chuloo (Pizza della Casa),* ☎ *01/324–114;* ⊠ *2/F, Time Center, Baga Toiruu (Ristorante della Casa),* ☎ *01/312–072. AE, MC, V.*

$$$$ ✕⊞ **Bayan Gol.** Each of this centrally located hotel's two red towers has its own reception: although more services are housed in the north tower, nearer Sukhbaatar Square, the south tower is more aesthetically pleasing, with plush dark-green rugs and diamondback gold coverlets. All rooms in both towers have balconies, many with good views of Nayramdal Park or the mountains south of Ulaan Baatar. The hotel's main restaurant, flanked by the twin towers, has a good-value, four-course prix-fixe menu, which might feature egg with caviar, cream of chicken soup, mutton goulash, and fruit salad, for example. Next door, the hotel's Singaporean-run restaurant/bar, Casablanca, has decent Western fare in a banker's lounge atmosphere. ⊠ *28 Chinghis Khan Urgun Chuloo, 49,* ☎ *01/328–869,* 𝖥𝖠𝖷 *01/326–794. 179 rooms, 21 suites. 4 restaurants, 3 bars, hair salon, business services, travel services. AE, MC, V.*

$$$$ ⊞ **Chinghis Khan.** A mirrored-glass and red-concrete tiered structure on the east side of the city, the Chinghis Khan has a huge empty foyer with a marble floor, a hanging crystal chandelier, and glass walls. The standard Western-style rooms have wooden desks, lounge areas, IDD phones, and cable TV. Although singles are roomy, the standard double rooms are slightly claustrophobic, and bathrooms in both are small. A post office counter, a bank, and a doctor are also available on site. But new plans for a mammoth shopping mall next door, if they work out, may help speed business again their way. ⊠ *5 Khukh Tenger Gudamj, east of the Selbe River, just north of Zaluuchuud Urghan Chuloo, 49,* ☎ *01/313–380,* 𝖥𝖠𝖷 *01/312–788. 196 rooms, 42 suites. 2 restaurants, bar, minibars, massage, sauna, gym, billiards, laundry service, business services, travel services. AE, MC, V.*

$$$$ ⊞ **Ulaan Baatar.** With an unbeatable location just east of Sukhbaatar ★ Square, the hotel has a plain, gray-concrete facade with pillars at its entrance that mask its small, homey interior. The lobby has leather settees and red wool carpets leading up a double staircase. All rooms have cable TV, IDD phones, and hair dryers. The first-floor restaurant serves both Mongolian and Western food and is popular with foreign travelers and expatriates. The room-service menu includes barbecued mutton and Mongolian milk tea. ⊠ *14 Sukhbaatar Sq. (off Enkh Tayvan Urgun Chuloo), 49,* ☎ *01/320–620,* 𝖥𝖠𝖷 *01/324–485. 165 rooms, 35 suites. 3 restaurants, minibars, hair salon, sauna, billiards, business services. AE, DC, MC, V.*

$$$-$$$$ 🏠 **Flower Hotel.** Popular with Japanese tour groups (guests bathe in the Japanese-style bathhouse), this white-brick hotel on the city's east side has small and functional standard rooms with blue-and-brown color schemes. Virtually no English is spoken here, though, and given the hotel's lack of amenities, the room rates may seem exorbitant. The hotel's Fuji Japanese restaurant serves chicken curry as well as ramen, sushi, and other Japanese standards. The Altai Restaurant has Western food, and the large Chinese restaurant serves set-price buffets; get there early, as many dishes run out. ☒ *12 Khukh Tengeriin Gudamj, up the hill east of Chinggis Khan Hotel, 49,* ☎ *01/458–330,* ☎ FAX *01/358– 330,* FAX *01/455–652,* WEB *www.mol.mn/flowerhotel. 56 rooms (without shower), 8 suites. 3 restaurants, bar, sauna. AE, MC, V.*

$$$ 🏠 **Bishrelt Hotel.** This small, friendly establishment dominated by an elegant central white spiral staircase has many facilities and services normally found only at larger hotels. All rooms have high ceilings, cable TV, and IDD. Smaller rooms come with balconies, while larger rooms are furnished with coffee tables, couches, and matching sofa chairs. The restaurant serves up a variety of cuisine that includes Hungarian beef goulash, fried chicken, cucumber soup, and ox tongue. A Continental breakfast is included in the rate. ☒ *Erhk Cholori Talbai (Liberty Sq.) 3/1, off Kuvisgalchid Urgun Chuloo, 43,* ☎ *01/313–786,* FAX *01/313–792. 20 rooms. Restaurant, sauna, bicycles, billiards, nightclub, business services, meeting room, travel services. AE, MC, V.*

$$$ 🏠 **White House Hotel.** A smiling doorman greets you as you enter a lobby decked out in red carpet, black leather sofas and chairs, and a white piano. Upstairs, the spacious rooms are decorated with gray-shelled drapes, bedspreads, and sofa covers, and they have cable TV, IDD phones, and comfortable beds. The White House is one of the best choices in town for comfort and value. ☒ *Damdinbazaryn Gudamj, 49 Amarsanaa St., southwest of Gandan Khiid, a few blocks north of Peace Ave.,* ☎ *01/367–872,* FAX *01/369–973. 14 rooms. Restaurant, nightclub, billiards, business services, travel services. AE, MC, V.*

$ 🏠 **Gana's Guest House.** If you're willing to forgo a few creature comforts, you can spend a night in a ger without leaving Ulaan Baatar. Down a residential alleyway 200 yards south of Gandan Khiid, Gana's has traditional-style gers, each outfitted with five beds, a washbasin, a table, and a wood-burning stove. Primitive outhouses and a foot-pump shower room are a few steps away. The restaurant is closed in winter. Gana also offers some of Mongolia's most reasonably priced travel services. ☒ *House No. 22, Ondor Geegen Zanabazaryn Gudamj; climb up the hill toward Gandan Khiid, turn east onto an unpaved alleyway flanked at the entrance by tourist stands, walk 2 mins, and look for the sign on the left-hand side, 49,* ☎ FAX *01/367–343. 5–8 gers, depending on season. Restaurant, travel services. No credit cards.*

$ 🏠 **Hunter Hotel.** A few hundred yards south of Gandan Khiid, this barebones hallway of a hotel offers budget travelers some of the cheapest housing in Ulaan Baatar. The tiny no-frills rooms have gray rugs, striped comforters, and clean cubicle-size bathrooms that have showers and 24-hour hot water. Dorm beds cost T9,000; a room with two beds costs T19,000. ☒ *Ondor Geegen Zanabazaryn Gudamj, 49,* ☎ FAX *01/360–375, 01/9918–1468. 5 rooms. Restaurant, bar, billiards. No credit cards.*

Nightlife and the Arts

THE ARTS

For traditional Mongolian song and dance, the main venue is the **Ulsyn Dramyn Teatr** (National Academic Drama Theater; ☒ Chinghis Khan Urgun Chuloo and Natsagdorj Urgun Chuloo, ☎ 01/323–490). The **Duur Bujgiin Balet Teatr** (State Opera and Ballet Theater; ☒ Skhbaataryn

Talbai/Sukhbaatar Square, east side, ☎ 01/320–357) stages Mongolian versions of classical ballets and operas. Ticket prices are T5,000. Fees of T3,000 for photographs and T30,000 for amateur video are charged.

NIGHTLIFE

Ulaan Baatar is home to several nightclubs. Some are safe and are happy to entertain tourists; others are dark, dangerous, and full of aggressive vodka-swigging men and prostitutes. If possible, avoid all nightclubs that aren't close to major roads: muggings (or worse) are not infrequent in unlit alleyways. **Fire** (✉ Microdistrict 3, just next to the post office, ☎ 01/360–731), is the current favorite among the young and trendy. Others still flock to the once-popular **Money Train** (✉ Enkh Tayvan Urgun Chuloo, at Amarsanaa Gudamj, ☎ 01/322–460). A slightly older crowd favors the live-music club **River Sounds** (✉ one alleyway south of Enkh Tayvan Ave., opposite the Opera House in Sukhbaatar Sq., ☎ 01/9915–8548). The dark-wooded **Chinggis Club** (✉ Sukhbaataryn Gudamj) and its sister establishment **Ikh Khuraldai** (✉ 2 Chinggis Avenue, ☎ 01/342–511 or 01/9919–7525), with live music on weekends, are popular among pub-crawlers.

Shopping

Knives, boots, traditional clothes, paintings of grassland scenes, and Buddhist art are among the items worth buying in Ulaan Baatar. Under Mongolian customs law, antiques must have an export certificate. Check that the shop can issue one before you buy. For a fine selection of beautiful handwoven Kazakh wall hangings, as well as ethnic clothing, carved chessboards, trinkets, woolen rugs, and leather bags, head to the small **Odyssey** (✉ 2/F, Aero Voyage Bldg., Khudaldaany Gubamj, next to Millie's Espresso, ☎ 01/9914–7902 or 01/312–378 [office]). Set up by a nongovernmental organization that works to rectify conditions in Mongolian prisons, many items in the shop were voluntarily made by prisoners participating in the NGO's program. All proceeds from the sales are used to improve their prison conditions. Up a flight of pale green stairs, the **Antique Shop** (✉ Baruun Selbe St., one block south of Liberty Sq., ☎ 01/317–839 or 01/9919–6825) has a small but fine collection of traditional copper-and-silver pitchers, ornamented teapots, silver jewelry, carved wooden boxes, and other objects, many of them genuine antiques. The **Fine Art Shop** (✉ Enkh Tayvan Urgun Chuloo) houses a collection of traditional paintings, felt dolls and wall-hangings, souvenirs, and art books. Kiosks outside the south and east gates of **Gandan Khiid** (✉ Zanabazar Gudamj) stock incense burners, hand-painted Buddhas, and thangkhas (painted cloth scrolls). The well-known local artist and newspaper cartoonist **Gulset** (✉ Chinghis Khan Urgun Chuloo, small cabin in front of Bayan Gol Hotel) sells watercolors, oils, copper teapots, brass Buddhas, thangkhas, and masks. Some of the paintings are his own work. The fourth floor of the city's largest shop, the **Ikh Delgüür** (State Department Store; ✉ Enkh Tayvan Urgun Chuloo, ☎ 01/324–311), is good for leather boots, Mongolian dhels and headgear, and souvenirs, including Mongolian chess sets and miniature yurts. A large shop inside the gate of the **Winter Palace Museum of Bogd Khan** (✉ Chingis Khan Urgun Chuloo, ☎ 01/342–195) has Mongolian teapots, knives, wool and cashmere, artwork, Buddhist items, and some antiques. **Avanchin Outfitters** (✉ M100 Building #112, Chingeltei District, one block west and south of the Museum of Natural History, ☎ 01/327–172) has quality camping equipment, including tents, boots, sleeping bags, flashlights, clothing, and sunglasses.

Manzshir Khiid

⑰ *1 hr by bus (46 km/29 mi) south of Ulaan Baatar.*

Manzshir Khiid is a unique combination of a ruined monastery, Mongolia's oldest nature reserve, and two small museums in a forested area among the Bogd Mountains. Founded in 1733 at the site of a healing spring, the grand monastery was once home to 20 temples and 350 lamas. Here, late autumn Tsam mask dances that reflected the shamanist roots of Tibetan Buddhism were held once a year to drive away evil spirits. Unfortunately, the site was all but annihilated by the Stalinist purges of 1937. In the late 90s, the main temple was restored and now houses a museum with photos of Manzshir in its former glory, as well as Buddhist art and fierce-looking Tsam masks. Among the objects recovered from the ruins is an enormous bronze cooking pot, cast in 1732, large enough to boil ten sheep and two cows. Behind the temple, you can climb up to a hilltop shrine strewn with old money, much of it from Mongolia's Communist era.

On the mountain slopes you can ride horses or hike through deer forests. Manzshir is easily accessible on a day trip: you can either book a tour through an agency, hire a vehicle to drive you there (a taxi should cost US$10–$15 one way), or take local transportation. Minivans leave hourly each day (8–6) from the long-distance bus station for the provincial capital of Zuunmod. From here it's a beautiful, easy 5-km (3-mi) walk to the monastery. If you want to stay overnight, there are yurt accommodations. ⊠ *Manazhir.* ☞ *Monastery and museums,* T1,000. ☯ *May–Oct., daily 10–6.*

Karakorum

⑱ *360 km (223 mi) southwest of Ulaan Baatar.*

Genghis Khan's 13th-century capital, Karakorum (Kharkhorin in Mongolian) was built on one of the ancient silk roads. The crosswinds of trade brought foreign traders, missionaries, warriors, and—on a journey that took a year from Rome—even the Pope's ambassador to this cosmopolitan city. The Franciscan monk William of Rubruk, the only Westerner to leave a contemporaneous account of the place, dismissed the capital as no bigger than the suburb of St. Denis in Paris. However, the Mongols brought the plunder of 20 kingdoms here, foreign and Mongolian currency were accepted as legal tender, and 12 religions were allowed to coexist with equal status.

The centerpiece of the city was the Khan's 7,500-square-ft palace, which was built like a church with a Chinese-style roof and crowned by a silver fountain so ingeniously constructed by a Parisian jeweler that wine, mare's milk, and other liquors poured forth from fabulous spouts shaped like lion's and snake's heads. Surrounding the palace were canals, and alongside a thriving foreign merchants' sector, Nestorian churches, mosques, and Buddhist temples could all be found fiercely competing for Mongolian souls. Although the area is Mongolia's richest historic site, the city actually served as the imperial capital for only 40 years; in 1264, Kublai Khan moved the capital to Beijing. After the demise of the Mongol empire, the city was razed by the vengeful Chinese Ming dynasty in 1388. Modern-day Karakorum is a small, modern town nearby.

In 1586 the **Erdenezu Khiid** (Erdenezu Monastery) was built using the fallen stones of the city, leaving just a few remains such as Turtle Rock, which marked one corner of the old city walls. Mongolia's largest monastery, Erdenezu housed 1,000 monks in 60 temples at its height. It was closed and damaged during the Stalinist purges of the 1930s but

now has seven active temples in the huge compound. Topped with 108 white stupas, the walls are said to be a smaller replica of the original Karakorum city walls. The temples are a mixture of flat-roofed Tibetan-style and Chinese-style wooden pillars, tiled roofs, and red walls. ⊠ *2 km (1 mi) east of the center of town.* 🎫 *T8,000; photo permit, T3,000.* ☉ *Daily 9–9; visitors are welcome to the temple Lavrim Sum's daily morning ceremonies (at around 11).*

Accessible on day trips from Karakorum are the ruins of an **ancient Uighur Muslim kingdom;** several **Turkish monuments** and inscriptions dating from the 8th and 9th centuries; the relaxing natural hot springs at **Khujirt;** and the **Orkhon Waterfall,** legendary birthplace of the Mongolian people. The relics are interesting if unspectacular, but on the way to them you pass beautiful unspoiled grassland scenery with horsemen using their urgas, marmot hunters, camel herds, isolated yurts, falcons, and foxes. There are also wolves and snow leopards in the area, though you're not likely to see them unless you go on a wildlife safari. Visits to local families and horseback riding give you an even better idea of the traditional Mongolian way of life. You normally get to sample airag, cheese, and milk tea boiled on a dung-burning stove. These trips are all best taken on a tour.

Dining and Lodging

$$ ⌸ ⚠ **Karakorum Yurt Camp.** You can stay in a real yurt without hav-
★ ing to rough it too much at this camp, set on open grassland within sight of old and new Karakorum. The yurts are in traditional style, with orange-painted posts and roof slats, wool rugs on the floor, small but comfortable wooden beds, and a wood-burning stove that is kept going for you by the staff. Each yurt sleeps up to four people. Bathrooms and showers (not always hot) are in a separate block 100 yards away. A giant yurt makes an evocative dining room and venue for song and dance performances. The set meals include buuz, mutton stew, and other Mongolian standards. Vegetarian or other special dishes can be ordered. The rate is for a bed (not the whole yurt), as well as meals. ⊠ *Karakorum. 12 yurts. Restaurant, horseback riding. No credit cards. Closed Nov.–Apr.*

Republic of Mongolia A to Z

To research prices, get advice from other travelers, and book travel arrangements, visit www.fodors.com.

AIR TRAVEL
Regular flights connect Ulaan Baatar to Beijing, Hohhot, Moscow, Irkutsk, Seoul, Osaka, and Berlin.

CARRIERS
The Mongolian airline, MIAT, and Air China run Ulaan Baatar–Beijing flights several times a week. MIAT also runs regular flights to Hohhot, Moscow, Irkutsk, Seoul, Osaka, and Berlin. Plans for a direct flight to Hong Kong in the summer months are under way. Air China, Aeroflot, and Korean Airlines also have offices in Ulaan Baatar. Opposite the MIAT building, Exc-El & Travel International Air Ticketing Service can provide tickets from all of the above airlines. In Beijing contact CAAC or MIAT.
➤ AIRLINES AND CONTACTS: **Aeroflot** (Natsagdorj Gudamj, Ulaan Baatar, ☎ 01/320–720). **Air China** (⊠ North of Flower Hotel, across the street from the central petrol station, Ulaan Baatar, ☎ 01/328–838). **Exc-El & Travel International Air Ticketing Service** (⊠ Baga Toiruu, Ulaan Baatar, ☎ 01/323–364, FAX 01/328–567). **Korean Airlines** (1/F, Chinggis Khaan Hotel, 5 Khukh Tenger St., Ulaan Baatar, ☎ 01/326–

643). **MIAT** (⊠ 8 Baga Toiruu, Ulaan Baatar, ☎ 01/322–273 or 01/ 322–144).

➤ AIRLINES AND CONTACTS IN CHINA: **CAAC** (⊠ Aviation Building, 15 Xi Chang'an Jie, Xidan District, Beijing, ☎ 010/6601–6667). **MIAT** (⊠ 1A Jianguomenwai Da Jie (west of the China World Hotel), Beijing, ☎ 010/6507–9297, FAX 010/6507–7397).

AIRPORTS

Buyant Uha Airport, the country's only international airport, lies 15 km (9 mi) to the south of town.

➤ AIRPORT INFORMATION: **Buyant Uha Airport** (☎ 01/320–221 or 01/ 313–163).

BUS TRAVEL

Buses run up to the border on both sides, but there are no direct buses from Hohhot to Ulaan Baatar. Minibuses do run between the railroad stations of the border towns of Zamin Uud and Erlian (T8,000, plus a border tax of Y6,000) but it's easier and far more convenient to take the rail direct to Ulaan Baatar from Hohhot or Beijing.

FARES AND SCHEDULES
Several useful routes run along Peace Avenue and past Sukhbaatar Square in Ulaan Baatar, but buses can be crowded and pickpockets abound. Mongol Teever is the main operator; a fleet of privately owned minibuses have also sprung up, following the same routes at the same T200 fare. Regular buses run to Karakorum and Manzshir. The 1-hr bus to Manzshir runs hourly each day 8–6 from the long-distance bus station (T700). The eight-hr bus to Karakorum runs three times a week and is much cheaper and slower than jeep travel—but can be more of an adventure. Quicker, privately owned micro-buses also run to both places daily, for a slightly higher fee, starting as well from the bus station square; signs to destinations aren't well-marked, but ask individual drivers. As in China, drivers often wait for all the seats to fill up before starting on their journey.

CUSTOMS AND DUTIES

Trains stop twice at the China-Mongolia border, at the Mongolian border town of Zamin Uud and also at the Chinese border town of Erlian for immigration and customs inspections. Your passport will be taken and stamped by officials from both countries; and you may have your bags checked as well. If you're exporting any antiques, you must have a receipt and a customs certificate from the store you bought it. Exporting fossils is illegal. Delays usually take from three to six hours, as the train wheels are also changed at the time. The train between Hohhot and Ulaan Baatar can be delayed for up to thirteen hours. Once you get your passport back, you can get off the train and wander through the border town. If you're traveling to Mongolia, you can stock up on a wide variety of food and beverages at Erlian; going the other way, the Zamin Uud station does not sell food.

EMBASSIES AND CONSULATES

➤ CONSULATES: **Canada** (⊠ Suite 56, Diplomatic Services Corp. Bldg., Ulaan Baatar, ☎ 01/328–281). **China** (⊠ Zaluuchuud Urgan Chuloo, Ulaan Baatar, ☎ 01/320–955, 01/323–940). **United Kingdom** (⊠ 30 Enkh Tayvan Urgun Chuloo, Ulaan Baatar, ☎ 01/458–133, FAX 01/358–036). **United States** (⊠ 59/1 Ikh Toiruu, Ulaan Baatar, ☎ 01/329–095, FAX 01/320–776, WEB www.us-mongolia.com).

EMERGENCIES

Most hospitals and clinics in Mongolia are chronically short of medical supplies and doctors; and medical training is often inadequate. If

you have a minor ailment that persists, ask your hotel to recommend a specific doctor in a hospital to visit. For more serious ailments, contact your local embassy for assistance in finding a Western doctor; you may also want to consider heading to Beijing for medical treatment. The places listed below cater to foreigners; unfortunately, English-speaking doctors are rare, and you will almost certainly have to bring your own translator.

➤ HOSPITALS AND CLINICS: **Arono Dental Clinic** (⊠ 300 ft north of the Winter Palace of Bogd Khan, ☎ 01/342–609). **No. 2 Hospital** (⊠ Enkh Tayvan Urgun Chuloo, next to U.K. Embassy, ☎ 01/458–250). **Yonsei Friendship Hospital** (⊠ Enkh Tayvan Urgun Chuloo, east of Sukhbaatar Sq., ☎ 01/310–945).

➤ POLICE: **Emergency hot line** (☎ 102). **Bayan Gol district** (⊠ Enkh Tayvan Urgun Chuloo, ☎ 01/361–734). **Sukhbaatar district** (⊠ Negdsen Undestniy, ☎ 01/332–0341).

INTERNET SERVICES

Major hotels offer Internet services, but it's not too hard to get a quick cyber-fix while you're out and about town. Several Web cafés have sprung up on Enkh Tayvan Urgun Chuloo and near tourist attractions. For a latte, milkshake, or desserts while on line, the clean, streamlined City Coffee has E-mail and other Internet services for T3,000 an hour. Fast on-line connections at T800 an hour are available at iCafé. The Mouse House has cyber-access for T800 an hour from 10 to 10.

➤ CONTACTS: **City Coffee** (⊠ in the same complex as Khan Brau, diagonal to the Bayan Gol Hotel, off Chinggis Khan Urghan Chuloo, ☎ 01/328–077 or 01/328–135. **iCafe** (⊠ Baga Toiruu, northeast side of the Ulaan Baatar Hotel, across the road from the Mongolian Technical University, ☎ 01/313–316. **The Mouse House** (⊠ Baga Toiruu, north of the State Department Store).

MAIL AND SHIPPING

The Mongolian postal system is very slow but usually reliable. Allow at least a few weeks for letters and postcards mailed from Ulaan Baatar to arrive; if you're en route to Beijing, you may want to post your mail from there instead. Parcel shipping is expensive, and slow as well. There are no mailboxes on the streets; post letters from the Central Post office at the southwest corner of Sukhbaatar Square. For express deliveries, courier services such as DHL and TNT offer door-to-door service.

➤ POST OFFICE: **Central Post Office** (⊠ Enkh Tayvan Urgun Chuloo). **DHL** (☎ 01/310–919). **TNT** (☎ 01/313–389).

MONEY MATTERS

ATMS

There are as of yet no ATMs in Mongolia.

CURRENCY

The unit of currency in Mongolia is the tugrik or tugrog, abbreviated "Tg." or "T". The exchange rate at press time was T1,097 to the U.S. dollar, T1,567 to the pound sterling, T712 to the Canadian dollar, T565 to the Australian dollar, and T455 to the New Zealand dollar.

CURRENCY EXCHANGE

Major hotels exchange U.S. dollars or traveler's checks. Some of the banks exchange cash and traveler's checks or provide cash advances on major credit cards. Find out the rates and fees before initiating your transaction. The redbrick Trade and Development Bank, open weekdays 9–12:45 and 2–3:30, accepts traveler's checks and credit cards (AE, MC, V). The entrance for currency exchange is to the left of the main entrance: look for the red Moneygram sign.

➤ EXCHANGE SERVICES: **Trade and Development Bank** (✉ Khuldaany Jie 7 Baga Toiruu, at Kuldaldaany Gudamj, ☎ 01/324–690 or 01/310–665).

PASSPORTS AND VISAS
ENTERING THE REPUBLIC OF MONGOLIA

In Beijing the Mongolian Embassy, open 9–11 and 2–4, issues 30-day visas for US$40. It takes four days. Next-day service is also available for an additional US$20. Letters of invitation or confirmation of hotel and/or tour booking are no longer required to visit Mongolia. Visas may also be obtained in Hohhot, at the consular office next to Zhaojun Huayuan (open 9–11:30 and 3–5:30), or at the Chinese border town of Erenhot Erlian (Erenhot in Mongolian), at the consular office in the Erlian Hotel, open 9–11. Both provide same-day service, though you may have to argue to obtain a 30-day visa rather than a seven-day visa, depending on the whims of local officials. One passport-type photo is required for all visas.

If you want to stay longer in Mongolia than your visa permits, you must register at the third floor of the State Centre for Civil Registration and Information. Stays of longer than 30 days require an accompanying letter from an official tour operator or an official work unit. Tourist registration fees are around T5000.

➤ CONTACTS: **Mongolian Embassy** (Menggu Dashiguan; ✉ 2 Xiushui Beidajie, Jianguomenwai, Beijing, ☎ 010/6532–1203). **Hohhot Consulate office** (Menggu Linshiguan; ✉ Zhaojun Huayuan, Xincheng Qu, 5 Wulan Xiao Qu, Hohhot, ☎ 0471/430–3266 or 0471/430–3254). **Erlian Hotel** (☎ 0479/752–1538 ext. 2307, FAX 0479/752–2194). **State Centre for Civil Registration and Information** (✉ Tsagdaagiin Gudamj, Ulaan Baatar, ☎ 01/327–182).

TAXES
DEPARTURE TAX

There is a T12,500 departure tax.

TELEPHONES
AREA AND COUNTRY CODES

The country code for Mongolia is 976. Drop the initial 0 in the city code when phoning from outside Mongolia. Major hotels all offer local and IDD services. You can also buy a phone card (for T5,000, 10,000, and 20,000) at the post office, and use a pay phone.

TRAIN TRAVEL

Although flying is much quicker, if you have the time, the 30-hour train journey from Beijing is one-fourth of the price, and worth making on one leg of your trip. On the way you pass the Great Wall and open grassland scenery and meet mainly Mongolian, Russian, and Chinese fellow passengers. Both classes of sleeper offer ample comfort.

Mongolia has only one main railway line, the Beijing–Ulaan Baatar–Irkutsk section of the trans-Siberian route. Trains run to and from Moscow and Beijing twice a week.

RESERVATIONS

In Ulaan Baatar, you can buy tickets at the International Railway Ticketing Office (weekdays 9–1 and 2–4, weekends 9–2); the two-story yellow building is a block north and west of the train station. Bring your passport. Reservations up to 10 days in advance can be made here, but over-booking is common during the summer months, so don't count on getting a ticket until it's in your hands. In Beijing, you can buy tickets at the international ticketing counter at the central railway station,

Beijing Zhan. Otherwise, CITS can book tickets. Contact Ulaan Baatar Railway Authority or the CITS in Beijing.

➤ CONTACTS: **CITS** (✉ Lu You Da Sha [Tourism Building], 28 Jian-guomenwai Da Jie, Beijing, ☎ 010/6515–8844 ext. 2110). **International Railway Ticketing Office** (☎ 01/94133, FAX 01/955–124). **Ulaan Baatar Railway Authority** (☎ 01/320–332).

TRANSPORTATION AROUND THE REPUBLIC OF MONGOLIA

TAXIS

Real taxis came to Ulaan Baatar in 2000, in the form of small yellow or light-blue vehicles, with a checkered "City Taxi" sign up top. If you don't see an official taxi coming, however, any vehicle—either inside or outside Ulaan Baatar—may be a taxi in disguise. Stand on the side of the street, wave your arm up and down, and before long someone is bound to stop.

FARES AND SCHEDULES

The standard rate is T210–250 per kilometer for local and long-distance journeys. Make sure the driver sets the odometer back to zero or make a mental note of the mileage before you head off. Most cab rides within the city shouldn't cost more than T1,500.

TRAVEL AGENCIES

In Mongolia's emerging tourism industry, at least 50 local operators are competing or cooperating with foreign tour companies. All offer tours, plane and train booking, and visa services. While prices vary depending on itinerary, services, and number of days, expect to pay US$300–$800 per person for a three-day trip to Karakorum, including a driver, meals, accommodation, and English-speaking guide. Longer excursions that require air transport range from $600 into the thousands of dollars. Prices go down depending on the number of people in your group; individual travelers may find it hard to join a group tour outside of high season. Going alone is possible; you'll just pay more.
➤ LOCAL AGENT REFERRALS: **Guchidhan** (✉ Box 49/411, Ulaan Baatar 46, ☎ 01/456–442, WEB www.mol.mn/guchidhan). **Juulchin** (✉ Chingis Khan Gudamj, 5B, Ulaan Baatar, ☎ 01/328–428, FAX 01/320–246; ✉ Room 4015, International Hotel, Jianguomenwai, Beijing 10005, ☎ 010/6512–6688 ext. 4015, FAX 010/6525–4339). **Khongor Guesthouse Tours** (✉ Apt. 15, Flat 6, 2/F, Enkh Taivan Urgun Chuloo, west of the Centrepoint Mall, Chingeltei District, Ulaan Baatar 38, ☎ 01/329–331, 01/9919–9923). **Monkey Business** (✉ No. 1 Bldg., Yu Lin Li, Room 406, Youanmenwai 2/F, Hidden Tree Bar, 12 Dong Da Qiao Xie Jie [at Nan San Li Tun], Beijing 100027, ☎ 010/6591–6519, FAX 010/6591–6517, WEB www.monkeyshrine.com). **Nature Tours** (✉ Room 212, Youth Federation Bldg., Baga Toiruu, Ulaan Baatar 10, ☎ 01/312–392, FAX 01/311–979). **Sand Dune Travel** (✉ Box 882, Ulaan Baatar 46, ☎ 01/367–343).

VISITOR INFORMATION

Ulaan Baatar, a Survival Guide is a tourist publication with maps and listings, produced each summer and sold by the main hotels. Ulaan Baatar also has two weekly English-language newspapers, the *Mongol Messenger* and the *U.B. Post*. Both are stocked by many kiosks and bookstalls along Enkh Tayvan Urgun Chuloo and west of Sukhbaataryn Talbai. They're a good source of information on entertainment and cultural events in Ulaan Baatar. On line, www.mongolart.mn offers helpful listings of current cultural and arts-related events, with some good links to other Mongolian English-language Web sites. The less useful www.mol.mn has more news-oriented items.

13 SIDE TRIP TO TIBET

ROOF OF THE WORLD

Welcome to a land that can't help but trade on its mystery. Turquoise-green rivers run through rocky terrain, which at times looks like moonscapes. A wall of towering, seemingly endless mountains surrounds the plateau, where the air is already thin. Wearing their waist-length braided black hair tied up in buns on top of their heads, men and women bejewelled with chunks of turquoise and coral still roam the land with nothing but dried yak meat and cheese for sustenance. Donning traditional clothing, the people, as much as the land, possess an enchanting aura that sadly is dying. Experience it now, while you still can.

By Nigel Fisher
and Lily Tung,
with Michael
Koeppel

Updated by
Kate Bryson
and Tom
Bryson

TIBET LIES ON A VAST PLATEAU as large as Western Europe, sandwiched between two Himalayan ridges whose peaks reach an altitude of 8 km (5 mi). The plateau is the source of all major rivers in South and East Asia: the Indus, Sutlej, and Brahmaputra from the far western highlands; the Mekong, Salween, Yangzi, Yalong, Gyrong, Yellow, Minjiang, and Jialing from the eastern region. Under the People's Republic of China the western half of the plateau has been designated the Tibet Autonomous Region, comprising the traditional Tibetan provinces of Ü (capital, Lhasa), Tsang (capital, Zhigatse), and Ngari (sometimes called Western Tibet). The remainder has been swallowed up by the Chinese provinces of Sichuan and Qinghai.

Until 1707, when Jesuit missionaries established themselves in Lhasa, the West had no serious contact with Tibet. Before then the Roof of the World, as this Himalayan land is poetically called, was isolated. Long, long ago, so one story goes, an ogress called Sinmo and a monkey named Avalokiteshvara were the only living creatures on the Tibetan plateau. In her loneliness, Sinmo lured the meditating monkey into her cave, where their combined efforts produced six offspring. These were to become the ancestors of Tibet's six main tribes.

Tibet did not become a nation until the 7th century, when a chieftain, Songsten Gampo, consolidated his rule by subjugating the ancient kingdom of Zhangzhung in the west. Songsten became the first true king of the unified Tibetan Empire, making Rasa (later renamed Lhasa) the capital. Many of the great palaces—including the Potala Palace—were initially built by Songsten.

For two centuries, the Tibetan Empire prospered, establishing advantageous treaties with its neighbors. Trade and knowledge were exchanged. The teachings of Buddha were brought to Tibet and received with enthusiasm by the ruling class. Elements of the shamanistic Bön faith, which the Tibetans had previously embraced, were incorporated into Buddhism. Riven by political and religious differences, the empire broke up in the 9th century. The influence of Buddhism diminished, and Tibet subsided into isolation for the next four centuries. When the Mongols swept through Central Asia in the 13th century, Buddhism experienced a rebirth in Tibet, as it did all over East Asia, and it became the country's official religion.

Tibet emerged again as an autonomous nation-state in the 15th century, when the monk Tsongkhapa rose as both a spiritual and a political leader. He established a new Buddhist doctrine, which emphasized moral and philosophical rigors rather than mysticism, and, in 1409, he renovated and enlarged the Jokhang temple and brought the Great Prayer Festival to Lhasa. He also founded three great monasteries: Ganden, Drepung, and Sera. This building frenzy was supported by the widening acceptance of Tsongkhapa's doctrine, which later was embodied in the Gelugpa order, or Order of the Virtuous Ones.

Though political power lay in the hands of the kings of Tsang, a Tibetan tribe that ruled out of Zhigatse, the country's second-largest city, the spiritual power now rested with the head lama of the Gelugpa order. This leader was (and still is) chosen from among newborn infants on the death of the previous head lama in the belief that the latter's spirit had entered the newborn. Eventually the division between the spiritual lamas and the temporal kings of Tsang became untenable. The Mongols sided with the lamas, defeating the king of Tsang and paving the way for Dalai Lama V (1617–82) to become both spiritual and tem-

poral head of state. Lhasa was once again securely positioned as the nation's capital and a theocracy was established.

As the next Dalai Lama, Dalai Lama VI, was ineffectual, the declining influence of the Mongols gave the Manchu Qing dynasty (1644–1912) its opportunity. Chinese troops moved into Lhasa, and the Chinese emperor Kang Xi declared Tibet a protectorate. Chinese control, sometimes manifest, sometimes latent, lasted until 1912.

In 1904 the British sent an expeditionary force into Tibet to combat the Chinese influence and guard against possible Russian encroachment, which could threaten British interests in India. At the fall of the Manchu dynasty in 1912, Tibet, with British support, gladly expelled all Chinese and declared the country's total independence. The withdrawal of the British from India in 1947 made Tibet vulnerable once again, and three years later 30,000 veteran troops of the new People's Republic of China attacked a defending force of 4,000 ill-equipped soldiers. The result was slaughter on a gigantic scale, culminating in the death of 1.2 million Tibetans and the destruction of virtually every historic structure. Tibet became a vassal state of China.

In 1959, to quell a massive popular uprising in Lhasa, the Chinese ruthlessly shelled the Sera Monastery and both palaces of the Dalai Lamas—the Potala as well as Norbulingka Palace and the crowds surrounding it. When a crowd of 10,000 sought sanctuary in the Jokhang, the Chinese bombarded that, too, and after three days of gunfire in the capital, some 10,000 to 15,000 Tibetan corpses littered the streets. Three days before the massacre, Dalai Lama XIV (the present Dalai Lama) had sought asylum in India, where he later set up a government-in-exile in Dharamsala. China then formally incorporated Tibet into the People's Republic, began a process of dissolving the monasteries and stripping Tibetans of their culture, and in 1965 renamed the land Xizang Zizhiqu (Tibet Autonomous Region; TAR).

In 1966 the Chinese Cultural Revolution reached Tibet. Virtually every sacred and cultural monument was damaged if not destroyed outright. Monks and Tibetan loyalists were jailed and tortured or simply killed. Not until the death of Mao did the havoc abate, and by then some 6,250 monasteries and convents had been destroyed or severely damaged, thousands of Tibetans tortured and killed, and another 100,000 herded into labor camps. The rest of the world virtually turned a blind eye. Eventually, in 1980, Deng Xiaoping's era of tolerance began. Some religious institutions have been restored and religious practices are now permitted—notwithstanding frequent crackdowns. Massive numbers of Han Chinese, encouraged with economic incentives, are moving west. It has been said that the late Deng Xiaoping will be remembered for making the eastern coastal cities more economically viable, while President Jiang Zemin's legacy may well be swamping the upstart western regions with Han Chinese—particularly the two vast provinces of Tibet and Xinjiang. The hope is to erase cultural distinctions and avoid a breakup à la Soviet Union by manipulating the demographics and simply outnumbering the minorities. The result, for now, is that Tibetans are indeed outnumbered. In some areas, like Lhasa, more than half the population is Chinese, but there is little integration.

Demonstrations still take place, and the call for Tibetan freedom is still heard. In 1988, 1989, and 1993, a series of bloody uprisings inspired by the monks challenged Chinese rule. Martial law was temporarily instituted. Discontent with the Chinese "invasion" continues, and the possibility of more demonstrations is always present. In December 1999

there were mass arrests after a boy, Urgyen Trinley Dorje, fled his monastery in Tsurphu for India; Beijing officials recognized that many Tibetan followers believe the boy to be the 17th Karmapa, the head of the Kagyu school of Tibetan Buddhism. Stepping up security following the Karmapa's escape, China also dismissed at least 29 tour guides, all of whom were educated in India, where the Tibetan government-in-exile is led by the Dalai Lama. Then, in May 2000, China reportedly recruited 100 Chinese tour guides who would tow the government line.

Since July 2000 all foreigners must travel with a guide who is trained at the Government Tourist Travel Bureau's so-called guide department. Read: If not Chinese, then Chinese-educated. Thus many of the old, experienced guides are blacklisted and no longer allowed to work in their profession. And while the price for hiring guides has now increased, the guides' salaries has decreased. Still, there is no way around this policy. Some backpackers try to go at it alone, bemused by thoughts of a windswept landscape and thrilling adventures. Just remember, if you go this route, you put everyone you encounter—from the guesthouse owner who chances it and rents you a room, to the restaurateur who unwittingly serves you a meal, to the pilgrim who points you in the right direction—at risk for arrest. While you may have a fascinating vacation, they may end up "re-educated." To avoid such consequences, even veteran travelers who have visited several dozen times now are certain to hire guides. If you plan to stay in heavily touristed regions and do not really wish to be guided, you should be able to find an official guide who will meet you at the airport, take you to your hotel, ask not to discuss political matters with you, leave you alone for your stay, and eventually escort you to the airport again.

Certain "closed" regions cannot be visited at all; others may be visited with a special permit, which your guide will obtain for you. Officials may suspend travel without prior notice by denying entry permits or by claiming all flights to Lhasa are "fully booked." Suspensions are most likely at politically sensitive times, such as the Tibetan New Year, the anniversary of the 1959 uprising on March 10, the anniversary of the 1989 demonstration in June, and International Human Rights Day in December. And, sadly, the slightest hint of public protest can prompt the Chinese to make a few more Tibetans disappear and deny foreigners permission to enter the TAR. To the casual observer Tibet may not seem to be a police state, but it is.

On the Roof of the World, people live at altitudes that average between 3,500 and 5,000 m (11,500 and 16,400 ft). At the higher elevations vegetation is sparse. Wild grasses in the mountain wilderness are covered by a blanket of snow in winter. Narrow gorges make passes between sky-scraping peaks, where billowy clouds are literally 4,500 m (15,000 ft) closer to the touch of the earthbound dweller. A few valleys are open to cultivation, and turquoise freshwater lakes perfectly mirror the color of the sky through the rarified air. Western sensibilities may often romanticize Tibet while also underestimating how frustrating travel here can be; yet ignore—if you can—the Chinese intrusion, the ugly modern buildings, the pollution, and the open-pit mines around the towns, and you'll journey along the top of the world knocking at the doors of the deities' heavens.

Pleasures and Pastimes

Architecture

Monasteries, some small, some vast, usually follow a similar layout: Entrance is through a portico, whose murals depict the Wheel of Re-

birth and the Four Guardian Kings, corresponding to the four directions of the compass. Often you will find the two gatekeepers, Vajarapani
and Hayagriya, and more murals showing protector deities of the
town or the monastery. Through the portico is the central hall, whose
size corresponds to the number of columns. Rows of seats in the hall
are for lamas attending ritual ceremonies—elevated seats are for head
lamas. Clockwise around the hall you usually find a series of murals
telling the story of the Lord Buddha or of other historical figures. Facing the entrance behind the elevated seats are rows of sacred images
and scriptures. In major temples there is usually an inner sanctum, where
the most revered images are kept. Also within the monastery complex
are *klangtsens* (residential units) with their own chapels and assembly
halls. Larger monasteries contain *tratsangs* (colleges), where Buddhist
precepts are studied.

The most common religious structure in Tibet is the Buddhist stupa,
called a *chorten,* which is built both as an act of merit and as a reli-
quary for the ashes of a religious leader. Every aspect of the chorten
holds spiritual significance. It consists of a square base, a dome, an ob-
long slab, a tiered triangular spire, and a small ornament, which represent, respectively, fire, earth, water, air, and space. The Potala Palace
has the most celebrated ones, containing the ashes of past Dalai Lamas.

On the domestic front, private houses have flat roofs and inward-lean-
ing walls built of brick. More picturesque are the yak-hair tents of the
nomadic shepherds, which are large enough to house a family. A hole
in the center of the tent acts as a chimney, but it doesn't provide
enough ventilation to keep the rank smell of yak butter from perme-
ating the tent.

Art
Tibet is an extraordinary repository of 13 centuries' worth of religious
art, especially illuminations, murals, and *thangkas* (painted cloth
scrolls; also known as *tankas*). Sculptures of deities and historic figures are mostly rendered in metal, clay, or stucco, though a few are
made of wood or stone. Despite destruction by the Chinese and the
persecution of artists since 1950, much of Tibet's art treasure remains.
In the new era of tolerance, Tibetans are relearning their art and actively restoring the masterpieces of their past.

Buddhism and all of its art forms arrived in Tibet from India at a time
when Buddhism was on the wane there, and soon Nepalese art began
to influence the Tibetan style. Chinese influence appeared in the 16th
century and was limited principally to the development of the landscape background in portraiture.

Images in Tibetan art are not meant to serve as lifelike representations
but as expressions of the Buddha mind, assisting the viewer in reaching higher levels of consciousness. The art nurtures meditation—most
images are intended to guide the meditator in communicating with a
particular deity, with the goal of assimilating the deity's attributes and
taking the next step to nothingness/completeness. Deities and historic
figures have been sculpted or painted from the 7th century onward;
alone the 1,000 rooms of the Potala house more than 200,000 images.

Dining
Tibetan cooking is simple: the staple is *tsampa* (roasted barley flour),
washed down with bowls of *soja* (butter tea). You are likely to eat tsampa
more than once only if panic hunger strikes. A more enjoyable dish is
momo, a steamed or fried dumpling filled with meat or vegetables, often
served with *then-thuk* (noodles). Other dishes include *lasha* (lamb

with radish), *gyuma* (black pudding), *thu* (cheesecake), and *dresi* (sweet rice). If you are invited to a Tibetan banquet, you'll have these and more—18 dishes in all.

With the explosion of tourism in Tibet, the quality and variety of food available in the region has improved greatly. In Lhasa, Tibetan and Chinese fare is supplemented by a competitive market of Western restaurants. Outside the capital, the variety of food leaves something to be desired, but in areas commonly visited by tourists you should be able to find a satisfying meal. You can even order a picnic from your Lhasa hotel before going on trips into the countryside.

Beer and soft drinks are available nearly everywhere. The local drink is *chang* (a fortified barley ale). Local water is not potable; it must be boiled or treated with iodine. In Lhasa and in other towns, however, bottled water is plentiful.

CATEGORY	COST*
$$$$	over $27
$$$	$21–$27
$$	$9–$21
$	under $9

Prices are per person for a three-course meal, excluding drinks, taxes, and tip.

Festivals

The most colorful times to visit Lhasa are during festivals, when pilgrims come into town and banners fly. Festivals occur according to the Tibetan lunar calendar, so the dates that follow are approximate. **Losar,** the Tibetan New Year Festival (February), is Tibet's most exciting celebration, with performances of Tibetan drama. During **Mönum** (the Great Prayer Festival; February) the image of Maitreya is paraded from the Jokhang temple around the Barkhor, which surrounds it. At the **Lantern Festival** (the Day of Offerings; February) huge sculptures made of yak butter are placed on the Barkhor pilgrimage route. **Buddha's Enlightenment Day** (May/June) draws many pilgrims, and there are outdoor opera performances. **Drepung Zöton** (Yogurt Festival; August) takes place at the monastery, with the hanging of a monumental thangka and dances by the monks. **Zöton** (August—two days after Drepung Zöton) is the popular Yogurt Festival; it starts at the Drepung Monastery and moves to Norbulingka, where operas and dances are held. **Labab Düchen** (October/November) commemorates the deities' coming to earth and attracts many pilgrims. **Paldren Lhamo** (November) honors the protective deity of Jokhang, whose image is paraded around the Barkhor.

Lodging

With Tibet's continued popularity as a tourist destination, the quality and variety of accommodations available have slowly improved. Although there may be no high-end hotels in Tibet, Lhasa does have several large hotels that are more than adequately comfortable. Most of Lhasa's hotels, large or small, offer rooms of varying quality and price. Ask and you may be shown rooms ranging from a depressing 20-person dormitory to a deluxe suite with private bath, balcony, and minibar. Outside Lhasa, in the major towns, there are bland Chinese hotels, about half of which have hot running water. You may prefer a Tibetan guest house, many of which are quite clean. The hospitality in these guest houses is warm and welcoming, but be forewarned that the shared bathing facilities are primitive.

CATEGORY	COST*
$$$$	over $102
$$$	$78–$102
$$	$54–$78
$	under $54

*Prices are for a standard double room with bath at peak season, excluding tax and service charges.

Shopping

The bazaars are fun. The Tibetans love to bargain, and they respect you for doing it, too. The best buys are traditional jewelry, metalwork, carpets, woodwork, and textiles. Appliquéd thangkas make superb wall hangings to take home. Government regulations require a permit to export antiques.

Trekking

Not all of Tibet is accessible by road, which makes trekking all the more thrilling. The best months for clambering over the Roof of the World are April through June and September through November, though the summer rainy season often is not that wet. Self-sufficiency is important, as resources are limited outside Lhasa. On the other hand, the high altitude respects those who pack light. You can rent or purchase decent trekking equipment in Lhasa, but don't expect the selection, quality, or prices you find in Kathmandu. You will most likely have to go with a guide; fortunately, trekking agencies have become more customer-friendly in the past few years and guides more experienced.

Exploring Tibet

Lhasa lies in central Tibet in the fertile Kyi-chu Valley, which extends north to its glacial origins in the Nyenchen Tanglha range. This region is the most heavily populated within the Tibetan Autonomous Region (TAR). South of Lhasa and central Tibet are the Lower Brahmaputra valleys, which pass into Assam (India) and Bhutan. The southern county of Dingri, known as the highland region, is bordered on the south by the high Himalayan range that includes Mt. Everest and the popular trekking routes around the Everest base camp. Western Tibet consists of the Upper Brahmaputra Valley, whose main city is Zhigatse. Far western Tibet, one of the least populated areas, has only recently been opened to foreigners and includes Tibet's holiest mountain, Kailash. Eastern Tibet, some 1,200 km (750 mi) east of Lhasa, is characterized by rugged mountains often topped with glaciers and broken by deep gorges. Less than half of this region is in the TAR. Outsiders rarely visit northern Tibet, or Jangtang, a vast lake-land wilderness with elevations ranging from 4,500 to 5,000 m (14,760 to 16,400 ft).

Great Itineraries

Numbers in the text correspond to numbers in the margin and on the Tibet and Lhasa maps.

IF YOU HAVE 4 DAYS
Spend your time in Lhasa following the Good Route described.

IF YOU HAVE 10 DAYS
Enter Tibet by land from Kathmandu, Nepal, and take two or three days to reach Lhasa. Give yourself three or four days to visit the sights in the capital city. During this time arrange to go on a tour: climbing into the Himalayas on the Nepalese border; visiting off-the-beaten-path monasteries such as Ganden, Samye, Tsurphu, or Sakya; hiking to lakes such as Nam-Tso or Yamdrok-Tso; or discovering the attractions of the gorges.

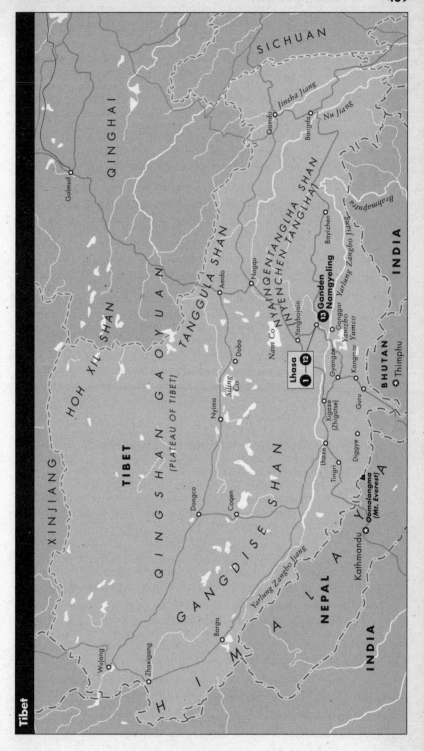

When to Tour Tibet

Winter temperatures can sink to −23°C (−10°F); in summer daytime highs reach 30°C (80°F). The best touring conditions occur from mid-April through June, but with pleasant weather come hordes of tourists. Summer sees a bit of rain, and often roads will be closed to popular tourist destinations, including the Everest base camp. If you can't make it in the spring, September through mid-November is another good option. Winter is frightfully cold, but the climate is dry and the skies perpetually blue. Cold weather also means fewer tourists, and travel is less restrictive as police at checkpoints are more concerned with keeping warm than turning back visitors.

LHASA

Lhasa, with a population of a little more than 160,000, is remarkably small considering its long history. Its major sights, both historical and architectural, fall into three eras: First, the 7th- to 9th-century building boom, which produced the first Potala Palace on Mt. Marpori (637) and the Buddhist-influenced Jokhang temple (641). Second, the 15th century, when Tsongkhapa renovated and enlarged the Jokhang temple (1409) and founded the three great monasteries: Ganden, Drepung, and Sera (1419). Third, when Lhasa again became the capital, and Dalai Lama V (1617–82) rebuilt (and expanded) the Potala on the foundations of the original. Over the next three centuries the lamas constructed the great Gelugpa monasteries and palaces, of which the Norbulingka Palace is the most notable.

Despite the Chinese invasion, the city still contains a generous amount of Tibetan architecture, art, and culture. The area known as Barkhor, which encompasses the Jokhang temple, remains a Tibetan enclave.

A Good Route

The high altitude of Lhasa will tax your stamina on your first day, so take it easy. Go down to the **Barkhor** ① for lunch and then spend the afternoon in the **Jokhang** ② temple. If there is time, you can visit the temple of **Meru Nyingba** ③ (adjoining the east wall of the Jokhang) and the **Ani Tshamkung** ④ nunnery, just south of the Jokhang. Nearby is the **Gyel Lakhang** ⑤, Lhasa's mosque. Or follow smells and sounds as you wander the streets of Barkhor. North of Dekyi Shar Lam is the 15th-century **Ramoche** ⑥ temple.

The monumental **Potala** ⑦ Palace should be your first stop on the second day. It will take the full morning to cover both the White and Red palaces. Spend the afternoon exploring the religious cave paintings and carvings on Chakpo-Ri, being sure to visit **Chogyel Zimuki** ⑧.

On the third day go out to the **Drepung** ⑨. Give yourself at least an hour and a half to inspect the monastery, then make the Drepung Linghor, the 90-minute pilgrimage walk around the monastery. The next stop is the **Nechung** ⑩ monastery, just southeast of Drepung. Then return to old Lhasa and shop around the Barkhor.

For the fourth day go out to **Sera Thekchenling** ⑪, northeast of Lhasa. Return to spend an afternoon at the **Norbulingka** ⑫ complex. If you have more than four days in Tibet, you can head out of town, possibly to visit the enormous **Ganden** ⑬ monastery, 40 km (25 mi) from Lhasa, or simply to get the feel of rural Tibet.

Sights to See

❹ **Ani Tshamkung.** The main temple at this nunnery was built in the early 14th century; a second story was added in the early 20th century. Before the Chinese invasion of Tibet, the nuns were responsible for light-

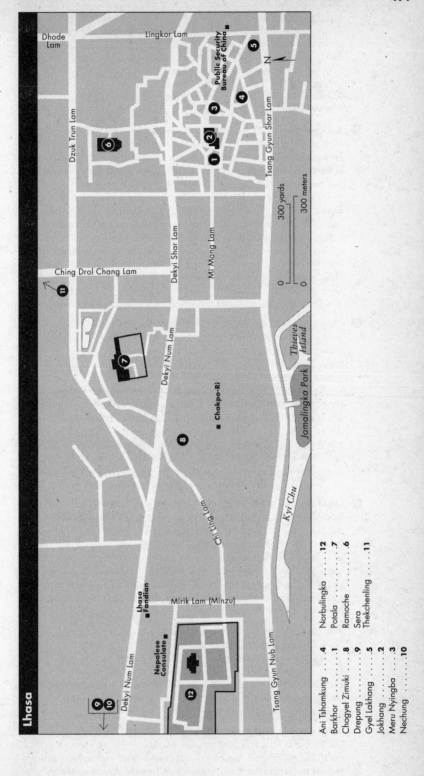

Lhasa

Dhode Lam

Lingkor Lam

Public Security Bureau of China

Dzuk Trun Lam

Ching Drol Chang Lam

Dekyi Shar Lam

Mi Mang Lam

Tsang Gyun Shar Lam

300 yards
300 meters
0
0

Dekyi Num Lam

Thieves Island

Jamalingka Park

Chakpo-Ri

Kyi Chu

Chi Ling Lam

Lhasa Fandian

Mirik Lam (Minzu)

Nepalese Consulate

Dekyi Num Lam

Tsang Gyun Nub Lam

ing the butter lamps in the Jokhang. Considerable damage occurred during the Cultural Revolution, but the nunnery was restored between 1982 and 1984 and now houses more than 80 nuns in this two-story residence. The chief pilgrimage site is the Tsamkung (meditation hollow) where Songsten Gampo concentrated his spiritual focus on preventing the flood of the Kyi-chu River. ⊠ *Waling Lam, southeast of Jokhang, look for a front entrance painted yellow.* ☒ *Y5 (additional Y20 for photos).* ☉ *Daily 8–6.*

❼ **Barkhor.** This plaza around the Jokhang temple, the spiritual and commercial hub of old Lhasa, is now the only part of the city that has not been overrun by the migrating Chinese. Properly speaking, the Barkhor is only the intermediary circumambulation surrounding the Jokhang, but the name is commonly used to refer to the heart of Lhasa. Join the pilgrims making the Barkhor circuit, and you will step back into the Forbidden City, passing monks sitting before their alms bowls and chanting mantras. The circuit is crammed with stalls where vendors sell trinkets, carpets, hats, prayer shawls, and just about anything else. The streets running north off the Barkhor walkway to Dekyi Shar Lam are shopping streets. Along the north wall of the Jokhang is the **Nangtseshak,** a two-story former prison that had more than its share of notoriety in the past. South of the Barkhor plaza are several notable buildings, including former residences of advisers to Dalai Lama XIV.

❽ **Chogyel Zimuki.** In caves scattered over Chakpo-Ri, a hill to the southwest of the Potala, are as many as 5,000 religious rock carvings and paintings. The oldest are thought to date from the 7th century. The most interesting are at **Chogyel Zimuki,** sometimes called Dragla Lugug, a grotto-style temple in which the inner sanctum is a cave. Beyond the temple's gate is a monastic building from which you can mount the steps of the two-story grotto chapel. On the second floor you'll find the entrance to the spherical cave, which has a central rock column. Three of the cave's walls and the column bear 71 sculptures carved into the granite, probably by Nepalese artists in the 7th to 9th centuries. ⊠ *Follow Mirik Lam south from Lhasa Fandian to dirt road along base of Chakpo-Ri facing Marpo Ri, hill on which Potala stands, to Chogyel Zimuki.* ☒ *Free.* ☉ *Daily sunrise–sunset.*

❾ **Drepung.** The largest of the Gelugpa monasteries was the residence for lesser lamas. Founded in 1416, it was enlarged in the 16th century by the Dalai Lama II. By the era of the Dalai Lama V (1617–82) it had become the largest monastic institution in the world, with 10,000 residents. During the Cultural Revolution it suffered only minimally because the army used the building as its headquarters and therefore didn't ransack it as much as other temples. The monastery was reopened in 1980 and the number of monks varies, as they are often sent away to be reeducated. About 570 monks were living here at press time.

The monastery's most important building is the Tshomchen, whose vast assembly hall, the **Dukhang,** is noteworthy for its 183 columns, atriumlike ceiling, and ceremonial banners. Chapels can be found on all three floors as well as the roof. In the two-story **Düsum Sangye Lhakhang** (Buddhas of Three Ages Chapel), at the rear of the Dukhang on the ground floor, the Buddhas of past, present, and future are each guarded by two bodhisattvas.

To set out on a pilgrimage around the monastery, the **Drepung Linghor,** leave from the corner of the parking lot. The walk takes about 90 minutes. The path winds west of the perimeter wall and uphill in the direction of Gephel Ritrö and then descends in the direction of Nechung. You can also walk 3½ hours up to the **retreat of Gephel Ritrö.** The re-

treat (now restored) was founded in the 14th century at the place where monks tended yak herds. The summit, **Gephel Ütse,** is another 2½ hours of steep climbing. ⊠ *Off Dekyi Num Lam, 7 km (4 mi) west of Lhasa center; take bus that passes Lhasa Fandian, get off at base of Gephel Ri, and walk 1 km (½ mi) north; or hire car or minibus taxi from town.* ☎ *Y25.* ⏱ *Daily 9:30–5; some chapels close noon–2.*

⑤ Gyel Lakhang. In perhaps the most Buddhist of cities, Gyel Lhakhang is a bit of an anomaly. It is Lhasa's largest mosque, for the city's approximately 2,000 Muslims. It was built in 1716 for immigrants who had arrived in the 17th century from Kashmir and Ladakh. ⊠ *Linghor Lho Lam, near East Linghor Lam.* ⏱ *Daily 8–5, except during prayers Fri.* AM.

★ ② Jokhang. Believed to be the land's first significant Buddhist-inspired temple, Jokhang is the most sacred building in all of Tibet. Day and night, Tibetans pay homage here. During the pilgrimage season long lines of devotees shuffle toward the inner sanctum, where they touch their foreheads on the sacred image of Jowo Sakyamuni (Buddha).

Built probably in 647, during Songtsen Gampo's reign, Jokhang stands in the heart of the old town. The site was selected as the geomantic center of Tibet by Queen Wengcheng, a princess from China brought to Songtsen Gampo as his second wife. Queen Wengcheng also divined that before the completion of the temple, the demon ogress needed to be pacified. This required the construction of 12 outlying temples, built on the "thighs," "knees," and so on, of the "supine ogress" to pin her down; the design entails three successive rings of four temples around the location of Jokhang.

Songtsen's first wife, Princess Bhrikuti from Nepal, financed the building of Jokhang. In her honor and in recognition of Tibet's strong reliance on Nepal, Jokhang's main gate was designed to face west, toward Nepal. Among the few bits of its 7th-century construction remaining are the door frames of the four inner chapels, dedicated to Mahakarunika, Amitabha, Sakyamuni, and Maitreya.

Over the centuries renovations have enlarged the Jokhang to keep it the premier temple of Tibet. Its status was threatened in the 1950s, when the Chinese Army shelled it and the Red Guards of the Cultural Revolution ransacked it. During this period of sacrilege, parts of it were used as a guest house and as a pigsty. About a third of the damage has since been repaired.

The Inner Jokhang has three stories and forms a square enclosing the inner hall, Kyilkhor Thil. Encircling the Inner Jokhang is the Inner Circumambulation, known as the Nangkhor. The Outer Jokhang, sometimes referred to as the western extension and constructed in 1409, contains the lesser chapels, storerooms, kitchens, and residences. The whole complex is encircled by the Barkhor Walkway and the old city of Lhasa.

Start your visit in the Barkhor. Look for the two willows flanking the stump of a willow tree planted by Queen Wengcheng. A wall now gives the stump some protection. Enter the temple through the portico supported by six fluted columns. Centuries of pilgrims prostrating themselves in the threshold courtyard have worn the flagstones smooth. Within the main courtyard is the assembly hall that Tsongkhapa had constructed for the Great Prayer Festival in 1409—an event that greatly enhanced Lhasa's position as the spiritual capital of Tibet. Along the outer walls are 19th-century murals, and in the inner hall are murals dating from 1648. On the north side is one of the residences of the Dalai Lamas.

Before entering the Inner Jokhang, you should walk the Nangkhor (Inner Circumambulation) in a clockwise direction. It's lined with prayer wheels and murals on the east side, which is also known for its series of Buddhist images. On the north side are several chapels of minor consequence. Outside the wall on the south side is the debating courtyard, renovated in 1986, which contains the platform where thrones for Tsongkhapa and other dignitaries were set up for the Great Prayer Festival. Enter by the **Zhung-go** (Main Gate), which has finely carved door frames from the early Tibetan period (7th–9th centuries). Left of the door is a painting of the future Buddha, on the right a painting of the past Buddha. A footprint of Dalai Lama XIII (1876–1933) is enshrined in a small niche. Continue on to the large Entrance Hall, whose inner chapels have murals depicting the wrathful deities responsible for protecting the temple and the city. Straight ahead is the inner sanctum, the three-story **Kyilkhor Thil**, some of whose many columns probably date from the 7th century, particularly those with short bases and round shafts.

The chapels on the ground floor of the Kyilkhor Thil are the most rewarding. In the west wing be sure to see the **Je Rinpoche Dakpa Namgye Lhakhang**, a chapel whose central image is Tsongkhapa flanked by his eight pure retainers. In the north wing, in the chapel **Mahakarunika Lhakhang**, is a reproduction of the image of the deity Mahakarunika. The most revered chapel of the inner hall is **Jowo Sakyamuni Lhakhang**, in the middle of the east wing, opposite the entrance. Here is the 5-ft statue of Jowo Rinpoche, representing the Buddha at age 12. It was brought to Tibet by Queen Wengcheng and somehow has survived, despite a history of being plastered over, buried in sand, and forced to endure the Cultural Revolution. ✉ *Barkhor.* 🎫 *Y25.* ☉ *Daily 9:30–12:30 and 3–6.*

❸ Meru Nyingba. The original version of this temple, built soon after the Jokhang, is where the Tibetan alphabet was finalized by the scholar Tonmi Sambhota. Within this 20th-century reconstruction are murals portraying many of the forms taken by Pehar, the chief guardian of the Gelugpa Buddhist sect. ✉ *Eastern wall of Jokhang off northern arc of Barkhor.* ☉ *Daily sunrise–sunset.*

❿ Nechung. This monastery is dedicated to the protector deity Pehar. From its construction in the 12th century, it has been home to important oracles whose political advice has been sought regularly. Today the current oracle resides in Dharamsala as an adviser to the Dalai Lama and his government-in-exile. Except for the gilded roofs and their embellishments, Nechung buildings largely survived the Cultural Revolution. The murals on the portico depict Pehar and his retinue. In the assembly hall murals show the *Deities of the Eight Transmitted Precepts,* and in the Jordungkhang chapel on the western side, you'll find more images of Pehar. There are two other chapels on the ground floor, two on the second floor, and a single chapel on the third floor. You can also visit the residence of the Nechung Oracle, behind the main building. ✉ *Dekyi Num Lam, 8 km (5 mi) west of Lhasa center, 1 km (½) mi southeast of Drepung Monastery.* 🎫 *Y20.* ☉ *Daily 9–noon and 2–4:30.*

⓬ Norbulingka. Dalai Lama VII (1708–1757), a frail man, chose to build a palace on this site because of its medicinal spring. In 1755, not content just to have a summer home for himself, he added the **Kelzang Podrang** to the southeast, a three-story palace whose ground floor is dominated by his throne, and had his whole government moved there from the Potala. The next Dalai Lama expanded the property, adding a debating courtyard, **Tsokyil Podrang** palace, a pavilion, and a library and retreat. The gardens were landscaped by Dalai Lama XIII (1876–

1933), who also oversaw the construction of a new complex, **Chensel Lingka Podrang,** to the northwest, containing three small palaces. The last addition, built by Dalai Lama XIV in 1954–56, was **Takten Migyur Podrang,** in the north, an ornate two-story building notable for Buddha images on the ground floor and a European-style reception room on the floor above. It turned out to be the place from which, disguised as a soldier, he fled to India on March 17, 1959, three days before the Chinese massacred thousands of Tibetans and fired artillery shells into every Norbulingka building. Only after searching through the corpses did they realize the Dalai Lama had escaped.

The work done to repair the damage in the aftermath of the March 1959 uprising is not of high caliber. The palace's 40 acres are divided into three sectors: the opera grounds (where Tibetan operatic performances are held during the Yogurt Festival), government buildings, and the palaces. The four complexes of palaces are visited by pilgrims in the following sequence: Kelzang Podrang, to the southeast; Takten Migyur Podrang, to the north; Tsokyil Podrang, in the center; and Chensel Lingka Podrang, to the northwest. ⊠ *Mirk Lam.* ☜ *Y25.* ☽ *Mon.– Wed. and Fri.–Sun. 9–12:30 and 3:30–5:30.*

★ ❼ **Potala.** Virtually nothing remains of the original 11-story Potala Palace built in 637 by King Songtsen. What you see today is a 17th-century replacement. The Dalai Lama V (1617–1682), anxious to reestablish the importance of Lhasa as the Tibetan capital, employed 7,000 workers and 1,500 artisans to resurrect the Potala Palace on the 7th-century foundation, using the original palace as its prototype. After eight years the White Palace was completed, in 1653. The Red Palace, the central upper part, was not completed until 1694, 12 years after the Dalai Lama's death, which was kept secret by the regent in order to prevent interruption of the construction. The Potala has been enlarged since then, mostly in the 18th century, and continually renovated, such as when the structural walls were strengthened in 1991. Once the headquarters of Tibet's theocracy, the vast Potala is now a museum.

The Potala was the world's tallest building before the advent of modern skyscrapers. Towering above the city from the slopes of Mt. Marpori, the structure is 117 m (387 ft) high; its 1,000 rooms house some 200,000 images. The outer section, the White Palace, was the seat of government and the winter residence of the Dalai Lama until 1951. In it you can pass through the Dalai Lama's spartan quarters. On either side of the palace are the former offices of the government. The Red Palace, looming above the White Palace, is the spiritual part of the Potala. Murals chronicle Buddhist folklore and ancient Tibetan life. Within the four stories that make up the functional part of the Red Palace are dozens of small chapels, where often a human skull and thigh bone are the only decoration. Interspersed among the chapels are eight golden chorten containing the remains of Dalai Lamas V and VII–XIII.

The eastern gatehouse is the main entrance used by pilgrims, who climb up from Zhol Square below. Other visitors usually reach the Potala at the rear drive-in entrance on the north side so as to avoid the climb. If you are entering from the north, you miss the ancillary buildings, including two printing presses dating from the 17th century.

Between the White and Red palaces is a yellow building that houses the Thangka Rooms, where huge thangkas (painted cloth scrolls) are kept. Once used in the Yogurt Festival, they are no longer displayed, although one was unfurled in 1994. Underneath the 13-story, 1,000-room fortress are the dungeons. Justice could be harsh—torture and jail time were the punishments for refusing to pay taxes, displaying anger,

or insulting a monk. The worst place to be sent was the Cave of Scorpions, where prisoners were the targets of stinging tails. ⊠ *Zhol.* 🖾 *Y40.* ☉ *Mon., Wed., and Fri. 8:30–noon; Tues., Thurs., and weekends 9:30–noon.*

⑥ Ramoche. This temple was founded by Queen Wengcheng at the same time as the Jokhang. Its present three-story structure dates from the 15th century. Despite restorations in the 1980s, it lost much of its former glory after the Chinese used it to house the Communist Labor Training Committee during the Cultural Revolution.

Ramoche was intended to house the most revered statue of Jowo Rinpoche. A threat of a Chinese invasion in the 7th century induced Queen Wengcheng to hide the statue in the Jokhang. Some 50 years later it was rediscovered and placed within the Jokhang's main chapel. As a substitute, Jokhang reciprocated with a Nepalese statue of Jowo Mikyo Dorje, which represented Buddha as an eight-year-old. It was decapitated during the Cultural Revolution and its torso "lost" in Beijing, but both head and body were later found, put back together again, and placed in a small chapel at the back of Ramoche's Tsangkhang (Inner Sanctum). ⊠ *Ramoche Lam, off north side of Dekyi Shar Lam, north of Tromzikhang Market.* 🖾 *Y20.* ☉ *Daily 8:30–5:30.*

⑪ Sera Thekchenling. This important Gelug monastery, founded in 1419 on 24 acres, contains numerous chapels, with splendid murals and icons. Originally it was a hermitage for Tsongkhapa and his top students. Within a couple hundred years, the community numbered between 5,000 and 6,000 monks. The complex comprises the *tsokchen* (great assembly hall), three *tratsangs* (colleges), and 30 *klangstens* (residential units).

On the clockwise pilgrimage route, start at the two buildings that will take most of your visit. **Sera Me Tratsang** (founded in 1419), which promotes elementary studies, has a *dukhang* (assembly hall) rebuilt in 1761 with murals depicting Buddha's life. Among the five chapels along the dukhang's north wall, the Ta-og Lhakhang is hard to forget, as its exterior is adorned with skeletons and skulls. The complex's oldest surviving structure, **Ngagpa Tratsang** (1419), is a three-story college for tantric studies whose dukhang is supported by 42 short and four tall columns. Here you find statues of famous lamas and murals depicting paradise.

Continue to the four-story-high **Sera Je Tratsang,** where you can take time out in the shaded courtyard, once the site for philosophical debates; today pilgrims come here to offer scarves and talismans. Other sites on the pilgrimage route are **Hamdong Khangtsang** (a principal residential unit), the **Tsokchen** (with 89 tall columns and 36 short columns), and Tsongkhapa's **hermitage** on Mt. Phurbuchok, which has a two-story chapel. ⊠ *5 km (3 mi) north of Lhasa at base of Mt. Phurbuchok.* 🖾 *Y30.* ☉ *Daily 9:30–4.*

Dining and Lodging

In an attempt to satisfy the tourist appetite, Lhasa has become inundated with Western-style cafés and restaurants. The Barkhor area is filled with reasonably priced restaurants offering Western and Asian menus. In western Lhasa the options are more limited; there your best bet may be your hotel. Many of the larger hotels offer a full meal plan, which can save you money but restricts your sampling of local fare.

$$$$ ✕ Lhasa Fandian. With five restaurants, you are sure to find a palatable meal here. At the Himalayan Restaurant you can try Tibetan spe-

cialties, including momos and *thukpa* (soup), as well as Nepalese dishes. Chinese cuisine is served at the Sichuan restaurant, and Western meals are on the menu in the, yes, Hard Yak Café. ✉ *Lhasa Fandian, 1 Minzu Lam,* ☎ *0891/683–2221. AE, DC, MC, V.*

$$ ✕ **Crazy Yak.** This restaurant offers well-prepared Tibetan, Nepalese, Chinese, and Western food that is reasonably priced. The Tibetan decor is inviting and there are traditional operatic and folk dance performances nightly at 7:30. ✉ *107 Dekyi Shar Lam, near Yak Hotel,* ☎ *0891/633–1999,* FAX *0891/632–9316. No credit cards.*

$$ ✕ **Kirey Mad Yak Restaurant.** The Mad Yak entices patrons with rooftop dining inside a Tibetan tent (more like a canopy than a Western enclosed tent) and folk dance performances downstairs in the main dining room. Order from an extensive menu or better yet, get together a group and try the banquet meal. As dancers entertain, your taste buds will be treated to such traditional items such as sautéed yak lung, cheese momos (dumplings), fried snow peas, and cold yak tongue. The dishes are much tastier than they sound. ✉ *105 Dekyi Shar Lam,* ☎ *0891/634–1071. Call ahead to arrange banquet meal. No credit cards.*

$$ ✕ **Snowlands Restaurant.** This cozy, colorful café with carpeted floors, small tables, and cramped booths, is a good choice for those looking to unwind after a long day of sightseeing. The kitchen turns out consistently tasty food and delicious baked goods, including cinnamon rolls, apple pie, and croissants. Combining the chicken sizzler and an order of garlic naan bread makes for a hearty meal. ✉ *4 Mentsikhang Lam,* ☎ *0891/632–3687. No credit cards.*

$$ ✕ **Yeti Café.** Curious about how Tibetan food is prepared? Then stop off at the Yeti, where you will find an English menu that indicates whether a dish is fried, steamed, braised, or boiled. The front dining area is crammed with couches covered by Tibetan rugs, and the rear of the restaurant offers plenty of private rooms for more intimate dining. The Shoguonomo, an appetizer of mashed potatoes filled with meat and deep fried, is recommended for those not adverse to oil and calories. ✉ *206-10 Dekyi Nub Lam, north of Lhasa Fandian,* ☎ *0891/633–0856. No credit cards.*

$ ✕ **Barkhor Café.** The Barkhor's covered outdoor patio is an ideal place to have a bite to eat while enjoying the views of the adjacent square and surrounding mountains. Chinese, Tibetan, and all of the usual backpacker favorites are available from their extensive menu. The large indoor seating area also houses several computers providing Internet access at Y10 per hour. The veggie burger is highly recommended. ✉ *Southwest corner of Barkhor Square, up a spiral staircase.* ☎ *0891/632–6892. No credit cards.*

$ ✕ **Makye Ame.** This artsy, hippie haven on the southeast corner of the Barkhor circuit is a perfect place for people-watching: you'll overlook the Barkhor kora from both the roof and the second-story corner. While the new management has done away with the infamous brownies, you can still chomp on good food ranging from chow mein to pizza to *thentuk* (beef stew). Try not to miss the spinach soup or the fresh apple juice, which tastes like a thinner version of apple sauce, a divine cool treat. Have a look at the gallery-quality black-and-white photos on the walls as you sway to the requisite Bob Marley tunes. Or surf the Internet for Y10 an hour. ✉ *Second floor, southeast corner of Barkhor Circuit. Look for the building with the big mural of Makye Ame,* ☎ *0891/632–4455. No credit cards.*

$$$$ 🏨 **Tibet Hotel.** Tour guides love to book big groups into this hotel. Note that if you're traveling in a small group, you are likely to be ignored by the management. The situation can be especially trying if you're hungry and the hotel restaurants are closed (they sometimes close when they should be open), since you'll be quite a ways from downtown.

Nevertheless, the rooms are bright, well-heated, and clean, thanks to dozens of busy-bee minions who keep them spick-and-span. If your tour plan includes breakfast in the hotel, be forewarned: it will likely be cold. For some reason, they don't bother to turn up the burners to heat the food. A small disco is the evening entertainment, although it caters more to the outside Chinese community than guests. ⊠ *221 Dekyi Nub Lam, Lhasa 850001,* ☎ *0891/683–3737,* FAX *0891/683–6887. 260 rooms. 4 restaurants, beauty salon, dance club, laundry service, business services, travel services. DC, MC, V.*

$$$–$$$$ ⊞ **Lhasa Fandian.** The Lhasa Fandian (formerly the Holiday Inn) is among the premier hotels in Lhasa, albeit not in Barkhor Square, the heart of the action. Bright, modern rooms come equipped with cable TV, IDD phone, comfortable sitting chairs, minibar, and even piped-in oxygen (to ease the stress of the altitude) in all but the most economical of rooms. The Hilsa health and recreation center has an indoor swimming pool and bowling alley. For evening entertainment, you can check out the karaoke bar. The hotel lacks Tibetan charm, but it does have a well-trained staff. ⊠ *1 Minzu Lam, Lhasa 850001,* ☎ *0891/683–2221,* FAX *0891/683–5796. 468 rooms, 12 suites. 5 restaurants, bar, minibars, room service, pool, beauty salon, laundry service, meeting room, business services. AE, DC, MC, V.*

$$ ⊞ **Grand Hotel.** A former government guest house that was converted into a hotel in 1998, the Grand is a large complex offering a wide variety of accommodations. The higher-priced rooms are nicely decorated with floral wallpaper, brightly colored bedspreads, and even Italian-made whirlpool bathtubs. On the other end of the spectrum, the economy rooms are a bit dark and dingy. Popular with Asian tourists, the Grand is attempting to capture a portion of the ever-expanding Western market. ⊠ *196 Beijing Zhonglu, Lhasa 850001,* ☎ *0891/682–4100,* FAX *0891/683–2195. 380 rooms, 20 suites. 6 restaurants, beauty salon, laundry service, business services, travel services. No credit cards.*

$$ ⊞ **Himalaya Hotel.** This nine-story building provides accommodation ranging from luxury suites to budget triples. Sliding glass doors open onto a lavishly appointed entrance defined by four grand columns, a marble floor, and a central chandelier. The rooms have fluffy carpet, big bathtubs, and TVs, albeit no cable. Ask for a room with a view of the Potala. The hotel stands near the Kyi River, a 10-minute walk from the Barkhor. ⊠ *6 Linghor Donglu, Lhasa 850001,* ☎ *0891/632–3888,* FAX *0891/633–2675. 116 rooms, 16 suites. 3 restaurants, massage, sauna, laundry service, meeting room, business services, travel services. AE, MC, V.*

$$ ⊞ **Kechu Hotel.** A small, charming hotel in the heart of the Tibetan Quarter, the Kechu veers away from the modern sterility of the other hotels in its class. Hallways with ornate ceilings and old black-and-white Tibetan photographs lead to rooms with traditional door frames, hardwood floors, dark-wood furniture, and thangkas on the walls. On the main floor is a small restaurant that offers buffet meals of Indian, Chinese, Western, and Tibetan cuisine. The lobby has a small sitting area, book exchange, and a well-stocked art shop near the front entrance. ⊠ *148 Dekyi Shar Lam, Lhasa 850001,* ☎ *0891/633–8824,* FAX *0891/632–0234. 17 rooms, 4 suites. Restaurant. No credit cards.*

$$ ⊞ **Shangbala Hotel.** This modern Barkhor Square hotel has clean, warm rooms with big bathtubs and steaming hot water. The soft thick carpet is luxurious to walk on and the beds are comfortable. Just like at the Fandian, the staff is professionally trained; the difference is that you'll pay half the price for a room at the Shangbala. If you are suffering slightly from the high altitude, try the Gao-Yuan-An Tibetan medicine tea offered in the minibar. It tastes like licorice and appears to work. The complimentary breakfast buffet includes real coffee—a rarity in Tibet. *No.*

1, Dan Jie Lin Road, Lhasa 850000, ☎ *0891/632–3888,* FAX *0891/632–3577. 70 rooms. Restaurant, minibars, room service, hair salon, bar, laundry service, business services. AE, DC, MC, V.*

$ ⌂ **Banak Shol.** A popular Tibetan Quarter choice with the backpacker crowd, the bright, monasterylike Banak Shol is built around a long, narrow central courtyard with several large trees reaching higher than the hotel's three stories. The rooms are basic but clean, and the all-Tibetan staff is incredibly friendly and helpful. The ground-floor restaurant with its outdoor seating is always a popular meeting spot to relax over a meal, a beer, and conversation. A computer is available for Internet access (guests pay per minute) and you can leave your belongings in a storage room before going on long treks. ☒ *43 Dekyi Shar Lam, Lhasa 850001,* ☎ *0891/633–8040,* FAX *0891/633–8040. 30 rooms, 2 suites, 2 dormitories. Restaurant, laundry service, Internet, meeting room, travel services. No credit cards.*

$ ⌂ **Pentoc Guesthouse.** Just one block north of Barkhor Square, the Pentoc is a clean and comfortable option for the budget-minded traveler. All rooms have colorful Tibetan-style bedcovers, dark-blue curtains, and either a love seat or chair. Rooms on the street side may be larger, but if you're a light sleeper the traffic noise below may wake you at dawn. Though the rooms tend to be cold, thick duvets will keep you warm in bed. The communal toilets and showers are immaculate. Videos are shown nightly at 8 PM in the lounge and a shop offers unique handcrafted souvenirs. ☒ *Tibetan Hospital Rd. #5, Lhasa 850001,* ☎ *0891/632–6686. 24 rooms. Business services. No credit cards.*

$ ⌂ **Snowlands.** Enter the inner courtyard of the Snowlands and you will soon forget the hustle and bustle of Lhasa's busy streets. This quiet hotel has comfortable rooms with walls painted in Tibetan designs, along with TVs and phones. Try to get a room with its own bath, since the communal bathrooms are very basic (although reasonably clean). A good-natured staff is always eager to please. ☒ *4 Mentsikhang Lam, Lhasa 850001,* ☎ *0891/632–3687,* FAX *0891/632–7145. 18 rooms, 2 suites, dormitory. Restaurant, bicycles, laundry service, travel services. No credit cards.*

$ ⌂ **Yak Hotel.** The Yak is the first choice for travelers on a tight budget who want to be in the Barkhor area. It offers a range of accommodations from doubles complete with bathrooms, phones, air-conditioning, and TVs, to immaculate six- to 10-bed dorms with shared bathroom facilities. Inspect the rooms before accepting, as they vary widely, from rather depressing to light, fresh, and comfortable. The Yak has a great roof area to lounge around on and its bar is a well-known meeting point for frequent Tibet travelers. ☒ *100 Delyi Shar Lam, Lhasa 850001,* ☎ *0891/632–3496. 28 doubles, dormitories. Bar. No credit cards.*

Nightlife and the Arts

Tibetan operas are performed at the **Lhasa City Academy of Performing Arts** and the **TAR Kyormolung Operatic Company.** Traditional Tibetan music is played at the **Crazy Yak, Himalayan** (Lhasa Fandian), and **Kirey Mad Yak** restaurants.

Shopping

Arts and Crafts

For Tibetan cloth tents and wall hangings try **Cuo Mei Lin Tent Factory** (☒ off Dekyi Shar Lam, down alley east of Yak Hotel, ☎ 0891/632–7904). The **Friendship Store** (☒ Yutok Lam) sells Chinese wares from across the Mainland. You are sure to get better deals elsewhere if you visit other parts of the country. The quaint **Lhasa Kitchen** (☒ 180 Bei-

jing Dong Lu) has a small arts-and-crafts window out front that sells handmade Tibetan paper products, including picture frames, hanging lanterns, and postcards. The shop also sells silver jewelry, including miniature prayer-wheel pendants, and door hangings—all great gifts at reasonable prices.

The **Pentoc Guesthouse Gift Shop** (✉ East Zang Yi Yuan Rd. #5) sells some of the more fascinating tourist knickknacks around, such as yak puppets. The staff here will let you know if a product was made in Nepal, where labor is cheaper and workers are often exploited. The **Potala Palace Art Gallery** (✉ outside entrance to Potala Palace, ☎ 0891/683–4854) sells traditional artifacts. Salesmen will bombard you with the pitch "Lookie! Lookie!" as you walk by. If you are looking for high-quality, award-winning Tibetan carpets and a guarantee that child labor wasn't employed in their making, consider the **Snow Leopard Carpet Industries** (✉ East Zang Yi Yuan Rd. #2), northwest of the *kora* circuit.

More Western-style paintings (i.e., on canvas) are available at the **Studio of Tibetan Folklore Oil Paintings** (✉ off Beijing Rd., near the Snowland Hotel, ☎ 0891/688–3106). You can chat with the artists at the gallery and buy directly from them at reasonable prices. The **Thangka Mandala Gallery & Workshop** (✉ Barkhor Circuit, South Side, Door 32) has a wide assortment of traditional-styled Tibetan paintings. Bargain hard here: this shop is catering to tourists with big bucks. **Tibet Da Peng National Arts Craft** (✉ outside entrance to Norbulingka, ☎ 0891/681–8066) sells carpets, thangkas, and jewelry. Bargain hard here; they have a steady flow of tourists.

Outdoor Equipment

North Col Mountaineering Shop (✉ West side of Potala Square, ☎ 0891/633–1111) has the best collection of outdoor equipment.

Side Trip to Ganden Namgyeling

★ ⑬   *45 km (28 mi) southeast of Lhasa.*

This enormous monastery was established by Tsongkhapa, the founder of the Gelugpa sect, in 1409. Unlike other monasteries, where abbots were often selected on the basis of heredity, this one was supervised by an abbot who was chosen for his worthiness and who served a term of seven years.

Of the six great Gelugpa monasteries, Ganden was the most seriously desecrated and damaged by Chinese using artillery and dynamite during the Cultural Revolution. Since the early 1980s, Tibetans have put tremendous effort into rebuilding the complex. Some 400 monks are now in residence; the Ganden community once numbered around 3,300 monks. Pilgrims come daily from Lhasa (buses leave the Jokhang at 6:30 AM) to pay homage to the sacred sites and relics.

The monastery comprises eight major buildings on either side of the dirt road. The most impressive structure is the **Serdhung Lhakhang** (Gold Tomb of Tsongkhapa) in the heart of the complex, easily recognized by the recently built white chorten before the red building. On the second floor is the chapel of **Yangchen Khang**, with the new golden chorten of Tsongkhapa. The original (1629), made of silver, later gilded, was the most sacred object in the land. In 1959 the Chinese destroyed it, although brave monks saved some of the holy relics of Tsongkhapa, which are now in the new gold-covered chorten. Be careful walking around this shrine: the buttery wax on the floor is thick and slippery. If you wish to take photos here it will cost Y20; video

costs a whopping Y1,500 for foreigners while inland visitors are charged Y750.

The **Assembly Hall** was repainted in 2001, so the murals are bright and shiny, but the old **Assembly Hall** exhibits more charm. From the second-floor balcony you can look down onto the two-story-tall Buddha statues. Walk downstairs to the main floor to see the old, dark murals. Be sure to climb up the particularly rickety ladder-stairs to see the ruling abbot's throne between the Buddha statues. At this shrine, you can admire the shoes of the 13th Dalai Lama. ✉ *36 km (22 mi) southeast on main Tibet–Sichuan hwy., then right onto winding road 9 km (5½ mi).* ✆ *Daily sunrise–sunset.*

TIBET A TO Z

To research prices, get advice from other travelers, and book travel arrangements, visit www.fodors.com.

AIR TRAVEL

CARRIERS

The easiest direct route is from Hong Kong, with a change of plane in Chengdu. China Southwest Airlines has twice-weekly nonstop flights from Kathmandu (with fantastic views of the Himalayas, including Everest) to Lhasa, and twice-daily flights from Chengdu. Both cost about $200 one way. Other flights to Lhasa include the weekly trip from Xian and Chongqing, and the weekly direct flight from Beijing. You must show your Tibet permit before leaving Beijing, Chengdu, Kathmandu, Xining, and Xian.

➤ AIRLINES AND CONTACTS: **China Southwest Airlines** (✉ ☎ 86/28–6668080, FAX 86/28–6710992, WEB www.cswa.com).

CAR TRAVEL

By road from Kathmandu, you can (usually) cross the border at Kodari. The Tibetan border guards have been known to grant individuals a permit at the border, though the law is for groups to enter on a prearranged tour. The 900-km (560-mi) route from Kathmandu to Lhasa takes two or more days to travel, traversing passes as high as 5,000 m (16,400 ft). Overnight stops are in Zhangmu and Shigatse. Minivans are available to shuttle you across the 8-km (5-mi) stretch between the two border posts—Kodari in Nepal and Zhangmu in Tibet. The cost from Zhangmu to Lhasa is about $55 in a minibus. Hiring your own four-wheel-drive vehicle with driver and unlimited passengers costs about $160. Exiting Tibet from Lhasa to Kathmandu is easier. The police do not stop you; the Nepalese frontier is always open, and a Nepalese visa is granted at the border.

Road travel from China into Tibet is tough. The inexpensive way most likely to meet with success is to cross the frontier by bus from Golmud, a sprawling town in Qinghai, at the end of the railway line from Xining. The distance is 1,115 km (691 mi), and the trip takes anywhere from 30 to 50 hours by bus (Y160); it can get very bleak and cold at night.

RULES OF THE ROAD

Foreigners are not permitted to drive in Tibet. All cars are hired with a driver and tour guide (Chinese law requires both). Rates depend on mileage, with a daily charge if the mileage is low. Daily rates start at $70 for a Landcruiser or Y3 per kilometer (plus permits), but will vary from agent to agent. Try the Lhasa Fandian and CITS to check rates and service.

CONSULATES
➤ NEPAL: **Nepalese Consulate** (✉ 13 Norbulingka Lu, Lhasa, ☎ 0891/632–2881).

EMERGENCIES
➤ CONTACTS: **Lhasa Fandian Clinic** (✉ 1 Minzu Lam, ☎ 0891/683–2221); **People's Hospital** (✉ Linghor Lam, ☎ 0891/632–2200).

HEALTH
CLIMBERS' ALERT

At the 3,600-m (12,000-ft) altitude, shortness of breath is the standard. You may experience mild discomfort—perhaps a headache or minor chest pains. These can be managed by an aspirin or two. Avoid exertion and drink plenty of nonalcoholic fluids, especially water. Severe altitude sickness should be brought to the attention of a physician—immediately. If you have high blood pressure, heart ailments, or respiratory problems, you may want to reconsider your route.

HOLIDAYS
Tibet has two sets of holidays: events observed by the People's Republic of China, which shuts down businesses and government offices on these holidays, and Tibetan Buddhist festivals, the celebrations of which are often shut down by the government. The lunar calendar determines the timing of many events.

MONEY MATTERS
CURRENCY EXCHANGE

The larger hotels all offer foreign exchange service. The main branch of the Bank of China, open weekdays 9–1 and 3:30–6:30, weekends 10:30–3, exchanges traveler's checks or cash into RMB and processes credit-card cash advances. A smaller branch office in the Barkhor area (1 block west of Banak Shol Hotel), exchanges traveler's checks and U.S. currency. You can also change traveler's checks at the Bank of China branches in Zhigatse, Zhangmu, and Shiquanbe.

➤ EXCHANGE SERVICES: **Bank of China** (✉ Dekyi Linghor Lam); (✉ Dekyi Shar Lam).

PASSPORTS AND VISAS
ENTERING TIBET

A visa valid for the People's Republic of China is required. The PRC embassy in Kathmandu will not issue these visas: you need to obtain one elsewhere—such as New Delhi, Bangkok, or your home country. That's standard; other requirements for entry are always in flux.

SAFETY
Don't openly talk politics with Tibetans. If they speak their mind, they may be charged with treason and receive a 20-year jail term. Do not photograph the people without first asking permission.

Public Security Bureau (PSB) personnel are everywhere, sometimes in uniform and sometimes in civilian clothes. The PSB monitors civil unrest, visa extensions, crime, and traffic. Beware the charming Tibetan who may be a secret policeman trying to entrap you into giving him a photograph of the Dalai Lama. Offices are in all towns and many of the smaller townships.

TIME
Tibet observes Beijing standard time, which is eight hours ahead of Greenwich mean time and 13 hours ahead of U.S. eastern standard time.

TOURS

BOOKING WITH AN AGENT

If you are required to join a tour in order to enter, many travel agents in Chengdu can arrange budget tours for independent travelers, and tour companies offer similar packages from Kathmandu. Quickly arranged three-day tours normally include round-trip airfare to Lhasa, all travel permits (which you may never see), three nights' accommodations, transportation to and from the airport, and a tour van with a guide for each day. When booking a tour, be sure to find out (in writing) what hotel your travel agent uses and other details. Often the only significant difference between travel agents is the quality of the guide in Lhasa, which, unfortunately, is hard to control.

Typically the cost of an organized tour for a week based out of Lhasa runs $1,000 to $2,000 plus airfare. Touring during a restrictive period may entail some frustrations. First, you'll have to spend time talking with tour companies and the PSB to uncover the "official" policy for independent travel outside Lhasa. Next will be numerous trips to travel agents around town to learn prices and itineraries. The better companies will provide you with a written contract that includes an itinerary and a list of services provided. Most tour companies will tailor a trip to meet your needs and budget.

➤ TOUR-OPERATOR RECOMMENDATIONS: **China Tibet Nature International Travel Service** (✉ 8 Tibetan Hospital Rd., Lhasa, ☏ 0891/633–8475); **CITS** (✉ Dekyi Nub Lam, Lhasa, ☏ 0891/633–6626; ✉ 208 Beijing Xi Lu, ☏ 0891/683–5046); **Mera Travels** (☏ 0852/391–6892, Hong Kong); **Tibet International Sports Travel** (TIST; ✉ Himalaya Hotel, Shar Linghor Lam, Lhasa, ☏ 0891/633–4082); **Tibet Ningchi International Travel Co.** (✉ Tibetan Hospital Rd., below Pentoc Guesthouse, Lhasa, ☏ 0891/634–1391);**Wind Horse Adventure** ✉ No. 1 North Minzu Lu, Lhasa, ☏ 0891/683–3009).

TRANSPORTATION AROUND TIBET

Lhasa is congested with taxis. You may call for service or ask at your hotel. A set fare of Y10 will get you anywhere within the city limits. Minibuses ply a fixed route with fares of Y2 or less. Bicycle rickshaws are also available for short trips and normally cost Y2–Y5.

➤ CONTACTS: **Taxi** (☏ 8091/683–4105).

VISITOR INFORMATION

➤ TOURIST INFORMATION: **Tibet Tourism Bureau** (✉ 18 Yuanlin Lam, Lhasa, ☏ 0891/683–4315 information; 0891/683–4193 to register a complaint).

14 PORTRAITS OF CHINA

CHINA AT A GLANCE: A CHRONOLOGY

400,000– **200,000** **years ago**	Early Paleolithic age: Fossil remains date Peking Man, which exhibits characteristics of modern Mongoloids. Evidence of use of stone tools.
800– **5000 BC**	Neolithic age: Beginnings of agriculture.
2205– **1766 BC**	Purported reign of Xia dynasty; no archaeological proof of its existence. Noted for use of fire, houses, and silk.
1766 BC– **1122 BC**	Shang dynasty: Beginnings of concept of "mandate of heaven," emphasizing good conduct of government and right of the populace to rebel against wicked leaders. Noted for highly developed bronze castings, carved jade ritual objects, and oracle bones.
1027 BC– **770 BC**	Zhou dynasty establishes capital near present-day Xian. Development of the feudal system. Writing used to keep records and for history and poetry books. Usage of coin currency.
607 BC– **487 BC**	Lifetime of Lao-tzu, philosopher who sought truth (dao) and utmost virtue in political relations and human nature, believing power should be in hands of people. Advisor to emperor. Purported author of *Tao Te Ching*. Founder of Taoism.
551 BC– **479 BC**	Lifetime of K'ung Fu-tzu (Confucius), teacher of moral principles of conduct and princely rule. Author of the *I Ching,* or Book of Changes. Stressed importance of humanity, courtesy, uprightness, honesty, and knowledge. Beginnings of Iron Age.
476–221 BC	Warring States period.
372 BC– **289 BC**	Lifetime of Meng-tzu (Mencius), proponent of living in proper relationships based on duty defined in social terms.
220 BC– **206 BC**	Despotic Qin Shi Huang Di (self-named "First Emperor") unites China and divides country into present-day 48 commanderies. Establishes capital and underground tomb with terra-cotta soldiers at Changan (Xian). Work begun on Great Wall to keep out nomadic tribes of north. Civil service exams instituted. Script, weights and measures, and coinage standardized. Books burned and Confucian scholars persecuted. Beginning of overland trade with Roman Empire.
206 BC– **AD 220**	Han dynasty. Gao-zu (202–195 BC) prevents attack from Huns by marrying daughter to Hun emperor. Wu Di (141–87 BC) encourages revival of Confucian studies; expands Chinese power to almost present-day position. Beginnings of papermaking. Collapse of Han dynasty and dissolution of the empire.
25–AD 220	Introduction of Buddhism from India. Silk Route developed.
265–420	Xin dynasty.
420–589	Division of China into Northern and Southern dynasties.
589–618	Empire reunified under the Sui dynasty. Grand Canal constructed, connecting northern and southern China. Development of gentry class. Reinstatement of civil service exams.

618–907 Tang dynasty. China's "Golden Age"; great flowering of arts and sciences under Xuan Zong (712–756). Notable poets: Du Fu, Wang Wei, Gao Shi, Bo Juyi, and Yuan Zhen. Coexistence of foreign religions. Rise of scholar-officials. Expansion of Buddhism and Confucian ethics. Paper and printing exported to West. Expansion of Buddhism and Confucian ethics. Only empress ever to rule China, Empress Wu (627–705), concubine to previous emperors, declares herself emperor in 690; orders ruthless persecution of opponents.

907–960 Instability following collapse of Tang dynasty leads to division of rule into Five Dynasties in north and Ten Kingdoms in south. Empire collapses and Barbarians invade north China. Beginnings of urban life and neo-Confucianism. Paper money and a primitive printing press are introduced, as well as the foot binding of women. First military use of gunpowder.

960–1280 China reunited under Song dynasty, capital established at Kaifeng. Coexistence with Jurchen, Khitan, and Jin rule. Flourishing of landscape painting. Genghis Khan defeats Jin in northwestern China in 1215.

1260 Mongol leader Kublai Khan, grandson of Genghis Khan, establishes Peking as his capital.

1279–1368 Mongol conquest of all of China and Tibet; founding of Yuan (Original) dynasty under "foreign" rule. Marco Polo reputed to visit China; serves under Kublai Khan (1275–1292). Rebellion instigated by White Lotus and Red Turbans groups leads to collapse of empire.

1368–1644 Ming (Brilliant) dynasty is marked by consolidation of power and institutional foundations of Chinese state. Capital moved to Nanjing until 1403. Beijing becomes capital again and Forbidden City constructed in 1421. Maritime expeditions across Indian Ocean.

1550 Europeans come to China seeking trade and Christian converts; Macau established as first European settlement in 1553.

1644 Manchu (Jurchen) conquest and founding of Qing dynasty. Capital returns to Peking. Pigtail forced on Chinese as sign of submission.

1662–1722 Kangxi Emperor, strong supporter of Confucian morality, consolidates the dynasty militarily. Taiwan reclaimed by China from Dutch.

1736–96 Qianlong Emperor presides over glorious period of pre-modern history. Emphasis on literature and scholarship in history, philosophy, and classics. Novels of the period include *Dream of the Red Chamber* (Cao Xueqin) and *The Romance of the Three Kingdoms* (Luo Guanzhong).

1794 First American ship arrives at Chinese port. Beginnings of Sino-American trade.

1773 To offset growing British demand for tea, and in response to restrictions on foreign trade, British begin exporting opium to Canton.

1839–42 Opium War. China orders complete halt of opium trade. British naval forces capture Fujian and Zhejiang.

1842 Qing emperor is forced to sign Treaty of Nanjing, which permits full resumption of British drug trade and exacts payments of indemnities from China.

1843 Treaty ports, allowing growth of Western commerce and culture and legal extraterritoriality for foreigners, grow from 5 eventually to 80 sites. Hong Kong ceded to Great Britain and China opened to Christian missionaries.

1853 Taiping Rebellion. The Taipings (Heavenly Kingdom of Great Peace), a peasant organization founded on Christian beliefs, take Nanjing and declare it their capital.

1856–60 Second Opium War. In retaliation against Chinese acts of protest against British and French, Treaty of Tianjin opens additional ports to foreign traders and grants extraterritorial privileges to foreigners.

1860 Chinese refuse ratification of Treaty of Tianjin. Anglo-French troops enter Peking and destroy Old Summer Palace.

1864 Final defeat of Taipings by combined Chinese and European forces.

1877 First group of Chinese students sent to Europe to study.

1883–85 Sino-French War, resulting in French control of Vietnam. Extravagant Empress Dowager Cixi (1835–1908), mother of the successor to the Qing throne, advises and exploits following three emperors. Under her direction, naval funds are squandered on reconstruction of Summer Palace.

1893 Birth of Mao Zedong to upper-level peasants in Hunan.

1894–95 China loses Korea, Taiwan, and Pescadores Islands in Sino-Japanese War.

1898 Hundred Days Reform seeks to remake the examination system, the administration, and government institutions in order to inaugurate a system of modern government.

1900–01 Boxer Rebellion, led by fanatical peasant secret societies, suppressed by by Eight-Power allied invasion (English, French, American, Japanese, Russian, and other forces). The Empress Dowager forced to flee, palace occupied. Russia invades Manchuria.

1901–11 Qing reforms: new school system, modern government departments, and abolition of old examination system.

1908 Death of Empress Dowager Cixi. Her son, two-year-old Emperor Pu Yi, inherits the throne.

1911 Republican revolution led by Sun Yat-sen (1866–1925) leads to fall of the Qing dynasty.

1912 Nationalist party (Guomindang; GMD) is formed. Yuan Shikai becomes president of the Republic and Beijing is declared capital.

1916 Death of Yuan Shikai. Beginnings of Warlord Era, during which Japanese, military commanders, and Communists compete in seeking to reform China.

1917 China declares war on Germany.

1919 China refuses to sign Treaty of Versailles, which cedes former German territories in Shandong province to Japan. Anti-imperialist sentiments give way to the May Fourth Movement, ushering in new ideas of science and democracy ringing with patriotism.

1921 Chinese Communist Party (CCP) founded in Shanghai.

1925 Death of Sun Yat-sen. May 30th Movement marked by anti-imperialist student demonstrations in Shanghai.

1926 GMD armies in the Northern Expedition, from Guangzhou to Yangzi valley, defeat warlord forces, including Japanese, in south China.

1927 GMD turns against CCP. Chiang Kai-shek establishes GMD capital in Nanjing.

1928 U.S. recognizes government of Chiang Kai-shek in Nanjing.

1931 Japan occupies Manchuria.

1934 Communists driven out of base in Jiangxi province by GMD and begin Long March, arriving in Yanan, Shaanxi province, some 6,000 miles and one year later. Only one-fourth of the 90,000 people survive the cross-country expedition.

1935 Mao Zedong becomes chairman and undisputed leader of CCP at Zunyi Conference.

1936 With encouragement from some Communist officers, Chiang Kai-shek is kidnapped by one of his generals in the Xian Incident and is released only when GMD agrees to cooperate with Communists against Japanese.

1937–45 Sino-Japanese War. GMD and CCP join forces against Japanese, but alliance ends by 1941.

1945 U.S. General George Marshall arrives in China to try to put together a coalition government between Communists and Nationalists.

1946 Full-scale civil war between GMD and CCP breaks out.

1949 People's Republic of China is established under Mao Zedong in Beijing. Nationalists, led by Chiang Kai-shek, flee with national treasures and entire gold reserves to Taiwan, leaving China bankrupt.

1950 China enters Korean War against United States. Marriage and agrarian reform laws passed. Sino-Soviet Treaty of Friendship, Alliance, and Mutual Assistance is signed.

1951–52 Three Antis Campaign against corruption, waste, and bureaucratism and the Five Antis Campaign against bribery, tax evasion, theft of state assets, cheating, and stealing of economic intelligence.

1952 Land Reform completed. Violent measures against landlords and local despots.

1953 Korean armistice. Beginning of First Five-Year Plan inaugurating transition to socialism by subordinating agriculture to industry.

1954 First National People's Congress adopts PRC state constitution. U.S. signs Mutual Defense Treaty with Nationalist government on Taiwan.

1955 Setting up of agricultural producers' cooperatives begins, in which peasants cultivate land together and share a common product in proportion to their pooled contributions.

1956 Mao Zedong makes Hundred Flowers speech inviting criticisms of cadres and the bureaucracy.

1957 Anti-Rightist Campaign purging erstwhile critics of regime who dared to speak out during Hundred Flowers period.

1958 Commune system established by amalgamating former agricultural producers' cooperatives. Great Leap Forward aimed at economic transformation in industry and agriculture. Chinese shell Nationalist offshore islands of Quemoy and Matsu.

1959   Resistance to occupation of Tibet suppressed. Dalai Lama flees to India. Chinese Defense Minister is dismissed for speaking out against Great Leap Forward.

1960   Soviet withdrawal of experts. Overambitious and misguided industrial targets of Great Leap result in devastating famine with an estimated 30 million deaths.

1960–62   Three years of natural disasters.

1962   Sino-Indian border war.

1964   China's first nuclear explosion.

1965   First signs of Cultural Revolution erupt in literary sphere in nationwide criticism of play, *Hai Rui Dismissed from Office*.

1966   Eleventh Plenum of Eleventh Central Committee formalizes the Cultural Revolution in move against Mao's critics, which leads to ousting of head of state Liu Shaoqi and general secretary of party Deng Xiaoping. Reign of terror and massive destruction ensue.

1967   Military is called in to restore order.

1968   Millions of urban youth sent to countryside to learn from peasants.

1969   Border clashes with Soviet Union. Ninth Party Congress names Defense Minister Lin Biao as Mao Zedong's closest comrade-in-arms and successor.

1971   Head of a powerful military faction, Lin Biao dies in mysterious plane crash over Mongolia. U.S. State Department abolishes travel restrictions to China, and U.S. table tennis team visits Beijing. Taiwan is expelled from UN, and China takes its seat on UN Security Council.

1972   President Nixon and Prime Minister Tanaka of Japan visit China. Shanghai communiqué is signed beginning process of normalization of relations between China and United States.

1975   Premier Zhou Enlai outlines program of four modernizations in agriculture, industry, science and technology, and national defense. Death of Chiang Kai-shek in Taiwan.

1976   Death of Zhou Enlai. First Tiananmen demonstrations against radical political line of Cultural Revolution. Severe earthquake measuring 7.5 demolishes city of Tangshan. Death of Mao Zedong is followed by arrest of Cultural Revolution protagonists, the "Gang of Four," led by Mao's wife.

1977   Deng Xiaoping returns to power.

1978   Sino-Japanese Treaty of Peace and Friendship is signed. Third Plenum of Eleventh Central Committee inaugurates socialist modernization and liberalized agricultural policies.

1978–79   Wall poster movement attacking Cultural Revolution and Mao Zedong evolves into Democracy Wall Movement.

1979   Resumption of formal diplomatic relations with United States. Deng Xiaoping visits United States. Sino-Vietnamese war. Democracy Wall is closed down and leading dissident Wei Jingsheng is arrested and sentenced to 15 years' imprisonment.

1980   Trial of "Gang of Four" and former military figures associated with Lin Biao. Opening of four special economic zones.

1981   Campaign against spiritual pollution and Western influences.

1983 Anti-crime campaign resulting in thousands of executions and deportations to countryside.

1984 Third Plenum of Twelfth Central Committee endorses broad economic and urban reforms.

1986 Student demonstrations begin in Hefei, Anhui province, and spread to Shanghai, Beijing, and 17 other cities.

1987 Party General Secretary Hu Yaobang is dismissed for failure to crack down on students. Anti-bourgeois liberalization campaign ensues against Western values and institutions.

1989 Death of Hu Yaobang leads to massive demonstrations in Beijing on Tiananmen Square for six weeks. Declaration of martial law does not quell crowds in Square. Military is brought in on June 4, resulting in thousands of deaths. General Secretary Zhao Ziyang is dismissed from office.

1992 Fourteenth Party Congress endorses concept of socialist market economy. First free elections in China.

1995 Chinese test-fire missiles off northern coast of Taiwan.

1997 Paramount leader Deng Xiaoping dies. Upon expiration of 99-year lease, sovereignty over Hong Kong reverts to China. Jiang Zemin becomes new chairman of the Republic.

2000 China attains "normal" trade status with the United States.

2001 U.S. spy plane collides with a Chinese fighter jet and makes emergency landing on Hainan Island. Pilot of Chinese fighter perishes; the 24 Navy crew members are held for 11 days while tension between two countries ensues.

— By Mielikki Org

UNDERSTANDING THE VISUAL ARTS IN CHINA

Since the Renaissance, in Europe and in the Americas the visual arts have generally been defined as works of architecture, painting, and sculpture. In pre-modern China, however, only one visual art held an esteemed status: calligraphy, the art of writing with a brush (*shu fa*). The design and making of buildings, the carving of images, many kinds of pictorial art, and crafts in general were simply not a part of definitions of "art." Their makers had no special status and these things were not the object of aesthetic discourse. In the 20th century, all of this changed. Collectors of Chinese art now amass paintings, hardwood furniture, porcelain, strange-shaped Taihu rocks, clay teapots, tomb figurines, rubbings, and much more. For practical purposes, art in China today is an eclectic mix, corresponding roughly to the concept of "material culture," all those things human beings have made with craft and creativity.

The most important artist in Chinese history was "anonymous." Much ancient art consists of durable objects—jades, ceramics, bronzes, stone carvings, and the like—and for all but recent periods the authorship of these works is simply unknown. Even when history is well documented, material culture emanated from workshops staffed with artisans whose names were rarely recorded. These workshops were often established for the imperial institution, and their quality standards were extraordinarily high. Only in the final century of the Eastern Han dynasty (2nd century AD) do we start to have the names of scholar-officials who were master calligraphers; famous named painters are known from a slightly later period. Outside the realm of calligraphy and painting, however, the makers of buildings, sculpture, and objects remain anonymous and their efforts collective. Thus, unlike the history of recent European and American art with its emphasis on famous masters, for much of Chinese art history attention is focused on long-lasting artistic traditions and on the particular periods when they flourished.

The "Son of Heaven," the emperor, was the most important patron in Chinese history. From the time of the Qin First Emperor (c. 221 BC) onwards, the imperial institution was responsible for almost all of the great public works and artistic monuments of China: from the Great Wall to imperial palaces, from Buddhist cave-chapels to pagodas. The emperors, through their court staff, dictated the designs of these sites, and officials charged with carrying out such projects could be held accountable with their life if they failed to satisfy their ruler's demands. In a very real sense, a tour of China becomes an overview of the remains of those strong, long-lasting dynasties—the Han (206 BC–AD 220) and Tang (618–906), the Ming (1368–1644) and Qing (1644–1911)—that left behind notable monuments. Imperial projects are characterized by their scale (the vastness of a Tang tomb), by their quantity (the myriad furnishings of the Forbidden City), by the quality of their materials and work (the images of the Great Buddha niche at the Longmen Grottoes, near Luoyang), and by their symbols of imperial power (most typically, dragons and phoenixes). No other institution or segment of the population in pre-modern China could challenge the imperial institution in the realm of art production and patronage.

Among the earliest arts to flourish in China were jade carving and pottery. These traditions have roots in Neolithic cultures of the 5th through 3rd millennia BC; jade, for example, was especially notable in the Hongshan Culture of modern-day Inner Mongolia and Liaoning and in the Liangzhu Culture of modern-day Shanghai, Jiangsu, and Zhejiang, both of which had disappeared by 2000 BC. The workmanship evident in Neolithic jades is displayed to great effect at the Liangzhu Culture Museum near Hangzhou (Zhejiang). The minute designs worked on the surfaces of these stones seem impossible in an age before sophisticated magnification and power tools. The Guan Porcelain Museum, also near Hangzhou, displays a Southern Song (12th–13th centuries AD) imperial kiln and tells the story of celadons (greenwares), one of China's most important ceramic traditions. The high volume and high quality of this and other imperial kilns anticipates the achievements

of sophisticated modern-day production. With both jade and ceramics there is a living connection to the remote past: the materials and processes of modern Chinese workshops and factories (often a part of tours) are not fundamentally different from their pre-modern antecedents. Jade carving continues to flourish in China today, using a great variety of hardstones and other attractive minerals. Many celadons offered for sale today—including Longquan, Guan, and Yaozhou wares—use the same clay sources and glaze recipes as their imperial-era prototypes. While excavated artifacts are not for sale and true antiques are very pricey, affordable replicas of both hardstones and ceramics are widely available.

The worlds of ancient and medieval China may be lost, but they are not utterly beyond our experience. A visit to a tomb (such as the Han tombs at Dabaotai near Beijing or the Tang tombs near Xian), a cave-chapel (such as the Yungang Grottoes near Datong), or the Forbidden City affords the visitor an experience akin to time travel with their prospects and natural settings, their volumes, spaces, textures, and colors. In this respect, a modern visitor is privileged as no pre-modern visitor ever was; only in recent times have these sites and monuments become public parks or museums. At such sites we can begin to appreciate the setting and context for objects now displayed in museum cases. Dragon robes take on new meaning once you have stood in the vast courtyard before the Hall of Supreme Harmony within the Forbidden City, where the Ming and Qing emperors presided over pre-dawn court gatherings. Tombs, temples, and cave-chapels offer the richest experiences of art in context for ancient and medieval times, while the former imperial palaces at Beijing, Chengde (Hebei), and Shenyang (Liaoning) are the most complete repositories for many of the arts of late imperial eras, after the 15th century.

In late medieval times, with the Northern Song (10th–12th centuries) period, scholar officials came to dominate Chinese society through their unique social status and the prerequisites of rank they enjoyed. They created their own arts for personal expression and relaxation. Calligraphy was preeminent, but painting, garden design, the collecting of antiquities and of objects for the scholar's studio were also significant. Modern-day museums display much calligraphy and painting by scholar artists ("literati," *wenren*)—men like Ni Zan, Shen Zhou, or Dong Qichang who were self-styled amateurs in the sense that they did not obtain their social identity through their artistic skills. A number of museums dedicated to individual artists have been established in recent years, usually at their native place. Garden design of the Ming and Qing is also largely a scholar's taste, designed to engage all the senses and to be savored in different ways at all times of the day and year. The many fine gardens in cities like Suzhou, Yangzhou, Nanjing, Hangzhou, and Shanghai were aped by imperial patrons in Beijing (as at Bei Hai and the Summer Palace). Idealized views of the Chinese past derived from the exquisitely harmonized settings of scholar's gardens (as in the 18th-century novel, *The Dream of the Red Chamber*) should be taken with the proverbial grain of salt. Only a small percentage of the population actually lived in such idyllic precincts.

Evocations of the natural world, especially the "mountains and waters" (*shan shui*) of the diverse Chinese continent, played an exceptionally large role in later Chinese arts. Paintings, garden design, porcelain decoration, and scholars' objects all took the eternal and ever-changing natural environment as their theme. This does not mean that Chinese artists or scholar-amateurs actually lived in nature or were devoted to the great outdoors. It does suggest the importance of the natural world as a source of Taoist and Buddhist imagery about life and the human condition. And because it can be appreciated without a specialist's knowledge of history or literature, landscape—both the real and the artistic—offers many rewards for the traveler. A tour of the Huang-shan mountains (Anhui) or Li River (Guilin) is a quintessential artistic experience as well as a nature lover's delight. The images of the natural world that you see from your train window are evoked in the gardens or museums you visit.

Because calligraphies and paintings were mounted as scrolls that were rolled up when not on view, it is very difficult to see the great works of the most acclaimed Chinese artists. Unlike the Mona Lisa, which is dependably on view in the Louvre, Chinese paintings are shown for limited periods only once or twice a year.

The superb Shanghai Museum, with its modern galleries and strong holdings in painting and calligraphy, is something of an exception. Painters of the Southern Song (1127–1279), Yuan (1279–1368), Ming, and Qing dominate Chinese museum holdings. If you are a fan of Ma Yuan's "one-corner" compositions (Ma was the scion of a whole family of Southern Song court painters), you will be able to see works of his period and style, if not necessarily works of his hand. Your chances to see the great names of later dynasties will increase considerably. The "Four Great Masters" of the Yuan, of the Ming, and of the Qing—artists who constitute one of the backbones of scholar painting—are regularly on display because they produced large numbers of works that in turn were collected avidly in later periods. With an artist like Shen Zhou (1427–1509) the lifetime output was so great and so diverse that, with diligent looking in museums, you can probably encounter the master repeatedly. Many literati works are ink monochrome and something of an acquired taste, like prints and drawings. Brilliantly colored works on silk produced for the Qing court—such as a large, impressive portrait of the Qianlong emperor (18th century) in armor on horseback—are well represented in Chinese museums. Until lately these were scorned by western art historians.

For the last thousand years or more, rulers and scholars in China have collected certain objects primarily for their historical value. The most prized objects, such as bronze ritual vessels and stone monuments, could be compared with the received historical record and Confucian classics because they carried inscriptions. Antiquarian study of relics preoccupied collectors, leading to the compilation of extensive illustrated catalogues of their holdings, and, not surprisingly, to a flourishing art market as well as considerable fakery. The collections of the Palace Museum (within the Forbidden City, Beijing) reflect these traditional interests and practices. Rich in archaic bronzes and jades, but poor in sculpture, the Palace collection was amassed by art-loving emperors starting in the Northern Song period (10th–12th centuries). Today it is not only one of the world's strongest collections of calligraphy and painting, it also houses the extensive furnishings of the Qing imperial court, from dragon robes to cloisonné and mechanical clocks sent as gifts by European powers. A fraction of the collections was moved to the island of Taiwan in 1949, but the bulk of its holdings remains intact and has been augmented in recent times by donations and discoveries. Visiting the Palace Museum can serve as a quick introduction to the kinds of things regarded as art in pre-modern China, as well as an immersion in the luxurious lifestyle of the ruling class.

A wider range of objects fills the many other museums in China. Most museums focus on history, using objects to tell the story of Chinese civilization from prehistory to modern times (c. 1840). These displays generally bring to mind exhibits in natural history and science museums, with their educational graphics, dioramas, models, and reproductions. Original works, including ancient jades, bronzes, ceramics, and other art, are installed amid these pedagogical aids. (Such display practices horrify some non-Chinese art curators, who place great weight on the unencumbered aesthetic experience of authentic art objects.) The preeminent example of this kind of presentation is the Museum of Chinese History, on Tiananmen Square in Beijing. The museum staff has gathered together many important new discoveries from around the country, and the galleries and cases are no longer in the drab Soviet style of a few years ago. The exhibits interpret the objects, which is useful both for the local population and for viewers who cannot read labels written in Chinese. Thus a visit to the Museum of Chinese History can provide a useful overview of Chinese civilization, albeit with history diced into neat dynastic segments under an overall Marxist framework ("primitive society, slave society, feudal society"). Most city and provincial museums depict the history of their own region, so the periods emphasized and the material displayed reflect the strengths and weaknesses of each area. The Shaanxi History Museum in Xian, an imperial capital for many dynasties, is thus correspondingly rich in tomb treasures and luxury goods from those epochs, and has some of the most modern facilities in all of China. Similarly, the Yunnan Provincial Museum in Kunming reflects the ethnic diversity of its peoples, both historically and in the present day.

Since 1950, the national government has made a notable commitment to archaeology, rescuing sites and artifacts from the path of bulldozers and carrying out extensive surveys and excavations in every province and region. The artistic and artifactual heritage as it is known today, a half century later, has caused scholars to rewrite the history of China from earliest times to the early imperial periods (beginning 221 BC). Virtually any volume written prior to the 1970s has been seriously compromised by its lack of these new data. While archaeology recovers a surfeit of data, only a small fraction makes its way into museum displays or publications. Many of the finest discoveries are, however, presented comprehensively through site museums—such as the Banpo Neolithic Village and the Qin First Emperor's Terra-cotta Army, both a short drive east of Xian, or the tomb of the Nanyue King in downtown Canton (Guangzhou). In these you can actually walk into an ancient site and see the artifacts in place, much as the archaeologists first encountered them. Many museums have galleries devoted exclusively to important local discoveries, such as the chime of 65 musical bells in the Hubei Provincial Museum (Wuhan) or the desiccated corpses in the Xinjiang Museum (Ürümqi). Don't be surprised if the most famous objects from a particular museum are not on display; they may be on loan to Beijing or abroad in a traveling exhibition.

Many fine art titles are now available at Chinese museums, sites, and bookstores, generally at bargain prices, although only a small fraction have English texts. Recent archaeology and expanding definitions of what constitutes serious topics for study have greatly enlarged the purview of "Chinese art history," and no one can command it all. Exhibition catalogues are perhaps the most useful guides to recent discoveries and their significance: *The Great Bronze Age of China* (Metropolitan Museum of Art, 1980), *The Quest for Eternity* (Los Angeles County Museum, 1987), *Son of Heaven: Imperial Arts of China* (Seattle, 1988), *Mysteries of Ancient China* (British Museum, 1996), *China: Five Thousand Years* (Guggenheim Museum, 1997), and *The Golden Age of Archaeology* (National Gallery, 1999). Two recent volumes also make good use of art and archaeology to introduce Chinese history and culture: Patricia Buckley Ebrey, *The Cambridge Illustrated History of China* (Cambridge, 1996), and Robert E. Murowchick, ed., *Cradles of Civilization: China* (University of Oklahoma, 1994). Laurence Sickman and Alexander C. Soper's *The Art and Architecture of China* (Pelican History of Art, Yale University Press, many editions) remains the best one-volume text, but covers only architecture, painting, and sculpture. Jessica Rawson, ed., *The British Museum Book of Chinese Art* (British Museum, 1992) is especially broad in its coverage.

DOING BUSINESS IN CHINA

If you're a business traveler in China, you probably still feel like a pioneer, even though it's been almost 20 years since Deng Xiaoping launched the "open door" policy and started inviting foreign investment into the previously isolated country. "We are learning how to compete in the market economy, and we need foreign expertise," a Chinese official or enterprise manager might tell you. But don't be misled into believing that you can come in with a plan this week and sign a contract next week, or that Western-style efficiency will be welcome in a joint venture with a Chinese company.

The Chinese, as every foreign business traveler quickly learns, have an elaborate, unwritten code of rules that apply to every aspect of business, from negotiating the contract to selling the product. A good way to prepare yourself is to read Sun Tze's *The Art of War*. The true author of this Chinese classic is unknown, but the best guess is that it was written by a brilliant military strategist who lived sometime around the 4th century BC. Sun Tze's basic principle held that moral strength and intellectual faculty were the decisive factors in battle, and today, these are the guiding factors in negotiating business deals. Not that you're dealing with adversaries. But from the days when the first foreign firms began to eye China's vast potential market of 1.2 billion consumers, the Chinese quickly realized that they had something the world wanted, so why not assure themselves a share in the capital that foreign ventures were sure to generate?

In recent years, a number of major Western companies have played hardball with Chinese officials and held their own. In 1996 for example, Disney was in discussions with the central government about distributing movies, selling merchandise, and building theme parks in China when Liu Jianzhong, director of the Film Bureau in the Ministry of Radio, Film and Television, warned that there might be no final approval for these projects if a Disney subsidiary went ahead with production of a film about the Dalai Lama, the Tibetan spiritual leader who is considered an enemy by the Chinese government. Disney refused to stop the film from being made and was blacklisted all over China. By 1999, Shanghai was in deep competition against Hong Kong wooing Disney to set up a Disneyland. According to *The Art of War,* you sometimes have to yield a city or give up ground in order to gain a more valuable objective. Although it might seem a good idea in the short run to bow to ideological pressure from China, it is probably best for a company's long-term goals and international image to hold out. There is dissension today within the ranks of China's government, and attempts to appease the authorities who make demands today may backfire if these people fall out of favor domestically, or if America's political relations with China deteriorate.

Furthermore, though the Chinese authorities may insist that their politics are none of our business, the lack of a clear rule of law in China can work against conducting business here. On a number of occasions business people have found themselves arrested and detained on trumped-up or nonexistent charges following a disagreement with a local partner or government authority over terms. Often the disagreement has to do with a city or provincial ministry's wanting an unreasonable share in the company. It is to the advantage of all foreigners living or spending time in China to push for political reforms that would incorporate due process of law.

This is all part of pioneering. In a country that had almost no modern roads 20 years ago, there are now huge swathes of concrete everywhere—and vehicles to run on them. According to World Bank figures, China's economy, before the Asian contagion, was the third fastest-growing in the world, with an annual average rate of 9.2% between 1978 and 1996. (Only Thailand and South Korea are ahead.) From being a country with virtually no capital, it has moved to among the top six nations in the world in terms of foreign exchange reserves. The people in the cities wear designer fashions, and construction cranes loom above almost every city or village street. Some observers think that as the market economy grows, a measure of democratic

reform will come. The Chinese people themselves are likely to demand a freer flow of information, if only to help them make financial decisions. In early 1997, for example, there was talk in China of a desperate need for the domestic news media to report responsibly and independently on the wild gyrations of the Shenzhen and Shanghai stock markets, so that the 21 million Chinese who own corporate equities can monitor their investments.

In spite of the economic reforms, this is still a centrally planned system called "socialism with Chinese characteristics." It is still a society with a thousand years of practice at handling foreign traders. Here are some fundamentals you should know before you go:

Your Team: If you're new to the place, retain the services of a China consultant who knows the language and has a strong track record. The nonprofit U.S. China Business Council (1818 N St. NW, Suite 200, Washington, DC 20036, tel. 202/429–0340, fax 202/775–2476, with additional offices in Hong Kong, Beijing, and Shanghai) is a good source for consulting services, referrals, and other information. Choose your own translator who will look out for your interests.

Know who you'll be meeting with in China, and send people with corresponding titles. The Chinese are very hierarchical and will be offended if you send a low-level manager to meet a minister. All of this ties into the all-important and intricate concept of "face," which can best be explained as the need to preserve dignity and standing.

Don't bring your spouse on the trip, unless he or she is involved in the business. Otherwise the Chinese will think your trip is really a vacation.

Attitudes Toward Women: The Chinese will take a woman seriously if she has an elevated title and acts serious. Women will find themselves under less pressure than men to hang out at the karaoke until the wee hours. This is partly because the party list might include prostitutes. (A woman will also avoid the trap that Chinese local partners sometimes lay to get rid of an out-of-favor foreign manager. They'll have a prostitute pick him up, then get the police to catch him so that he can be banished from the country for a sexual offense.)

Business Cards: Bring more than you ever thought you'd need. Consult a translator before you go and have cards made with your name and the name of your company in Chinese characters on the reverse side.

The Greeting: When you are introduced to someone in China, immediately bow your head slightly and offer your business card, with two hands. In the same ceremonious fashion accept your colleague's business card, which will likely be turned up to show an Anglicized name.

Be there on time. The Chinese are very punctual. When you are hosting a banquet, arrive at the restaurant at least 30 minutes before your guests.

The Meeting: Don't make plans for the rest of the day, or evening, or tomorrow or the next day. And don't be in a rush to get home. Meetings can go on for days, weeks, whatever it takes to win concessions. Meetings will continue over a lavish lunch, a lavish dinner that includes many toasts with mao tai, and a long night at a karaoke, consuming XO cognac from a showy bottle. To keep in shape for the lengthy meetings, learn the art of throwing a shot of mao tai onto the floor behind you instead of drinking it down when your host says "ganbei." (Chances are he is not really drinking either.)

Gifts and Bribes: Yes, a local official might ask you to get his child into a foreign university or buy your venture partner a fleet of BMWs. A few years ago a survey by the Independent Commission Against Corruption in Hong Kong found that corrupt business practices may represent 3%–5% of the cost of doing business in China, a factor that respondents (Hong Kong firms) claimed was bearable and not a disincentive. However, the Chinese government has been campaigning against corruption and business fraud. American companies have the added constraint of the Foreign Corrupt Practices Act, which prohibits offering or making payments to officials of foreign countries. The law can be a good excuse for not paying bribes. However, you may find yourself faced with a great many arbitrary fees to be paid to the city and county for everything from your business license to garbage collection. It is hard to avoid paying these.

To win friends in a small but legal way, give small gifts to the people you meet. Bring

a shipment of such items as pens, paper-weights, and T-shirts emblazoned with your company logo. And, before you leave town, host a banquet for all of the people who have entertained you.

Communication: Gestures that seem insignificant on the surface will help make or break your efforts to gain entry into China. Escort a departing visitor to the elevator as a way of giving him face, for example. To make a visitor feel particularly esteemed, walk him all the way to the front door of the building. And don't "have other plans" when your Chinese associates invite you out. As in many Asian countries, personal relationships are more important than the contract. The people you are dealing with may not tell you what they really want from a partnership with you until you're out eating and drinking.

There are many ways of saying "no" that may sound like "yes" to foreigners. If you hear that your proposal "is under study" or has arrived at "an inconvenient time," start preparing a new one.

A manager of a local factory in search of a foreign venture partner might tell you that the deal can be done, but that doesn't mean it will be. Make sure you meet with the officials in charge of your sector in the city, those who have the authority to approve the deal. If someone says he has to get the boss's approval, you should have a hearing with the boss—even if it means getting your boss there on the next flight to meet with his counterpart.

Early on, you may be asked to sign a "letter of intent." This document is not legally binding; it serves more as an expression of seriousness. But the principles in the letter, which look like ritual statements to the Westerner because they lack specific detail, may be invoked later if your Chinese partner has a grudge against you. He'll say you have not lived up to the spirit of mutual cooperation and benefit initially agreed upon.

How to Compromise: You will have to give your Chinese partner something he wants. He might, for instance, want your capital to go into lines of business other than what you had in mind. You might have to agree to this if establishing a presence in China is important to your business. Take the example of John C. Portman III, vice chairman of the Atlanta-based architecture firm John Portman & Associates. Portman spent the early 1980s courting the Shanghai government. Besides volunteering suggestions for redeveloping the city, he set up a trading company that brought an exhibition of goods from Shanghai to Atlanta. Not his usual line of business, but in the end the friendships he'd cultivated netted his company the coveted contract to design and develop the $200-million Shanghai Centre, which houses the Portman Ritz-Carlton Hotel, and China now accounts for about half of the company's total business.

Know when to be flexible, but for important details such as who actually has control of the venture and its operations, hold out, even if it takes a year or more. There are ways to make sure of who is really in charge of a joint venture, even though for matters of face and power the Chinese partner will probably want to provide the person with the loftiest title. You will also want to own the controlling share, because it means quality control, profitability, and decision-making power over matters for which your company is legally liable. Often an inside deal is worked out, whereby the foreign party provides the general manager, who actually is in charge of day-to-day operations, while the Chinese partner brings in the chairman, who works with a board of directors and has authority only over broad policy issues.

Don't go to China and tell your prospective partner you want to start production by a certain date. Expect your Chinese associates to drive their hardest bargain just when you thought it was safe to go home. They know that once rumors of a concluded negotiation become public, you will not be able to back down from the deal without having to make difficult explanations to your investors and headquarters.

Demand that your contract include an arbitration clause, which stipulates that if a dispute arises the matter will be tried by an arbitrator, preferably in the United States or a third country. However, even in China, there are arbitration centers that comply with international standards and are well ahead of the court system.

Being There: Saddled with 50 employees from the state-owned enterprise and you don't even have a customer in China? That's the way things have been done.

You will have to make changes slowly and be prepared to train people for new skills. Profits may be equally slow to roll in, but remember the corporate axiom that has become the main China strategy: We're in it for the long haul.

If you're trying to break into the China market with a product or service, learn more about the consumers you're targeting through a focus study. These have become popular among prospective consumers, who have proved willing to sit through sessions lasting as long as three hours. (Focus panels generally last only 40 minutes in the United States.) Test the name in different cities, because meaning can vary according to the local language. As the *Economist Intelligence Unit* reported recently, one company had a name for a butter product that meant "yellow oil" in one city, "engine oil" in another, and "cow fat" in a third.

The Law in China: China works on civil law—that is, laws are passed by the National People's Congress and implemented. Quickly. Hong Kong's legal structure is based on common law (the same as Britain's and the United States'), which develops through judicial decisions (case law). The heart of Hong Kong's existence, "One Country, Two Systems," is that both judicial systems exist side by side. But sometimes they clash in China, particularly when it comes to business. In 1999, 29 Hong Kong businessmen were being detained in China. About half languished under house arrest in hotels or actually behind bars because a business deal had gone sour. Many actually are citizens of other countries. The aggrieved party, which sometimes turns out to be officialdom, just grabs the person as a hostage until the money, which they see as theirs, is handed over. In at least two cases, the hostages were not released even after court rulings in China so ordered.

Will Feng Shui Help Your Prospects? The 7,000-year-old art of placing objects in harmony with the environment and the elements is virtually mandatory in Hong Kong and Taiwan—it always had a stronger influence in southern China. In other areas, it's officially considered feudalist superstitious nonsense, but of course, if it facilitates business. . . . If there's any doubt in your mind, by all means call a geomancer.

While China speeds along toward overtaking the United States as the world's largest economy—the World Bank forecasts that will happen in the year 2020—any number of factors may make or break your efforts to reap some of the benefits of this dizzying growth. Barring serious political upheaval, you'll probably want to stay here and make constant—i.e., day-to-day—adaptations to the changing demands of the market. Like armies, companies in China have to figure out when to advance their presence, when to scale back, when to retreat to another location. And with each new strategy, be prepared to negotiate, feast, and sing karaoke songs.

— By Jan Alexander

Updated by Saul Lockhart

BOOKS AND VIDEOS

Books

For general overviews of Chinese history from the 1600s to the present, start with *The Search for Modern China* (Jonathan Spence, Norton, New York, 1990) or *The Rise of Modern China* (Immanuel Hsu, Oxford University Press, New York, 4th edition, 1990). To explore deeper roots, with essays on specific cultural topics, read *An Introduction to Chinese Civilization* (John Meskill, ed., D.C. Heath, Boston, 1973). The story of Hong Kong is presented in *A Borrowed Place: The History of Hong Kong* (Frank Welsh, Kodansha, New York, 1994). An excellent book on Tibet is *High Peaks, Pure Earth: Collected Writings on Tibetan History and Culture* (Hugh Richardson, Serindia, London, 1998), by the foremost Western Tibetan scholar.

A number of memoirs have been published in recent years that provide not only personal stories, but also intimate windows on China's vast socioeconomic changes. *Wild Swans: Three Daughters of China* (Chang Jung, Simon & Schuster, New York, 1991) covers much of the 20th century in its look at the author's family. *A Single Tear* (Ningkun Wu, Atlantic Monthly Press, New York, 1993) traces the travails of a patriotic, U.S.-trained scholar who returns to China in 1950. *The Private Life of Mao Zedong: The Memoirs of Mao's Personal Physician* (Zhisui Li, with Anne Thurston, Random House, New York, 1994) combines the doctor's personal history and an intimate, controversial focus on the PRC's founding father. For a portrait of modern China, try *Behind the Wall* (Colin Thubron) and *China Wakes* (Nicholas D. Kristoff and Sheryl Wudunn, Vintage Press).

The United States and China (John K. Fairbank, Harvard University Press, Cambridge, MA, 4th ed., 1983) is a good primer on bilateral relations, while *The Great Wall and the Empty Fortress: China's Search for Security* (Andrew Nathan and Robert Ross, Norton, New York, 1997) is a solid analysis of China's foreign policy concerns. A thoughtful collection of essays on current U.S.–China relations can be found in *Living with China: U.S.–China Relations in the Twenty-First Century* (Ezra Vogel, ed., Norton, New York, 1997). Among the scores of excellent books on Chinese politics are *Politics of China* (Roderick MacFarquhar, ed., Cambridge University Press, New York, 2nd ed., 1993) and *Sowing the Seeds of Democracy in China: Political Reform in the Deng Xiaoping Era* (Merle Goldman, Harvard University Press, Cambridge, MA, 1994).

At the juncture of politics and the economy is *China's Second Revolution: Reform After Mao* (Harry Harding, Brookings Institution, Washington, DC, 1987). *One Step Ahead in China: Guangdong Under Reform* (Ezra Vogel, Harvard University Press, Cambridge, MA, 1989) probes deeply into the changes in southern China since 1978.

One of the best windows into contemporary Chinese society is by the Chinese journalists Sang Ye and Zhang Xinxin, titled *Chinese Lives: An Oral History of Contemporary China* (ed. by W.J.F. Jenner and Delia Davin, Pantheon, New York, 1987). Western journalist Orville Schell has written several books that track China since the mid-1970s, the latest being *Mandate of Heaven: The Legacy of Tiananmen Square and the Next Generation* (Simon & Schuster, New York, 1995). *China Pop* (Jianying Jha, The New Press, New York, 1995) is a superb look at popular culture in the PRC today. *In the Red: On Contemporary Chinese Culture* (Geremie R. Barme, Columbia University Press, New York, 1999) is an important and insightful look at Chinese literature, society, and politics just before and after the Tiananmen Sqare massacre. For the bottom line on dissident expression—including art, culture, and politics—see *New Ghosts, Old Dreams: Chinese Rebel Voices* (Geremie Barme and Linda Jaivin, Times Books, New York, 1992). *Tiananmen Papers* (Andrew Nathan, Public Affairs Press, 2001) is a controversial anthology of documents that reveal the inner struggle of the party leadership during the student protest in Tiananmen Square in 1989.

For a taste of historical Chinese literature, spend some time with *Story of the*

Stone; it's also known as *Dream of the Red Chamber* (Xueqin Cao, trans. by David Hawkes, Penguin, New York, 1973). Any book or essay by author Lu Xun will give you a taste of China's painful path from dynastic rule through early Communist rule; try *Diary of a Madman and Other Stories* (trans. by William Lyell, University of Hawaii Press, Honolulu, 1990). *Bolshevik Salute* (Meng Wang, University of Washington Press, Seattle, 1989) is one of China's first modern novels translated into English. Of the collections of Chinese literature and poetry both ancient and modern, check out *An Anthology of Chinese Literature: Beginnings to 1911* (Stephen Owen, ed. and trans., Norton, New York, 1996) and *From May Fourth to June Fourth: Twentieth Century Chinese Fiction and Film* (David D.W. Wang and Ellen Widmer, eds., Cambridge University Press, New York, 1993).

A number of the works of Gao Xianjian, 2000 Nobel Laureate for Literature, have been translated into English. He's best known for *Soul Mountain* (HarperCollins, 2000) and *The Other Shore* (Chinese University Press, 1999). Anchee Min's bestselling *Red Azalea* (Berkley Books, New York, 1995) is a memoir of life during the Cultural Revolution. *Katherine* (Berkley Books, New York, 1996), about a young woman and her seductive American English teacher, and *Becoming Madame Mao* (Houghton Mifflin, 2000), about the powerful Jiang Ching, are other popular works of Min's. Ha Jin, who began writing by a fluke, is the author of *Waiting* (Vintage Books, New York, 2000), which won the 1999 National Book Award and the 2000 PEN/Faulkner Award for Fiction. The story tells of one man's frustration at the hands of the bureaucracy as he tries to marry the woman he loves.

Videos

Among Chinese directors, Chen Kaige captures the beauty of the Chinese countryside in his mysterious, striking *Life on a String* (1991). He also directed an epic story of the artistic and personal commitment of two Peking opera stars, *Farewell, My Concubine* (1993) and *Temptress Moon* (1997). Tian Zhuangzhuang directed the controversial *The Blue Kite* (1994), a story of the travails of a young schoolteacher under communism in the 1950s and '60s. (It is currently not allowed to be shown in China). The outstanding films of director Zhang Yimou, such as *Red Sorghum* (1987), *Ju-Dou* (1990), *Raise the Red Lantern* (1991), *Shanghai Triad* (1995), *The Story of Qiu Ju* (1992), and *To Live* (1994) all star the excellent actress Gong Li, whose roles range from a glamorous mob mistress in 1930s Shanghai to a rural worker.

Any film by Ang Lee is a sure delight. He was feted for his 2001 *Crouching Tiger, Hidden Dragon*, which won four Academy Awards. Lee's earlier films are also worth seeing; *Eat Drink Man Woman* and *The Wedding Banquet* are amusing looks into modern-day Chinese relationships.

An American filmmaker of Chinese descent, Peter Wang, looks wryly at contemporary China in *A Great Wall* (1986). Director Ann Hui's *Song of the Exile* (1990) follows a young woman returning home to Hong Kong after graduating from a British university.

A Western take on Chinese history is presented in Bernardo Bertolucci's *The Last Emperor*, filmed in China. Three documentary films by Ambrica Productions (New York), *China in Revolution 1911–1949* (1989), *The Mao Years 1949–1976* (1994), and *Born under the Red Flag 1976–1997* (1997), depict the political and social upheavals that followed the death of the last emperor. They are available from Zeitgeist Films (☎ 800/255–9424). The Long Bow Group (Boston) has produced *The Gate of Heavenly Peace* (1996), a documentary film about the Tiananmen Square protests; it is available from Naata (☎ 415/552–9550).

CHINESE PLACE NAMES

Chapter 2, Beijing

Pinyin	English	Chinese Character
Běijīng	Beijing	北京
Bādálǐng Chángchéng	Badaling Great Wall	八达岭长城
Gùgōng	Forbidden City	故宫
Jiètàisì	Temple of the Altar	戒台寺
Lúgōuqiáo	Lugouqiao (Marco Polo Bridge)	芦沟桥
Míng Shísānlíng	Ming Tombs	明十三陵
Mùtiányù Chángchéng	Mutianyu Great Wall	慕田峪长城
Qīngdōnglíng	Eastern Qing Tombs	清东陵
Sīmǎtái Chángchéng	Simatai Great Wall	司马台长城
Tiānānmén Guǎngchǎng	Tiananmen Square	天安门广场
Yíhéyuán	Summer Palace	颐和园
Yúnjūsì	Yunju Temple	云居寺
Zhōukǒudiàn Běijīng Yuánrén Yízhǐ	Zhoukoudian Peking Man Site	周口店北京猿人遗址

Chapter 3, North Central China

Pinyin	English	Chinese Character
Tiānjīn	Tianjin	天津
Dū Lè Sì	Du Le Temple	都乐寺
Pānshān	Pan Mountain	攀山
Héběi	Hebei	河北
Běidàihé	Beidaihe	北戴河
Chéngdé	Chengde	承德
Shānhǎiguān	Shanhaiguan	山海关
Shānxī	Shanxi	山西
Dàtóng	Datong	大同
Xuánkōng Sì	Hanging Monastery	悬空寺
Yīngxiàn Mùtǎ	Yingxian Timber Pagoda	应县木塔
Yúngāng Shíkū	Yungang Grottoes	云冈石窟
Hénán	Henan	河南
Huáng Hé Youlan Qu	Yellow River Park	黄河公园
Luòyáng	Luoyang	洛阳
Shàolín Sì	Shaolin Monastery	少林寺
Zhèngzhōu	Zhengzhou	郑州
Zhōngyuè Sì	Temple of the Central Peak	中岳寺
Shāndōng	Shandong	山东

Jìnán	Jinan	济南
Láoshān	Mt. Lao	崂山
Qīngdǎo	Qingdao	青岛
Tàishān	Mt. Tai	泰山

Chapter 4, Northeastern China

Pinyin	English	Chinese Character
Heilongjiang	Heilongjiang	黑龙江
Hārbīn	Harbin	哈尔滨
Jílín	Jilin	吉林
Běidàhú Huáxuě Chǎng	Beidahu Ski Resort	北大湖滑雪场
Chángbáishān	Changbaishan Nature Reserve	长白山
Chángchūn	Changchun	长春
Sōng Huā Hú	Song Hua Lake	松花湖
Liáoníng	Liaoning	辽宁
Dàlián	Dalian	大连
Jīn Shí Tān	Golden Stone Beach	金石滩
Shěnyáng	Shenyang	沈阳

Chapter 5, Northwestern China

Pinyin	English	Chinese Character
Shǎnxī	Shaanxi	陕西
Gùyuán	Gu Yuan	咕原
Gǔzhōngkǒu	Guzhongkou	滚钟口
Huáshān	Huashan	华山
Níngxià	Ningxia	宁夏
Qīngtóngxiá Zhen	Old Qingtonxia	青铜峡
Tóngxīn	Tongxin	同心
Xīān	Xian	西安
Xīxià Wánglíng	Western Xia Tombs	西夏王陵
Yínchuān	Yinchuan	银川
Zhōngweì	Zhongwei	中卫
Gānsù	Gansu	甘肃
Bǐnglíng Sì Shíkū	Thousand Buddha Temple and Caves	炳陵寺石窟
Dūnhuáng	Dunhuang	敦煌
Jiāyùguān	Jiayuguan	嘉峪关
Lánzhōu	Lanzhou	兰州
Maìjīshān Shíkū	Maijishan Grottoes	麦积山石窟
Xiàhé	Xiahe	下河
Yáng Guān	Southern Pass	阳关
Yùmén	Jade Gate	玉门
Qīnghaǐ	Qinghai	青海
Géěrmù	Golmud	格尔木

Hóngaízǐgoū	Dek Tser	红崖子沟
Niǎo Dǎo	Bird Island	鸟岛
Qīnghǎi Hú	Qinghai Lake	青海湖
Riyuè Shān	Sun Moon Mountain	日月山
Tǎ'Ěr Sì	Ta'Er Monastery	塔尔寺
Tánggǔlā Shānkǒu	Tanggula Mountain Pass	唐古拉山口
Xīníng	Xining	西宁
Xīnjiāng	Xinjiang	新疆
Āsītǎnà Gǔmù	Atsana-Karakhoja Tombs	阿斯塔那古墓
Bózīkèlǐkè Qiānfó Dòng	Bezeklik Thousand Buddha Caves	柏孜克里克千佛洞
Gāochāng Gǔchéng	Ancient city of Gaochang	高昌古城
Jiāohé Gùchéng	Ancient city of Jiaohe	交河故城
Kāshí	Kashgar	喀什
Pàmǐ'ěr	Pamir Mountains	帕米尔
Pútáo Goū	Grape Valley	葡萄沟
Saì Lǐ Mù Hú	Sayram Lake	赛里木湖
Tiānchí Hú	Heavenly Lake	天池
Tǎshíkùěrgān	Tashkurgan	塔什库尔干
Tǔlǔfān	Turpan	土鲁番
Wūlǔmùqí	Ürümqi	乌鲁木齐
Yīníng	Yining	伊宁

Chapter 6, Shanghai

Pinyin	English	Chinese Character
Chén Xiàng Gé	Chen Ziang Ge	陈香阁
Dàjìng Gé	Old City Wall	大境路老城墙
Dōngtaí Lù Gudaì Chǎng	Dongtai Road Antiques Market	东台路古代场
Shànghǎi Pǔdōng Fázhǎn Yínháng	Former Hongkong & Shanghai Bank	上海浦东发展银行
Fúyóu Lù Gudaì Chǎng	Fuyou Road Antiques Market	富有路古代场
Hǎiguān Loú	Customs House	海关楼
Hépíng Fàndiàn	Peace Hotel	和平饭店
Huángpu Gōngyuán	Huangpu Park	黄埔公园
Waì Tān	The Bund	外滩
Yùyuán	Yu Garden	豫园
Húxīntīng Cháshì	Midlake Pavilion Teahouse	湖心亭茶室
Zhōngguo Yínháng	Bank of China	中国银行
Dà Jù Yuàn	Grand Theatre	上海大剧院
Dà Shìjiè	Great World	大世界
Guójī Fàndiàn	Park Hotel	国际饭店

Huā Niǎo Shìchǎng	Bird and Flower Market	花鸟市场
Jìngān Gu Sì	Jingan Temple	静安古寺
Rénmín Gōngyuán	People's Park	人民公园
Rénmín Guáng Chǎng	People's Square	人民广场
Shànghǎi Bówùguǎn	Shanghai Museum	上海博物馆
Shànghǎi Měishùguǎn	Shanghai Art Museum	上海美术馆
Shànghǎi Zhánlán Zhōngxīn	Shanghai Exhibition Center	上海展览中心
Yúfó Sì	Jade Buddha Temple	玉佛寺
Fúxīng Gōngyuán	Fuxing Park	复兴公园
Lónghuá Gu Sì	Longhua Temple	龙华古寺
Lánxīng	Lyceum Theatre	兰心大剧院
Shànghǎi Gōngyì Měishù Yànjiūsuǒ	Shanghai Arts and Crafts Research Institute	上海工艺美术研究所
Sóng Qìnglíng Gùjū	Soong Chingling's Former Residence	宋庆龄故居
Sūn Zhōngshān Gùjū	Song Yat-sen's Former Residence	孙中山故居
Yàndàng Lù	Yandan Lu Pedestrian Street	雁荡路
Xújiāhuì Dàjiàotǎng	Xujiahui Cathedral	徐家汇教堂
Zhōnggòng Yīdàhuìzhi	Site of the First National Congress	中共一大会址
Bīngjiāng Dà Dào	Riverside Promenade	冰江大道
Dōngfāng Míngzhū	Oriental Pearl TV Tower	东方明珠
Jīnmào Dàshà	Jinmao Building	金茂大厦
Pudōng Mǎtóu	Pudong Ferry Terminal	浦东码头
Shànghǎi Lìshi Bówùguǎn	Shanghai History Museum	上海历史博物馆
Shànghǎi Zhèngquàn Jiāoyìsuo	Shanghai Securities Exchange Building	上海证券交易所
Lu Xùn Gōngyuán	Lu Xun Park	鲁迅公园
Móxī Huìtáng	Moshe Synagogue	摩西会堂
Huǒshān Gōngyuán	Huoshan Park	火山公园

Chapter 7, Eastern China

Pinyin	English	Chinese Character
Jiāngsū	Jiangsu	江苏
Nánjīng	Nanjing	南京
Sūzhōu	Suzhou	苏州
Wúxī	Wuxi	无锡
Zhènjiāng	Zhenjiang	镇江
Ānhuī	Anhui	安徽
Héféi	Hefei	合肥
Huángshān	Huangshan	黄山

Zhèjiāng	Zhejiang	浙江
Hángzhōu	Hangzhou	杭州
Fújiàn	Fujian	福建
Chóngwǔ	Chongwu	崇武
Fúzhōu	Fuzhou	福州
Méizhōu	Meizhou	湄洲
Quánzhōu	Quanzhou	泉州
Wǔyí Shān Fēngjǐngqū	Wuyi Mountain Nature Reserve	武夷山风景区
Xiàmén	Xiamen	厦门
Yǒngdìng	Yongding	永定
Jiāngxī	Jiangxi	江西
Jǐngdézhèn	Jingdezhen	景德镇
Jǐnggāngshān	Jinggangshan	井冈山
Jiǔjiāng	Jiujiang	九江
Lúshān	Lushan	庐山
Nánchāng	Nanchang	南昌

Chapter 8, Southeastern China

Pinyin	English	Chinese Character
Guǎngdōng	Guangdong	广东
Cháozhōu	Chaozhou	潮州
Cuihēng	Cuiheng	翠亨
Fóshān	Foshan	佛山
Guǎngzhōu	Guangzhou	广州
Jǐn Xiù Zhōng Huá	Splendid China	锦绣中华
Shàntóu	Shantou	汕头
Shékǒu	Shekou	蛇口
Shēnzhèn	Shenzhen	深圳
Zhōng Huá Mínzú Wén Huà Cūn	China Folk Culture Villages	中华民族文化村
Zhōngshān Shì	Zhongshan Shi	中山市
Zhūhǎi	Zhuhai	珠海
Hǎinán	Hainan	海南
Hǎikǒu	Haikou	海口
Sānyà Shì	Sanya	三亚市
Tōngzhá	Tongzha	通什市

Chapter 10, South Central China

Pinyin	English	Chinese Character
Húběi	Hubei	湖北
Shénnǒngjià	Shennongjia	神农架
Wǔhàn	Wuhan	武汉
Yíchāng	Yichang	宜昌

Pinyin	English	Chinese Character
Húnán	Hunan	湖南
Chángshā	Changsha	长沙
Héngyáng	Hengyang	衡阳
Sháoshān	Shaoshan	韶山
Wǔlíngyúan	Wulingyuan	武陵源
Yuèyáng	Yueyang	岳阳
Guǎngxī	Guangxi	广西
Guìlín	Guilin	桂林
Líng Qú	Ling Qu	灵渠
Liǔzhōu	Liuzhou	柳州
Lóngshèng	Longsheng	龙胜
Nǎnníng	Nanning	南宁
Wúzhōu	Wuzhou	梧州
Yángshuò	Yangshuo	阳朔
Zuǒjiāng	Zuo River	左江
Guìzhōu	Guizhou	贵州
Ānshùn	Anshun	安顺
Guìyáng	Guiyang	贵阳
Huángguǒshù Pùbù	Huangguoshu Falls	黄果树瀑布
Kǎilǐ	Kaili	凯里
Xīngyì	Xingyi	兴义
Zūnyì	Zunyi	遵义

Chapter 11, Southwestern China

Pinyin	English	Chinese Character
Yúnnán	Yunnan	云南
Dàlǐ	Dali	大理
Dàměnglóng	Damenglong	大勐龙
Hǔtiaò Xía	Tiger Leaping Gorge	虎跳峡
Jǐnghóng	Jinghong	景洪
Kūnmíng	Kunming	昆明
Lìjiáng	Lijiang	丽江
Lúgū Hú	Lugu Lake	泸沽湖
Měnghǎi	Menghai	勐海
Shígǔ	Shigu	石鼓
Shāpíng	Shaping	沙坪
Shí Lín	Stone Forest	石林
Xīshuāngbǎnnà	Xishuangbanna	西双版纳
Xīzhōu	Xizhou	西州
Yuán Shǐ Yǔ Lín Gōngyuán	Primitive Rain Forest Park	原始雨林公园
Zhōngdiàn	Zhongdian	中甸
Zhōuchéng	Zhoucheng	周城
Sìchūan	Sichuan	四川

Bādōng	Badong	巴东
Chéngdū	Chéngdū	成都
Chóngqìng	Chongqing	重庆
Dàzú	Dazu	大足
Dūjiāngyàn	Dujiangyan	都江堰
Éméishān	Emeishan	峨眉山
Fēngdū	Fengdu	丰都
Gězhōu Bà	Gezhou Dam	葛州坝
Jiǔzhàigōu	Jiuzhaigou	九寨沟
Kāngdìng	Kangding	康定
Lèshán	Leshan	乐山
Qútáng Xiá	Qutang Gorge	瞿塘峡
Shíbaǒzhài	Stone Treasure Stronghold	石宝寨
Sōngpān	Songpan	松潘
Wū Shān	Wu Mountain	巫山
Wū Xiá	Wu Gorge	巫峡
Xīlíng Xiá	Xiling Gorge	西陵峡

Chapter 12, Inner Mongolia and the Republic of Mongolia

Pinyin	English	Chinese Character
Nèi Méng Gǔ	Inner Mongolia	内蒙古
Hū Hé Hào Té	Hohhot	呼和浩特

CHINESE VOCABULARY

Many of the pronunciations for the *pinyin* below appear to have two syllables. Actually, there are two separate sounds, but they move smoothly from one into the other and make but a single sound when said correctly. For example, the *pinyin* "dian" is pronounced "dee-**en**," with a slight emphasis on the second part of the word: this should be a single sound, as opposed to what you would hear if you said separately the letters "D" and "N." Below, only the words with hyphens in them are pronounced this way. All other "spelled sounds" (a literal translation of the word *pinyin*) should be pronounced as indicated.

English	Pinyin	Pronunciation

Basics

English	Pinyin	Pronunciation
Yes/there is/to have	yǒu	yoh
No/there isn't/ to not have	méi yǒu	**may** yoh
Please	qǐng	ching
Thank you	xiè xie	**shay** shay
Excuse me	má fan nǐ	mah fahn nee
Sorry	duì bù qǐ	**dway** boo chee
Good/bad	hǎo/bù hǎo	how/**boo** how
Goodbye	zài jiàn	dzy jee-**en** (y as in why)
Mr. (Sir)	xiānshēng	shee-**en** shung
Mrs. (Ma'am)	fū rén	**nyoo** shuh
Miss	xiǎo jiě	shee-**ao** jee-**ay**

Days of the Week, Time Expressions

English	Pinyin	Pronunciation
Sunday	xīng qī rì/	shing chee **dz**/
	xīng qī tiān	shing chee tee-**en**
Monday	xīng qī yī	shing chee ee
Tuesday	xīng qī èr	shing chee **ahr**
Wednesday	xīng qī sān	shing chee **sahn**
Thursday	xīng qī sì	shing chee **sih**
Friday	xīng qī wǔ	shing chee **woo**
Saturday	xīng qī liù	shing chee **lee**-o
Week	xīng qī	shing chee
Month/moon	yuè	yway
Year	nián	nee-**en**
When	shén me shí hóu?	shun muh shur ho?
Night/evening	wǎn shàng	wahn **shahng**
Yesterday	zuó tiān	zwo tee-**en**
Today	jīn tiān	jeen tee-**en**
Tomorrow	míng tiān	ming tee-**en**

Numbers

1	yī	ee
2	èr (used as a numeral)	ahr
2 of . . .	liǎng	lee-**ahng**
3	sān	sahn
4	sì	sih
5	wǔ	woo

6	lìu	**lee**-o
7	qì	chee
8	bā	bah
9	jĭu	jee-**o**
10	shí	shur
11	shí yī (10 + 1)	shur **ee**
15	shí wŭ	**shur** woo
20	èr shí (2 10)	**ahr** shur
21	èr shí yī (2 x 10 + 1)	**ahr** shur ee
30	sān shí	**sahn** shur
50	wŭ shí	woo shur
100	(yī) băi	(ee) by
200	èr băi/liăng băi	**ahr** by
500	wŭ băi	woo by
1,000	(yī) qiān	(ee) chee-**en**
first/second/third . . .	dì yī/dì èr/dì sān . . .	dee ee/dee **ahr**/dee **sahn**

Useful Phrases

Hello/How are you	nĭ hăo/nĭ hăo ma?	**nee** how/ nee how mah?
Do you speak . . .	nĭ huì shuō . . .	nee **hway** shwo
. . . English?	. . . yīng wén ma	**yeeng** wen mah?
I don't understand.	wŏ bù dŏng	woh **boo** dohng
I don't know.	wŏ bù zhī dào	woh **boo** jer dow
I am lost.	wŏ mĭ lù le	woh mee loo luh
What is this?	zhè shì shén me	juh shur **shun**-muh
Where is . . .	. . . zài năr?	. . . **dzy** nahr?
the train station?	huŏ chē zhàn (zài năr?) . . .	who-**oh** chuh jahn
the subway station	dì tiĕ zhàn . . .	dee tee-**ay** jahn . . .
the post office	yóu jù . . .	yoh jew . . .
the bank	yíng háng . . .	**yeeng** hahng . . .
the hospital	yī yuàn . . .	yee yoo-**en**
my hotel	wŏ de bĭn guăn . . .	woh duh **been** gwahn . . .
I am American	wŏ shì mĕi guó rén	wo **shur** may gworen
British	yīng guó rén	**yeeng** gwo ren
Australian	ào dà lì yà rén	ow dah lee **yah** ren
Canadian	jiā ná dà rén	jee-**ah** nah **dah** ren
Where are the . . . rest rooms?	cè suŏ zài năr?	**tsuh** swoh zy nahr?
Left (side)	zuŏ (biān)	zwoh (bee-**en**)
Right (side)	yòu (biān)	yoh (bee-**en**)
In the middle	zài zhōng jiān	zy johng jee-en
I'd like a room	wŏ xiăng yăo yī ge fáng jiān	woh shee-ahng yow ee guh **fong** jee-en
I'd like to buy . . .	wŏ xiăng măi . . .	woh shee-**angh** my
How much is that?	ná duō shăo qián?	nah **dwoh** shao chee-**en**?

A little	yī diǎn	ee dee-**en**
A lot	hěn duō	hun **dwoh**
More	duō	**dwoh**
Less	shǎo	shao
I feel ill	wǒ bù shū fu	woh boo **shoo** foo
I have a problem	wǒ yǒu yī ge wéntì	woh yoh ee guh **wen** tee

At the Restaurant

Where can we find a good restaurant?	Zài nǎr kěyǐ zhǎodào yìjiā hǎo cānguǎn?	**dzy** nahr kuh yee jow dow **yee** jee-ah how tsahn gwahn?
We'd like a(n) . . . restaurant.	Wǒmen xiǎng qù yì gè . . . cānguǎn.	woh mun shee-**ahng** chew **yee** guh . . . tsahn gwan.
elegant	gāo jí	gow jee
fast-food	kuàicān	**kwy** tsan
inexpensive	piányì de	pee-**en** yee duh
seafood	hǎixiǎn	hy shee-**en**
vegetarian	sùshí	soo shee
Café	Kāfēi diàn	kah fay dee-**en**
A table for two	Liǎng wèi	lee-**ahng** way
Waiter, a menu please.	Fúwùyuán, qǐng gěi wǒmen càidān.	foo woo ywen, cheeng **gay** who mun tsy dahn.
The wine list, please.	Qǐng gěi wǒmen jiǔdān.	cheeng **gay** who mun jee-o dahn.
Appetizers	Kāiwèi shíwù	ky way **shur** woo
Main course	Zhǔ cài	joo **tsy**
Dessert	Tiándiǎn	tee-**en** dee-**en**
Can you recommend a good wine?	Nǐ néng tūijiàn yí ge hǎo jiǔ ma?	nee nung **tway** jee-**en** yee guh **how** jee-o ma?
Wine, please.	Qǐng lǎi diǎn jiǔ.	cheeng ly dee-**en** jee-o.
Beer, please.	Qǐng lǎi diǎn píjiǔ.	cheeng ly dee-**en** **pee** jee-o.
I didn't order this.	Wǒ méiyǒu diǎn zhè gè.	woh **may** yoh dee-**en** juh guh.
That's all, thanks.	Jiù zhèxie, xièxiè.	Jee-o juh shay, **shay** shay.
The check, please.	Qǐng jiézhàng.	cheeng jee-**eh** jahng.
Cheers!/Bottoms Up! To your health!	Gānbēi! Zhù nǐ shēntǐ jiànkāng.	**gahn bay!** Joo nee **shun** tee jee-**en** kahng.

INDEX